Y0-BVQ-486

Global City Regions

Global City Regions

Their emerging forms

Edited by
Roger Simmonds
and
Gary Hack

London and New York

First published 2000
by Spon Press
11 New Fetter Lane, London EC4P 4EE

Simultaneously published in the USA and Canada
by Spon Press
29 West 35th Street, New York, NY 10001

Spon Press is an imprint of the Taylor & Francis Group

Designed and typeset in Baskerville and Gill by Keystroke, Jacaranda Lodge, Wolverhampton
Colour separation by Tenon & Polert Colour Scanning Ltd
Printed and bound in China

British Library Cataloguing in Publication Data
A catalogue record for this book is available from the British Library

Library of Congress Cataloging in Publication Data
Global city regions: their emerging forms / edited by Roger Simmonds and Gary Hack.
p. cm.
Includes bibliographical references and index.
1. Metropolitan areas. 2. Metropolitan government. 3. Cities and towns—Growth. I. Simmonds, Roger, 1940– . II. Hack, Gary.
HT330.G55 1999
307.76—dc21 99-16491
CIP

ISBN 0-419-23240-0

Contents

Notes on contributors

Gilda Collet Bruna Since 1995 she has been the Director and President of EMPLASA (Empresa Metropolitana de Planeamiento do Gran São Paolo). Between 1990 and 1994 she was Professor and Director of the Faculty of Architecture and Urbanism in the University of São Paulo. Today she is the coordinator of the Architecture and Urbanism Course in the University of Mogi das Cruzes in São Paulo.

José María Ezquiaga He is Professor of Town Planning and Urban Studies at the School of Architecture at Madrid University. As a consultant he is CoDirector of the master plans for Cordoba, San Jose de la Rinconada (Seville) and is producing strategic plans for the corridors of Henares-Guadalahara and North Toledo. He was Head of the Planning Department of the City of Madrid 1985–88 and Director General of Urbanism and Urban Planning of the Madrid Region, 1988–95. He has a PhD from the School of Architecture, Madrid.

Rosalind Greenstein She is Senior Fellow and Director of the Land Use and Regulation Program at the Lincoln Institute of Land Policy, in Cambridge MA. Her work focuses on the economic and social forces that shape and define metropolitan regions. Prior to working at the Lincoln Institute, she taught urban and regional planning at the University of Wisconsin-Madison, directed the research and evaluation activities for the Massachusetts Industrial Services Program, and was a senior regional economist with DRI/McGraw-Hill. She has a BA in economics from the University of California at Santa Cruz and a PhD in city and regional planning from the University of North Carolina-Chapel Hill.

Utis Kaothien He is Assistant Secretary General of NESDB (the National Economic and Social Development Board, Office of the Prime Minister), Thailand. He sits on a number of National Boards, for example the National Housing Authority, the Ministry of the Interior, and the Ministry of Defence, and is an advisor to a wide number of agencies. He has been a lecturer in the Faculty of Social Sciences since 1979 in Kasetsart University, Bangkok. He has a PhD from Cambridge University (UK), a Master's degree in environmental planning from the University of the Philippines, and a BArch. from the Far Eastern University, the Philippines.

Nein-Hsiung Kuo He is the Director of the Comprehensive Planning Department, Construction and Planning Administration, Ministry of the Interior, Taiwan. His department defines, administers and reviews regional plans in Taiwan.

Francisco Sabatini He is an Associate Professor in the Institute for Urban Studies at the Pontificia Universidad Católica de Chile. He is a sociologist working as a consultant to public agencies on the themes of urban segregation, conflict and public participation and with public and private firms on the theme of local business and the community. He published *Barrio y participacion* in 1996 and *Environmental Conflicts* in 1997. He has a PhD from the University of California—Los Angeles (UCLA).

Michael J. Stepner He is now Dean of the Newschool of Architecture in San Diego. Previously, from 1971 to 1997, he was in the employ of the City of San Diego in a number of roles, including City Architect, Urban Design Coordinator and Assistant Planning Director. He has a BA in architecture from the University of Illinois and is a registered architect and town planner. He has lectured at numerous universities on planning and urban design.

Leo J. M. Tummers He is Associate Professor of Town Planning at the Faculty of Architecture, Delft University of Technology, the Netherlands. He has carried out a number of studies with the National Spatial Planning Agency in The Hague, including an extensive comparative study of spatial structures in Western metropolitan areas, particularly in relation to their systems of open spaces. This work was carried out with his wife, J. Zurmond, who is a professional town planner for the Dutch Ministry of Housing, Spatial Planning and the Environment. They published *Het land in de Stad* in 1997.

Yuichi Takeuchi He is Director of the Social Systems Research Department, Institute of Behavioral Studies, Tokyo, and has worked for the institute since 1971 on city planning and transport-related themes. He has a BA and MSc in city planning from the Department of Urban Engineering Tokyo University.

Anne Vernez Moudon She is Professor of Architecture, Landscape Architecture, and Urban Design and Planning and Associate Dean for Applied Research at the University of Washington, Seattle. She is currently Director of the Cascadia Community and Environment Institute for Interdisciplinary Education in the College of Architecture and Urban Planning. She works as a consultant to communities nationally and internationally and was on the faculty of Berkeley and MIT. Her published work includes *Built for Change* (1986), *Public Streets for Public Use* (1991), and *Urban Design*, edited with Wayne Attoe in 1998. She has a PhD from the Ecole polytechnique fédérale of Lausanne and a BArch from the University of California—Berkeley.

Stephen Walker He is University Reader in Property Economics and Finance and Director of Research in the Department of Town Planning, Oxford Brookes University, UK. He has led multidisciplinary teams on European Union, World Bank, and UK government-sponsored projects, covering economic development, tourism, and energy efficiency studies. He has completed eight studies for central government departments in the UK, including *The Effectiveness of Green Belts* (1993), *The Supply of land for Housing, The Use of Planning Agreements* (1992), and *The Operation of Compulsory Purchase Orders* (1997). He has a BA in economics and geography, and an MPhil and MSc in macroeconomic modelling and forecasting.

Douglas Webster He is the Senior Urban Planning Advisor to the National Economic and Social Development Board, Prime Minister's Office, Thailand. He is on leave as Professor of Planning in the Faculty of Environmental Design, University of Calgary, Canada, where he was previously Director of the Urban and Regional Planning Program. He has been Professor of Natural Resource Planning and Manager of the CIDA Program, Asian Institute of Technology, Bangkok. He has spent the last 20 years providing advisory services in urban and regional development to governments, the World Bank, and UN agencies in South East Asia and many other parts of the world. He has a BA in geography from the University of Toronto, an MA in regional and resource planning from the University of Waterloo, and a PhD from the University of California—Berkeley.

Gary Hack He is Professor and Dean of Fine Arts at the University of Pennsylvania. Previously he was professor in the Department of Urban Studies and Planning at MIT. He was head of the DUSP, 1983–87. For a decade he was a partner in the firm of Carr Lynch Hack & Sanyall, responsible for projects like the plan and program for the regeneration of New York's West Side and many planning and urban design projects. In recent years he has been involved in major projects in Tokyo, Beijing, and Bangkok. His best known publication is the regularly updated *Site Planning*, which he once co-authored with Kevin Lynch. He has a BArch and MCP and a PhD from MIT.

Roger Simmonds He is a lecturer in the Joint Centre for Urban Design at Oxford Brookes University. He was chair of the JCUD, 1989–93. He has worked as a planning consultant in Europe, North America, Africa, and the Middle East, and has been project director or principal researcher on six major research projects: for the Mellon Foundation, the Nuffield Foundation, two projects for the National Endowment for the Arts (Washington DC), and two for the Lincoln Institute of Land Policy. He has a BArch from Leicester College of Art and Design, an MA from Yale University, and a PhD from MIT, where he has been a visiting professor and research associate on a number of occasions.

David Barkin He is Professor of Applied Economics at the Metropolitan Autonomous University in Mexico City, where he works on alternative sustainable development strategies in Third World countries. His latest books include *Monarcas y campesinos* (in Spanish) and *Distorted Development* (in English, Japanese, and Spanish). He has a PhD from Yale University.

M. Christine Boyer She has been Professor of Architecture at Princeton University since 1991. Her best known publications are *Dreaming the Rational City* (1983), 'Cities for Sale' in *Variations on a Theme Park* ed. Michael Sorkin (1992) and *Cybercities* (1996). She has an BA in mathematics from Goucger College, an MSc in computer and information science from the University of Pennsylvania, an MA in urban studies and a PhD from MIT.

Ralph Gakenheimer He is a Professor at MIT and has worked on problems of urban planning in some 16 countries. He was a visiting scholar at the World Bank on the theme of rapid motorization in the developing world and is currently researching the broad theme of "mobility: in search of solutions attractive to all stakeholders" for the Automotive Board of Governors. He has written several books and articles on these themes. He has a BES in engineering and planning from Johns Hopkins University, an MRP from Cornell, and a PhD from the National Engineering University of Peru and the University of Pennsylvania.

Stephen D. N. Graham He is a principal lecturer at the Centre for Urban Technology (CUT), University of Newcastle upon Tyne. Among many recent publications he has a book with Simon Marvin, *Telecommunications and the City* (1996). He has a BSc in geography from Southampton University, an MPhil in town and country planning from

Newcastle University and a PhD in technology policy from Manchester University.

Simon Marvin He is the United Utilities Professor of Sustainable Urban and Regional Development and Co-Director of The Research Centre for Sustainable Urban and Regional Futures at the University of Salford, UK. Among many recent publications, he co-authored with Stephen Graham, *Telecommunications and The City* (1996). He has a BA in geography/sociology from the University of Hull, an MA from the University of Sheffield, and a PhD in technology policy from the Open University in Manchester.

Pedro Ortiz Castaño He is Director General of Urbanism and Regional Planning for the Madrid regional government. Previously he was Director of the Strategic Plan for the City of Madrid, 1990–94, and a Madrid city councilor, 1991–95. Among many articles and publications are *Madrid no te olvida* (co-authored in 1992), *Punto y seguido* (1991), and *Los parques de Madrid* (1990). He has a *baccalaureat français*, a BA in architecture from Madrid University, and an MA in urban studies from Oxford Brookes University.

Agustin Rodriguez-Bachiller He has been Senior Lecturer in the School of Planning at Oxford Brookes University since 1975, especially interested, since his PhD, in location theory and modelling, with an award-winning article on discontiguous urban growth. Other areas of research have included town planning education (author of a book on the subject in 1988). Recent work has included expert systems in town planning and geographical information systems for environmental impact assessment. He has a first degree in architecture from Madrid University, an MSc in urban and regional planning studies from Reading University, and a PhD in geography, also from Reading University.

Saskia Sassen She is Professor of Sociology at the University of Chicago. Her most recent books are *Globalization and its Discontents* (1998) and *Losing Control?* (1996). Her books have been translated into several languages: *The Global City* has appeared in French (1996), Italian (1998), and Spanish (1998). She has just completed *Immigration Policy in the Global Economy*, sponsored by the Twentieth Century Fund. She continues work on two projects: "Cities and their Crossborder Networks," sponsored by the United Nations University, and "Governance and Accountability in a Global Economy." She is a member of the Council on Foreign Relations and has just been invited to be a Fellow of the American Bar Foundation.

Melvin M. Webber He is Professor Emeritus of Planning at the University of California—Berkeley. A series of his early essays explored the effects of increasing ease of communication and transport on urbanization, social relations, and economic development. They included "Order in Diversity" (1963), "The Urban Place and the Nonplace Urban Realm" (1964), and "The Post-city Age" (1968). In more recent years he has been exploiting those technological trends to promote development in America and Europe, as well as in developing countries of Africa, Asia, Latin America, and the Middle East.

The Lincoln Institute of Land Policy's interest in *Global City Regions*:

How are metropolitan regions organized? What are the forces that lead to existing patterns of development and the variation in these patterns across the globe? Who gains and who benefits as a result of these patterns? Is the community interest thereby served? If intervention is needed, what is the nature of that intervention? Which interventions are likely to be most successful? What lessons can be learned and transferred under what conditions? When this project first began a number of years ago, these and similar questions motivated our interest. Today, we may have slightly better information on the forces—ranging from global, to national, to local—that influence the development patterns of metropolitan regions. However, we do no better at evaluating the costs and benefits in human terms nor in devising effective responses to the physical effects of social, environmental, economic, and political forces that shape city regions. We believe that inventories and assessments of existing assets, followed by analyses of the paths that led to the existing development patterns, are crucial for the effective management of city regions. We hope this effort by scholars from around the world motivates more work on such topics.

PART 1

Assumptions and Objectives

1 Introduction

Roger Simmonds and Gary Hack

CHANGING URBAN STRUCTURE

Most urban regions around the world have experienced dramatic change during the twentieth century. They have grown in size and population, in many cases spectacularly so, but they have also changed their economies, population character, and spatial form. This book is concerned with these "structural" changes in city regions around the world at the end of the century.

What cities are becoming will in large measure determine what they can be like. But we take it as a premise that, within limits, citizens can create the cities of their choice. Much of the data in the following chapters is evidence for this. Cities are, after all, remarkably varied in their form and character. They will only continue to be, however, if citizens and urbanists understand and work effectively with the forces and trends which are prevailing.

GLOBALISM AND REGIONAL CHANGE

In this book, the significant unit of study is the "city region" defined by the spatial extent of closely linked economic activity, rather than the "city", or jurisdictional definition of the settlement. Most city regions contain dozens, hundreds or even thousands of political subdivisions. Nonetheless, city regions are becoming a new political force out of necessity. Many of the problems which settlements face call for region-wide policies and coordinated action across many jurisdictions.

Globalization has had much to do with the growth in the potency of regions. The end of the nation state is often exaggerated, but throughout the world national governments have ceded much of their control over capital flows across their frontiers, and in the process have diminished their influence over the location of new investment. Motorization, the emergence of branding on a global scale, the spread of international symbols of affluence and pleasure, and the widespread adoption of land-extensive development forms such as the production line factory, the shopping center and single family housing subdivisions, have all been made possible, or have been aided on their way, by international capital flows and the lowering of trade barriers.

Central city governments, usually have limited capacity to enlarge their boundaries, and they have seen their influence wane as an increased fraction of economic activity takes place beyond city lines. The new anchors of regional development—airports and their peripheral development, new universities and associated science parks, recreational theme parks, wholesale marketing areas, and even new office and financial centers—are often located on the urbanizing fringe. Cities have become the sprawling, formless conurbations forecast by Mumford, Gottman, Doxiadis, and dozens of other prognosticators half a century ago.

In a few regions of the world, national or state governments have sought to align the boundaries of urban governments with the extent of the built-up urban area, or have created special authorities for particular urban functions that have jurisdiction across local government boundaries. In many more countries there is a devolution of responsibilities to local and regional governments, creating new patterns of planning and of delivering infrastructure and services. There is much to be gained by reviewing the results of these efforts, and by revisiting the efforts at regional planning in many more cities around the world. The spatial reality of regional cities, fueled by global trends, demands new forms of governance and management.

RAPID GROWTH AND CHANGE

Much of the rhetoric of urbanism through the twentieth century has focused on the huge growth rates of land occupancy and population in city regions. "Stemming the flood tide of urbanization" has been the call to action of dozens of national urban policies. But in most parts of the world, high growth rates are a symbol of the success rather than the failure of urban areas. By casting off traditional cultural accommodations, and installing new forms of social and economic institutions and infrastructure, cities became attractive magnets to those struggling in the countryside. And, as we shall argue later, it is far more productive to ask how the forces of modernization can be directed to improving the form of regional cities than to limit their growth by diverting activity elsewhere.

The technologies of economic modernization carry with them a preference for urban forms. First the telephone, then the motorized vehicle, more recently electronic communication—each altered the necessities of location. But none broke the bonds of urbanization entirely by eliminating the need for cities. The result, instead, has been a spread of urban functions over wide geographic regions. The traditional nineteenth century city remains, but as a specialist component, often for entertainment and consumption rather than as a zone of industrial production.

A NEW URBAN EPOCH

Now, at the end of the century, most urbanists and influential social scientists working in the field argue that we are in the midst of another period of dramatic structural change that will transform cities just as surely as industrialization and its artifacts. But there is little agreement about what will emerge to take the place of what we now call cities.

Ulrick Beck,[1] speaking of the experience in the West, argues that we know only that we are immersed in a moment of change and that the old institutions under which we have lived have largely collapsed or been transformed. This feeling is most clearly revealed in our use of the term "post-" to describe the present condition. We live in the "post-industrial city", with a culture of "post-modernism", under the regime of a political economy often called "post-Fordism". The urbanist Edward Soja[2] has recently coined the phrase "post metropolis" to describe the city region of today. At least, from the point of view of the practitioner, we know what we are not but we do not yet know what we are or where we are going.

The purpose of this book is to bring the evidence of recent history to bear on the search for new paradigms for understanding and managing urban growth and development. Few revolutions occur without advance warning, and in many the broad outlines could be discerned by observing closely the circumstances before the change. By looking carefully at how cities, spread across four continents, have evolved in recent decades, and by keeping a special eye out for consistencies, the direction of change can become clearer.

It remains to be seen whether change will come as a radical departure from the forms of cities we now know, or as simply an acceleration of processes currently under way. But in at least one sense the current moment differs from the past: cities throughout the world are facing the same forces of change at the same moment in history. The variation of today's cities speaks to the fact that they evolved on their own time scale, within a unique condition of national events and the national economy, and with local cultural traditions in the forefront. Today instantaneous communications leave no city isolated from global cultural and economic forces. Yet each region brings its own particular strategies and mix of advantages and disadvantages to the global marketplace, and is likely to benefit and be affected in different ways. But most of all, and for the first time, this is a shared moment of change.

AIMS AND CONTENT

The aim of this book is to take stock of what has been happening to the socio-economic and spatial structure of a selection of urban regions around the world over the past 30 years, and to identify the underlying societal dynamics. The book takes two main forms:

- Detailed analyses of the evolving form of 11 city regions, compiled by teams of the Global Cities Consortium in each of the regions.
- Essays by knowledgeable observers of urbanization, technological and social trends.

The book is the product of two international symposia given by members of the Global Cities Consortium[3] and invited experts. Each symposium focused on one phase of data assembly and analysis by the consortium.

City regions selected for the consortium and included in this volume are indicative of urban conditions around the globe, rather than a carefully crafted representative sample. They have been chosen to reflect a range of population sizes (from less than 3 million to 32 million), levels of income (from lower income countries to the wealthiest), and ages (from old European settlements to the newly emerging cities). Three (Bangkok, Taipei, and Tokyo) are in Asia, but all are industrial cities or rapidly becoming so. Three are in Europe, one a strongly centered city (Madrid) and two of them multi-city conurbations (the Randstad, Holland, and the West Midlands, UK). The three North American examples include one of the oldest cities on the continent (Boston), and twentieth century cities (Seattle and San Diego). The two South American cities (Santiago and São Paolo) are sprawling metropolitan areas in the most advanced countries.

However, in other senses, the 11 regions were selected because they conformed to certain specifications. Each global city region:

- Is diverse economically—no single industry cities such as free-standing national capitals, resort cities, or resource-based cities.

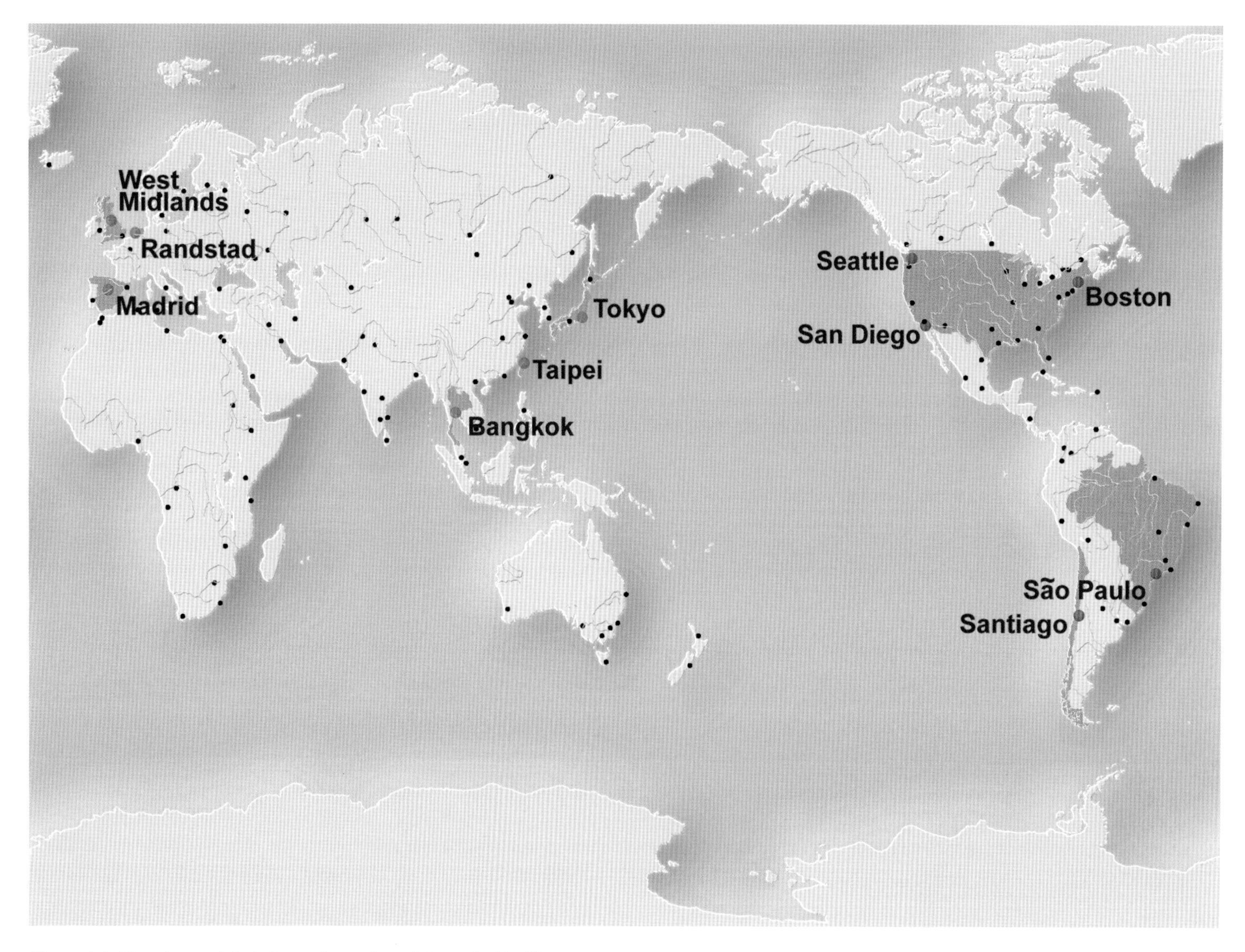

Figure 1.1 The eleven global city regions, viewed from the Pacific

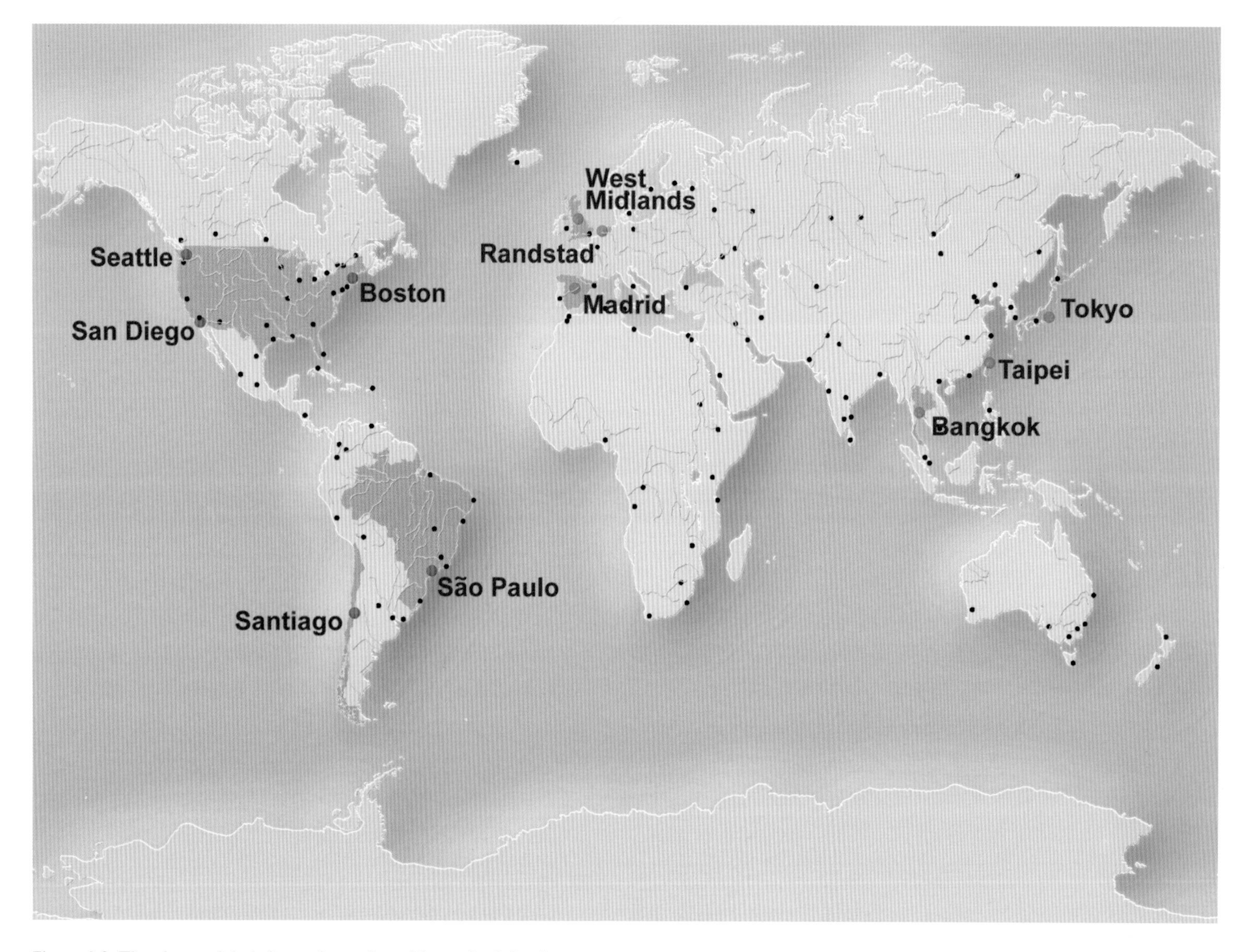

Figure 1.2 The eleven global city regions, viewed from the Atlantic

- Is undergoing economic transformation—either developing a manufacturing economy for the first time, or shifting to a service economy.
- Has experienced significant growth over the past two decades—no declining cities.
- Has developed in a country with a significant private sector economy—no socialist cities or tightly controlled economies.
- Has a history of attempts to deal with regional form and development.

In selecting the regions, there was also an attempt to reach out beyond those cities with well documented experiences in regional planning and development—Paris, London, New York among them—to enlarge the field of knowledge. These three regions are discussed, to some extent, in the following chapter.

Part 2 of the book contains 11 chapters which describe the evolution of each of the 11 city regions over a 30 year period, from 1965 to 1995. As far as possible, the information covers the complete city region, extending to the limits of the linked urban area. Data on key social, economic, and spatial indicators are presented at 10 year intervals. The accompanying narrative describes and interprets the policies and action programs of relevant agencies in the city region over the same time periods.

The information on the 11 regions is intended to allow the reader to make comparisons between them and between them and their own region and, in the process, form conclusions about several important questions:

- What evidence do we find for the general claim that most city regions have been passing through a moment of shared discontinuity or rapid transformation during this 30 year period?
- What trends, if any, can we discover in the changing social, economic and physical form of city regions around the world?
- Is a new kind of human settlement emergent?

Some of these questions are addressed in Part 3, which follows the 11 chapters. The evolving physical form of the cities has been compared along a number of relevant dimensions, including density, dispersal and location of major groups in the city. The cultures of governance and regional management have been similarly examined, bearing in mind the broad differences in cultural influences which have a profound bearing on political organization.

Finally, Part 4 includes a variety of essays, some interpretive, others provocative, on the subject of change in global city regions. These cover the interrelated questions of how the global economy affects urban prospects, technologies and their impacts on urban transport and urban form, the advantages of compact as opposed to distributed city forms, and the wider issue of city space and cyberspace.

Global cities are inevitably also regional cities. The ties between globalism and regionalism are, as we said earlier, the central preoccupation of this book.

NOTES

1. Ulrich Beck, *Risk Society: Towards a New Modernity* (English Language version), London: Sage, 1992.
2. Edward W. Soja, "Six Discourses on the Post Metropolis", in S. Westwood and J. Williams (eds), *Imagining Cities*, London: Routledge, 1997.
3. The first Global Cities Symposium was sponsored by the Lincoln Institute of Land Policy and held in Cambridge MA in September 1995. Gary Hack, Roger Simmonds, and David Barkin acted as chairpersons. Representatives of 12 city regions and other invited speakers gave presentations. The second symposium was held in El Escorial, Spain, in July 1997. It was sponsored by the Comunidad de Madrid (the autonomous regional government of Madrid), the Lincoln Institute of Land Policy, and the Universidad Complutense. Pedro Ortiz and Roger Simmonds acted as chairpersons. Representatives of the 11 city regions and other invited speakers gave presentations.

2 Planning the city region

A short history of Western practice

Roger Simmonds and Gary Hack

Though the character of city regions and their political context have changed dramatically over the last century, the aims of Western governments, with the exception of one brief period in the 1960s, have remained remarkably constant. None the less there has been an ongoing debate between two ways of thinking about city regions: between various "radical" models which have wanted to see the city region as a new type of human settlement and a "conservative" model which wanted to retain much of the earlier integrity of city regions as hierarchies of relatively free-standing and self-sufficient settlements clustered around a major urban core; the dominant paradigm. It is a complex ongoing debate and each of us has taken different sides of it in our time. Previously, the debate was much more heated in Europe than in the United States, where, until recently, the issue of the social or built form of regions has not generated much interest. In the United States each local community has spread at will and there was no strong pattern of existing local centers to be engulfed or protected. Today all this has changed and regional "growth management" has become a major public preoccupation in the United States.

The term "regional planning" is often used in the English-speaking world to refer to attempts by governments, national or provincial, to manage the growth and form of regions, which may be more or less intensely urbanized, usually to achieve more general social and economic ends. But "regional planning" is also used to refer to a potentially quite different set of practices; namely, efforts by national governments to even the spread of wealth throughout the country. Often this has involved infrastructure investments designed to enable weak regions to compete with strong ones, incentives to employers to move from strong to weak regions, restrictions on the growth of strong regions, and so on.

"Regional planning" became a term referring to both kinds of activity because, in the earliest examples, they were deeply interconnected. In Europe, at least, both were generally carried out by the same central government agency. As time has passed they have become much less connected, as various forms of regional government have emerged to take over regional management. At the same time national governments have been forced to recognize the importance of having at least one strong economic region which can compete in the global economy. The uneven spread of wealth within a given country is, thus, often accepted today as a cost which must be paid in the achievement of this aim. Our focus in this book is planning the global city region, whether or not it is linked with achieving a more even distribution of wealth across a national geography.

Another common term since the middle of the century, and overlapping with the focus of this book, is "metropolitan planning". The defining characteristic of the "metropolis" was considered to be the movement patterns of workers. The pattern was assumed to be radial, from the periphery to the center, or centers, where the jobs were located. The metropolis was invariably defined by some form of "commuter shed", including all those villages, suburbs and surrounding towns which sent more than a certain proportion of its residents to work in the main centers of employment. Today there would be no point in defining what we are calling the "city region" in this way in the West because the major employers are scattered across the region and the movement pattern of workers is much more complex. To avoid confusion with earlier definitions of the "metropolis", we also avoid using the term in these introductory chapters, except in a historical sense. However, it is still in good currency in many quarters, and we defer to others' use of it in the book.

We use the term "city region" because it is more neutral and carries less historical baggage. It does, however, raise considerable difficulties of boundary definition. Most of the 11 regions in Part II are based on boundaries which are historical or which have been drawn recently for pragmatic reasons to facilitate the management of the nation state. The detailed city region studies ahead are focused on the main urbanized area within these administrative regions, defining the boundaries of the "city region" informally in terms of the level of economic activity contained within it.[1]

As this book is about attempts to manage or plan these city regions, we are often forced into looking at plans made by the governments of geographic entities which do not coincide with the urbanized region we are interested in.

Sometimes, however, national governments have set up commissions to study these denser areas of interaction and make recommendations specifically about them. In some locations this area has come to have its own political system with elected councilors—the so called "Metro Model" pioneered in France in the late 1960s. Other regional systems, particularly in the United States, tend to take the form of councils of governments (or COGs) to which the independent municipalities of the region send representatives. In the Seattle region all elected municipal members also automatically become members of the regional COG. Greater London moved from being the subject of a government commission, to being run by the Greater London Council (a Metro Model), to being a COG (after the GLC was abolished in 1985), and its government is now being redefined once again. The story of the West Midlands (UK) ahead is very similar. It shows the great importance which the public has begun to attach to this subject in the last 30 years.

EARLY PRACTICE

The Berlin city region had clearly defined boundaries and an administrative structure by 1905, but the first comprehensive plan for a modern city region appears to have been the 1909 plan of Chicago. It was prepared by Daniel Burnham and Edward Bennett, some 15 years after the World Columbian Exposition had created aspirations for the City Beautiful. Drawing upon a host of European examples of parks and boulevards, and laced with the pragmatics of reorganizing railroads and accommodating motorized vehicles, it promoted a regional vision of the city, extending well beyond its political boundaries. A remarkable illustration in the front piece to the plan, drawn by Jules Guerin well before it was possible to see the city from the air, illustrates a 200 square mile region: "Bird's Eye View, Showing the Location of the City on the Shores of Lake Michigan, together with the smaller Surrounding Towns connected with Chicago by radiating Arteries" (Figure 2.1).

The difficulty proved not to be the vision but the political accommodations necessary to carry out plans

Figure 2.1 The 1909 plan for Chicago and its region. ***Illustration*** **Jules Guerin**

such as this for city regions. Aspects of the Chicago plan which were carried out were the park system, through the creation of a new special district (with taxation powers), and eventually building regulation and infrastructure planning under the banner of the Chicago Plan Commission, another new entity. The Regional Plan for New York and its Environs, published in 1931, suffered a similar fate: its accomplishments were the result of many entities acting together, rather than of the creation of a single multipurpose entity capable of carrying out the plan. The Regional Plan Association of New York and New Jersey remains an important advocacy group, and has published two subsequent plans updating the vision for the region, but it has no official powers.

By the end of the Second World War, four decades after the Chicago plan, there were still only about 10 regional city governments in place in the West, most of which were run as commissions of central governments. Now, at the end of the century, there are perhaps 150 regional city planning and management entities in place around the world, with a great variety of structures and powers.

H. van der Camman,[2] on the basis of studies of regional plans drawn up for Paris, London, the Ruhr, and the Randstad in the 1930s, suggests that their aims can be grouped under three headings:

- To carry out programs of reconstruction and rationalization to prevent the exploding nineteenth/early twentieth century city from destroying itself.
- To prevent the larger and faster-growing city regions, often the national capitals, from drawing investment and workers away from other regions of the country, thus creating large wealth differentials between one part of the country and another.

- To ensure that the national resources which were put into the fast-growing city region were coordinated and used efficiently.

Much of this thinking took place during the Depression, when there was little pressure from development and this may explain how it is that city regions with very different powers and administrative systems in Europe ended up with very similar strategies for how to achieve their aims. In broad terms these were:

- Reduce congestion in the urban center by reducing the density of housing and rationalizing land uses into distinct land use zones.
- Build a system of major new roads, including one or two orbitals, to manage the shift of activity, especially freight, from rail to road and to reduce the traffic going through the center.
- Most regions in Europe had some notion of constraining further peripheral growth by introducing some kind of a green belt or green girdle on the fringe.
- Deal with the huge projected population overspill by building new and expanded towns beyond the current city limits and the green belt, if one was proposed.

The most extensively implemented of these plans were those for the London region of 1943 and 1944 by Patrick Abercrombie. This esentially "conservative" paradigm remained unchallenged as a model of good practice until 1965, when the master plan for the Paris region emerged.

The Abercrombie plans adopted the strategies just mentioned, including an orbital, not built for 30 years, and a green belt. Beyond that, they appear to have been inspired in part by the desire to conserve and recreate the regional landscape inherited from an earlier historical period. It was a landscape whose spatial logic could have been summed up in its time by Central Place Theory, with an attempt to create a hierarchy of free-standing settlements around a central core. The main characteristics of the plan were that London would be virtually recreated by turning it from a mononuclear to a polynuclear region of relatively autonomous physical "communities". The overspill population would be taken in free-standing and largely self-sufficient new towns, located beyond the green belt and 25 miles from the edge of the city region as it then existed.

The plans had three other key ingredients. One was the belief that the emergence of "community" depends in large part on a settlement being identifiable in space—in this case by being surrounded by open countryside wherever possible. A second ingredient was the belief that it should be possible to create settlements which were functionally semi-autonomous, as indeed were the towns of a previous epoch, without the tendency for them to specialize and thus become functionally interdependent with other towns in the region. A last ingredient appears to have its origins in the garden city movement at the beginning of the century. This movement developed complex ideas about how settlements could be designed to contain the best qualities of traditional "town" and "country". Over time these ideas became embodied in quite simple government policies which were aimed at little more than guaranteeing residents of urban settlements access to the countryside. This was often achieved through limiting the size of settlements, preventing settlements merging together and ensuring that new settlements were freestanding in countryside and not tacked onto existing areas, unless these happened to be very small.

At the same time as these more deliberate European efforts to plan the city region, the federal government and state highway departments in the United States, where car ownership levels were much higher than in Europe, had programs to build relief roads and orbitals which eventually became linked into a national expressway grid. These were to have a great impact on the eventual built form of regions. In 1955 the state of Massachusetts laid out and built the now famous Route 128. Its main purpose was to divert traffic between Maine and points south from passing through the center of Boston. The road was heavily criticized at the time—called by one well known commentator "the road to nowhere".

Yet Route 128 opened up cheap land to the national highway grid and it remained cheap because towns along it competed with each other to attract investment. This plentiful land, close to the suburban housing areas and connected to high level financial services downtown and to a local technical university, Massachusetts Institute of Technology, became the focus of an electronics-based employment boom, the so-called "Massachusetts Miracle" of the late 1980s. Once Route 128 was full, development leapfrogged 20 miles out to the next Boston orbital, Interstate 495 (see Figure 4.1). This is, of course, a common story in the United States and Europe, but maybe the story and the lessons drawn from it became so closely associated with Boston because of the startling transformation of the region within a few years from industrial wasteland to electronics-based boom region.

The prime lesson, of course, was that where transport infrastructure is laid down, especially where there are junctions, development will eventually follow, whether or not it is formally contained in land use plans. Several regional plans of the same period used investment in mass transit as a major organizing structure for the region. The best examples are probably Stockholm, Perth, and Toronto. This idea is currently going through a substantial revival, most notably through the work of Peter Calthorpe in California, where "transit-oriented development" (TOD) is offered in reaction to formless automobile sprawl.

Because of the huge and initially unintended impact of national road investment programs on the location of development in a region, the US federal government tried to package its transport grants in such a way as to aid in the realization of the growth strategies of the towns it impacted. At the same time, the aim was to ensure that efficiencies and cost savings in better coordinated road building, transit building, etc., could be diverted to pay for local programs which required modest physical development of some kind. The better known examples have been the Tri State Transport Commission in the New York region, and the Boston Transportation and Planning Review of the mid 1970s.

Eventually, the federal government attached a requirement that, before federal funds could be spent on regional infrastructure, some form of regional entity must be created to review and coordinate it with local programs and other regional initiatives. These agencies have been the seeds from which a more substantial regional administrative system is growing in the United States. This is particularly the case on the west coast, where the San Diego and Seattle regional administrations, discussed in Part II, are particularly interesting examples.

The majority of these early regional planning initiatives in Europe were based on a single old industrial city expanding into its hinterland, with governments often making plans to turn the region from a mononuclear to a polynuclear structure, as discussed. We should not leave this chapter, however, without recognizing that there has been another version of this process most clearly revealed in the planning associated with the Ruhr in Germany, the Randstad in Holland, and the West Midlands Region of the UK. All three regions were made up of a number of largely independent cities and small towns, which were seen to be growing in interdependence to form a larger polycentric whole. The early initiatives in all three regions, however, were not so much to grasp creatively the emergence of this new whole and make plans and programs for its emergence as to protect the integrity of the existing settlements. Just like the other early European plans, they were "defensive" in their objectives and still tend to be so.

It is interesting to compare the changing forms of the Madrid region and the Randstad over the past 30 years. Madrid, once a classic monocentric region, has exploded into being polynuclear (see Figure 5.1). The Randstad, originally an agglomeration of independent towns and cities, has become more of an integrated whole (see Figure 6.1). The result is that in broad outline they have grown to be surprisingly similar. Because the major green zones of the Randstad, however, are in the center (the Green Heart) and those of the Madrid region are on the periphery, one is in a sense the obverse of the other.

A NEW KIND OF SETTLEMENT

The 1965 master plan for what had then become officially the Paris Region represents a bold break with the aims and practices of earlier planning in Europe. It was also given the kind of support from the French government which was needed to translate planning ideas into a vigorous program of action on the ground.

The master plan, while following many of the earlier programs, discussed above, adopted the attitude that the city region should be thought about as a new kind of human settlement or, at the least, should be planned to allow a new kind of social and economic settlement to emerge. In contrast to the conservative and defensive character of earlier thinking, it was radical and open-ended and it took the offensive.

The aims of the plan for the Paris Region[3] were:

- To prepare the region of Paris for its future.
- To shape it into a more efficient economic tool, by meeting the needs of industry and the new service sector.
- To bring about the unity of the urban region by providing a transport infrastructure which meant that "any necessary journey" was possible.
- To highlight the region's established beauty and to create new beauty.

It continued to believe in the policies of deconcentration, contained in all earlier plans, proposing the following strategies for action:

- Build seven new towns intended to take 3 million of the projected overspill population. The new towns which were eventually built have become the best known feature of the master plan, if not its most successful.
- Continue with the reduction of residential and industrial employment densities in the center of Paris and the upgrading of historical infrastructure.
- Given the complex and changed lifestyles of Parisians, provide maximum choice of residence, work, leisure, and culture. The result has been the best regional transport system in the world: 500 km of motorway

have been built, including 11 radials and two orbitals, a regional express system, the extension of the existing metro to the suburbs and upgrading of the surface rail system. It is interesting that there was so little planning for air transport in such a far-sighted and transport-oriented plan.

- Create a range, not really thought of as a hierarchy, of different centers. Some would be the centers of the new towns, others, like La Défense, would be created independently outside the traditional urban center. Smaller centers were expected to grow close to the orbitals and form new suburban centers of some substance.

The effect would be to transform the Paris Region from being monocentered to multicentered. Earlier plans, particularly the Abercrombie plans for London, were clearly antimetropolitan, in the sense of being preoccupied with disaggregation and the self-sufficiency of the parts. The Master Plan for Paris was pro-metropolitan in the sense that it was concerned with integration and specialization of the parts. The city region would grow as an integrated whole settlement. The new towns, for example, are major extensions of the existing built-up area not loosely connected and largely self-sufficient small satellites, 25 miles away across a green belt, as the London and Randstad new towns were at the time.

At the same time, the 1965 plan took quite a different approach to social change. The plan would provide citizens with maximum choice out of which new, and as yet unpredicted, social forms were expected to grow. This also contrasted with the Abercrombie plans, where the attempt was to re-engineer "traditional community" through physical planning.

The ideas contained in the 1965 Master Plan for Paris became the dominant approach in the West to planning the city region and it was the platform from which earlier plans, like the Abercrombie plan for London, were fiercely attacked. The creation of the Paris Region, later to be called the Ile de France Region, with its own directly elected government, was also a model copied by many countries in Europe. Well known examples were the creation of the metropolitan counties in the UK, including the Greater London Council and the West Midlands (sometimes known as the Birmingham region), which is described in Chapter 13. Madrid is another example from the chapters ahead. The Paris plan inspired a brief period in which most Western countries expected what often came to be called the "regional city" to become a recognizably different kind of human settlement, with its own institutions, political structures, and modes of social control (including, of course, land use planning). For many urbanists at the time, the late nineteenth and early twentieth century city was dead. "Long live the regional city."

The same kind of radical optimism appears in the book *Explorations into Urban Structure*.[4] It reflected the leading edge of academic thought when it was published in 1964, a year before the Paris plan. It contributed to breaking the mold of thinking about the city and its region. First it criticized the tendency to dwell on the city as a physical object and focused attention on the social and economic form of cities in general. Then, in the famous chapter by Melvin Webber, "The Urban Place and the Non-place Urban Realm", the book put forward the claim that the social and economic form of cities, facilitated by new forms of transport and communications, was going through such a radical transformation that one could only conclude that a new type of human settlement was emerging.

An Anglo-American conference held in 1964, whose proceedings were published in a book, *The Regional City*,[5] took this last claim as its premise. Derek Senior, the editor of the book, says of it, "the assumption behind this seminar is that the urban region represents a new form of civilization, with its own distinct possibilities and problems." Peter Self at the conference argued "the urban framework has continued to become still broader and more loose jointed, to rest on greater mobility, and to entail further specialization of activities. Some consider that a new environment for our civilization, which may be called the 'urban region', is in the making."

POST-OIL CRISIS REVISIONISM IN THE WEST

The 11 chapters in Part 2 begin their comparative maps and social and economic indicators around 1960, just before the Paris plan was started. The chapters on the six Western regions ahead thus take up the story in greater detail from 1965 on. However, this important date is quickly followed in many commentators' minds by something which is critical for understanding practices in the West during the last 30 years of the century. The oil crises of the 1970s and the recurrent economic recessions which accompanied them led to a substantial revision in the attitudes of urbanists and, in time, to a return to conservative paradigms in the West. Suddenly it seemed clear that the huge growth projections which were made in the 1960s for large city regions would not now happen. People from the inner cities continued to leave for the suburbs in large numbers, often following employment by this time, but the real difference was that very few people or companies were moving into the old centers to replace them. Suddenly, the task was less one of how to accommodate hordes of people being relocated from overcrowded urban centers than one of the threatened collapse of these urban centers through depopulation and disinvestment.

This exodus of population was accompanied by a number of other serious problems for cities. In the 1970s national and local governments in the West began to lose the little power they had to shield local companies from the full blast of global competition. And by the 1980s in the United States, in particular, "global trade" had become the prevailing ideology. At the same time, changes in political support for location "subsidies" and the changing demands of productivity forced many local companies into closure and forced others to seek the most cost effective locations they could for their businesses. Those whose work force could afford personal transport moved out to new and cheaper sites close to the new expressway systems. With them went a significant section of the major retailing which had once dominated downtown activity. This trend increased to a flood through the prosperous 1980s, increasing the crisis of most old city centers.

For the first time, growth on the periphery was seen to be not just bad for the countryside but for the old city centers as well. It was a moment in the United Kingdom when the "unholy alliance" which had long existed between the country landowners on the right of the Conservative Party, who wanted to prevent development in the countryside, and the left wing of the Labour Party, who wanted to divert investment to the inner cities, was never stronger. The first rumblings about the "cost of sprawl" began to emerge at the same time as awareness of the impact of automobiles on air quality.

But they were only rumblings. The crisis of the inner cities was so severe that governments began to focus solely on the inner city problem. Earlier schemes of "urban renewal", involving demolition and rebuild, had been unpopular and, anyway, there were no funds now for such ambitious projects. A new design paradigm had been emerging which valued the traditional city, and in the English-speaking world a new paraprofessional, the "urban designer", emerged to translate these sentiments into a set of practices for urban regeneration.

An important dimension of these regeneration practices became the involvement of employers and residents of neighborhoods in decision making and active rehabilitation on the grounds that this involvement gave them a stake in the area and encouraged them to stay and make it their operational base or home. The Model Cities Program in the US and other programs in Holland and Germany became recognized good practice, and they have since been widely adopted by other Western countries. Along with the grass roots organizations formed in the so-called "environmental movement", they became the seeds from which a much wider movement towards participatory government in cities and the building of "social capital" at the local level has now emerged.

In the process, the traditional late nineteenth and early twentieth century city became desirable again and even a model for new settlements. Central government money, although limited, was applied to recuperating the city. In this environment the idea of the "regional city" became less important. The idea of the Randstad, for example, fell from favor and the Dutch began talking again of south-western Holland as little more than a carefully conserved hierarchy of traditional cities, towns and villages.

At this time also the UK government heaved a huge collective sigh of relief that it would not now have to spend the vast amount of money on infrastructure for the London region which the French had spent on Paris a decade earlier. However, in 1985 the Ministry of Transport finally made the decision to build, in the green belt, the M25 London Orbital, which it has been widening ever since. At the same time, however, the UK government disbanded the metropolitan counties, which had been inspired by the Paris experiment. The stated grounds, though there were others, were that they were inefficient and their land use plans drove up the prices of land and other essentials, rendering the region unable to compete for new investment with independent towns and districts. There was very little protest at the time.

France's own city regions faced the same kind of crisis. But the French government persisted with its directly elected regional governments and with the spirit of the 1965 master plan for the Paris Region. Its scale was greatly reduced, however, and there was a sharp move from government-led to market-led programs of action:

- The number of new towns was reduced from seven to five and the population expected to live in them was reduced from 3 million to 1 million.
- The new centers would now include only La Défense and the new towns. Other centers would be allowed to emerge as US-style shopping malls at major transport interchanges.
- Three radial motorways were dropped and the planned number of lanes on the others was halved.
- The regional underground express trains were forced to run on existing tracks wherever possible.
- Added to the plan were the "Zones of Natural Balance", a conveniently less expensive but significant program to manage the countryside and wilderness areas beyond the built-up areas.

CURRENT THINKING

The 1980s building booms reawakened public and professional interest in the periphery, where "growth management", in the 1990s, became a key phrase in the language of modern urbanism. In the 1980s offices also began to desert the central city, and two-thirds of all new office space in the United States was built on the fringe, while the peripheral centers attracted a vast amount of new manufacturing investment. New "edge cities", often bigger than the original central city area, and usually outside the control of existing city governments, emerged in about a 10 year time span.

The building booms of the late 1980s and the sprawling edge cities produced by them resulted in, for most professional urbanists at least, a new attachment to the old urban centers, now recognized to be in fierce competition with these new areas and with each other for the limited amount of government and international investment. Some centers grew spectacularly, like Boston's (see Chapter 4), providing financial services to the vastly increased number of companies on the periphery and entertainment for an increasingly prosperous and sophisticated regional population. In the dash to create or conserve a distinctive image in the name of creating cultural continuity with the past, and in the hope of drawing in international and regional tourists, traditional townscapes have been preserved and commodified. This has involved the conservation of old buildings and the production of strict design codes and design guidelines, largely to ensure that new build reflects the essence of local traditional townscape. In this way some old urban centers have moved from being what Sharon Zukin[6] calls "centers of organized production" to become "centers of organized consumption". As the public and private managers of these districts learn their techniques from the entertainment industry these districts increasingly evoke the practices and ethos of the "theme park".[7] In this way the theme park, an urban form type which first emerged on the periphery, has been successfully imported into traditional centers.

In spite of these invasions, the traditional nineteenth and early twentieth century city, that object of conservation and commodification in the downtown areas, was increasingly being held up as the model of how new settlements should be designed on the periphery. At the scale of the region, though not at the scale of building and street design, where he favored "modernist" layouts, Patrick Abercrombie and his Greater London plans of 1943 and 1944, so vilified in the 1960s and early 1970s under the influence of the Paris plan, were once again the models of good practice.

FUTURE ISSUES

Ironically, it is two issues that have dogged planners throughout the century which have again attracted public attention to regional development. The first is congestion—not the inner city congestion that motivated earlier decentralization plans, but today's suburban congestion. Suburbanites find themselves stuck in traffic moving between suburbs, and the spread of activities at the regional scale creates a nearly insoluble problem. Roadway infrastructure between outlying activity centers is badly lacking and is extraordinarily costly to construct. Most cities have no effective circumferential transit systems. Today the residents of outlying areas are forcing discussion of regional issues, and in many cities new regional plans begin with the issue of this new kind of congestion relief as a central theme.

While the London new towns, 25 miles away across a green belt, may have achieved the quality of semi-autonomy imagined for them, this does not appear to be true of subcenters which have been designed or emerged spontaneously closer to the main transport infrastructures on the periphery. Here there is evidence of new kinds of specialist areas, often building around information-intensive activities, emerging and being planned—like "just-in-time production zones" near the airport, technopoles or planned science cities close to a technical university or government research institute, entertainment districts close to a major theme park, business districts near the airport or on the airport road to the city, wholesale and distribution districts, media production districts, etc. The data ahead will give us some idea how much evidence there is for these claims. If they are justified, it will go some way to explaining the congestion on the urban fringe, because the specialist areas will, inevitably, be generating movement between each other. We already know that the spread of employment into suburban areas has greatly contributed to this congestion, at least during the rush hours, as people try to move back and forth across the region rather than in and out of the old metropolitan center(s).

There is evidence here that the modern city region is generating the desire for grid-like movement patterns, in contrast to the radial forms of most transport systems, which were built in response to the radial patterns of movement of the past. Largely in response to this problem, but also so that the London subcenters can be accessible to a wider public, enabling them to specialize and survive economically, the latest plan for the London region is seeking to transform its radially and hierarchically structured rail system into a net. It aims to achieve this by taking trains, which previously terminated at some 12 stations on the edge of the inner city, through the center in tunnels and out to the other side of the city region. The latest plan for the Madrid region seeks to transform its hierarchical and radially structured road system into a net for similar reasons. This is discussed in Chapter 21.

The second ascendant issue is the effect of urbanization on the regional environment, also not a new topic. The early regional plans of the 1920s were motivated by the need to secure regional open space, and protect regional watersheds, and in many cities these remain motivating factors. But there is a wider movement today aimed at ensuring environmental sustainability on a regional scale. Many city regions, the San Francisco Bay Area among them, have used "sustainability" as a wedge into broader questions of development form and character.

The question of how specialized new regional nuclei are becoming also impinges on the theme of sustainable regional form. It has generally been accepted that a region made up of semi-autonomous, relatively dense, and free-standing towns, as advocated by Abercrombie, is the most sustainable regional form. Now critics are beginning to examine this claim a little more closely. If the free-standing settlements are not semi-autonomous but specialist, a growing tendency, then this is not a sustainable form in regions where car ownership levels are high, because it will generate car trips accross open land between all the specialist centers. Indeed, under such conditions the conservative model might turn out to be highly "unsustainable". In the cases ahead it is clear that alternative built form policies are beginning to be advocated today on congestion and sustainability grounds, including the idea of the "regional net", already discussed, and the "growth corridor", under serious consideration by the UK government. In this sense the running debate throughout the century between what we called at the beginning the "conservative" and the "radical" attitudes to macro urban form is far from settled.

Environmental policies have widespread public appeal throughout most developed countries, and even in less developed countries practical necessities such as the prevention of flooding, groundwater pollution, subsidence and landslides have elevated sustainability to an important plane. Another event to compound this theme, and relating to policies for achieving sustainable open space, has been the industrialization of agriculture. Providing access to a countryside of craft-based farming production has been a major theme of the "conservative" model in Europe, though it is only a shadow of the ideas originally advocated in the garden city movement, as discussed. But guaranteed access to the industrialized landscapes of agribusiness is not such an attractive option. In place of such policies we find local groups today advocating much more vigorous programs of linked regional scale public open space. Industrialized agriculture, is contributing to this by producing the surplus-to-needs land on which such open space programs will depend, even in Europe, where the Common Agricultural Policy has considerably slowed down the impact of agricultural industrialization. This increasing amount of "green" public open space appears to suffer from underinvestment all over the world and awaits, perhaps, new forms of participatory management by local people. Meanwhile, most global city regions have become patchworks of bits of urban development interspersed with bits of poorly maintained open land, as the chapters ahead will show The main exception to this trend is where the old craft-based countrysides have been subjected to the same kind of conservation programs which have been popular in traditional urban areas in the West.

Another quite different set of pressures on regional governments in the West is being generated by high-profile social scientists with a special interest in urban settlements. Their claims, almost without exception, are that a new urban epoch, global in its scope, is in the making. This new epoch is resulting in new forms of urban management and production. Theorists from different disciplines and traditions, however, disagree about the nature of this change and how great a transformation it represents. For Manuel Castells,[8] for example, the transformation to an "informational" mode of production in industrial and service sector activity is quite as profound as the earlier shift to "industrial" modes of production early in the nineteenth century in Europe and North America. For David Harvey,[9] focusing on the change from one form of capitalism to another, this moment ranks as one of the two major moments of transformation in the history of capitalism. At the same time sociologists like Ulrich Beck[10] and Anthony Giddens[11] define their own versions of this moment of transformation. They focus on processes of ongoing institutional construction and deconstruction, for example in response to globalization or perceptions of the environmental crisis, leading to a new era of "reflexive" or "high" modernity.

Writers like Beck and Giddens are often popular with urbanists because they seem to offer a mature way of overcoming the latent "scientism" which has dogged conventional urbanism for so long and yet leave the conventional technical role model of urbanism itself surprisingly untouched. Much more difficult for urbanists to digest have been the proclamations of "postmodern" thinkers about the city. Edward Soja, in his *Six Discourses on the Post Metropolis*,[12] opens up a more complex set of questions for urbanists to deal with—including how to respond to the ever expanding pluralism of contemporary societies and the way this threatens to undo at every turn the initiatives and programs which traditional urbanism would like to put on the table.

How regional governments and politicians respond to these different claims by social scientists will depend a great deal on the climate of the times. The Paris plan of 1965 was, to a significant extent, a creature of its time. It emerged at a moment of optimism about the future. It was also a time, like the present, when claims were being made about major structural changes taking place in social and economic practices. In a period of relative prosperity and confidence, the Paris planners took a particularly bold and open-ended stance to the future. The conservatism of the Abercrombie plans can, perhaps, be explained by the fact that they were produced in the middle of the Second World War. Today, though many in the West are living through a moment of unprecedented prosperity, most have ambivalent attitudes to the fast changing world. A significant minority see globalization as a new form of colonialism either by the United States or by what John Friedmann calls the "transnational elite".[1] This time round they feel sure that they are going to be the ones who are colonized and they are openly hostile to it. Many urbanists in the West are uneasy about the scale of deconstruction which seems necessary if a region is going to be able to attract the outside investment it needs or, alternatively, if it is to develop the social capital it needs if it is to help itself.

In light of the above, and driven by the neotraditionalist concerns of the latest wave of conservative urbanism in the West, a final issue for regional management is the view that globalization threatens regional identity and that all regions will end up culturally and spatially like everywhere else, unless the plan conserves established cultural and spatial features. This view has been supported, off and on, throughout the century in Europe, by a mixture of liberals and intellectuals from the extreme left and right. A counterclaim is that it is the accelerated process of globalization itself which has created this heightened sense of regional identity. It is only because they are now much more conscious of the differences between their region and others that citizens or market makers are so concerned to build on that difference.

Again, however, it is the so-called, "postmodernists" who are asking the difficult questions about this apparently straightforward policy issue. When we speak of regional identity in the increasingly fragmented societies of today, from the point of view of which social or interest group are we seeking to understand it? And, even if we can answer that question, how can decisions be made about what is "authentic" material on which to build such an identity when the distinction between myth and reality, or between virtual and real, becomes ever more blurred?

The 11 chapters which follow in Part 2 provide insights into how these issues of globalization, social and economic change, suburban congestion, regional sustainability, and the cultural identity of regions are being played out in other parts of the world today as well as in the West. Variations on these basic themes will be discovered as well as quite different perspectives, often with more explicit social policy objectives than tend to be found in the West today.

NOTES

1 John Friedmann defines "world cities" as "large urbanized spaces of intense social and economic interaction." (*Where We Stand: A Decade of World City Research*, Discussion Paper D9304, Los Angeles CA: UCLA Graduate School of Architecture, 1993.)

2 H. van der Camman (ed.): *Four Metropolises in Western Europe*, Assen and Maastricht: Van Gorcum, 1988.

3 Jean-Pierre Lecoin, "Paris and the Ile-de-France Region," in H. van der Camman (ed.) *Four Metropolises in Western Europe*, Assen and Maastricht: Van Gorcum, 1988.

4 Melvin M. Webber, "The Urban Place and the Non-place Urban Realm," in Melvin M. Webber (ed.) *Explorations into Urban Structure*, University of Pennsylvania Press, 1964.

5 Derek Senior (ed.) *The Regional City: An Anglo-American Discussion of Metropolitan Planning*, London: Longman, 1966.

6 Sharon Zukin, *Landscapes of Power: From Detroit to Disney World*, Berkeley CA and Oxford: University of California Press, 1991.

7 Michael Sorkin, "See you in Disneyland," in Michael Sorkin (ed.) *Variations on a Theme Park: The New American City and the End of Public Space*, New York: Hill & Wang, 1992.

8 Manuel Castells, *The Informational City*, Oxford: Blackwell, 1989.

9 David Harvey, *The Condition of Postmodernity*, Oxford: Blackwell, 1989.

10 Ulrich Beck, *Risk Society: Towards A New Modernity*, London and Newbury Park CA: Sage, 1992.

11 Anthony Giddens, *The Consequences of Modernity*, Stanford CA: Stanford University Press, 1990.

12 Edward W. Soja, "Six Discourses on the Postmetropolis," *Urban* (Madrid) 2, 1998.

PART 2

Studies of Global City Regions

The research consortium. We set up the consortium, with funds from the Lincoln Institute of Land Policy, in 1995. Senior figures from 11 selected regions around the world were invited to join. Their role would be to manage the phases of the research for their region, make presentations at international conferences, and work with us to define successive phases of study. The research, which is recorded and interpreted in the following 11 chapters, was carried out in two phases of work, each culminating in an international conference. The first was held in Cambridge, in the Boston region, in September 1995 and the second in El Escorial, in the Madrid region, in July 1997. By the time the book is published we plan to be into a new phase of study with an international conference planned in another of our participating regions.

The research. Both phases of research were conducted according to strict specifications aimed at providing answers to a number of agreed research questions, outlined in Chapter 1. The strictness of the protocols had the aim of maximizing the potential for generating ideas by contrasting and comparing the data from the 11 regions. Graphic material was put on a GIS at MIT and, in phase 2, at Oxford Brookes to serve as a basis for future work and to guarantee that graphics could all be rapidly produced to the same scale, using the same symbols, whenever needed.

Though we knew well the problems of assembling comparable statistics across international boundaries, the social and economic indicators contained in Table 1 on the next page do not cover as wide a field as we intended. A number of efforts to assemble comparable figures, particularly related to the take-up of new technology, had to be abandoned.

The data which are presented, other than those which are produced as a matter of course on an annual basis in each country, should be treated as an approximation. In the case of the land occupancy maps, for example, if a map of land occupancy was produced within five years of the stated date (say 1965) it has been treated as approximately equivalent to that date and no attempt to recreate a more exact map of the period has been made. In cases where the date of maps is further than five years from the stated date, some attempts at interpolation between that and an earlier or later date have been made. The same is true, but in a different way, with statistics, such as the percentage of national income earned by the top and bottom 20 percent of income groups. Here the specification was that only salaries, wages, pensions, and unemployment payments would be considered here but for many regions this statistic was not available or certainly not in this form. Some teams have found sufficient data from which to construct an approximation for the figure while others have been unable to do so. In light of the approximate nature of much of the data, the interpretation of statistics by the relevant research team in the chapters ahead is even more important than usual.

The comparative statistics. The comparative data take two forms: graphic data, which are presented in each of the chapters ahead, and statistical data, which are presented here in Table 1 on p.19.

Table 1 INDICATORS FOR THE ELEVEN GLOBAL CITY REGIONS

		Bangkok	Boston	Madrid	Randstad	San Diego	Santiago	São Paulo	Seattle	Taipei	Tokyo	West Midlands
Total population	1960	3,312,000	3,651,031	2,510,217	5,144,700	970,700	2,133,252	4,791,245	1,512,979	1,380,010	15,928,189	5,046,000
	1970	4,529,500	4,092,305	3,781,348	5,636,000	1,262,804	2,871,060	8,139,730	1,938,899	3,846,526	22,424,349	5,179,000
	1980	6,644,400	4,153,634	4,684,895	5,789,000	1,736,100	3,735,399	12,558,725	2,240,264	4,627,200	27,365,972	5,176,000
	1990	8,589,900	4,387,986	4,947,555	6,066,000	2,348,417	4,518,057	15,416,416	2,748,895	5,704,400	30,607,845	5,294,900
As % of nation	1990	16	2	13	40	1	34	10	1	28	25	9
Net migration	1960–70	–	62,367	266,429	–	160,115	383,660	1,977,901	244,246	1,389,696	3,136,018	–
	1970–80	–	(50,034)	158,657	–	350,239	285,231	2,263,103	174,678	369,426	1,257,084	–
	1980–90	–	(12,954)	34,068	–	391,883	78,266	274,696	297,812	474,396	1,268,582	–
Growth rate	1960–70	–	0.01	0.04	0.01	0.03	0.03	0.05	–	0.11	0.03	–
	1970–80	0.04	0.00	0.02	0.00	0.03	0.03	0.04	–	0.02	0.02	–
	1980–90	0.03	0.00	0.01	0.00	0.03	0.02	0.02	–	0.02	0.01	–
Agriculture/extraction as % of employment	1960	–	1.1	3.8	8.0	0.8	–	4.5	0.14	21.0	8.7	3.1
	1970	16.9	0.8	1.0	1.0	0.9	–	2.9	0.12	8.0	4.3	1.4
	1980	8.9	0.7	0.5	1.2	0.9	4.3	1.3	0.06	5.0	2.6	3.0
	1990	1.7	1.0	0.2	1.3	1.1	5.8	1.2	0.06	2.0	1.6	1.6
Manufacturing as % of employment	1960	–	32.6	25.9	40.0	37.7	–	68.8	36.26	36.6	40.7	25.9
	1970	22.5	26.8	33.5	33.5	25.2	–	65.6	30.85	35.0	40.6	33.5
	1980	32.6	24.4	25.2	25.6	20.1	28.0	64.3	20.74	38.0	34.6	25.2
	1990	32.5	17.5	24.0	23.0	15.6	29.0	58.2	18.25	36.0	31.7	24.0
Services as % of employment*	1960	–	26.9	70.3	53.0	61.5	–	8.7	63.60	43.0	50.6	37.2
	1970	60.6	34.7	65.5	65.0	73.9	–	12.0	69.03	56.0	54.9	41.9
	1980	58.3	39.4	74.3	73.2	79.0	67.7	17.3	79.20	57.0	62.6	43.1
	1990	65.8	45.4	75.8	75.7	83.3	65.2	18.8	81.69	62.0	65.8	49.2
Regional per capita GDP estimates	1960	–	–	–	–	–	1,279	–	–	–	1,209	–
	1970	–	–	–	6,039	5,155	1,662	5,295	–	–	2,541	–
	1980	2,105	–	–	15,372	12,300	1,617	6,753	–	–	10,693	–
	1990	5,468	–	13,422	22,509	23,789	–	–	–	10,202	30.847	–

*Boston, São Paulo and the West Midlands did not include wholesale/retail, transport services and utilities and public administration in their service calculations.

continued overleaf

Table 1 INDICATORS FOR THE ELEVEN GLOBAL CITY REGIONS

		Bangkok	Boston	Madrid	Randstad	San Diego	Santiago	São Paulo	Seattle	Taipei	Tokyo	West Midlands
National	1960	274	2,838	883	1,748	2,838	837	521	2,838	349	860	1,901
per capita	1970	586	4,933	2,211	3,536	4,933	1,436	915	4,933	829	2,835	3,184
GDP	1980	1,700	11,889	5,728	8,837	11,889	3,080	3,332	11,889	3,416	7,809	7,993
(1992 US$)	1990	4,270	21,827	11,765	16,096	21,827	5,279	4,792	21,827	9,850	17,625	15,741
% of national income earned by bottom 20%	1990	7.2	–	7.3	6.0	4.0	4.9	4.7	5.2	7.5	8.3	–
% of national income earned by top 20%	1990	45.6	–	40.9	38.0	–	56.4	52.7	42.2	38.6	38.2	–
Number of	1960	–	1,011,057	–	397,830	32,199	–	–	–	589,713	1,003,000	–
automobiles	1970	–	1,402,912	336,425	949,000	644,452	103,225	483,104	853,762	91,350	4,240,701	1,345,000
	1980	657,000	1,980,158	1,345,030	1,888,000	1,022,778	240,483	1,654,677	1,271,176	300,964	7,997,007	1,577,000
	1990	2,128,000	2,520,681	1,812,002	2,201,000	1,396,505	342,327	3,090,416	1,726,564	1,048,206	14,902,698	2,116,000
Population	1960	–	3.61	19	–	–	6.6	–	–	127	27	5
per	1970	–	2.92	11	6	6	28	17	2.29	42	5	4
automobile	1980	10	2.10	3	3	3	16	8	1.90	15	3	3
	1990	4	1.74	3	3	3	13	5	1.68	5	2	2
Average	1990	–	24 mins	–	–	19 mins	–	45 mins	–	–	–	–
commuting time	1995	105 mins	–	–	–	21 mins	22 mins	–	24.6 mins	45 mins	41 mins	23 mins
% of	1970	11.92	86.9	–	42	91	17.9	–	88.5	3.93	–	42
households	1980	26.09	92.4	77.6	75	93	22.7	31	90.4	19.01	–	75
with	1990	49.02	95.8	91.7	88	97.7	36.7	39	95.05	40.04	100	88
telephones	1995	54.34	98.0	–	93	99	96.2	74.0	97.3	100	100	95
Cellular phones per 100 Pop.	1995	6.23	15.3	1.9	–	–	15	1.41	–	3.61	8.13	5.9

Table 1 *Continued*

		Bangkok	Boston	Madrid	Randstad	San Diego	Santiago	São Paulo	Seattle	Taipei	Tokyo	West Midlands
No.PCs in use per 100 pop.	1995	2.7	45% (access to computers)	8.5	–	60	3.33	–	–	8.3	15.38	25
No. connected to the internet per 100 pop.	1995	0.53	8.07	–	–	16	–	–	–	1.6	0.13	7.9
% of households connected to cable TV	1995	3.8	80	5	–	70	–	–	–	76.6	23.08	4.1
% of households with satellite TV receivers	1995	2.2	13.8	5	–	–	–	–	–	–	14.51	14.7

Key to the illustrations in Part 2 (chapters 3–13)

Landuse/Landcover

- Pre 1960s urban
- Post 1960s urban
- Marsh
- River
- Water
- Green Belt (area of restricted development)
- Forest
- Parkland

Political and administrative boundaries

- International boundary
- Regional / State boundary
- District boundary

Transport

- Airport
- Proposed airport
- Ferry
- Railway station
- Minor railway station
- Proposed railway station
- High speed railway
- Proposed high speed railway
- Main railway
- Proposed main railway
- New railway
- Proposed new railway
- Other railway
- Proposed other railway
- Highway
- Proposed highway
- Limited access road
- Proposed limited access road
- Other road

Communication

- Main supplier fiber optic cable coverage
- First competitor fiber optic cable coverage
- Second competitor fiber optic cable coverage
- Main supplier fiber optic cable
- First competitor fiber optic cable
- Second competitor fiber optic cable
- Main supplier fiber optic transfer station
- First competitor fiber optic transfer station
- Second competitor fiber optic transfer station
- Satellite receiver

Social Indicators

- High income
- Low income
- Academic
- Commercial
- Industrial

Note:
While we have tried to be comprehensive and consistent, not all of the information contained in the key is supplied on every relevant drawing.
Neil McIntosh and Caroline Older supplied the maps in Part 2.

3 The Bangkok region

Utis Kaothien and Douglas Webster

Bangkok is over 200 years old. Founded by King Rama I in 1782, it rapidly developed along both banks of the Chao Praya River, Thailand's main avenue of commerce and communication, before motor vehicles usurped this function. Bangkok has been called the Los Angeles of Asia. Not only is it known locally as the "City of Angels" but, like Los Angeles, development patterns are primarily driven by the road network, rather than by land use regulations or development controls. In recent years an increasingly extensive expressway network has had a profound effect on the city's development, strongly contributing to low density, corridor aligned sprawl.[1] Bangkok was not always this way. Prior to the middle of the twentieth century, it was a city of tree lined canals, "The Venice of the East"; but most canals were filled in to provide rights of way for roads after World War II.

Bangkok is currently in a period of transition. The city is enhancing its role as a knowledge center while manufacturing is dispersing to suburban areas, and increasingly, even farther afield in the Extended Bangkok Region. The current official population of Bangkok Metropolis (BMA), is over 8 million; however, the Extended Bangkok Region (EBR), which includes BMA, contains over 17 million people. The EBR accounts for over 90 percent of the value of manufacturing in Thailand, and a similar proportion of high level professional, business, and producer services.

Growth of suburban and exurban areas in the extended region has been driven to a considerable extent by congestion in the core, which encourages residents and businesses to disperse, and by government policy, e.g. the infrastructure-led Eastern Seaboard (ESB) initiative. Many areas in the core city are losing population, although

Figure 3.1 Bangkok's Silom Business District—one of several highrise 'downtowns'

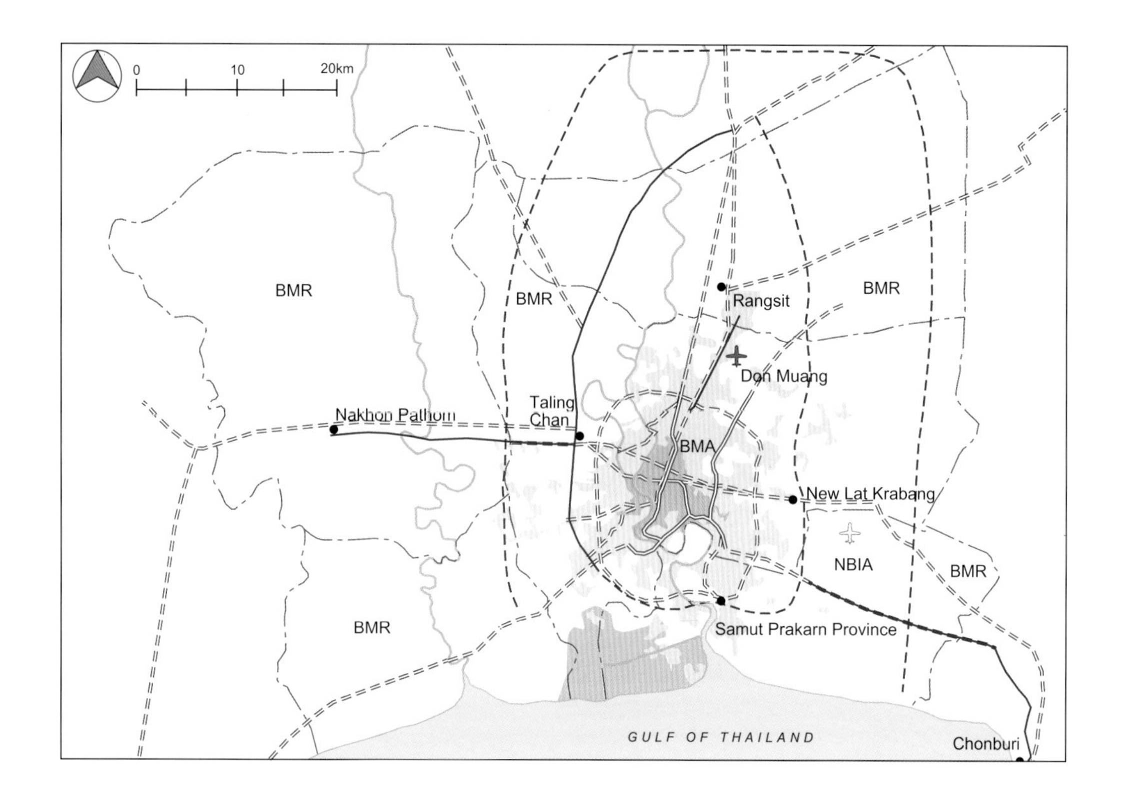

Figure 3.2 The Bangkok region, 1995

Figure 3.3 The location of the Bangkok region

daytime populations are growing with increased office activity. (Daytime populations are at least 1 million greater than night time in BMA.) Is there a danger that the center will be "hollowed out" too much? Much of Bangkok's character is defined by its intense street life. Have government policy makers put their foot down too hard on the "dispersal accelerator"?

To visitors, Bangkok is obviously unique—nowhere in the world are temples, postmodern buildings, and street vendors arrayed along traffic jammed arteries the way they are in Bangkok. And this is just the physical dimension—the distinct culture, manifest in cuisine, lifestyle, entrepreneurship, quality service, and design, intensifies the city's individuality. The goal of those who are trying to improve the city is to maintain its dynamism, cosmopolitanism, and individuality, while at the same time addressing its major problems: traffic jams, air and water pollution, and limited public (including green) space.

There are signs of improvement. New expressways have, surprisingly—even to their advocates—improved the flow of traffic. A recently opened 24 km elevated mass transit system serving the multinodal core is making travel in the city center much easier—for those who choose to use it. And, helping preserve the ideal world of intense activity in the core—along with accessibility and ease of movement. Water pollution should be considerably reduced by the early twenty-first century as six new sewerage systems deliver benefits as promised. Efforts by the current governor to reduce particulate matter in the air, particularly from construction, are beginning to bear fruit. Introduction of unleaded gas has resulted in ambient airborne lead concentrations at about 25 percent of late 1980s levels.

GOVERNANCE

The BMA is a unique urban area in Thailand—it is the equivalent of a province, with considerable autonomy to plan and manage its affairs. Bangkok has enjoyed this status since 1985. The governor is elected for four years and appoints four deputy governors. The city is divided into 50 districts; district counselors are elected to advise the district directors. Increasingly, BMA is successfully exercising a wider variety of powers, for example in mass transit, the urban environment, urban planning, and social programming.[2]

BMA, along with five immediately surrounding provinces, forms the Bangkok Metropolitan Region (BMR). However, the BMR is a fragile entity. Its only planning mechanism was the BMR Committee chaired by the current Prime Minister but it is now defunct. Under some national governments, it never met. The only other manifestation of its existence is statistical—data are aggregated at the BMR scale. Since development spills over into the surrounding provinces, e.g. the airport corridor into Pathum Thani to the north, and heavy industry into Samut Prakarn, immediately to the east—more effective mechanisms to coordinate services and infrastructure with regionwide importance and consequences (and economies of scale in delivery) are needed. Of equal concern is that local government within the adjacent provinces often consists of numerous small "tambons"—forms of government ill equipped to handle the complexities of rapid urbanization in a large metropolis.

The Extended Bangkok Region exhibits the same shortcomings in terms of governance as the BMR. The EBR approximately corresponds to a special economic programming region termed Eastern Seaboard II (ESB II). The National Economic and Social Development Board (NESDB) has responsibility for coordinating development among key line Ministries in this area through its Center for Integrated Planning Operations (CIPO). Attempts by the NESDB to "spin off" this function through the creation of a regional coordinating authority, or similar institution, have never been accepted by the political establishment.

In summary, the Bangkok region consists of three tiers: BMA, BMR, and EBR. Only the BMA has a local government system that has the capacity to handle large scale urbanization. Yet population in urbanizing areas of the EBR outside BMA will grow faster than in BMA over the next 15 years—new mechanisms obviously need to be developed to coordinate development in the EBR.

At the same time, the technical, managerial, and financial capabilities of the BMA itself need to be strengthened. For although BMA's population growth, currently slightly under 2 percent annually, will continue to slow, its importance in Asia, and the world, as the site of important private, public, and international functions will continue to grow, driving significant socioeconomic change as well as physical redevelopment. This new role will require BMA to take on new functions, particularly related to increased amenity.

CHANGING ECONOMIC PATTERNS

Until recently, the economy of the BMR has grown at an annual rate about 3 percent higher than the national economy. During the mid 1990s, until the economic crisis of mid 1997, regional domestic product grew at over 11 percent per year. During the overheated economy of the late 1980s and 1990, the economy grew at an extremely fast 17.5 percent per year—probably the fastest growing urban economy in the world at that time. For the first time in many decades, Bangkok's economy is probably growing (or actually declining) at a slower rate than the national economy, for it has been the Bangkok based financial and property sectors which have been hit hardest, and first, by the mid 1997 economic crisis.

Incomes in Bangkok are much higher than in the country as a whole—about 3.4 times as high. This disparity is reflected within Bangkok itself, where, as described by the indicators, the highest one-fifth of earners accounted for 45.6 percent of income, the poorest one-fifth 7.2 percent. Based on the comparative indicators, however worrying, this is a worldwide phenomenon. Bangkok is a middle income urban region; mean income was US$5,468 in 1990, which rose to close to US$9,000 before peaking in mid 1997.

The structure of the region's economy varies greatly between BMA (the core) and the five surrounding suburban provinces. BMA has a well balanced economy in which manufacturing accounts for about one-third of economic product, while (1) wholesale and retail trade, (2) business and personal services, and (3) construction and infrastructure services sectors account for approximately 20 percent each. On the other hand, the five suburban

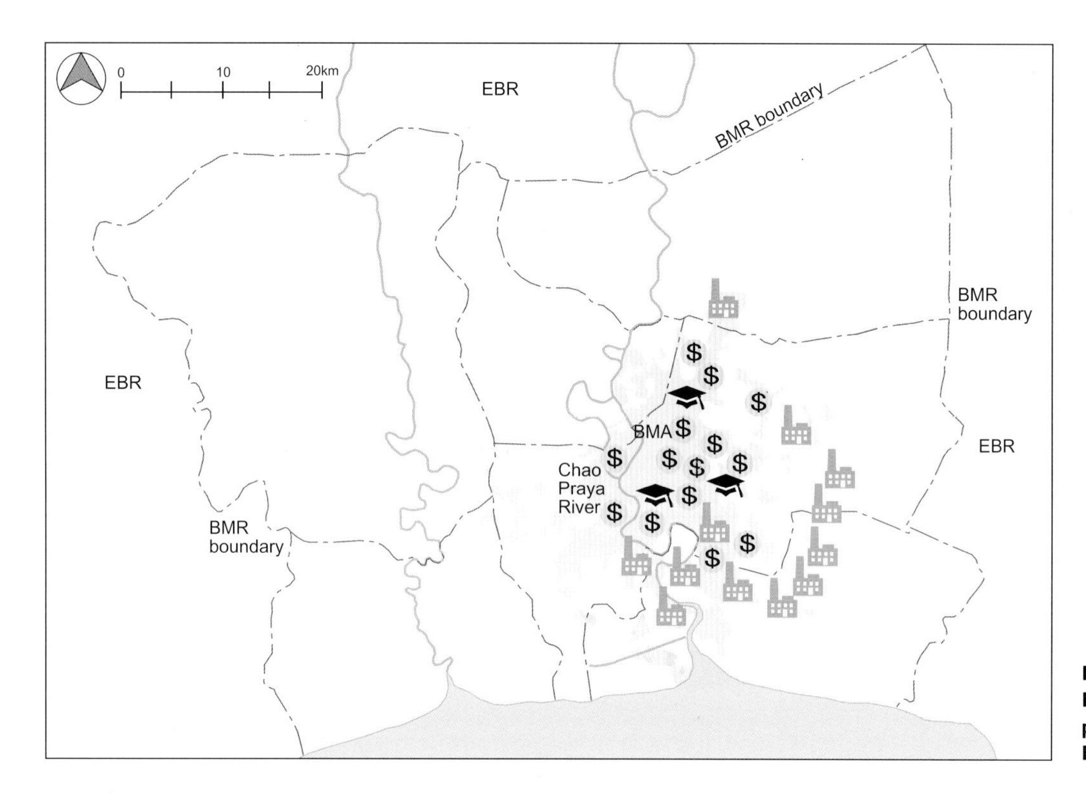

Figure 3.4 Economic patterns in the Bangkok region

provinces are overwhelmingly dependent (66 percent) on manufacturing. Although some knowledge services are suburbanizing, the future health of the economy in suburban areas will, to a considerable extent, be dependent on attracting or developing higher value manufacturing (given low priced competition from China and other emerging producers) and the development of the New Bangkok International Airport (NBIA), 30 km to the east of Bangkok's center, which will inject US$10 billion in investment and attract 650,000 people to that suburban area.

The growth in the value of business and professional services in BMA has been dramatic—161 percent between 1989 and 1993. In BMA this sector has replaced manufacturing as the "engine" of the economy. However, the "knowledge" sector was hit hard by the 1998 economic crisis—nevertheless, if needed reforms are implemented, it is expected to regain its health and fast growth. Key "knowledge" activities in BMA include financial services, technical services (e.g. computers, engineering), international governance (e.g. the UN, ESCAP), education and culture, domestic and international media, advertising, fashion, and design. It will be the ability of BMA to deliver such services cost effectively and to state-of-the-art quality that will largely determine its economic future in a rapidly globalizing world.

The main constraint on even faster economic restructuring, and associated growth, in the Bangkok area is human resources. Although Bangkok has a high literacy rate, there are very significant shortages of technical and professional personnel in fast growing fields such as computer science, accounting, engineering, design, etc. The second constraint relates to infrastructural backlogs, particularly in transport. This problem is most manifest in terms of vehicle congestion (which costs the region US$4 billion per year); average commuter times are 105 minutes—over twice as long as in other urban regions, see Table 1 on p.19.

CHANGING SOCIAL PATTERNS

Bangkok is experiencing rapid social change, as are virtually all large city regions in the world.[3] Change agents include increasingly diverse information and entertainment systems (e.g., multichannel television, videos, the internet); increased education; changes in labour force activities and participation rates; the decrease in the importance of the extended family; and the personal, family, and community stresses associated with long hours spent commuting. As is common elsewhere, young people are frequently at the vanguard of such change.

One of the most important underlying changes is the decline of the extended family. For example, only 22 percent of families in the BMR are extended, 67 percent are nuclear, and 11 percent "nonconventional". Another important social characteristic of Bangkok is the high female labour force participation rate—among the highest in the world—probably exceeded only in Chinese cities.

Given the inequality of income, and the relatively low wages earned by many workers in the informal sector, slum housing is home for approximately 1.3 million of Bangkok's people. Slums are being upgraded throughout the urban region through programs such as the Urban Community Development Office. While the number of slums, and of people living in them, is declining in the core area, new slums are emerging in suburban areas, particularly in industrial areas to the east. This "suburbanization" of slums is the result of market forces (the high value of land in the core), decentralization of employment (particularly manufacturing), and upward socioeconomic mobility from older slums in the core, as a result of the very high economic growth experienced from 1985 to 1995.

In the past, unlike in most cities of the world, social classes were highly intermixed within neighborhoods. For example, in core Bangkok, a representative *soi* (see below) might contain the house of a very wealthy individual, several middle class houses, and a mini-slum—all along a road less than 0.25 km in length. However, residential suburbia generally consists of privately developed multiple unit developments ("mubans") with dozens to hundreds of similarly priced housing units found inside self-contained (often gated) communities. Thus suburbanization, particularly to the north and east, is resulting in increased spatial segregation by social class. The boom in condominium construction, particularly in the core, is having a similar effect; in this case "secured" vertical developments tend to attract people of similar socioeconomic class.

Priority social concerns in the Bangkok region include:

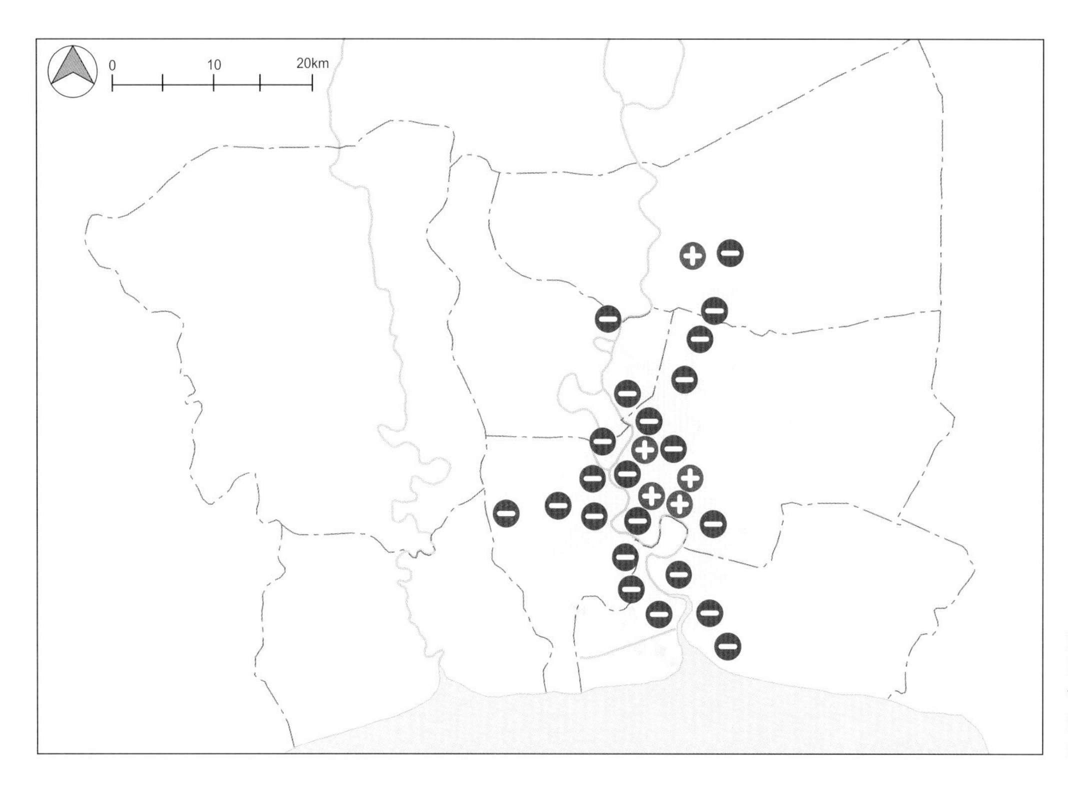

Figure 3.5 Residences of the wealthiest 20 percent and the poorest 20 percent

- Increased alienation among teenagers, associated with behaviour such as drug use (particularly amphetamines and "designer" drugs), motorcycle racing, etc.
- Increased family discord and, in some cases, breakdown, because of modernization stresses, such as long commutes.
- Decline in community and religious values, often replaced by more individualistic and/or materialistic values.
- The persistence of poverty despite, until recently, very rapid economic growth rates in the BMR and virtually no open unemployment. Between 1980 and 1989 the poverty rate in Thailand's cities fell only slightly, from 7.5 percent of the population to 6.7 percent.
- Relatively high income disparity.
- Stress and anxiety associated with rapid economic and social change linked with globalization

Income inequality has been exacerbated by the economic crisis, which has resulted in unemployment across a wide spectrum of activities ranging from the informal sector (e.g. taxi drivers), through construction work to financial workers. The result has been increased stress levels as measured by visits to mental health clinics, suicides, etc.

CHANGING SPATIAL PATTERNS

The official city, centering on the monarchy, was located near the Grand Palace; this area, known as Rattanakosin, is still the government center of Thailand. International trade and settlement focused on the New Road (Charoen Krung) area, which has since moved outwards to become one of the region's main commercial and banking centers (Silom). Chinatown grew up on the edge of the Rattanakosin area, to serve the official city. Over time, the land between the international trading and government areas has been completely urbanized, enveloping Chinatown, resulting in a multidimensional and multinodal cityscape in the core.

Suburban areas have developed primarily along key arterial roads extending from the core of the city. Beyond suburbia, the exurban settlement pattern is one of more recent corridor development along roads, complementing historical settlement along canals. The micro pattern of development in suburbia is often linear, running at right angles to roads and canals, reflecting the historical long narrow lot patterns which enabled more farmers to have canal frontage.

Bangkok is an urban region whose structure is in flux. Many of the change dynamics it shares with other large urban regions, for example suburbanization characterized by malls, "big box" stores, and a rapidly growing edge city shaped by office/commercial complexes at major road/expressway interchanges, and industrial complexes/estates within corridors along major roads. This industrial corridor development is clearly evident as are the suburban commercial shopping nodes. Commercial shopping complexes are linear in the core city but nodal (at key intersections) in suburbia.

Other changes are more specific to Bangkok. As noted, slums are suburbanizing and exurbanizing. However, in some areas, particularly in the northern corridor, the formation of slums has been preempted by the market supplying modern, affordable "walk up" worker rental housing near major industrial areas.

New "downtowns" emerge on a regular basis. To some extent this reflects the constraints on redeveloping older commercial areas because of small lot sizes, etc. At present the BMA, in conjunction with several major corporations, is supporting development of a new downtown in the Rama III area. The BMA has used infrastructure as the instrument to accomplish this objective. For example, it is constructing a US$100 million sewage system to serve the area and built a road in 1996 to connect the Rama III and existing commercial areas. A 12.5 km light rail system to link the Rama III area with the dominant existing city center is being considered.

A major determinant of future spatial structure in the region will be the New Bangkok International Airport at Nong Ngu Hao. (See Figure 3.6.) The Democrat Party government (installed in late 1997) has announced that it will "fast track" the airport to open in 2004. This will result in the eastern corridor superseding the northern corridor as the major axis of Bangkok's suburban and exurban growth.

The future of Bangkok's port is a big "if" in terms of spatial structure. It is government policy to move most port activity to the modern container port of Laem Chabang on the eastern seaboard. If this is accomplished, the Klong Toey area, where the port is located, can be redeveloped. Redevelopment of the area will need to take into account that the area contains Bangkok's largest slum (containing approximately 100,000 people), and BMA's pronounced strategy of reclaiming the river front for the people to enjoy ("a water friendly eco-city").

Probably the biggest driving force that will shape Bangkok's future spatial structure is the opening of two mass transit rail systems over the next several years. (The BMA system opened in 1999.) These systems will create points of high accessibility, especially where lines cross, e.g. at Siam Centre, through which approximately 1.5 million people will flow daily. Large scale design work is under way to exploit these opportunities. For example, Chulalongkorn University has produced a redevelopment scheme for its large land holdings in the Saphan Lueng area, while the NESDB and the State Railway of Thailand (SRT) are currently holding a design competition related to the redevelopment of railway land in the Makasan and Bang Sue areas.

However, much of the above may be tempered by the current substantial oversupply of residential and commercial property. There are approximately 500,000 vacant residential units in the EBR while approximately 30 percent of office space is vacant. It could take six or more years to clear this surplus real estate, effectively slowing redevelopment in the urban region.

INFRASTRUCTURE INVESTMENT IN THE BANGKOK REGION

Thailand's rapid economic growth during the "golden age of manufacturing", which lasted from 1985 to 1995, resulted in high growth in vehicle ownership and in demand for industrial support infrastructure, and telecommunications services. With increasing affluence, public pressure emerged for a higher quality environment in Bangkok. Given the pace of growth, and Thailand's conservative fiscal policies, substantial bottlenecks resulted in most infrastructure sectors. In 1992 the royal Thai government passed a Bill in Support of Private–Public Cooperation in the Delivery of Public Services in an attempt to encourage private sector investment in the infrastructure. Virtually all investment attracted under this policy occurred in the EBR. Nevertheless, significant infrastructure backlogs continue.[4]

Roads

Figure 3.6 describes existing and planned expressways and limited access highways. Road development accelerated rapidly in the 1950s. This marked the beginning of the "superblock" mode of road/land development, a pattern which continues to the present, extending 30–40 km from the original city center. "Superblocks" can be as large as 20 km^2.[5] Superblocks are the product of the fact that most side roads (*sois*) dead end within large rectangular areas bounded by a few major roads. Thus *sois* add more traffic to the main roads, but do not serve through traffic.[6] BMA has indicated that reducing the number of dead end *sois* to alleviate the superblock problem is a major priority.[7]

The First Stage Expressway, the first limited access toll road in Bangkok (and Thailand) was completed in 1987 by the Expressway and Rapid Transit Authority of Thailand (ETA).

By 1995 the Department of Highways (DOH) was actively upgrading approximately 450 km of interprovincial highways (non-toll) in the Bangkok study area as part of Phase 1 of its Divided Highway Program.[8] In addition, approximately 400 km of limited access highways (mainly toll roads) have been approved for construction (or are under construction) in the study area by the ETA, the DOH, and the SRT.[9] These modern four, six, and eight lane highways are designed to support economic growth in outlying areas (particularly the fast growing north and east corridors), as well as to relieve traffic congestion in BMA.

The spatial hierarchy of roads consists of a concentric series of ring roads superimposed upon the upgraded radial roads, with local traffic being carried on the roughly rectangular grid of 200 major (arterial and secondary) urban roads. The Inner Ring Road (Rachadapisek Road) and the Outer Bangkok Ring Road are both only partially completed. Despite the high level of automobile ownership in the Bangkok area (see Table 1 on p.19), and the current lack of rapid transit alternatives, only 9 percent of the land in core Bangkok is used for automobile related functions, falling to 3–5 percent in suburban areas.

The SRT, Second Stage Expressway, and Don Muang expressways have been contracted out to private firms on a concession basis. However, the ETA may reverse its privatization policy and operate toll roads directly, as it

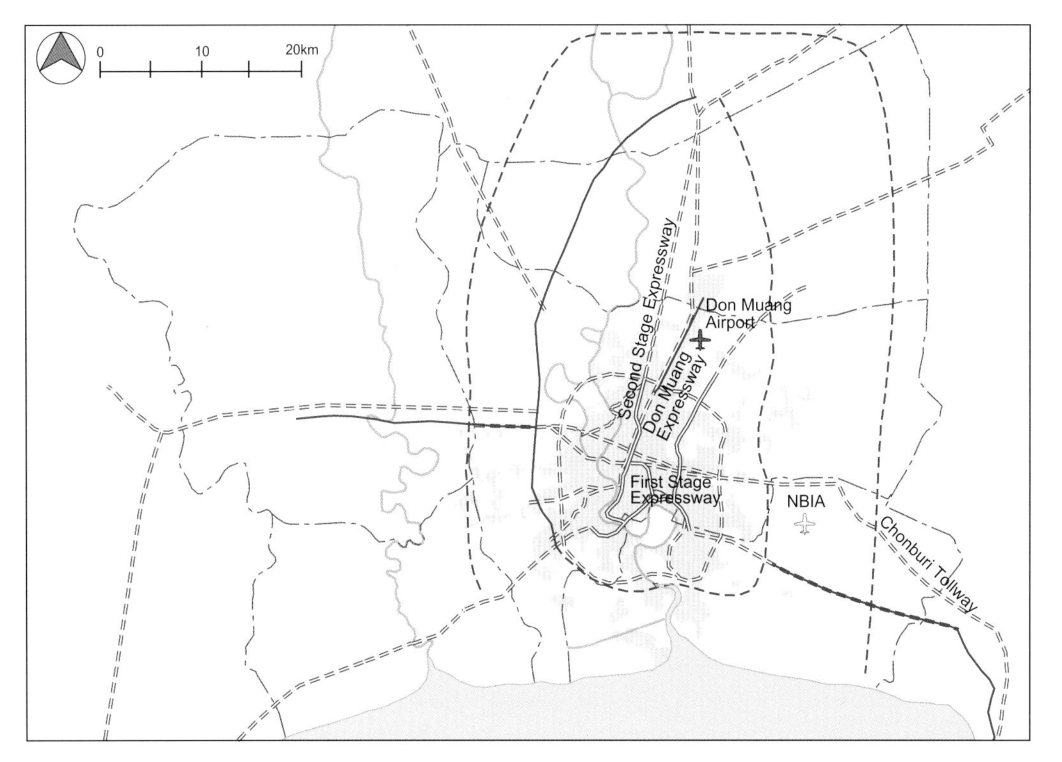

Figure 3.6 Main roads and airports in the Bangkok region, 1995

does the First Stage Expressway.[10] The tollway from Bangkok to Chonburi (linking Bangkok with the fast growing ESB) will be operated directly by DOH. (See Figure 3.6 for locational details.)

As indicated in Figure 3.6, there are two major corridors radiating from core Bangkok—one to the north serving the existing Don Muang airport and another to the east serving the ESB and the proposed New Bangkok International Airport. (The eastern seaboard is the fastest growing regional economy in Thailand and is rapidly emerging as the industrial heartland of Southeast Asia.)

Road infrastructure along the eastern corridor is rapidly being upgraded with the Bangna Trad highway being double-deck (the upper deck will be a tollway) and construction of a tollway to Chonburi. Along the northern corridor, a double-deck toll road is in operation (operated on a concession basis by the Don Muang Tollway Company), and it has been extended to and beyond the Don Muang airport. Plans have been approved to build toll roads to serve the slower growing western and southwestern corridors.

Assessment. The new controlled access and multilane radial and ring roads are encouraging further sprawl beyond the present built-up area as they open up new areas for housing and industrial development. If Thailand's urban areas continue to spread out instead of densifying, in 30 years, as the cost of automobile commuting soars, it will be difficult to extend rail mass transit systems into vast, low density suburban and exurban areas. The effective population density should be much greater than BMA's present 3,550 persons/km^2 for a regionwide mass transit rail system to function effectively.

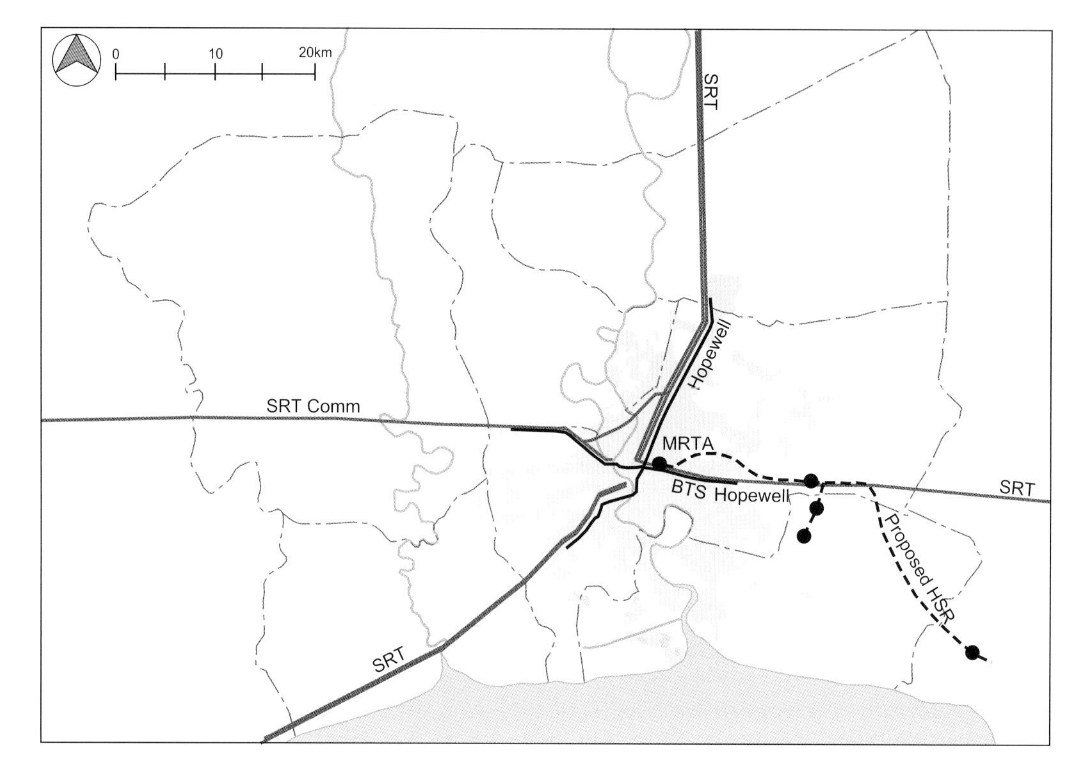

Figure 3.7 Railways in the Bangkok region, 1995

Rail

Figure 3.7 describes the existing and planned SRT network. In effect, these lines serve a commuter function; however, few dedicated commuter services are in operation. Fare paying commuting passengers averaged over 75,000 trips per day in 1993 within the BMR.[11] However, the service is slow because much of the system is still single track, there are numerous level crossings at which vehicles are given priority over trains, the rolling stock is outdated, and trains are crowded during rush hours. The highest priority proposed commuter rail route would follow the SRT line to the east; the north and west lines are second and third priorities (see Figure 3.7).

A 60 km US$3.7 billion Hopewell commuter rail system, only 20 percent complete, but contracted to open in 1998, has recently been cancelled by the royal Thai government. However, the government will invite other private parties to take over construction. The system is designed to take advantage of the existing SRT network, which approximately corresponds with areas of highest suburbanization.

The Hopewell project illustrates the lack of coordination in rail and overall infrastructure planning.

Although SRT granted Hopewell a concession to develop expressways as part of its system, this concession conflicts with exclusive rights to toll road development along the northern corridor already granted by DOH to the Don Muang Tollway Company. Similarly, the fact that Hopewell was granted a monopoly on commuter rail service in the Bangkok region effectively precluded the SRT developing its own commuter services (which would extend farther out from the core), for example a service to the east to Chachoengsao as recommended by Japan International Cooperation Agency (JICA).[12] (See Figure 3.7 for locational detail.)

In May 1990 the government unveiled the concept of a 218 km long high speed rail (HSR) service (160–200 km/h) on a new line that would link Bangkok with the eastern seaboard, utilizing electromotive trains on standard gauge HSR track. However, its fate is uncertain; the economic situation, plus questions concerning its financial viability, have clouded the project's future.

Traffic congestion in core BMA is compounded by the lack of mass transit systems. Two rail systems are being developed to serve core Bangkok, the BMA elevated line and the MRTA underground Blue Line. Figure 3.7 describes mass transit rail systems under construction or planned.

The competing systems are uncoordinated in terms of fare structure and physical connections. However, efforts are under way by NESDB and BMA to improve the situation and, as noted, to take advantage of high mass transit accessibility areas to develop high density, mixed use complexes on a public–private partnership basis. Even if all three systems are built, total trackage will be less than the trolley network which was dismantled in the 1950s.

BMA's elevated "BTSC" (Bangkok Transit System Corporation) project is now operating after several false starts because of financing difficulties. The 24 km network will link major commercial nodes in Bangkok's core.

The Blue Line, which will serve the eastern perimeter of the core area, has a long history. Attempts at construction of an elevated electric rail system along this route in the early 1990s, the original "Skytrain", were plagued by environmental,[13] financial, and contractual difficulties under the ETA,[14] as well as frequent changes of government. As a result, the Metropolitan Rapid Transit Authority (MRTA), a state enterprise in the Prime Minister's Office, was established in 1992 with authority to build the Blue Line system.

The Blue Line is to be completely financed by the MRTA, and will run underground within the 25 km^2 area of downtown Bangkok. Despite the increased routing flexibility that an underground system allows, the Blue Line will follow the original above-ground route of the Skytrain.

Bangkok's three mass transit systems will have the following peak passenger capacities after their first phases are completed:

- MRTA Blue Line: 40,000 riders per hour.
- BMA (BTSC) Green Line: 50,000 riders per hour.
- SRT (Hopewell/BERTS) Red Line: 60,000 riders per hour (construction stopped).

According to the Mass Rapid Transit Systems Master Plan, developed by the Office of the Commission for the Management of Road Traffic,[15] *after* the various color lines have been constructed, another 106.5 km of rail will be needed to meet mass transit demands.

Assessment. The Bangkok Plan[16] is based on the premise that the development of rapid transit systems over the next ten years will be the most important factor affecting Bangkok's spatial structure since roads replaced canals as the dominant transportation mode. Since only the Hopewell lines will serve the suburbs, if they are not developed, the potential of the rail based mass transit system to reshape urban form may be limited.

Airports

Figure 3.6 describes the location of the existing (Don Muang) and future (NBIA) international airports.

The Royal Thai Air Force (RTAF) built Don Muang in 1913. Don Muang is Thailand's dominant aviation hub. It is a convenient transit point for Asian, European, and North American airlines, especially because of its strategically important location and the fact that it has no noise abatement curfew. Recent major renovations to Don Muang, including the construction of a second international terminal, have increased its capacity to 20 million to 25 million passengers per year. (Current use is approaching 20 million passengers.)

Despite recent improvements, aircraft movement and apron congestion at Don Muang continue. Ground traffic management procedures are being improved to increase capacity;[17] the fact that the RTAF retains half the airfield for exclusive military use inhibits expansion.

With the postponement of the opening of the NBIA to 2004, the RTAF has agreed to relinquish some of its space for additional taxiways and parking. This could increase Don Muang's capacity to 45 million passengers by 2000, although the current Democrat government has indicated that this order of magnitude of expansion may not be necessary if NBIA can be opened in 2004. Air cargo facilities were modernized in 1995. Cargo capacity has been increased to roughly 1.38 million tonnes per year, which should meet demand until 2003–05.[18]

The NBIA will be located on a 35 km² site at Nong Ngu Hao. It will be built in four phases over a 30 year period. By 2004, when the first phase is expected to be completed, the NBIA will be handling 21 million passengers per year, with a maximum capacity of 30 million passengers per year. Additional phases have been planned which will expand the capacity to 100 million passengers and 6.5 million tonnes of freight. The NBIA will be operated by a new state enterprise, the New Bangkok International Airport Corporation. Capitalization will be based on privatized operations.

Don Muang will remain a major airport with the completion of the NBIA, although it is unclear how roles will be divided. A committee has been established to address this question. No ground transportation projects have been approved to link the two sites, even though they are less than 30 km apart.

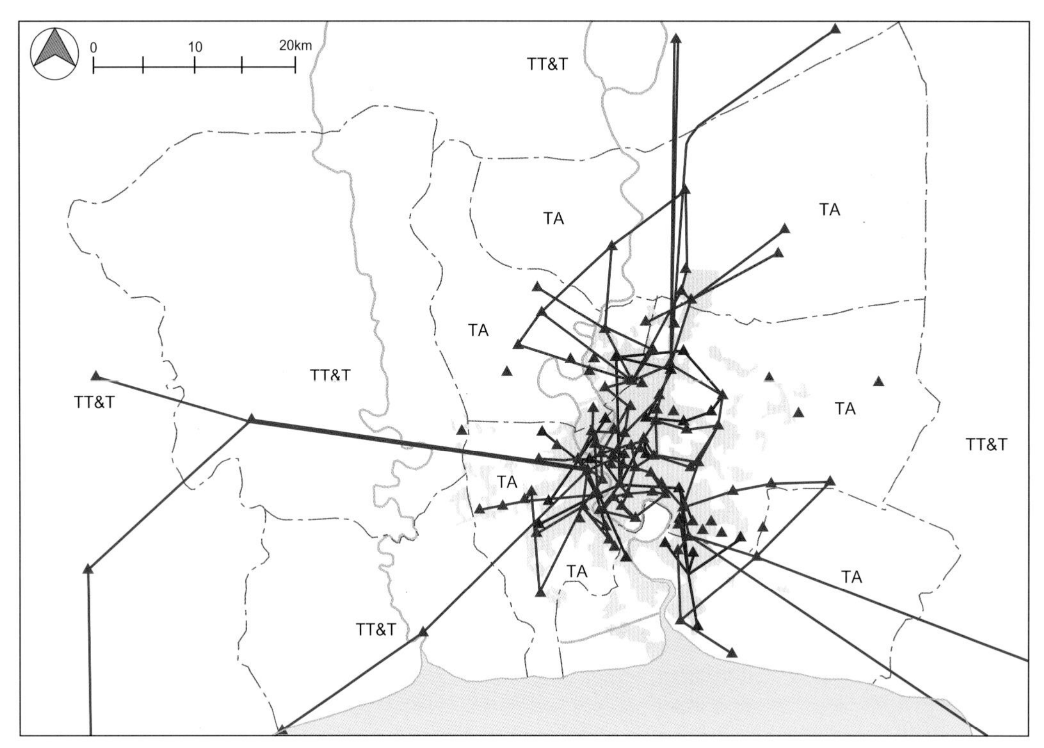

Figure 3.8 Fiber optic systems in the Bangkok region, 1995

Telecommunications

Telephone line shortages, formerly Bangkok's greatest infrastructure deficiency, have largely been overcome through partial liberalization of the sector. Table 1 on p.19 indicates the rapid growth of telecommunications services in the Bangkok area. In 1960 there were only 0.7 telephone lines per 100 people; in 1990, 49.02. Even in late 1993 existing lines were congested, and there were 1,860,470 customers on the waiting list, which averaged four years.

Unable to meet the growing demand, in 1990 the Telephone Organization of Thailand (TOT) concluded a 25 year concession agreement with Telecom Asia (TA) to install 2.0 million new lines in the Metropolitan Telephone Area (BMA, Samut Prakarn, Pathum Thani, and Nonthaburi). In addition, TOT concluded an agreement with Thai Telephone & Telecommunication (TT&T) to install 1.1 million new lines "up country", which included Nakhon Pathom and Samut Sakhon Provinces, which are part of the EBR. By 1995, after liberalization, projects to install new lines were well under way, and the MTA service density was 22.63 telephone lines per 100 people.[19]

The concessions include the construction, operation, and maintenance of network, switching, and transmission equipment, and customer service. Using fiber optic trunk lines, a high capacity digital network for voice, data, and video transmission is being developed. The concessions also include control over the lucrative "value added" services possible with digital lines, such as PIN Phone 108 credit cards, Subscriber Identification Module (SIM) cards, used in "roaming" mobile phones, and cordless phones.

The concession agreements were expanded in early 1996 to add 600,000 lines to the TA concession for

Bangkok and 500,000 lines to the TT&T concession for "up country" service. The TOT won permission from the government in mid 1996 to install and operate 800,000 lines itself, 200,000 in the BMA and 600,000 "up country". By 1996 the waiting list had nearly been eliminated.

A 1996 study by the Thailand Development Research Institute indicated that installation of 6 million more lines (as proposed in the Eighth National Development Plan, 1996–2001) would cause an oversupply until 2005. The demand projection was based on an 8.6 percent average annual GDP growth rate; the Thai economy is currently growing at 4–5%.

TOT introduced an integrated data communications network (ISDN) to Bangkok in 1991 in support of multimedia. Commercial services began in 1994. At least eleven commercial companies in Thailand now offer ISDN services in the Bangkok area.

The Ministry of Transportation and Communications (MOTC) and the Public Relations Department of the Prime Minister's Office are expected to give non-exclusive rights to use these fiber optic cables (plus direct satellite and microwave links) for a range of new multimedia subscription services to individuals and businesses, including home shopping, video-conferencing, and teleworking. Telecom Asia and several other companies are planning to offer these services in Bangkok.

Pay television in the Bangkok area exclusively utilized microwave technology until 1996—the prime provider was the International Broadcasting Corporation (IBC) (230,000 subscribers in 1997). However, true cable television, utilizing the TA fiber optic system (see Figure 3.8) was introduced by UTV. UTV had over 120,000 subscribers when they merged with IBC and adopted a system-wide true cable network. The future would seem to lie with fiber optic cable television systems because of better picture quality, particularly in the rainy season, and in areas with high rise building interference.

Assessment. As indicated by Figure 3.8, the fiber optic network in the BMA is extensive and growing, and compares favourably with networks in other global cities. Given this situation, there is little obvious spatial impact on urban form within the contiguous built-up area, which is thoroughly covered by the fiber optic network. Outside the core area, in exurban areas, since planned fiber optics development will/does follow major arterial roads (or rail lines), linear patterns of urban development will be (and are being) reinforced. This may be a short to medium run phenomenon—fiber optic networks are likely to become more widespread in suburban and exurban areas.

However, policy challenges remain, especially related to Bangkok's aspiration to be a global knowledge center. Rates for comparable service are higher than in competing cities such as Singapore as a result of inefficiencies and oligopoly. On the other hand, relatively high domestic long distance rates, although declining, contribute to Bangkok's primacy. Partial liberalization has increased the number of telecommunication providers, but geographic or type of service based oligopolies are still the norm.

Conclusion

Overall, Bangkok appears to be making progress in catching up with infrastructure backlogs. New expressways have noticeably reduced traffic congestion in many areas, telecommunication line shortages no longer exist, and one mass transit rail system is operating and another is under construction. The economic slowdown has helped, slowing demand for transportation and communication services. In addition, several major infrastructure projects commenced during the boom period have, or will shortly, come on stream to improve the infrastructure of the Bangkok region.

LAND USE PLANS AND OTHER PUBLIC SECTOR INITIATIVES

Institutional factors and regional form

In attempting to influence urban form and function, planners distinguish between explicit urban planning instruments—e.g., city plans, development controls, zoning ordinances—and implicit mechanisms, e.g., piped water or rapid transit line routing decisions. In the case of the Bangkok region, the most potent public sector forces shaping urban and regional form are implicit in nature, particularly those related to infrastructure.

Although BMA has had an approved (since July 1994)[20] comprehensive plan, there are no effective implementation instruments tied to it. At any rate, most of the suburban areas (where most demographic growth is occurring) are uniformly designated "low density residential". Thus the BMA comprehensive plan has very little influence in shaping urban form. The plan advocates homogeneous, segregated land uses (there is no mixed land use category) yet Bangkok is characterized by, and known for, mixed land use. The city's congestion problems are largely related to intensity of development, and the relationship among infrastructure, economic activities, and residence rather than land use *per se*.

In general, Thai public sector (government and state enterprise) institutions enjoy considerable autonomy, with no oversight institution effectively able to coordinate their actions which affect urban form and function. Good vertical coordination often exists within organizations; however, horizontal coordination is usually poor. Thus individual organizations have sectoral plans for activities in the urban region, sometimes well prepared, but almost invariably uncoordinated with the plans of other organizations. To give an example, the ETA makes plans for expressway systems with limited involvement of the BMA; a similar situation exists in respect of the Metropolitan Waterworks Authority. The Bangkok area, from a public sector management perspective, is essentially the product of autonomous organizations operating in the context of their own programs rather than an overall plan or vision of the future urban region.

As noted earlier, outside BMA the situation becomes more serious, given the lack of effective BMR and EBR development/planning coordinating mechanisms, and the large number of technically and financially weak local governments within Bangkok's suburban and exurban areas.

Urban and regional planning

Early Bangkok was well planned—under the guiding influence of royalty. Rattanakosin still reflects careful master planning. (Unfortunately, few tourists visit this attractive area of Bangkok.) Bangkok remained relatively small until after World War II. In 1947 the population of Bangkok and Thonburi (the urbanized area across the Chao Praya river) was a little over 1 million, living in an area of approximately 65 km^2.[21] The immediate post-World War II city still strongly reflected the Rattanakosin, international trading settlement, and Chinatown urban form described above.

Beginning in the 1950s, and especially in the 1960s and 1970s, with the war in Vietnam, the city changed dramatically, economically, socially, and physically. (In 1960 the characteristic manufacturing unit in Bangkok had only 8.5 employees.)

The Greater Bangkok Plan 2533 was produced by Litchfield & Associates in 1960; it aimed to establish land use zoning and directions for urban growth for the following 30 years. By the time of the commencement of the Litchfield project Bangkok had already made the transition to an automobile and road based city. While the consultants acknowledged the significance of the *klongs* (canals) as drains for storm water, fire protection, the disposal of sewage, and bathing, their plan was predicated on the model of the modern Western city.[22] Interestingly, the canals have become important for transportation again, carrying over 30,000 commuters (and rising) per day; restoring their former esthetic qualities and recreational function is a high priority of BMA.

Although Bangkok did not officially adopt a comprehensive plan until 1994, various plans, such as the "Litchfield plan", were prepared over the preceding 25 year period which were not officially adopted.

In reaction to the increasing congestion in Bangkok in the 1970s, the Eastern Seaboard concept was introduced, with a development plan for the area completed in 1982. The principle underlying the ESB was to decentralize population and economic activity (especially port and manufacturing) within the EBR. As noted, NESDB, through CIPO, continues to be responsible for implementing the ESB program. The original ESB program stressed economic production over social and community issues—consistent with Thailand's developmental focus on economic growth in the 1980s and early 1990s. An ESB II development strategy has been developed which will place more emphasis on community, quality of life, and amenity, in addition to measures to further strengthen and restructure the region's economy.

The BMR lacks an up-to-date regional plan; the Department of Town and Country Planning (DTCP) produced a general land use plan for the BMR area in 1984 which has not been updated. Constituent provinces of the BMR lack up-to-date land use plans; plans have been prepared for major urbanized areas in the BMR by DTCP in its Bangkok office. These municipal (and immediate surroundings) plans vary in terms of their up-to-dateness; they are general land use plans that do not necessarily relate systematically to the larger settlement system in the BMR, and are not linked with effective implementation mechanisms.

In 1995 the metropolitan regional structure study (Chao Phraya Multipolis Structure Plan) was completed —it covers 18 provinces, including BMA, all of the BMR, the eastern seaboard, the Upper Central Region, and the Western Region. The concept has been approved by the Cabinet. However, it will have impact only to the extent that line agencies, e.g., DOH, put its recommendations into effect.[23] The metropolitan regional structure study is based on a vision of the extended region as a system of well-planned and compact communities, interacting through state-of-the-art transportation and communications infrastructure to form a single socioeconomic system. Considerable green space would be preserved between communities for agriculture, water retention, floodways, recreation, etc. Controlled access highways and good rail service would encourage compact settlement near highway interchanges and railroad stations.

The Massachusetts Institute of Technology and the EC Urban Planning Project worked with BMA to produce the "Bangkok Plan". This plan advocates the use of innovative implementation instruments; it focuses on intensity of use rather than land use *per se*, and emphasizes jobs/ housing balance. The plan advocates relatively high density communities based on employment/residential balance, and mixed land use/good urban design both in selected suburban locations (suburban centers) and at key multimodal transit stations in the core area of the city. This type of development pattern, if implemented, would contribute to a lessening of congestion problems in Bangkok and provide structure to the urban fabric.

The Bangkok Plan was an important input into a new comprehensive plan for Bangkok which will come into effect in 1998. The new comprehensive plan stresses the important role of district centers and neighborhood development within the urban system.

CONCLUSION

Bangkok in 2010 will be a multinodal urban region extending 200 km from its current center. It is expected that the EBR will contain approximately 23.7 million people by 2010, 11.5 million of whom will live in BMA and another 5 million in the adjacent suburban BMR provinces.[24]

Bangkok's future: the official vision

Based on current long range plans and vision statements, the *core area* of the city will continue its dynamic development as a global information/knowledge center. The population of the core is unlikely to be much larger than it is today despite significant construction of condominiums, especially in high amenity areas such as along the Chao Praya river. Land readjustment, and related mechanisms, would be employed to acquire land for medium to high density housing for some of the lower income workers employed in the core area. Historic and official areas would be conserved and restored. Based on public support and significant investment, the quality of the urban environment will be much higher than today.

Suburban development will increasingly be to the east. A major infrastructure objective will be to provide more "through" secondary and feeder roads in suburbanizing areas to reduce superblock problems. A second objective would be to make suburban neighborhoods more self-sufficient in basic services such as social facilities (for which land would be reserved), shops, and services, to reduce travel demand. Preferably, these services would be grouped around community centers.

The function of *exurban* sub-areas will vary. For example, airport related functions will emerge near the NBIA, while, farther to the east, manufacturing will dominate. To the north, key educational and research complexes will propel some communities (e.g., the Thammarsat/AIT/science complex in Rangsit), while cultural functions and tourism (e.g., Ayutthaya) will provide the *raison d'être* for others. Where possible, exurban communities, often containing populations of 100,000–300,000, will be separated from each other by green space.

Issues and challenges

If the above vision is to be realized, key issues/challenges need to be addressed, in particular:

- Effective mechanisms need to be established to coordinate development in the BMR and EBR regions. The existing *ad hoc* system is not adequate to coordinate rapid development that will result in a population increase of over 3 million by 2015 in these areas. Second, within the BMR and EBR regions, local government areas need to be enlarged, and measures taken to increase their technical, managerial, and financial capacities.
- BMA has demonstrated that autonomous urban government can work well in Thailand, and several important initiatives have, and are, being successfully championed and implemented by BMA. However, there is little horizontal coordination, even within sectors such as expressways, among provider institutions, and with the BMA government itself. This results in oversupply in some areas and lack of services in others, plus routing and site conflicts, and avoidable externalities. Measures need to be taken to ensure better horizontal coordination between the BMA government and the key national government and state enterprises that are so important in shaping the urban landscape. Within Bangkok, BMA could act as a focal point for the coordination of infrastructure development. If BMR and EBR were strengthened, they could play a similar role for the larger region.
- More attention needs to be paid to obtaining agreement/understanding of stakeholders, working out

design details, and participatory processes during the planning stage of major infrastructure projects. At present, long delays are the rule (sometimes 10 or more years) in obtaining approval to commence implementation of infrastructure projects. This is the weak point in the system—once project implementation commences it usually proceeds rapidly and efficiently.

- Virtually all of BMA's 3.5 million population increase over the next 15 years will occur in suburban areas, particularly to the east. It is crucial that these suburban areas be developed on an infrastructure led, community centered basis. The superblock problem can be pre-empted, as can the need for long travel for everyday goods and services.
- It is essential that key transportation initiatives now under way, in particular the MRTA rapid transit lines, be completed as soon as possible. The stalled Hopewell project should be revived, under a new concession or by a government agency, to provide fast growing suburban areas to the north and east with mass transit service. In addition, longer range commuter rail service should be implemented in the EBR, particularly to the east (NBIA and ESB), as soon as possible.
- Early completion of the NBIA is essential. The vision of an interacting extended region, growing fastest to the east, is based on the NBIA acting as a key node in this system.
- Large amounts of capital will be required to fund major infrastructure projects in the Bangkok area. The region has been successful in attracting capital for rail and expressway systems, using innovative mechanisms such as BOT (build, operate, transfer). However, much more capital needs to be attracted for priority region shaping and environmental improvement projects. In particular, public–private joint ventures should be encouraged and promoted.
- Progress is being made, especially by BMA, in improving the urban environment, particularly in reducing air and water pollution, green space provision, and improving public spaces. Although they are expensive, more such initiatives should be undertaken, and present ones expanded and accelerated. Not only will an improved urban environment improve the quality of life of Bangkok's residents, but increased amenity is essential in attracting high value economic activity, particularly in the knowledge sector, to the region.

NOTES

1 D. Webster, "Mega-Urbanization in ASEAN: New Phenomenon or Transitional Phase to the 'Los Angeles World City'?" in T. G. McGee, and I. M. Robinson, *The Mega-urban Regions of Southeast Asia*, Vancouver BC: UBC Press, 1995.

2 For more information on the governance of Bangkok see J. Ruland and M. L. B. Ladavalya, "Managing Metropolitan Bangkok: Power Contest or Public Service?" in J. Ruland (ed.) *The Dynamics of Metropolitan Management in Southeast Asia*, Singapore: Institute of Southeast Asian Studies, 1996.

3 For more detail on this topic see: A. Poungsomlee and H. Ross, *Impacts of Modernization and Urbanization in Bangkok: An Integrative Ecological and Biosocial Study*, Bangkok: Mahidol University, 1992; P. C. Koanantakook, "Urban Life and Urban People in Transition," *Proceedings of the TDRI Conference: Who Gets What and How? Challenges for the Future*, Chonburi: TDRI, 1993; Government of Thailand, *Thailand National Report: World Summit for Social Development, Copenhagen, Denmark, March 1995*, Bangkok: Royal Thai Government, 1995; M. Askew, *Interpreting Bangkok: The Urban Question in Thai Studies*, Bangkok: Chulalongkorn University Press, 1994.

4 For more detail see U. Kaothien, D. Webster, and V. Vorathanyrakit, "Country Report of Thailand" in R. Brockman and A. Williams, *Urban Infrastructure Finance*, Manila: Asian Development Bank, 1996.

5 R. Archer, *Network Infrastructure for the Sustainable Development of Asian Cities: Implementing the Formula L + P + F + NI = SUD*, Working Paper 53, Bangkok: HSD Program, Asian Institute of Technology, 1994.

6 For more detail see K. Suwarnarat, "Urban Infrastructure Development of Bangkok, 1997," *Proceedings of the Second International Expert Panel Meeting on Urban Infrastructure, Bangkok, December 1997*, Nagoya: UN Center for Regional Development, 1998.

7 Ibid.

8 The former "National Toll Motorway Network." Charging tolls was abandoned after complaints by the citizenry. However, the reintroduction of a national controlled access highway system is now being reconsidered. Selected DOH highways will be operated on a toll basis, the Bangkok–Chonburu highway in particular.

9 The SRT's "Hopewell" project, officially the Bangkok Elevated Rapid Transit System (BERTS) includes an elevated toll road sharing the rail deck.

10 Space does not permit analysis of the systems used to deliver/finance major infrastructure projects in the Bangkok area. For details see Kaothien *et al.*, "Country Report of Thailand." Also see D. Webster, C. Borden, R. Archer, C. Suwanmala, and K. Lookruk, *Urban Development under the Eighth and Ninth Plan Periods: Assessment Report*, Bangkok: World Bank, 1997.

11 This is a high estimate because it counts anyone boarding or leaving a train within BMR. Figures for commutes to/from the central city are as low as 38,000 trips per day.

12 JICA/NESDB/SRT, *An Improvement Plan for Railway Transport in and around Bangkok Metropolis in Consideration of Urban Development*, Bangkok: NESDB/SRT, 1995.

13 Khunying Chodchoy Sophonpanit of "Magic Eyes" led a successful movement to have all future rail mass transit projects underground within the downtown area.

14 The "Skytrain" was canceled, then a nearly identical contract was let to the Bangkok Land Company, but Bangkok Land could not raise enough capital and defaulted; the project is now government-financed.

15 OCMRT is located in the Prime Minister's Office.

16 BMA/MIT, *The Bangkok Plan* (Draft Final), Bangkok: BMA, 1996.

17 It is possible that with state-of-the-art aircraft handling procedures the capacity of Don Muang, even given the existing space constraints, could be doubled.

18 However, a late 1996 survey reported a shortage of warehouse space at Don Muang.

19 TT&T's 1995 installation figures were not available for those two provinces; however, service densities are probably higher than the MTA service densities. (In 1993 the BMA had 73 percent of the BMR's population, with only 54 percent of its telephone lines.)

20 Before that date no official plan existed for BMA.

21 Askew, *Interpreting Bangkok*, p. 7

22 Ibid.

23 To some extent this may be happening. DOH is commissioning consultants to examine the feasibility of highway route alignments similar to those advocated in the Metropolitan Regional Structure Plan.

24 NESDB/Norconsult, *A Spatial Development Framework for Thailand*, Bangkok: NESDB, 1997, table 4.2.

4 The Boston region

Rosalind Greenstein and
Jemelie Robertson

The relationship between the Boston metropolitan region and the global economy is strongly influenced by the region's political economy and social structure. These, in turn, are shaped by the region's history and institutions. The region derives its considerable strengths from the attributes that allow it to compete successfully in a highly competitive economy. At the precipice of the twenty-first century that means a depth and breadth to its high-technology and knowledge-intensive labor force. Historically, it has meant a sort of tenacity that allows economic prowess to emerge from economic malaise.

The region is split, however. Not all sectors of the economy are competitive in the international market. Not all residents are prepared to reap the benefits of a high-technology, knowledge-intensive regional economy. Not all residents benefit from the gains that accrue to the public sector from the wealth generated in the private sector. To understand how the region can expect to fare in the international market of the twenty-first century, one first needs an understanding of the forces which have led to the current regional conditions and how the physical structure of the region constrains and informs these conditions.

A city's shape is largely formed by the supply and character of the land on which it sits. However, the mode of transportation and the means of communication also exert a powerful influence on city form and city character. It is not different for the Boston metropolitan region, whether one examines its early eighteenth century mercantilistic roots, its mid nineteenth century industrial base, or its late twentieth century knowledge-intensive network. The city's port location meant that expansion to the east was limited. As demand for city locations outstripped supply, however, Boston builders were able to increase land supplies by filling bays and leveling hills. Much of this land reclamation occurred between 1850 and 1900, with the more ambitious projects increasing land supply in the Back and South Bays (Warner, 1962).

It was not only the supply and shape of land that formed the city, but also its genesis as a walking community. Through the eighteenth century the city extended two to three miles out from the center that was a reasonable one-hour walk. The transportation and communication technology of the day meant that commerce and affairs of state were carried out face-to-face. Later the city adapted to new innovations, and, with each subsequent round of technological advancement, the city grew. Horse and buggies, stagecoaches, steam-powered railroads, electric trolleys, and the nation's first subway system all left their imprint on spatial patterns within the city, the shape of the city as a whole, and the relations between the city and its hinterland.

During the nineteenth century the city's land supply was effectively increased in three ways. In real terms, the landfill projects actually created more buildable sites. Second, the 1860s and 1870s saw Boston annex the independent towns of Dorchester, Roxbury, Brighton, Charlestown, and West Roxbury. Furthermore, technological innovations in transportation and communications increased the feasible area of commuting. In the 1850s a street-level rail service connected Harvard Square in Cambridge with Union Square in Somerville, while another line linked downtown Boston with the suburbs of Roxbury, West Roxbury, and Dorchester.[1] By the 1890s the area of dense settlement had reached six-mile radius from City Hall (Warner, 1962).

While it is true that politics, land supply, transportation, and communication networks can partially account for Boston's urban form, the city was also shaped by larger economic and industrial forces. From its founding in 1630, Boston played an important commercial role for the developing nation despite competition from New York and Philadelphia. In comparison with these more southern colonial outposts, Boston was relatively isolated and less well endowed with productive farmland in its hinterland.[2] However, its port and port-related activity did much to enrich the region. Spin-off activities included shipbuilding, rope and sail making, warehousing and docking, re-export trade, brokering, insurance, and banking. It was these latter activities that were to play a significant role in facilitating the expansion of the burgeoning manufacturing sector (North, 1961).

Boston's position as the commercial center of New England was strengthened as the interdependence between the city and its hinterland grew. Boston supplied financial and legal services for production centers through-

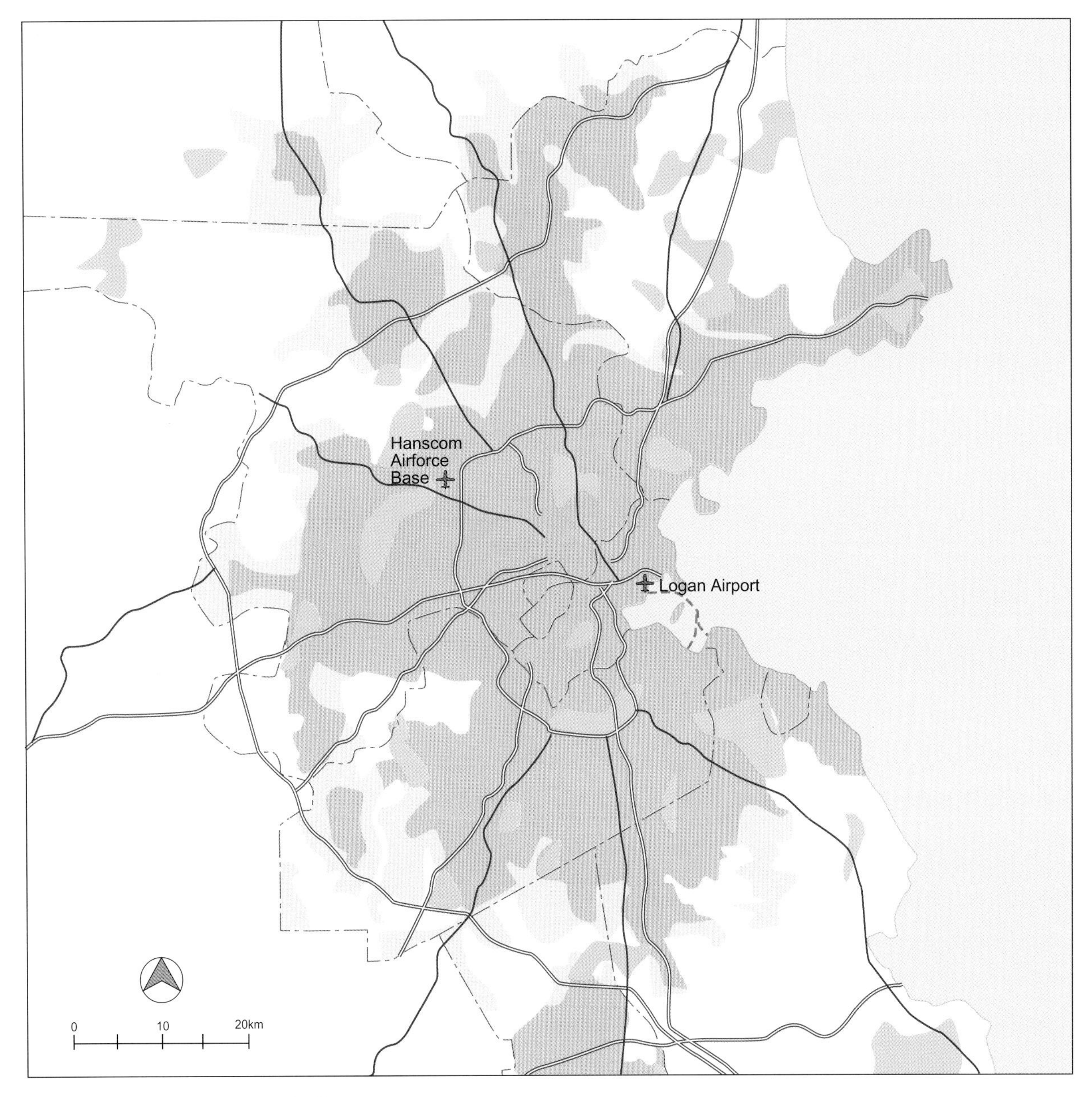

Figure 4.1 The Boston region, 1995

Figure 4.2 The location of the Boston region

out eastern Massachusetts as well as providing links with markets to the west and south. This relationship was reinforced by a rail network which connected the city center with the outlying manufacturing centers, such as Waltham, Lynn, Lawrence, and Fall River. Additionally, the gains Boston's financiers and merchants garnered from expanding western markets and a lucrative trade with China provided sufficient local capital to finance the growing industrial sector in surrounding areas.[3, 4]

Also contributing to the growth of the industrial sector was the great influx of European immigrants, who provided an ample supply of low wage labor for the textile, shoe, and leather factories that dotted the landscape beyond Boston. At the end of the nineteenth century eastern Massachusetts had specialized manufacturing centers where groups of immigrants—and descendants of immigrants—tended to cluster. For example, immigrants from southern Europe and French Canada worked in the shoe factories and mills in cities such as Lowell and Lawrence; Chinese laborers arrived from California to work on Boston's Pearl Street Telegraph Exchange; fishermen from Portugal and the Canadian Maritimes settled in New Bedford and Gloucester; Irish immigrants, and their descendants, worked in and around Boston's seaport, as well as in factories in Boston and surrounding towns such as Somerville, Cambridge, Charlestown, and Revere. Boston's upper class tended to be drawn from those who had immigrated in the colonial period and were now engaged in the legal and financial fields and resided in the affluent neighborhoods of Beacon Hill and the Back Bay.

Yet changes that occurred beyond the region reverberated in eastern Massachusetts. The population of the United States was moving west, so producers found that their markets had also shifted. Furthermore, infrastructure investments in New York State—in the form of canals and railroads—proved to limit Boston's western and southern expansion. Technological changes also had important effects. While cheap hydro-power once gave New England's mills and factories a competitive advantage, steam power increased the economically competitive production sites beyond river locations. If population movement to the west shifted the demand for the region's manufactured goods, the use of railroads for long haul transport of Pennsylvania coal increased the feasible supply of locations for factory production. Meanwhile, the US south was faced with a labor surplus as technology increased farm productivity and lowered the demand for workers.

Figure 4.3 Illustration of the Boston region
Source Alex S. MacLean ©1997 Landslides Aerial Photography

By the 1930s New England's factory owners began to look for cheaper production sites. Three sets of forces came together—high costs in New England, technological changes, and the population shifts that moved markets—and led to a drop in industrial production in eastern Massachusetts and an increase in the rural south. Just as there was a structural shift in demand for locally produced goods, the Great Depression added a sustained drop in orders that was only relieved with World War II generated demand.

World War II provided not only a reprieve to the ailing textile and shoe industries, but also supplied a foothold to engineering, electronics, physics, and related fields thanks to links developed during the pre-war period between the Massachusetts Institute of Technology and the Washington establishment. Thus, scientists working at, or trained at, MIT were well poised to intensify these connections when the US entered the war on December 8, 1941. Today much of the Boston region's high-technology industry traces its origins to this turn of events.

CHANGING ECONOMIC PATTERNS

During the first half of the twentieth century the region's employment was dominated by old-line manufacturing, largely producing consumer goods (e.g., clothing, sugar and confectionery products, printing and publishing) for local consumption, and intermediate goods (i.e. machine tools) for the region's factories. However, like the rest of the nation, much of the region's industry needed the demand of World War II to recover from the Depression.

While prior to World War II there was little federal money for basic research, early ties between the US military and Massachusetts companies would profoundly affect the future direction of the region's economy. There were two important military projects linked with MIT. The first occurred during the war when the US military established the Radiation Laboratory at MIT to co-ordinate the development and production of magnetrons[5] for the Royal Air Force. This project gave Raytheon, then a radio tube manufacturer, a tremendous advantage in the post-war period, as it received the production contract for the magnetron. The second project came about in the 1950s when the US Air Force established the Lincoln Laboratory as a nonprofit laboratory, operated by MIT, which would design and build a national air defense system. An electromagnetic computing machine—that is, a computer—was at the heart of the project.

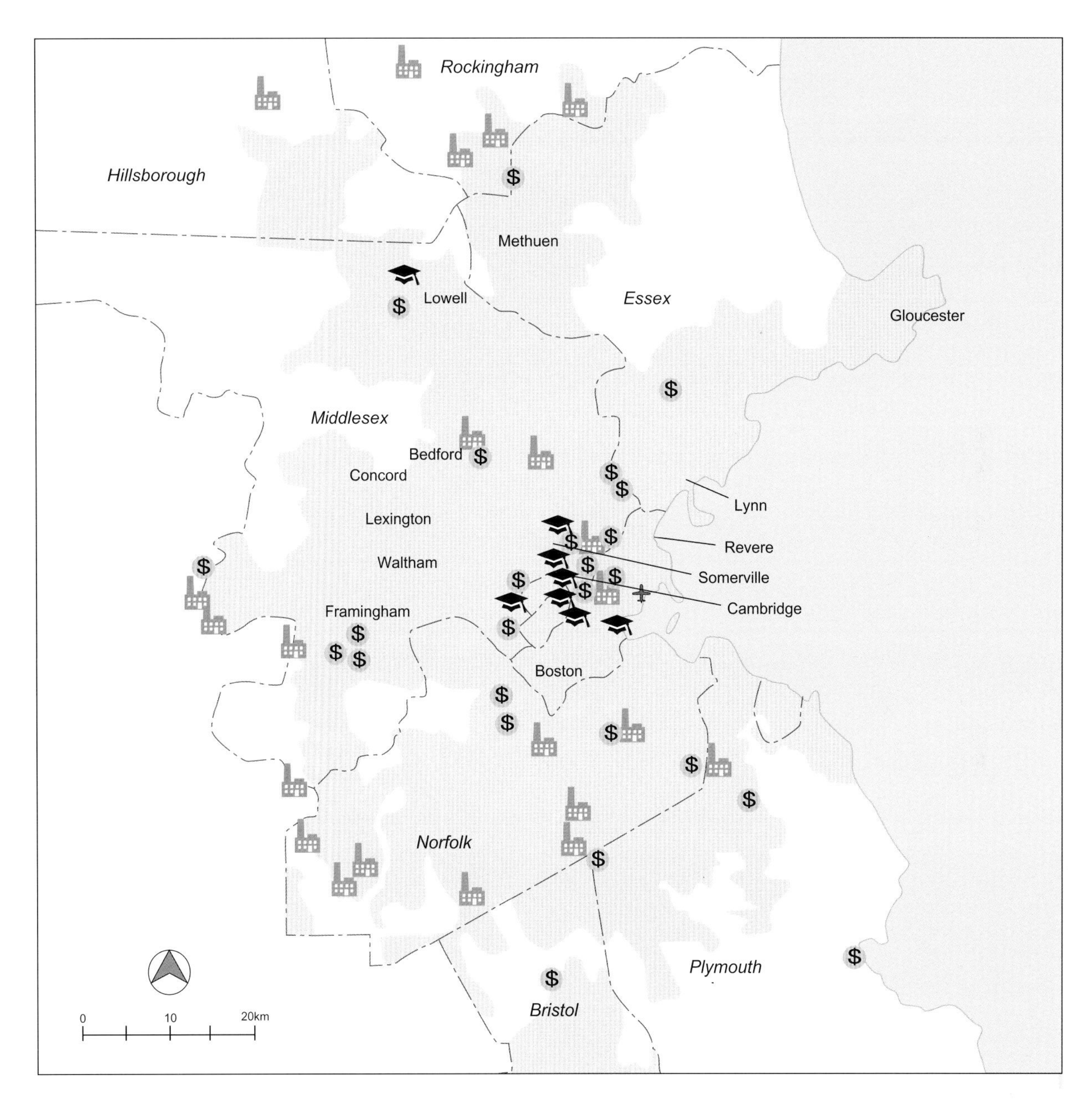

Figure 4.4 Economic patterns in the Boston region

This collaboration between the US government, MIT, and private industry would have far-reaching implications for industry as a whole as well as for Boston's industrial landscape. Boston's prior industrial strength and the uniqueness of MIT goes far in explaining why Boston succeeded in the development and production of the newest technological advances of the time, but the alliance between government, academic, and industrial sectors also proved extremely influential in how production facilities were arranged in space.

Take, for example, the US Air Force's location at Hanscom Field,[6] which straddles the suburban towns of Lexington, Bedford, and Concord and lies just beyond Route 128, Boston's first circumferential highway.[7] (See Figure 4.1.) Located just outside the gates of Hanscom Air Force base are Lincoln Labs; down the street from Lincoln Labs is Raytheon; and up the street a mile or two is MITRE Laboratories, another nonprofit lab funded by the federal government.

Out of the seeds that the US government and MIT sowed at Lincoln Laboratories grew the US minicomputer industry. In fact some 50 companies were spun off from Lincoln Labs alone during the 1950s and 1960s. Perhaps the most famous spin-off was Digital Equipment Corporation. Ken Olsen, its founder, was an MIT engineering graduate who worked at Lincoln Labs before going out on his own in 1957. Olsen started his company in Maynard, an old mill town located about midway between Route 128 and Boston's second beltway, Route 495. Six years earlier An Wang started Wang Laboratories, which then moved to Lowell, right on Route 495, in 1976.[8] Wang played a significant role in attracting other high-tech firms to Lowell, and was thus one of the important elements in Lowell's shift from a depressed and abandoned textile town in the 1950s to a model of industrial revitalization in the 1980s (Flynn, 1984). A great deal of entrepreneurial activity was spawned by the demand created by the US military for advanced electronic and avionics systems. Moreover, these producers found suburban locations when the central part of Boston had been largely built up.

Boston suffered greatly in the aftermath of the oil crisis induced recession, with unemployment hitting double digits in 1975. High technology played an important part in pulling the region out of its economic recession. One estimate is that Massachusetts' high-tech employment increased by more than 30 percent from 1975 to 1979,[9] a pace that is twice as fast as the rate for the state's total employment. The minicomputer industry played an important role in the expansion of the 1980s. In turn, with minicomputer firms largely located out by Route 495, new job growth was occurring outside Boston's traditional core.

In an analysis to desegregate employment growth over the 1980s Torto and Wheaton (1994) found that the rate of employment expansion in the suburbs exceeded that of the city of Boston. However, even in these higher growth areas, and despite the strength within the manufacturing sector, the suburbs actually lost manufacturing jobs. As high-end electronics replaced older manufacturing, the way that production was organized in the Boston metropolitan area underwent a profound change. In product cycle terms, production for mass markets (e.g. the former General Motors plant in Framingham or the former Shraft's sugar refinery in Charlestown) was being replaced by new products for a more limited customer base (e.g. DEC's minicomputers or Raytheon's missile guidance systems). Fewer production employees were required under this new regime. Thus minicomputers could still play an important role in the region's industrial base, even as the suburbs saw manufacturing employment decline by 8.5 percent during the 1980s. What is really striking about the employment data is the great rise in high-end services, including finance, legal, and business services. Even these industries, which saw growth in the city of Boston, grew at a far greater pace in the suburbs.

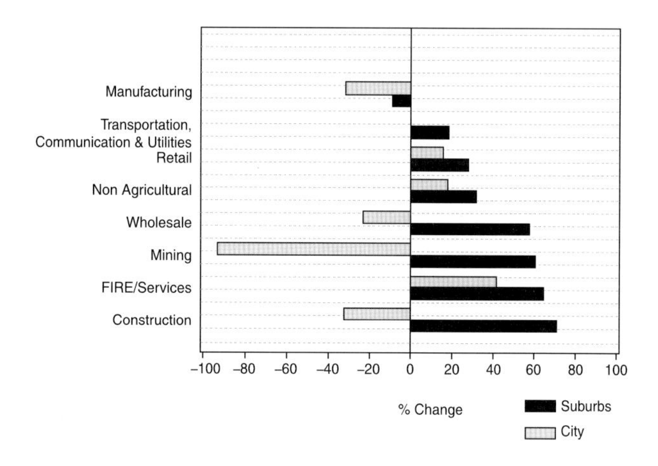

Figure 4.5 Boston area employment change, by industry sector, 1980–90.
Source Torto and Wheaton (1994)

To fully understand the Boston spatial structure, however, one must link this industry structure with the physical form of the city by examining the effects on the region's income structure and the resulting arrangement of economic classes across the landscape.

CHANGING SOCIAL PATTERNS

At the end of the 1990s metropolitan Boston is highly integrated into the world economy. To the extent that other places follow Boston's lead, the region can foreshadow the economic and social ramifications of globalization.

Since 1960 metropolitan Boston has become increasingly dependent on the production of services, while the production of manufactured goods has become less important to the economic well-being of its residents. In 1960 somewhat more than 32 percent of all workers in the region were employed by firms in the manufacturing sector; despite an increase in total employment of 59 percent over these three decades, manufacturing employment dropped to under 18 percent by 1990. Estimates for 1995 support this trend, with employees in the manufacturing sector decreasing by another 16 percent in the region.

For high school graduates entering the labor market in the post-World War II years, manufacturing employment provided an *entrée* into the middle class. Nevertheless, even within manufacturing, the fate of workers varied. Those employed in Massachusetts' declining industries—like the shoe factories of Lynn and Lawrence or the textile mills of Fall River—saw their livelihoods threatened as owners found lower cost production sites in the non-metropolitan counties of the US south and in developing countries around the world. Production workers in industries where US manufacturers still held competitive advantages, such as those at the former General Motors plant in Framingham or General Electric's turbine plant in Lynn, fared far better, even well into the 1970s. Union wages provided these workers, typically white men with high school diplomas, with median incomes above the state average.[10] However, the combination of increased competition from goods manufactured outside the US, as well as the cyclical nature of US defense spending, both contributed to the long-term decline in Boston's manufacturing sector.

The changes in the manufacturing sector were accompanied by changes in the service sector. Many well paying jobs opened up in the financial and business services portions of the labor market that typically required college and advanced degrees. However, structural change in social organization has also affected employment trends. While New England always had higher female labor force participation rates than the national average, changes in household organization drove many tasks that were formerly done within the household outside. Thus the US census reports an increase of over 60 percent in employment in restaurants and pubs from the mid 1970s to the mid 1990s for the Boston region. Similarly, as young adults moved from labor market to labor market in search of employment, extended family and kinship networks weakened. This, coupled with increased longevity, has created demand for caretakers for children, on the one hand, and for the frail elderly on the other.[11]

Together these forces have meant that, for those with only high school diplomas, employment in the service sector was largely restricted to jobs such as food service worker, home health aid, or cashier. Jobs in these occupations typically employ those without advanced training and offer less stable employment, less generous employee benefits, and do not provide a family wage. The result of this industrial transformation meant a slight increase in an already highly unequal income distribution.

However, these structural economic changes occurred along with demographic changes. The increase in poverty has been disproportionately borne by the new immigrants. In particular, since the 1970s, there has been an increase in immigrants and refugees from Southeast Asia and Central America who found their way to urban centers in the region, including the cities of Boston, Lawrence, and Lynn. Indeed, if the Boston region's rising technology-intensive industry can be seen as one of the benefits of US military dominance, then the increase in the immigrant population in the 1970s and 1980s can be seen as the human cost of US military incursions.

Table 4.1 Share of aggregate household income in the Boston region, by income strata, 1960–90 (%)

%	1960	1990
Bottom 20	5.8	3.5
Top 20	47.7	46.8
Top 5	17.4	19.4

Source *Data calculated from US Bureau of the Census.*

CHANGING SPATIAL PATTERNS

Boston's spatial pattern has changed dramatically since the days when its settlement reached only two to three miles beyond City Hall. On a regional level, Boston was center to its hinterland, with commercial and rail links to the industrial cities of Lowell, Waltham, and Fall River. Indeed, within these settlements, far from Boston, the same constraints of transportation and the topography of the land defined spatial patterns, and residential location was limited by the demands of the daily commute.

Overall, the pace of the region's land consumption has increased over the last two or three decades.[12] However, access to automobiles, alone, cannot explain this. Certainly the movement of industry out to Route 128 and beyond since the 1950s meant that residential locations could also move farther from the city of Boston. Demographic changes coupled with profound changes in the labor market also have contributed to the increase in suburbanization. Urban economists have long held that residential location can best be understood by a model that assumes workers choose housing to minimize their commute (Alonso, 1970). The underlying assumption is that in each household only one adult is working in the paid labor market. Moreover, because of the costs of relocation, there is a high expectation that that one employed adult will have a multi-decade relationship with their employer. However, in an era when so many households include two workers, and when workplace attachments are far weaker, the assumption that workers choose housing to minimize commutes is far more difficult to accept.

Perhaps the residential location decision should be thought of as a *household location decision.* Adult workers, then, may prefer a residential location that will increase access to the labor market over a location that minimizes the commute of one household worker to the present job. If this alternative hypothesis is reasonable, households will find locations on the fringe of metropolitan areas as optimal over the long run.

Another aspect of Boston's spatial patterns is the region's economic segregation. Within the metropolitan region, 1980 median single-family house prices showed significant variation by submarket (Case & Mayer, 1995). The high-end submarkets have always served as bedroom communities to neighboring industrial centers; these submarkets form a golden crescent along Route 128. The low-end submarkets were the center of Boston's old industrial complexes.[13] These three submarkets are scattered across eastern Massachusetts and are part of industrial era Boston's industrial hinterland.

Future work on the spatial patterns of the Boston region needs to make the link between industrial structure and residential location more explicit. For example, for some in Boston's high-technology sector, the 1990s were a period of great economic gain. Start-ups were able to find venture capital and the stock market provided powerful incentives for private firms to take their ventures public. In doing so, a great deal of wealth was created. Boston's finance industry also generated employment and wealth for the region. For example, while total employment for the metropolitan region increased by 59 percent from 1960 to 1990, in the combined finance, real estate, and insurance sector the growth was 156 percent (US Bureau of the Census, 1993). A major contributor to this growth was Fidelity Investments, an international company that manages over $475 billion in assets and currently employs more than 11,000 workers in the metropolitan region, representing somewhat less than half of the domestic work force.

When, in the eighteenth century, Boston merchants and financiers grew wealthy off of their involvement in Far East trade and the western expansion, they used their wealth to invest in Boston's next wave of economic expansion in the form of mills and factories in the region's industrial hinterland. Boston's twentieth century entrepreneurial engineers and mutual fund managers may have used their wealth to bid up the price of housing in some of the region's wealthiest communities. For the Boston metropolitan area the price of single-family houses rose 117 percent as compared with 66 percent for the US as a whole during the 1980s.[14] Moreover, the trend to increasing consumption of residential real estate is taking a new twist at the end of the 1990s. In some of these already overheated submarkets, home owners are purchasing houses that are considered modest within the context of these suburbs, only to tear them down and build what the real estate industry calls "executive mansions". For example, in Wellesley, one of the region's priciest suburbs, average house size increased more than 20 percent to 3,500 ft^2 from 1980 to the mid 1990s (Knight, 1997).

Segregation by class is apparent across the metropolitan area. However, to see segregation by race and ethnicity requires a closer examination of spatial patterns within the city of Boston itself. Historically, Boston has been a city highly segregated by race and ethnic group. For example, Irish immigrants and their descendants tended to cluster around South Boston while Italians would cluster in the North End. And, as was true in many of North America's cities, the Roxbury section of Boston saw successive waves of ethnic groups settle. In the early part of the century Russian and Eastern European Jews settled in Roxbury. However, by the 1960s Roxbury would come to be known as Boston's black neighborhood.

From the 1960s through the 1990s the influx of new ethnic and racial minorities changed the face of Boston's neighborhoods. Data collected by the Boston Foundation (Sum, 1993) shows that the effect of this influx of minorities was quite uneven across the city. Some neighborhoods, such as the North End, Charlestown, and West Roxbury, remained white enclaves during these three decades of change. Other neighborhoods, such as the South End, Dorchester, and Mattapan, which had significant minority populations in the 1970s came to be dominated by these "minorities" by 1990. Other areas, including East Boston, Allston, and Jamaica Plain experienced moderate integration during this period, but remained primarily white.

As was the case in many urban centers, groups that once had been excluded from economic and political power have achieved the heights of influence. The last three Boston city mayors have their roots in these ethnic communities (Kevin White and Raymond Flynn from the Irish community and Thomas Menino from the Italian community). Since the 1970s Boston's immigrant population has increased rapidly, with an influx from the Caribbean, Latin America, and Asia. In 1960 only 4 percent of the region's population was of a racial or ethnic minority; by 1990, this number had increased to 15 percent. There is evidence that the number continues to rise.

With high-paid professionals bidding up the cost of housing, and with the elimination of rent control in the cities of Brookline and Cambridge in the mid 1990s (the last two municipalities in the commonwealth to eliminate this income subsidy) the impoverished in the region are increasingly confined to substandard housing. And, in the Boston region, poverty is highly correlated with race and ethnicity.

Table 4.2 Poverty rates by race and ethnicity, city of Boston, 1989 (%)

Hispanic	46
Black	23
White	8

Source *Data calculated from Boston Foundation (1989).*

INFRASTRUCTURE INVESTMENT

Transportation planning and investments for the Boston region are carried out under the auspices of the Boston Metropolitan Planning Organization (MPO), a public agency with representation from federal, state and local governments.[15] Current long-term plans are designed to meet large increases in travel demand. For example, automobile and transit based trips are projected to increase about 15 percent to 20 percent over the 30 year period of 1990–2020 (Boston MPO, 1997). However, what may have the greatest impact on the quality of life of the region's residents is that vehicle miles traveled are expected to rise even more (26 percent) and vehicle hours still more (35 percent). More trips by more cars traveling more time means less control over one's time.

In contrast to transportation planning and investment, telecommunications are largely a private sector function, where coordinated planning and implementation are rare. Furthermore, the fragmented nature of local government in Boston (indeed, in all of New England), coupled with weak county governments, means that franchises for telecommunications are parceled out for relatively small geographic areas.

Roads

Boston is served by a network of interstate roads that link Boston with the northern New England States and Canada, west to upstate New York, and south to the southern New England states and New York City. In addition, the region is served by two ring routes: Route 128 and Route 495. This network provides great mobility for people and freight. Indeed, the planning agency responsible for transportation places the highest premium on mobility.[16] Such a goal translates into conditions that favor metropolitan area residents with access to automobiles over those with limited or no access to private vehicles. Because of residents' travel behavior, the demand for highways has been steadily increasing, even outpacing population increases as growth in suburban employment outpaces employment growth in the region's core.

As employment centers have increased in the suburbs, so too has the residential population; as a consequence, journey-to-work trips are increasingly suburb-to-suburb rather than the traditional commutes of in-town location to in-town location or suburb-to-central city. Indeed, according to the Boston MPO (1997), journey origins and destinations, for the transport of both people and freight, now extend beyond eastern Massachusetts to include the neighboring states of Connecticut, Maine, New Hampshire and Rhode Island.

Table 4.3 Population households, and vehicle miles traveled, Boston metropolitan region, 1980 and 1990

Variable	1980	1990	% change 1980–90
Population	2,861,322	2,922,934	2.2
Households	1,035,191	1,110,900	7.3
Vehicle miles traveled	41,401,000	51,341,000	24

Source *Boston Metropolitan Planning Organization (1997).*

Currently Boston is in the midst of the largest infrastructure project in the commonwealth's history. The Central Artery/Third Harbor Tunnel involves not simply depressing the existing elevated highway (expected completion is 2004) and adding the Ted Williams Tunnel (opened for commercial traffic in July 1995) to link Logan Airport and East Boston to the downtown but a number of related improvements as well. Some of the roadway improvements include removing elevated ramps and increasing open space in Charlestown and a Boston-to-Cambridge crossing over the Charles river.

In addition, 17 other highway projects located outside the city of Boston are listed in the transportation plan, with anticipated completion dates ranging from 1999 to 2010. These projects have been designed to either improve safety or ease congestion for suburbanites, while retaining the dominant hub–spoke structure of the road system. Transportation technology is also expected to ease some of the system's congestion, though the plans appear to be

Figure 4.6 Main roads and airports in the Boston region, 1995

modest. Currently they include automatic vehicle identification and real-time travel information.

Other improvements advance the MPO's goal of multimodalism, and the regional plan pays some attention to pedestrian and bicycle travel. While bicycle and pedestrian travel advocates have long endorsed these alternatives to single-occupancy vehicles, the federal money funneled through the Intermodal Surface Transportation Efficiency Act has provided incentives for transportation authorities to listen to this voice. The 1997 transportation plan calls for a number of bicycle trail feasibility studies. Most of these proposed bicycle trails would place new trails in abandoned rail beds in suburban communities. The MPO advocates increasing the use of bicycles for the journey to work and claims that "all new roadway projects and all reconstruction projects should provide increased safety and mobility for all users, including people who walk or bicycle" (1997). However, among the public commentators to the plan were those who argued that the MPO's support of "rails to trails" was misplaced, since most of the trail users were recreational users who drove cars to the bike trails. Additional support for the bike trails came, the citizen commentator argued, from residential abutters to the trails who wanted to make sure that the abandoned rail beds did not get revived for train use (1997).

Rail

While some of the region's abandoned rail beds are slated for bicycle paths, others will see new life as commuter rail lines. In the fall of 1997 rail services reopened after a 38 year hiatus to residents in the South Shore. The Old Colony line cost $537 million to rebuild. Demand for the service has been great; only two months after beginning its operation the two lines of the branch had exceeded the Massachusetts Bay Transit Authority's (MBTA) projections for the year 2000, with approximately 12,300 passengers riding the train during the average weekday commute. Already this increased accessibility to public transportation has contributed to rising house prices and further development along the line. Regardless of its success, the return of the railroad has not been trouble free as public officials deal with related traffic snarls, limited parking capacity and safety issues. Although the demand for commuter services is great, and such investments tend to increase property values, the proposed third line of the Old Colony service has generated a substantial amount of public protest. Residents in the town of Hingham claim that the rail service would conflict with their historic preservation goals for the downtown. Furthermore, Hingham residents are joined by others who object to the large number of level crossings.

Other less ambitious commuter rail projects are also planned, which, typically, extend existing service. These projects include the extension of the Attleboro line to New Bedford and Fall River; the extension of the Ipswich line to Newburyport; the extension of the Framingham line to Worcester. (See Figure 4.7.) However, work is also planned to improve run times and frequencies.

Within the urban core there are plans for rail improvements and additions as well. For example, Phase I of the South Boston Piers Transitway project is scheduled for completion in 2002. It will provide a fixed guideway, dual mode bus system that links the South Station rail and bus terminal to newly developed areas in South Boston. However, this proposal remains somewhat controversial, as the South Boston Pier planning and development process is coming to the attention of the public. Concerns

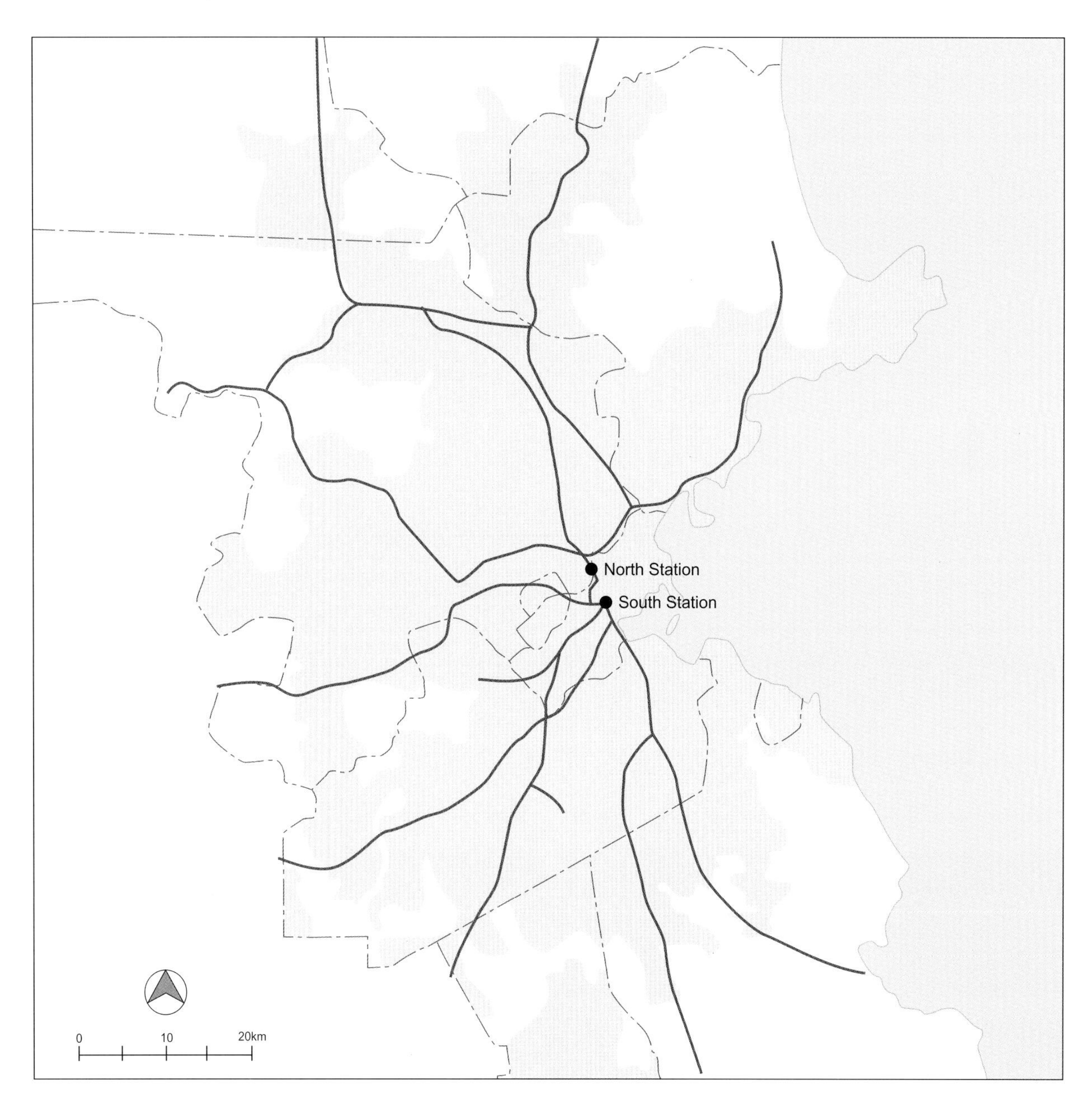

Figure 4.7 Railways in the Boston region, 1995

about keeping the waterfront accessible to pedestrians as well as making the links between a planned convention center and South Station may cause some reexamination of transit plans in the area. Improvements to South Station were completed in 1995, with North Station improvements expected to be completed in 2001. Along with North Station improvements is the shifting of Green Line trolley tracks from above-ground location to underground, improving the streetscape just beyond the entrance to North Station.

However, critics of the mass transit system argue that jobs are scattered beyond the central business district while mass transit service (excluding the commuter rail) is concentrated in the city core. For example, Somerville, an inner-ring suburb adjacent to Boston and Cambridge, is Massachusetts' most densely populated municipality, yet the MBTA has only one subway stop for 76,500 people living on 4.11 square miles of land. Employment in Somerville, Logan Airport, and other centers just beyond the borders of the city of Boston is approximately equal to that in downtown Boston. Yet workers in these centers are under-served by mass transit. A coalition of mayors in the separate jurisdictions that surround the city of Boston have begun to float the idea of an Urban Ring. The concept would entail building a new system linking neighborhoods in the inner ring suburbs and connecting to the current centrally focused rail lines. With these proposed additions the system would provide net-like coverage for the area, thereby encouraging the use of public transit and reducing commutes for residents. The MBTA is spending $278,000 to study the Urban Ring. A more limited solution to the Urban Ring service is in operation, with three limited-stop bus routes that link Cambridge with Boston's Longwood Medical Area and Roxbury; South Boston with the Longwood Medical Area; and Cambridge with Boston's South End.

Beyond the metropolitan region itself, the nation's investments in Amtrak will provide benefits to Boston. At current speeds, express trains take four to five hours to travel from Boston's South Station to New York City's Pennsylvania Station. In addition, passengers typically have a 20 minute layover in New Haven, Connecticut, while engines are switched. When the Northeast Corridor Electrification project is complete, downtown-to-downtown travel time will compete favorably with air travel, particularly when one considers roadway congestion at Logan and New York's airports. New high-speed trains are in production that will allow the nation's first high-speed rail cars to travel the highly traveled Washington DC–Boston corridor at 150 mph. The electrification project is expected to be completed by 1999. A second Amtrak project will restore rail service from Boston to Portland, Maine, and will use existing commuter and freight rail lines; operation is also expected for 1999.

Air and seaport

Air travelers coming into Boston fly over Boston harbor, and are afforded views of the distinctive topography of Cape Cod, the construction activity that includes the Boston harbor clean-up, historic Boston landmarks such as the Custom House tower,[17] as well as the city's modern skyline, largely shaped by the real estate boom of the 1980s. Massport is the commonwealth's agency responsible for the construction and maintenance of port facilities, both air and sea. As such, Massport is responsible for the Logan Airport modernization program. The program is intended to relieve congestion on the airfield, at the terminals, and on surrounding roadways. To do this, links between Logan and the region's public transit system will be improved. Currently, transit users headed for the airport typically transfer one or two times before reaching the bus that shuttles passengers from the MBTA's Blue Line to their airline terminal. Alternatively, a high-priced water taxi shuttles passengers from a hotel near the financial district across the harbor, where a bus once again transports passengers to their airline terminals. Planned connections from Logan to the Blue Line and South Station will partially alleviate these hurdles. These improvements, along with those to the airfield, terminals, and fuel distribution system are expected to cost $1 billion.

Outside Logan International Airport, the nation's thirteenth-busiest airport, the region's air travelers have few choices; however, those choices will expand. Hanscom Field, located in Boston's northwestern suburbs (see Figure 4.6), not only serves the US Air Force, but is also base to some 500 business and private aircraft. While demand for Hanscom to serve as overflow to Logan traffic is present, the airfield is surrounded by wealthy suburbs whose residents oppose increases in air traffic. Thus the fate of Hanscom to serve as a second regional airport is ambiguous. Just beyond the region's western boundary lies the city of Worcester. This troubled industrial city is attempting to revitalize Worcester Airport as an economic development tool. Massport is involved in this development with an eye to providing relief to Logan. At this stage their efforts include joint marketing and promotional efforts.

While Massport is attempting to work in collaboration with nearby Worcester, the T. F. Green Airport in Providence, Rhode Island, is in competition with Logan for air travelers. Providence is an hour's drive from downtown Boston, making the airport competitive, particularly for

South Shore residents flying at peak commuting times. Small airlines that are offering cut-rate prices on selected flights are helping to increase the prominence of the Providence airport.

Massport is also spending money on improvements at the Port of Boston. Two hundred million dollars' worth of capital improvements are in progress. However, despite these improvements, cargo handling costs, which are the northeast's highest, will continue to deter shippers from using Boston's port and are not likely to increase the current shipping traffic from the two cargo ships per week that now come to call. Other port improvements include a $67 million dredging project to deepen the port so that it can handle larger cargo ships. However, the lack of agreement between the Longshoremen's Association and Massport is unlikely to alter the cost structure of handling cargo; thus, despite costly improvements, the role of the port in Boston's transportation system will remain limited (*Boston Globe Online*, 1998).

If Boston harbor has limited potential for cargo traffic, there is room for expansion in commuter traffic. Ferries now provide service from South Shore communities to downtown Boston and Logan Airport. Massport expects expanded commuter boat service within the harbor to be completed in 1999. These services include boats linking the North Station rail terminus with the World Trade Center and Logan Airport, and the Charlestown Navy Yard to downtown and South Station. (See Figure 4.1.)

Telecommunications

During the latter part of the 1980s and the 1990s access to cable, wireless technology, computers, and the internet increased tremendously. As cellular networks expanded so too did use. For example, from a base of just over 5 million subscribers in 1990 nationwide, cellular phone subscribers increased to over 55 million by 1997. Similarly, the same type of explosive growth is evident in connections to the internet, where the number of internet hosts in the United States jumped from approximately 200,000 to just under 20 million during the same time period.[18] This tremendous surge in use can be accounted for by a number of factors, including increases in disposable income, technological innovations, and market deregulation. The deregulation of the market began in earnest in 1984 with the break-up of AT&T. A second round of restructuring occurred 12 years later. The Telecommunications Act of 1996 hurled the US telecommunications industry into the midst of tremendous upheaval and readjustment. The Bill was intended to open up the industry to market forces, eliminate the monopolistic structure that had dominated for the past century, and ultimately allow the general population more options, better rates, and increased access to technology. While the new regulations are intended to increase consumer options, technological advances have required some market restructuring. The first round of deregulation split AT&T's long-distance from its local service and allowed other long-distance carriers to compete with AT&T. This gave the local carriers (the so-called 'Baby Bells') territorial monopolies. Just as AT&T had an advantage in long-distance competition with upstart companies like Sprint and MCI, the Baby Bells now have an advantage in competing with companies interested in providing a variety of telecommunication services such as local phone, cable television, internet access, and the like. If the second round of deregulation is successful, no longer will a small number of large incumbent companies control entire market segments.

The deregulation process is still in its early stages, and most services rely on existing telecommunications infrastructure, which the incumbent companies are mandated to lease to smaller competitors. The competitors may be local or long-distance telephone carriers, cable television companies, internet providers, or some hybrid of these. Companies that are used to operating in a monopoly or regulated market are now faced with the dual pressures of rapid technological change coupled with seismic market restructuring. Some in the industry warn that the massive increases in voice and data traffic will cause a virtual "meltdown"; others argue that the phone carriers are failing to invest in bandwidth, which will place the US at a disadvantage with regard to international competition (Harris, 1997). Regardless, while the market adjusts to the new institutional structure created by the Telecommunications Act, the fight for market share is keeping prices low for consumers.

Within this national institutional structure, the Boston metropolitan area continually shows high growth for computer access, internet connections, and wireless communications. In part this is due to the high concentration of high-tech industries in the area, but also, and in some cases more importantly, because of the number of colleges and universities. Indeed, Middlesex County was ranked fourth in the nation in 1997 for number of internet connections—a distinction for which Harvard University is primarily responsible (Matrix Information and Directory Services, 1997).

However, in an area where educational, industrial, and service industries alike rely on information technology to remain competitive and efficient, individual access remains highly dependent on income levels. Thus, while making physical distances less significant in people's personal and professional lives, these same advances can create barriers to those in lower income groups and increase social stratification based on information availability.[19] The Telecommunications Act was intended to help rectify this situation by lowering costs through competitive forces, but another option would be to create programs that would allow access to these technologies for those who cannot afford ownership.

Conclusion

Infrastructure in the Boston region both reflects and reinforces the metropolitan area's social structure. The hub-and-spoke configuration of the transportation infrastructure is reflected in the core-and-satellite relationship between the central city and its residential suburbs. Once, the region's commuter rails moved suburbanites into the city center where the majority of its high-wage jobs were located. However, a number of factors, including the region's circumferential highways, have contributed to drastic changes in commuting patterns. Now suburbs are home to Boston's lawyers and financiers as well as to the owners, investors, and employees of the new knowledge-intensive and high-technology firms. Public transit, however, is inadequate to the task of moving workers along the newer commuting paths created by this change in the industrial landscape. Consequently, single-occupancy vehicles are the modal form of transit, and bumper-to-bumper peak-hour commutes are common on the region's most traveled commuter routes.

Infrastructure investments in the city of Boston are evident (even intrusive during the current phase of construction) as the Central Artery/Third Harbor Tunnel project continues to consume huge sums. Nevertheless, central city residents face crowded subway cars and difficulty making simple cross-town trips. It would be wrong, however, to argue that circumferential highways alone increased the low-density suburban development in the region. But, as the region's propulsive high-tech industries provided employment opportunities for engineers and other technically trained workers in the suburbs, public investments reflected social and political strength.

Regional land use plans and other initiatives to manage regional form

In the Boston metropolitan region there is an absence of formal regionwide planning to shape the built environment, and there are no effective mechanisms in place to do so even if the will existed either in the public or in the private sectors. This is largely due to a transportation policy dedicated to increasing mobility as opposed to access,[20] a highly decentralized form of governance—even in comparison to other US regions—and private developers' decisions, which are made chiefly on a piecemeal basis. In all of New England the direct participatory form of democratic governance is deeply entrenched, and eastern Massachusetts is no different. While there are many variations, tradition and size play a large part in determining the precise form of governance in each town. Most localities follow the town meeting form of government,[21] with either meetings open to all registered voters or elected meeting representatives. In addition, the "home rule doctrine" allows local governments to carry out any function, except those specifically denied by the commonwealth's constitution or the legislature.[22] This government structure does a lot to give residents a strong sense of place and connection with local institutions; however, it also tends to create institutional barriers to regional thought and action.

While the public sector is limited in its ability to think and act regionally, the market is indifferent to city and town boundaries. Certainly, finance capital has a long tradition of seeking the highest returns on investment regardless of borders. While it is far easier to move capital over distances, increasing labor mobility can be seen through the prism of the history of transportation and telecommunications. Improvements in public transportation meant that workers could seek employment beyond the range of intracity public transit. While capital and labor markets both have relatively long geographic reaches, land markets are fixed in space.

One result of these differences is that while the capital and labor markets partially determine both the supply and the demand for developed land, there is no market mechanism for expressing community preferences. In the Boston region the political mechanism for expressing community preferences is largely via town governance structures that do a relatively good job of allowing citizens to influence decisions made locally that have an effect on institutions such as schools, parks, police and fire protection. However, the relatively small size of each of these local governments, coupled with the popular impression that local control would be lost were regional governance structures strengthened or created,[23] leaves communities free to be shaped by powerful market forces that, in fact, have significant "local" effects. The irony is, of course, that joining in some sort of regional compact could conceivably result in *less* of a loss of local control than the *status quo*.

In light of these conditions groups of citizens have turned to a variety of nongovernmental initiatives to manage urban form, including a variety of local small-scale initiatives in the Boston region that represent citizens' attempts to improve the environment in which they live, in the expectation that improvements in the quality of their lives will follow. These initiatives are motivated by a variety of concerns, from esthetic to ecological to an interest in how the fabric of individuals' lives is shaped, formed, and transformed by the built environment. These examples vary from experiments in housing, in community based urban economic development, in community based suburban redevelopment, and in agricultural preservation. Some focus on themes of empowerment and target excluded social and economic groups, while others seek a radical transformation in personal relationships as the necessary first step in the radical transformation of political relationships. They are grass roots attempts by citizens to create and shape institutions through which groups can define and express community values when existing political and economic institutions fall short.[24]

CONCLUSION

The story of the spatial structure of the Boston metropolitan region is a story of the invention, acceptance, and obsolescence of products and services for local, national, and international markets; of how this production is organized in space; of how the profits of one industrial era exert their influence over the spatial structure in the next, and how the spatial structure is both created by this process and itself shapes it.

Despite the central role that market forces have played in the Boston metropolitan region, one cannot understand the region without understanding the strong role that the government played. Beginning with the Bay State Colony's first settlements that were grants from the King of England, to the US government's assistance to MIT via the Morrill Land Grant Act, to the role that the federal government played in the region's high-technology industry during World War II as well as during the Cold War, Boston has excelled in harnessing the contributions from a variety of sources to yield what appears to be a more powerful economic force.

Technological and social forces are exerting a centrifugal force on the region. Route 128 has been replaced by the Route 495 ring road as the defining limit of the Boston region. Telecommunications served to promote further growth outside the city of Boston. However, disinvestment by both the private and the public sectors, in terms of physical as well as social construction, also contributed to the central city population declines.

In the first quarter of the twenty-first century the Boston region is likely to be a globally competitive region driven by its strength in technology, financial services, and medical science. The degree to which it is a city that the residents of other global cities want to emulate may well rest on the continuing creativity and tenacity of its citizens, organized into place based communities to make modest changes in the landscape. These efforts can be understood as attempts by communities not to get lost in the force of global processes that require metropolitan areas to compete on a global scale yet, ironically, leave them looking more alike than before and less able to differentiate themselves one from another.

NOTES

1. See Warner (1962) for an in-depth study of these three Boston suburbs.
2. The seeds of Massachusetts' highly fragmented local government may be traced to this era. Conzen and Lewis (1976) report that "[t]he Massachusetts Bay Colony spread settlement inland by setting up highly independent 'towns' that, in the early stages, traded relatively little with Boston."
3. Hekman, John S. and John S. Strong (1981) attribute a great deal of the available capital for industrial investment in this period to the "mercantile profits made in the China trade during the halcyon period from 1793 to 1807" (p. 44).
4. See North (1961: chapter 12) for a wonderful description of the economics of this time and place.
5. The magnetron was the center of the newly invented radar systems that the British were using against the German bombers.
6. In 1953 the US Air Force became the legal owner of Hanscom Field.
7. Route 128 was the nation's first limited access circumferential highway and was intended to provide recreational access to the Atlantic Ocean north and south of the city of Boston.
8. Wang did his advanced training in physics outside MIT's immediate orbit; he was at Harvard's Computation Lab before going out on his own.
9. Nancy S. Dorfman (in Lampe, 1988) uses a definition of high technology that includes a variety of industries, from computers to drugs, from guided missiles to household appliances. Despite the breadth of industries included in her definition, in 1979 almost 65 percent of Massachusetts' high-tech employment was accounted for by only five industries: electronic components and accessories; office computing and accounting machines; communications equipment; measuring and controlling instruments; and guided missiles and space vehicles.
10. Average earnings of unionized workers were 11 percent higher than those of non-unionized workers in the commonwealth (Bureau of National Affairs, 1997).

11 For example, the US Bureau of Labor Statistics (1995) identifies home health aides, human service workers, and personal and home care aides as the nation's fastest growing occupations for the 1995–2000 period.

12 One measure of this increasing land consumption is the falling density rates. However, while the region as a whole has seen land consumption increase, within the area that the Boston Metropolitan Planning Organization defines as its region (excluding some of the farthest reaches of our definition of the region) the pattern of density decline is somewhat unexpected. For example, densities have been falling in the "inner core" while slight increases have been recorded for suburbs located in subregions to the west, southwest, and on the South Shore (Boston, MPO, 1997).

13 1980 median single family house values for top three and bottom three submarkets (Case & Mayer, 1995):

Rank	*Submarket*	*Value 1980 ($)*
1	Concord, Wellesley, Weston, Carlisle, Acton, Wayland, Sudbury, Dover, Sherbom, Westwood	96,430
2	Belmont, Winchester, Newton, Lexington	83,360
3	Andover, North Reading, Tewksbury, North Andover, Dracut, Chelmsford	65,360
25	City of Boston	33,330
26	Worcester*	35,500
27	Fall River, New Bedford	33,330

* Worcester is an old industrial city, just outside the Route 495 belt, and is excluded from our definition of the Boston region

14 Data are for the Boston Metropolitan Statistical Area for the median price of existing single-family houses, 1982 to 1990, McGraw-Hill/DRI, US Regional Service.

15 Transportation planning for the region is done in accordance with the federal 1991 Intermodal Surface Transportation Efficiency Act (ISTEA) and associated planning regulations. A key feature of ISTEA is that transportation planning occurs within the context of an established MPO that meets the federal goal of intergovernmental co-operation. Prior to ISTEA, Boston's MPO had operated with a rather heavy hand from the commonwealth. Representatives from state-level agencies (e.g. Port Authority, Turnpike Authority, Highway Department) are joined by representatives from the Federal Highway and Transportation Administrations. At the regional level, the Metropolitan Regional Planning Council (which represents 101 cities and towns in the region) is included, as is the city of Boston, all as permanent members of the MPO's Central Transportation Planning Staff. In addition, three representatives are elected from the region's cities and three from the towns. The process is still quite new.

16 According to the Boston MPO, "It is the vision of this Transportation Plan to maintain, manage, and operate a multimodal transportation system in the Boston region that provides a high level of mobility for all people and economic activity consistent with environmental and fiscal resources." Some critics of the plan, as noted in the public comment section of the plan, take issue with the MPO's focus on mobility over accessibility. For example, in criticizing the existing project evaluation criteria (e.g. cost effectiveness; change in vehicle miles traveled; change in productivity; change in accidents) the Environment Department of the City of Boston argued that comparisons should be made among projects, rather than on the project basis used by the MPO. In another comment by the Massachusetts Sierra Club the MPO plan was criticized for continuing the *status quo*, defined as "a continuing reliance in the region on the widening and reconstruction of roadways in an attempt to accommodate peak hour traffic volumes consisting mainly of single occupancy vehicles" (1997).

17 The evolution of the Custom House marks some of the important transitions that Boston has experienced. In 1847 the then $1 million Greek Revival-style Custom House was built; in 1914 the federal government, in need of more space, added a 495 ft Italian Renaissance tower. In 1986 the city of Boston paid the federal government $11 million for the building. The tower results in a relatively small floor plate, and renovations that respected the historical integrity of the building were difficult. The building was vacant until the city sold it for $6 million to private developers and the Marriott Corporation. After a $26 million renovation the Marriott Corporation is selling time shares (Miara, 1997).

18 The term "host" is defined simply as a computer connected to the internet. It does not represent the number of people using that computer.

19 For example, correlation between household income and computer use for adults 18 years or over (US, 1993, %):

Family income	*Uses computer anywhere*	*With computer at home*
Up to $10,000	11.4	6.8
$10,000–$14,999	15.2	8.4
$15,000–$19,999	23.0	12.5
$20,000–$24,999	27.7	15.3
$25,000–$34,999	36.5	21.2
$35,000–$49,999	46.3	31.3
$50,000–$74,999	60.3	45.9
$75,000 and over	65.4	61.7

Current Population Survey, October 1993.

20 "The MPO's overriding vision for the region is 'to maintain, manage, and operate a muiltimodal transportation system in the Boston region that provides a high level of mobility for all people and economic activity consistent with environmental and fiscal resources'" (1997). This is in contrast to a concern about increasing access, or shaping the urban form, or other possible policy goals.

21 Local governments in Massachusetts are either cities or towns. Within the Boston region designated here there are 202 cities and towns in Massachusetts as well as New Hampshire. Cities have mayors and elected city councilors; the mayor serves as the chief executive while the city council provides district representation. Towns have "boards of selectmen" who are elected to represent districts. Towns convene town meetings at least once a year. The moderator is elected to run the meeting. The town's professional staff are hired by the town's operating officer, either a town manager or an administrator, each having somewhat different statutory responsibilities. The chief operating officer serves at the pleasure of the board of selectmen.

22 Despite home rule, additional constraints are placed on Boston by the state legislature that prohibits the city from acting independently on a variety of issues, both large and small.

23 Indeed, county level government was all but dismantled. On July 11, 1997, Governor Weld signed legislation that abolished Middlesex, Worcester, and Hampden Counties. The entire system is likely to be abolished.

24 The examples range from the Dudley Street Neighborhood Initiative (DSNI) in the Roxbury section of Boston that has led redevelopment in this urban neighborhood to cohousing experiments in the city of Cambridge and the metro-west suburb of Acton; to community supported agriculture in Ipswich that combines a farm and pre-school; to the Cape Ann Sustainable Community Project (CASC) in Gloucester that has opened up its home to homeless families as one aspect of an attempt to radically recreate the relationship of care; CASC has gone on to build housing on land held by the community in trust. There are many more examples across the region.

BIBLIOGRAPHY

Alonso, William (1964) *Location and Land Use*, Cambridge MA: Harvard University Press.

Boston Foundation (1989) *In the Midst of Plenty: A Profile of Boston and its Poor*, Boston MA: Boston Foundation.

Boston Metropolitan Planning Organization (1997) *Transportation Plan for the Boston Region*, Boston MA: BMPO.

Bureau of Labor Statistics (1995) http://stats.bls.gov

Bureau of National Affairs (1997) *Union Membership and Earnings Data Book, 1990s: Compilations from the Current Population Survey*, Washington DC: BNA.

Case, Karl E., and Mayer, Christopher J. (1995) "The Housing Cycle in Eastern Massachusetts: Variations among Towns and Cities," *New England Economic Review*, March–April, pp. 24–40.

CATV Cyberlab (1997) "Detailed Industry Statistics: State Data." http://www.catv.org

Cellular Telecommunications Industry Association (1996) *State of the Cellular Industry*, Washington DC: CTIA. http://www.wow-com.com

Consumer Electronics Manufacturers' Association (1996) "Consumer Electronics and the US Economy: Factoids Online." http://www.cemacity.org/govt/cefiles/page5.htm

Conzen, Michael P., and Lewis, George K. (1976) *Boston: A Geographical Portrait*, Cambridge MA: Ballinger.

Eisner, James (1997) "Distribution of Intrastate and Interstate Telephone Revenue by States," Washington DC: Industry Analysis Division, Federal Communications Commission.

Harris, Blake (1997) "Economic Development: the Race for Bandwidth," *Government Technology* 10 (13), pp. 126–30.

Heckman, John S., and Strong, John S. (1981) "The Evolution of New England's Economy," *New England Economic Review*, March–April, pp. 35–46.

"Importance of Port of Boston seen Slipping," *Boston Globe* Online, 14 January. http://www.boston.com/globe/

Knight, Deborah (1997) "Make Way for Mansions," *Boston Sunday Globe Magazine*, 19 October, p. 16.

Lampe, David (1988) *The Massachusetts Miracle: High Technology and Economic Revitalization*, Cambridge MA: MIT Press.

Massachusetts Department of Telecommunications and Energy (1996) "Massachusetts Cable Statistics." http://www.state.ma.us/dpu/catv/catv.htm

Matrix Information and Directory Services (1997) *Matrix Maps Quarterly* 4 (2), p. 4.

Miara, Jim (1997) "Custom Housing: Renovation of Boston Landmark Completed: Mariott Markets Units," *Boston Business Journal*, 25 August. http://cgi.amcity.com/ boston/

National Center for Health Statistics (1960–90) *Vital Statistics of the United States*, Washington DC: Government Printing Office.

Network Wizards (1998) Internet Domain Survey. http://www.nw.com/

Nielsen Media Research (1996) *Home Technology Report*, New York: Nielsen.

North, Douglass C. (1961) *The Economic Growth of the United States, 1790–1860*, Englewood Cliffs NJ: Prentice-Hall.

Stein, Charles (1997) "Economic Divide of Races is Cited: Massachusetts Study finds Split on Jobs, Pay," *Boston Sunday Globe* Online, 26 October. http://www.boston.com/globe/

Sum, Andrew, *et al.* (1993) *White Poverty in Boston*, Boston MA: Boston Foundation.

Torto, Raymond G., and Wheaton, William C. (1994) "Downtown/Suburban Competition for Jobs in the 1990s: Economic Policy Implications for Boston," Boston MA: John W. McCormack Institute of Public Affairs.

US Bureau of Economic Analysis (1977) "Gross State Product: New Estimates for 1993–94 and Revised Estimates for 1977–92," press release BEA 97–15. http://www.bea.doc.gov/bea/gsp0697c.prn

US Bureau of the Census (1993) "Use of Computers at Home, School, and Work by Persons eighteen Years and older," *Current Population Survey*, October, Washington DC: Government Printing Office.

Warner, Sam Bass (1962) *Streetcar Suburbs: The Process of Growth in Boston, 1870–1900*, Forge Village MA: Harvard University Press and MIT Press.

5 The Madrid region

José María Ezquiaga with
Eva Cimadevilla and Gemma Peribáñez

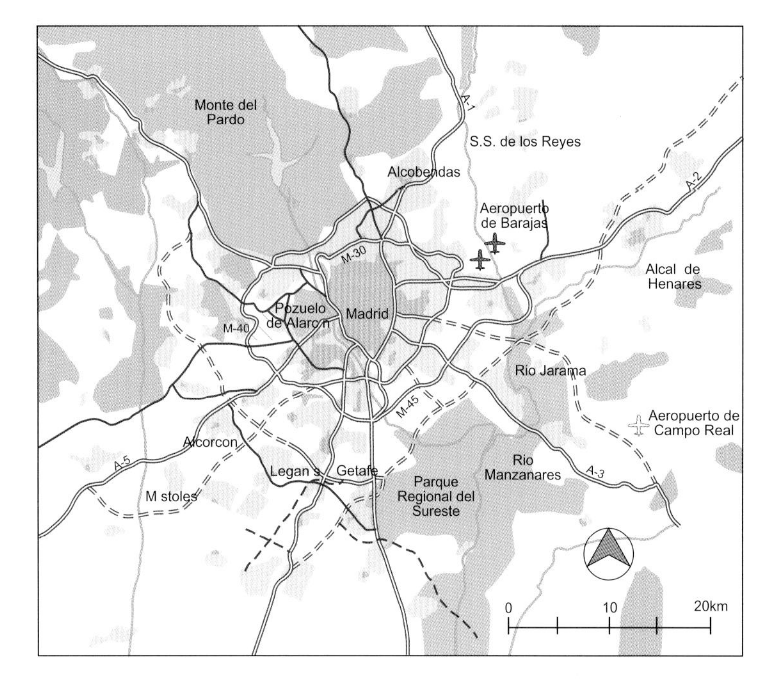

Figure 5.1 The Madrid region, 1995

The metropolitan area of Madrid has its origins in the fact that Madrid has been the state capital since the sixteenth century. Although as a whole the territory tends towards a high degree of functional integration, four important areas can be differentiated for explanatory purposes:

- The urban core, which can be understood as the area of the historic city, known as the Casco Antiguo (Old Town), and the successive amplifications of the nineteenth and twentieth centuries within the M-30 ring road. It constitutes a compact and dense urban fabric of 41.7 km^2 and 990,679 inhabitants (20 percent of the regional total), in which the major part of the capital's functions and most important tertiary activities are concentrated.
- The municipality of Madrid is understood to be the urban core and a first periphery area made up of neighborhoods, which were originally independent municipalities that with the passing of time have been swallowed up in the expansion of the city. It has an area of 605.8 km^2 and 3,010,492 inhabitants (60.85 percent of the total).
- The "metropolitan crown", understood to be the 26 municipalities (apart from Madrid) closest to and functionally most integrated with the capital. In the main, they are included in the body of the metropolitan area of Madrid, which was created in 1963 and ended with the creation of the Autonomous Community. Its area is 1,336 km^2 and it has a population of 1,582,077 (31.98 percent of the total).
- The Community of Madrid coincides with the administrative limits of the province of the same name, which was established in 1833, covering an area of 8,027 km^2. It constitutes one of the Autonomous Communities into which the state was organised territorially under the 1978 constitution. As a result it has institutions of

self-government and a directly elected parliament. Its current population stands at 4,947,555 (12.7 percent of Spain's total population).

During the last decade Madrid, like many other European metropolises, has experienced profound transformations in its economic structure and territorial organization.

It is a long time since the old metropolitan model of the 1960s was in use. Rigidly hierarchical and functionally specialised, best summed up by the image of a potent urban center which concentrated the major proportion of population and employment, and was surrounded by successive peripheries in a constellation of dormitory nucleuses. Alternative tendencies have appeared which move towards the construction of a more articulated territory in which the new territorial processes cover over the old inherited pathology which belonged to the period of the formation of the metropolitan area.

Figure 5.2 The location of the Madrid region

The traditional relationships of dependence between the centre and the periphery appear to have altered substantially owing to the appearance of new urban centers in areas previously considered to be peripheral and the existence of worrying processes of congestion or social and environmental decline in the old central neighborhoods. A strong tendency to residential suburbanization has appeared, and recently economic activity has also begun to move into the suburbs. These processes imply levels of occupation of territory on a scale never known before and a huge increase in the demand for transport. To sum up, the tendency towards the replacement of the old metropolitan scheme—which was similar to a solar system—by a reticulated territorial structure with new urban poles, yet still marked by strong socieconomic disequilibria (inequalities?) and environmental risks, appears to be clear.

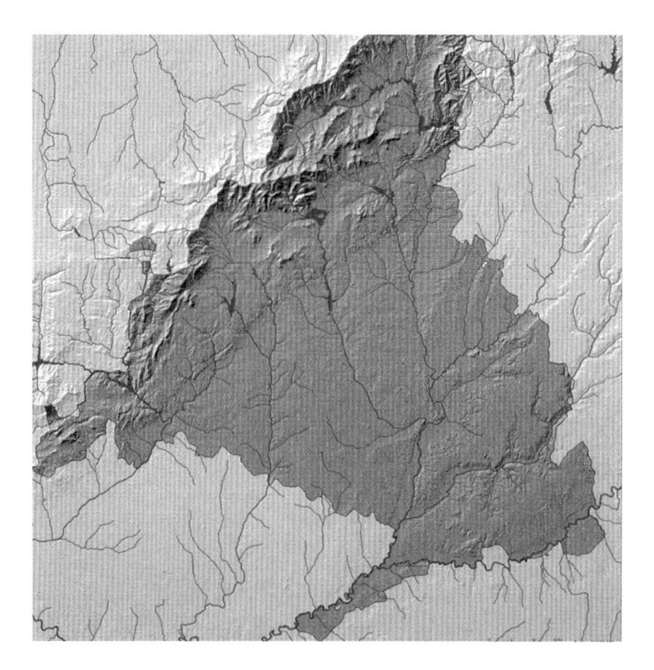

Figure 5.3 The Autonomous Community of Madrid

The first legitimate question which may be asked is whether these tendencies will help to overcome in a positive way the problems and structural disequilibria of the inherited metropolitan scheme, or whether, on the contrary, they could signify a new factor to aggravate the existing imbalances and pressures. The answer will depend a great deal on the strategies which the region is able to develop to redirect these spontaneous tendencies towards territorial restructuring.

Apart from this, the complexity of the new territory demands integrated action, which can come only from a coherent and ample Territorial Project. Isolated action on any one of the distinct problems could well be neutralised by the overall scale of the problems, or generate a "frontier effect" by simply moving the site where the problems manifest themselves.

CHANGING ECONOMIC PATTERNS

The basic sectors of the economy of the region of Madrid are service industries and, in particular, services focused on sales and industry, followed by construction, with an agrarian sector that has hardly any quantitative importance in relation to total production.

In terms of employment, the high degree of tertiarization in the economy of Madrid can be confirmed by the process of economic specialization that has been visible in recent years. The increased importance of the service sector can be explained by the city's role as the state and

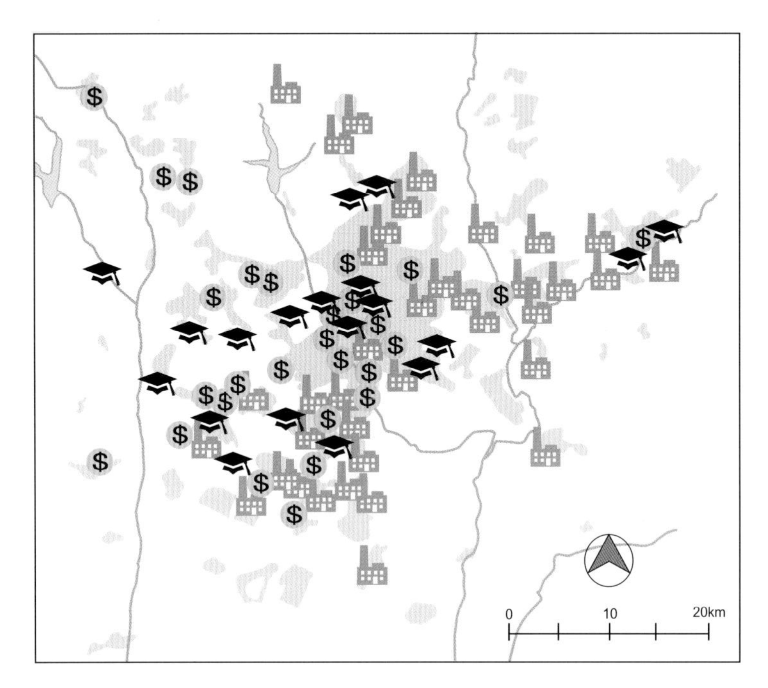

Figure 5.4 Economic patterns in the Madrid region

financial capital of the country and as the site of the head offices of major national and international companies. Its central geographical position is also a determining factor, above all in the radial structure of its road network and the flow of passengers and goods by rail and air. In combination these factors have converted Madrid into a nerve center of transport and communications within the Iberian peninsula.

Table 5.1 Value added by areas of economic activity, 1991–95 (pta billion)

Economic activity	**Autonomous Community of Madrid**					**Spain**
	1991	**1992**	**1993**	**1994**[a]	**1995**[b]	**1995**[b]
Agriculture	14.5	16.8	17.9	20.3	19.0	2,041.3
Energy	211.8	220.4	234.1	244.4	249.4	3,812.0
Manufacturing	1,395.8	1,397.8	1,404.4	1,486.0	1,589.9	13,016.4
Construction	757.4	789.9	809.9	826.2	920.3	5,736.2
Sales-related services	4,911.5	5,348.2	5,643.4	5,955.9	6,347.5	35,701.7
Services unrelated to sales	1,316.8	1,473.1	1,531.5	1,622.2	1,772.1	9,580.3
Total	8,607.8	9,246.2	9,641.2	10,155.0	10,898.2	69,887.9

Notes [a] *Provisional data.* [b] *Advance information.*

Source Contabilidad regional de España. Base 1986. INE..

Table 5.2 Employment by economic sector (%)

	Autonomous Community of Madrid					**Spain**
Sectors	**1992**	**1993**	**1994**	**1995**	**1996**	**1996**
Manufacturing	27.1	26.0	25.2	25.2	23.3	31.2
Construction	10.4	9.6	8.9	8.8	8.4	9.6
Services	62.5	64.3	65.9	66.0	68.2	59.2
Total	100.0	100.0	100.0	100.0	100.0	100.0

Source Encuesta de Coyuntura Laboral, Secretaria General Tecnica, Ministerio de Trabajo y Asuntos Sociales.

Industry

Within the industrial arm of the economy, the most significant contributions in terms of financial value are, in order of importance, the branches of the metalworking industries, machinery and electrical goods, the chemical industry, food, drink and tobacco, paper and the graphic arts, and transport equipment. We have seen expansion in the chemical industry, food and drink and transport equipment. The region specialises, by comparison with the rest of Spain, in high-technology equipment (electronic equipment, precision and optical instruments and office machinery) and also in some consumer goods (printing and publishing and pharmaceutical products).

Industry is concentrated in the Corredor de Henares and in the municipal areas of the south within the first and second municipal ring (see Figure 5.4). These locations are supported by the capital's population and the excellent communications with Barcelona, Toledo and Andalucia.

One of the most important characteristics of industry in Madrid is the process of diffusion from the center towards the periphery, known as the "frontier effect", which involves the movement of industrial sites beyond the boundaries of the region, in response to the lower price of floor space and subsidies from the local authorities.

Services

The service sector contributes 74.5 percent of the earnings of the region's economy and is clearly concentrated in the center of the metropolitan area, as it is the most effective place to reach a potential market of 5 million inhabitants. Nearly all public services are located here and occupy a quarter of the total available floor space.

Within the service sector, the most important activity is the "business to business" subsector, whose constant growth has led it to exceed the floor space requirements of the financial sector, the traditional occupant of the floor space used by the tertiary sector in Madrid.

As in the industrial sector, services have witnessed a drastic change in their requirements for physical space, with an important demand for equipment and quality of environment.

CHANGING SOCIAL PATTERNS

The concentric territorial structure of the metropolitan area of Madrid, together with the strong rates of population growth experienced owing to the intense migratory flows from other provinces and natural settlement have been the determining factors for the last twenty or thirty years. They have produced the type and structure of population which is characterized by strong territorial disequilibria.

After the era of growth, a period of reduction in natural growth rates and the ageing of the generations who were responsible for the heavy migration was experienced. This was accompanied by the enforced movement of young adults towards the periphery as a result of the tertiarization of the residential space of the center.

This movement clearly characterizes the reality of the center of the metropolitan area, which is occupied primarily by government and immersed in a process of population ageing and loss. In contrast, the different zones of the metropolitan ring, occupied by groups of young people, find themselves at the end of their stage of rapid natural growth and at the beginning of a process of ageing. The western area differs from the general trend because of migration from the center of the metropolitan area.

This population dynamic corresponds to factors of urban development, the location of economic activities and the existence of transport infrastructure. It reflects the geographical distribution of income. In this way, the Madrid municipal area is the most important, receiving more than two-thirds of the regional income, with a per family level clearly above the regional average. The metropolitan ring presents large differences, being the area to the west with the highest level of income, followed by the north and east. The municipal areas to the south have the lowest levels of income. (See Figure 5.4.)

The spatial distribution of the population

In 1975 more than 75 percent of the Madrid regional population lived in the capital. In 1991, the percentage was 61 percent. In the last few years, in the middle of a continuing process of deconcentration, it has hardly reached 50 percent. The municipalities that have been favoured by this phenomenon are those situated outside of the metropolitan area, those in the west, where there is a predominance of single-family dwellings, and to a lesser extent those to the north and east.

In contrast to the evolution at the beginning of the 1960s, it is now the municipalities of the south that are experiencing a slowdown in population growth. The municipal areas of Madrid, Alcorcon and Mostoles are the ones experiencing a relative decline in their importance, while the rest of the large municipalities are maintaining relative stability.

Lifestyles

At the end of 1994 the average family size was 3.2 members, less than in the past but still above the European average. It has been projected that in the year 2006 the average size will be 2.6 people.

The vast majority of homes are nuclear—couples with their children, it being normal for the latter to remain in their parents' house well into adulthood. More than a third of those between the ages of 30 and 34 remain in their parents' homes as a consequence of the problems of access to work and housing.

CHANGING SPATIAL PATTERNS

The process of formation of metropolitan Madrid has been characterized by the contradiction between the ideal schemes for urban expansion and the actual expansion of the metropolis since the beginnings of urban planning in the nineteenth century. The ideal model of urban expansion as a spreading "oil stain" was substituted for the uneven development of suburban peripheries, producing waves which colonized urban rings farther and farther out, leaving a great deal of empty space which later, when its value was realized, became the object of redevelopment.

This uneven growth, conditioned by minimum investment in the creation of new infrastructure, had to support itself on the radial road network that connects Madrid with the rest of the country and on the weak infrastructure and urban morphology of the primitive rural centers in the orbit of Madrid. In this way a very heterogeneous territory was laid down, characterized by the functional and social differences between the diverse radial sectors in which the capital was organized.

After 1929, in the face of the impossibility of keeping to the original plan of urban development, a change of direction in thinking and urban planning was produced. The resulting model was characterized by:

- Growth to the north, supported by a new central area.
- A limit on the expansion of the main area by several green belts.
- The organization of new settlements around ring roads designed to ease traffic congestion.

The *Plan General* of 1946 was the first to look beyond the limits of the city of Madrid and proposed a transport network for the adequate organization of the territory. To fulfill this aim, an infrastructure, whose basic design has lasted until the present day, was based upon the combination of successive orbital motorways and new radial connections.

While the plan was in force (1946–63), the heavy demographic growth due to the massive influx of in-migrants to the capital outstripped the forecasts of the planners. This situation necessitated, in the *Plan Metropolitano* of 1963, a more pragmatic approach to planning, based on an extension of the area where building was permitted in a network towards the east, new green belts and orbital motorways farther from the city center.

Meanwhile, outside of the plan, the process of "suburbanization" was being initiated. The capital city failed to reach the population levels predicted in the plan, while the metropolitan population easily outstripped the most extreme predictions.

The municipality of Madrid underwent a qualitative transformation during this period. The central "almond" readapted its morphology to new tertiary activities and the growth of the public administration. This tendency, combined with the migratory flows, produced a territory which was functionally specialized and socially fragmented. An arc from southeast to southwest took industrial employment (see Figure 5.4), and the population with lower income, for the most part rural in-migrants, formed the system of dormitory towns on top of the existing pattern of rural settlements

Owing to the lack of transport, growth continued to gravitate to the existing routes, leading to a radial unit form, deformed by the weight of the population of the south and the dynamism of the Corredor del Henares towards the airport and the east.

By 1971 this had resulted in an area prematurely congested and conditioned by:

- Functional and social fragmentation.
- Dependence on the metropolitan center.
- Lack of a collective transport system.
- Precariousness of the basic infrastructure.
- Rigidity in the housing market, with an absence of rented accommodation which would permit residential mobility closer to the place of work.

After 1971 the adoption of the *Esquema Director Regional* constituted the first attempt to replace the traditional radial-centric scheme with a linear scheme based upon the potential of the northeast axis in the direction of Barcelona, where the airport is situated. Thus in 1972 an arterial road network consisting of three complete orbital motorways (M-30, M-40, M-50) was incorporated into the *Plan Metropolitano*, which reinforced the radial-centric model.

The urbanism of the 1980s was characterized by acceptance of the impossibility of changing the inherited metropolitan structure in the short term. Instead, as a strategy Madrid opted, as did many western regions, for the transformation of the city on a local scale. The *Plan General del Municipio de Madrid de 1985*, faced with the reality of the fragmented urban periphery, set as an immediate objective the attainment of physical continuity and rebalancing the integral parts of the city.

This attempt to overcome the old hierarchical and functionally specialized metropolitan model has resulted in a progressive transformation to a more complex space with the following tendencies:

- The generation of new centers in zones previously considered to be peripheral.
- The appearance of new forms of suburbanization of residential activity and the occupation of peripheral space for economic activity.
- A strong increase in demand for mobility, in both public transport and private vehicles.

The main features of the metropolitan region at present can be synthesized in the following points:

- The city center has conserved its vitality as a cultural and "directional" center, although with a tendency towards displacement to the north of the central "almond". In this area saturation levels are being reached.
- The Old Town is beginning a period of decline, which is affecting the different neighborhoods in different ways. While some are welcoming the return of the suburban population with greater income, others are experiencing a process of environmental degradation and social marginalization.
- The metropolitan periphery formed over the old rural centers which forms the second and third metropolitan rings has got over the initial lack of facilities and is now taking part in the growth of economic activity, evolving towards the construction of a pattern of more balanced cities.
- The urban southern periphery of the municipality of Madrid is experiencing a progressive decline in living conditions and environmental quality due to the formation of areas of chronic unemployment and the resulting social marginalization.
- The suburbs of low density in the west are growing in size and are rapidly extending towards the Sierra de Guadarrama, with a great increase in tertiary installations and large commercial shopping areas. This is in an area characterized by high environmental quality.
- New centers of activity and new residential enclaves are crystalizing around the points of maximum accessibility to the public transport system and the metropolitan road network.

The sum of these processes has meant an increase in the use of land area on a scale unknown since the 1960s. Initiating a period of expansion without demographic growth which has had no precedent until now.

INFRASTRUCTURE INVESTMENT

The tendency towards the "decentralization" of economic activities is the style of growth which characterizes the mature period of metropolitan agglomeration. It generally follows the phase of suburbanization of residence. The saturation of central spaces, the diffusion of accessibility and the technologies of telecommunication, and the presence of territorial opportunities make for a growing number of services, industrial installations and suppliers who prefer the relative costs of distance to the diseconomies of a central site. However, this process also presents risks: on the one hand, territorial dispersion increases the pressure on land; on the other, the process of deurbanization could lead to the rundown of the city center or even produce the phenomenon of inner city break-up.

In the case of Madrid this tendency is favored by the transition from the radial system of communications to a radial-centric model, given the recent construction of the metropolitan distributing motorways (M-40, M-45, M-50). In the absence of a more extensive road network, the new orbital roads have opened up a "new metropolitan frontier". This fact has tended to generate new areas of low density suburbanization, today concentrated in the west but also emerging among the rural populations of the northeast and the south, which will probably lead to the spontaneous formation of urban centers at the junctions of the principal radial roads.

Policies to coordinate the metropolitan public transport system

The territorial organization of Madrid makes a metropolitan system of transport based on the use of cars unsustainable in the long term, given the diseconomy of congestion and the high cost of infrastructure and energy that it requires.

The public transport system consists of the local railway network, which has eight lines, is 259 km in length and has 79 stations, a metro of 112 km and the urban bus routes. Until a short while ago, the main problem was lack of coordination between the various transport services. For this reason, in 1985 one single authority, the Regional Transport Partnership (Consorcio Regional de Transportes) was set up as an autonomous body of the Autonomous Community of Madrid. The policies developed by the Consorcio are:

- The co-ordination of the various transport networks through the creation of large "interchange" stations, which facilitate interchange between the various means of public transport.
- The reorganization of the surface rail lines to rationalize the service and eliminate duplication between the metro and rail networks.
- The financing of the operating deficit and new investment required by the system through a contract program, agreed with the central government, which subsidizes a proportion of the cost of every passenger journey.

Regarding the construction of new infrastructure, an important step was taken in the 1990s with the improvement of the metro, both in the sense of extending lines to new centers of population or neighborhoods previously without service and as regards better connections between existing routes. To this end, a key factor has been the joining up of the circle line on the metro and the opening of new stations where people can change from the main-line railway to the metro network at the heads of the large metropolitan corridors. In metropolitan centers which are not connected to the railway and new construction is not viable in the short term, lanes reserved for buses and multiple occupancy vehicles are being contemplated, with the aim of compensating for the time penalty which the user of public transport currently suffers.

Table 5.3 Indicators of road transport

	Autonomous Community of Madrid				Spain
Indicator	**1993**	**1994**	**1995**	**1996**	**1996**
Total network/km^2 of surface	0.42	0.42	0.42	0.42	0.32
Total network/1,000 inhabitants	0.66	0.66	0.64	0.64	4.01
Vehicles/total network	762.79	778.69	820.71	850.01	120.55
Vehicles/1,000 inhabitants	502.22	514.84	526.79	547.57	483.00

Source *Anuario Estadistico DG de Programación Económica y Presupuestaria Ministerio de Formento.*

Roads

The present system of roads is the result of a major investment program over the last 20 years in the realization that the integration of the Madrid region with the principal centers of European growth depended upon an adequate transport infrastructure permitting efficient external communications. With this in mind, the radial network of roads and the improvement in connections with Portugal, France and North Africa through Algeçiras are of vital importance.

As regards the requirements of internal mobility, these are conditioned by the tendency of population to move out from the center towards the periphery and by the congestion which the interior of the metropolis suffers. These two factors have resulted in heavy demand for mobility which, given the organization of the region, generates multiple displacements, both in private vehicles and in public transport.

Table 5.4 Demand for public transport: tickets issued (millions)

Mode	1993	1994	1995	1996
Urban transport in Madrid				
Metro	390.8	392.4	397.2	534.0
Buses	501.1	513.9	521.5	409.9
Metropolitan transport				
Interurban buses	175.6	181.4	191.6	207.8
Local rail network	142.5	147.7	126.0	130.3

Source *Consorcio Regional del Transporte.*

With the aim of providing roads for private transport and goods vehicles, the Madrid region has returned to the development of the inner ring roads, the M-30 (finished during the first half of the 1970s) and M-40, as fundamental elements in the distribution of internal traffic (see Figure 5.6) as well as the future M-50, of which only two sections are as yet open—the first in the south, designed to bring continuity and cohesion to the urban centers which form the first urban ring. The other section is in the west of the region, between the municipalities of Las Rozas, Majadahonda, and Pozuelo de Alarcon, which constitute the third band of the metropolitan ring.

Rail

As a means of connecting the region with the rest of Europe rail transport has traditionally faced the problem of different track gauges, which has been an obstacle to the normal flow of goods and passengers. Given the economic impossibility of a complete change of gauge, the development of the high-speed train will absorb the bulk of expenditure on the transport infrastructure in Madrid

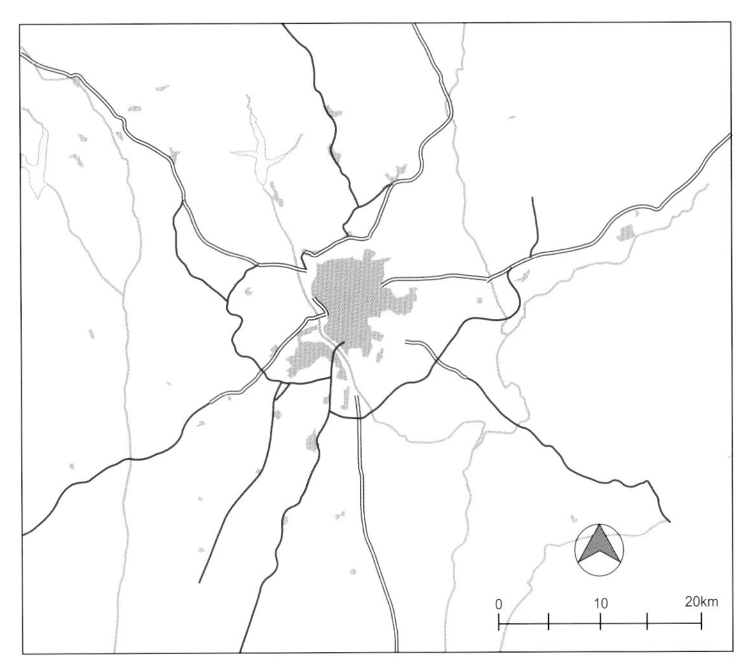

Figure 5.5 Main roads in the Madrid region, 1965

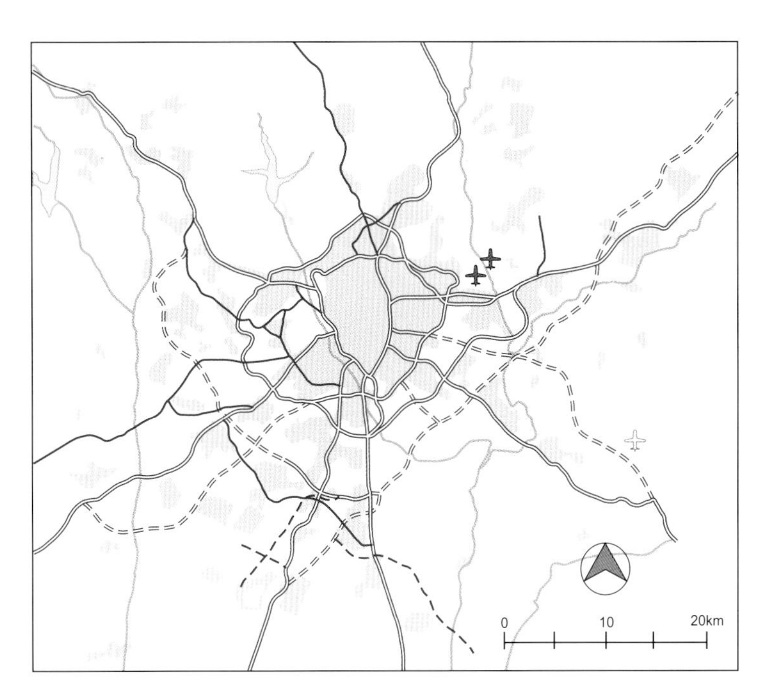

Figure 5.6 Main roads and airports in the Madrid region, 1990

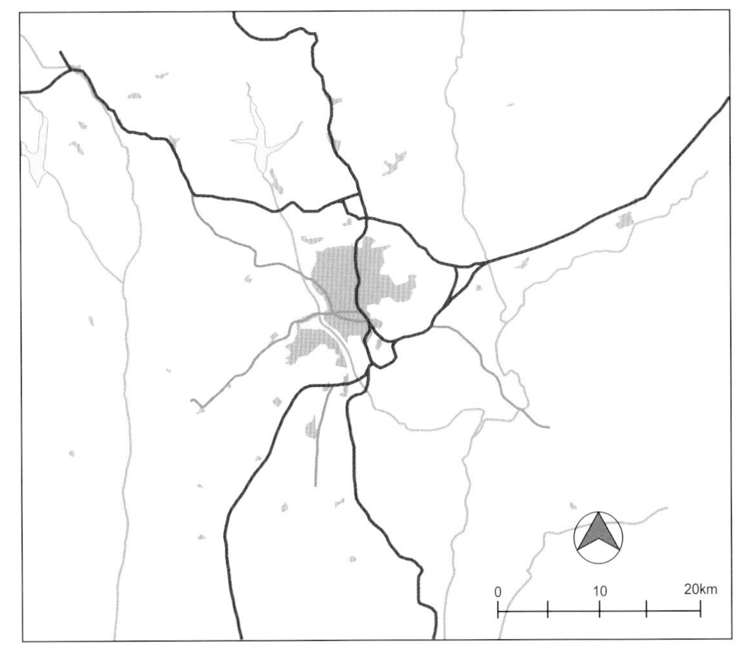

Figure 5.7 Railways in the Madrid region, 1965

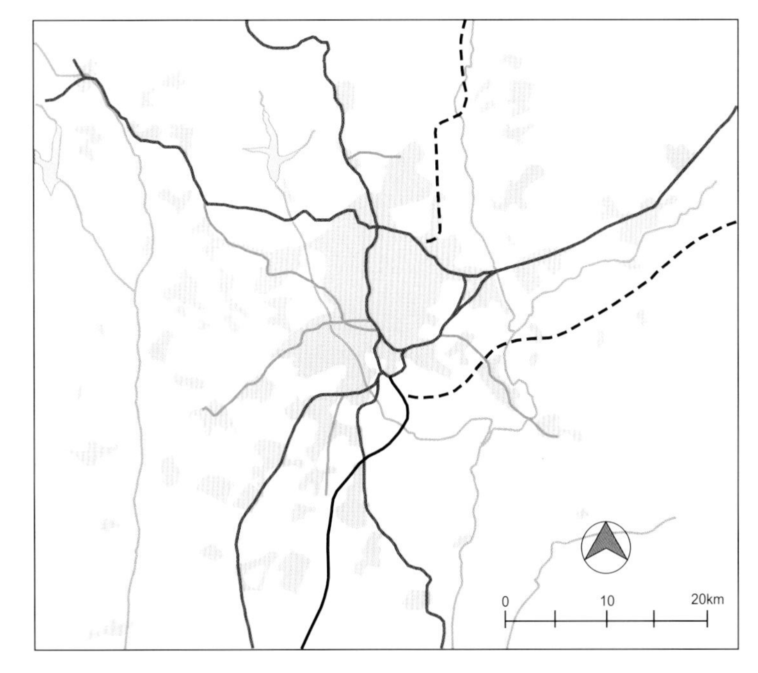

Figure 5.8 Railways in the Madrid region, 1990

over the next few years. It will be supported by the central government. So far the high-speed line between Madrid and Seville is operational. A second line linking Madrid via Valladolid with Barcelona and on towards France is planned (see Figure 5.8). The network of local railways also represents a key element in intraregional mobility in as much as it forms part of the system of public transport which connects the city of Madrid with the metropolitan municipalities and those zones on the peripheries of the region.

One of the most obvious weaknesses in the infrastructure has been the lack of a public transport connection from Barajas airport to Madrid which has sufficient capacity, bearing in mind the airport's increasing importance and the rising number of passengers forced to use taxis as the only way of reaching Barajas. The solution to this deficiency is the construction of a light railway which will connect with the city's metro network. It is due to enter service in 1999.

In contrast to what is happening with the high-speed train, the burden of financing the local rail network falls on regional government, except in the case of the line to the airport of Barajas, which will be completely financed by funds from the European Union. At the moment, the extension of the metro and local railway lines to the airport's present and future terminals is under consideration as an alternative solution.

Barajas airport

Madrid's airport has a key role in the development of the region. Its strategic importance is indisputable if we consider the growing importance of accessibility as a key element in the structure of relations between urban regions. Its importance for Madrid is derived from the peripheral position of the metropolis in respect to the most dynamic centers of economic activity. Its character as a key part of the transport infrastructure is complemented by the possibility of being configured as an advanced point of diffusion and development of policies of territorial restructuring.

For this, it is necessary to increase the potential of the airport on three levels.

- From the point of view of transport and logistics.
- As an element in the requalifying of its surroundings. It has to be made accessible by means of motorways and the development of public transport.
- Environmental integration of the airport, through a policy of regeneration and reducing its environmental impact.

The airport is situated 13 km northeast of Madrid's city center. The principal means of access are the Nacional II and the second ring road, the M-40. Alternative secondary roads are the Carretera de Alcobendas, the M-110, and the Avenida de Aragon. In spite of the fact that it is relatively well off in terms of access by road, Barajas needs an alternative system of public transport to the bus—which accounts for only 7 percent of journeys—and taxis, which account for 57 percent.

The airport extends over an area of 1,600 ha. It has two runways which cross each other and three buildings dedicated to the processing of passengers. It also has a cargo terminal with a floor area of 38,000 m^2 as well as other areas dedicated to hangers, workshops, etc. The airport is operating at the limit of its capacity, the principal deficiencies in its configuration being:

- Inefficient design of the airfield.
- Insufficient passenger loading/unloading bays.
- Inadequacy of the passenger terminals.
- Limited capacity of the cargo terminal.
- Saturation of car parking.
- Limited access by public transport.

This situation called for a series of measures aimed at adapting the installations to the forecasts of air traffic expected by the year 2012: 40 million passengers a year, 700,000 tons of freight a year, and 400,000 operations a year.

The measures were divided into two phases: the first lasted until 1995 and involved the modification of the airfield, the enlargement of the passenger loading/ unloading bays and the extension of the passenger terminals. The second phase, with a horizon in the year 2012, envisages:

- A new area of terminals to the north of the present one.
- A new runway (under construction) and another under consideration.
- New stations for aircraft and taxiing areas.

In parallel, with the aim of transforming Barajas into a powerful combination of infrastructure and services linked to the functioning of a major airport, the above-mentioned activities would be completed by:

- Improvements in access through a connection with the third ring road, the M-50, and new public transport systems. In particular the construction of a light railway between the city and the airport, with connections to the metro.

- Making land available to encourage complementary activities and a residential population attracted by the nearness of the airport or by the conditions of the area, such as the reservation of open spaces and green areas.

Telecommunications

The last component of the infrastructure is telecommunications, also known as the "invisible infrastructure". It is a key element in attracting companies which need to integrate information and commercial practices for their strategies in a global economy. Given its situation at some distance from other centers of decision making, the development of communications is fundamental if Madrid hopes to become integrated into the world system of cities. Despite the fact that the region is the most developed in the country, it finds itself clearly lagging behind the rest of Europe and above all the United States as regards the level of new information technology found in companies and in the home.

FROM URBAN TRANSFORMATION TO THE REGULATION OF THE REGION

From defensive planning to a general debate about the city

The peculiar situation of Spanish cities—and of Madrid in particular—at the moment of the constitution of the first democratic town councils in 1979, meant that urban policies had to attend to the serious deficits in basic infrastructure, homes, materials and transport which had built up throughout the period of expansive growth of the 1960s and around which an important neighborhood movement had crystalized. Significantly, these movements expressed themselves in terms of sectoral demands, which in turn reflected the segmentation of responsibilities in the administration, formulating in this way a deep lack of confidence in the capacity of the instruments of projection/planning to come up with solutions.

The credit for taking the step from the initial defensive planning to the articulation of a global debate about the city capable of supporting concrete urban interventions is due to to the *Plan General*, drawn up between 1980 and 1985. It is interesting to point out the new understanding of the plan as an instrument oriented to the design of urban intervention. As such it meant abandoning the exclusively normative treatment of the neutral expansion of the city for the alternative: planning the strategic selection of interventions capable of making the transformation of the city a reality.

The intervention transforms: the first generation of urban redevelopment

The first generation of large projects coincided with the structural operations of the plan. However, their gestation and beginnings preceded the conclusion of the structural operations. In spite of the variations in their contents, it is possible to extract a series of characteristic features common to them all:

- They have as an objective substantial benefits or contributions to the urban infrastructure, reviving and expanding the traditional concept of "public works".
- They enjoy widespread public support and the direct backing of the municipal and central administration in their fulfillment.
- They are motor elements in the transformation of the overall urban structure of the city, capable of taking action on the redefinition of their immediate surroundings.
- They concede priority attention to the configuration of public space, both as a civic institution and key element of the city.

"Operation Atocha" represents the flagship model of the new city project promoted in the plan and the implementation of its model of urban intervention. With this aim, the project stresses the effort to give an integrated answer to the requirements dictated by Atocha Station's structural role as the major point of interchange in the public transport network of the city, and its symbolic role as the first radical step in the regeneration and beautification of a particlar public space.

Operation Atocha, together with San Francisco el Grande, Parque Tierno Galvan and the restoration of the river Manzanares, constituted what became to be known as the "Key of the South" (*Llave del Sur*). This idea covers the common locality of these initiatives around an intermediate area between the centre and the periphery. As such it sets objectives such as the "reconstruction" of every urban unit and the modification of the spontaneous ecology of the city. In this way it extends the environmental qualities of the urban center towards the south.

The second generation of urban initiatives

Even though no break exists in the continuity of the first generation projects, a series of different features in relation to those previously discussed can be identified in the projects initiated in the second half of the 1980s.

- The objective of the interventions diversifies, incorporating new themes such as the formalization of the new centrality, the transformation of areas of poverty and the home.
- They divide the areas of urban intervention, which confine themselves to the ordering of parts of the city and infrastructural intervention that can be considered logical functions.
- They expand the areas of intervention of the consolidated city, to the prevision of new action in the periphery.
- They introduce new criteria for economic viability and the incorporation of the private sector in the management and execution of certain projects.

An important group of projects is directed towards the creation of new centers of tertiary activity in a critical period of high demand for office space and spiraling rise in their price.

The story of every one of these projects is different. The tertiary area of the Estacion Sur de Autobuses, the southern bus station, south of the orbital M-30 motorway, is integrated with Operation Atocha and provides a center of interchange between (long-distance) buses and urban transport. It complements that already established at Atocha and takes advantage of the particular features of the connection to form another 'central distirct' which counterbalances the concentration of offices in the north of the city.

The initiative setting up the new Commercial Exhibition Centres in the vicinity of Barajas airport is intended for commercial exhibitions in the strictest sense. The complementary service area, the Campo de las Naciones, incorporates a science park and a large suburban park designated for recreational and general use. This operation embodies two relevant innovations. It implies one of the first movements towards decentralization, that is to say, the creation of a new center of activity, alternative to the urban center, in a strategic location in the periphery. Secondly, it represents a new model of intervention on a large scale, derived from strategies of natural economics. The center of gravity in this type of action is displaced by themes such as the selection of the most innovative functions, and the promotion or design of special formulas of management.

The Pasillo Verde Ferroviario (Green Rail Corridor) exemplifies both the transformational aims of the first-generation interventions and the new forms of mixed management introduced since. In synthesis, the operation responds to two basic objectives. In the first place, to take advantage of the existing railway stations in the district of Arganzuela in the south of the city, to strengthen their role as points of interchange between modes of transport, and to turn the space freed from railway use into green areas, for the benefit of the public, and tertiary enclaves. Secondly, taking the opportunity afforded by the modernization and the rationalization of the railway to relocate the tracks underground. A new avenue along the line of the route which would link up the stations. This solution would also overcome the physical barrier of railway lines bisecting on the district.

Finally, the South Madrid and Valdebernardo projects are a response to the demands of the Autonomous Community of Madrid for the creation of space destined for the construction of homes. As urban interventions they were two innovations: on the one hand, they oriented from the start towards residential objectives; on the other, they were intended to redefine the habitual relationship between new expanding areas and the already consolidated city. In reality, although we are speaking in terms of new residential extensions, neither project is limited to domestic housing. Both also attempt to meet the more ambitious objective of reequipping and improving the urban periphery.

The problem of the large scale: focus on the organization of the territory

On a regional scale, the spatial transformations of the Madrid region have coincided with a period of important institutional changes, which in turn have led to innovations in the focus of planning. Within the framework of the new decentralized organization of government, the Autonomous Community of Madrid was founded in 1983, which among its other responsibilities assumed those relating to planning and controls which had previously been reserved to central government.

In its initial stage the community developed a policy which can be described as 'defensive' in the sense that it prioritized action aimed at solving the most serious problems and imbalances inherited from the period when the metropolitan area was being formed.

The first law on regional organization was passed in 1984 and took the form of *Directrices de Ordenacion del Territorio* familiar in the metropolitan area several years previously. The most significant contribution of the regional law lay in its recognition that spatial planning and the allocation of economic resources should respond to demand and changing circumstances. It was considered appropriate to differentiate between the specific forms in the framework of regional organization with directives (*directrices*) and the establishment of programs of investment (*programas coordinados de actuacion*).

The first directives, drawn up in the period 1984–85, were conditioned by the economic crisis and the 'defensive' focus that was dominant in municipal planning at the time. Their conclusions were oriented towards formulating a strategy for the conservation of the countryside and rural spaces and for the improvement of the infrastructure, beginning with the most basic aspects: water, sanitation, waste disposal and transport.

The first stirrings of economic recovery highlighted the need for a change of focus. From 1988 the organization of the region was reformulated as an incremental process, based on the design of 'territorial strategies' for the sub-regional area over large centers of metropolitan development. These strategies were more strongly committed to the restructuring of the territory, oriented towards the prioritization of positive public action.

The experience of managing a series of large public works during the period 1988–92 highlighted the inadequacy of the existing legal framework. The normal planning mechanisms worked well enough in specific activities involving both the autonomous community and the municipalities where the degree of precision in the programming and urban content were high. However, the lack of legal instruments limited the scope for planning long or medium term projects of regional transformation, with a greater order of magnitude and time scale.

For this reason, in 1995 a new law of Regional Policy, Land and Urbanization was passed by consensus. It constitutes a new focus on the question. The 1995 law recognizes that the government of the territory of the metropolitan region is a shared responsibility between the autonomous community and the municipalities. It defines the respective areas of responsibility and puts the emphasis on overcoming any eventual conflict by means of shared management and reaching a compromise in the event of difficulties. The Regional Strategic Plan is the new form to which the duty of establishing the basic elements in the organization and structure of the regional area is entrusted. It therefore constitutes a reference point for the other instruments of planning. The most relevant innovation is that the new form extends the 'normative' focus, beyond the remit of the old *directrices*, with a strategic dimension, making them selective and binding in action. Its contents thus include traditional elements of direct urban planning (or at second level), where resolutions are implemented only at the level of municipal projects, as well as to the most innovative elements which encompass and authorize, within certain conditions, large scale projects with an impact on the whole region.

6 The Randstad

Leo J. M. Tummers and
Pieter M. Schrijnen

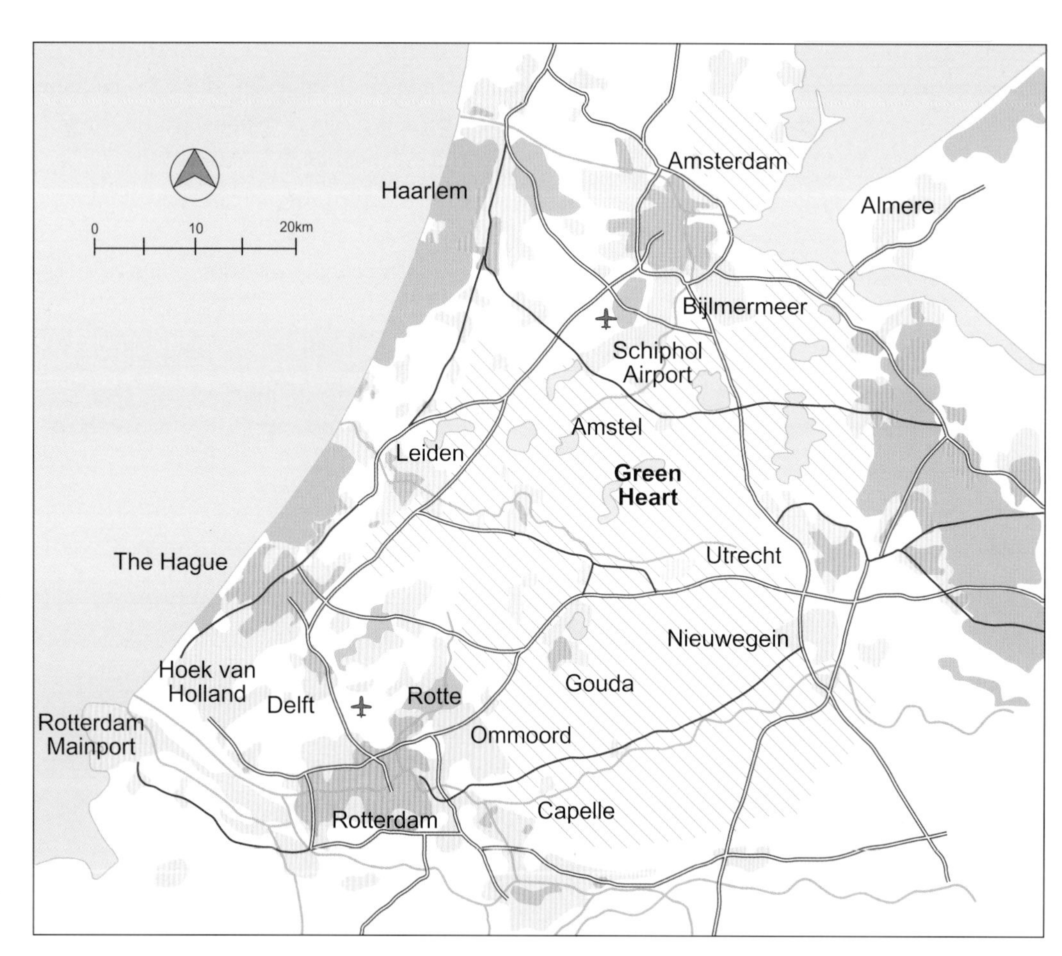

Figure 6.1 The Randstad, 1995

The Randstad city region is the business and national center of the country. The population density of the Netherlands is fairly high, with almost 14.5 million people in 1988 inhabiting 33,945 km^2, producing an average density of 425 inhabitants per square kilometer.

The agglomeration of the Randstad is the most highly urbanized area of the Netherlands. Forty-five percent of the population occupy only one-quarter of Dutch territory, which means around 6 million people at an average density of more than 1,000 inhabitants per square kilometer. The Randstad is also the area in which about 50 percent of employment is concentrated. The Randstad area of around 6,000 km^2 is the site of 70 percent of the head offices of the 100 biggest Dutch companies, 65 percent of R&D activities and high-tech companies, 93 percent of foreign services and 80 percent of foreign commercial enterprises. The coastal region of the Netherlands plays an

Figure 6.2 The location of the Randstad

important part in international tourism, while just behind the line of dunes are to be found three of the biggest vegetable and flower markets in the world. The Randstad maintains major links with other economic centers in the world through its harbors and airports. This is especially true of the port of Rotterdam, which is the largest transshipment center in the world, and of Amsterdam Schiphol Airport, ranking fourth in Europe. The Randstad has seven universities. Furthermore, the four major cities, Amsterdam, Rotterdam, The Hague, and Utrecht, excel in social and cultural amenities, museums, theaters and conference centers.

Both the Randstad and Holland have their origins in the delta of the Rhine estuary, the Rhine being the main river of the Western European mainland. The center of Holland has a natural western boundary formed by dunes. This natural boundary of the dunes was linked up with manmade dikes along the river branches to secure the central area of the country, which evolved into the Randstad of today.

Amsterdam and Rotterdam were both named after rivers, the Amstel and the Rotte. These were both dammed and then connected by locks to the bigger lakes and bays of Holland which in turn were connected to the North Sea. Geographically, historically, and economically, both Amsterdam and Rotterdam became the cornerstones and the core cities of the Randstad. The twentieth century saw a boom in modern urbanization and modern agriculture in the west of the country, which today makes up the whole rural–urban complex known as the Randstad.

The Randstad took shape in the Middle Ages as a region of cities. Those already established at the onset of urbanization in the twelfth century have names like Haarlem, Dordrecht, Gouda, and Delft; besides Amsterdam and Rotterdam and The Hague and Utrecht these older cities are also of great historical interest. In the Middle Ages a modern democratic urban culture was born in Flanders and Holland, with an economic background in textile production and trade.

In this context of rising urbanism and democracy the Dutch state took form. A location for the central government was needed. None of the existing cities could force its will upon the others. None of the larger cities was awarded the favour of hosting this institution. Instead, a hunting lodge in the dunes was chosen to house the States General, 's-Gravenhage, "the garden of the count", today internationally known as The Hague.

The seventeenth century, the national Golden Age, saw the rise of Rotterdam, and to a greater extent Amsterdam, based on strong worldwide international trade. This coincided with the birth of the nation of the Netherlands, achieved after freeing itself from Spanish rule under Philip II. After this period, the national history records a long period of stagnation while other leading European nations were involved in the industrial revolution of the eighteenth and nineteenth centuries.

After 1945 the modern urban history of the Randstad made a new start. It is in this post-war period that the name Randstad was coined; it rapidly became popular in the Netherlands and abroad. From 1945 to 1960 national economic growth and population increase were focused on the Randstad. As soon as these phenomena occurred, political reflection on national planning set in, with the main intention of limiting further growth in the Randstad.

The Randstad can be characterized as a polynuclear city region, a ring of cities and medium-sized towns interlinked by a rail and road infrastructure and grouped around a central open space, the Green Heart of the Randstad. Literally translated, Randstad means "rim city". The cities of the Randstad are located on the rim of what is called the central open space and, at the same time, there is the rim to the sea coast and to the oldest sea dikes of Amsterdam and Rotterdam, which still define the outer boundaries of the central Randstad area.

The area's importance internationally is not only economic but also ecological. The delta of the Rhine is ecologically a highly diverse area, interspersed with river foreshores, a variety of freshwater lakes, transitional fresh and salt water areas and the North Sea coast. The Randstad is surrounded by lakes and wetlands that lie on the route of migrating birds.

In the last 30 years several attempts have been made to

Figure 6.3 The Hague, from the North Sea

reorganize the local and regional legal institutions together with their boundaries in the Randstad region. Up to this date no major administrative institutions have been established.

Until 1988 physical planning was aimed at siphoning off the expected urban growth in the Randstad to other areas in the Netherlands to avoid congestion. In the new global economy and amid European competition, the Randstad was rediscovered as a natural growth pole between other European urban regions. Infrastructure investment and urban expansion made their come-back in Randstad policies.

The fact that the Randstad region is, strictly speaking, an example of 'weak' government is to a certain extent offset by the fact that, in a country as small as the Netherlands, there is great concern about the Randstad from the various national Ministries and from the national government. Of course, the national government is a type of "strong" government, and is deeply involved in the crucial decisions on investment and land use relating to the Randstad.

CHANGING ECONOMIC PATTERNS

The Randstad has developed into a global city region from Holland's background as a seafaring and agricultural nation. Logistics around harbor, airport, and road transport are a vital characteristic of the Randstad economy. In the Randstad today services make up 70 percent of employment, being strongly connected with trade and industrial production, which together make up 25 percent of the available jobs. The Randstad has seen, in the decades under consideration, an important loss of industrial employment, from the demise of the shipbuilding industry to the loss of the aircraft manufacturer Fokker. Fishing activity and dairy produce have been restricted as a result of European quotas. Fishing activity, agriculture, horticulture, and food industries are strong internationally, but have a limited position (5 percent) in the employment indicators of the Randstad. Nevertheless agribusiness in the Randstad is so omnipresent and important that in many places there are conflicting interests in land use planning and the creation of expansion possibilities for the industry.

Each of the four main Randstad cities has its own specialization. *Amsterdam* is a financial and air transport center, flanked by a harbor complex and steel mills. The stock exchange is based in Amsterdam, and most Dutch banks and a number of multinational companies have their headquarters in the city. Most editors of national newspapers are based in Amsterdam, just as are the most important Dutch museums, orchestras, and theaters.

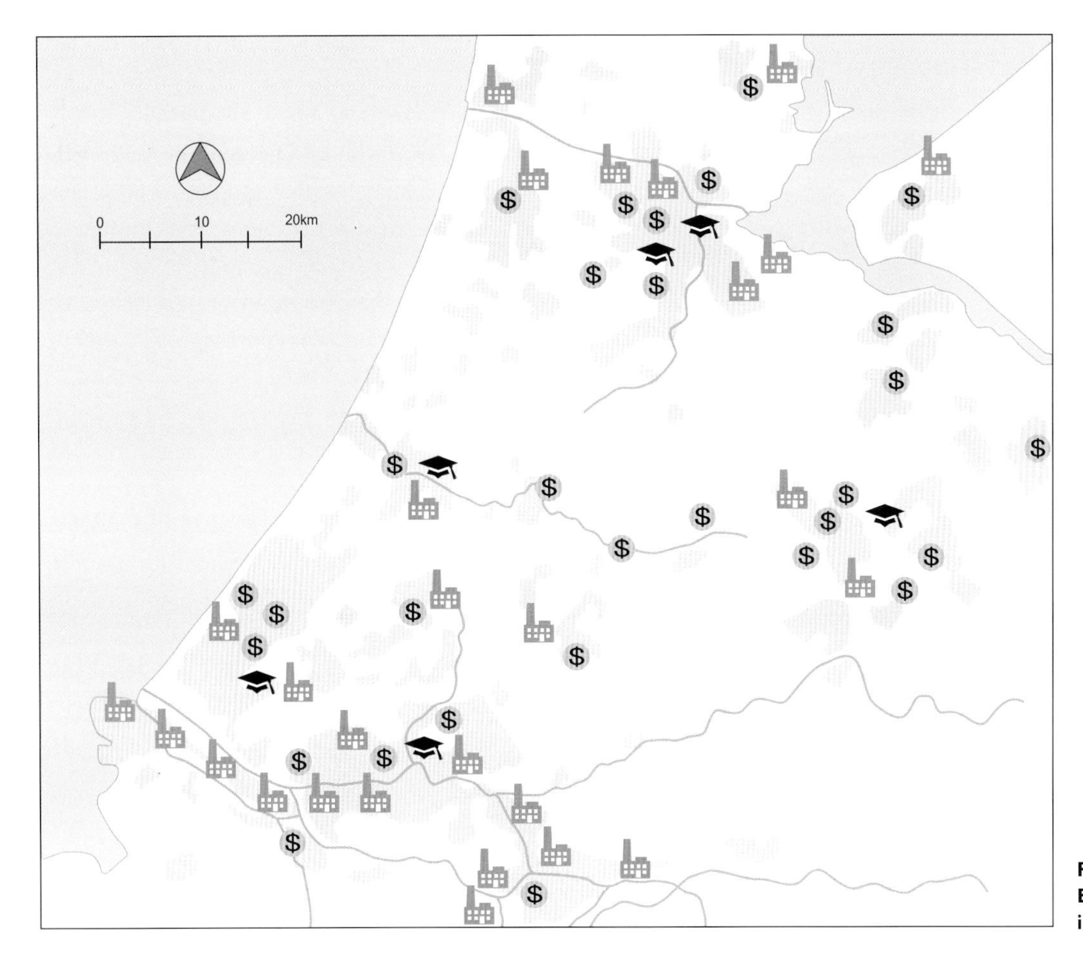

Figure 6.4 Economic patterns in the Randstad

Schiphol developed further into an international airport as the home of Royal Dutch Airlines (KLM). A logistics base including many banks is concentrating around Schiphol Airport. Steel furnaces, chemistry, metallurgical, and food industries concentrate around the North Sea Canal from Amsterdam westwards.

Rotterdam is the largest seaport in the world. It plays a major role in the transshipment of raw materials, semi-manufactured products and consumer goods to Germany, the United Kingdom, and Belgium. The economic structure of the Rotterdam area is based on these flows. The quays, depots, petrochemical, metallurgical, and food industries and distribution activities extend for 60 km from the Hook of Holland along the Nieuwe Waterweg to the river banks southeast. The shipbuilding industry has been cut back in size, while offshore activity is rising. In recent decades Rotterdam has been developing its cultural and university facilities.

The Hague is the government center and here there has been growth in the civil service, in diplomatic establishments, in non-governmental organizations, and in international institutions. Moreover, The Hague is the home of the head office of multinational enterprises, like the Shell oil company. Office employment is still growing in the Hague.

Utrecht is the hub of the national rail network and therefore became an important center for services. Utrecht acquired important institutions such as the Jaarbeurs trade fairs, the head offices of the Dutch railways, transport industry, and major insurance offices and software firms. The university grew to become one of the largest in the country.

On the national scale the Randstad still holds its strong position in the Dutch economy, although the areas in the east and south of the Netherlands have grown somewhat faster in the past decade. A growing problem for the Randstad economy is the loss of employment in the lower income brackets.

CHANGING SOCIAL PATTERNS

The Netherlands has a strong tradition of searching for social equilibrium. The levels of pensions and social security are relatively high. The lowest 20 percent of households earn 6 percent of the national household income, whereas the highest 20 percent earn 38 percent. The lowest bracket consists mainly of the elderly, students, and single parent families. The extremes are widening, with the wealth in the top 5 percent rising quickly, whereas enduring poverty is the prospect for the lowest 5 percent.

Figure 6.5 Rotterdam center, with the new Erasmus Bridge

Distributive policies are also applied to spatial policies and housing. Until recently, national government subsidized 60 percent of newly built homes. Large subsidies still support the urban renewal process. Also, rent subsidies are given to low income households. Together, these policies result in a quite diverse population composition for most districts. More newly built districts on the urban fringes and in the suburbs are not inhabited only by wealthier families; lower income groups are encouraged to move into these areas as well. Creating a diverse population structure is an important feature of urban renewal policies. Experiments are being made with economic free zones in the older districts, to enhance entrepreneurship among immigrants.

Few large cities are free of poverty; the Randstad is no exception. The pattern is a familiar one: new immigrants tend to flock to the older districts, which are also the poorest. The poorer areas are relatively small, however, certainly in comparison with such districts in most other countries. Immigration and unemployment are spread evenly over the larger cities in the region.

After a few decades of focusing primarily on welfare, Dutch policies are increasingly redirected toward supporting the supply side: contractors, investors, builders. Thanks to a shift in policy, more housing for middle and high income groups is being built. The concept behind this policy shift is that building for these groups not only serves the wealthy, but also gives rise to movements in the housing market that favour lower income groups.

None the less, even the most improved policies cannot alone eradicate segregation. The differences between the immigrants and the native people are growing, and the social diversity is rising. Those who can afford it move into areas where people live who have a similar income level and similar social and cultural preferences. The relatively small distances between very different urban and rural settings in the Randstad and the high level of car ownership allow people to search in a vast area for neighborhoods that suit them best. The result is a tendency towards monocultures in the social realm, albeit on a relatively small, dispersed Dutch scale.

CHANGING SPATIAL PATTERNS

The original landscape of the Randstad is an extremely flat and open array of polders (land reclaimed through the ages from the sea). Cities, villages, and windmills are clearly visible from great distances. Amsterdam and to a lesser degree the other Randstad cities were built at extremely high densities and the boundary between town and country was clear-cut. On the Randstad map of 1960 the spatial pattern still responds to the image of a very spacious landscape with a small number of dense cities. Only in the northeastern corner of the 1960 map do we find the pattern of a wooded landscape interspersed with urban settlements.

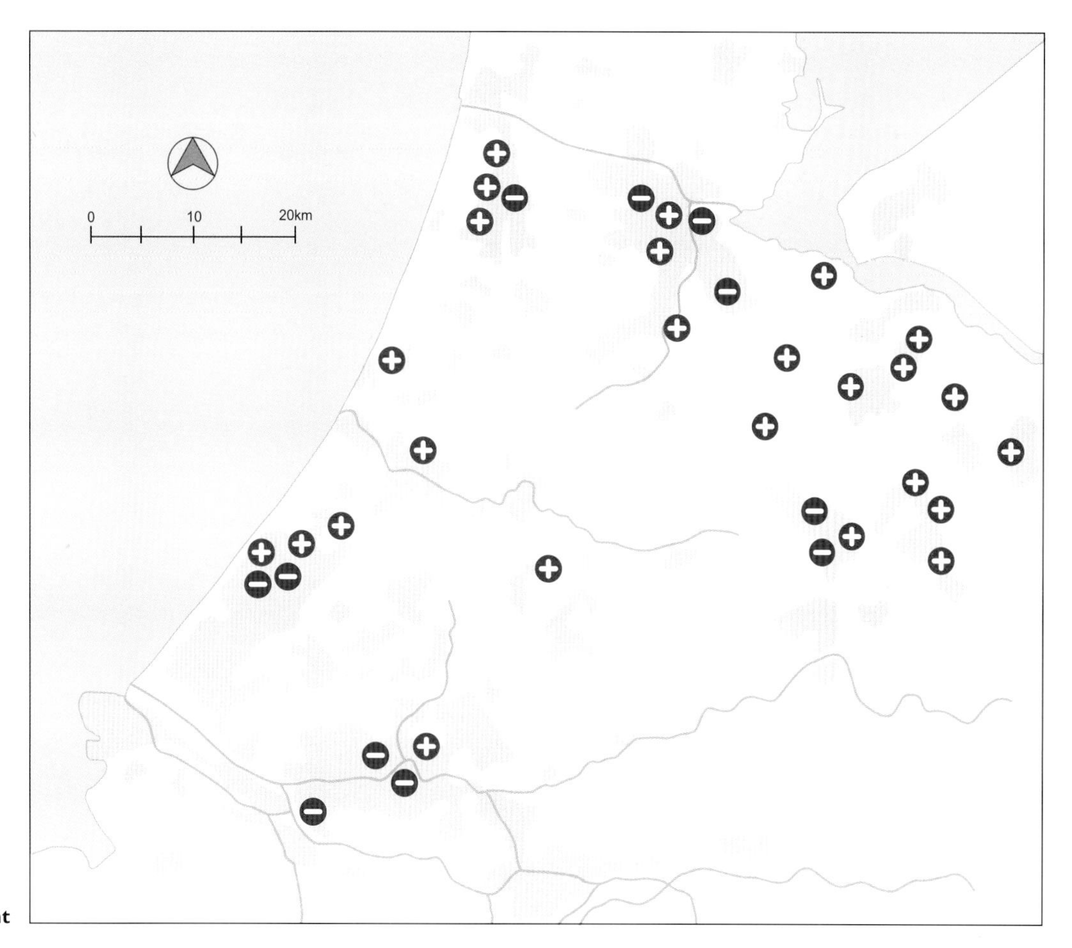

Figure 6.6 Residences of the wealthiest 20 percent and the poorest 20 percent

From 1960 onwards, spatial patterns suggest that the Randstad is following the typical Western process of urbanization. Increases in population and rising affluence have provided the financial and thereby the technical means to overcome the formerly prohibitive threshold of the polder subsoil conditions that previously limited urban sprawl. Dutch spatial planning policies have over the years in different ways tried to restrain this process or to guide it in particular directions. We deal more specifically with the spatial policies channeling the urban growth in Randstad in the section after next.

The results of this confrontation between market forces and governmental spatial policies can be seen on the map. Each decade shows an increasing surface of built-up areas and infrastructure as densities diminish. Since the 1960s the spatial patterns increasingly reflect the effects of national planning policies in their different successive stages.

First the overspill locations for Amsterdam and Rotterdam were chosen as far out as 30 km from the Randstad. These distances unintentionally emphasized the imbalance between work force and job opportunities in the isolated new towns of that period. The awareness of the disadvantages of an open urban system with distant satellites caused a turning point in planning policies. From that moment new policies were introduced so that densities and distances would allow crisscross movements between job locations and housing within the Randstad.

The 'Green Heart' as a central landscape reservation gradually became more formalized in the national planning approach. Since 1990 it has been defined in the Green Heart national planning document, approved by Parliament. Like the London green belt the Randstad's Green Heart is a clear example of reliance on a large scale spatial effect to contain urban growth in the whole of the Randstad. The Green Heart literally forms the inner ring of the Randstad: it prohibits urbanization inside this boundary.

The various urban renewal policies have favored increased density in the existing built-up areas. After 1990 plans were made to locate future new housing areas on the edges of the major cities. At the same time, urban developments outside the Randstad in other parts of the country, where spatial patterns were more inviting to private initiative, outranked growth in the Randstad itself. Very significant investments in infrastructure and building new landscapes are now undertaken to encourage future growth in the Randstad.

Within most conurbations new economic location patterns emerge. Most Dutch city centers have a medieval or Renaissance background, not really equipped for the location of larger scale business centers. The older centers hold their role in public administration, culture, and services. But along the highways the modern edge cities arise. Especially around Amsterdam, a very large shift from city center towards the 'southern axis' can be seen. Many businesses, among others the major Dutch financial companies, established their head offices around the southern ring roads. Also around The Hague and Utrecht new business districts develop around the suburbs. The historic center of Rotterdam was destroyed in World War II. The reconstruction offered opportunities to concentrate business in the former center. Restructuring older industrial areas and harbors also offers many inner city locations for offices.

INFRASTRUCTURE INVESTMENT

Dutch physical planning policies are formally concerned with a comprehensive view of the total scope of planning, housing, and the social and environmental aspects of cities and rural areas. But infrastructure policies are facilitating market forces through generating transport demand. Both policy fields influence city structure, through the spatial choices of households and industries, in a counteractive way. Infrastructure offers access, to land, jobs, and market opportunities. As long as access to such resources is limited, infrastructure nodes attract the settlement of families and firms. As soon as infrastructure offers a wider range of choice, it supports dispersion of activities. This often contradicts the goals of Dutch planning policies.

Infrastructure for land protection and reclamation

In the Randstad people are used to a dynamic relationship with the forces and the gifts of nature. The Randstad lies in the delta of the Rhine and Meuse rivers. The terrain consists mostly of clay and peat. Dunes, dikes, and flood barriers are needed to protect the land against floods from the sea, whereas water management is needed to control inland groundwater and surface water levels. Unfortunately this water management leads to shrinking soils. According to the latest insights, extra areas of surface water are needed to protect the fertile land against subsoil saltwater pressure from the sea. At the same time, growing peak discharges from the Rhine and Meuse demand higher dikes along the rivers and more space to absorb peak flows.

The ability to control the water systems allowed the Dutch to reclaim large areas of land from the sea, though only small areas have been reclaimed recently. Debate continues over new extensions, for port and industrial activities near Rotterdam and for new housing areas near Amsterdam. The tradition of solving land-bound problems by gaining new land from the sea may finally have come to an end now that the natural and economic values of open water systems are recognized.

Roads

At the beginning of the century the *Rijkswegen*, the state roads, linked cities. They interconnected with the radial inner city road systems. Long-distance traffic before the days of the motorway system had to pass through all cities along these roads. In the 1930s the first steps were taken to develop a system of limited access roads between the larger cities, bypassing minor towns and villages. The first national highways linked up with the radials of the larger agglomerations. Only since the 1950s has the main road system been conceived of as a tangential freeway system. In the period 1955–85 the national motorway system was completed, making the whole country more or less equally accessible. A fine meshed network of motorways in the Randstad has put more than 90 percent of the population within 20 driving minutes from a freeway.

Accessibility through the freeway system was one of the policy aims to support the economy on the periphery of the Randstad. However, the success of this policy was considerably compromised by the roads also opening up sites closer to existing cities. The tangent system that diminished the pressure from through traffic in towns automatically improved access to suburbs. In a time when locations for larger scale offices and industries within the cities were scarce, the new road system gave access to suburban and peripheral locations. A strong dispersion of households and enterprises was enhanced by the freeway system, from the former central cities to the broadening belt of the Randstad, mostly to locations not accessible through public transport.

During the 1980s the extent of the environmental crisis became clear. This has put a temporary restraint on car use and road building, especially within cities themselves. In the same period a more precise notion of the impact of infrastructure on economic development arose. The costs of congestion in an area could be measured and could be compared with the cost of road building. This comparison showed road investment in the peripheral parts of the country to be far less effective in macroeconomic terms than investment in the larger cities and ports.

In the same decade the European Union started to open up borders, and an awareness of global competition

Figure 6.7 Main roads and airports in the Randstad, 1995

arose. So good links with the international network became more important in improving the competitive position of Dutch enterprises. The result is that infrastructure policy is bent in the direction of investing in the economy of the Randstad. Large investments are being made to improve the road system around Rotterdam port area in the south of the Randstad and the Schiphol Airport area in the north. The links between the main economic centers and the hinterland are being improved as well. The main corridors, Amsterdam–Germany, Rotterdam–Germany/Belgium, get priority in the investment schemes and a new level in the hierarchy of the road system may be emerging. With these building efforts go attempts to control the use of the car. Taxes on fuel rise slowly. Toll systems around the larger towns and on the corridors are being discussed. Experiments will eventually start with special lanes for freight or for paying users. Although these measures will improve access to the main ports, all locations along the main corridors will also benefit.

Public transport

In the Netherlands public transport is not seen as merely an old-fashioned instrument to create social welfare. It can play an important role in creating the conditions for a thriving city economy in tandem with the improvement of the quality of city life. The means for achieving this are very limited, however, because public transport investments are mainly deployed at the wider national level.

The railway networks in the Netherlands and in the Randstad reached their greatest density in the 1930s. The railways connected the larger towns by train and areas within a region by a mix of train, tram, subway, and buses. In that period very little private motor traffic existed. The first suburbs arose along the rail lines around the major towns.

When private car use grew, the use of public transport declined. Between 1950 and 1970 hardly any new investment was made. The regional tram system was gradually abandoned and replaced by bus services. Many of the smaller stops on the railway system were closed down. New city quarters and suburbs were served by bus. After 1970, within and around the four largest cities in the Randstad, new links were constructed, as the development increments show : in Amsterdam a subway to the Bijlmermeer and a railway to Almere and Lelystad; in Rotterdam a subway to Hoogvliet and Spijkenisse and a light rail

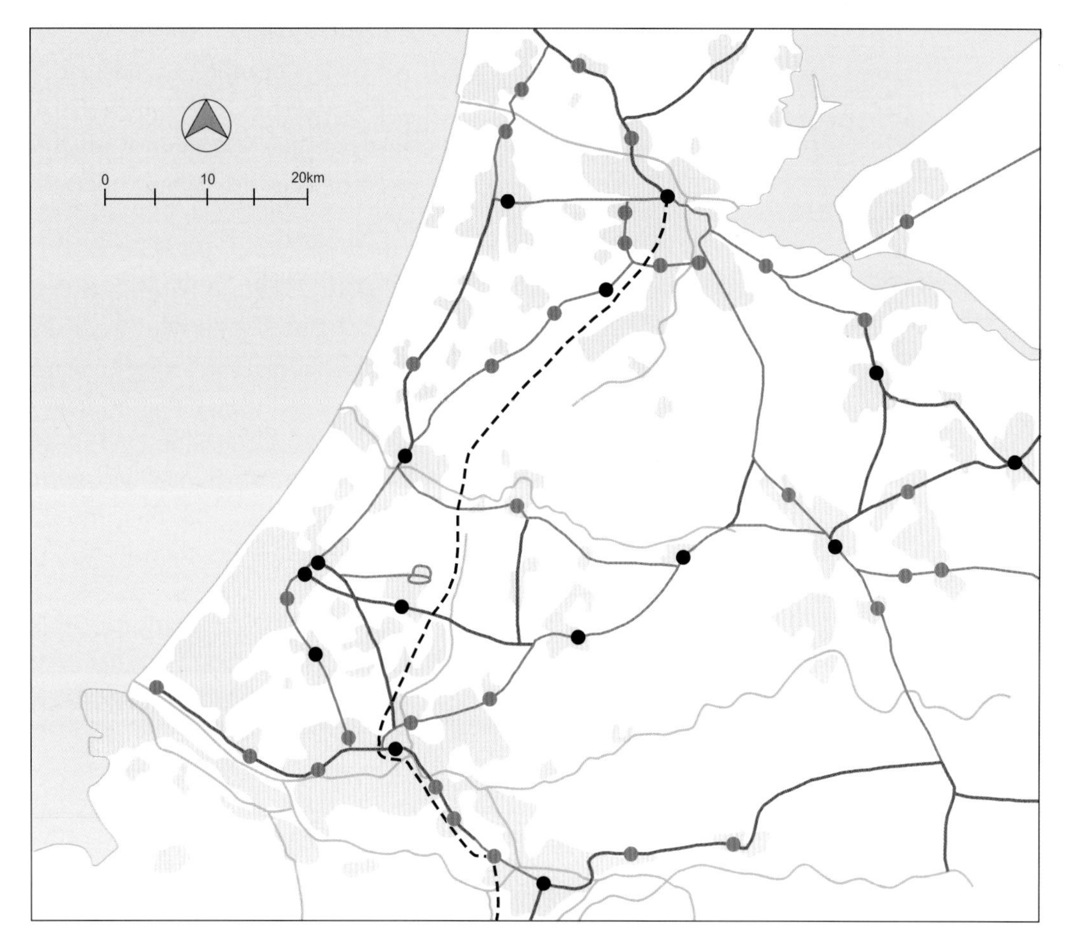

Figure 6.8 Railways in the Randstad, 1995

to Ommoord and Capelle; The Hague got a new railway line to Zoetermeer; Utrecht got a light rail connection with Nieuwegein. Also in the 1970s a new rail line connected Amsterdam directly with The Hague and Rotterdam, serving Schiphol Airport at the same time.

During the 1980s public transport received more attention. In relation to the policy of improving the economic output of the infrastructure system, railway development has been seen as a means to improve the accessibility of city centers, to reduce congestion on the road system and, through that, to create macroeconomic benefits and to improve the environmental performance of the whole transport system.

Yet in this decade government policies towards public services changed focus. Government spending turned from subsidizing public transport companies to new investments in national and international long-distance rail links. Within the Randstad competition is encouraged in the public domain, to reduce dependence on subsidies and to improve the productiveness of companies. New private rail companies got permission to use the railway infrastructure to serve their customers.

The causes of congestion in the road system lie, above all, in the traffic in and around the agglomerations. Yet government investment in public transport systems primarily goes to the upper segment of the market, to the longer-distance trains that can be exploited without state subsidies. Investments in new tracks are made for high speed trains to France and Germany, and in longer distance connections within the country. On the most intensively used parts of the rail network the tracks are in the process of being doubled and at places tripled. Schiphol Airport, Amsterdam and Rotterdam are the focal points of the new or improved connections.

New physical planning after 1990 concentrated the expansion of larger cities in a limited number of locations within the agglomeration. New quarters need good public transport facilities. Budget constraints, however, limit the investments to a few light rail lines in the larger agglomerations. Around smaller cities buses have to serve as the only means of public transport, usually on infrastructure shared with the private car. Rotterdam and Amsterdam can expand their subway systems, within the existing cities, in order to improve access to the existing centers. Here the economic importance of the city centers gained them ground in the competition for more government spending.

Seaports and airports

The focal points of the Dutch infrastructure policies are the two main ports, Amsterdam Airport Schiphol and the Port of Rotterdam. The ports form major hubs in the global and European networks of passenger and freight transport. From both ports dense multimodal networks connect with markets in Europe. Both ports play an important role in the structure of the Dutch economy. According to the national government they deserve the best possible infrastructure services. In particular, links in the hinterland are to be improved, in order to attract new international transport flows to the Randstad.

High-speed railway lines to France and Germany may well bring new passengers to Schiphol Airport and create a different modal split in the future between air and rail passengers. These high-speed railways will form the top segment of the Dutch railway system. Likewise the hinterland road connections must give very reliable links for freight transport and business traffic to neighboring countries. A new railway line is planned exclusively for international freight traffic, linking Rotterdam with Germany.

Schiphol Airport is developing fast, with annual growth rates of more than 5 percent in the markets for passengers and freight. Schiphol ranks fourth for passengers and third in freight among European airports. Its share of transfer passengers is high. The airport is enlarging its terminal facilities and has permission to add another runway. Capacity is rising towards 60 million passengers a year. Environmental and safety concerns, however, lead to public debate on the location of the airport, and on the prospect of additional runways. Around the airport business is concentrating, especially transport and trade, logistics, and distribution. The center of the trade in fresh flowers is located near the airport, in Aalsmeer. Complete control over the logistic process from glasshouses or cropland to the florist is an absolute essential for this delicate trade. Just-in-time delivery is the key factor. Excellent cooperation between producers, transport companies and retailers, and the vicinity of Schiphol, has helped produce a strong Dutch position in markets abroad.

The capacity of the existing roads around Schiphol is being extended to facilitate traffic movement. A new underground line is planned between the airport and Amsterdam to improve connections. New links are added to the national railway network in order to provide direct connections between the major Dutch cities and Schiphol. The southern part of Amsterdam improves its accessibility by these new links.

The port of Rotterdam has a market share of 40 percent of all harbors from Le Havre, France, to Hamburg, Germany. The port authorities have a strong tradition of facilitating navigation, logistics and large scale industries. Every 10 years new areas for shipping facilities, storage, distribution, and industry are constructed—each time on a larger scale, located farther out into the sea. Feasibility studies have been started on new extensions, some 17,500 acres, westwards into the sea. Large investments are made to keep the port area accessible to all kinds of inland traffic. Rivers and canals are widened, and a special freight-only railway line to Germany is being built, as mentioned. The road system is being extended, with special lanes for freight on existing routes and some new roads. Pipelines connect the port with industrial centers in Holland, Germany, and Belgium.

Telecommunications

The telecommunications infrastructure in the Netherlands offers many opportunities, in the economic sectors, and in research, education, and culture. Not only traditional copper, but also mobile telephone and competing fiber optic networks, are available, in many parts of the country. Recently the telecoms market has been opened for competition. This market is very dynamic, in terms of infrastructure, services, and prices.

The former national telephone company (PTT Telecom, now KPN) is constructing a fiber optic network for national and international data transmission. In the year 2000 this network will cover 80 percent of Dutch business locations. KPN Telecom already offers ISDN connections on any location in the country. KPN is also active in the fields of mobile communication, PABXs, the internet and other IT services. New telecommunication companies started their activities in the markets for mobile phones, international communication, data transmission, and IT services. The new companies already have two separate fiber optic networks available in the Netherlands. The national railway company (NS) cooperates with British Telecom in Telfort, and uses the fiber optic network that NS has built alongside the railway tracks. The Dutch energy distributors cooperate with the local and regional distributors of radio and television signals through cable, in Enertel. The cable distributors have a large number of local fiber optic networks at their disposal, that penetrate almost all neighborhoods. Eighty-eight percent of all households are connected to this network. Internet is already available through the fiber optic network to private households in some parts of the country; probably the whole Randstad region will be covered by the year

2000. Telephone services through the new cable networks will follow. A wide range of IT services will also follow.

The telecommunication infrastructure is widespread. The networks do not discriminate between regions or districts within the country. Only very specialist functions, like remote sensing through observation satellites, depend on the vicinity of the ground stations. Most other IT-using companies are footloose.

Concluding challenges for regional planning

The average time people spend on traveling appears to be constant. In different cultures, at different levels of wealth, people tend to travel some 75 minutes a day. Within this constant time budget, growing incomes lead to a shift towards faster means of transportation, and to higher mobility. So history shows ever increasing mobility, of people, commodities, and services. Information is now moving with the speed of light, capital is moving almost as fast on the global level. Access to global resources is increasing at an amazing speed. The daily realm of people and organizations is rising steadily.

These are important reasons for economic processes to speed up. The business cycle, for example, is shortening fast. On the global markets, the time to market, the time a company needs in order to develop and introduce a new product or a new way of producing it, is reduced to a minimum. Business activities are being transformed and rearranged in the global space. Companies can settle at any place where all types of infrastructure are available. Within those limits, economic activities become footloose.

Spatial planning concepts have (or had) a much longer life cycle. Most cities are organized around centripetal concepts of coherence and compactness. The growing mobility, the speed of the economic cycles, and the free market system are centrifugal forces. New types of services arise, new kinds of relations or arrangements between companies and clients develop, each time with other spatial projections. The importance of traditional centers is changing, within cities like Amsterdam and Rotterdam, within the Randstad as a whole. As we have seen, suburban locations form new focal points in the economic structure of the Randstad, as do the nodes of infrastructure around the main ports.

The questions for research and political consideration are whether there can be, or should be found, some kind of coherence between spatial structures, business cycles, and growing mobility, or whether the spatial structures can show and should show more continuity, as a solid backbone for the dynamics of the markets. In the Randstad, this discussion is focusing around a few themes:

- Growing mobility and demand-oriented infrastructure planning will have more impact on other spatial patterns than most planning agencies have contemplated. Spreading processes will continue; the degree of diversity within the city region, and between city region and periphery, will diminish. The open country will come under even more pressure. Is mobility to be facilitated or to be restrained and redirected into public transport systems?
- Former city centers are under pressure, because road infrastructure and market forces tend to create new business zones in the suburban fringe and around smaller towns. The traditional centers of economic, cultural, and social meaning lose their position. Are there any convincing planning concepts available that can suit city life and market forces at the same time?
- The Green Heart is under pressure from the widely available infrastructure. The main ports and the larger cities tend to use all open land for their next extensions and for their infrastructure. Brokers and developers see many opportunities for new housing projects in the open landscape. The qualities that the Green Heart can offer to city life are not yet integrated into this fragmented planning process. Can there be a restraint upon accidental sprawl? Can a way be found to develop the conurbations and the landscapes in a unifying concept? Should the Randstad extend outwards or inwards?

Stronger planning concepts used to be restricted to the level and scale of cities and agglomerations. Planners also used to focus on housing, on city centers, and left business zones and infrastructure to the market sector or to other policy fields. In the Netherlands initiatives are emerging to create more coherence between various policy fields—to create an understanding of all relevant forces on the spatial markets, to create a kind of coordination between them. The interests are very different, so the chances of implementing integrating concepts are low. Yet it is important to note that the dialogue has started, as a beginning.

REGIONAL LAND USE PLANS: FROM A REGION OF CITIES TO A CITY REGION

The Netherlands has a long tradition of strong local government. Although the Physical Planning Act formally speaks of a hierarchical three-tier system, only municipalities can draw up building regulations and binding legal land use plans. The disposition to consensus is also a

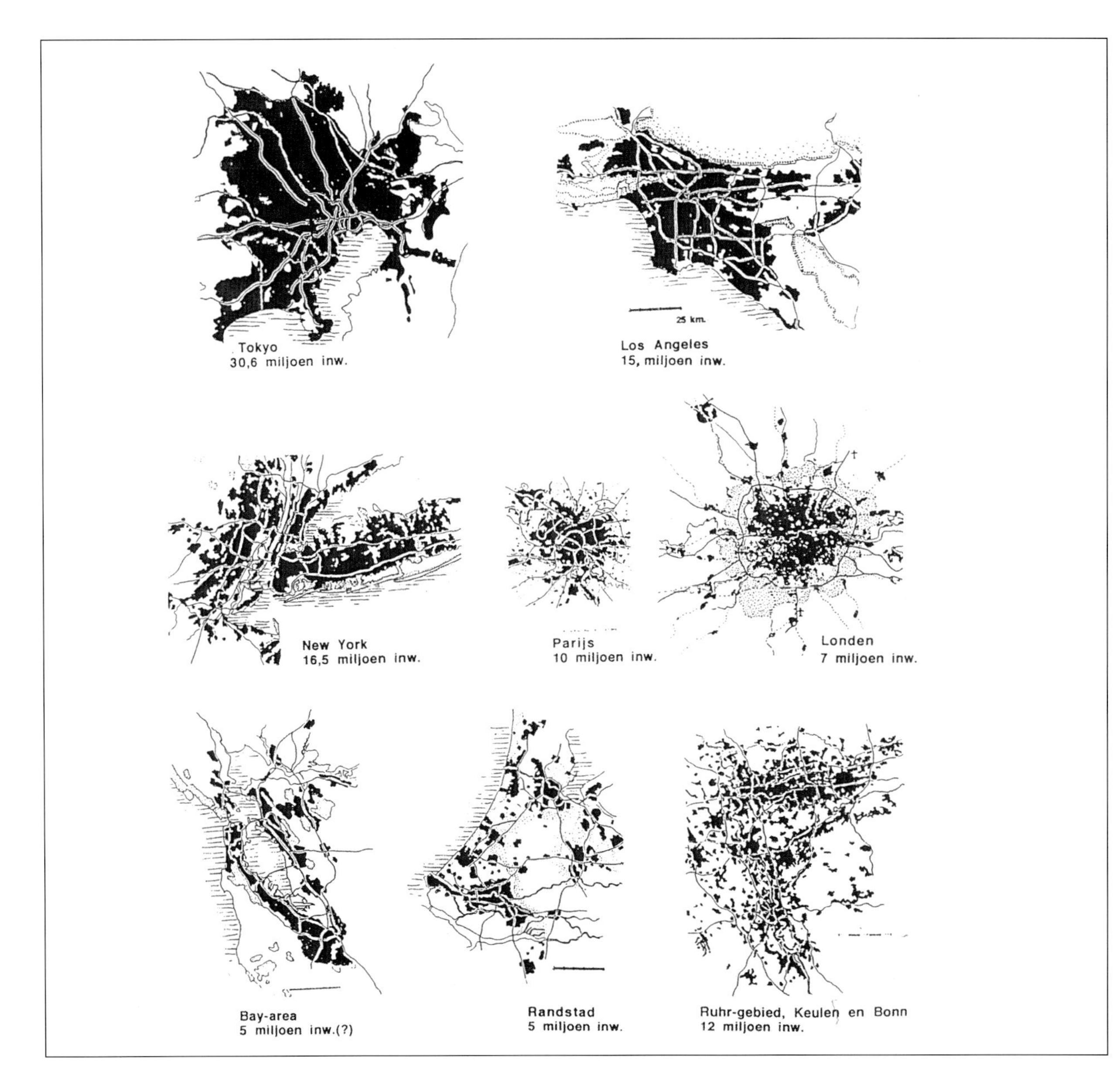

Figure 6.9 City regions compared.
Source L. M. Tummers and J. Zuurmond, *Land in de stad*, 1998

characteristic of Dutch policy making. The central government, the 12 provinces and the 548 municipalities are in continuous debate over the directions of change. Since the 1980s the market forces in land and real estate have entered into the debate. But even today the planning processes in the country correspond to the political conditions of the 'polder model', based on consensus by deliberation and restraint on the part of all actors.

The Randstad itself comprises four provinces and some 170 municipalities. A specific regional planning board comprising the Randstad, as such, does not exist. The most important plans for the region as a whole stem from the Ministry of Planning and Housing. Spatial planning and environmental policy generally developed in harmony with the authorities from the larger cities. Infrastructure planning, agriculture, and nature conservation were mainly under the control of other government agencies.

National planning policies have delayed the changeover from a region of cities to a city region on the scale of the Randstad. Since 1960 four National Memoranda on Physical Planning have sought to restrain urban sprawl, to control suburbanization. The area of the Green Heart, presented in Parliament in 1996 and designated in 1997, defines boundaries to spatial development at the regional level of the Randstad as a whole, but no such legislation on intermediate open spaces is as yet available to regulate the growth of the various conurbations. Here the landscape is still a vulnerable part of the conurbation and the infrastructure in the urban Randstad is increasingly congested.

From 1958 on, the Dutch government has tried to guide the spatial processes in the country. The decades since 1960 have witnessed a number of successive policies and strategies in planning matters. The binding concepts about the nature of urban entities and views on decentralization have varied during these years, while the focus of the schemes has shifted from housing to the environment and the economy.

The first Memorandum on Physical Planning (1960) sought to learn from the experience of Great Britain concerning the growth and containment of London. The Netherlands initiated a strategy of decentralization of urban growth from the natural magnet of the Randstad to outlying regions, and to a number of post-war new towns. According to this memorandum, the cities in the Randstad ought to function as more or less independent entities, with the distance between new towns and older cities being large.

The Second Memorandum (1966) was concerned with the increase in affluence and the vast quantity of housing still to be built. Car ownership and mobility were growing fast. The scale of planning was becoming larger. The agglomeration became the unifying space for urban functions. Another range of new towns was chosen, nearer the central cities, with buffer zones in between.

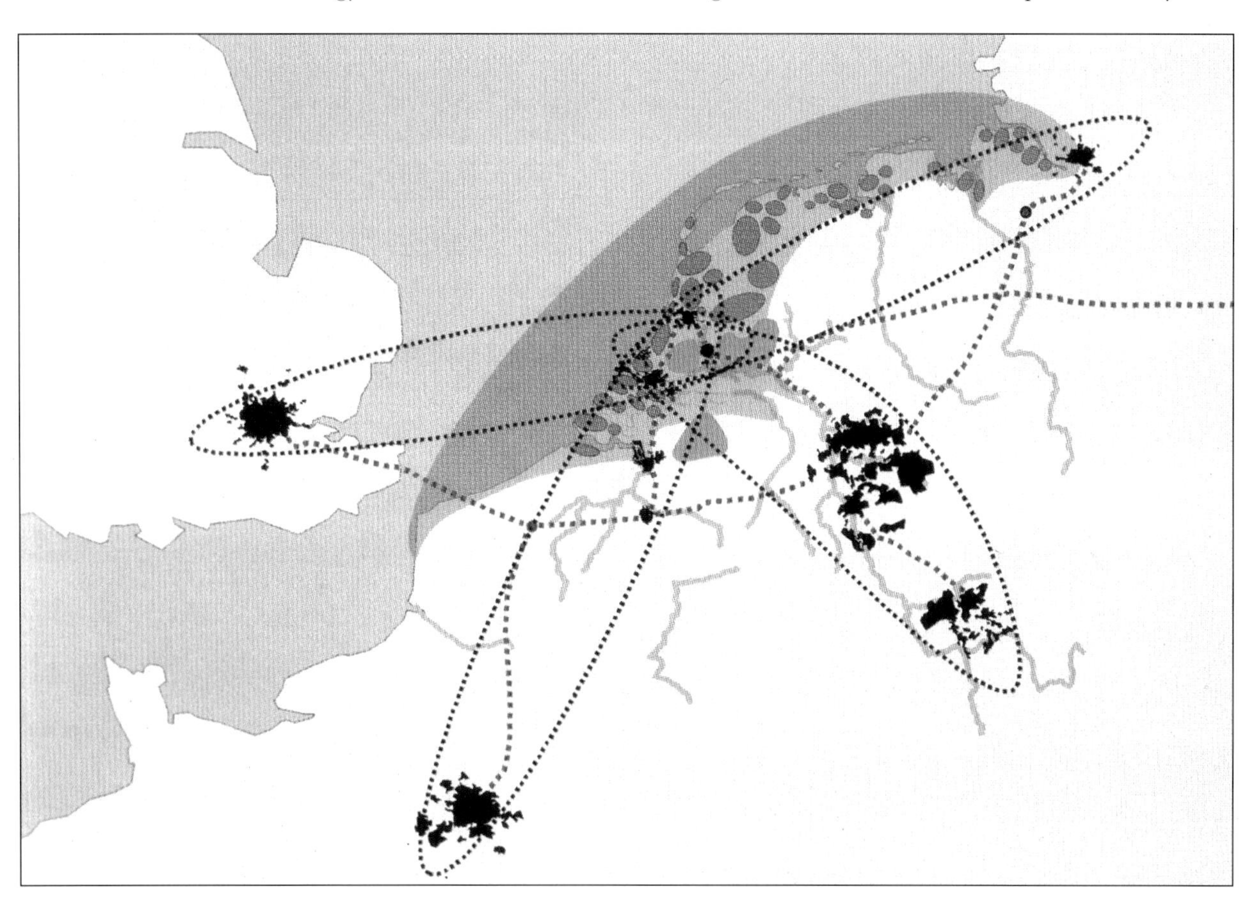

Figure 6.10 Randstad in the European urban scene

In the 1970s the urban renewal process set in. Environmental problems demanded increased attention. Although population growth ebbed somewhat, rising wealth created a shift in interest from urban multifamily housing projects to single family houses in a green setting. At the same time market forces made themselves felt in facilitating suburbanization in the whole rim of the Randstad. The scale of the planning was criticized in the Third Memorandum (1973). In the *stadsgewest* or conurbation a larger town and its suburbs had to provide houses and services for its population and business zones for its firms. The map of the Randstad showed seven conurbations, to be separated by green buffer zones.

The concept of decentralization was dominant in Dutch planning schemes until the 1980s. First at city level, later at the national level too, a countercurrent of preference for concentration became manifest. The Fourth Memorandum (1988) aimed at a positive approach to metropolitan urban growth in the Randstad. The focus of planning changed from the housing aspects to the economic aspects of city life. The scale of the planning concept split in two: the Randstad had to compete in the European urban scene and infrastructure networks must connect the economic nodes of the Randstad into a metropolis. Locations for new housing projects and industries ought to be found in or near the largest cities. Enough locations are still available around the conurbations, although the scheme puts a severe strain on the green wedges in the conurbations.

As stated in the previous section, planners are currently

debating which directions to follow in the future: either occupying the Green Heart, extending the rim of the Randstad, or building in corridors towards the periphery. The fact that nowadays so many options are still open must be explained by the early nationwide planning activities, which connected the potential for natural growth in the Randstad with planned locations in a larger part of the Netherlands.

A picture of the Randstad region in the 1990s centers around metropolitan concepts and the many related aspects of urban strategy. The major conurbations of Amsterdam and Rotterdam, with a population of 1.5 million each, and of The Hague, with a population of 1 million, are revitalizing and gaining momentum economically. The conurbations are involved in debates about and experiments with the reorganization of public administration, in order to centralize planning power at the conurbation level. The outcome is as yet unclear. The power of the smaller municipalities and the cultural identification of people with their own local governments are defying the wishes of the central administration to control the planning process.

The overall development of urban planning concepts for the Randstad, however, proceeds without any specific regional administrative unit within the Randstad, other than those of the four provinces which comprise the Randstad. These provinces are now shifting to a much more proactive position, whence they initiate ideas, visions, and plans. Their traditional field is not so much the control of the major Randstad cities as the control of the whole scope of the province, including its villages, agricultural areas, nature reservations, and ecological networks. Since 1990 a stream of publications has flowed from the four provinces on the subject of the Randstad. They show initiatives for the formulation of green belts, regional public transport networks, and recreational policies. For the national government the cooperating provinces form a counterforce of growing importance.

These provinces may become the administrative power to ensure a balanced development of urban areas and green networks, of infrastructure and economic nodes. In the 1980s they formulated active strategies to create a Randstad Green Structure. Particularly within the conurbations this is a very challenging issue. It may be the key to initiating a strategy of integrative urban–rural planning on the conurbation level.

CONCLUSION

The Randstad and its Green Heart arose as a mighty metaphor in the course of the twentieth century. While the Green Heart has been politically formalized, the urban Randstad is developing further without altering its long-standing legal institutions. Amsterdam and Rotterdam are the two main cities of the Randstad, dominating a wide ring of separate urban units, ever more woven together in a single region of cities.

As a city region the spatial structure of the Randstad belongs to an emerging special type of conurbation: highly decentralized from the beginning, folded around a green heart, bounded on the outside by the shores of the North Sea and the many rivers and lakes. Its physical structure bears more resemblance to, for instance, the San Francisco Bay Area in northern California than to more classical cities such as London or Paris, let alone the giant cities of today such as Tokyo or Los Angeles. As a country the Netherlands is densely populated; it is full up. As a city region the Randstad is hardly dense at all.

In the Green Heart and the connecting spaces the Randstad possesses a unique asset: regional landscapes that safeguard their scenic and ecological values. This system of open spaces must provide the 'countermold' to organize the growing agglomeration around it. But there are also some prominent agricultural areas within the Randstad of great economic importance. Urban pressures on future land use in the Randstad are confronted with the demands of a very successful agribusiness complex.

In the 1990s battles have been fought over the pressure of infrastructure planning on urban regions. Harbors, new rail lines and airport extensions meet with opposition from the conservation lobbies. While the Randstad has the special character of an extremely deconcentrated conurbation, further deconcentration on a national scale may, in the long run, prove to be detrimental to the national well-being. The synergy of the urban cores in Randstad is already handicapped by the existing distances between them. It is thus evident that planners need a comprehensive vision and scope that encompass the different planning sectors involved in city region planning: infrastructure, open spaces, and agglomerative developments. While some outstanding architecture is involved in inner city plans, the site planning for areas to be developed by market forces is lagging behind in design quality.

The 'polder model' as a successful mix of public–private planning initiatives appeals to the new item of 'governance' in spatial physical planning. European competitiveness and infrastructure planning speed up the debate on Randstad planning. The unresolved issues are the ones where quality is involved. Quality of life in the social field and the issue of sustainability in checking the growth figures against the ecological standards of today.

7 San Diego and Tijuana

MICHAEL STEPNER AND PAUL FISKE

The San Diego global city region, in reality, is a binational region consisting of two cities—San Diego, California, in the United States, and Tijuana, Baja California, in Mexico—as well as suburbs on both sides of the border. Together, the region has a population of over 3.5 million and 1.5 million jobs; and, the county of San Diego is expected to grow by 1 million residents by 2020. The Tijuana region may grow by a similar amount in the same period. Many issues and problems are common to both areas and require joint planning and solutions. Both cities are at the edge of their countries. San Diego is at the southwest corner of the United States—south of southern California—a distinction that is very important to its residents. Tijuana is at the northwest corner of Mexico and bears little resemblance to the interior cities of Mexico. As a region, both cities see themselves as the gateway to Mexico and to the United States and jointly as a principal location on the Pacific Rim.

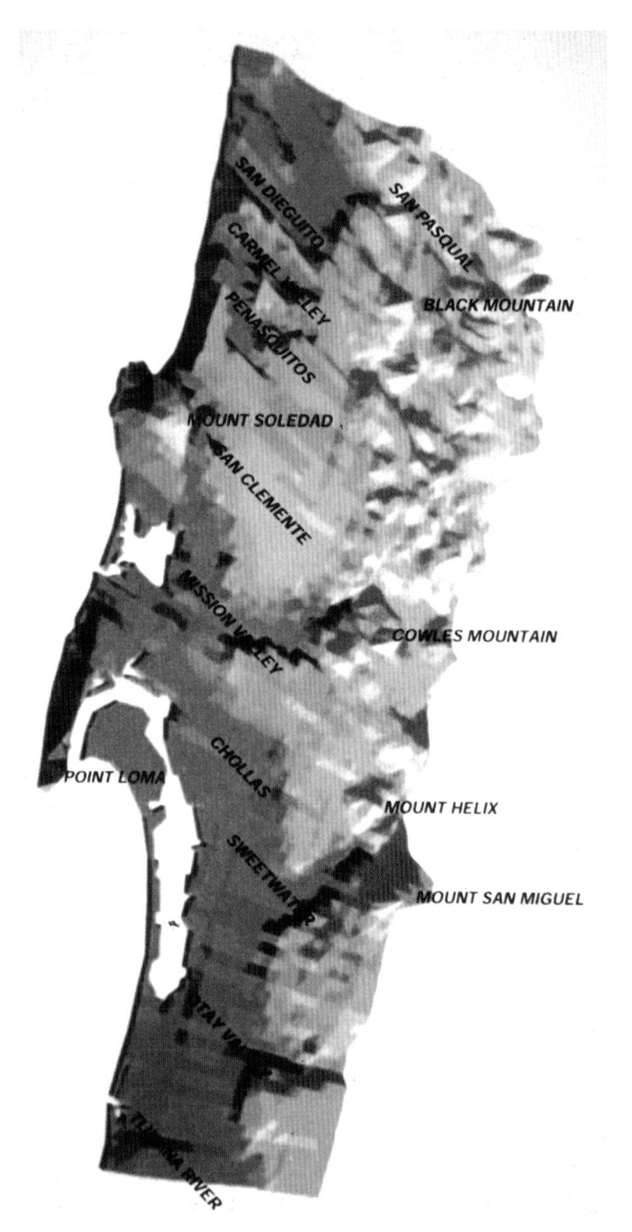

Figure 7.1 The San Diego–Tijuana region city link
Source Adèle Naudé Santos and Assoc. with Andrew Spurlock Martin Poirier Landscape Architects

The metropolitan area of San Diego is a geographically distinct area bounded by two natural boundaries and two that are manmade. To the east are the mountains and desert—one of the most biologically diverse areas in the United States—and to the west is the Pacific Ocean. To the south is the "walled" but permeable border with Mexico; to the north is the "armed" border, the Camp Pendleton Marine Corps base, San Diego's line of defense against the encroachment of Orange County and Los Angeles (southern California).

The San Diego–Tijuana region, on the US side of the border, is fiscally conservative, which results in the provision of adequate infrastructure and services falling further and further behind. How to deal with community concerns—such as loss of neighborhood character, loss of sensitive resources, inadequate public facilities and services, and traffic congestion—was and is the paramount issue facing the decision makers.

In Tijuana, the issues are similar but are surpassed by the question of how to provide even a minimum level of infrastructure and public services. This is, in large part, due to the country's economic problems and to the nature of the political system, which is very centralized in Mexico City.

San Diego is a low-density city and by the year 2010 it will have run out of raw, undeveloped land that is suitable and designated for residential development. By contrast, Tijuana is a much higher-density city and is spreading out in an unplanned and, in some cases, in an unpermitted manner. Basic services, such as water and sewers, may not reach some of these areas for many years if at all.

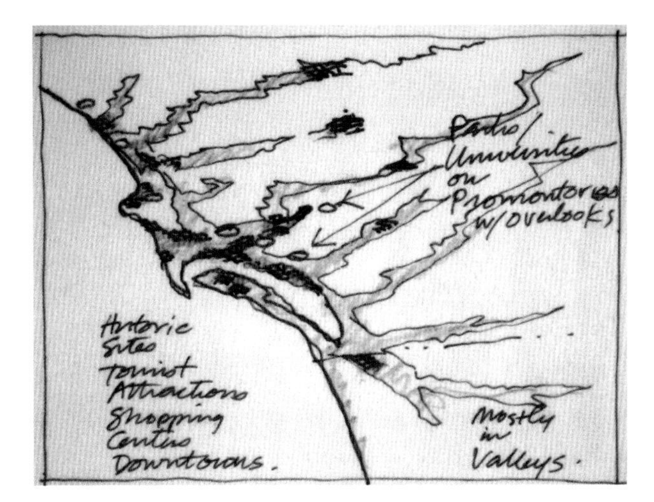

Figure 7.2 San Diego: regional features

The city of San Diego is expected to grow by 300,000 people between 2000 and 2010. This forecasted population is based mostly on natural increase and reflects the demographic trends of an increasingly diverse citizenry. The creation of high-paying, defense-related jobs fueled in-migration in the late 1980s, but today's challenge is in providing the emerging generation of city residents with good schools, good neighborhoods, and good job skills so they can compete successfully in the changing job market.

The municipality of Tijuana contains almost 1,400 square miles. The official population is approximately 800,000 but unofficial estimates put the city's population at anywhere between 1 million and 2 million people. Tourism and manufacturing are important in the economy.

While the region is dominated by the two major cities of San Diego and Tijuana—which sit next to each other at the border—there are 17 other cities on the US side of the

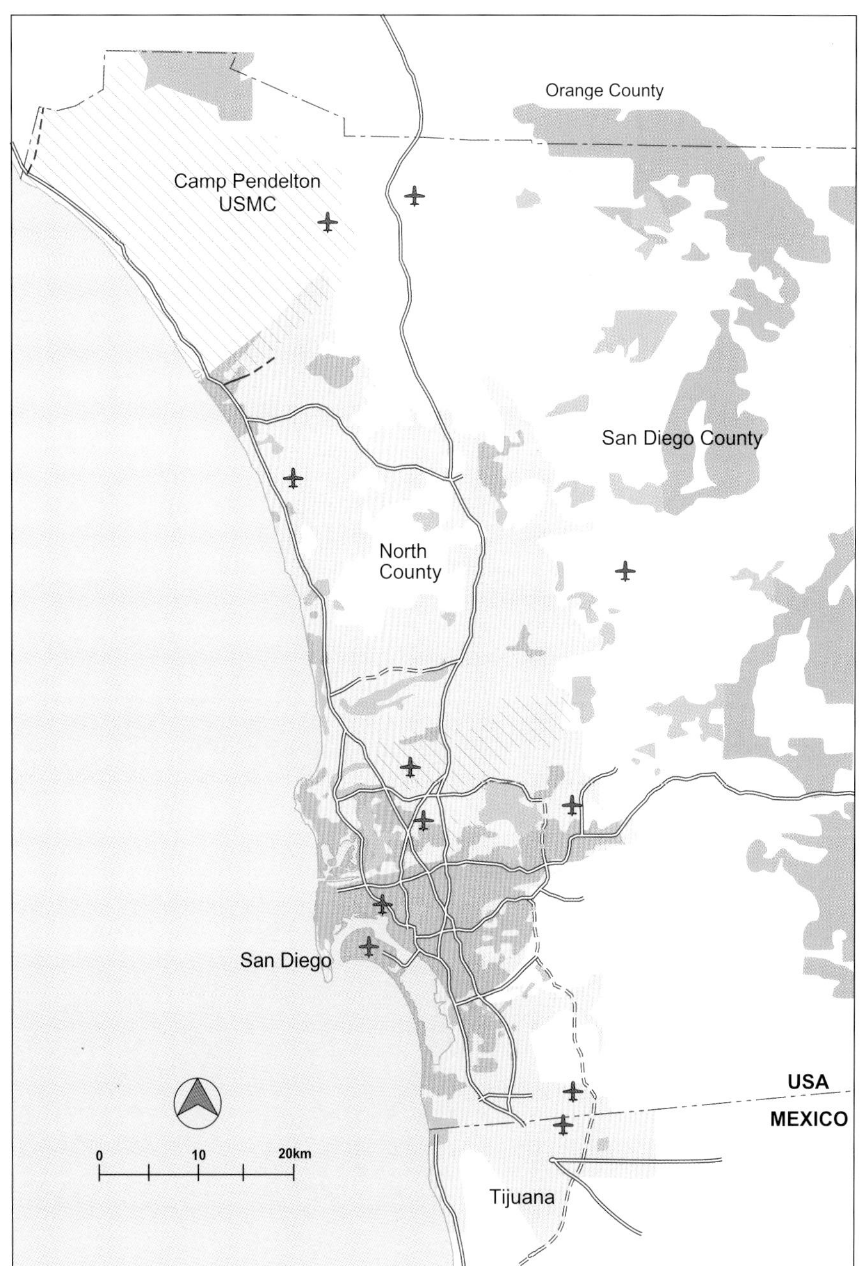

Figure 7.3 The San Diego region, 1995

Figure 7.4 The location of the San Diego region

border and one (the newly formed city of Rosarito Beach) on the Mexican side of the border. There are also large unincorporated, urbanized areas on both sides of the border. In addition to the 20 cities in the region, there are also the county of San Diego and 158 special districts of various kinds on the US side. These agencies are not always in agreement, seeing things from the perspective of their own turf and immediate needs.

The San Diego Association of Governments (SANDAG) is the agency responsible for preparation of the Regional Growth Management Strategy as well as addressing issues of population growth, transportation, environmental management, fiscal management, economic development, and criminal justice. While SANDAG has little actual authority to direct other government agencies,

Figure 7.5 Economic patterns in the San Diego region

it has served as a forum to bring together not only the 18 cities and the county but also key state and federal agencies. The city of Tijuana now sits on the SANDAG board as an ex-officio member as a result of the changing nature of local government administration in Mexico. When SANDAG was first formed, Mexican cities had little local decision-making or administrative powers. All of this was centralized in Mexico City and, to a lesser extent, at the state level, including land use planning and its implementation. All of this began to change about 1990 as the Mexican government began to devolve authority to the local government administrations. This has resulted in the creation of a stronger municipal structure in Tijuana and closer cooperation regionally. It also enabled the mayors of Tijuana and San Diego to sign a binational planning agreement in 1993, which reaffirms the increasing interdependence of the region and the need for supportive and collaborative efforts across the border.

CHANGING ECONOMIC PATTERNS

The evolution of the region's economy over the last two decades of the twentieth century has resulted in an increase in the ratio of lower paying jobs to higher paying jobs. Between 1980 and 1990 the number of service sector jobs increased from about 172,000 to over 316,000 (an 84 percent gain). Services are now the largest and fastest growing job sector. Unfortunately, service jobs pay wages averaging as much as 60 percent less than jobs in manufacturing and health services (SANDAG). Now, one in three jobs is in services. If the region's job base continues to change in this direction, *per capita* income will drop 20 percent below the state and national average between 2000 and 2020.

Problems have resulted from a slow national recovery: the real estate, savings and loan, and banking foreclosures of the early 1990s; defense expenditure cutbacks; and the inability to more fully participate in the growing international trade marketplace. In addition, governments at all levels (federal, state, and local) are experiencing expenditure overruns or revenue shortfalls. Locally and statewide, population growth has continued to be relatively strong throughout the economic downturn. The combined impact of these economic problems and population growth makes it more difficult for the region to regain the economic ground and stability it has lost. SANDAG recommends that the region:

- Ensures a rising standard of living for the region's residents that is equal to or above that of comparable metropolitan areas.
- Encourages the enhancement and development of regional capital facilities (infrastructure) that are necessary to encourage the expansion and retention of local businesses.
- Ensures a more productive labor force by properly educating, training, and preparing new entrants. Initially, success in increasing labor force productivity can be measured by the ability to reverse the rising trend of births to unwed mothers, the school dropout rate, and the number of crimes committed per 1,000 residents.
- Encourages the expansion of locally owned businesses to create job opportunities that require skilled labor.
- Reduces the rise in the region's cost of living to a level equal to or below that of comparable metro regions.
- Maintains the cost of local government facilities and services at a level equal to or below those of comparable metro regions. This can be measured as a percentage, determined by the ratio of local government expenditures *per capita* over personal income *per capita*.

CHANGING SOCIAL PATTERNS

The trend of the 1970s and 1980s was rapid population growth composed predominantly of in-migration from other states and from other parts of California. This was fueled by the economy and growth in defense and related industry. Since 1990 such jobs have been drastically reduced, with San Diego employment now comprised of about 15 percent manufacturing versus approximately 35 percent in the 1960s. As a result, real median household income in the San Diego region dropped by 13 percent between 1990 and 1995.

The region's population growth in the 1990s has averaged 1.8 percent, down from the 3.0 percent average of the previous decade (April 1996, SANDAG). Despite this, the region continues to become more ethnically diverse. Between 1990 and 1995 Hispanics and Asian and other races (per census terminology) have increased 20 percent compared with 9 percent for the black population. Growth in the non-Hispanic white population has been low by comparison, increasing by 3 percent. Changes in age groups have also occurred, with persons under age 15, between ages 35 and 54, and 75 years and older having increased at least twice as fast as the total population. The number of persons between 20 and 34 has actually declined.

The city and region are faced with a decline in the average standard of living unless effective steps are taken to provide infrastructure and social and health care services;

Table 7.1 Changing social patterns, San Diego

- The city of San Diego is the United States' seventh largest city in population and eleventh largest in land cover.
- San Diego County is the fifth largest county.
- The county has the eleventh largest Native American (American Indian) population, with 20,066.
- The county has the seventh largest Asian population, with 198,311.
- The county has the eighth largest Hispanic population, with 510,781.
- The city is fifty-fifth in percentage of residents age 65 or older.
- The city is fifty-ninth in African-American population percentage.
- The city is ninth in Asian population percentage.
- The city is twenty-second in Hispanic population percentage.
- The city is thirteenth in foreign-born percentage.
- The city is eighteenth in percentage of families who do not speak English in the home.
- The 1991 crime rate of 8,537 crimes per 100,000 population ranked fifty-seventh out of seventy-seven cities. Atlanta was first with 18,953 and Los Angeles was fortieth with 9,730.
- Over 51 percent of all homes in the city are occupied by renters.
- San Diego taxes collected amount to $335 per resident—sixtieth out of 77 cities. Washington DC ranked first at $3,978.

By the year 2010, San Diego will have:

- An aging population and there will be no majority racial or ethnic group.
- A further decline in public revenues and increased demand and need for public facilities.

Note Similar data not available for Tijuana.

Figure 7.6 Residences of the wealthiest 20 percent and the poorest 20 percent

to educate and train the labor force; and to reduce teenage births, the school dropout rate, and the crime rate among youth. Tied to these factors, it is important to encourage the expansion of local businesses requiring skilled labor, provided affordable housing, revitalize neighborhoods, and maintain the cost of local government facilities and services.

The binational nature of the region must also be recognized in order to address goals fully for the future. The county of San Diego (approximately 4,200 square miles) and the municipality of Tijuana, together, occupy about 5,600 square miles of land, forming a natural region despite the international boundary that divides it. Based on the 1990 US and Mexico census data, San Diego and Tijuana had over 3.25 million people. In 1990–2000 San Diego County population increased 34 percent. The population of Tijuana grew 62 percent in the same period, with a median age of 21 years, compared with a median age of 31 years in San Diego County. The goal of "sustainable economic development" is equally applicable to both cities and success in achieving that goal may depend increasingly on coordinated planning to fulfill common objectives.

CHANGING SPATIAL PATTERNS

Twenty years ago, San Diego was provided a compelling view of its present and future by two internationally renowned land planners. Kevin Lynch of the Massachusetts Institute of Technology and Donald Appleyard of the University of California, Berkeley, conducted a "regional reconnaissance" of the San Diego area. The perceptive observations were assembled in a 50 page illustrated document, entitled *Temporary Paradise?*

Temporary Paradise? called for the preservation of the region's remaining undeveloped valleys and canyons. It recommended that parts of the valleys should become ecological preserves or areas for public enjoyment. The canyon fingers could be linked by a series of trails for walking, cycling, and horseback riding. There has been moderate success in achieving this vision—certainly more success than was typified by the canyon and river valley development common in the 1950s and 1960s. On the other hand, a large amount of native plant and animal habitat as well as rural and agricultural land was lost during the last two decades. This was due largely to the continued high influx of people to the region and the continuing demand for low-density, detached housing during the 1970s and 1980s.

Demographic and economic factors have played a major role in the continuation of the trend toward relentless urban sprawl. The maturing of the post-World War II "baby boom" generation in the 1970s and 1980s drove housing demand. Many in this generation apparently internalized the housing goals of their parents as the desirable norm for their own household formations and opted for suburban, low-density housing. During a seven-year, high-growth period in the 1980s, population increased 22 percent; but San Diego freeway traffic increased approximately 50 percent.

Development patterns have been established for most of the areas that comprise the western one-third of the county. The city of *San Diego's Progress Guide and General Plan* (current version first adopted in 1979) promoted urban revitalization over urban sprawl. Through the early 1980s there was a high amount of new residential development in the older established urban areas, mostly in the form of redevelopment and infill apartment and town house construction. With the economic boom of the mid 1980s, combined with reduced residential mortgage rates, there was a return to the high levels of low-density suburban development that characterized the three previous decades. However, now there was in place the beginnings of an urban light rail transportation system. This transportation option had not been available to San Diegans since the streetcar system was dismantled soon after the Second World War. Voters countywide approved a 0.5 percent transportation sales tax passed in 1988. This tax, which will be applied through 2008, apportions one-third for transit, one-third for highways, and one-third for local streets. Long-range light rail transit plans call for a north coastal extension to the University City urban node, an area that includes a regional shopping center, extensive medium and higher-density residential development, major hotels, and the University of California, San Diego.

Perhaps the biggest challenge in revitalizing the older urban areas of San Diego is availability of public funds for the maintenance and operation of infrastructure and services. The severe restrictions placed on property tax rates by the 1978 passage of state Proposition 13 (Homeowners' Tax Relief) have resulted in insufficient funding for fully adequate maintenance of streets, parks, libraries, schools, and related public functions. The extended economic recession affecting southern California during the first half of the 1990s also dampened private reinvestment, critical to maintaining and enhancing the livability of many of the older urban areas as well as some of the post-war suburban communities.

Progress has been made in establishing the foundation for an enhanced urban environment. Expansion of the San Diego Trolley LRT system is a prime example. A growing challenge to local government is its ability to serve the needs of an increasing and relatively recent immigrant and minority population in the urban areas. This group reflects a rapid rise in both Asian and Hispanic population groups that began in the 1970s and continues to grow as a percentage of the population.

Based on the current general plans of the 18 cities and the county, the region will begin to run out of vacant, residentially designated urban land soon after 2005. Increasingly, future housing opportunities will need to come through redevelopment, including densities that will support the transit corridors and nodes now being built and planned. This pattern of compact development will be increasingly necessary based on the projected population growth as well as restrictions resulting from the region's sensitive wildlife habitat. In 1997 the city adopted the Multiple Species Conservation Program (MSCP), which will conserve almost 165,000 acres of habitat. Close to 100 species would be protected and acquisition costs over a 30 year period are estimated to be between $400 million and $750 million. This effort is considered necessary to meet federal and state environmental protection requirements while, at the same time, contributing to the region's continued economic development.

INFRASTRUCTURE INVESTMENT

For the region, today's challenge is in providing the emerging generation of city residents with good schools, good neighborhoods, and good job skills so they can compete successfully in the changing job market. In many ways, the region is at a crossroads. Actions we take or defer today will affect how well the city delivers for its citizens on the principles of economic opportunity, individual responsibility, sense of community, commitment to quality education, equality for all, and the ability to pursue personal goals free of crime.

Provision and maintenance of infrastructure and public facilities have been severely strained in the last two decades. The limitations are felt particularly in the older urbanized areas as the combination of limited property tax revenues and shifts of local taxes to the state have occurred. Just since 1990, the effect of state repeals of previous subventions to local government have resulted in a 16 point drop in the percentage of cities' and counties' combined share of the local property tax dollar (from $6.8 billion or 46 percent in 1990 to $5.9 billion or 30 percent in 1995).

In 1987 development impact fees (DIF) were enacted in the urbanized communities to assure redevelopment would pay a portion of the cost of facilities needed to maintain existing levels of service to the community. These fees have been used to offset a small portion of the effects of limited property tax revenues. Because the percentage of new development is much lower than existing development, facilities cannot be fully funded by DIF. Additional sources of funding must be identified.

Roads

The modern history of major road building in San Diego began in 1956, with the Federal Interstate Highway Program, a system that is now 90 percent complete in San Diego County. A heavy infusion of federal funds began in the late 1950s and continued at a high level through the 1970s, with less funding in the 1980s and 1990s.

In 1958 the first of the San Diego freeways (the east–west Interstate 8) crossed through the dairy and grazing lands of Mission Valley, located three miles north of the downtown business district. The new freeway facilitated the growth and development of suburban residential "bedroom communities" located east of the pre-1950s trolley-line communities of North Park and Kensington. Interstate 8 also facilitated regional retail shopping center and office development in the previously agricultural valley. The old trolley service ended in the late 1940s, and the new San Diego Trolley that initiated service from downtown to the border in 1981 is now being expanded east and parallel to Interstate 8 in Mission Valley.

By the 1960s the Interstate 5 coastal freeway was under construction, providing a high-capacity link from the US–Mexico border. Improvements continued, providing a full freeway for over 100 miles through northern San Diego County and into Orange County and the city of Los Angeles. This freeway became a major route for trucks from the Los Angeles metropolitan area as well as a prime conduit for daily cross-county commuter traffic and weekend recreational travel to and from Los Angeles and Orange counties.

The region's population nearly doubled from 1960 (1.03 million) to 1980 (1.86 million). During that time the number of motor vehicles approximately tripled from 454,000 to 1.3 million. This era coincided with the height of the region's highway building. In 1997 the population stood at 2.7 million. The remaining major unbuilt freeway is the north–south inland State Route 125, proposed as the first private venture toll highway in the region. It is planned to serve the inland (Otay Mesa) international border crossing.

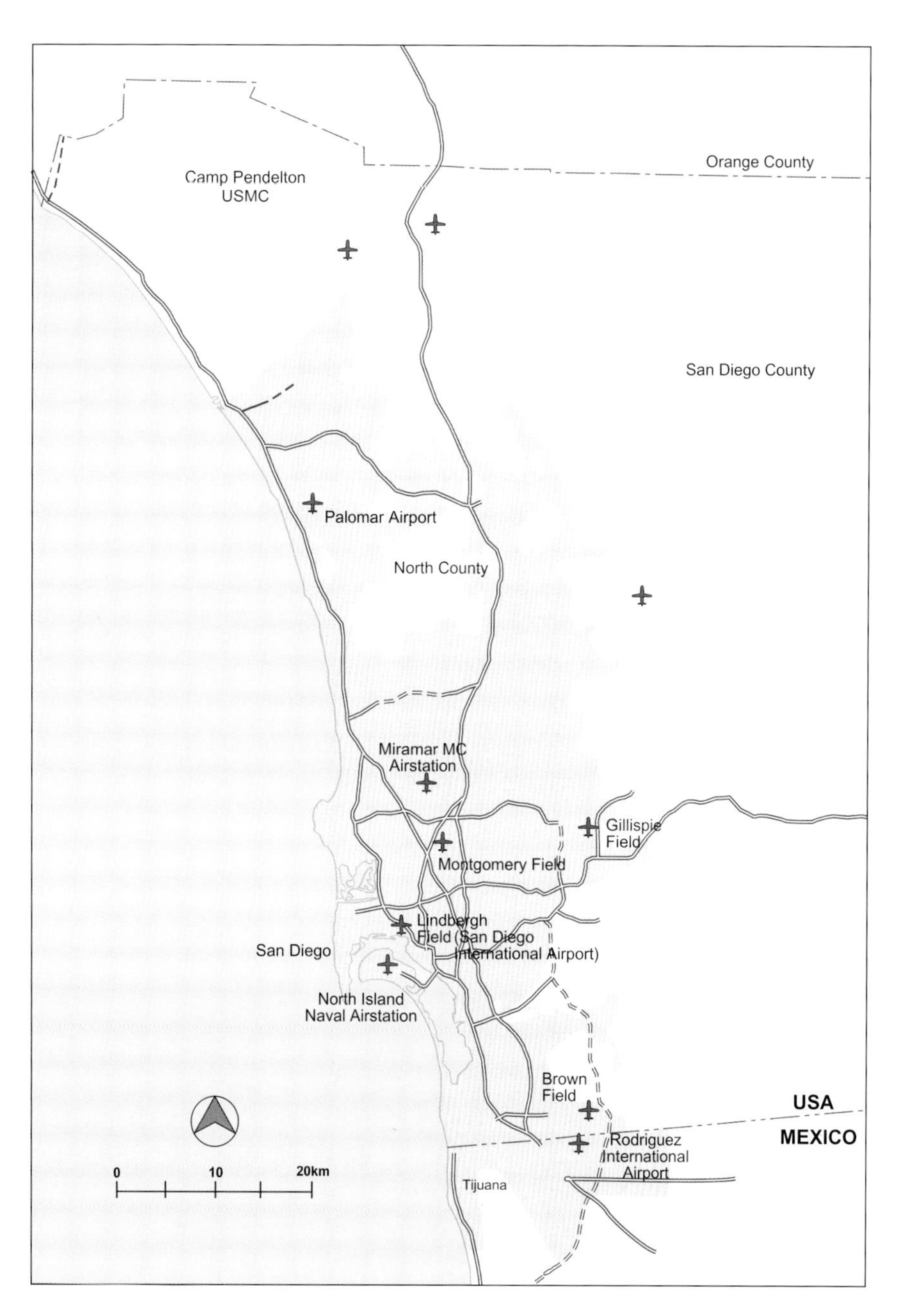

Figure 7.7 Main roads and airports in the San Diego region, 1995

Rail

Significant progress has been made in providing light rail transit within the San Diego region only since 1981. Very few mainline rail improvements and no light rail construction took place from 1960 to 1980. An attempt was made in the mid 1950s to attract more passengers back to mainline trains by Santa Fe, the corporation operating the line to Los Angeles and east from there through the Rocky Mountains and Great Plains to Chicago. The addition in 1955 of new passenger coach service at rates competitive with the airlines did not compete well after the early 1960s and the advent of faster jet airline service to destinations outside San Diego County. Through the 1960s and 1970s, major interstate highway construction also made passenger car travel and truck transport beyond the region more feasible and attractive as an alternative to the aging north–south rail infrastructure. However, in recent years, traffic congestion between San Diego and Los Angeles has made intercity rail travel more attractive. Amtrak, the national passenger rail service, now operates 10 round trips daily from San Diego to Los Angeles and points north.

The San Diego & Arizona Eastern (now San Diego & Imperial Valley) freight line, which served since 1919 to link with the agricultural Imperial Valley 80 miles to the east, was heavily damaged by storms and bridge fires in the early 1980s. A 1996 study of the cost to reopen this line to Imperial County and link service east via the Southern Pacific Railroad and south via the National Railroad of Mexico is estimated at $100 million or more. A public/private financing strategy for restoration has been recommended by the region's advisory council of governments (SANDAG). The feasibility of financing the freight line, however, remains to be resolved.

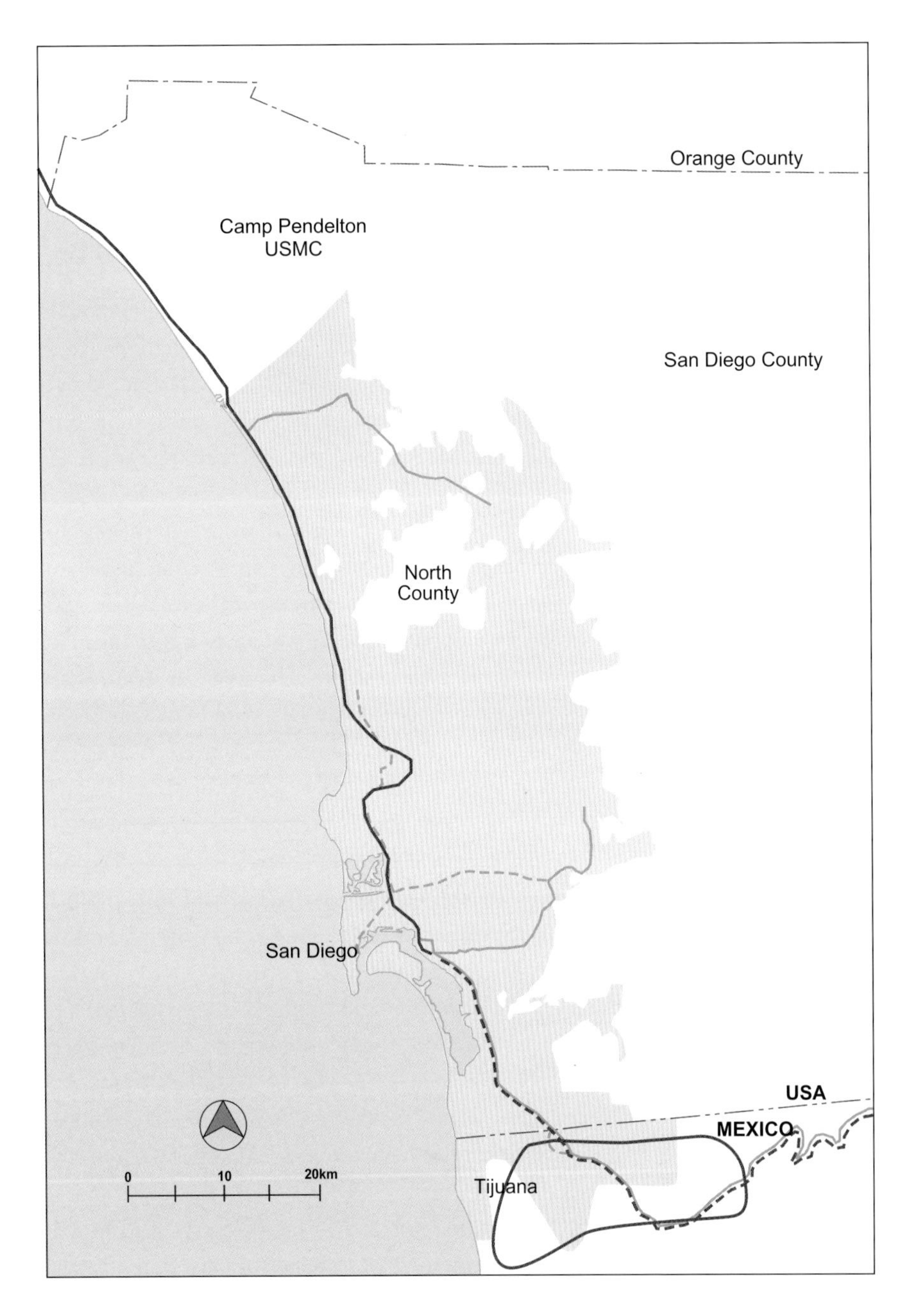

Figure 7.8 Railways in the San Diego region, 1995

In the late 1970s the first urban rail transit to operate since streetcar service ended in the 1940s was proposed and funded. Commonly known as the San Diego Trolley, this electric rail system began operating in 1981 with the first 16 miles from the Mexican border to downtown San Diego. This link, as well as the East Line of 22 miles to the city of Santee, was built within the right of way of the existing San Diego & Arizona Eastern railway. By doing so, substantial savings were realized, making these lines feasible.

In 1997 an extension of the light rail transit line was completed east from the Old Town link into the Mission Valley mixed use area, which is comprised of regional retail, office, and residential development, and a major sports stadium. This Mission Valley West line is further proposed for extension east to serve the 30,000 student San Diego State University. It would connect with the more southerly existing East Line, thus completing a loop back to downtown San Diego.

The Mission Valley East segment of approximately six miles is proposed to be funded by the region's 1988 voter-approved 0.5 percent addition to the sales tax. This funding mechanism collects over $130 million per year for local transit, highways, and streets. The current tax will expire in 2008, and the willingness of the electorate to renew it may affect this and other planned transit extensions. The Mission Valley West segment of six miles (9.7 km) was a $220 million project, owing to numerous grade crossings of major roads, highways, and water areas. This link included developer funding assistance through right-of-way dedications and financial participation in construction.

New coastal commuter rail service was begun in 1995 along the upgraded (continuous weld rail) Santa Fe line, 43 miles (69 km) from downtown north to the city of

Oceanside. This diesel locomotive "Coaster" commuter service, funded by California voter-approved rail funds and the local 0.5 percent transportation sales tax, uses two-level (double-deck) coaches to transport workers to the downtown business district and other business centers.

The city of Tijuana is proposing a trolley system to be constructed in five phases. The first phase of the LRT is expected to commence in late 1997 and to be completed in 1999. A convenient connection at the San Ysidro trolley station is planned.

Airports

The San Diego–Tijuana region is a center for military aviation with Miramar Naval Air Station (now a Marine Corps air station), North Island Naval Air Station, and Imperial Beach Naval Air Station. There are a number of general aviation airports located throughout San Diego County (two—Montgomery Field in San Diego and Palomar/Carlsbad in North County—also have limited commercial commuter flights). There are two "international" airports in the region—Rodriguez International Airport in the city of Tijuana and San Diego International Airport (Lindbergh Field) in downtown San Diego. Both airports are limited in size, are geographically and topographically constrained, and both are undergoing limited expansion.

Lindbergh Field, at 464 acres (188 ha), is the smallest major commercial airport in the United States (approximately one-fiftieth the size of Denver's new airport). Since the Second World War the planning agencies in the region have conducted numerous studies to try to determine where a new airport could be located in the region. Almost on a biannual basis, studies have been undertaken to determine airport needs. Each study has shown that Lindbergh Field is or will be obsolete and that no alternative site in the region is "acceptable."

The most recent studies reexamined the concept of a joint facility with Tijuana, linking Rodriguez Field and Brown Field at the border in San Diego. Brown Field is constrained for large planes by topography and proposed residential development to the west; Rodriguez is not. In combination, it was believed, they could serve the region for the foreseeable future. The plan was not adopted, owing to questions of international sovereignty and traffic impact in the southern part of the county.

A study has been commenced that steps back and looks at what the region's air travel needs will be in the future. There is a strong constituency that believes an expanded airport is crucial. There is also an equally strong constituency that believes it is not. One alternative that will be looked at in the current study is the feasibility of a 75 mile long high-speed rail connection to Orange County, where recently closed El Toro Marine Corps Air Station is being considered. In the meantime, both Rodriguez and Lindbergh fields are being expanded. In Tijuana expansion will accommodate increased flights to the interior of Mexico and, also, international flights.

Expansion at Lindbergh Field is under way with new terminals adding about 18 gates. This expansion is being accommodated on land acquired from the recently closed Naval Training Center and is expected to serve the airport for the next 15–20 years. The first airport master plan in the airport's 80 year history is now complete. The plan looks at the use of adjacent industrial land (approximately 100 acres, 40.5 ha) next to the airport. It also looks at acquisition of land for a second taxiway from the adjacent Marine Corps Recruit Training Center. Proposals for a $500 million upgrade of Brown Field as a general aviation and cargo port are also under consideration.

Furthermore, there is discussion of another attempt at a binational airport with Tijuana, with only a terminal this time on the US side and all airport operations in Mexico. Development of a new airport is a 15–20 year building project. Therefore the region must improve and expand the facilities it now has.

Telecommunications

In 1960 the telecommunications network was essentially the Bell Telephone public utility. At that time nearly 84 percent of households had telephones, steadily increasing to almost 98 percent in 1990. A slight drop to 96.2 percent by 1995 may be due largely to the region's prolonged recession (which was not overcome until late 1995), as well as the increasing availability of alternative telecommunication means prevalent by the mid 1990s (e.g. wireless phones addressed to a business rather than a residence).

The *status quo* in 1960 was altered over the next three decades by two forces: first, the rapid pace of technology; second, by a federal court ruling that during the 1980s required the "divestiture" by the century-old Bell System (American Telephone & Telegraph, AT&T) of its several telephone companies providing local service to multistate regions of the United States. Long distance telephone service was opened to market competition, resulting in a substantial share of such service (about 35 percent by mid 1997) being provided by companies other than AT&T.

By 1995 approximately 15 percent of the population utilized cellular wireless telephones with digital technology emerging as the next step toward improved wireless voice quality. The use of personal computers grew from a small percentage of users in 1990 to about 60 percent of the population by 1995. That percentage has somewhat leveled off for the time being. Ownership is highly income-dependent, with initial costs for a complete system typically between $2,000 and $3,000, plus the added cost of periodic system upgrades necessary to avoid obsolescence. In households earning over $100,000, personal computer (PC) ownership is 65 percent, while only 12 percent of households earning less than $30,000 own PCs. Nationwide, about 16 percent of the population (42 million people) have access to the internet.

Cable television service is utilized by approximately 70 percent of the households in the San Diego region, a level 5–10 percent higher than nationally, probably owing to the foothill and canyon topography that makes reception difficult in many areas. Across the border in Tijuana, the Television por Cable de Mexico company provides service and has a link with one of San Diego's largest servers, Cox Communications. The cable services in San Diego each provide at least one Spanish language channel as well. In May 1997 Cox Communications, which serves central and eastern San Diego, announced an $8 million grant partnership that would name a new public 12,000 seat sports and concert arena at San Diego State University (enrollment 30,000 students) the "Cox Arena at Aztec Bowl." In addition SDSU will receive additional fiber optic hookups to Mexico and two-way video to local schools. This represents significant corporate-supported progress for the 100 year old public university, which was dedicated at its present location in 1931 with the encouragement of a Spanish official in attendance who characterized the facility as "the finest example of Spanish architecture outside of Spain."

The city of San Diego and SDSU both have actively promoted expansion of the fiber optic network to foster a knowledge-based region seeking to compete globally.

Conclusion

The San Diego–Tijuana region is in the midst of major infrastructure building and rebuilding. This includes a number of high profile projects: expansion of the light rail transit system in San Diego, construction of a new rail transit system in Tijuana, new freeways and expansion of existing freeways in both cities, expansion of San Diego's convention center and stadium, and multibillion dollar upgrades and replacements of the sewer and water systems. This latter not only to incorporate new technology but, perhaps more important, to correct years of deferred maintenance.

The focus is not only on major projects but on existing neighborhoods as well. This includes new schools, parks, libraries, police and fire stations, and increased maintenance. Even so, these new projects and efforts are well short of neighborhood needs caused by lack of public investment in projects and maintenance—a shortfall that was estimated at $700 million in 1990.

The state of the infrastructure in the San Diego–Tijuana region can be described best, perhaps, in the following excerpts from a special newspaper section in the *San Diego Union-Tribune* on August 20, 1995, written by staff writer Roger Showley.

> There is growing recognition that failure to reinvest in San Diego's infrastructure could threaten the region's economic viability.
>
> "We're losing ground vis-a-vis the rest of the state and nation," said regional planner Michael McLaughlin. "We need to make those investments necessary to bring back higher value-added, higher-paying jobs."
>
> Meanwhile, at least as much work is needed south of the border. Mexican planners acknowledge that much of the population lacks basic sewer and water service, paved streets, decent housing, sufficient health care, uncrowded schools and park and recreation facilities.
>
> A 1993 study indicated that Mexican infrastructure investment fell short by as much as $5.4 billion in the 1980's. The total no doubt far exceeds that figure today.
>
> As officials throughout the country proudly cut the ribbons on new trolley stations, schools and libraries, they turn their backs on many existing facilities that are falling apart at the seams.
>
> The neglect, euphemistically referred to as "deferred maintenance," totals about $200 million in the city of San Diego, the county and the San Diego Unified School District alone.
>
> Despite all its building plans, San Diego still ranks 55th among the nation's 77 biggest cities in spending per capita . . .

REGIONAL LAND USE PLANS AND OTHER INITIATIVES TO MANAGE URBAN FORM

Problems facing the region are due to several factors, most of which are tied to the need to respond more effectively to rapid population growth. The wide-ranging distribution of urban/suburban development that encompasses much of the 1,400 square mile western county area places great demands on the supply and distribution of imported water. The added sewage and solid waste generated also impose high system demands and create high costs for adequate disposal. Work commute trips have increased as development patterns have steadily spread outward from urban centers.

Pervasive regional problems include the cost of housing, opportunities for good jobs, the provision and maintenance of public facilities and services, and efficient transportation options and their acceptance by commuters. Revitalization of declining neighborhoods and the protection of diminishing native plant and animal habitat are also critical for the future. The development trends of the last 30 years have tended to work against many of these factors, especially the last two. If the region is to reverse these declines, gains will have to be made in public acceptance of more compact residential development. If new development and redevelopment can be created that will achieve a high degree of livability, it should become increasingly acceptable and even desirable to the region's growing population.

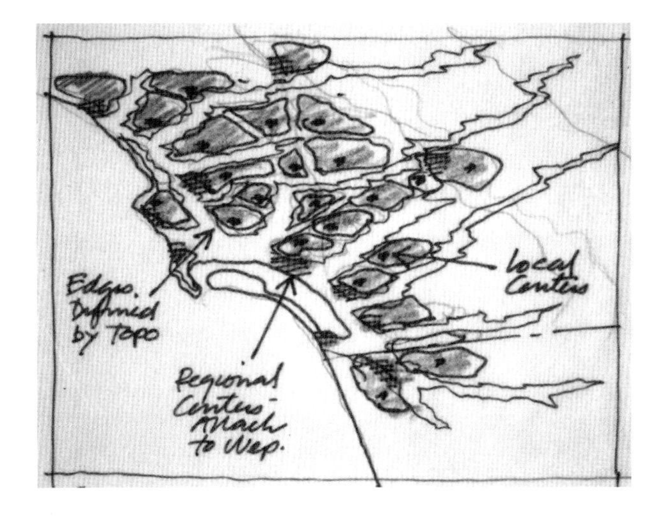

Figure 7.9 Communities in the San Diego region

The San Diego–Tijuana metropolitan area lies at the extreme southwest border of the United States. None of the topographic features within the border area bears any relation to the international border. Mountains extend across the border and a system of rivers and canyons crosses it in many places. A large flat mesa and the coastal plain also exist both north and south of the border.

The main source of employment on both sides of the border is in the service and commerce sectors. In San Diego County, 82 percent of the population older than 25 years has graduated from high school and more than half have an education beyond high school. More than half of the population in Tijuana over 15 years of age has more than a primary school education and the literacy rate is among the highest in Mexico at 94.5 percent.

There are two border crossing facilities connecting Tijuana and San Diego. The San Ysidro crossing has the distinction of being the world's busiest port of entry. In 1994 more than 45 million persons crossed at the San Ysidro port.

Transborder connections

Historically, San Diego and Tijuana have not been closely connected from a political or commercial standpoint. Traditionally, the official maps of both jurisdictions went blank at the border. Newspapers on either side, generally, have given very little space to what is happening on the "other side." To some extent, the poor political connection between the two cities has resulted from the problem of heavy illegal immigration that is focused on the San Diego–Tijuana border. This problem has led to strained relationships at the local, state, and federal levels. For years Tijuana has been recognized as the major staging area for northbound migrants in search of employment in the United States. In the past, several hundred thousand migrants have been apprehended annually and returned to the area south of the border. Recent efforts by the US government have greatly stemmed the northbound migration.

Two major programs are improving the commercial and political ties across the border. At the national level, the North American Free Trade Agreement (NAFTA) was approved by Canada, Mexico, and the United States. This agreement is dramatically changing the economic interaction between the three countries. The agreement eliminates tariffs and other barriers to the movement of goods, services, and investments among the three countries. In the San Diego–Tijuana region NAFTA appears to be stimulating the manufacturing sector, especially on the south side of the border. Dramatic increases in the movement of products between Mexico and the United States are also being noticed.

At the local level, in April 1993, the mayors of San Diego and Tijuana mounted a joint effort to deal with issues and problems that affect both cities, culminating in an agreement to cooperate in future binational planning and coordination. Current activities between the two cities address such issues as the traffic flow at border crossings, public works issues, environmental protection, coordination of public safety, technology transfer, emergency management, and city planning.

City and regional planning

In the area of city planning, the staffs of the two cities are continuing to meet regularly to exchange information, to cooperate on the development of specific planning projects, to identify and resolve planning issues, and to coordinate staff development. SANDAG includes Tijuana as a liaison member.

San Diego and Tijuana have begun work, also, on a collaborative project to develop plans for the improvement of the areas surrounding both the San Ysidro and Otay Mesa ports of entry. The primary focus of this effort is on the San Ysidro port. The proposal is to prepare a unified transborder specific plan that includes both sides of the border in the vicinity of the crossing. The plan is proposed to address: (a) multimodal transportation terminals and linkages, (b) direct and safe pedestrian crossings, (c) infrastructure needs, (d) land uses and opportunities for revitalization and redevelopment, (e) mitigation of environmental problems, and (f) urban design considerations.

New forms of development

During the period from 1960 to 1990 dramatic changes occurred in the development form of San Diego. The 1950s and early 1960s were the start of the major post-war period of suburban growth. New low-density subdivisions spread out on to agricultural and other undeveloped land. The first shopping centers were built following the construction of new freeways. Then the decline of retailing in downtown and the older commercial centers began.

The older parts of San Diego were built primarily on the flat mesa tops. Building that did occur on hillsides was done in small increments and was sensitive to the natural form of the land. New development pushed beyond the mesas to the foothills. Mass grading techniques, in the absence of regulations, allowed the flattening of hills and the filling of canyons, dramatically changing the form of the city.

The early 1970s were marked by the environmental movement. At the state level, voters approved Proposition 20, the Coastal Protection Act, to ensure public access and that new development is appropriate and compatible with the coastal environment. The state legislature also enacted requirements for several mandated general plan elements, including housing, conservation of resources, energy, scenic highways, and open space preservation.

At the local level, the voters in the city of San Diego approved Proposition D, a 30 ft (9.15 m) height limit in the coastal zone. Also, in recognition of the invasions of the natural environment by mass grading, the city enacted design and grading regulations for slopes, prepared an open space plan, and, subsequently, passed acquisition bond measures. A mid 1970s building boom that completely overwhelmed the region's ability to provide services and facilities led the cities in San Diego County, the county of San Diego, and the regional agency (SANDAG) to revise their general plans to direct and guide growth. The city of San Diego adopted a general plan that divided the city into four tiers or development categories: Urbanized, Planned Urbanizing, Future Urbanizing, and Open Space.

The Urbanized category is characterized as the central, older, developed, urban core of the city. The Planned Urbanizing category is outlying, newly developing communities. The Future Urbanizing category is open or vacant land, primarily zoned agricultural, and was

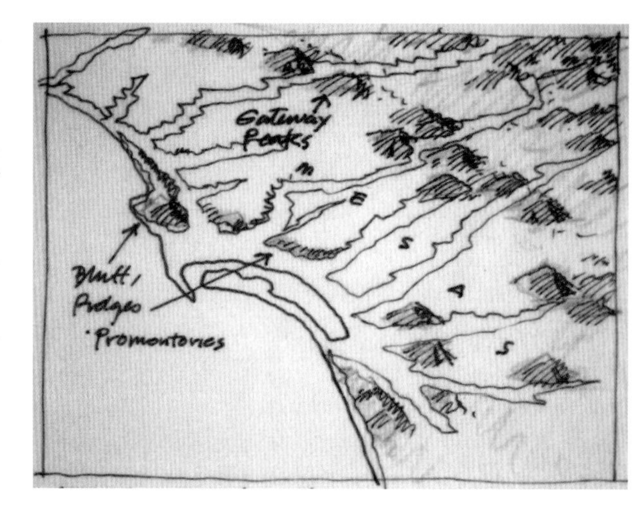

Figure 7.10 The urban forms of the San Diego region

not expected to be needed for development before 1995. This established the growth limit line. The Open Space tier is that land, primarily hillsides and canyons, to be preserved in its natural state as park preserves or regional parks.

The phased development categories are intended to serve as planning tools to guide development. The purpose of the Future Urbanizing category is to set aside an urban reserve of undeveloped land to be released on an as-needed basis for future development. By categorizing this land, it was hoped that planning would occur in a logical, coordinated fashion that would preserve natural resources and prevent undue strain upon the public infrastructure and transit systems.

New infrastructure in the Planned Urbanizing communities has to be provided on a "pay as you grow" basis. In the Urbanized communities the city's general fund would pay for infrastructure.

In the late 1970s and early 1980s a development slow down, coupled with the new plan requirements, channeled most development into the urbanized neighborhoods. This generally consisted of multifamily development replacing single-family housing in areas zoned for higher intensity uses. The new developments were characterless stucco boxes, surrounded by surface parking, built to the maximum density possible. The design and density of these new developments created a demand for wholesale downzonings across the city.

This combined with the continued inability of the city to keep up with public facility needs led to the imposition of development moratoriums. In 1988 four citizen-initiated ballot measures designed to manage or reduce growth in San Diego County, primarily by limitations on housing starts, were defeated. In the wake of community rejection of the measures, the City Council adopted five policy statements that were aimed at finding solutions to the identified growth problems. These were:

- Preservation of sensitive resources.
- Preservation of neighborhood character.
- Reduction of traffic congestion.
- Provision of adequate infrastructure.
- Greater regional planning cooperation (the subject of the one growth-related measure that did pass).

These policies reflected the concerns of the neighborhoods and, also, City Council recognition that simplistic building permit caps and development moratoriums (in the absence of real solutions to the underlying problems) were ineffective at best and, at worst, could be destructive to the community.

To implement the policies, a number of programs were undertaken by the city. There were also a number of complementary programs by other agencies. One of these programs is Land Guidance, which is based upon the linkages between land use, transportation, and air quality. The goal of Land Guidance is to reshape the city's urban form to reduce automobile dependence and to encourage alternative forms of transportation while minimizing impacts on existing community character. In addition, the goals and objectives of Land Guidance complement affordable housing and sensitive land protection programs through accommodation of density in designated areas.

In 1992 the city adopted its Land Guidance policies based in large part on Transit Oriented Development (TOD) Design Guidelines prepared for the city by Peter Calthorpe. Since the TOD Design Guidelines were approved by the City Council in August, 1992, efforts to implement them have focused on the recently completed update of the Zoning Code and the Street Design Manual. In addition, they have been adopted as part of the regional plan prepared by SANDAG, the Air Pollution Control District's policies, and the plans of the Metropolitan Transit Development Board.

San Diego has always approached dealing with planning and development issues at both the broad policy level and the project level simultaneously if the opportunity presented itself. Policy recommendations regarding design, circulation, and neighborhood development have been part of the city's general plan since the 1970s —policies reflective of what we are today calling transit-oriented developments or neotraditional developments or urban villages. For the current efforts, there are two overriding design concepts:

- You should be able to walk around the block comfortably and safely.
- You should be able to send your 10 year old to the store for a loaf of bread and a quart of milk.

The major goal has been to build neighborhoods rather than buildings. This has been the focus of the city's planning policies. Unfortunately, these policies have been implemented more on a case-by-case basis than in a consistent manner.

CONCLUSION

The San Diego region has experienced incremental yet steady changes in the quality of life it has offered over the past 30 years. In the 1960s *per capita* income exceeded national averages while housing costs were below the norm. As discussed above, these factors began to reverse by the late 1970s. The region's overall affordability has decreased dramatically. This trend has been more pronounced in San Diego than in the state or the nation as a whole. In most measurable categories, such as work commute distances, overall traffic congestion, crowding of public recreation areas (e.g. beaches, camp grounds), and other population-driven factors, the quality of living has been reduced. There are some unexpected gains, such as improvements in air quality since the 1970s due to regulation and advancing air pollution technology.

There are clearly gains in the quality of living in terms of the arts, entertainment, education, and recreation as compared with 1960. Quality of life in San Diego has changed from being simple, relatively inexpensive, and somewhat limited in terms of the arts and entertainment to being more complex, diverse, and vibrant. However, the new vibrance has been added at a cost some cannot afford to pay. In a maturing urban region, housing costs in the more desirable residential areas have risen, some of the older urban areas have experienced economic and physical decline, and homelessness has become more common and more visible. In order to reverse some of the negative trends, additional investment in education and in public capital projects appears needed. The ability to do this will depend largely on the success of the local economy.

San Diego is at a point where there is interest in doing something. Perhaps it is a recognition that things are changing or a recognition that things are not as they should or could be or a recognition that we cannot run away from the urban problems facing our cities. And there are efforts being undertaken locally. Initiatives—such as the mayor's Livable Neighborhoods Strategy or the citywide diversity programs—all point to an understanding of the need to work at creating a good city. All these efforts recognize the connection of all the elements—physical, economic, and social.

There is a recognition that crime and public safety are not a police problem; that air quality is not a technology problem; that homelessness is not a housing problem. But we have to guard against being lured into a solution based on technology. San Diego is a high-tech city and we all want to get on the information superhighway. But, we must be careful. Like the auto superhighway, the info superhighway can allow us to disconnect from our surroundings and the people in those surroundings. Once we opt totally for virtual reality over reality, we have lost the battle to maintain our quality of life. Fortunately, humans are not creatures of isolation, so cities and our physical surroundings are being rediscovered.

A question San Diegans have been asking themselves since the city began is "What do we want to be when we grow up?" And as a city with a long history of planning, they have answered that question many times with the finality described in *San Diego Union Tribune* Editor, Neil Morgan's quote: "San Diego has a head start on urban quality because we recognize that a quality city must be continually nurtured."

8 The Santiago region

FRANCISCO SABATINI

The Santiago urban region (SUR) includes the city of Santiago, the capital of the country, with a population of some 4.5 million (34 percent of the national population), and in addition a series of smaller cities and towns with populations under 50,000.[1] Santiago is located in the middle of an extremely long and thin country: more than 5,000 km in length and of an average width of 150 km.

Since its foundation by the Spanish conquerers in 1541, Santiago has been the political, military and economic center of the country. Chile is recognized as one of the most centralist countries in Latin America. Economically, despite the dynamic process of expansion of regional export economies in the last two decades, 47 percent of the gross internal product was produced in the SUR in 1992. This percentage consistently increased between 1985 and 1997, a period in which the Chilean economy grew at an average rate of around 7 percent.

The SUR is located in a valley with dimensions of roughly 80 km by 35 km, surrounded by mountain ranges, of which the Andes cordillera, with peaks of over 6000 m, and the coastal cordillera stand out. Air pollution in the valley, which reaches levels comparable to those experienced in Mexico City, is due to a large extent to this topographical situation, which impedes the circulation of air masses.

With a semiarid mediterranean climate, a long dry season, a winter of high rainfall (average annual precipitation is 366 mm) and an irregular topography, the SUR is exposed to erosion processes and flood risk in years of particularly high rainfall. In addition there is the seismic threat present throughout the entire country. The last severe earthquake affecting Santiago occurred in 1985, with previous earthquakes in 1971 and 1965.

Two characteristics in which Santiago differs from many other urban regions in the world are its ethnic and cultural homogeneity and its compact form, despite the fact that trends of change to both these characteristics have been noted in the last 15 years. There is a growing immigrant population, coming from distant countries, such in Asia, as well as neighboring ones, even though these are still minority populations.

Of greater importance is the change in urban form, a process which includes the "exurbanization" of medium and high-income families in "leisure homes" (*parcelas de agrado*). This is a process which has come to affect all of the region surrounding the city, but for which currently no statistics or land registers exist; the maps in this chapter do not include the information. None the less, Santiago shows a relative delay in the formation of an "urban region" in comparison with the other major cities covered by this book. The explanation lies in the low rates of car

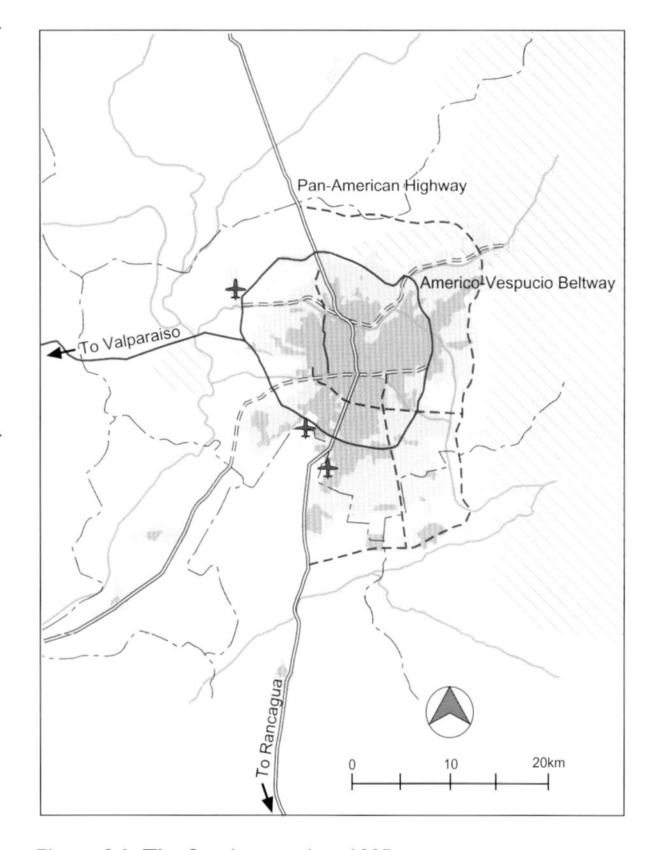

Figure 8.1 The Santiago region, 1995

ownership (see Table 1 on p.19) and, in general, the low level of development of the country. (Tables 8.1–4 include various social and economic statistics for Chile and Santiago.)

Another important change in the urban form of Santiago, which is distinct from other urban regions, especially in Europe, concerns the patterns of social segregation of space. Until the beginning of the 1980s, Santiago was characterized by a high level of geographic segregation of

Figure 8.2 The location of the Santiago region

social groups. Practically all the high-income households were concentrated in the eastern sector of the city, while in the south and west there was a considerable agglomeration of poor families. Since then a new and vigorous private real estate sector is changing this pattern through residential developments for medium and high-income families in traditionally poorer zones of the city, and the construction of modern commercial and service centers. The trend is towards reducing the geographic scale of social segregation, although a strongly regressive distribution of income still persists (Table 8.1), considered one of the worst in Latin America (CEPAL, 1995).

The importance of both the state and the private market stands out in the evolution of the urban form of Santiago since 1960. The former operated particularly

Table 8.1 Chile: social and economic indicators, 1960–90

	National population (000)	**Urban population** (%)	**Labor force** (000)	**Unemployment** (%)	**Exports** (US$ 000)	**Imports** (US$ 000)
1960	7,585	68.2	2,495	8.0	470	555
1970	9,368	75.2	2,932	5.7	1,112	956
1980	11,104	81.2	3,636	10.4	4,705	5,469
1990	13,177	84.5	4,676	5.7	8,310	7,065
1960–90	173.7	–	187.4	–	1,768.1	1,273.0

Variation (1960=100)

Household consumption distribution (%)

	Poorest 20	**Poorest 40**	**Poorest 60**	**Richest 20**
1960	–	–	–	–
1970	7.6	19.4	35.0	44.5
1980	5.2	14.5	28.1	51.0
1990	4.4	12.6	25.3	54.6

Household poverty (%)

	Extremely poor	**Poor**	**Not poor**
1960	–	–	–
1970	8.4	20.1	71.5
1980	11.7	24.3	64.0
1990	14.9	26.3	58.8

Daily calorie consumption of the 40% lower income population

1960	–
1970	2,019
1980	1,751
1990	1,629

Illiteracy (over 14 years old)

1960	16.4
1970	11.0
1980	9.2
1990	5.3

Life expectancy at birth

1960	58
1970	64
1980	70
1990	72

Residential construction (no. of dwellings)

1960	30,697
1970	26,231
1980	46,284
1990	77,261

Infant mortality (per 1000)

1960	119.5
1970	82.2
1980	33.0
1990	17.5

Hospital beds per 1000 inhabitants

1960	4.0
1970	3.8
1980	3.4
1990	3.4

Source Díaz (1991).

Table 8.2 Chile: economic indicators, 1987–96

GDP per capita (US$) **1996**	**Gross domestic investment** (US$ millions) **1996**	**Gross domestic saving** (% of GDP) **1996**	**GDP per capita: average annual growth rate 1987–1996**	**GDP: average annual growth rate 1987–1996**	**Consumer prices** (twelve months' variation) **up to July 1997**
3,440	27.7	25.5	5.4	7.1	5.3

Source *IDB estimates from National Accounts (Central Bank of Chile) on internet (November 7, 1997):* <http://iadb60000/http/INT_lib/basicpub.html>

Table 83 Educational indicators for the Chilean population

	Social coverage of educational services (%)		**Education (approved years of study)**	**Illiteracy rate** (%)
	Basic education[a]	**Intermediate**[a] **education**		
1970	93.3	49.7	4.3	11.0
1982	95.3	65.0	7.8	8.9
1992	98.2	75.1	9.2	5.2

Source *Mizala and Romaguera (1995a).*
Note [a] Basic education includes eight years of study; intermediate education, the following four years.

Table 8.4 Santiago: employed population, by educational level, 1966–88 (%)

	1966	**1970**	**1980**	**1988**
No education	4.7	3.0	1.5	1.1
1–4 years	20.2	15.3	9.5	7.5
5–8 years	37.1	36.6	32.1	25.1
9–12 years	32.2	36.1	44.3	50.8
1–4 years university	1.9	3.9	5.6	5.5
5+ years university	3.7	5.0	7.0	9.7
No data	0.2	0.1	0.0	0.3
Total	100.0	100.0	100.0	100.0

Source *Mizala and Romaguera (1995b).*

through investment in urban infrastructure works which formed part of the master plan of 1960, called the Santiago Intercommunal Regulatory Plan (SIRP). The latter operated especially since the radical liberalization of land markets and the weakening of urban planning which occurred around 1980. Paradoxically, the real estate sector emerging from the liberalization has contributed to the achievement, after 30 years' delay, of some of the principal objectives of the master plan, particularly that related to the decentralization of the urban structure into subcenters. These have emerged spontaneously in almost the same locations anticipated in the SIRP of 1960.

Neither the city of Santiago nor the SUR has sole authority. The principal urban authority is the municipal government, which designs and administers "regulatory plans," which combine zoning and building regulations. The city of Santiago is comprised of 34 municipal authorities. Until the 1970s the city was divided into 17 *comunas* and the (national) Ministry of Housing and Urban Development exercised more or less complete control of the peripheral growth of the city through a regulation on "urban limits." With the liberalization policies (1979), which included the elimination of the "urban limits," and a new definition of the municipal districts (1981), Santiago's 17 *comunas* (municipalities) were further subdivided, into a total of 34, and the city enjoyed considerable freedom to expand. In addition to the difficulties of coordination, which this large number of municipal authorities presents, there is also the unofficial dispute regarding the future of Santiago between the Ministry of Housing and Urban Development, formally responsible for urban planning, and the Ministry of Public Works, whose decisions have had a great impact on the development of the SUR.

CHANGING ECONOMIC PATTERNS

From the economic point of view, two main processes explain the evolution of the SUR from 1960 to 1990: the industrialization process based on import substitution which began in the 1940s, and the neoliberal modernization initiated with the 1973 *coup d'état* that overthrew the socialist government of Salvador Allende (1970–73) and imposed a military regime.

From 1960 to 1990, when the military regime ended, the Chilean economy changed from one based primarily on import substitution and single commodity export to a stable, competitive, and open economy with a growing and diversified export sector.

The reliance on foreign technologies designed for economies of scale beyond the small Chilean domestic market in the import substitution oriented process of industrialization helps explain the spatial concentration of economic activity in Santiago during the twentieth century. Urban concentration made it possible to meet requirements for production processes related to economies of scale, capital intensity, and technological indivisibility. Other causes of urban concentration are cultural, sociopolitical, and historical. Outstanding among these is the considerable concentration in Santiago of military forces and staff, during both the colonial period and the new republic. This was in order to deal with three centuries of fierce resistance from the Mapuche indians (mid sixteenth century to mid nineteenth). Chile was a country occupied militarily from Santiago, a trait which to a certain extent is still expressed in strong political centralism.

The liberalization of the Chilean economy since the mid 1970s contributed to the establishment of new economic activities throughout the country, mostly linked to the export sector and, specifically, to the exploitation of natural resources. Exports currently account for nearly 40 per cent of gross domestic product (GDP). When liberal economic reforms were implemented in the 1970s, severe stagnation and social problems hit Santiago as a consequence of the previous concentration of industrial development in the capital.

Yet the manufacturing sector has remained concentrated in the SUR. Moreover, the steady growth of the economy since 1985 has resulted in a return to the geographic concentration of economic activities in the SUR, whose share of GDP increased from 42 percent to almost 47 percent between 1985 and 1992.[2]

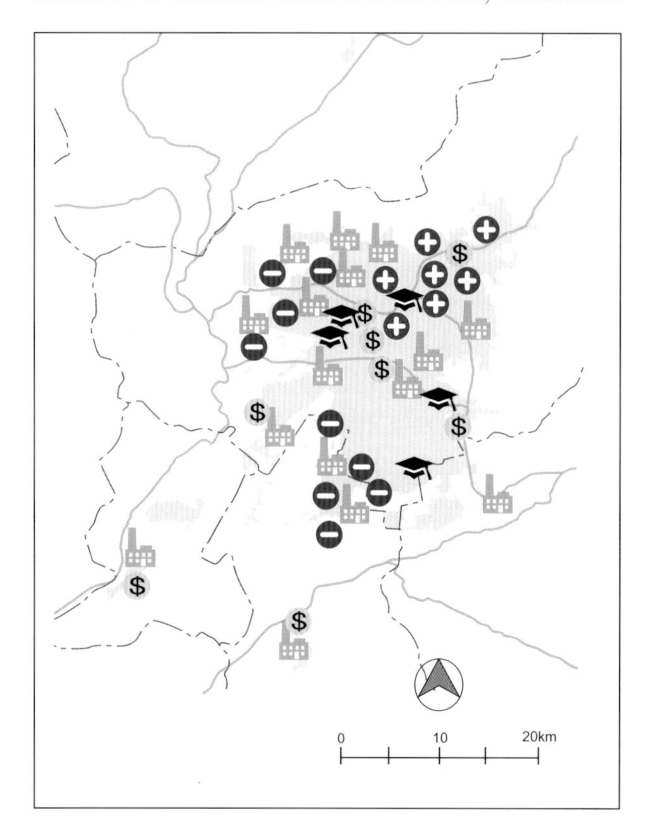

Figure 8.3 Economic patterns in the Santiago region

The increasing importance of the service sector is a major structural change observed since 1985. The extension of market mechanisms thereafter favored the growth of a non-financial services sector whose output consists of productive services tightly connected with the manufacturing sector. Services exports increased from 8.9 per cent to almost 20 per cent of total exports (Díaz, 1995). The most dynamic sectors of the economy, with the exception of the primary activities, centralize their location and decision-making processes in Santiago, which seems to be emerging as an international financial and investments metropolitan center (De Mattos *et al.*, 1995).[3]

CHANGING SOCIAL PATTERNS[4]

The principal change in the social structure of Santiago between 1960 and 1990 was triggered by the policy of liberalization of land and property markets applied by the military government after 1979. In a favorable economic and urban environment, the liberalization stimulated the creation of a dynamic sector of real estate promoters. Through projects of considerable size, and in their search for land rents, these private agents are contributing to the reduction of the marked geographic scale of social segregation which came to be characteristic of Santiago. Residential segregation seems to be getting stronger at a low geographical scale—mainly, through the building of gated communities—at the same time it is weakening at a higher geographical scale.

This effect arises through two principal routes: the location of medium and high-income residential projects in areas where the most probable future was their occupation by neighboring low-income families—as much in the urban periphery as in areas undergoing urban renewal—and the construction of shopping centers on the medium and low-income urban periphery. The average physical distance of poor families from urban centers of activity and from higher-income neighborhoods is decreasing. The benefits can be considered as of two types: functional, especially in terms of reducing the length of daily trips; and social, particularly through strengthening a sense of social integration which could help counter behavior often described as "social pathologies," such as juvenile vagrancy, family disintegration, drug addiction, and adolescent pregnancy.

The emergence of high-income residential developments outside traditional areas is making apparent a basic change in Chilean society: the creation of a new high-income stratum made up of professionals and new entrepreneurs not linked with traditional elite groups. This morphological change has also had an effect on the search for contact with nature in the "exurbs."

The policies of liberalization of urban markets were accompanied by an effort to socially restructure the city and a novel social housing policy. These three lines of public action and their effect on the city can be summarized as follows:

1. The liberalization of real estate markets, particularly through the implementation of a new regulatory framework introduced in 1979, was based upon the curious idea that urban land is not a scarce resource. This policy assumed state regulations were the main source of scarcity of urban land and associated problems. Regulations were therefore relaxed or banned. Rules on "urban limits" were abolished, resulting in the designation of a huge area for urbanization. In 1982 the government defined this area as some 60,000 ha, while the urbanized area of Santiago was of approximately 40,000 ha.

In 1994 the democratic government amended this policy, redesignating 40,000 ha from the areas open to urbanization to the tracts of land defined in 1979 as not suitable for development, citing agricultural soil fertility, slope gradient or ecological value as reasons. This was done as an indirect way of reinstating the "urban limits" regulation and policy. As Table 8.5 shows, the city has now occupied virtually all the area legally subject to urbanization (close to 60,000 ha). Yet the market has surpassed this new *de facto* urban limit: the modern industrial area in the northern part of the city (which is discussed later) has grown well beyond it. The same has occurred with the (urban) residential leisure homes in rural areas surrounding Santiago within an 80 km radius of the city center. These trends show that private urban dynamics prevail over state regulations. Well known international firms have built plants or offices in this industrial area in the northern part of the city, despite the fact that they are violating zoning regulations. It is a common assumption that the regulations will eventually be adjusted to accommodate the new developments.

2. The series of actions aimed at reestablishing urban segregation, which had been challenged by the urban social movements of the Allendes' socialist period (1970–73), included a vast program of eradication of shanty towns from areas of "real estate interest," as officially declared (1979–85 period). They also included the restructuring of the size and administrative limits of the municipalities to constitute socially homogeneous areas, a criterion at odds with what most urban planners seek in other countries. Social homogeneity was defended as a way to avoid the concentration of local government's scarce resources in the hands of those residents with more lobbying influence, usually the wealthiest.

3. The new social housing policy (1981), still in effect, shifted state subsidies from builders to families. The state distributes vouchers to the applicants according to criteria that include family savings, housing necessity, and family size. The amount of the subsidy is inversely proportional to the price of the dwelling that the beneficiary buys in the market. Direct construction of social housing by public agencies, a tradition in Chile that in some periods accounted for approximately 60 per cent of the dwellings built in the country, almost disappeared with this new policy.

The effect of this policy in urban terms is, on one level, the same as previous social housing policies: to continue locating poor families where other poor households live,

Table 8.5 Santiago: urbanized area and population, 1960–96

	Urbanized area* (ha)	**Urbanized area** (annual growth %)	**Population** (000)	**Population** (annual growth %)
1960	21,383.11		2,133.2	
1970	31,571.34	3.97	2,871.1	3.02
1982	41,462.71	2.30	3,937.3	2.67
1992	49,240.00	1.73	4,756.7	1.91
1996	57,180.00	3.81	5,068.5	1.60

Sources INE-Chile (population data), and GIS Laboratory, Instituto de Estudios Urbanos, Pontificia Universidad Católica de Chile (geographic data).

contributing to the spatial concentration of poverty. But there is something new: by offering multifamily solutions and setting very low standards—the "basic" housing unit is approx. 40 m^2—there is no possibility of house extension. As a result this policy produces a "ghetto effect": the progress of each family becomes tied to their chances of leaving such areas, rather than working towards their improvement. The social benefits and functions which can be derived from the reduction of the scale of social segregation are difficult to achieve for the poor families who receive housing under this policy.

CHANGING SPATIAL PATTERNS

Up to recent years Santiago was a contiguous city with a geographic density that did not change much. Nowadays its spatial structure is undergoing substantial modification, in both the city itself and its surrounding region (Table 8.5).

The changes in the internal structure of the city of Santiago have occurred particularly since 1985 with the emergence of subcenters for services and industry, and with new residential developments which are reducing the geographic scale of social segregation, as mentioned.

Figure 8.3 shows the beginning of the vigorous emergence in 1990 of the modern industrial area in the northern sector of the city, both along the length of the Pan-American highway towards the north and along the length of the Américo Vespucio beltway, joining the main high-income area in the northeast with the international airport towards the west. After 1990 various shopping centers arose, especially where this orbital road crosses radial access routes to the city, which increasingly are complemented by office development and public services. Downtown Santiago has also been revitalized and old commercial sectors have been modernized, including the recent opening of a mall in the city center. Similarly, the rundown areas around the center are experiencing a significant process of residential urban renewal under the influence of the dynamic real estate sector and public incentives at both the municipal and national levels.[5]

In addition to contiguous peripheral growth, the SUR exhibits new important trends of scattered suburbanization, satellite-type growth, and the formation of industrial corridors. These phenomena have increased since 1990 owing to the rise of car ownership and improvements in roads and communications technology, and the development of interurban public transportation services (Table 8.5).

Scattered suburbanization consists of the subdivision of agricultural land into leisure homes for upper and high middle-income families. It is an "informal" type of urban development. It makes use of a regulation which defines the minimum size of an agricultural property as 5,000 m^2 (1.235 acres). Private clubs, schools, and sports facilities are proliferating with this type of suburbanization pattern, spread throughout the SUR. Linked with the use of private cars, the leisure homes are tantamount to an "informal city" for the wealthy. Increasing pressure is being exerted upon public agencies for the provision of urban facilities and services.

Satellite-type growth takes place in existing towns and small cities, preferably those within 80 km of downtown Santiago. This is an old trend generated by the growth of exports in agricultural and agro-industrial activities of the central administrative regions of Chile since the mid 1970s, a process which became more marked after 1985. These agro-industrial activities, located along the length of Santiago's access roads, especially towards the south, are contributing to the formation of urban corridors.[6]

INFRASTRUCTURE DEVELOPMENT

Investment in the infrastructure has had a major effect on the development of the urban form of Santiago since 1960,[7] basically in two forms: (1) the reduced amount of such investment has significantly precluded the international trend of cities to "explode" into surrounding areas, thus maintaining Santiago´s "inkstain" type outline; and (2) investment in infrastructure works undertaken since 1960, especially highways, constitutes one of the determining factors in the profound changes in the internal structure of the city which took place in the 1990s. These changes include the decentralization of activities, a reduction in the scale of social segregation of space and the initiation of the "explosion" of the city into the surrounding region. Liberalization of the land and housing markets, economic growth, and increased congestion have driven these changes.

Roads

The construction of urban roads (expressways, limited access roads, and major roads), the responsibility of the Ministry of Public Works (MOP), has had a great influence on the evolution of urban form in Santiago. Since the introduction of automotive transport after the Second World War, the construction of radial roads has made possible the peripheral and contiguous low-density growth which came to be a dominant characteristic in the development of the city.

Particularly in the eastern sector, where higher-income suburbanization was concentrated, these investments were linked with real estate speculation and business. Traffic congestion was another determining factor in deciding where to implement the investments. As the congestion

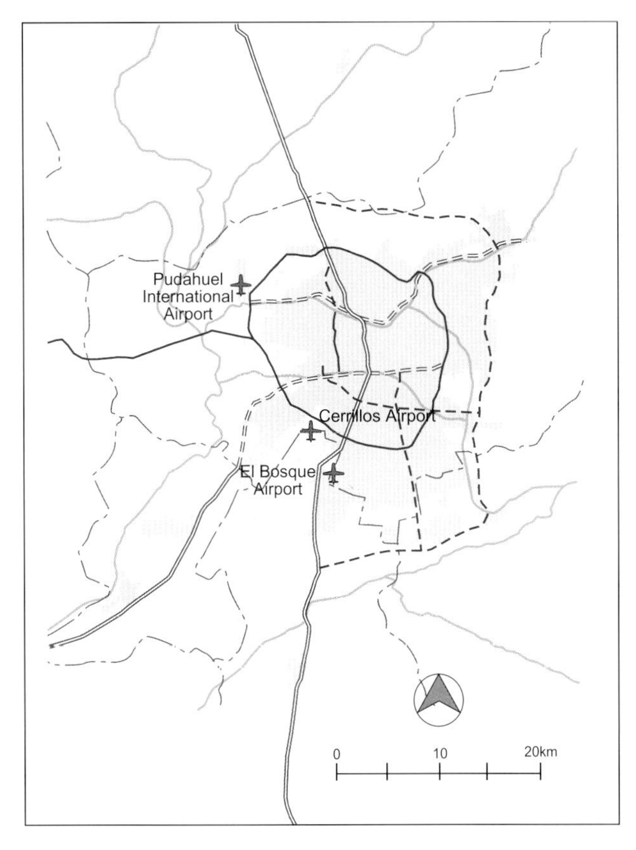

Figure 8.4 Main roads and airports in the Santiago region, 1995

was greater in areas where car ownership was concentrated, investment tended to focus on the eastern sector of Santiago. One estimate indicates that 42 percent of total investment in urban road works of "communal importance"—that is, excluding access roads to the city and the Américo Vespucio beltway—undertaken between 1965 and 1975 was made in the high-income *comuna* of Las Condes, which then represented approximately 8 percent of the city's population (Geisse and Sabatini, 1977).

Without doubt, the principal road project of this period was the beltway Américo Vespucio, 70 km in length and constructed over 36 years, beginning in 1960. The SIRP of 1960, unquestionably the most important urban plan of the period, proposed this beltway as a major construction work which was designed to improve accessibility to the interior of the city and also to promote the generation of subcenters of activity in order to break up the centralization of Santiago. It also naively attempted, in accordance with the theories of the period, to contain urban growth as if the Américo Vespucio were a "green belt," in which it certainly failed. Far from slowing growth towards the periphery, the new infrastructure made possible and encouraged such growth, despite the availability of important tracts of land inside the projected beltway.

Recently completed as a full circuit in 1996, this road has been key to the more recent emergence of commercial, industrial, and service subcenters located at the intersections with the principal radial access roads to Santiago. These subcenters have contributed to a reduction in the length and quantity of commutes; and they also encourage an attitude of social integration, especially among the poorest.

Due to the country's increased economic activity, roads in the region of Santiago have been steadily improved, especially access routes to the city, including those connecting with the principal ports of the country. These works have encouraged the phenomenon of leisure homes previously commented upon, as well as the linear development of industrial activities. The improvement of access to the city with works on some regional roads, favoring rapid access to the center and to the east, and the construction of a second beltway can be found in the principal future plans. (The section of the latter project already confirmed is marked on Figure 8.4 with dashed lines.)

In the 1990s the MOP has adopted a policy of "private concessions" consisting of putting the construction of roads, tunnels and ports out to tender with private companies, granting them subsequent administration of tolls for a determined period. A program of urban concessions has been initiated especially for the construction of sections of the new beltway in high-income areas, where the possibility of private business exists.

The metropolitan region—60 percent of which is covered by the area of this study—has 100,000 km of national and regional principal and secondary roads, although 19.7 percent of them are unpaved. Approximately two-thirds of the national budget of MOP for road works is designated for road conservation, in spite of a 70 percent increase of that budget in the last five years.[8] There is a noteworthy scarcity of roads in the country, a problem which has become more acute with economic growth. Hence the importance of the policies of private concessions.

Rail

The traditional railway system in Chile suffered important losses and physical and economic deterioration in 1980–2000. Lines have ceased to operate, such as the passenger service between Santiago and two of the country's major ports, Valparaíso and San Antonio. The deterioration of the track has caused a significant drop in average traveling speeds, among other problems. The rolling stock is old and badly maintained.

The service of cargo transport previously managed by the powerful and monopolistic State Railway Company

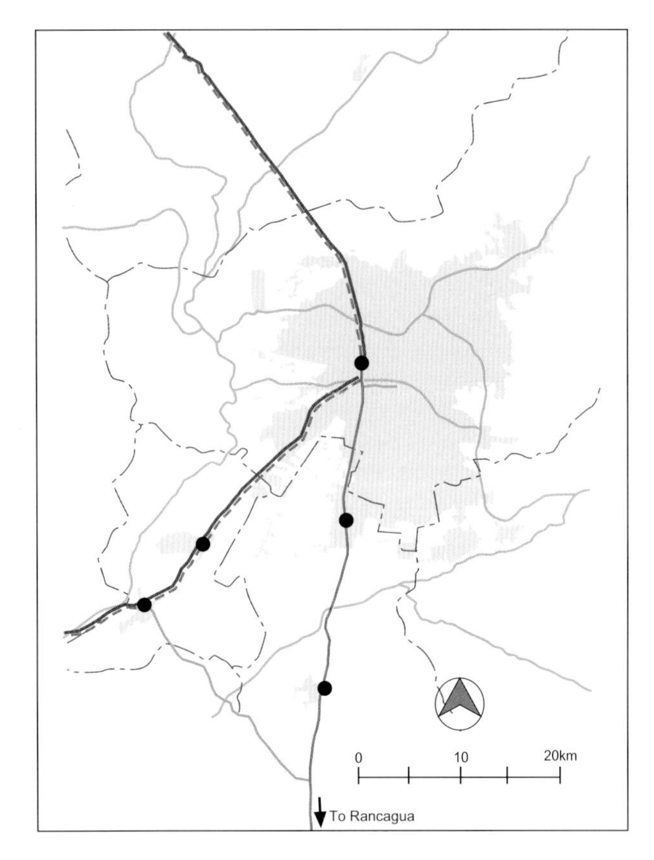

Figure 8.5 Railways in the Santiago region, 1995

was privatized four years ago, and the complete privatization of the company (including passenger services) is currently being prepared. The company sustains significant annual losses.

The only significant exception to this situation is the Santiago–Rancagua Metro Train,[9] with lines approximately 90 km in length. In operation since 1990, the Metro Train has grown considerably, and competes with the intercity buses. The railway lines on this stretch are the best maintained in the country. In increasing numbers, the residents of "leisure homes" in the south of the urban region are combining the use of the Metro Train and car for their daily commute to the city. This service has allowed an increase in the number of people living in Rancagua and working in Santiago, and vice versa, although this is still a relatively small number of people. In 1994 the Metro Train carried 1.8 million passengers, compared with the 167.3 million carried by the Metro network. The latter has 27.3 km of line. However, a recent study carried out by the Metro company concluded that the demand exists for a Metro Train service between Santiago and Rancagua which cannot be met owing to the lack of train availability and the low level of service offered.[10]

A project exists for the construction of two other Metro Train lines towards the north and the west of the city, respectively, as is indicated in Figure 8.5. They will operate in conjunction with the Metro, as the service to Rancagua currently does. There is coincidence between the conventional railway lines and the improved system. Moreover, one of the networks planned for the Metro coincides with conventional lines and, in part, with the Metro Train planned for access to west Santiago. The urban impact of the Metro Train services is similar to that of roads: it facilitates urban growth in zones relatively distant from Santiago; however, it promotes a discontinuous form of development around the stations, and not a continuous one, as the roads do.

The first section of the Santiago Metro (subway) began service in 1975. Between 1987 and 1996, when the network consisted of two lines with a total line length of 27.3 km, the number of passengers increased 31.6 percent. In 1991 the total number of trips made in Santiago on a workday—excluding those to and from areas outside the city—was 8.37 million, while those made on the subway were some 0.54 million; that is, 6.4 percent. Since April 1997 the Metro of Santiago has operated with a third line, increasing the total route length to 37.6 km. A series of projects for the extension of existing lines and the construction of new lines are planned.

Beyond contributing to the relative decongestion of various intensely used zones in the city, the Santiago Metro has reinforced the two principal alternative subcenters to central Santiago, which were also the first to emerge in the east and south of the city. The Metro has contributed to extending the market areas of these sub-sectors, and to reinforcing their "centrality."

Airports

The SUR relies on only three public airports with paved runways; two of these, Cerrillos and El Bosque, are military facilities. The third is the international airport of Pudahuel, opened in 1967 with a runway 3,200 m in length. Prior to this the international airport was Cerrillos (with a 2,242 m runway).

The Pudahuel airport has had a new passenger terminal since 1994 and its landing systems have been further improved since then. Since the construction of Pudahuel there have been no major investments in terms of runways.

Many years after its construction, the location of the present international airport has turned out to have driven one of the greatest urban changes in the last few decades. One of the last sections of the Américo Vespucio beltway to be completed was La Pirámide in 1990. This incline joins the high-income eastern sector of Santiago with the airport and with various other major access routes to the city, including the highway to Valparaíso, the country's principal seaport, 100 km west of Santiago. Since then the industrial zone to the north of the city (mentioned above) has been developed at such an accelerated rate that it is perhaps the most modern in the country, and likewise has been developed into residential suburbs with leisure homes and, more recently, a business center with offices and services, including financial services. This road development has enabled the creation of the urban trilogy which one sees in various major cities of the world: international airport, high-tech industrial park and residential suburbs for highly qualified managers and professionals who work in these industries. The importance of environmental aspects, quality of life, and desire to avoid traffic congestion and pollution for these groups has been one of the driving factors in this change.

Telecommunications

Chile was one of the first countries to adopt the multicarrier system (1994) after the privatization of the telecommunications sector was completed in the 1980s. The two traditional state monopolies—CTC for local service and ENTEL for national and international satellite communication—were privatized, and presently there are five carrier companies (CTC-Mundo, Entel, Chilesat, Bellsouth Chile, and a holding company formed by the first three), as well as a relatively small competitor company to CTC for the local telephone market (Manquehue Telephones). Cable television is undergoing rapid expansion, and is dominated by two companies (VTR and Metropolis Intercom).

Trends towards market penetration by foreign capital, economic concentration, and integration of sound, data, and image transmission services can be seen in the sector.

In tandem with these changes the quality and coverage of services have increased considerably and costs have dropped. These improvements in telecommunications are important for a city such as Santiago, which should lead the challenge of the globalization of the Chilean economy but which suffers from serious environmental problems and rapidly increasing traffic congestion.

However, the impact of telecommunications infrastructure development on the urban form is not significant. Investments tend to follow localized demand, both for the local telephone market (of greater social coverage) and for cable television and fiber-optic lines (more concentrated in productive and tertiary areas and in high-income suburbs). The effect, if any, is to reinforce the current structure of land use.

Conclusion

Investments in infrastructure, particularly road works, have been influential in the evolution of the urban form of Santiago. In the context of the globalization of the Chilean economy, increasing rates of car ownership, sustained economic growth, liberalization and modernization of the urban real estate sector, and increasing congestion, the current and new road works, and, to a lesser extent, the Metro are driving radical changes in the urban form of the region.

Both the city's access and internal roads, whether existing, improved or new, have significantly contributed to modifying accessibility and mobility within the city limits and the SUR. This has stimulated changes in the urban form: the decentralization of activities towards subcenters, the "exurbanization" of high and medium-income groups, and the development of virtual urban corridors which include smaller old cities, industrial development, and new residential developments.

REGIONAL LAND USE PLANS

The 1960–90 period can be categorized into two phases concerning urban planning: a "planning phase" (1960–70) and an "anti-planning phase" (1973–90), with the three-year Allende period dividing them.

The first phase evolved around the ideas and proposals contained in the 1960 master plan for the capital city, the SIRP. With the exception of the Metropolitan Transportation Plan (1967), which included a subway system, the most important urban projects carried through since then in the SUR were those included in the SIRP: (1) the Américo Vespucio beltway; (2) a new international airport (Aeropuerto Pudahuel); (3) the improvement or opening up of major radial roads; (4) several subcenters on the periphery of the city, most of them located at the intersection of the orbital highway with radial roads; and (5) several "industrial areas."

The construction of the Santiago subway was initiated in 1969. Three of the five lines of the original project have been built, albeit with some modifications; the third in 1997. Forthcoming projects include the extension of Metro lines in the form of Metro Trains to the region surrounding the city.

It must be noted that all of the important urban projects of the period 1960–90 were designed and initiated in this first "planning phase" (1960–70). The first three on the list, as well as the subway, correspond to public works that were built or initiated in this period. The industrial areas as well as the subcenters were expected to emerge from urban development, given the favorable context represented by the other urban projects in conjunction with certain regulations or actions, such as the reserve of land in the case of industries.

A second phase started with the military regime at the end of 1973. During the period 1973–90 no new significant urban project was designed or built by the government; only the completion of existing projects was undertaken. Other crucial developments resulted from the spontaneous evolution of market forces, yet were clearly favored by the public urban projects of the SIRP. This is the case with the new subcenters on the periphery of Santiago, which include shopping centers, offices, and industries.

Perhaps the most important urban project carried out by the Pinochet government was the completion in 1990 of a part of the Américo Vespucio route, discussed earlier, in the northeast of the city, which crossed a hilly area. This investment was undertaken after an economic assessment proved its social profitability. Although no urban criteria were used in the study, an important spatial transformation was initiated, including the emergence of the industrial development in the north of Santiago.

Planning authority has rested mainly with a large number of local municipalities (17 before the 1981 administrative reform, 34 since then). The city lacks a single urban authority. As early as 1881 local municipal governments formulated and applied their own zoning ordinances (*planos reguladores*) and authorized land use changes, including peripheral land conversion and building projects. Since its creation in 1965 the Ministry of Housing and Urban Development has been formally responsible for the planning of the city as a whole. Yet the action undertaken by this Ministry in relation to urban Santiago has been a weak second priority as compared with the goal of reducing housing shortages. Housing programs have captured almost all the energies of the Ministry.

The SIRP was designed and implemented by the Ministry of Public Works, and since 1990 this Ministry has been implementing a well designed public works plan for the SUR, consisting mainly of road infrastructure. The plan has had and will have an influence on the urban evolution of the SUR which easily surpasses that of the urban policies of the Ministry of Housing and Urban Development.

These two agencies are not only uncoordinated as regards their policies for the SUR but frequently even contradict one another. The Ministry of Housing and Urban Development, created in 1965, formulated the *Plan Regulador Metropolitano* (PRM-1994), which replaces the SIRP-1960 as the master plan for the SUR. The PRM-94 seeks to limit urban expansion and raise the average population density in the city by over 50 percent, with the aim of reducing the average costs of urbanization and journey distance. The latter would also reduce congestion and air pollution. These plans have been subject to much criticism. One, relevant to our interest in the urban form, is that daily commuting distances are possibly more dependent upon the city's internal structure than upon its spatial coverage.

It can be seen that the authorities lack clear proposals and a development policy for the main urban region of the country, upon which rests, to a significant degree, the competitiveness of the economy.

The SIRP-1960 should be considered as a partially successful exercise in urban planning, especially as regards the influence that the Américo Vespucio beltway has exerted over the evolution of Santiago's urban form to the present day. More recently the Ministry of Public Works has designed, based on a transportation and land use model, a new orbital road to Santiago with an approximate extension of 130 km (compared with the 70 km of the Américo Vespucio beltway). The construction of part of the beltway is being negotiated with private investors under a form of franchise.

The beltway project appears to be clearly in conflict with the PRM-94. It forms part of the MOP's ambitious long-term infrastructure plan, designed to improve internal accessibility in the central macro-region of Chile, which includes the metropolitan region as well as Regions V and VI (with capitals at Santiago, Valparaíso and Rancagua, respectively). It is most likely that the plan of MOP will be put into action, stimulating low-density growth closer to the discontinuous morphological pattern of other urban regions of the world. In fact, the improvements already made to regional and national roads within the area of study are stimulating an expansion of "leisure homes."

CONCLUSION

We are witnessing the historic rupture of the morphological pattern of the city of Santiago. From a monocentric city, spatially continuous and socially segregated on a large geographic scale, we are moving to a polycentric city which is beginning to "explode" into the surrounding region in a discontinuous form and to generate corridors of development, and which exhibits a trend of reducing the geographic scale of social segregation.

These trends of change are, however, varied. They are notable in relation to the decentralization of the city's internal structure and the break-up in the pattern of social spatial segregation; but they are vaguer and weaker in relation to changing from the model of a contiguous city, an aspect in which the SUR is lagging behind the emerging patterns in the majority of other urban regions examined in this book.

These changes in the urban form of Santiago have been, and are being, driven since the early 1980s by a combination of direct factors, contextual factors, and long-term causes. Outstanding among the direct factors are the policies of liberalization in land and property markets which have favored the emergence of a vigorous property sector capable of radically modifying land use in the city. Among the contextual factors are economic growth, increases in household income and car ownership, and worsening traffic congestion problems. Lastly, a long-term cause of these changes lies in the investments in infrastructure works, especially those envisaged in the master plan of 1960.

The design and implementation of these types of works, particularly urban roads, is seen to have more influence on the evolution of the urban form than actual urban planning. At a time of growing conviction about the difficulty of planning the development of these urban regions, the case of Santiago offers some clues in considering this subject. At least two points appear relevant in this sense: the long-range influence that decisions made more than 30 years ago concerning the infrastructure have had on urban development; and the fact that this influence, far from having diminished with policies of liberalization and privatization, actually reached its peak under the new conditions. As such, the evolution of Santiago suggests that planning and the market are not alternative or exclusive policies, but that both can be important in the introduction of urban public management schemes which are more sophisticated, more eclectic, and have greater chances of success.

ACKNOWLEDGEMENTS

The author is grateful to those who contributed to this study: to Luis Delcorto and Franz Kroeger, who collected and prepared graphical information; to Sandra Lerda, for her help with economic analysis and statistics; and to Laura Mullahy, who translated the text from Spanish to English and in the process provided editorial comments, helping to improve the chapter.

NOTES

1 For the purposes of this study, Santiago refers solely to the city of Santiago and SUR refers to the whole urban region, including the city.

2 Information from the Central Bank of Chile, elaborated by the Ministry of Planning and Coordination. In reality, these figures refer to the metropolitan region of Santiago, one of the 13 administrative regions into which Chile is divided, and which includes the SUR. However, the difference between the SUR and the metropolitan region of Santiago is not significant economically, and even less so when one is simply interested in evaluating a trend.

3 In its annual ranking of 1997 *Fortune* magazine selected Santiago as the Latin American city which offers the best conditions to do business.

4 A more in-depth discussion of the contents of this section is presented in Sabatini (1998, 1999).

5 The residential developments inside the city, both in the new suburbs for the poor and in renovation of rundown areas, are not indicated on the maps, and neither are subcenters which have grown up since 1990.

6 Because they consist of industrial plants of small size or concentration, these emerging corridors do not appear on Figure 8.3.

7 The urban form or structure includes two dimensions: the silhouette or border and the internal structure of the city. The outline can differentiate a contiguous city (or inkstain type) from a city which breaks into the surrounding region. The internal structure defines cities according to the level of decentralization of its activities, the scale and degree of social or functional segregation, and density of land occupancy.

8 Minutes of Ministry of Public Works of Chile.

9 The city of Rancagua, situated to the south of Santiago, is the capital of the VI Region of Chile and in 1992 had a population of 179,638.

10 Minutes of Metro de Santiago.

REFERENCES

Comisión Económica para la América Latina y el Caribe (1995) *Informe de desarrollo socioeconómico 1995*, Santiago: CEPAL.

De Mattos, Carlos, Sabatini, Francisco, and Soler, Fernando (1995) "Globalization and Urban Form: the Case of Santiago, Chile," paper presented at the thirty-sixth annual conference of the Association of Collegiate Schools of Planning, Phoenix AZ, 1995; published in Spanish as *Globalización, territorio y ciudad: el caso de Chile*, Documentos serie Azul 7, Instituto de Estudios Urbanos, Pontificia Universidad Católica de Chile, 1996.

Díaz, Alvaro (1991) "El capitalismo chileno en los 90: crecimiento económico y desigualdad social," PAS Workshop, Series of Analysis Documents.

Díaz, Alvaro (1995) *La industria chilena entre 1970–1994: de la sustitución de importaciones a la segunda fase exportadora*, Santiago: CEPAL/CIID, LC/R 1535.

Geisse, Guillermo, and Sabatini, Francisco (1977) "Propuesta de investigación sobre problemas y políticas de tierra urbana en Santiago," Internal document, Santiago: Instituto de Estudios Urbanos, Pontificia Universidad Católica de Chile.

Mizala, Alejandra, and Romaguera, Pilar (1995a) "Capacitación y características educacionales de la fuerza de trabajo: el caso chileno," second version of paper presented at the seminar on "Flexibilidad laboral y mercado del trabajo," Santiago: CIEPLAN, 6 January.

Mizala, Alejandra, and Romaguera, Pilar (1995b) "Flexibilidad laboral, sector informal y fuerza de trabajo secundaria," draft of paper presented at the seminar on "Flexibilidad laboral y mercado del trabajo," Santiago: CIEPLAN, 6 January.

Sabatini, Francisco (1998) *Liberalización de los mercados de suelo y segregación social en las ciudades latinoamericanas: el caso de Santiago, Chile.* Documentos del Instituto del Estudios Urbanos, Serie Azul 14, Pontificia Universidad Católica de Chile. Paper presented at the XX International Congress of the Latin American Studies Association, LASA, Guadalajara, México, April 1997.

Sabatini, Francisco (1999) *Tendencias de la segregación residencial urbana en Latinoamérica: Reflexiones a partir del caso de Santiago de Chile.* Documentos del Instituto de Estudios Urbanos, Serie Azul 29, Pontificia Universidad Católica de Chile. Paper presented at the seminar "Latin America: Democracy, Markets and Equity at the Threshold of a New Millenium," Uppsala University, Sweden, September 1–3, 1999.

9 The São Paulo region

GILDA COLLET BRUNA

Urban growth and its particular transformations in the final decades of the last century are a worldwide phenomenon. Metropolitan São Paulo with 16.4 million inhabitants is part of it, and it is now facing the challenge of becoming a global city region. São Paulo metropolis has been widening its geographic area of influence and strengthening its polarization through the development of more specialized functions. Over time a new profile has been designed through the development of production-oriented activities like sophisticated information and financial services. As the state's main urban agglomeration, the metropolis comprises 39 municipalities, stretching over 8,051 km^2 (3,108 square miles). In 1991 its total built-up area was 1,771 km^2 (684.0 square miles). This metropolitan region is the main business center of South America. It concentrates a major share of domestic and international offices and houses the headquarters of the 20 largest banks operating in Brazil, as well as 65 percent of the commerce and service buildings of the whole state of São Paulo.[1]

Figure 9.1 The São Paulo region, 1995

This steady growth of the metropolitan region achieved higher rates than the hinterland of the state until 1980, when the transformations started to be felt, with a gradual decrease in the population growth rate, which in 1991 was 1.9 percent, while the hinterland grew at 2.3 percent. A sample of the 1996 Brazilian census confirmed a national trend towards a decreasing growth rate, from 2 percent in 1991 to 1.38 percent in 1996, indicating that probably it will be zero in 2030. Besides, the population as a whole is aging, with some 6 percent of the total inhabitants being 65 years old and more, while, during the 1980s there were only 3 percent. The slowing down of the population growth rate is higher in the metropolitan regions of São Paulo and Rio de Janeiro. São Paulo's demographic expansion was only 0.40 percent in 1992 97, compared with 1.16 percent in the period 1989–91.[2]

From 1980 to 1990 São Paulo's migration rate was 0.10 while the Santiago and Madrid rates were respectively 0.10 and 0.13. The growth rate as a whole was practically the same in many city regions if one compares the figures in Table 1 on p.19. This rate was at a minimum in the decade 1980–90, when Tokyo and Madrid had 0.01 and Taipei, São Paulo and Santiago 0.02, with San Diego, Bangkok and Ankara 0.03. As part of these transformations, there was almost no internal migration[3] toward the São Paulo metropolitan region during this period, and some 274,000 inhabitants left. This demographic transformation meant also changes in activities, with the loss of traditional manufacturing jobs, from 68.8 percent in 1960 to 58.2 percent in 1990 (Table 1) followed by the generation of new high-tech jobs and the increase of jobs in the tertiary sector. So service jobs grew from 8.7 percent in 1960 to 18.8 percent (Table 1). The other city regions studied had higher proportions of service employment growth, like San Diego, with 61.5 percent in 1960 and 83.3 percent in 1990. Also in the city of São Paulo the population growth was mainly static but higher in some municipalities registering more than 500,000 inhabitants like Guarulhos (with the international airport), Osasco, and Santo André.[4]

What, then, happened with the distribution of population in the hinterland of the state of São Paulo, which resulted in a change in its local and regional government? Population increased on the areas adjacent to São Paulo metropolis, as other bordering metropolitan areas within the state began their institutional process, like the new metropolitan region of Santos on the Atlantic Ocean. It was approved by the state parliament and also by the state governor as a metropolitan region in 1996. Campinas region to the northwest of São Paulo is now starting its institutional metropolization process, and other regions are thinking of it also, like the Paraíba river valley region around the municipality of São José dos Campos on the east side of São Paulo, and Sorocaba on the west.

Nowadays, being a "metropolitan region" means for the municipal governments to agree to participate in a Metropolitan Development Council, then instituted, both in terms of working together with the state and taking decisions about the public metropolitan functions of shared interest. It means contributing to the Metropolitan Fund. This is created to financially support the studies and public works needed.

This is a complete transformation of the regional government of the past, as the new federal constitution gave the states the power to create micro-regions, urban agglomerations and metropolitan regions. It is a management process which is totally different from that of the past military period of the 1970s, when the decisions were taken by the upper levels of government and imposed on the lower ones. Nowadays, in the state of São Paulo, metropolitan regions take decisions by consensus, thus reinforcing the voluntary system of participation. This is also already happening at Santos metropolitan region. Also the Metropolitan Development Council can create special commissions which will last for the time needed to bring solutions to shared problems, and in which civil society is called on to participate.

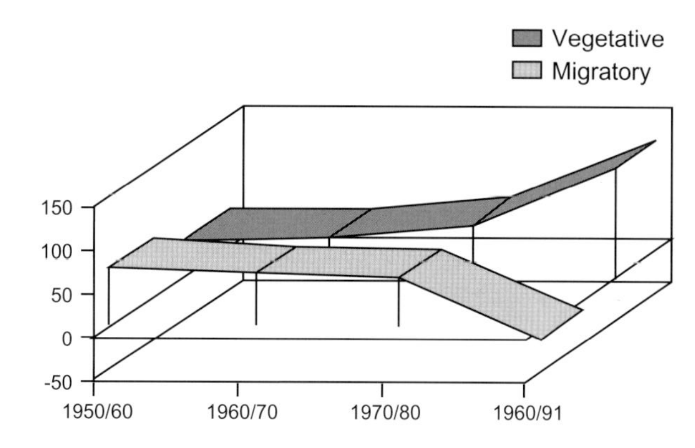

Figure 9.2 Demographic growth in the São Paulo region, 1951–60 to 1991–96.

Source IBGE/SEADE in Emplasa, PMDI-94

This also is a completely different picture from the one which existed 30 years ago. Financial and economic difficulties are being faced by the federal, state, and municipal governments, which are searching for innovative measures to be adopted for budget control. This context is favoring governmental policies that encourage the participation of the private sector as a potential investor in projects of social interest. Thus privatization, concessions, and other forms of partnership, like BOT (Build, Operate, and Transfer, where private sector companies build and operate for a 20 or 30 year period and then transfer the facility to the public), are encouraged. These have become the solution for many urban and regional problems. In this case the state of São Paulo maintains its role as controller, stabilizing the patterns and standards to be provided by the services, leaving to the private sector matters related to

Figure 9.3 The location of the São Paulo region

the operational and financial aspects peculiar to each project. To achieve these goals, the rationalization of investments became very important. Planning and production of specialized information regarding reurbanization, development of public transportation, and other facilities to improve regional performance and living conditions became an important strategic focus.

Both the physical and the socioeconomic environment rank metropolitan São Paulo in a good position as an investment location, with the potential to strengthen the South American market, and participate in other ways in the market globalization movement.

These changes will demand innovative actions in services, public works, and management. It is the challenge to be faced at the beginning of the twenty-first century.

CHANGING ECONOMIC PATTERNS

São Paulo metropolitan region always had a high share of the domestic product at both state and national levels. Nevertheless, there is a changing pattern indicating that other regions of the state of São Paulo and even of Brazil are becoming more productive. The metropolitan region's

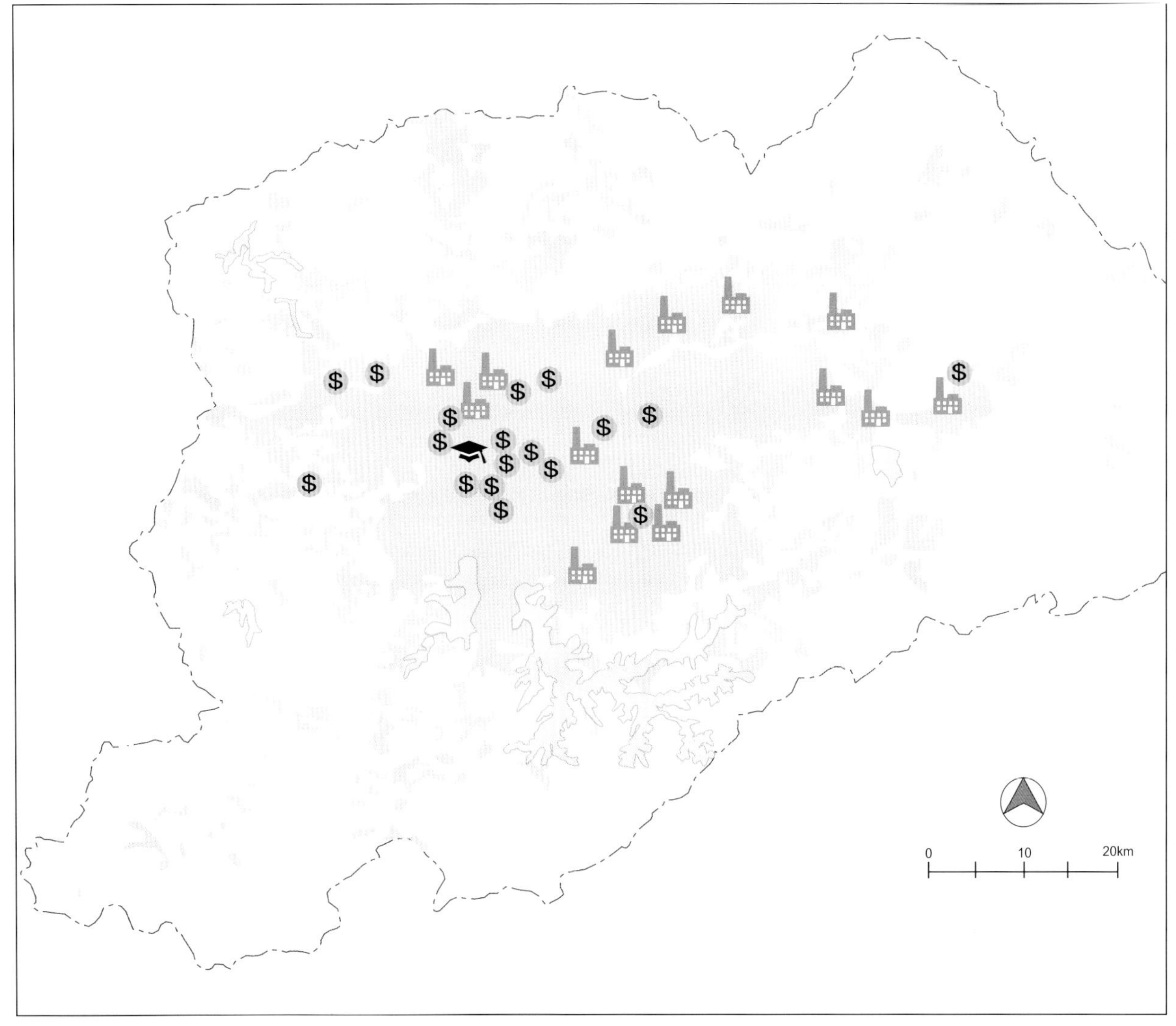

Figure 9.4 Economic patterns in the São Paulo region

share of the total state domestic product was about 65.3 percent in 1970, 60.0 percent in 1980, decreasing to 51.7 percent in 1985 but staying around 51.9 percent in 1994.[5] This change reflects a slow shift over the years of manufacturing moving from the metropolitan region to the hinterland of the state, increasing its production, jobs, and population. This shift of development is responsible for the creation of other regions, discussed above. Similarly there were shifts of activities at the national level, indicating the development of other states and their regions, as shown in Figure 9.5. São Paulo metropolitan region's share of total national domestic production fell from 24.5 percent in 1970 to 22.9 percent in 1980, 19.9 percent in 1985, and 18.5 percent in 1994.

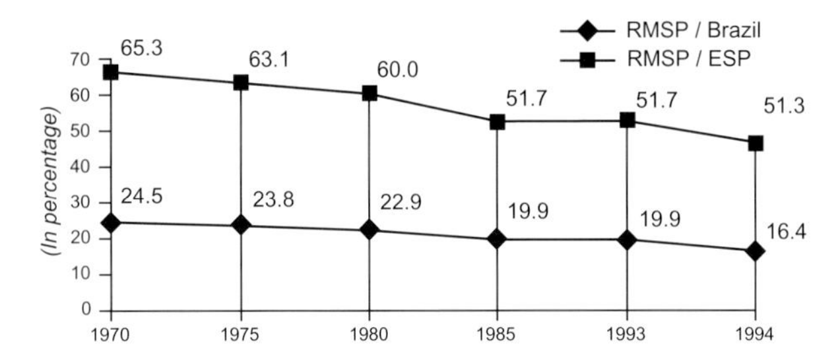

Figure 9.5 The São Paulo region's share of gross domestic product, 1970–94.

Sources IBGE/FGV plus Emplasa's estimates, November 1995

Despite all these transformations, São Paulo metropolitan region continues to keep an almost steady share of the state value added. It was 60 percent in 1980, dropping somewhat during the periods of change and recession, reaching 52.4 percent in 1985, 48.2 percent in 1991, and recovering to about 51.9 percent in 1994. (See Figure 9.6.)

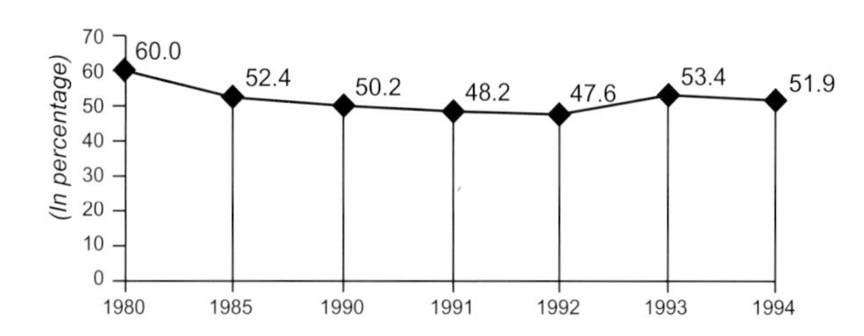

Figure 9.6 The São Paulo region's share of value added, 1980–94.

Sources State Treasury secretariat and SEADE, November 1995, special table

During the last decades São Paulo metropolitan region's activities have changed, with manufacturing slowly decreasing from 1985 to 1995 and other activities, such as commerce and services, increasing. This is shown by Figure 9.7. The level of workers formally employed is slightly lower compared with the 1980s, but the level of "informal" workers is growing considerably as shown in Figure 9.8. This means that there are more jobs for inhabitants. Although what the country needs now, perhaps, is a new set of fiscal deregulations. Between 1990 and 1996 the number of registered employees dropped 11 percent, while productivity grew 7 percent, according to the Brazilian Institute of Geography and Statistics (IBGE). This may be due to the option to work at home. Within the metropolitan region of São Paulo, one in 20 workers (representing 5 percent of the total) have their office at home.[6]

These changing economic patterns are leading to the formation of new central places, not only within the region of São Paulo but also on a wide adjacent area that is being called the "macro-metropolis", relating all the metropolitan regions of the state, as well as the other bordering regions described above.

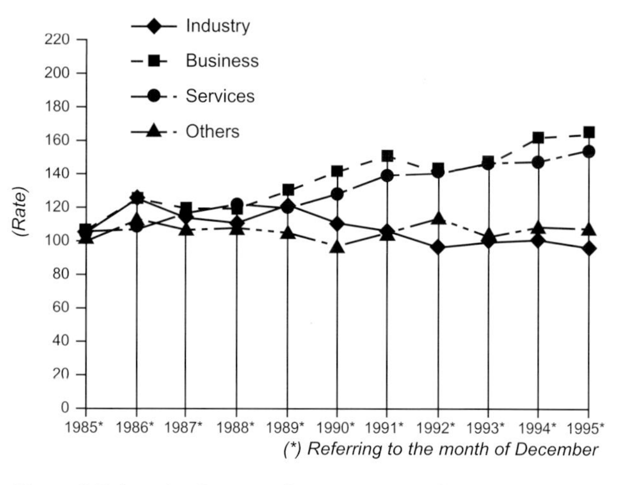

Figure 9.7 Levels of occupation per economic sector in the São Paulo region, 1985–95.

Source SEADE, PED 1985–95

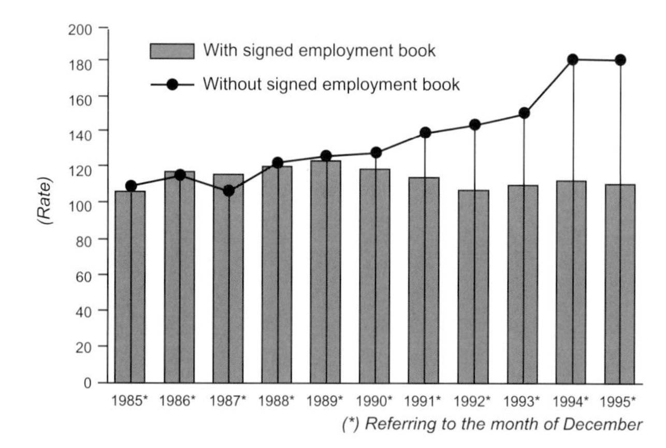

Figure 9.8 Level of private sector workers in the São Paulo region, 1985–95.

Source SEADE, PED 1985–95

CHANGING SOCIAL PATTERNS

The quality of life has changed faster during recent years with the implementation of the federal government monetary program which created the real (the Brazilian currency today). From 1985 to 1995 there was a real increase in the income of all family categories. This was particularly so for low income families, as shown in Figure 9.9. Also, it is possible to see the situation of the head of household per groups of income (1991) , as shown in the related Figure 9.10. The lower group with income varying from 0 to 2 was 24 percent of the total for São Paulo metropolitan region. The following group of families from 2 to 5 was 36 percent. Considering this last group and adding the group with income between 5 and 10, representing 19 percent of the total income groups, it is possible to discover that a huge new consumer group is emerging.[7]

Thus between 1994 and 1996 there was economic growth driven by the expansion of durable consumption goods. The government's aim has always been to phase in this demand, in order to keep it in pace with sustainable growth.[8] Figure 9.4 shows the spatial distribution of these groups in the São Paulo metropolitan region. It is possible to see an extensive area of low to medium income east and west of the city, and a higher one in the municipality of São Paulo, the central nucleus of the metropolitan region.

Owing to the rise of medium income groups it is expected that retail sales and retail outlets will grow. The estimates are of an increase of 5 percent over those of 1995. Department stores, variety stores and electronics stores will be responsible for almost half the growth.[9] This points to a strong change in the quality of life, once the domestic market can offer products of good quality. On the other

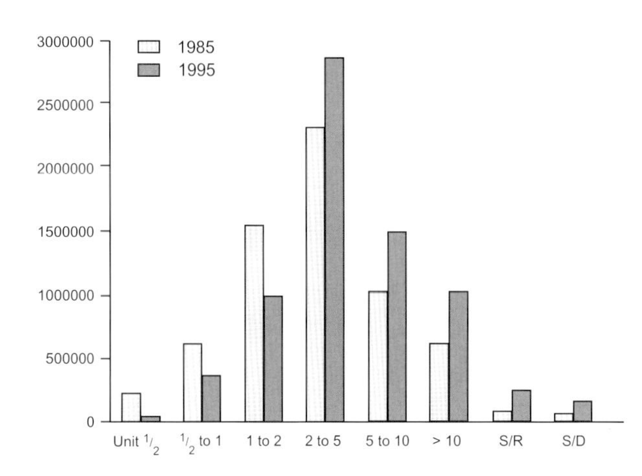

Figure 9.9 Number of people in each income bracket, 1985–95.

Source IBGE, PNADs 1985, 1995

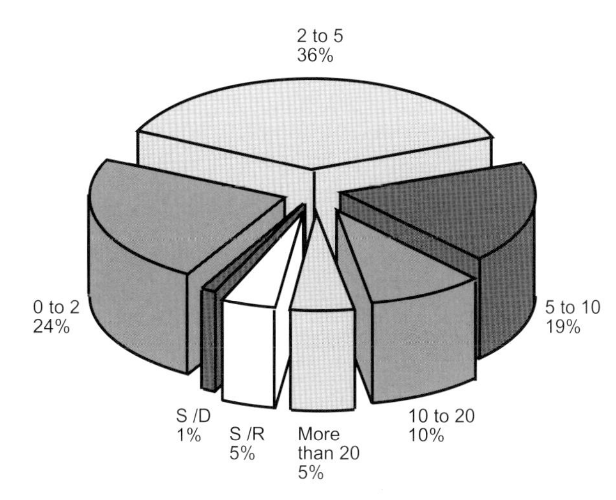

Figure 9.10 Heads of household by income bracket, 1991.

Source IBGE, PNADs

hand the attention is caught by a constant increase of jobs in the production of hardware for the generation of electrical energy, civil construction, and agriculture.

CHANGING SPATIAL PATTERNS

According to the many metropolitan plans for São Paulo city region, the expansion of the urbanized area should occur west and east but never to north or south, where the Cantareira range of mountains and the complex of water reservoirs are situated respectively. Instead, what we find is a wide sprawl of land occupation both north and south. The plans also always pointed to the need to modify the basic radial-centric road system to a road network which included ring roads. This has been slowly taking shape over the years.

The danger of water pollution is very high, as poor families squat areas around the Guarapiranga and Billings dams, living without sewers, and producing solid waste which is thrown at the water's edge. The São Paulo state and municipal governments are working together to urbanize these areas, offering treated water and sewer solutions for the population involved.

Globalization has shaped an urban form reflecting the different resources available to different sectors of the society. In other words it has shaped a fragmented city with many focal places, both for the poor and the rich. Low income families try to live near job opportunities. This means behind the houses of rich families, who are able to offer housekeeping jobs, or close to large or small employment areas. There are low income housing estates, self-built family housing areas and whole shanty towns. Other problem areas are vacant industrial land and districts prone to flooding, erosion or landslides.

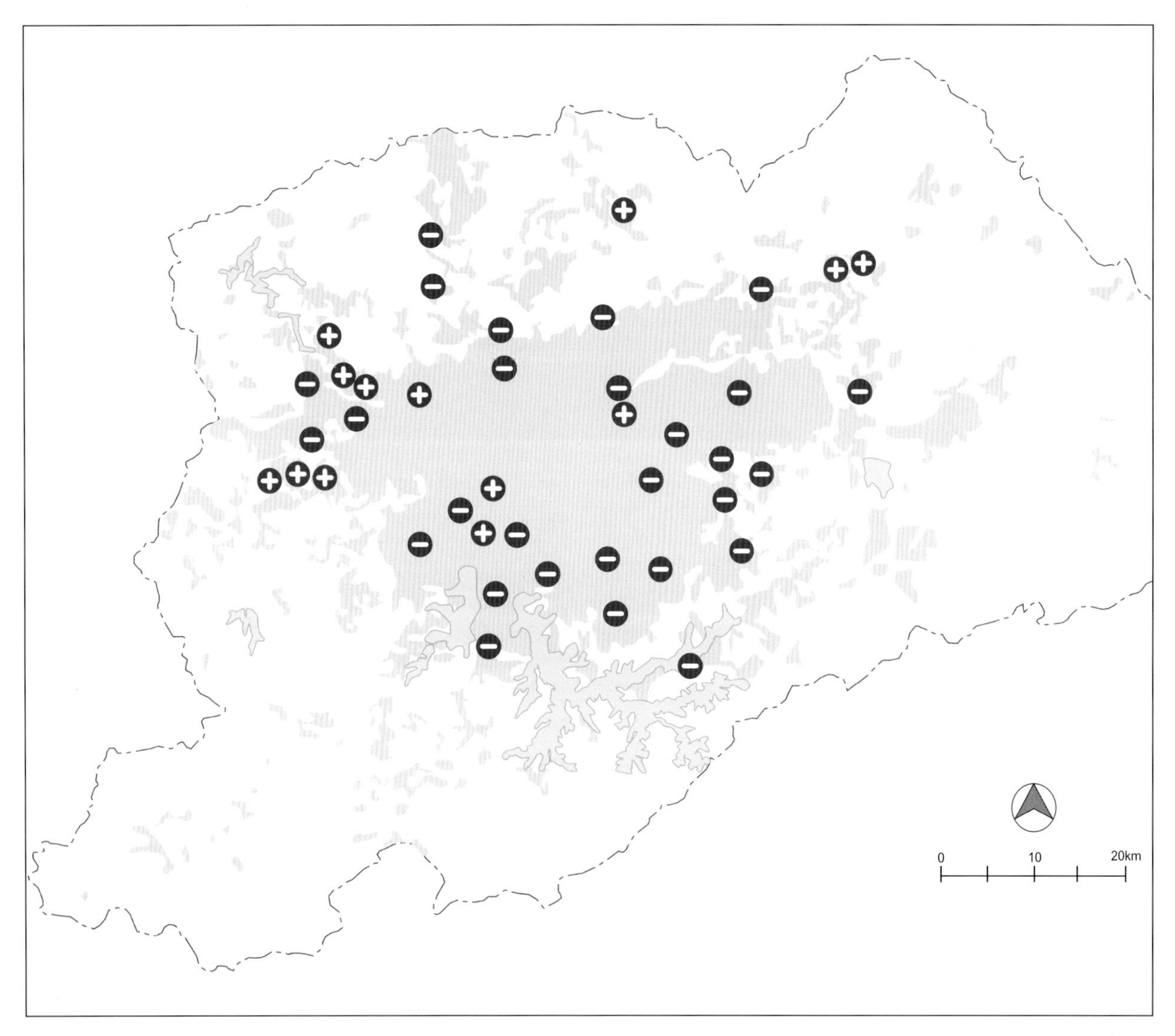

Figure 9.11 Residences of the wealthiest 20 percent and the poorest 20 percent

These areas are intermixed in the continuing tissue of the region, and are being targeted by public power policies like the Guarapiranga and Billings Project, the High Tietê River Basin, and other basin projects which rely on the participation of the state, the relevant municipalities, and the local community. Basin commissions and subcommissions are being created for the purpose. They are required to work with the Sanitation Council of the state of São Paulo. Its commissioners will work together with those of the river basin regions. All the projects for low income people, who have settled in the preservation areas, aim to reurbanize the poor neighborhoods, taking to them the facilities they need.

The vacant manufacturing areas are already, spontaneously, turning into new tertiary employment areas. Much of the vacant or unoccupied land nearby is state-owned so that the state government is engaged in many projects of reurbanization. This involves creating new centers of commerce and services connected with residential areas, like the project connected with the old Matarazzo Industry, now vacant on the west of the city. Together with the public transportation improvement by the state, this rail shore area has a high potential for new employment investment.

The advantages of globalization trends, in their turn, have set a complete transformation in motion, in the form of the tertiarization of the metropolis. There are many shopping malls, modern estates for medium and high income families, and manufacturing areas still productive. There is a huge conservation area, mainly to protect water resources. The central metropolitan area is split in many districts, like the Paulista Avenue, the Faria Lima, and Luís Carlos Berrini Avenues, with other centers on the metropolitan west side, as well as on the east side.

The changing patterns of the São Paulo region reflect also the general improvement in the purchasing power of the low income families, as described above. This social condition enables the restructuring of all these new metropolitan central places. The integration of public transportation, discussed below, will bring to the metropolis

300 km of integrated rail (suburban trains plus subway) associated with dedicated corridors of municipal and intermunicipal buses. Mass transportation will thus be offered to a wide section of population. This will reinforce changes in existing centers, which are also being driven by the improved economic and social conditions discussed above.

INFRASTRUCTURE INVESTMENT

The state government has a very difficult task in improving the rail system because it was practically abandoned in terms of investment and maintenance during the last third of the twentieth century. So, when the newspaper says, "There was a delay in rail traffic on the northwest-bound CPTM [Metropolitan Train Company] line between the metropolitan cities of Francisco Morato and Paranapiacaba, causing degradation and an increase of the number of accidents on road SP332,"[10] it is clear that this rail problem is like a snowball rolling downhill and growing all the time. Since the 1950s, there has been no investment in railways, as roads had priority. The railways became outdated, with slow traffic and frequent delays. They serve passengers during the day and at night they carry freight. There is almost no maintenance.

As a consequence, the passengers using the railway system are poor and a large number of them escape the controls and travel without paying. In the rush hours the trains are full of people, like food packed in cans, with fearless young people travelling by grasping outside the train's doors. Others become the railway's "surf boys" balancing on the roof.

This slow ruining of the railways over the years contrasts dramatically with the logic of road construction which began with radial roads following the old demolished streetcar lines. Some planners still lament the failure to complete the radial road plan of 1930, which they still see as "the utopian city of the future, as in the '30s, when he [the mayor, Engineer Prestes Maia] issued his plan for a city with trees but already prepared for the automobiles".[11] The story of the systems of circulation of the São Paulo region shows a megacity requiring the best attention from the public authorities to solve its problems. Congestion grows each day "indicating that it is time for intervention before it becomes too late and the city collapses."[12] It is astonishing that in a metropolitan region of about 16.4 million inhabitants (1991 census) some 50 percent of the population circulates on foot, with the other half motorized. Of these only 25 percent use individual vehicles while 75 percent use public transport. Of these, about 30 percent ride local transportation and the remaining 70 percent use metropolitan.[13]

In terms of passengers transported within the metropolitan region, 25.2 percent take rail (18.1 percent subway and only 7.1 percent suburban railway). Bus trips represent 74.8 percent of the distribution of passengers (52.7 percent use municipal buses and 22.1 percent inter municipal). Intermunicipal buses are managed by the State Metropolitan Urban Transportation Undertaking (EMTU in Portuguese).[14] In spite of low levels of car ownership, the percentage of people using cars is now enough to make traffic jams adding up to some 120 km daily.[15]

In terms of telecommunications, foreign enterprises which were attracted to the region gave birth to the first national enterprises and services related to the development of software, in a new business park now fully occupied.[16] To begin with there was some concern about national security and commercial balance, but it was a consensus that no country would be able to develop successfully if it did not have an information technology sector, including local projects, the manufacture of hardware, and the development of local services like software applications.

The model of import substitution enabled the country to create the necessary skills to master the technology. The PCs arrived, finding the users anxious to be free of the data processing centers, analysts, and other specialized services. From 1984 to 1992 government import controls and incentives assured the telecommunication sector some protection from outside competition so that national enterprises could invest with some degree of tranquility. On the other hand this phase also gave rise to a high level of smuggling.

From the 1990s onward, to counteract these consequences of market rigidity, flexibility was introduced through the reduction of taxes and the importation of hardware, so that production grew and quality improved. Today an increase in the number of joint ventures and other forms of international cooperation is predicted, assisted by the growing market for such products.

With these assumptions, we can now focus on the relations between infrastructure and urban form, pointing out problems and presenting the proposals being implemented by the government of the state of São Paulo. It is important to remember that all three spheres of government have concurrent powers—meaning, for instance, that all of them have their own plan of public transportation, education, health, and so on. Therefore, from an institutional point of view, it is a must to have agreements on every sector, so that implementation can occur without the usual insoluble bureaucratic problems.

Roads

During the 1950s the road system continued a radial-centric form, as shown in Figure 9.12. Nevertheless a new road structure, also largely hierarchic in form, was being built over the years. This is still incomplete. At the end of the 1960s the new plans proposed a road network of about some 450 km of expressways, but these could not be paid for by the city.[17] Many other plans have been formulated since, but the basic principles remain the same.

The zoning law that still is responsible for the city form, also in terms of volume, dates back to 1972, although it has been modified through many resolutions of the local government. Therefore, until today, São Paulo metropolitan region is a sprawling predominantly radial-centric road system, being composed of many urban centers that grew until they became part of the conurbation. Some of these centers are very important for their specialization, bringing new inputs to the system.

Today, to improve living conditions within the metropolitan region, the state government is working to implement the outer ring road, which would act (like a beltway) to receive all the through traffic and direct it to its destinations without it entering the city. This ring road is also a better location for intermodal freight terminals, especially when they are near the railway system. In another sense, the ring road is also seen as an organizer of a road network, that will change, to a significant extent, its radial-centric form.

As the state cannot afford these projects, partnerships are being set up with the private sector. The first ring road section will link the Anhanguera and Bandeirantes roads in the north (the major roads going northwest into the hinterland of the state of São Paulo) to the Regis Bittencourt road in the southwest area of the metropolis. (The Regis Bittencourt road links the metropolis to the southern states of the country.) There are many factors being studied, such as how to design the ring road crossing the water reservoir preservation areas at the south, or how to design the links with the major roads that reach the city. The state govern-

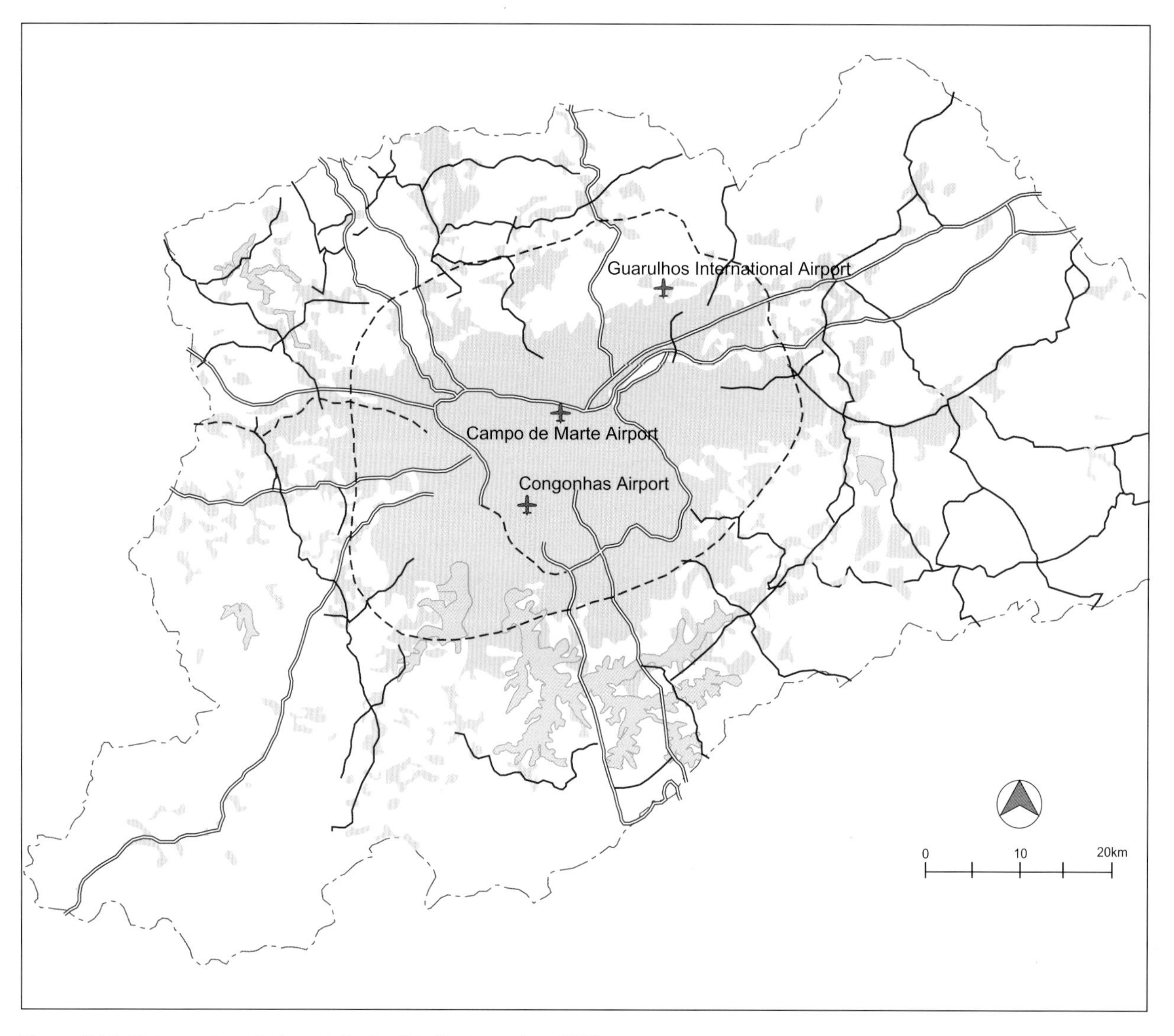

Figure 9.12 Main roads and airports in the São Paulo region, 1995

ment has already signed a convention with both the federal government and the municipality of São Paulo, so that not only the private sector but also all the three levels of government will contribute financially with funds to build this belt road. All the citizens of the metropolis seem to want the road built.

The road system also is a provider of the state bus corridors linking different municipalities. Many of them are in the process of setting up a concession. They not only run within the São Paulo metropolitan region but also are making connections into Santos metropolitan region. (Santos metropolitan region was instituted with nine municipalities. Santos, the larger city on the Atlantic Ocean, is the main harbor of the country.) These intermunicipal buses are projected to run in trunk dedicated corridors whenever possible, like the one linking the municipalities of Diadema and São Paulo in the southeast area of the metropolis. Essentially their mission is to collect people from the periphery (like Diadema) and take them to the main terminals, connecting with the rail system, suburban trains or the subway. There is a computer-operated system to keep the regularity of trip intervals at the rush hours. Equipment is very clean and efficient. The state is planning, through concession contracts, to exchange in five years the types of buses now running on diesel or gasoline to electricity or gas. This is being called the Blue Project, because the sky will become bluer without the pollution.

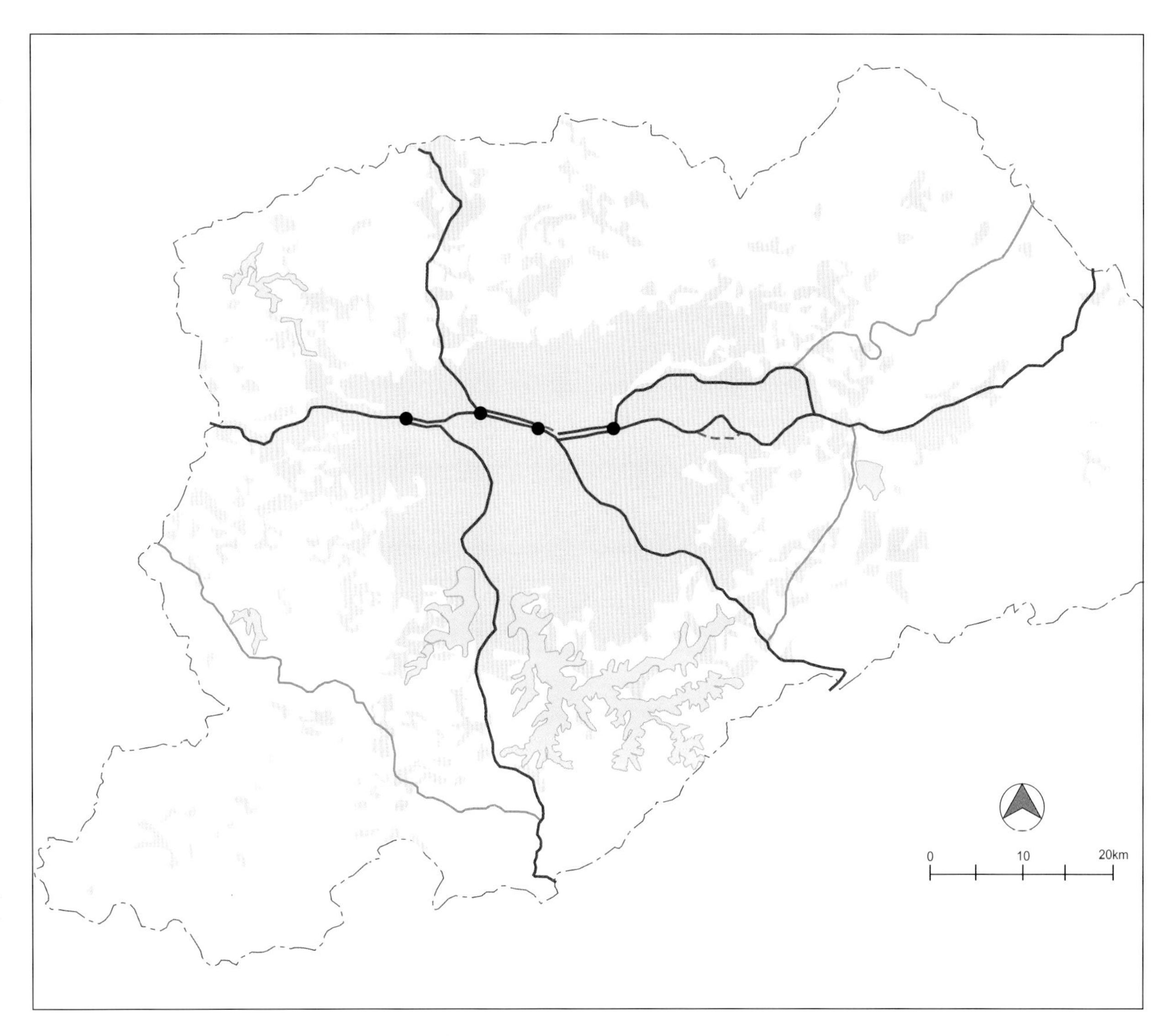

Figure 9.13 Railways in the São Paulo region, 1995

Rail

Remembering the snowball rolling down the hill, mentioned earlier, how can the government stop it if it doesn't have enough resources to implement the projects which are necessary? The answer the state of São Paulo government came up with was to begin to implement the subway project which was stopped by the last two governments. This indeed is the first priority for the State Metropolitan Transportation Secretariat (which is implementing a comprehensive plan of urban transportation during this administration, the *Plano Integrado de Transportes Urbanos*—PITU—in Portuguese).

First, they recovered previously promised international aid and are building the subway expansion northward. Second, they are preparing a concession in terms of BOT (Build, Operate, and Transfer) for the fourth and fifth subway lines. Third, the railway system is being improved through investment in maintenance. This involves rebuilding the old parts of the lines, buying and renting new trains, building new stations and connecting some of them with the subway system.

The main east railway project will allow the organization of a dual transportation system toward the east area of the metropolis, a once poor area of the city whose citizens have taken initiatives to upgrade it. This dual system will have the railway as express train, connecting passengers straight from the central area (Roosevelt Station) to the periphery (Itaquera and Guaianazes), while the subway system will stop at each station.

The implementation of government priorities will allow the metropolitan region to count on some 300 km of rail infrastructure (interconnected subway and railway). This will bring poor, median, and high income people from the periphery to the inner areas at a low fare, with a new system of ticketing, including interchanges with both state metropolitan and municipal buses.

The improvement of the rail system means bringing the whole system up to the quality which the subway already has, both on its inner and outer areas. This is being carried out by the suburban railway system itself, through better surveillance, cleaning of the spaces, and control of people who take the train without paying.

Airports

São Paulo City International Airport is located in the municipality of Guarulhos, northeast of the central area of the metropolis. During the last decades Guarulhos has had a higher growth rate, most probably because the airport location is a strong factor of attraction for new uses like manufacturing and wholesale. The international airport is being expanded through the construction of another runway. The other airports within the metropolis are smaller in surface and are totally locked in by the urbanized area. Congonhas Airport, located at the municipality of São Paulo, is being used for small airplanes, making mainly domestic connections. Campo de Marte, an old military airfield, is now used mostly for training and also for private ultra-light airplanes, sail flights and helicopters. The state government has studied some alternatives for the reurbanization of the area around Campos de Marte Airport, opening the possibility of a partnership with the private sector, as well as with the federal government, which is responsible for air transportation, and the municipality of São Paulo, which controls land use.

Viracopos Airport, in the northwest of the region, has become a valuable freight facility similar to Santos harbor in the metropolitan region of Santos. Besides these modes of circulation, it is important to remember that the state of São Paulo is using the hydroway system of the rivers Tietê and Paraná, already with more than 1,600 km of navigable extension. This hydroway enables freight traffic to come from the central and northern areas of the country up to near Piracicaba municipality, to be shipped or flown abroad or to other southern regions, or by the railway or road systems without entering São Paulo metropolitan region.

Telecommunications

Most probably there is a straight relation between urban form, the nature of the infrastructure, and the concentration of activities. The city cannot live without infrastructure and it must achieve a size large enough to attract, through economic agglomeration, specific types of technology investment.

The greater the city centrality, the greater the investment by certain kinds of high-technology, financial, and management services, and the more the associated jobs. These are, also, areas for particular types of research and development.

The study of the location of telecommunications shows that the information handling enterprises of the country are highly concentrated in the metropolitan region of São Paulo (75 percent) and, of these, 70 percent are in the municipality of São Paulo. The more dynamic segments, in terms of financial and innovation capacity, are represented by a few leading enterprises within their own market cluster.

In the case of public sector data processing, 50 percent is located in the metropolitan region of São Paulo, and the other 50 percent is distributed throughout the remaining states. Micro and median computers have their spatial concentration in company headquarters in the municipality of São Paulo, amounting to 66.77 percent of the country. Others are distributed within the metropolitan region of Rio de Janeiro.

The concentration of financial management facilities for the 40 largest companies in the country is only 33 percent in the municipality of São Paulo,while in the metropolitan region of Rio de Janeiro it reaches 47.3 percent. Analysis of these data shows that this bias is due to the presence of IBM in Rio de Janeiro metropolitan area, with the largest billing of Brazil, while the municipality of São Paulo concentrates the headquarters of the largest number of information handling enterprises in the country.

Both the municipality of São Paulo and the metropolitan region of São Paulo have a high concentration of the headquarters of the main enterprises of the telecommunications sector, with 60 percent and 62.5 percent respectively. The hinterland of the state of São Paulo has 10 percent while the metropolitan region of Rio de Janeiro has 15 percent, and the other states 12.5 percent. All the headquarters of facsimile and radio communications companies are in the municipality of São Paulo. It also has 49 percent of the data communication enterprises.

Conclusion

In Brazil, infrastructure building programs were predominantly in the hands of the central government mainly until the 1970s. States and municipalities had to go to the central government for financial resources. The dominant pattern today, as discussed previously, is that of "concurrent powers", by which it is meant that the federal, state, and municipal governments have their own plans of public transportation, education, health, and so on. Therefore, at the institutional level, agreements are needed in order to get a program implemented. During the 1970s the federal government used to set conditions and, without their acceptance, no financial aid would be released. Now in the 1990s, at a time of budget difficulties, decentralization is in practice.

REGIONAL LAND USE PLANS AND OTHER INITIATIVES OF REGIONAL GOVERNMENT

The main regional initiative was the institutionalizing of metropolitan regions as the business of each state, not the federal government, as discussed above. This implies the creation of a Development Council, where state members and the municipal members meet voluntarily to take care of common interests.

This tends to take the form of consensus building. State and municipal members, by decision of the Development Council, create temporary special purpose commissions to solve some problems like those to do with the environment. The metropolitan regions also will have an investment fund to which all the metropolitan municipalities as well as the state will contribute. An administrative agency composed of members of the municipalities and the state also will be created in each metropolitan region. (Both the fund and the administrative agency still have not been created in the metropolis of Santos.) With this frame other metropolitan regions will be created in the state of São Paulo, as mentioned. Therefore a mega-metropolis network is growing around the São Paulo region, distributing production and jobs outside the region, and taking the state to a different balance in terms of the generation of domestic production.

Similarly, in the country as a whole, the share of São Paulo city is not so high as it was in the 1960s and 1970s, demonstrating that new developments are growing outside the region and in other states. This is generating production and jobs and, therefore, making it possible for this huge country to be more balanced in economic and social terms.

CONCLUSION

The main opportunities in the short term will favor low income families, offering them public transportation of about 300 km of rails and more buses at low cost and even at no cost to senior citizens and to those employees who receive from their employers monthly transport vouchers. The rail services will be to the same high quality as the subway and the intermunicipal buses. It is anticipated that the transportation system will work without the usual risks of vandalism as people come to respect such a high quality of service. Median income families also will be attracted by this comfortable public transportation system. It is hoped that many will leave their cars in the garage, thus easing road traffic.

Partnerships with the private sector, mainly in the form of concessions like that of the subway system BOT, where the state in the near future will recover its power over the system, are promising. Similar partnerships are occurring in other areas, like the reurbanization of the state areas along the rail shore, and other state services. For bus corridor construction it is necessary to sign conventions with the municipalities, as they run the local roads, and the state has to share the roads with them. Bus concessions have been part of the municipal administration for a long time, with good results. Nevertheless there are still some groups operating informal microbus services, and pressing the municipalities to admit them to the formal sector.

In general the main centers are more attractive to the telecommunication servers, enabling the enterprises located there to have quality control, flexible production, just-in-time processes, and also to restructure themselves into new spin-off companies, thus generating new economic activity. It is important to understand that, nowadays, there are public bids to open the provision of telecommunications services to national and international firms.

The new urban patterns that are emerging in the south, southwest, and west areas of the metropolis are urban expansions, taking the form of horizontal residential condominiums. They are built on the existing and already congested road system, mainly the Presidente Castelo Branco Road and the Raposo Tavares Road. In order to deal with this congestion, construction of the outer belt road of the metropolis, to be built in partnership with the private sector, will be open to public bid.

Major urbanization poles already structured in the São Paulo region are attracting new development, like the municipality of Guarulhos (northeast of São Paulo), with many new manufactures and other activities linked to the fact that the international airport is located there.

In terms of the growing spatial pattern, there is a deep transformation occurring in the east zone of the metropolis. This was traditionally a poor area which is now a median income area, as by hard work and improved national economic circumstances the former population has increased its prosperity. Nowadays the new generation can go to university, most to private ones. Tatuapé subway station, is part of the new spatial pattern for centers, represented by many high rise buildings for median and high income people, with a new shopping center inaugurated in1997. In terms of changing spatial patterns, all the east side of the metropolis is becoming in general a median class area, where existing families are reinvesting in new development.

Regional form is also being transformed in areas with good road access, like those areas along the Nações Unidas Avenue, on the edge of the Pinheiros river, and the Berrini Avenue parallel to it. This, connected to the Faria Lima Avenue, has created an urban area attractive to reurbanization. For example, in 1998 the municipality of São Paulo approved the Faria Lima Avenue Project. It means to link the Pinheiros neighborhood to the Itaim Bibi one and reaches Berrini Avenue. This was part of old plans for the city of São Paulo that tried to build transverse roads in some areas, so that it would start to form a network of roads instead of the dominant radial-centric structure. This project issued a kind of special bond allowing entrepreneurs to build beyond the allowed indicators of built-up-area, both for parking and for other uses. The road forms a new piece of the metropolitan road network, breaking the earlier strong radial-centric structure of the central area.

Also, the railway along the Pinheiros river is a target for improvement with the construction of new train stations. This will be part of the whole upgraded 300 km rail system already mentioned.

Along the railway shore there are many vacant parcels of land, some state-owned and many the sites of industry which has moved out of the city. Therefore there is room to densify, to reurbanize, and to enable a new urbanization where the population can have both services, the trains and the subway routes, integrated into one system. These reurbanizations are examples of how new urban tissue is being shaped, connected to a public system of access and counting on the partnership of the private sector for its implementation.

The huge number of company headquarters attracted telecommunications companies to the region. There is a continuous growth of employment in the sector. It was steady during the 1980s, even, when the country went through a long period of recession and economic instability. The 1990s brought changes as a result of the policy of opening the market to the internationalization of products, prices, and quality. This was initially followed by a small decrease in the level of employment.[18] Although the generation of information-related jobs has been continuous, analysis shows a concentration in the municipality of São Paulo (70 percent of information handling and 60 percent of telecommunications). Still there is room to grow, with good salaries, constant training, innovations in methods, and also in terms of production.

The municipality of São Paulo also contains 49 percent of the productive enterprises in those sectors which are intensive in science and technology. Those engaged in production activity in this sector represented something like 57 percent of the work force. In 1992 there was a shortage of some 27.39 percent of jobs for qualified personnel, mainly in engineering and management. Only 7.48 percent of employed people had been to college. These data show the situation in 1992 when the country was in the middle of a process of employment adjustment, due to the end of the domestic market reservation. This meant a decrease in local production and employment, favoring the increase of imports.

São Paulo metropolitan region is a huge market in which to offer services. Thus upgrading trends are in motion to service the median and high income family residential areas, and to improve the living conditions of low income families. There is room to densify these areas, resulting in a new type of spatial urban pattern, discussed above. These areas may tend to specialise in the future, meaning, for example, that special production locations will be attached to the telecommunications network. Around these locations the trend seems to be a higher socioeconomic growth, bringing higher production and new jobs.

NOTES

1 Emplasa, *Projects and Planning*, 1996, p. 22.
2 "Diminui crescimento demográfico no Brasil," *Gazeta Mercantil*, June 8, 1997, p. A6.
3 In fact, migration continues toward the metropolitan periphery although at a slower pace.
4 Emplasa, Data and Information section.
5 Brazilian Institute of Geographical Studies (IBGE) and Getúlio Vargas Foundation (FGV), plus Emplasa estimates, November 1995.
6 "Administration and Marketing: the Option to Work at Home Grows," *Gazeta Mercantil*, August 7, 1997, p. C8.
7 IBGE, Demographic Census, 1991, data on minimum wages.
8 "Economy goes to Sustainable Development," *Gazeta Mercantil*, August 22, 1997, p. A4.
9 "Retail awakes External Capital Interest," *Gazeta Mercantil*, August 7, 1997, p. C1.
10 "Falta de trem faz crescer acidentes em via" (Absent Trains increase Road Accidents), *Folha de São Paulo*, April 16, 1997, pp. 3–8.
11 "São Paulo chega a 2000 com o projeto de 1930" (São Paulo at 2000 with 1930 Project"), *Folha de São Paulo*, April 16, 1997, pp. 3–16.
12 "São Paulo: nove idéias para fazer o trânsito andar" (Nine Ideas for keeping the Traffic moving), *Veja*, 10 April 1996.
13 Empresa Metropolitana de Transportes Urbanos (EMTU).
14 Cia do Metropolitano de São Paulo, *Relatório da Diretoria de Operação*, São Paulo, 1995, p. 11.
15 "São Paulo: nove idéias."
16 More on this in Campos Rui, Diretor de Mercado, Fenasoft, Feiras Commerciais Ltda, "Informática no Brasil: fatos e números" (Data Processing in Brazil: Facts and Figures), 1996.
17 Prefeitura do Município, *Plano urbanístico básico de São Paulo*, São Paulo, 1968.
18 Emplasa/Campus Rui, "Informática no Brasil."

ACKNOWLEDGMENTS

The research could not have been done without the dedication of the EMPLASA team but any errors are my responsibility. For all the work, attention, and commitment I want to express my gratitude to the following. For data and information handling: Cecília Maria Rodrigues Nahas, Leonelo Fernando de Camargo, and Eugênio Senese Netto. For cartography development: Priscila May Jalasny Masson, Lúcia Rodrigues Serpa Panzolda, and Claudionor Macedo Flores. For information complementing: Zilton Luiz Macedo. For financial research: Ivani Moreira, Janice Yunes Perin and Janet Yunes Elias. For graphics, maps and final composition: Enéas Nucci Júnior.

10 Seattle and the central Puget Sound

ANNE VERNEZ MOUDON AND
LEROY A. HECKMAN

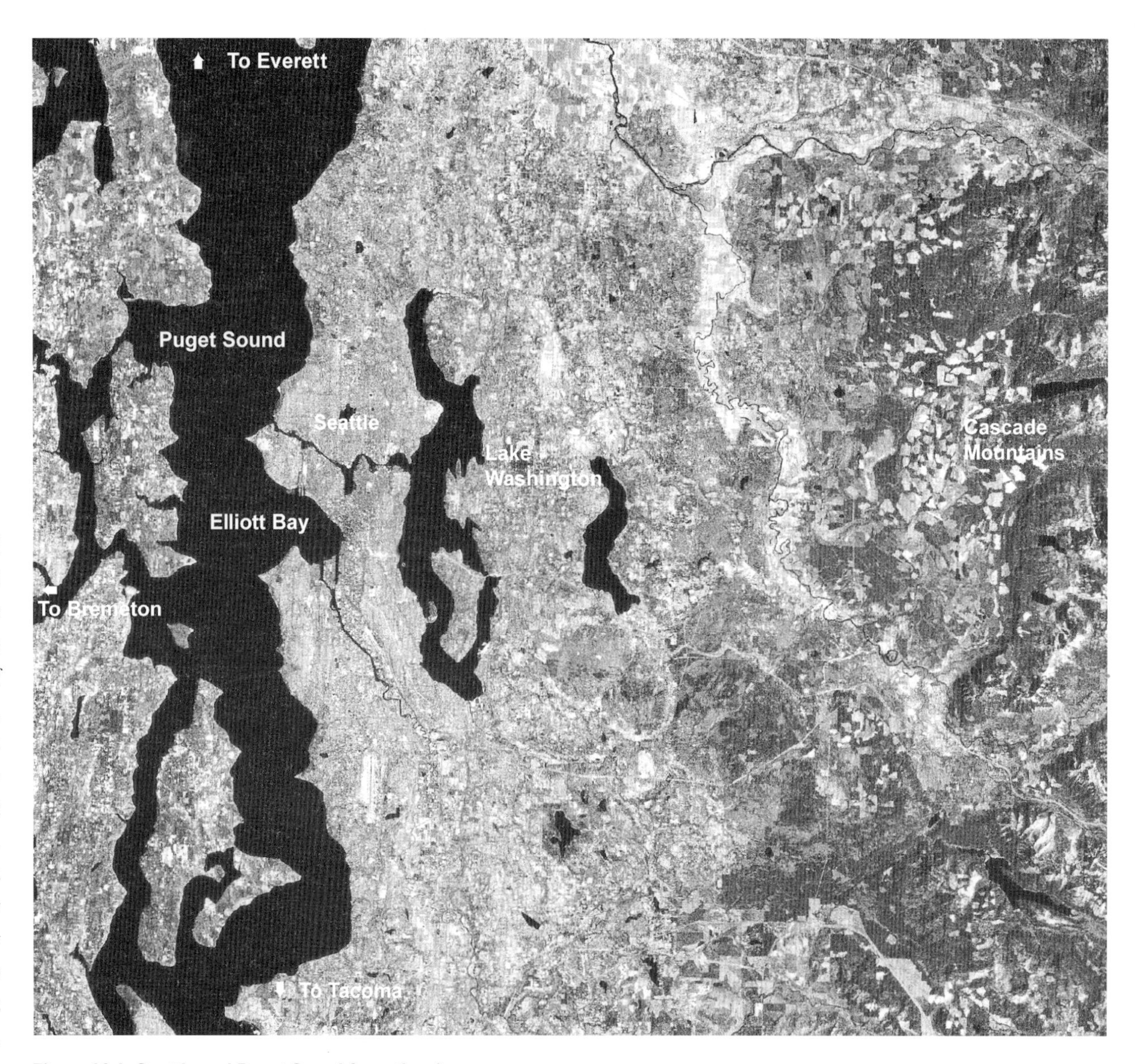

Figure 10.1 Seattle and Puget Sound from the air

Celebrated in movies and music, home of Boeing and Microsoft, Seattle has been underwritten as the potential "shock city" of the twenty-first century, much as Manchester was hailed as the prototypical city of the industrial revolution or Los Angeles as the embodiment of the modern city. On postcards and television clips, Seattle's symbolic being takes the form of a typical, albeit glittering, high-rise downtown flanked by the city's landmark, the Space Needle, amidst an attractive waterfront and a spectacular snow-topped volcano, Mount Rainier. In reality, the city of Seattle proper is the lone flagship of a sprawling region consisting of four counties (King County dominates, though Snohomish and Pierce are rapidly developing to the north and south, and with Kitsap County to the west), two additional central cities (Tacoma and Everett), and some 70 incorporated suburban cities. Like most US central cities with roots in the nineteenth

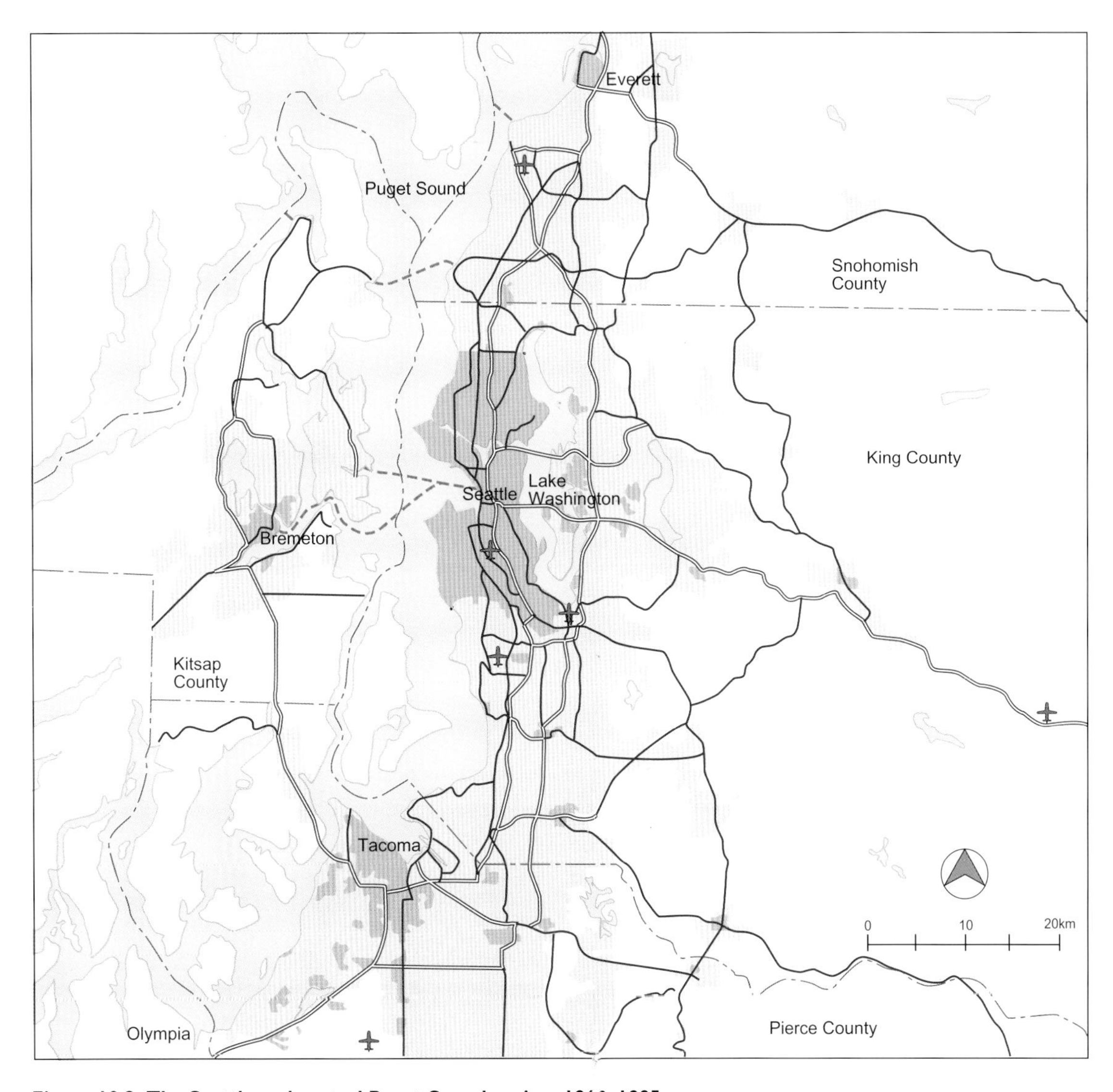

Figure 10.2 The Seattle and central Puget Sound region, 1960–1995

century, the city of Seattle has lost population since the 1950s, and today it houses less than one-fifth of the region's population on one-tenth of its land. Further, Seattlelites, as they are called, differ greatly from their more conservative suburban counterparts, the former consistently clashing with the latter on issues such as the environment, transportation reform, equal rights for gays and lesbians, and gun control. Powerful industries such as Boeing have grown in many locations away from the city of Seattle. Bill Gates, the famed chairman of Microsoft, and himself a native Seattlelite, moved both company and family outside of the city limits.

A representative name for the shock city of the twenty-first century has yet to be found. "Pugetopolis" was tagged as a potential descriptor in the 1960s as metropolitan growth away from the central city became obvious. The "City of Puget Sound" was proposed more recently before settling on the less urban, and hence more appropriate, "central Puget Sound" to describe the four-county planning region, framed by a boundary defining an "urban growth area." A word that even natives have difficulty pronouncing, "Puget" is the name of one of George Vancouver's lieutenants, which the captain selected to attach to the enormous area west of Seattle where water and land intermix before giving way to the Pacific Ocean. Though not much easier than "Puget" on the Asian or European tongue, Seattle remains, and probably will continue to remain in spite of local mistrust for the mother city, the region's key word to the outside world—much as San Francisco continues to represent the more anonymous Bay Area.

Central Puget Sound indeed resembles the San Francisco Bay Area as it was a few decades ago: some 3 million people spread in a large, low-density urbanized

Figure 10.3 The location of the Seattle and central Puget Sound region

region which emerged out of the conurbation of the two older port cities of Tacoma and Seattle, and of many small and even tiny towns around them (Figure 10.2). The analogy between the two regions stops in their position relative to their home state. While San Francisco continues to compete with the megalopolises of southern California, Seattle and the central Puget Sound constitute the only major metropolitan area in the state of Washington, with 60 percent of the state's population (3 million out of 5 million) and 60 percent of its employment base (1.5 million out of 2.5 million jobs). Virtually all of Washington state's connections with the nation and to the world take place in the central Puget Sound's air- and seaports. In a state which is highly dependent on international trade—total exports *per capita* are twice the national average—these figures illustrate the primacy of the Seattle urbanized area. They do not, however, lessen the constant frictions and inequities which continue to exist in state politics dominated by rural interests. These interests, coupled with frictions and inequities between the urban and suburban factions within the central Puget Sound itself, make things difficult and indeed cloud some of the area's future prospects.

Enlightened leadership has turned to neighboring states to promote the potential of the region as a world economic power (Figure 10.3). The concept of an international bio-economic region called Cascadia has been given credence and has spurred interesting programs. Cascadia—from the Cascade Mountain range separating the coastal areas from the eastern plateaus—covers the Oregon Territory, and combines the Canadian and US northwest continental corner. It is a bio-region with similar geological structure and climate, and an economic gateway to the Pacific Rim. Air routes over the North Pole make the Pacific Northwest equidistant to Japan and northern Europe, both of which are indeed important trading partners. Cascadia's "Main Street," a 300 mile stretch along the Pacific Ocean, runs from the city of Vancouver, British Columbia, to Eugene, Oregon. Six million people strong, it houses 75 percent of British Columbia's, Oregon's, and Washington's populations. Within Cascadia, the central Puget Sound dominates in population size, economic activity, and ease of communication with both southern and northern partners. However, the central Puget Sound lacks the national prominence given to Vancouver, British Columbia, as Canada's single major port on the Pacific. Moreover, it lacks the concerted and sustained state-level support of the Portland metropolitan area.

Central Puget Sound is characterized by a continued strong dependence on national defense policy and on aerospace manufacturing production. The pre-World War II historical dependence on resource exploitation has waned, replaced by serendipitous growth in the computer technology and communication sectors. Washington state's agricultural and food processing activities also greatly impact the demands made on the region's ports. The region's population is relatively young, educated, and primarily Caucasian. Steady growth since a major recession in the early 1970s has provided a sound economy which is projected to continue into the twenty-first century.

CHANGING ECONOMIC PATTERNS

Since 1967 the number of jobs in central Puget Sound has expanded faster than in the nation as a whole in spite of significant roadblocks. During this time, the dominant lumber, paper, and pulp industries have had to restructure to confront a changing market. Aerospace manufacturing, the other dominant industry in the 1960s, suffered a major setback in the early 1970s. Boeing cut one-half of its work force; as a result, 60,000 jobs were lost, putting the region's economy on hold for most of the decade. Although manufacturing today remains a strong component of the local economy, it fell from holding almost 40 percent of the jobs in 1960 to only 19 percent in 1990; further, although both manufacturing and non-manufacturing gained in employee numbers from 1980 to 2000, the non-manufacturing sector now accommodates 10 times as many employees as manufacturing (at 600,0000 versus 60,00 jobs, respectively). Traditional industries such as lumber, paper, and pulp have stabilized, though further loss in this sector's jobs is expected. The overdependence on

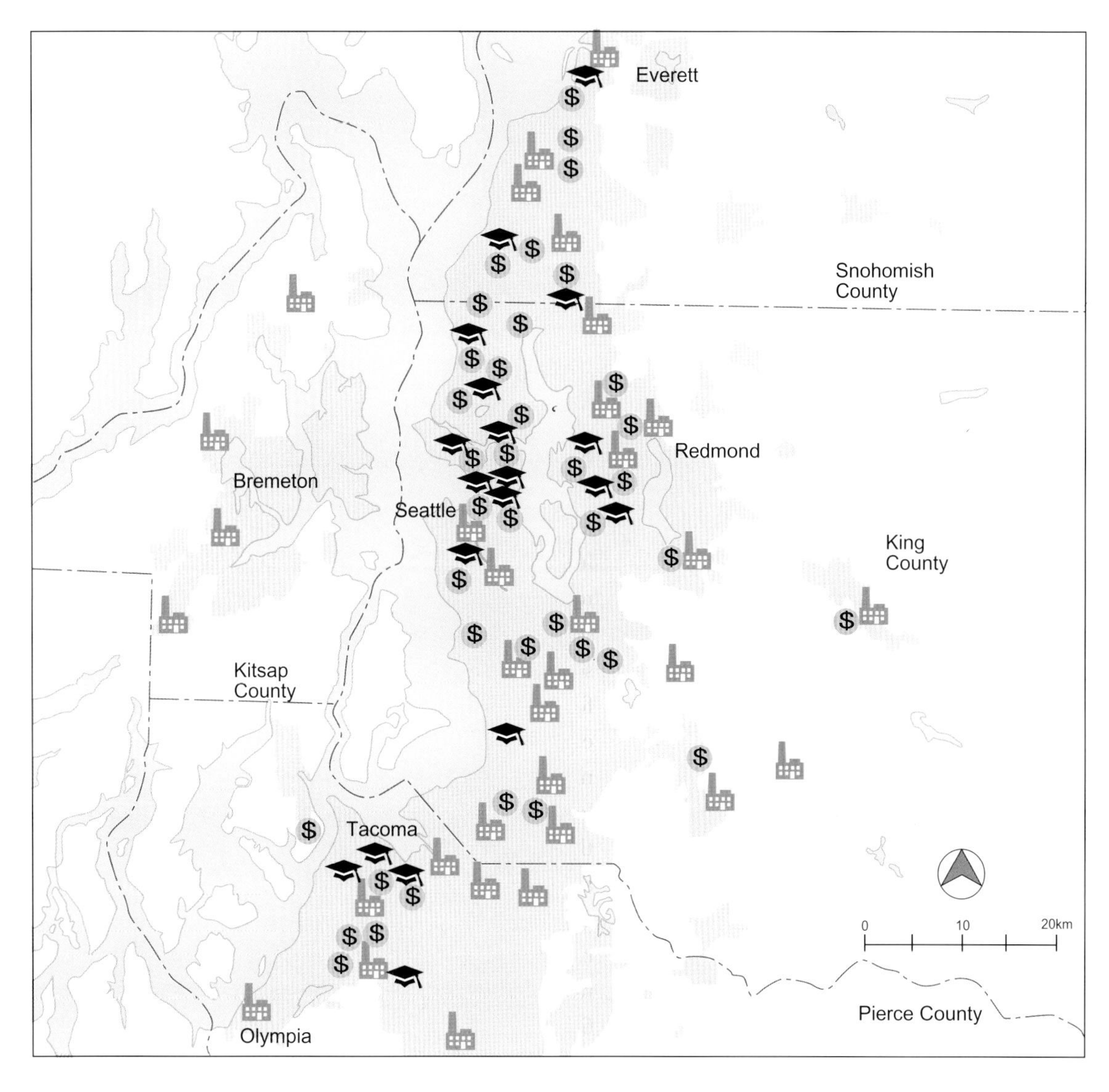

Figure 10.4 Economic patterns in the Seattle and central Puget Sound region

aerospace manufacturing which led to the 1970s recession has been remedied with further diversification in trade, transportation, communications, and utilities (Figure 10.4). Also, historically difficult labor relations have subsided, with union membership dropping to one-fifth of the manufacturing jobs.

Today, almost half of the employment in manufacturing (slightly more than 9 percent of all area jobs) is in aerospace industries, with Boeing accounting for more than 8 percent of the region's jobs. Boeing's strong international markets, and its merger with McDonnell-Douglas, offer an optimistic outlook for the region's future. The industry has a multiplier effect of 3.14 on jobs in the region. Other manufacturing activity includes ship and truck building (the former related to the US Navy), paper-related products, apparel, and bio-medical instrumentation.

Services accounted for 30 percent of the jobs in 1990, an increase from 19 percent in 1960. Growth has been experienced in producer services (finance, insurance, real estate, business and professional services) for which 36 percent of business is now conducted interregionally. Non-producer services are also strong, including health, consumer and social services, and tourism; the last is the fourth largest industry in the state, employing some 100,000 people.

Government accounts for almost 16 percent of the region's jobs. The two least populated counties in the region depend heavily on military activities—Washington being the fifth most military-dependent state in the nation. The University of Washington has 1.6 percent of the region's jobs, most concentrated in the city of Seattle. City and county governments also are a significant source of government jobs. (State government, located in Olympia, is outside the central Puget Sound Region.)

The remaining 30 percent of employment falls into the categories of transportation, communications, and utilities (6 percent of jobs), retail and wholesale trade (17 percent), resource-based industries (lumber, fishing, and food with 2 percent) and construction (5 percent).

Steady economic growth over the past 20 years has been particularly beneficial in a state which relies on sales, business, and property taxes for revenues. Businesses in Washington state pay a larger share of total taxes than in other states. Generally, the state is eleventh in the United States for *per capita* taxes, second for *per capita* sales tax, sixth for gasoline tax, and twenty-fifth on property taxes. This is against a state ranked ninth for *per capita* personal income. Top revenue-producing firms with more than US$ 2 billion in the mid 1990s are Boeing, Price Costco (discount warehouse), Weyerhaeuser (lumber), Microsoft, Paccar (heavy equipment), Nordstrom (apparel retail), Safeco (insurance and finance), and McCaw Cellular, now part of AT&T. Other wealth-producing but comparatively lower-employment industries are Microsoft (15,000 employees), Paccar (11,800), Safeco (7,400), and McCaw (5,800).

Overall, one in five jobs in the state now depends on international trade. The two top-trading international partners of both Washington and the central Puget Sound are Japan and Great Britain. Generally, one-third of the region's exports go to Europe, and two-thirds to Asia.

CHANGING SOCIAL PATTERNS

Population is unevenly distributed in the central Puget Sound: King County houses 55 percent of the people, followed by Pierce at 18 percent, Snohomish at 12 percent, and Kitsap at only 5 percent. King County also holds 70 percent of the jobs, compared with 14 percent in Pierce

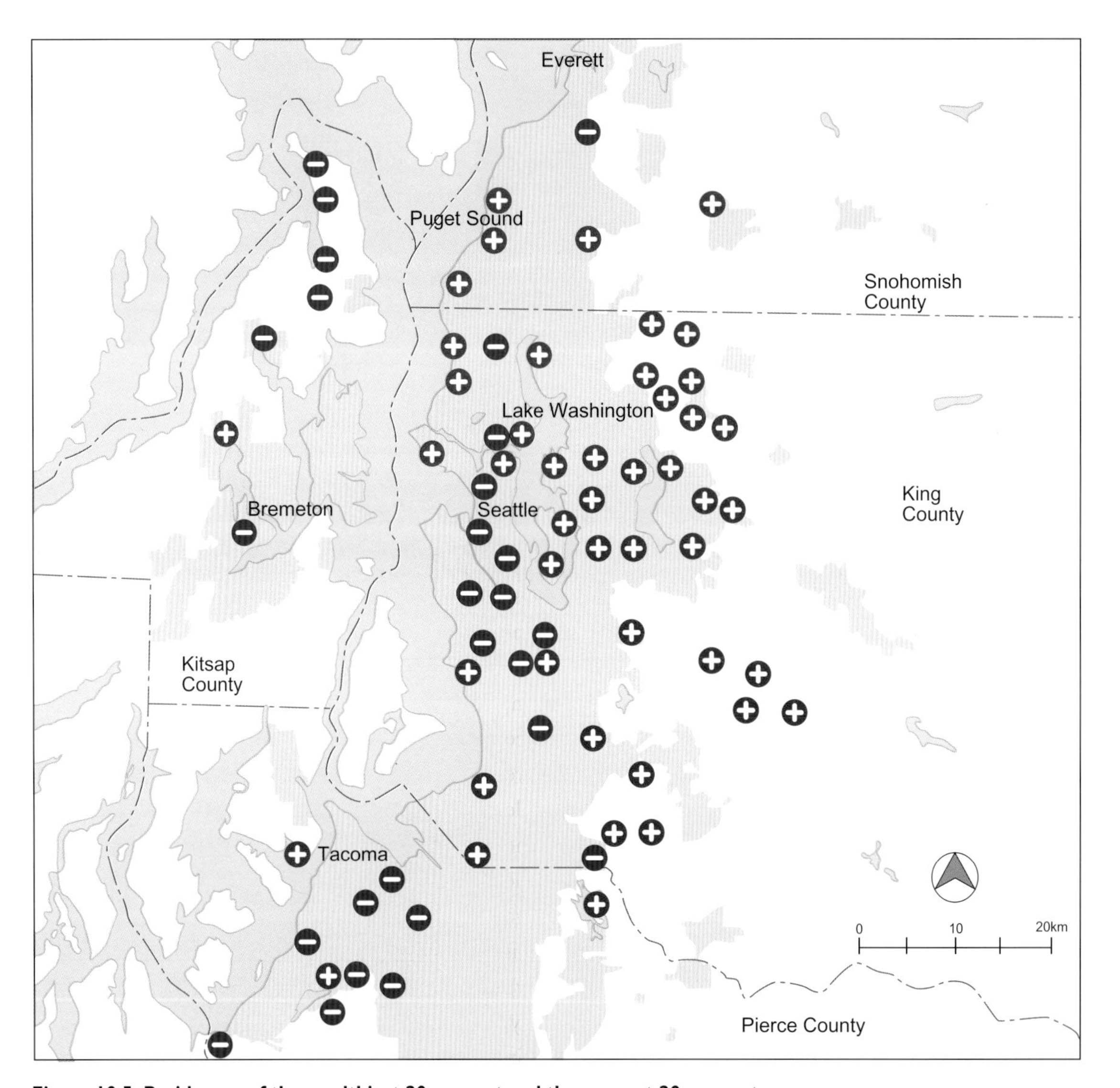

Figure 10.5 Residences of the wealthiest 20 percent and the poorest 20 percent

County, 12 percent in Snohomish, and 5 percent in Kitsap counties. Approximately 70 percent of the population live outside of the central cities of Seattle, Tacoma, and Everett. Further, one-third live outside either central or suburban cities in the counties' unincorporated areas. Residents' median age is relatively young at 33 years. Education levels are high: 88 percent of the population over 25 years hold a high-school diploma, and 33 percent have a Bachelor's or higher degree.

Early migration from northern Europe established the area's social character beginning in the late 1800s. A doubling of the population since 1960 brought little change to the region's racial and ethnic profile. Whites constitute more than 85 percent of the central Puget Sound population—compared with 55 percent in the San Francisco Bay Area and 63 percent in the San Diego area. Asians represent 6.7 percent of the population, African-Americans 5 percent, and Hispanics 3 percent. Interestingly, the state just elected the nation's first Chinese-American governor, and King County (the most populated and urbanized county) elected an African-American chief executive.

The region's distribution of minorities is also uneven, with half of the population of color living in the three central cities. Two counties, Kitsap and Snohomish, have only 10 percent and 7 percent of their population as people of color, respectively. Average *per capita* money income is $16,700, against $14,400 for the nation. Only the population of Pierce County has a below-national-average income. The number of people living in poverty is comparatively low at 8.5 percent (13.1 percent nationally). The percentage of families with children living in poverty, however, is substantially higher than the US average in Kitsap and Pierce counties. Pockets of poverty exist as well in Seattle's, Tacoma's, and Everett's Asian and African communities. The more affluent households are now found in the newly developed suburbs east of Lake Washington as well as along the region's many waterfronts (Figure 10.5).

Population growth in the region has averaged 2 percent per annum since the 1960s. This growth has been closely related to economic development: it decreased from 2.5 percent between 1960 and 1970 to 1.5 percent between 1970 and 1980. These rates are high compared with the national average of 1 percent but remains lower than California's at 2.4 percent, Florida's at 3.1 percent, or Arizona's at 3.3 percent (each for 1980–90). Annual population growth from 1980 to 1990 was lowest in King County at 1.73 percent and highest in Snohomish at 3.26 percent. Growth patterns are expected to continue expanding the region, with the largest share of population increases occurring outside of King County.

Net migration now accounts for slightly more than half of the population growth, with 30 percent of the newcomers arriving from the states of Oregon and California. Figures are lacking for migration from outside the US, but estimated at less than 20 percent of net migration, with most immigrants arriving from Southeast Asia or China.

CHANGING SPATIAL PATTERNS

The central Puget Sound urbanized area covers almost 950 square miles (2,500 km^2), stretching over 80 miles (130 km) north–south along the Sound's shore. Anchored by the three older, formally industrial cities of Tacoma in Pierce County (1990 population 170,000), Seattle in King County (520,000), and Everett in Snohomish County (80,000), the urbanized area more than tripled in size over the four decades 1960–2000. The planning region delineated by the Urban Growth Boundary now includes approximately 22 percent of King (458 square miles), 12 percent of Pierce (186 square miles), 9 percent of Snohomish (180 square miles), and 30 percent of Kitsap (117 square miles).

Only during and after World War II did the construction of roads and bridges across Lake Washington facilitate eastward expansion and accommodate the wave of suburbanization which has swept this, as well as all US cities, since. Westward expansion across the Sound to Kitsap County continues to be discussed, though dreams of new bridges are likely to remain such for the foreseeable future.

With suburban development engulfing second-growth timber land and agricultural fields, regional population densities loom low, now around 3,000 people per square mile. As in other US cities, retail was first to follow residential suburbanization. Two large suburban shopping centers were built in the 1950s and 1960s north and south of downtown Seattle. Today, the region contains at least 16 regional malls and countless local shopping centers. Office development followed the retail trend by a decade, with some 30 clusters, most of which range between 1 million ft^2 and 5 million ft^2 of leasable space. One suburban city, Bellevue, has become the region's recognized "edge city," with 100,000 residents and 90,000 jobs, 24,000 of which are located in the downtown area. While additional edge cities are expected to emerge in the future, they are likely to exclude office skyscrapers and focus instead on becoming mixed live–work communities.

Fierce competition from suburban employment growth has been fought successfully by downtown Seattle, which, contrary to many other US central cities, remains extremely healthy. With 165,000 jobs, the central business district holds 35 percent of Seattle's and 10 percent of the entire region's jobs. The loss of housing stock experienced in the 1960s and 1970s is being remedied: the 20,000 people now living in or near Seattle's downtown are expected to double by the first decade of the twenty-first century. With only a few glitches, downtown retail has continued to thrive, to include a preserved farmers' market, a renovated nineteenth century historic area, major department stores and formerly suburban chain stores moving in. In contrast, Tacoma's downtown has been struggling, with little if any retail, and only 30,000 jobs; much the same situation faces Everett. However, recent and continuing development of a branch campus of the University of Washington in Tacoma may herald a renaissance of this historically significant downtown.

Industrial land supply has increased along with population growth. While many of the flat lands close to the Port of Seattle are now brownfields (contaminated areas) under environmental litigation, industrial development has taken over most of the flat agricultural lands extending south of the port. Industry also followed development along new high-capacity roads to the north and the east sides of the region. Boeing's main plants in Renton (south) and Everett (north), as well as scattered office locations, have led the way to opening up a substantial supply of industrial and commercial land throughout the region. The rapid growth of suburban cities starved of revenues also has facilitated the process of converting land for industrial and commercial uses. Adequate servicing of new industrial land, however, remains in question.

INFRASTRUCTURE INVESTMENT

Regional transportation is the number one issue in the central Puget Sound. The current regional transportation infrastructure is largely the result of decisions and actions taken prior to the 1960s. Forty years later, regional systems operate at or above capacity—hardly a surprising situation, given the doubling of the population, compounded by a more than twofold increase in *per capita* miles traveled and the number of trips taken using automobiles.

The roots of the problem provide the best basis to consider options for the future. First, this region, as many others in the US, made the inherently risky decision to invest almost exclusively in private automobiles as a means of transport. By 1960, as streetcars and passenger rail had been replaced by personal automobile travel, public transit ridership had dropped by two-thirds, and to this date only 3 percent of transportation expenditures are directed at public transit—corresponding almost exactly to the share of persons using transit as an alternative mode of transport. Over the years, voters consistently rejected options presented by the region's leadership to develop a state-of-the-art transit system, even at times when it would have been heavily subsidized by the federal government.

Second, the region's habits in funding transportation can no longer work. Most large investments made since the 1960s relied on significant support from federal revenue sharing and grants for automobile travel. Since then, however, budgets for expenditures and capital improvement have dropped by as much as one-third owing to shifts in national priority funding. Further, new environmental regulations and community activism have severely limited infrastructure development. This bleak situation is rendered even worse by considering the region's suburban land use patterns, which, perpetuated since their adoption in the 1960s, are characterized by very low densities and large areas in single use.

Less prominent than transportation in the public arena, yet no less problematic, is the region's supply of both water and electricity. Hydropower and water supply and treatment infrastructures are operating at capacity with, again, little relief in sight because of limited budgets, new environmental regulations, and public resistance. Agencies are responding with improved management of current resources, campaigns for conservation, and pricing increases.

Roads

The physical and financial hardship of bridging over the Sound or over the deep alpine waters of Lake Washington historically posed regional transportation problems, limiting east–west regional linkages. In response, and to cater to the region's dependence on resource exploitation, especially the logging industry, waterways dominated transportation policies until the 1920s. Major engineering works were completed in the late 1910s connecting Lake Washington with Seattle's harbor in Elliott Bay via Lake Union, which required the lowering of waters by 17 ft on Lake Washington. Establishing the history of dependence on federal generosity, the Montlake Cut, Ship Canal, and Hiram-Chittenden Locks all benefited from support by the US Corps of Engineers. To date, these passages continue to serve the construction and fishing industries as well as the popular pleasure boating activities. The most used remnant of the focus on waterborne transport is the elaborate Washington state ferry network which connects Seattle with the islands in the Puget Sound, and the Kitsap

Figure 10.6 Main roads and airports in the Seattle and central Puget Sound region, 1997

County peninsula to the west and the northwest. As most of these are car ferries, this network now acts as an extension of the road system. The recent growth of the region and resulting increase in travel time make the ferries a viable daily transportation system for an increasing number of people who seek a semirural setting within reach of the city. Proposals to extend the waterborne transit system with water taxis or buses are made regularly, and may indeed become a viable way to diversify modes of transport in the region. Seaplanes are not only the privy of the rich but also the basis of a small commuter industry to the islands.

Regional road building began in earnest in the 1920s with the construction of a north–south parkway along Seattle's portion of the original Pacific Coast Highway. Part of the Federal Work Project Administration programs, the road retains a historical character with bridges and overpasses built in the parks design tradition. However, the original viaduct built along downtown Seattle's old seaport area constitutes today a serious barrier to waterfront redevelopment in the downtown area.

High-capacity "freeways" (their being "free" remains a serious public policy issue to date) replaced existing highways as part of the extensive post-war national program to improve the interstate road network. Several such freeways were completed in the late 1960s (Figure 10.6). Interstate 5 (I 5), serving the entire west coast from Mexico to Canada, more than doubled the north–south capacity. It runs on the eastern edge of Tacoma's downtown and carves through Seattle's center with a twelve lane structure with four reversible lanes to accommodate directional traffic. Interstate 405 (I 405) serves as a half ring road to the east of Lake Washington, linked to I 5 at both the southern and the northern edges of the lake.

The major east–west connection, Interstate 90 (I 90), was first built in the 1940s as a state-of-the art floating bridge crossing two deep channels of Lake Washington. It became a high-capacity freeway only in the 1990s. Flanked by an elaborate system of retaining walls, bridges, and tunnels, all with lavishly landscaped parks, I 90 is now touted as the nation's most expensive highway stretch ever built, likely using some of the last federal subsidies for such roads. A second floating bridge and limited access road, State Road 520 (SR 520), was built in the 1960s, and funded locally through tolls charged over a period of some 20 years. Contentious debate continues to this date on whether or not to increase SR 520's capacity or to build a third bridge over the lake.

As in other US metropolitan areas, public resistance to building additional freeways developed quickly after the 1960s. In downtown Seattle, mindful citizens immediately took steps to mitigate the impact of the gap created by I 5 between the downtown and its east side neighbors. Several bridges were built, one of them combined with a park, to reconnect the two sides with a continuous street network. Plans for secondary freeways within Seattle were shelved. Today, a few years after the completion of the I 90 multi-lane mammoth, some of the same citizens are working on the "Sound to Mountain" project to insure a green corridor along some of the freeway's path.

Since the late 1970s Washington state road planning and building brought in secondary high-capacity roads which insured and continue to insure regional sprawl. The Valley Freeway (SR 167) doubled the north–south capacity along the southern industrial corridor and supported east side development. Several state roads have also been built in south King, Pierce, and Snohomish to support east–west development.

To date, the region has a total of 16,700 miles (26,720 km) of roadways, 3,000 of which are federally owned, 1,200 owned by the state, and 12,500 by cities or counties. The annual costs of transportation are estimated at $7,000 *per capita*, which represents more than 25 percent of personal income. Private out-of-pocket expenses cover more than 85 percent of these costs, or more than 35 percent of the median household income. These figures include the costs of congestion and environmental impacts, estimated at 5 percent of the total costs.

Rail

The region's heavy rail network reflects investments made between the 1880s and 1920s to connect the developing west with the country's East Coast and Midwest. It remains a diesel fueled system. The first Northern Pacific line arrived in Tacoma in 1885 in response to the rapid growth of that industrial city. Eight years later, the Great Northern entered Seattle—a catalyst expediting the dominance of that city in the region for years to come. These lines carried both passengers and freight. Access to Tacoma's and Seattle's harbors quickly became a priority to support the region's lumber industry. The half-dozen competing private lines which developed the network have now consolidated into two, Burlington Northern and Union Pacific. They continue to retain possession of major land holdings acquired in compensation for financing this infrastructure. To date, they serve every major industrial park concentration in the region and link them with the seaports of Tacoma and Seattle. (Fifty percent of the out-of-state rail traffic now originates in the ports of Seattle and Tacoma.) (Figure 10.7). However, some of the older routes have been abandoned as industry consolidates in suburban locations and adapted to new uses such as bicycle and walking trails.

Interstate passenger service provided by the national company, Amtrak, handles but a small fraction of the central Puget Sound passenger travel, reflecting national priorities given to automobile and air transport. With service available in Tacoma, Seattle, and Everett, it provides connections to Oregon and California, Vancouver, British Columbia, Chicago, and beyond. Improved passenger car technology has recently allowed some reduction in the time distance between Cascadia's three main cities. However, the low level of service, combined with poor inner-city connections to the stations and the stations' own antiquated state, still severely restricts the market potential of the system.

A regional passenger rail system existed in the form of streetcars in and around the region's central cities until the Second World War, when it was dismantled. Only partially replaced by "rubber" transit or buses, the loss of regional rail announced the demise of public transit as a means of transport for the middle classes and up. Since then few improvements have taken place in the system. Electric trolley buses now serve the densest areas of Seattle. In the 1980s a federally subsidized tunnel was constructed under downtown Seattle to facilitate express bus service to suburban areas. As an experiment in improving the performance of bus transit and addressing the pollution problems of the region's primarily diesel-fueled bus fleet, the project introduced more expensive vehicles which were powered by electricity inside the tunnel and by diesel outside of it. The upshot is that these dual-fuel vehicles required fuel transfer stations—which demanded space and added travel time at both ends of the tunnel. The project's ambiguous place in the region's transit system is

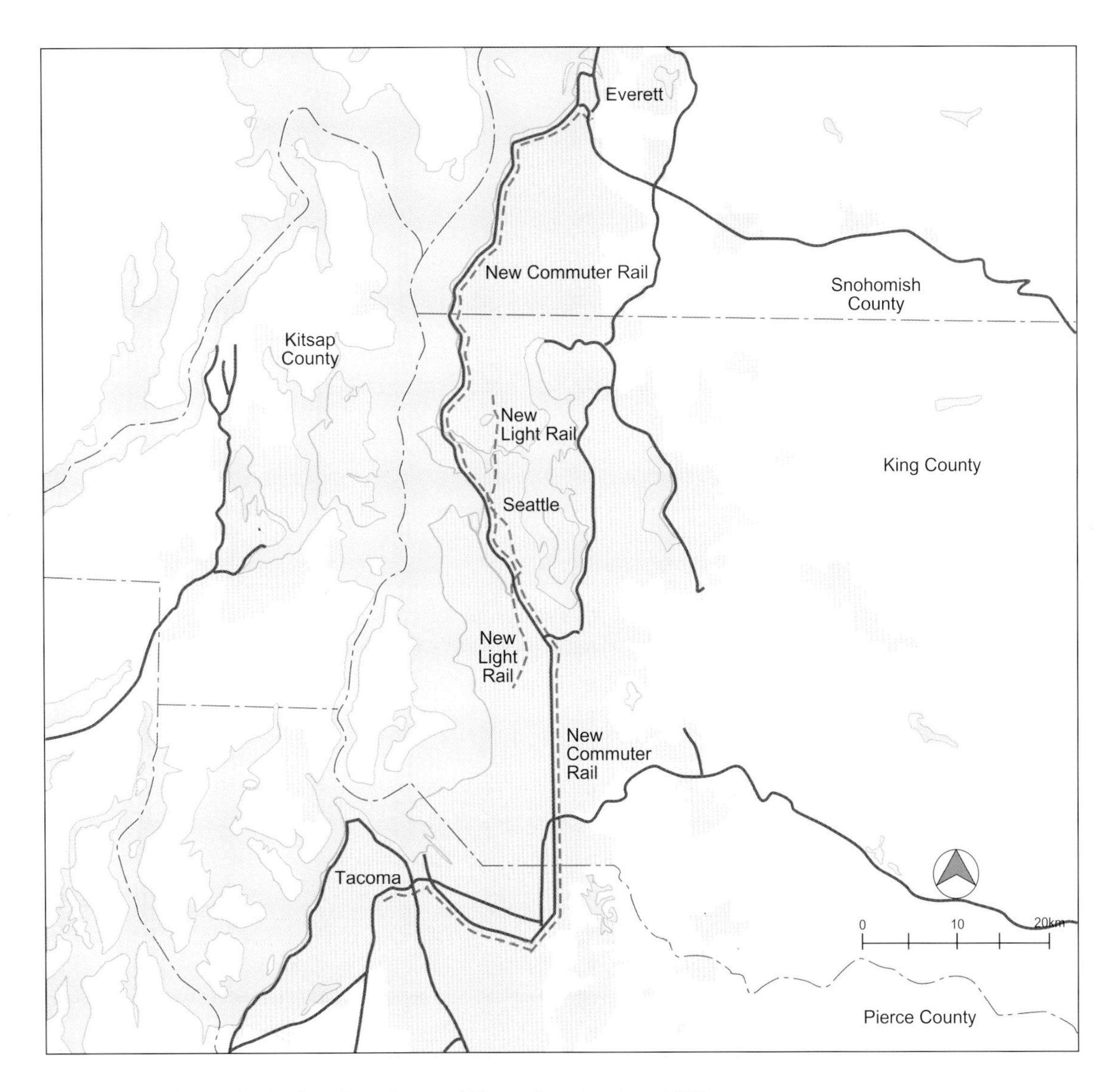

Figure 10.7 Railways in the Seattle and central Puget Sound region, 1997

best illustrated by the fact that, after much controversy, rails were installed in the tunnel in anticipation of a future regional rail system.

A short electric monorail route linking Seattle's downtown with a neighborhood two miles north was built as part of a 1962 World's Fair exhibit. Though of limited use, the train holds a special place in the heart of Seattle-lites. A recent initiative to extend this system throughout the city was passed easily. This initiative leaves Seattle's public officials in a quandary: not only does it lack any consideration for funding, but it lies outside the region's first comprehensive transit plan which was recently approved by voters.

A four-county Regional Transit Authority (RTA, recently renamed Sound Transit) was created in the early 1990s to prepare a regional transit plan. A $3 billion scheme was finally approved in 1996 which includes several elements. It reinstates commuter rail from Lakewood (approximately 10 miles south of Tacoma) to downtown Everett; this commuter rail service is expected to use existing rail lines almost exclusively. Rush-hour service between major employment centers will rely heavily on bus connections and park-and-ride facilities. The plan also calls for a new light rail system to run from SeaTac Airport, south of Seattle, to the university district, a major employment center four miles north of downtown Seattle. With seven-day service at less than 10 minute intervals, the light rail will replace some of the best used bus service of the region. However, its connection with the airport through areas with good potential for development south of downtown Seattle promises to affect the city's future profile.

Rail and bus transit investments will be complemented by the completion of the regional high-occupancy-vehicle

(HOV) lane network. The network will stretch along I 5 from Tacoma in the south to Everett in the north, loop along I 405, and run some 15 miles eastward along I 90. The most promising aspects of the RTA plan lie in a single-fare, coordinated regional bus and rail transit, as well as in the integration of express bus services and HOV lanes.

Ports

Two large seaports serve the region, one in Tacoma and one in Seattle. Managed by two competing quasi-public authorities—the legacy of the historically intricate relationship between the ports and rail companies—they have none the less come together to share the region's main airport of SeaTac.

The seaports themselves were modernized in the 1960s to accommodate containerized cargo. A fully automated port-to-destination system was put in place in the mid 1980s, including a double-stacked container rail service. Containerized cargo business increased by 15 percent annually in the 1980s, and now handles nearly 85 percent of the region's $32 billion annual import/export business. Indeed, the only competitors on the West Coast are the ports of Long Beach, California, and Vancouver, British Columbia.

SeaTac International Airport, the region's primary airport, currently handles 18 million passengers per year (triple the number in 1970, and these numbers are expected to triple again by 2020). Ten percent of this traffic is international; there are over 30 daily passenger and cargo flights leaving for foreign destinations. The region has four additional jet airports: Boeing Field (previously the city of Seattle's municipal airport, now used primarily by Boeing); Paine Field near Everett in the north and Renton Field south of Seattle (both with modern navigational aids and owned and operated by Boeing); and the McChord Air Force base. Of the four, Paine Field is the only airport other than SeaTac allowed to handle passenger traffic—for emergency landing in case of bad weather conditions at SeaTac, or for a few charter flights.

A third runway is currently under planning for SeaTac Airport to augment capacity and reduce dependence on weather conditions. Opposition on the part of adjacent neighborhoods is slowing the project down and has pushed civic leaders to consider alternative locations for yet another airport. Yet others continue to argue for high-speed rail links along the Cascadia Main Street Corridor, which would help the three internationals airports of Vancouver, British Columbia, Portland, Oregon, and SeaTac, Washington, to operate collaboratively and efficiently.

Telecommunications

National laws regulating the communications industry exercise a great influence on local infrastructure development. By abolishing the monopoly enjoyed by local telephone companies, the Telecommunications Act of 1996 substantially altered the provision of telecommunication services. In both expected and unexpected ways, it is also affecting the authority of states in their control of highway rights.

Fifty private telecommunication industries are estimated to operate in the greater Seattle area, and more than 120 in the region as a whole. Nationally, more than 97 percent of households lease a telephone line. The region's urbanized area is also well served by cable television—with either airborne or underground cables, wireless cellular, and satellite communication infrastructure. Fiber optic cables are also being installed by both telephone and cable television companies. Local jurisdictions lease air or ground space for cables which are integrated with the existing utility network. Cable companies are usually granted franchises to operate in given neighborhoods or parts of towns.

Jurisdictions also grant permits for ground stations and transmitter sites, whether they are located on public or on private property. The Federal Telecommunications Act bars state and local governments from unreasonably discriminating against any of the companies competing to provide these services. However, problems have arisen regarding the location of facilities needed for telecommunications. For example, local residents have opposed the intrusion of cellular towers into their neighborhoods, fearing potential health hazards or disliking the appearance and disconnecting juxtaposition of tower and community character. While the Act preserves local zoning powers, it prohibits their use to regulate access to the services. Consequently, owing to local residents' resistance to siting antennas, several jurisdictions, including King County and the city of Tacoma, have declared temporary moratoria while they devise plans to accommodate these services in a socially acceptable manner.

Beyond the regulators and the utility companies, the public agency most involved in local communications is the Washington State Department of Transportation (WSDOT). The national Intelligent Transportation Systems program (ITS) has helped to develop the existing information infrastructure to manage freight and passenger traffic flows as well as to enhance safety and emergency response systems. An innovative Surveillance, Control, and Driver Information (SC&DI) network was completed in the mid 1990s, with fiber optic and analog video cables installed along most of King County's freeways. The SC&DI system will extend along the region's freeways into Snohomish and Pierce Counties by the end of the millennium. Ironically, the WSDOT is prohibited by state law from installing infrastructure for non-transportation purposes; hence it is now investigating ways in which it can rent the considerable unused capacity of its fiber optic cables. Such restrictions are now being reconsidered, as different levels and units of government do not want to rely on privately installed capacity for their own use.

Overall, the region's telecommunications infrastructure appears to be reasonably well developed, although the highly competitive climate in the private sector, combined with the complexity of coordinating public entities, makes it difficult to assess either its effectiveness or its possible impact on future development.

Conclusion

Insufficiencies in land transportation infrastructure will continue to plague the region for the foreseeable future. Current economic strength has provided a few windows of hope for uncovering local sources of funding. In the early 1990s the state passed several laws on growth management which mandate that jurisdictions adopt plans to govern public spending and to insure that growth takes place where infrastructure exists or is built at least at the same time as development occurs (the concept is called "concurrency"). Impact fees are also being assessed for new development to assume some of the infrastructure costs. Further, cities are either passing or considering levies for needed road repairs. Also, the $3 billion RTA plan is proof that a positive economic outlook, combined with readily tangible congestion, are moving the electorate to raise local sales tax and motor vehicle excise tax to improve transportation.

At the state level, however, heated debates have failed to bring agreement on increasing the gasoline tax as an appropriate means to cover current budgetary shortfalls. Finally, while cultural and legal conditions prevent certain pricing measures from being effective, traffic management techniques, including increased charges for parking and campaigns to modify behaviors, have been moderately successful in changing aspects of transportation demand.

REGIONAL MANAGEMENT

Urban planning has been high on the region's agenda following the passage of the State Growth Management Act in 1990–91. A powerful set of laws, the Act emanated from widespread concerns for preserving the quality of the state's natural environment and for controlling the cost of new infrastructure while also accommodating robust economic growth. Modeled on similar legislation in Florida and Oregon, these laws call for restraining further sprawl by monitoring growth, maintaining the current urban service structure, and reinforcing existing activity centers. Counties, and the fastest-growing jurisdictions within them, are to adopt comprehensive plans for future development based on infrastructure "concurrency," and to address issues shared by and overlapping the different jurisdictions. Each city's or county's plan must address transportation, land use, capital facilities, economic development, housing, and utilities together, and in the way they affect each other. The plans must also be consistent with adjacent areas of neighboring jurisdictions. Finally, the operating expenditures of a given jurisdiction must be consistent with its plan—part of a Strategic Capital Investment Plan.

As a result of the Act, the four counties and primary cities in the central Puget Sound adopted "Vision 2020," a growth and transportation "strategy," to guide the management of the region's future with the goals of conserving forests and farmland, keeping existing cities and centers vital, and facilitating more efficient provision of transportation and other services. An urban growth area (UGA) was agreed upon to establish limits on sprawl and to "bound" the land supply for development over the next 20 years. Urban Centers were also designated to serve as loci of concentrated future development. The 21 centers so identified represent the primary nodes of activity already existing in the region, and include the centers of many suburban jurisdictions. There are 12 Urban Centers in King County (five in Seattle alone), three in Snohomish (one in Everett), five in Pierce (two in Tacoma), and one in Bremerton, the major urban area in Kitsap County. Occupying less than 1 percent of the region's land area, the centers currently house almost 5 percent of the population and nearly 30 percent of all jobs. They are expected to incorporate 8 percent of the population growth and 32 percent of the employment growth projected between now and 2020.

The region's future clearly depends on successfully enforcing the mandates of the State Growth Management Act. In principle, the focus on existing multiple cores, together with the current freeway network, provides a strong and workable structure for further development. The RTA/Sound Transit plan further reinforces the region's growth strategy. The region's counties and most of its cities now have completed their jurisdictional plans, all of which are reviewed and approved for compliance with the Act. This state of affairs is an important accomplishment in its own right and unique in the nation (with the exception of Portland, Oregon). Issues are emerging, however, regarding how these plans can or will actually affect eventual development.

First, the plans address long-term goals and projections for the region which are difficult to control in the short and medium terms. Generally, the long-term emphasis of the plans provides so many options in locating infrastructure and private development in the short term that regional imbalances are likely to occur. At this point, for example, only a few Urban Centers are experiencing high pressures for development (as is the city of Redmond, Microsoft's headquarters). Many are stagnating. Likewise, housing development pressures continue at the region's fringe, while only a few Urban Centers are successful in attracting residential facilities. Hence increasing differences in the relative importance of the designated Urban Centers raise new questions about infrastructure provision, with congestion in the successful centers and overcapacity in others. Further, institutional constraints and short-term political struggles tend to steer infrastructure development in areas which are not necessarily in tune with the logic of the plans. For example, while the RTA plan calls for the completion of the high-occupancy-vehicle lanes in King County as the core of the region, short-term WSDOT plans for the expansion of limited access highways now appear to equalize the distribution of resources between counties: current Capital Improvement budgets schedule Pierce County to receive as much as King County, even though it represents 20 percent of the land area within the UGA—versus 49 percent for King. Snohomish County to the north will receive about half of King County's allocation. Hence state programs now work to "even out" the distribution of transportation infrastructure in the region at a rate which is faster than the one anticipated by the long-range plans, and, as a result, to support development away from the "core" of urbanized central Puget Sound earlier than planned.

Secondly, the proliferation of jurisdictions in the region greatly complicates regional management as intended by the plans. For example, water, sewers, and transportation continue to be administered at the county, multicounty, or state level, and, in theory, to remain somewhat immune to the numbers and types of jurisdictions within these units. In reality, however, managing these services entails collaborative arrangements which are very sensitive to the number of jurisdictions involved.

The number of new suburban cities incorporating has continued to rise since Seattle stopped annexing in the 1950s. Today counties and cities form almost 80 jurisdictions in the central Puget Sound. Over the past six years alone, eight suburban cities undertook incorporation, and 12 others performed large land annexations, for a total of 172 square miles and 380,000 people opting for autonomy from their county. Suburban incorporations and annexations often work to weaken the regional "good." While at the outset they aim to gain control over such services as police and fire, they also often discourage "unwanted growth" in the form of non-single family, medium density residential development, and to unduly increase their supply of revenue-producing commercial and industrial land. Indeed, the low densities of recently incorporated or annexed areas—2,000 people per square mile against 3,000 for the region—suggest that the Growth Management Act's goal of restraining sprawl will be harder to pursue in the future.

Finally, increases in the number of financially independent jurisdictions work to increase competitive forces in the region and eventually support short-term, market-driven development patterns. The growing supply of commercial land reinforces the propensity for small employment centers to emerge outside of the existing Urban Centers. Many small activity centers already exist, and are continuing to form beyond the designated centers. These small centers further diffuse travel patterns and therefore weaken the region's transportation framework.

CONCLUSION

Will the shock city of the twenty-first century retain its luster in the long run? Answers to this question are necessarily tainted by the excessive optimism generated by the economic boom at the turn of the millennium. In taking stock, the first step is to recognize that the region exhibits special, positive features which will remain relatively independent of the fluctuations of the economy.

- Overall population projections are comparatively low, even in the long run, and—unlike California's, for example—include a limited number of foreign immigrants.
- The region's employment base is serendipitously anchored in what are considered promising and non-polluting industries.
- Its vast, first-class natural environment is likely able to sustain some of the worst assaults of even unchecked urbanization.

These are the region's inherited "lucky charms." Beyond

them, however, two features emanating from local wisdom also help to paint a bright future.

First, the region's acceptance of and energetic response to the Growth Management Act clearly is an excellent and commendable first step in addressing growth in a coordinated fashion. Resistance to the Urban Growth Boundary remains relatively tamed and most jurisdictions have acquiesced and managed to develop comprehensive plans. A second and unique aspect lies in the strength of Seattle as the region's vibrant central city and in the leadership that the city has been able to provide in the arena of environmental and social responsibility. If these two attributes, a vigorous flagship city and the will to coordinate regional development, continue, then the central Puget Sound has a chance to retain its aura of being a good place.

Less positive prospects can be detected in the provision of infrastructure. The dependence on automobile travel, the increasingly limited budgets available for transportation infrastructure, and the public's reluctance to invest in the long term could significantly affect mobility and accessibility, which in turn will affect productivity and trade. State politics will play an important role in securing a brighter future in this regard, yet it is not clear that the tensions between rural, suburban, and urban interests can be sorted out.

Affordable, quality housing was an important part of the region's draw until the 1980s. The current geographic spread, combined with transportation congestion, demands innovative approaches to both urban and suburban housing. Yet only a few jurisdictions have been able or willing to promote such approaches. Housing affordability is becoming the second issue, after transportation, affecting employers' competitiveness. Regional approaches to affordable housing are lacking, and public awareness among the general population is so low that this element could well become the region's greatest weakness as the twenty-first century progresses.

Similarly, a lack of funding for public education, combined with a lack of coordination between regional planning and education policy, may undermine the region's future. This aspect of infrastructure cannot be addressed in detail within the confines of this text—suffice it to note that the lack of attention will continue to plague residential location choice and quality of life.

In summary, we can safely predict that growth and densification will take place in the central Puget Sound, yet it is not possible to anticipate whether this growth will yield the planned integrated mixed-use cores and whether the Urban Growth Boundary will remain. Most likely, further "Los Angelization" of the urbanized region will take place, along with further consolidation of urbanized and urbanizing centers, principally in King County, and near Seattle. This mixed scenario can be influenced as well by whether or not the concept of Cascadia evolves into an economic and physical reality. Cascadia likely offers the greatest and yet untapped potential for the central Puget Sound to enter the twenty-first century. Geography, culture, trade, and travel patterns suggest that perhaps the most promising investment in infrastructure will be the provision of high-speed rail along the Cascadia Main Street corridor. The 300 mile stretch, with Seattle almost exactly half way between Portland, Oregon, and Vancouver, British Columbia, could be traversed in time distances of less than two hours between each of the three metro areas. Reaching out to neighboring urbanized regions in the Cascadia basin will help to address some of the issues facing international trade, to promote tourism, and to provide access to a broader range of services—including sea- and airport facilities and higher education—without having to duplicate them.

BIBLIOGRAPHY

Artibise, Alan, Moudon, Anne Vernez, and Seltzer, Ethan (1997) "Cascadia: an Emerging Regional Model," in Robert Geddes (ed.) *Cities in our Future*, Washington DC: Island Press.

Brambilla, Roberto, and Longo, Gianni (1979) *Learning from Seattle*, Washington DC: Partners for Livable Places.

City of Seattle (1991) "Seattle's Character," Office of Long-range Planning, April.

City of Seattle (1994) "Toward a Sustainable Seattle: a Plan for Managing Growth, 1994–2014." Adopted July 25.

David Evans & Associates (1996) "Statewide Communications Strategic Plan, Final Report" prepared for the Washington State Department of Transportation, March.

Findlay, John M., and Coates, Kenneth S. (eds) (forthcoming) *On Brotherly Terms: Canadian–American Relations West of the Rockies*, Seattle, WA: University of Washington Press.

Hammer, John, and Chapman, Bruce (1993) *International Seattle: Creating a Globally Competitive Community*, Seattle WA: Discovery Institute.

Morrill, Richard, and Hodge, David C. (1991) "Myths and Facts about Growth Management," University of Washington, Department of Geography, January.

Moudon, Anne Vernez, Wiseman, Bill, and Kwang-joong Kim (eds) (1990) *Master-planned Communities: Shaping Exurbs in the 1990s*, Seattle WA: University of Washington College of Architecture and Urban Planning.

Moudon, Anne Vernez, Ryan, Dennis, Schmidt, Eric, and Sidener, Jack (1981) "Seattle, Washington," in *Case Studies of Ten Cities*, Environmental Design Administration, US Department of Housing and Urban Development, Office of Policy Development and Research, September.

Pivo, Gary (1990) "The Net of Mixed Beads: Suburban Office Development in Six Metropolitan Regions," *Journal of the American Planning Association*, autumn, pp. 457–69.

Puget Sound Regional Council (1993) *Foundation for the Future: An Economic Strategy for the Central Puget Sound Region* I, *An Economic Profile: Our Jobs, People and Resources*, Puget Sound Regional Council, October.

Puget Sound Regional Council (1996) "The Costs of Transportation: A Report for the Transportation Pricing Task Force of the Transportation Policy Board," Puget Sound Regional Council, October 10.

Puget Sound Regional Council (1997a) "Regional Review: Monitoring Change in the Central Puget Sound Region," Puget Sound Regional Council, September.

Puget Sound Regional Council (1997b) "Urban Centers in the Central Puget Sound Region: A Baseline Summary and Comparison, Winter 1996–97," Puget Sound Regional Council.

Sale, Roger (1978) *Seattle, Past to Present*, Seattle WA: University of Washington Press.

Other sources

Trade Development Alliance; *Puget Sound Business Journal*; State of Washington, Office of Financial Management, Forecasting Division; US Census.

11 The Taipei region

NEIN-HSIUNG KUO

The Taipei metropolitan area is located in the northwestern section of Taiwan, facing the Taiwan Strait (see Figure 11.1). It is the political, economic, and cultural center of Taiwan. With an area of 1,895.53 km^2, or 5.25 percent of the total area of Taiwan, the Taipei metropolitan area consists of Taipei City and 24 neighboring cities and towns that are highly dependent on the main center. Under the guidelines of the Northern Regional Plan it has developed into an integrated, multifaceted, metropolitan area (see Figure 11.2).

It is connected by the national motorway network (Sun Yat-sen Freeway) to the port city of Keelung, which is 25 km away to the northeast. About 80 km away, to the southeast, lies Ilan City. Upon the completion of the planned Taipei Ilan Freeway, the travel time between the two places will be reduced to 50 minutes, which is expected to expand the boundary of the metropolitan area and bring more prosperity to the cities and towns on the Ilan plains. Going west on the Sun Yat-sen Freeway, one will find the Chiang Kai-shek International Airport 40 km away from Taipei City center. Farther south, the Hsinchu Science-based Industrial Park, a community where most of the high-technology industries in Taiwan concentrate, is 75 km away.

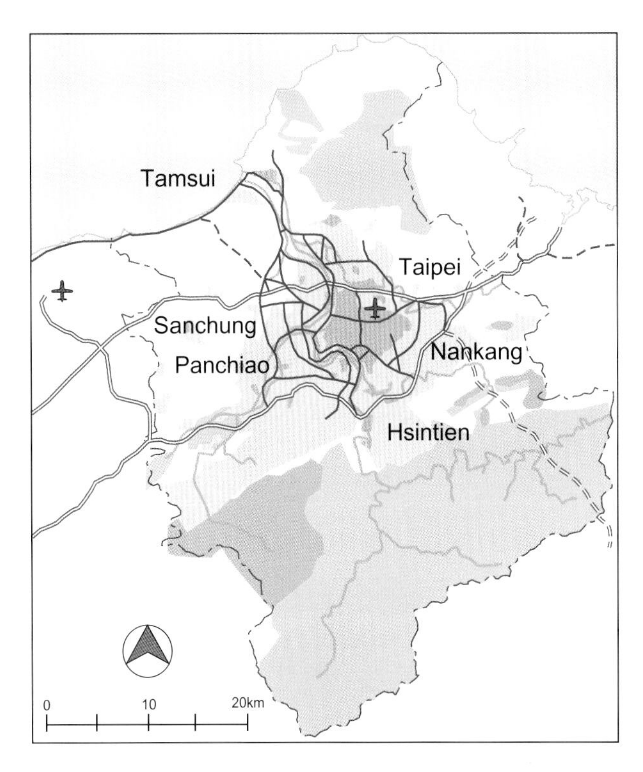

Figure 11.1 The Taipei region, 1995

The land use character of the metropolitan area is composed of mixed uses downtown. Because of the mix of living and commerce, day and night city activities never stop. There is little racial and income segregation, owing, some would say, to the Chinese cultural character. Lack of parking lots and related public facilities, like parks and open spaces, is due to development along main streets. This impacts road functions and environmental quality, but has, perhaps, some benefits for the average commuting time in Taipei metropolis, which was 38.1 minutes in 1993. The results of mixed land uses probably reduce trips and traffic volumes and result in less demand for parking spaces.

Figure 11.2 The location of the Taipei region

From 1985 to the present, the government of the Republic of China has been actively engaged in the promotion of national construction projects. These and other important construction projects are discussed below.

Figure 11.3 The Taipei region from the air

CHANGING ECONOMIC PATTERNS

As an island located in the west Pacific, Taiwan enjoys a favorable geographical location and it is logical that foreign trade has become the main sector of its economy. From the beginning, more effort was put into promoting exports to increase foreign currency reserves. These grew from US$20.6 billion in 1971 to US$76.2 billion in 1991, at the average annual growth rate of 6.8 percent. On the other hand, with the rise of income, more local demand has emerged, raising imports to US$62.8 billion. The surplus of foreign trade has risen from US$216.4 million in 1971 to US$13.3 billion in 1991, at an average annual growth rate of 9.4 percent (see Table 11.1).

Table 11.1 Value of foreign trade in Taiwan (US$000)

	Exports	Imports	Balance	GDP
1971	2,060,393	1,843,938	216,455	6,592,000
1981	22,611,197	21,199,551	1,411,646	48,218,000
1991	76,178,309	62,860,545	13,317,764	179,370,000
1995	111,659,000	103,550,000	8,109,000	260,175,000

The growth of commerce and industry in this area naturally attracted the other sectors of economy, for instance banking and other services. This has led to tertiary industries concentrating mostly in the Taipei metropolis and becoming the most important business in the area. As a proportion of the whole economy it has risen from the 58 percent in 1971 to the 60 percent in 1995 (see Table 11.2). This has also made Taipei an economic, financial, trading, and service center. In terms of industrial development, automation technology has contributed to the slowing down of employment rates in the secondary

Table 11.2 Industrial structures in the Taipei metropolitan area

	Primary industry			Secondary industry			Tertiary industry			Total		
	People	**Proportion**	**Annual growth rate**	**People**	**Proportion**	**Annual growth rate**	**People**	**Proportion**	**Annual growth rate**	**People**	**Proportion**	**Annual growth rate**
1971	129,517	(13%)	–	300,605	(29%)	–	595,565	(100%)	–	1,027,457	(100%)	–
1981	114,038	(5%)	–1.26%	786,653	(38%)	10.10%	1,185,729	(57%)	7.13%	2,086,420	(100%)	7.34%
1991	41,000	(1.8%)	–9.72%	877,000	(38.2%)	1.09%	1,380,000	(60%)	1.52%	2,298,000	(100%)	0.97%
1995	31,000	(1.2%)	–6.75%	889,000	(35.4%)	0.34%	1,591,000	(63.4%)	3.62%	2,511,000	(100%)	2.24%

Source *Urban and Regional Development Statistics 1971–91*, CEPD, Executive Yuan, Republic of China.

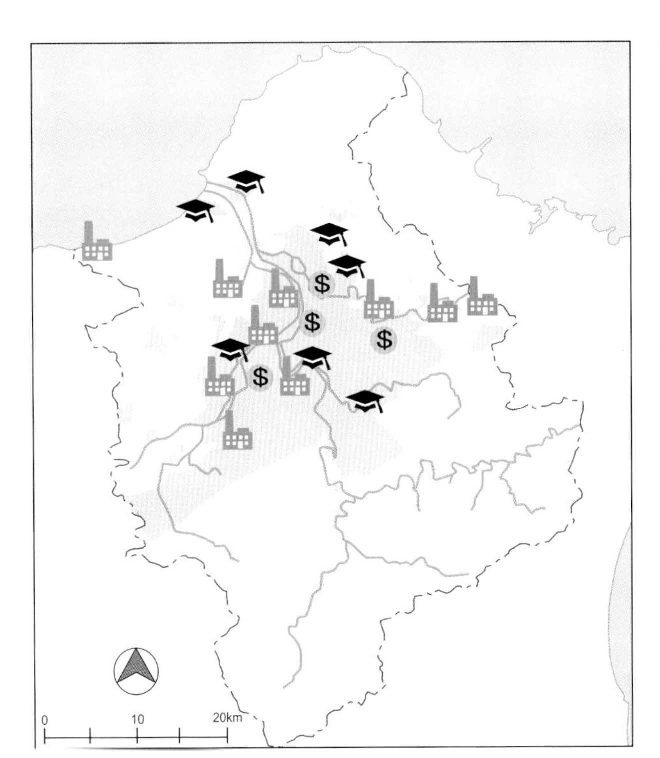

Figure 11.4 Economic patterns in the Taipei region

Table 11.3 Average annual income per household (US$)

	Taipei city	**Taipei metropolitan area**	**Taiwan areas**
1971	7,075	6,250	4,875
1981	12,613	12,504	9,922
1991	35,571	31,544	26,548
1995	43,131	36,792	32,069

Notes [a] Calculated according to the purchasing power of the currency in 1991. [b] Exchange rate in 1971: US$ = NT$40.00; in 1981: US$ = NT$36.79; in 1991: US$ = 26.82; in 1995: US$ = NT$26.49.

industries. There was a decline from 10.10 percent average growth in the 1980s to 1.09 percent in the 1990s. Major industry has changed from being labor-intensive to technology-intensive.

The average annual family income has risen from US$6,250 in 1971 to US$36,792 in 1995 in the Taipei metropolitan area. In Taipei City itself the figures are US$7,075 in 1971 and US$43,131 in 1995. The numbers are significantly higher than those of the rest of Taiwan and the relative prosperity and wealth of this region are clear. Table 11.3 shows annual average income for the three areas.

CHANGING SOCIAL PATTERNS

The proportion of the population in the Taipei metropolitan area to that of the whole Taiwan area has increased from 19.7 percent in 1971 to 28.2 percent in 1991, indicating a trend of population concentration in the Taipei metropolitan area.

The population in the Taipei metropolitan area grew from 2.96 million in 1971 to 5.79 million in 1991, and 5.92 million in 1995. That is, the population grew 2.83 million during 20 years, at an average annual growth rate of 3.42 percent. On the other hand, the annual growth rate shows a steady decline over the same period, from 4.1 percent in 1971 to 1.15 percent in 1991. At a closer look, the rate of natural increase dropped to 1.09 percent in 1991 as a result of the promotion of family planning and rapid urbanization.

Table 11.4 Population growth and motor vehicles in the Taipei metropolitan area

Items	Areas	1971	1981	1991	1995
Population	Taipei city	1,804,605	2,270,983	2,717,992	2,632,863
	Suburban areas	1,155,261	2,281,428	3,079,074	3,285,948
	Taipei metropolitan area	2,959,866	4,552,411	5,797,066	5,918,811
		(20.8%)	(25.1%)	(28.2%)	(27.8%)
	Taiwan area	14,257,543	18,135,508	20,556,842	21,304,181
POP annual growth rate (%)	Taipei city	3.78	2.19	0.18	
	Suburban areas	4.55	4.01	2.00	
	Taipei metropolitan area	4.10	3.12	1.15	
POP natural growth rate (%)	Taipei city	2.04	1.57	0.94	
	Suburban areas	2.50	2.19	1.23	
	Taipei metropolitan area	2.23	1.89	1.09	
POP social growth rate (%)	Taipei city	1.74	0.62	-0.76	
	Suburban areas	2.05	1.82	0.77	
	Taipei metropolitan area	1.87	1.23	0.06	
Motor vehicles	Taipei city	158,756	614,249	1,178,717	1,350,274
	Taiwan area	957,295	5,413,407	10,611,037	13,204,478
Motorcycles	Taipei city	113,268	406,140	662,721	735,015
	Taiwan area	826,492	4,541,547	7,439,081	8,517,024
Car ownership	Taipei city	8.8%	27.0%	43.3%	51.2%
	Taiwan area	6.7%	29.8%	51.6%	62.0%

Note Percentage figures are based on the proportion of population in Taipei metropolitan area over the country as a whole

Table 11.5 Age structures of population in Taipei metropolitan area (%)

Age structure	1971	1981	1991
0–14	37.6	31.7	26.7
15–65	59.8	64.5	67.5
Over 652.6	3.8	5.8	

Table 11.6 Top 20% and bottom 20% income groups in Taiwan area

Income groups	1966	1975	1983	1993	1995
Top 20%	41.45	38.63	37.54	38.66	38.99
Bottom 20%	7.90	8.84	8.61	7.13	7.30
Top 20% / bottom 20%	5.24	4.37	4.36	5.42	5.34

The growth rate of the in-migrating population (i.e. the rate of social increase) has dropped from 1.87 percent to 0.06 percent in 1991, showing the slowing down of the concentration. At the same time, within the whole metropolitan area, the percentage of people in the city has also declined from 61 percent in 1971 to 47 percent in 1991. All this shows the changing trend of population concentration and the move toward the suburban areas.

The figures in Table 11.5 clearly show the trend that the Taipei metropolitan area is developing into an ageing society. In Table 11.6 it is clear that the relative earnings of the top 20 percent of income earners have remained roughly the same over 40 years.

CHANGING SPATIAL PATTERNS

In the past 40 years, with the large investment in public facilities, urban planning, and rapid industrial development, the pattern of population settlement has also changed. The spatial structure of the Taipei metropolitan area has transformed from a single-core to a multicore model.

1945–67

The railroad was the main transportation system until the 1970s. In each city, development was centered around the train station and moved outward. Upon the restoration of Taiwan in 1945, the majority of the population in Taipei Hsien concentrated on Panchiao and Jui-fang. The new generation after the Second World War mainly resided in Hsin-tien, Chung-ho, Yung-ho, San-chung, and Panchiao. In 1962, in order to tear down the buildings without license and rehouse the residents, public housing was built in the southern area of the airport and Keelung Road. There were major improvements in the quality of new buildings during the 1960s. In 1967 Taipei City was upgraded to a national city and deservedly enjoyed its position as the center of political, economic, and cultural activities, while Taipei County mainly accommodated manufacturing industries, suburban housing areas, and inexpensive settlements for immigrants from the countryside.

1967–85

Between the 1970s and the 1980s the main transportation system in Taiwan became the highways. The successful completion of many transportation projects, including the Sun Yat-sen Freeway in 1978, the electrification of the longitudinal railroad in 1979, and the opening of CKS Airport in 1979, were all the result of the full-scale effort to improve the transportation systems. The new freeway resulted in much more convenient transportation in the western corridor. In cities, where the main commercial areas had been gathered around the train station, the development now turned to the areas along the main highway routes. After Taipei was upgraded to the status of national capital in 1967, with the ability to manage the development of the towns and suburbs in Taipei County, it began to turn into a modern and highly developed international metropolis. Private cars gradually became the major means of transportation in the city. The traffic systems in the metropolitan area, like the main and arterial road system, the overpass system, the underground railroad lines, and the planning for the MRT system, were all important projects in this period, which changed the nature of the core city (Taipei).

1985 to the present

In the 1980s, upon the imposition of a new construction floor space index in Taipei City, many construction companies built houses in the neighboring towns and cities of Taipei County to avoid the limitation. This caused a rapid growth in the number of housing units in Taipei County and attracted more new immigrants. Due to the frequent disputes over labor and environmental protection in this period, many manufacturers closed their factories to erect high-rise housing or office buildings for sale. Many buildings in the new industrial zones were also used as offices or warehouses.

Examining the migration process from the rural to the urban areas, it is clear that, in the case of Taipei County, the labor-intensive factories in cities like San-chung, Hsin-chuang, Panchiao, Chung-ho, Yung-ho, and Hsin-tien attracted most immigrants. In the 1970s, when the factories moved out to towns in the outskirts, such as Shu-lin and Wu-ku, the new country migrants also moved toward those places, resulting in some of the fastest growing populations in these areas. On the other hand, there is also a trend in the past few years where dwellers in Taipei City are moving out to cities and towns in Taipei County. The main reasons may be the insufficient space in the urban areas, the high housing prices, and the moving of some service industries into the neighboring areas. The overall social increase rate in Taipei metropolitan area has declined since the 1970s but, in comparison with other cities and towns in Taiwan, it is still one of the highest. This suggests that the peak of migration into the city is over but the Taipei metropolis still attracts a large number of new immigrants every year.

The concentration of population in the metropolis in recent years is quite different from that in the 1970s. By examining the change of the population growth rate and the size of population between 1986 and 1991, it can be found that Taipei metropolitan area and the six adjacent cities like Panchiao, San-chung, etc., which enjoyed the highest population growth rate in the past, now are all witnessing a decline in the population growth rate. On the other hand, with the completion of some new construction projects, like the second freeway in the northern region and the MRT system, some towns and cities on the outskirts, like Hsi-chih, Shenkeng, Sanhsia, and Tamsui, are attracting more migrants. The spatial structure of population distribution in the metropolitan area has also undergone dramatic change and the sphere of influence of the metropolitan area is expanding.

INFRASTRUCTURE INVESTMENT

Taiwan entered the railroad era in 1900, before which waterway transportation dominated. In terms of marine transportation, the initial construction of the Keelung harbor was completed in 1900. In the period of Japanese occupation (1895–1945) the first priority was to actively engage in transportation construction for the purpose of military control and economic exploitation.

As a result of World War II (the Pacific War), Taiwan was intensively bombed by the Allies at the end of the Japanese occupation. All transportation infrastructure was affected to a great extent. Recovery did not gather pace until after the central government of China relocated to Taiwan at the end of 1949 and US aid began to arrive in Taiwan from 1952. At that time, all investment in transportation came from US loans or aid. During the period when US aid poured into Taiwan (1951–65), however, major development in the transportation infrastructure did not occur because capital was invested in production activities. Only investment for the minimum and absolutely necessary transportation construction was made. Since this period, however, many major infrastructure projects have been implemented, as will be discussed.

Roads

In 1945 everything was waiting to be raised from the ruins after World War II. Road construction focused on the principle of rebuilding existing roads to their original functions. There was little improvement in terms of engineering standards or construction technologies. After Taipei was designated as a provincial city after 1945, the grid pattern of the road system remained what it was during the Japanese occupation. With the old town as the center, development went eastward and so did roads, although the roads maintained a chessboard formation.

When the central government of China was relocated to Taiwan, Taipei became the temporary location for the central government with the result that the population increased dramatically. The number of construction projects also increased rapidly. By 1967 the population surpassed the million mark.

By 1960 Taipei had become the political, military, cultural, economic, and financial center of Taiwan. In 1967 the central government announced that Taipei would be directly under the jurisdiction of the central government. In 1968 the six towns of Neihu, Nankan, Mucha, Chingmei, Shihlin and Peitou were annexed by Taipei to support the requirements of city construction and development.

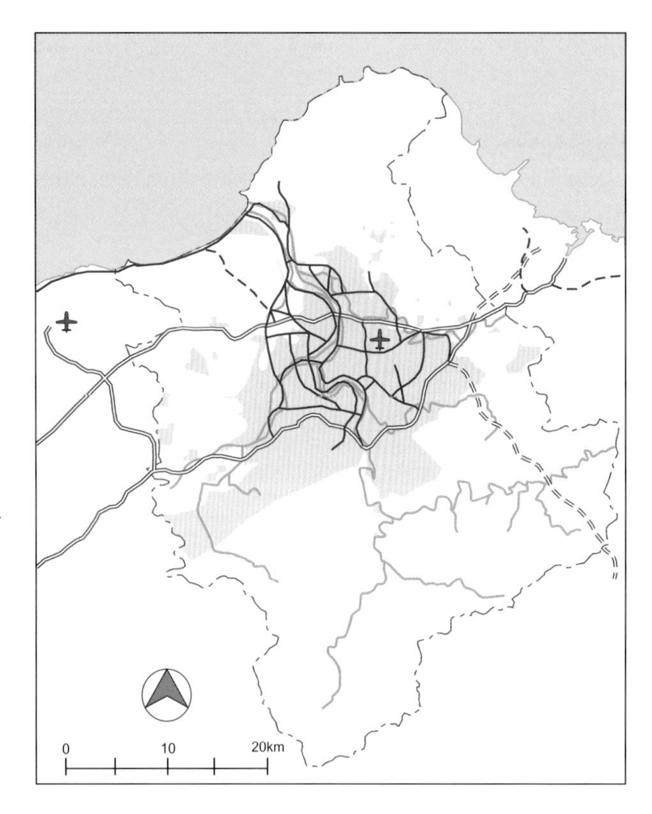

Figure 11.5 Main roads and airports in the Taipei region

During the 1970s road construction began to evolve from two-dimensional development to three-dimensional elevated expressways. The elevated Huanho South Road was built in 1972; the North Gate elevated expressway was completed in 1978; the Cheinkuo expressway was completed in 1983; the Hsinghei elevated expressway was completed in 1989. As for roads connecting regions outside the city, six major transportation corridors were formed between Taipei and neighboring towns: Keelung, Tamsui, Taoyuan, Shanshia, Chungho, and Hsintien.

Because of the spatial barriers, such as the Tamsui river system in the southeast and the basin characteristics, the progress of Taipei's metropolitan expansion and growth can be characterized by the construction of bridges. In addition, the construction and renovation of the bridges connecting Taipei and neighboring towns accelerated the mobilization of population and the development of these neighboring towns. For example, there was only Chungcheng Bridge between Taipei and Chungho and Yung-ho. Later on, the Fuho Bridge (1973), Hwachung Bridge (1976), and Yongfu Bridge (1984) were built, which accelerated the development of Chungho and Yung-ho to become two of the satellite cities of Taipei.

The road system in the Taipei metropolitan area has expanded in the form of a net which, although the road system had already adopted a grid pattern in the urban planning of 1937, is more informal in the surrounding townships where new roads were not fully supervised and controlled. The growth in *per capita* income and automobile ownership has continued to push up the demand for transportation facilities, though the construction of public facilities in Taipei County is far slower than that enjoyed by Taipei City. Road construction fails to satisfy the demand of transportation, which causes traffic quality to deteriorate in the suburbs of the metropolitan area.

In the past, both the provincial and municipal governments had devised development projects concerning expressway systems but effective integration and coordination in the operations of provincial and municipal projects were often lacking. There are still a number of problems in the overall development of expressway systems, and the overall road network structure is far from perfect. The standards of planning and installation are inconsistent; connecting points among the road network are not effectively integrated; traffic control systems have yet to be planned and established for greater support; and the lack of a budget leads to delayed construction schedules. These problems are yet to be solved. To facilitate the comprehensive development of the entire expressway system, initial planning for the overall development and construction projects of expressway systems in Taipei metropolitan area was devised in 1996 so as to integrate and facilitate the construction of expressway systems (see Figure 11.5).

Rail

Except for the section from Keelung to Hsinchu, which was 102.7 km in length and built by the Ching Dynasty, most of the railroads in Taiwan were built by the Japanese government. After the restoration of Taiwan, however, there were several major developments of new lines.

The various tasks of the electrification of rail began in 1974. They were listed as one of the ten National Construction Projects at the time. The entire line from Keelung to Kaohsiung started operation on July 1, 1979, ushering in the modernization era of Taiwan rail. In 1979 another rail project among the Ten Construction Projects, the North Loop Rail, began operation. It runs from Nanshenhu Station in Ilan in the north to Hsincheng Station in Hwalien in the south. It connects important points between two major lines in the east and west, playing a major role in development and tourism in the east and even in national defense. In 1992 the South Loop Rail, among the Twelve Major Construction Projects, was completed, which realized the dream of an around-the-island rail route.

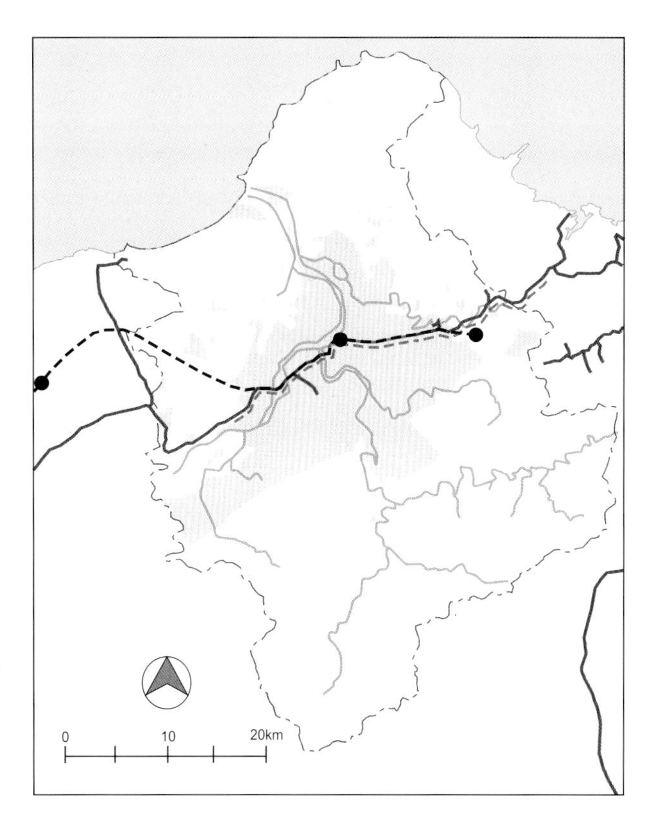

Figure 11.6 Railways in the Taipei region

The north–south high-speed rail construction project was approved on June 25, 1992. The planned route totaled 345 km (double track), starting from Shichi in Taipei and ending at Tzuoyin in Kaohsiung. A total of seven stations were designated along the line, including Taipei, Taoyuan, Hsinchu, Taichung, Giayi, Tainan and Kaohsiung (see Figure 11.6).

The total construction budget of HSR is estimated at around NT$441.9 billion. The government plans to finance NT$251 billion, and the rest will come from capital investment by the private sector through the means of BOT (build, operate, and transfer). The first stage of bidding for private investment was officially announced in October 1996. Private investors are required to complete the construction project and begin operation by July 2004.

The underground rail project in Taipei metropolitan area was carried out in stages from July 1983 to support overall city development, to eliminate the barriers produced by level crossings, relieve the city of traffic bottlenecks, and support the MRT system and HSR. The project includes the underground construction of Taipei Station, Songshan construction project, Wanban construction project and Nankan project planning operations.

In December 1977 the Committee of Transportation Planning of the Ministry of Transportation and Communication completed the initial planning of the MRT system for Taipei metropolitan area, and devised the MRT network in 1981. During the same time, the Taipei government planned to introduce a medium capacity rapid transit (MCRT) system to assist a high-capacity system. The Taipei government officially established the Department of Rapid Transit Systems (DORTS) in 1987 to take over the planning, design, submission of amendment alternatives to the TRTS lines. Meanwhile, controversial sections of the approved network were further studied to present eight lines (the Tanshiu, Hsintiene, Nankang, Panchiao, Chungho, Muchas, and Neihu lines and a maintenance line). The project totaled 86.8 km with 79 stops. The Mucha line (12.9 km) and the first section of the Tamsui line, between Tamsui and Chungshan Station (22.8 km) are now operational.

The budget required for the initial network is estimated at NT$440 billion, 50 percent of which comes from the central government and the other 50 percent from local governments (36.875 percent from Taipei City government, and 13.125 percent from the provincial government).

An assessment of the later development network of the TRTS was completed in 1991, which includes Hsinyi, Songshan, Hsinchuang, Luchou, MCRT Loop, Nankang east extension line and Tanhei New Town line. These routes have yet to be approved.

To substantiate the government policy of developing the CKS International Airport into an Asia-Pacific operations center, the central government has decided to funnel private capital into the construction of the transit network from Taipei to the airport by means of a BOT scheme. The goals are to meet the demand of large volume transportation, provide passengers with a comfortable and convenient public transit system, and shorten the journey time between the airport and Taipei. At present, this transit network is still in the planning stage. The target year envisaged is 2021.

Airports

After relocating to Taiwan in 1949 the central government designated Taipei Sungshan Airport, built during the Japanese occupation, as the international airport, and opened Tainan Airport as an auxiliary international airport. The volume of air travel grew 30 percent between 1960 and 1970. In view of the rapid growth of air travel and the limited capacity of the Sungshan Airport runway, the government started to look for a place to build an international airport in the northern region in 1967. Construction of CKS Airport was officially begun in July 1974. By February 1979 the first phase of the project was complete and open to traffic. Taipei Sungshan Airport was then changed into a domestic airport.

The CKS international airport is about 40 km away from downtown Taipei. The maximum take-off and land per hour is 60. At present, the number applies only during peak hours. There are 22 passenger plane aprons and 12 cargo plane aprons, all of which can accommodate wide-body jets. The passenger terminal covers an area of 144,000 m^2. The annual capacity is 12 million persons, with 4,000 persons passing through the terminal during peak hours. The cargo terminal covers an area of 62,000 m^2, with an annual capacity of 400,000 tonnes, and is well equipped with state-of-the-art facilities.

The original master plan of the CKS Airport was meant to be implemented in three phases, including three parallel runways, three passenger terminals and a cargo terminal. The CKS Airport expansion project includes the construction of the second phase passenger terminal (expected passenger volume at 20 million persons annually), the expansion of the existing cargo terminal (expected cargo volume at 1.41 million tonnes annually), with the construction of aprons and connecting stop ways. All are scheduled to be completed and open to traffic in 1999.

The proposal of central government is to build the CKS Airport into the Asia-Pacific Air Transport Center. Taiwan is located at a strategic position between Southeast Asia and Northeast Asia, boasting the best geographical position to serve as the Asia-Pacific Transit Center. In addition, the CKS Airport is the most distant airport in the Far East a long-distance flight from the west coast of the United States can reach without refueling. (Flights to Hong Kong need to refuel at the CKS Airport in the winter.) Direct flights from CKS Airport can reach the west coast of the United States and Canada, New Zealand and Australia. The goals of the planning for an air transport center include:

- In the short term (1997) develop the CKS Airport into an air cargo transit center, at first based on existing facilities.
- Attract multinational corporations to establish their operation headquarters in Taiwan to bring momentum to the development of related high-value-added manufacturing and service industries, and in the mid term (2000) develop and expand the facilities for flight passenger transit.
- Establish the prestigious position of Taiwan as an air transit center.
- In the long term (2005), in conjunction with the project of becoming the cargo and passenger transit center, develop the CKS Airport and the surrounding area into airport cities by combining the long development of the airport with the industries and transportation infrastructure in the surrounding area.

Telecommunications

During the 1970s Taiwan reached the goal of a "telephone in every village". Between 1970 and 1980, owing to rapid economic growth, the number of local phone calls increased 68.16 percent, while that of long-distance phone calls increased 121.15 percent and that of international calls increased 61.32 percent. However, being a state-owned business in Taiwan, the telecom company was limited by its budget and the obligation to remit profits to the Treasury.

To catch up with the information age and provide better service quality, the telephone exchange units in cities are mostly digital. An integrated service digital network was completed in northern Taiwan in 1994. Under the policy of replacing copper cables and same-axis cable systems with fiber optic communication networks, high-tech fiber optic telecom technologies and equipment have been introduced to domestic long-distance communication systems. By the end of 1994 a total of 134.368 km of fiber optic network was already completed. The percentage of the use of fiber optics is as high as 95 percent, and set to reach the goal of 100 percent by 1997. Figure 11.7 shows the distribution of fiber optic systems in Taipei metropolis.

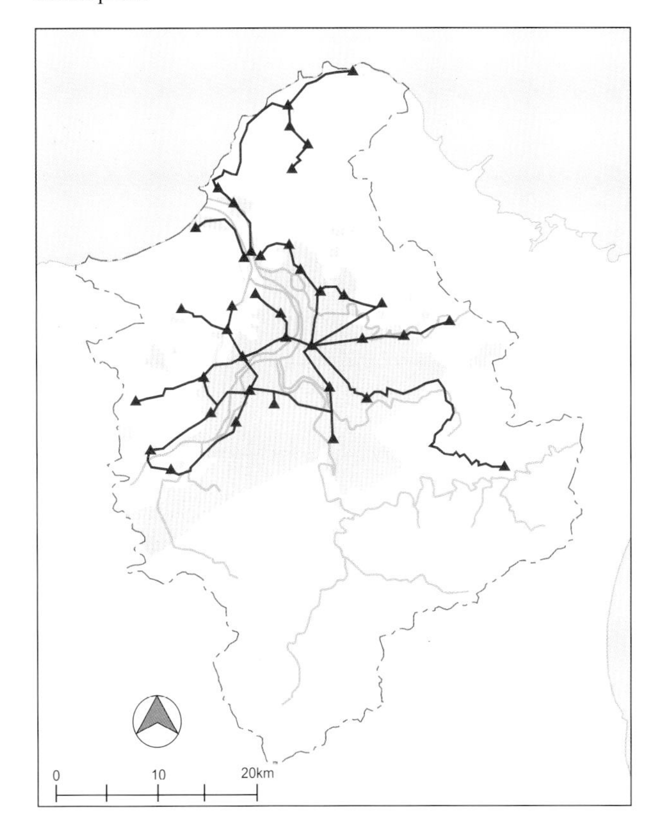

Figure 11.7 Fiber optic cable coverage in the Taipei region

In view of the importance of information to the development of science and technologies, the Directorate General of Telecommunications installed domestic and international networks connected to the internet for applications by industry, entitled Hinet. The services provided by Hinet include Telnet, e-mail, file transfer protocol (FTP), title designation and installation related to domain name service, installation of file servers related to public domain service, exchange of Netnews, and providing an international indexing database, and a domestic academic network database.

To support the government policy of building an Asia-Pacific Operations Center and increasing service quality, the telecoms business was transferred from government agency to the state-owned Chunghwa Telecom Company in 1996. A number of businesses were also gradually transferred to the private sector to reach the final goal of complete privatization. The contents of liberalization policy consist of the liberalization of end user equipment, liberalization of network use, and liberalization of business operations.

A NII (National Information Infrastructure) Promotional Task Force was established to facilitate economic growth in Taiwan, increase the competitivity of the entire country and improve the standards of living. The goal of this task force is to allow any interested party to use any kind of interactive multimedia information services through the network whenever and wherever they are. The entire information telecom project includes the establishment of seven major networks: high-speed digital exchange network, packaged exchange network (Pacnet), information acquisition network (Amnet), Hinet special line network, integrated service digital network, with a cable television visual network as part of the fiber optic infrastructure. Table 11.7 gives the indicators for telecom infrastructure.

Table 11.7 Indicators of the development of the telecom infrastructure

Indicator	1970	1980	1990	1995
% of households with telephones (number of telephones/100 persons)	3.93	19.01	40.04	55.1
ownership of mobile phones per 100 persons			0.41 person	3.61 person
ownership of personal computers per 100 persons			4.7 person	8.3 person
number of connection to the WWW network per 100 persons				1.6 person
% of households with cable TV subscriptions				76.6%

Conclusion

The above developments took place over four distinct phases during the latter half of the twentieth century: the period of American aid and system restoration (1952–64), the Period of system saturation (1965–72), the period of major construction projects (1973–81), the period of construction transformation (1982–today).

The Taipei metropolitan area has developed in radial

corridors. Home–work trips in the metropolitan area are mostly centered on the central city (about 50 percent of total passenger trips). This has resulted in some serious traffic problems on those corridors. Besides, as motor vehicles increase rapidly in number, the growth rate of motor vehicles greatly exceeds the growth rate of the road area. Take Taipei City, for instance. The growth rate of motor vehicles was 11.26 percent between 1971 and 1991 but that of the roads was only 3.51 percent. There are also some problems in the development of transportation systems, such as the fact that a complete MRT system must be built to meet the needs of developing the metropolis into multiple cores, parking spaces are insufficient, and illegal parking causes great inconvenience and affects the traffic flow. Future prospects for the construction and completion schedule of the major transportation projects in the metropolitan area are summarised in Table 11.8.

As the information industry continues to prosper, the development of telecoms will tend toward liberalization and privatization to meet social demand. In the aspect of telephone use, better communication quality will be provided; the rates for domestic long-distance calls and international calls will be further reduced. The establishment of NII can support Taiwan in realizing the goal of becoming the Asia-Pacific operations center, financial center and transit center. It can also help facilitate the elevation of the domestic information telecoms industry. Government agencies can also use the popularization of information technologies to provide all kinds of information services. In the near future, information acquisition will become easier and easier. People will access a large amount of data without running all over the place. As far as the entire Taipei metropolitan area is concerned, the number of journeys can be reduced.

Table 11.8 Future prospects of transportation systems in the Taipei metropolitan area

	Road	Rail	Air
1999	completion of the Taipei-Tocheng section of the Taipei-Ilan Freeway		completion of the Expansion Project for CKS Airport and beginning operation
2001	construction of the East-West Expressway between Pali and Hsintein		
2003	construction of the West Coastal Expressway	completion and operation of the High Speed Rail	
2006		completion of the relocation of Rail Underground in Taipei metropolitan area	
2012	completion of the Expressway systems in Taipei metropolitan areas	plan the initial phase network and long term network of Mass Rapid Transit systems in metropolitan areas, completion of the Rapid Transit Line between Taipei and the CKS Airport	

REGIONAL LAND USE PLANS AND OTHER INITIATIVES TO MANAGE REGIONAL FORM

In 1968 the Council for International Economic Cooperation and Development produced the Taipei–Keelung Metropolitan Regional Plan, to be the outline plan for the development of the region.

By 1979 Taiwan had experienced accelerated economic development but had failed to implement a plan for its population and economic activity distribution. The lack of planning in essential facilities resulted in the concentration of population and industrial activity in the north and south of the island. Housing, industrial, and agricultural sectors vied for available land. The public infrastructure failed to cope with economic development, thereby becoming a retarding factor. Finally, pollution degraded the living environment. In an attempt to improve the above deficiencies, the Council for Economic Planning and Development (CEPD) formulated the National Comprehensive Development Plan (NCDP) for Taiwan. The plan is mainly intended to provide space allocation and a development plan for population, industry, essential facilities, and natural resources. The Comprehensive Development Plan was a goal-oriented, guided, long-range plan, beginning in 1977 and ending in 1997.

Since the implementation of the NCDP for Taiwan, several issues in social, economic, and environmental development emerged. Hence, in July 1993, the Executive Yuan approved the implementation of the Economic Promotion Bill, which directed the CEDP to study and amend the NCDP, as well as draft a National Development Planning Law. The NCDP was aimed at accommodating the different aspects of the country's socioeconomic development, such as providing proper space allocation for population, industry and public infrastructure as well as being the basis for the planned allocation of land, water, and natural resources. It is a goal-oriented, strategic, long-range development outline, planned up to the year 2011.

Regional plan

The implementation of the NCDP for Taiwan was announced in 1979. The plan divided Taiwan into four regions, north, central, south and east. The Taipei metropolitan area is located within the regional plans for northern Taiwan. The regional plan is directed by the Ministry of the Interior (MOI), and the Regional Plan for Northern Taiwan is formulated by the Construction and Planning Administration (CPA), MOI. Regional planning means the comprehensive development plans made for certain regions that are grouped because of features of geography, population, resources, economy, and social activities. In 1992 the Taipei Metropolitan Area Physical Plan was produced by the CPA, MOI, as the blueprint for the global construction of Taipei metropolitan area.

The continued implementation of major developments and constructions, such as the Six-year National Development Plan, the Economic Promotion Bill and the Asia-Pacific Operations Center has led to giant improvements in the condition of the region's transportation, urban development, and industries. These had a major impact on regional land use. As a result, the regional plan was reviewed and reevaluated between 1995 and 1997. The main points of the amendments included the definition of environmentally sensitive areas, criteria for the nature and intensity of land development, and the designation of the non-urban land use.

Urban planning

Urban planning belongs to the lower level of the national land planning system of Taiwan; it is able to concretely specify the plan for a district's development. The principal objective of this plan is to provide a reasonable plan for land use. Urban planning is directed by the city or township governments on all levels, which means the reasonably planned development of a particular area in terms of its economy, transportation, health care, security, education, and recreation which influences the land use and zoning control of urban land. According to Section 9 of the Taiwan urban planning law, there are three types of urban planning: the town plan, the country and town plan, and the special district plan. The Taipei metropolitan area includes 39 urban planning zones, with an area of 143,180 ha, or about 76 percent of the whole metropolitan area.

Land use planning

To ensure the adequate permanent utilization of land resources, areas are designated as "Constrained Areas" or "Developable Areas," according to the regional plans. There are minimum standards set up to monitor the polluting activities. Zoning control is also implemented to require permits for development so as to govern the development and upgrade the quality of the environment.

Guidelines for land use. Taking into account the characteristics and developmental needs of each area, regional planning must take into consideration the objective and the subjective points of view. The land is designated as either of the following categories:

- *Constrained Area.* The land of this category includes nature conservation for water supplies, ecological conservation areas, steep land preservation zones, forests, movable faults, relics, and other land designated as such by law.
- *Developable Area.* The land, other than that listed in the first category, which is feasible for development. However, any development project is still subject to review and approval by the authorities concerned. The environmental factors to be considered in granting the permits are whether the land belongs to one of the following areas: areas of groundwater recharge, sloping land with potential for disaster, water conservation areas, flood areas, and with subsidence of ground, nuclear power plants in nearby areas, air traffic noise areas, highly fertile agricultural land, and other land designated as such by law.

Zoning control. Table 11.9 shows the actual and percentage amounts of permitted land use for Taipei City and for Taipei metropolitan area.

Other initiatives to manage regional form

Taiwan is densely populated, and its land resources are limited; different sectors compete for the use of land. However, there is a lack of thorough land resource allocation planning. The pressure for development in the remote areas or environmentally sensitive zones is great. Land resources are being used over their limit; hence effective planning controls become necessary. In areas where population is concentrated in the cities, development and facilities are not well coordinated. Then there is the need to improve the quality of the townscape, a development that calls for better planning and design.

Table 11.9 Areas of urban development land in plans for the Taipei metropolitan area

Zones	Residential		Commercial		Industrial		Public facilities		Total	
	ha	%	ha	%	ha	%	ha	%	ha	%
Taipei city	3,862.04	36.4	553.93	5.2	479.05	4.5	5,726.96	53.9	10,621.98	100.0
	40.5	14.8	55.3	2.1	12.0	1.8	49.8	22.0	40.8	40.8
Beyond Taipei city	5,673.46	77.9	446.93	5.8	3,525.24	32.9	5,771.14	73.3	15,416.77	100.0
	59.5	21.7	44.6	1.7	88	13.6	50.1	22.1	59.2	100.0
Total in Taipei metropolitan area	9,535.50	36.6	1,000.86	3.8	4,004.29	15.4	11,498.10	44.2	26,038.75	100.0
	100.0	36.6	100.0	3.8	100.0	15.4	100.0	44.2	100.0	100.0

The national and city governments do not have long term planning objectives. As a result, areas where development is sluggish need better infrastructure. Then there is the social problem caused by the absence of effective co-ordination between public infrastructure and private construction. As the problem is a burden to the government, there is a need to see to the full-scale implementation of development permits and increase the budget as necessary. There has been a wild outbreak of land utilization violations, making evident the need for effective countermeasures and the creation of a national land information system that can lay the foundations of plan submission, decision making, and development management. A complete plan and effective management measures are strongly needed for the solution of improper coastal zone development and excess soil dumping caused by the urban construction sites in the metropolitan area.

CONCLUSION

The developmental issues in Taipei metropolitan area embrace the following familiar subjects: the review of flood prevention plans, the construction of metropolitan transport systems, the construction of public facilities and utilities, the preservation of environmental quality, and the provision of housing.

The population in the Taipei metropolitan area will reach 6.5 million by the year 2005, accounting for 30 percent of the total population of Taiwan by then. Immediate action must be taken lest the urban problems, discussed above, get out of control. By way of conclusion, and based on the major physical constructions in the Taipei metropolitan area which have been discussed, the future directions for development in the regional plans for northern Taiwan are to:

- Consider the limit of available resources and develop a reasonable size of population in the metropolis, so as to achieve reasonable growth in population and industries.
- Enhance the developmental functions of the multicores and establish a hierarchical multicored spatial structure.
- Improve and create a pleasant living environment.
- Accelerate and integrate the construction of transport systems to meet the needs of the multicored development and commuting patterns.

The concepts of dots, lines, and the flat are the factors that should be considered in designing the future developmental structures of the Taipei metropolitan area. The dots are the important points of development; the lines are the axes of transportation; and the flat means the adequate categorization of the areas of similar functions and characteristics. Based on this, it is possible to classify the whole Taipei metropolitan area into eight sections, namely: the metropolitan circle, the primary urban center, the secondary urban centers, the local centers, the main corridors, the secondary corridors, the dependent areas, and the satellite cities. This is an overall urban system that determines the spatial structures of the Taipei metropolitan area.

Based on the above discussion, the concept of three rings, six axes, and six centers is developed as follows:

- The three circles include the inner circle for residence, consisting of the core city and six adjacent cities; the middle circle for industries, and the outer circle for the natural environment. The inner circle for residence is ideal for settlement. The middle circle for industries is to develop different kinds of industries based on their distance from the inner circle, with technology-intensive industries staying close to the inner circle while the labor-intensive ones usually stay far from the core city. The outer circle for the natural environment may be designed for water or mountain activities.
- The six axes are the corridors between Taipei and Tamsui, Sanchung, Panchiao, Chungho, Hsintien, and Nangkang.

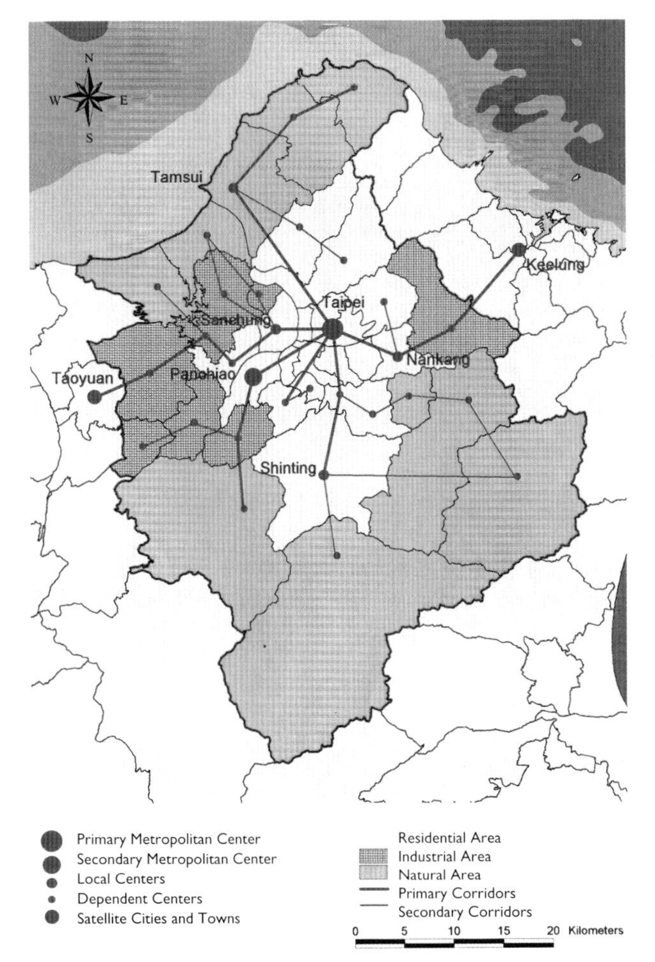

Figure 11.8 Spatial structure of the Taipei region

Table 11.10 Planned functions of the six spatial planning zones in the Taipei metropolitan area

Spatial planning units	Primary functions	Secondary functions	Range
The core of Taipei district	Regional center for commerce, finance, and administration	Residential (higher density)	Sungshan, Taan, Kuting, Shuangyuan, Lungshan, Chengchung, Chiencheng, Yenping, Tatung, Chungshan
Tamsui-Sanchih district	Residential (medium and low density), and recreational	Local commercial center, farming, fishing	Shihlin, Peitou, Tamsui, Sanchih, Shihmen
Sanchung-Hsinchuang district	Industries (technology-intensive), residential	Local commercial center, recreational	Sanchung, Hsinchuang, Luchou, Wuku, Taishan, Linkou, Pali, Kueishan
Panchiao-Chungho district	Secondary regional commercial center, Residential (high density)	Industries (technology intensive), recreational	Panchiao, Yung-ho, Chungho, Shulin, Yingko, Tucheng, Sanhsia
Hsintien-Mucha district	Residential (medium and low density), recreational	Local commercial center, farming	Mucha, Chingmei, Hsintien, Shenkeng, Wulai, Pinglin, Shinting
Nankang-Hsichih district	Industries (technology-intensive), residential (medium and low density)	Local commercial center	Neihu, Nankang, Hsichih

- The six centers are the core centers of Taipei City, the secondary metropolitan centers at Panchiao, and four local centers at Tamsui, Sanchung, Hsintien, and Nangkang.

As for the separation of functions of the spatial planning zones in the Taipei metropolitan area, shown in Table11.10, Taipei City is definitely the major center of politics, the economy, and culture of the whole of Taiwan. It serves commercial, financial, and administrative functions and plays the role of central management.

REFERENCES

The following texts and journal articles have been drawn on to a greater or lesser extent in writing this chapter.

General of Budget, Accounting and Statistics (1995) "Report on the Study of Family Income and Expenditure in the Taiwan area of the ROC", GBAS, Executive Yuan, R.O.C.

Council for Economic Planning and Development (1979) *The Evaluation and Review of Ten Construction Projects*, CEPD, Executive Yuan, R.O.C.

Council for Economic Planning and Development (1996) *The Comprehensive Development Plan for Taiwan*, CEPD, Executive Yuan, R.O.C.

Coordination and Service Office for Asia-Pacific Regional Operations Center (1996) *The Plan to develop Taiwan into an Asia-Pacific Regional Operations* Center, CEPD, Executive Yuan, R.O.C.

Ministry of the Interior (1995) *The Regional Plans for Northern Taiwan*, Construction and Planning Administration, MOI.

Taipei City Government (1992) *The Comprehensive Development Plans for Taipei City*, TCG, R.O.C.

Taipei County Government (1993) *The Comprehensive Development Plans for Taipei County*, TCG, Taiwan province, R.O.C.

Construction and Planning Administration (1992) *The Practical Planning for the Taipei Metropolitan Area*, CPA, MOI.

Ministry of the Interior (1996) *1995 Taiwan-Fukien Demographic Fact Book*, MOI, R.O.C, Taipei, Taiwan.

Department of Budget, Accounting and Statistics (1997) "The Statistical abstract of Taipei City", DBAS, Taipei City Government, R.O.C.

Department of Statistics (1996) *Statistics Abstract of Transportation and Communication 1995 R.O.C*, DOS, Ministry of Transportation and Communication, R.O.C.

Directorate General of Telecommunications (1995) *White Paper on Telecommunications*, DGT, Ministry of Transportation and Communication, R.O.C.

Institute of Transportation (1995) *The Long-term Development Planning Update of the Overall Transportation System in the Republic of China on Taiwan, 1995–2020* IOT, MTC, R.O.C.

Editing Committee of the *Transportation and Communications Yearbook* (1973–1997) *Transportation and Communication Yearbook 1996*, ECTCY, MTC, R.O.C.

Ministry of Transportation and Communication (1991) *The History of Transportation and Communication, ROC*, MTC, R.O.C.

Jaw Jye-Chian (1983) *The Developmental Strategies of Transportation*, United Economics, Taipei.

Department of Housing and Urban Development (1995) "The Construction Project of the Road Systems in the Living Perimeter of Taipei (Taiwan Province)", HUD, Taiwan Provincial Government.

Bureau of Taiwan High Speed Rail (1997) "The Abstract of the Construction Project of High Speed Rail in the Western Corridor of Taiwan", BTHSR, MTC, R.O.C.

Feng Cheng-Min (1990) "The Impact Analysis of the Construction of High Speed Rail in the Aspect of Regional Development in Taiwan", Institute of Traffic and Transportation, National Chiao-Tung University, Taiwan.

Feng Cheng-Min (1994) "The Beneficial Evaluation of the Construction of High Speed Rail in the Aspect of the Development of Economics in Taiwan", Institute of Traffic and Transportation, National Chiao-Tung University, Taiwan.

Taipei City Government (1997) "Report on the Systems of Expressway Construction Projects in Taipei City", TCG, R.O.C.

Institute of Transportation (1992) *The Trip Investigation for the Traveling of the Household in the Taipei Metropolitan Area*, IOT, MTC, R.O.C.

Construction and Planning Administration (1980) "Taipei Seminar on Metropolitan Development Planning", CPA, MOI, R.O.C.

Institute of Transportation (1995) *Transportation Policy White Book*, Institute of Transportation, MTC, R.O.C.

Institute of Transportation (1995) *The Overall Transportation Planning for Taiwan Province*, IOT, MTC, R.O.C.

Institute of Transportation (1996) *Initial Planning for the Overall Development and Construction Projects of Expressway Systems in Taipei Metropolis*, IOT, MTC, R.O.C.

Construction and Planning Administration (1996) *Construction and Planning Policy White Book*, CPA, MOI, R.O.C.

Department of Rapid Transit Systems TMG (1996) *An Introduction to the Rapid Transit Systems of the Taipei Metropolitan Area*, DRTS, Taipei City Government, Taiwan.

Taiwan Area National Freeway Bureau (1995) *Annual Report 1995*, TANFB, MTC, R.O.C.

Engineering Office of Taipei Railway Underground Project (1995) "Taipei Railway Underground Project Introduction".

Institute of Transportation (1992)" The Seminar on Impact Assessment of Large Scale Transportation and Development Projects, 1992", IOT, MTC, R.O.C.

Council for Economic Planning and Development (1985) "The Study of Urban and Regional Development in Taiwan Area: The Evolution of Urban Growth and Spatial Structure", Department of Housing and Urban Development, CEPD, Executive Yuan, R.O.C.

Construction and Planning Administration (1996) *Land Development Regulations*, CPA, MOI, R.O.C.

12 The Tokyo region

Yuichi Takeuchi

In today's world, populations, along with economic, social and cultural institutions, are centered in urban districts, resulting in the formation of large city regions worldwide. Many of these cities have populations in excess of 1 million. The Tokyo metropolitan region is an area of more than 31 million people, and as such is a conurbation on a scale without precedent in human history. The Tokyo metropolitan region is situated on the wide expanse of the Kanto plain, in the geographic heart of Japan (see Figure 12.2). At the center of the region is Japan's capital, the city of Tokyo itself. Japan's administrative, economic and social institutions are concentrated in Tokyo, which is also the center of the nation's road and railway network and the terminus of the Shinkansen rail routes and expressways.

The Tokyo metropolitan region consists of Tokyo and the adjacent prefectures of Ibaraki, Chiba, Saitama and Kanagawa. The conurbation extends outwards over a radius of 70 km from central Tokyo to occupy most of the flatland areas of these administrative units. To reach the outer limits of this conurbation takes about an hour and a half by train from the center of Tokyo. The region itself comprises a single living environment with close internal links.

The study of world cities has been a popular topic ever since the 1980s. Interest has been shown especially in urban areas which constitute centers of operations for multinational corporations, international finance, international organizations and telecommunications, and which often have an influence within the global economy on a par with or indeed ever greater than that of most countries. Tokyo is often cited as an example of such a city, along with New York, London and Paris. In other words, Tokyo is not merely a vast urban area with an enormous population: it functions within the international community as a global city, that is to say, a center of global economic, social and cultural institutions. But in comparison with New York, London or Paris, Tokyo has a status as a global city primarily because of its concentration of economic functions. The center of Tokyo is indeed an economic and financial center of global distinction, but the Tokyo metropolitan region consists of a vast conurbation stretching out over a radius of 70 km. Quite apart from the concentration of urban functions within the city center, this wider area also is influenced by the phenomenon of globalization.

It was in 1868 that the Japanese capital was moved to Tokyo, or Edo, as it was then still called. Until the early 1900s Tokyo was where financial institutions including the Bank of Japan located. It was also the base for state-run corporations and factories involved in areas such as railways and steel manufacture. Many related companies, especially those active in heavy industry and the chemical industry, were fostered in this environment. These companies served as the propelling force of economic development during the period of Japan's industrial revolution. They pushed forward the urbanization of Tokyo and it was these industries that were largely responsible for rapidly extending the urban area of Tokyo.

Two catastrophic events befell Tokyo during the three decades from 1920. The first was the great Kanto earthquake of 1923 which resulted in loss of 44 percent (33 km^2) of the Tokyo area due to fire. The other event was the Second World War in which Japan was embroiled between 1938 and 1945 and which resulted in the loss of 28 percent (158 km^2) of the ward area of Tokyo. These two events stimulated Tokyo's outward advance into the suburbs, the city gradually expanding along the railway lines of Japan National Railways centering on Tokyo Station and of the private railway companies operating primarily in the suburbs. The upshot was the vast urban region extending outwards from the center. By 1990, whereas the Tokyo area accounted for only 3.6 percent of the national territory, 24.8 percent of the Japanese population lived in this area. More and more companies have been setting up in Tokyo in order to take advantage of the city's core administrative and global economic functions. Population is concentrating in Tokyo and workers with high educational levels are being absorbed from all over the country.

However, this process of urban expansion is by no means infinite in scope. The concentration of population and economic functions and the expansion of urban areas are having the effect of worsening the environment, aggravating traffic congestion, and increasing the risk of major disasters. The rapid flow of population into the

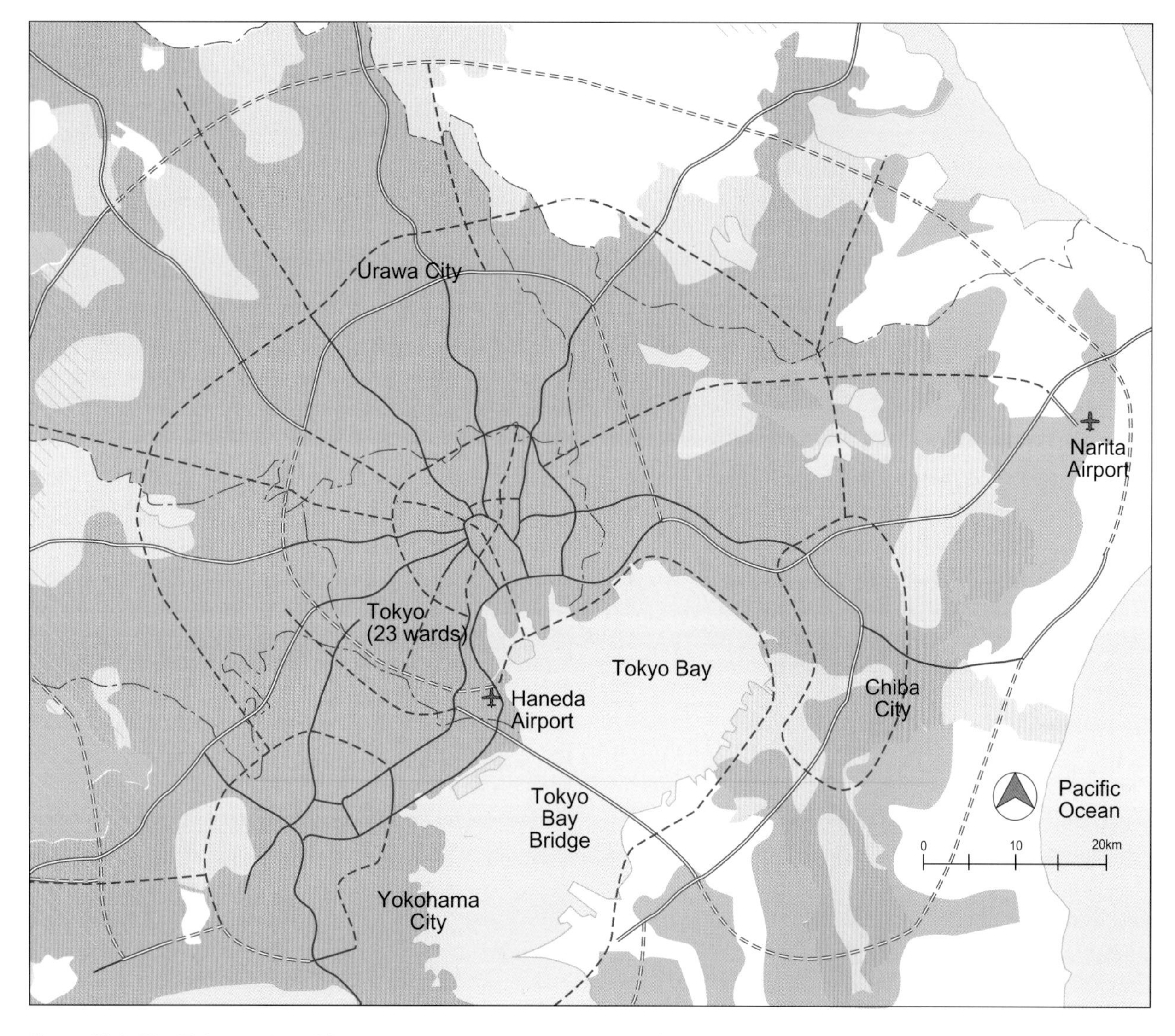

Figure 12.1 The Tokyo region, 1995

Tokyo metropolitan region continued between 1960 and 1985, but the trend subsequently leveled off, and after the entry into the 1990s the disadvantages of being based in Tokyo came to outweigh the benefits, as reflected in the fact that more people began to move out of the city than into it.

As suggested by the fact that Tokyo is considered to be a global city mainly because of its economic functions, Tokyo has none of the political and historical weight of London, none of the beauty or cultural traditions of Paris, and none of the dynamism of New York. Housing is by no means of high quality, the streets are congested and drab, and there is the constant risk of earthquakes. On the other hand, within this concentration, the trains run on time and with immaculate service. Electric power and water are supplied with complete reliability. Such facilities are supported by the massive and versatile infrastructure which exists in Tokyo. It is this infrastructure that has enabled Tokyo to grow into the vast city it is today.

Modern Tokyo is supported by this accumulation of infrastructure, but there has frequently been concern about the inadequacy of the infrastructure owing to rapid increases in demand. This inadequacy has brought about congestion and deterioration in the environment, and the risk of disasters has increased. It is the infrastructure which has made Tokyo what it is today but it is this same infrastructure which has also brought about the urban problems which the city now has to face.

CHANGING ECONOMIC PATTERNS

The Tokyo metropolitan region is located on the Kanto plain, at the front of which is the fine natural harbor of Tokyo Bay. The area benefits from plentiful supplies of water and electric power and is the center of a transport network which includes railways and roads. Manufacturing industries have concentrated in this area because of these factors since before the Second World War. There is also a concentration of tertiary industries, including finance.

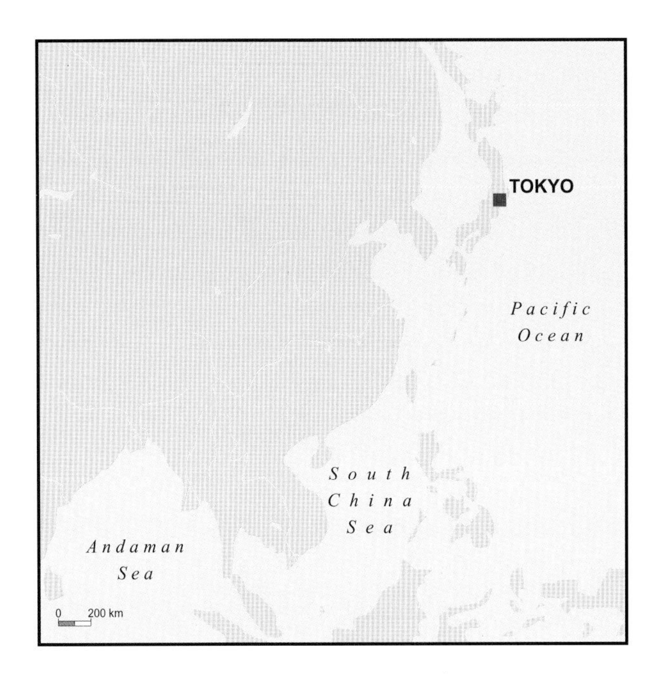

Figure 12.2 The location of the Tokyo region

The industrial section of the Tokyo metropolitan region is located facing outward toward Tokyo Bay in a prime location, and has been the propelling force behind Japan's high-level economic growth since the 1960s. A large number of higher educational institutions are also located in the Tokyo metropolitan region and supply a high-quality labor force. A quarter of the Japanese labor force is in fact concentrated in the Tokyo metropolitan region. Since the late 1970s there has been a gradual move away from heavy and chemical industries in the direction of the automobile, electrical and electronics industries as the leading industries in the Japanese economy. It should be mentioned also that the proportion of manufacturing industry for Japan as a whole which occupies the Tokyo metropolitan region has decreased slightly from 28.6 percent in 1960 to 24.8 percent in 1990.

Changes in manufacturing industries in the Tokyo metropolitan region have been accompanied by a rapid increase in the importance of service industries, especially in the financial sector. Looking at the figures for gross production per prefecture, the proportion of secondary industries in the Tokyo metropolitan region in 1960 was 42.7 percent and of tertiary industries was 53.6 percent. The proportion of secondary industries on a nationwide scale was 37.3 percent, while that of tertiary industries was 50.6 percent. In contrast, the same proportions for the

Figure 12.3 The Tokyo metropolitan area

Tokyo metropolitan region in 1993 were 30.1 percent and 69.5 percent. The figures for the country as a whole were 34.0 percent and 64.4 percent. The growth of tertiary industries in the Tokyo metropolitan region was highly conspicuous. In terms of numbers employed, the figures in 1960 were 8.7 percent for agriculture, 40.7 percent for manufacturing industries, and 50.6 percent for service industries. By 1990 the figures had changed respectively to 1.6 percent, 31.7 percent and 65.8 percent. (See Table 1 on p.19.) A large proportion of the increase in service industries can be accounted for by the growth of international industries such as finance and by information-related industries and the entertainment industry. Such changes in the industrial structure have brought about a concentration of companies in the Tokyo metropolitan region: 67.3 percent of the 1,772 listed companies in Japan have their head offices in the Tokyo metropolitan region. Economic links with other advanced countries have grown stronger: there are 2,710 branches of foreign corporations with offices in Tokyo, making the city one of the world's major business centers.

A feature of the economic pattern of the Tokyo metropolitan region is that the concentration of multinational corporations, vast conglomerates, and the companies providing services to these corporations has made Tokyo the economic center of Japan and indeed of the world. On the other hand, small and medium scale manufacturing industries with plentiful technical development capacity are also concentrated in this area, with the result that Tokyo has one of the highest concentrations of manufacturing industries of any of the world's major cities. The products created by these small and medium scale industries play an important role on both the Japanese and the global markets.

CHANGING SOCIAL PATTERNS

The Tokyo metropolitan region absorbed large numbers of people from all over Japan during the period of high economic growth. There was therefore a large proportion of young people among the city's population during the 1960s and 1970s. However, the inflow of population into the city began to decrease during the 1980s and there was a dramatic increase in the proportion of people aged 65 and over. This phenomenon of aging is particularly noticeable in the city center. There has also been an increase in the number of elderly people living alone. Other features of the population structure in the Tokyo metropolitan region are the small size of households, the high level of education of residents, and the fact that the population consists almost entirely of Japanese nationals. Of the 20 million or so people aged 25 or over living in the urban region, 5.7 million, or about 29 percent of the population, are university or college graduates. This labor force with its high educational levels is the source of Tokyo's dynamic economic activity. The proportion of foreign residents is, however, only 0.6 percent, and residents other than Japanese are a small minority in this environment.

The *per capita* GDP of the Tokyo metropolitan region continued to rise during the period of economic growth, exceeding US$30,000 by 1990 (see Table 1 on p.19). There is relatively little difference between the incomes of the richest and the poorest segments of society, and income levels have risen through the urban region as a whole. Unemployment rates are also very low: the figure of 1.3 percent for 1970 rose, but only slightly, to 3.3 percent in 1985.

There were 10.3 million households in the Tokyo metropolitan region in 1988. That same year there were 12.75 million residential units, meaning that demand for housing was in overall terms being satisfied. There is a high rate of home ownership, 53.3 percent of householders owning their own homes in 1985. The average floor area of residential accommodation has increased steadily, exceeding 80 m^2 by 1988. Nevertheless, about 10 percent of all households experience excessively cramped conditions.

Although the Tokyo metropolitan region has undergone changes in industrial structure and the formation of suburbs like other of the world's major cities, it has relatively few of the inner-city problems experienced by other cities. Indeed, there has been a redevelopment boom in the city center. But the invigoration of economic activities in the city center brought on by redevelopment has resulted in the decay of traditional residential quarters and the collapse of communities. Aging is a particular problem in these areas, and the question of how such communities are going to be revived in the future is likely to be a major one.

In the past three decades people have seen an increase in the amount of free time available to them. Daily activities now take place around the clock, there has been an increase in night work, and consumption has become more varied in line with the increase in the amount of free time. Employment has also become more diversified, ever increasing numbers of women are in work, and lifestyles are rapidly changing. Features of life in the Tokyo metropolitan region today include the expansion of the suburbs, increasing reliance on the automobile, and "Americanization," all of which are advancing exponentially.

CHANGING SPATIAL PATTERNS

Concentration of population and companies in the Tokyo metropolitan region was especially noticeable during the period of 30 years between 1960 and 1990. For example, the population of the region in 1960 was 15.93 million, a figure equivalent to 16.9 percent of the total Japanese population. However, by 1990 the population had risen to 30.61 million, or 25 percent of the national population (see Table 1 on p.19). Population increase in the country as a whole during these years was about 30.19 million, meaning that the increase in the Tokyo metropolitan region accounted for 48.6 percent of the national increase. Looking at the spatial structure of the Tokyo metropolitan region over these 30 years, there has been no significant change in the tendency toward geographical centralization with central Tokyo at the hub, but internally there has been a tendency toward both centralization and decentralization. The population has expanded outward at a low density, resulting in the so-called doughnut phenomenon, while employment has been characterized by growth in central Tokyo and by rapid expansion in the central parts of neighboring areas such as Yokohama, Kawasaki and Chiba. This combined tendency toward centralization and decentralization is a feature of these decades.

By 1960 the commuter belt of central Tokyo had extended almost 70 km to the present borders of the urban region, but as the influx of population continued into the region, so the built-up conurbation expanded outward, meaning that by 1990 the area up to a radius of 70 km from the center consisted entirely of built-up urban areas. Large-scale housing developments, intended to cope with the increase in demand for housing, were built in the vicinity of small and medium scale towns which had long existed in the suburbs, especially in the vicinity of the railway lines extending out radially from the city center. These spatial patterns were formed basically by the railways. However, the spread of the automobile has brought about an increase in the amount of land being used for the construction of residential accommodation along the main roads most suited to use by private cars.

Motorization and road building have increased since the 1960s. Industrial estates have been built along the major trunk roads; the automobile, electronics and electrical appliances industries have built factories inland, as have also distribution centers. The consequence is that the suburbs of urban areas are increasingly coming to be used as industrial sites dominated by factories, distribution centers, and research and development facilities.

On the other hand, restructuring on the part of manufacturing industries is resulting in factories moving out of existing urban areas and the Tokyo Bay area, with a consequent increase in the proportion of service industries. The head offices of Japan's leading companies along with financial and international institutions are concentrated in the Marunouchi and Otemachi areas, where major companies first began to congregate during the Meiji era, resulting in the formation of one of the world's main economic centers. During the 1980s offices concentrated also in the vicinity of the city center, in metropolitan subcenters such as those of Shinjuku, Ikebukuro and Shibuya which are also important railway termini, and in areas along the Yamanote line which have easy access by subway. The upshot of this development was that the whole area within Japan Railways Yamanote line came to be regarded as the center of the Tokyo metropolitan region.

This concentration of commercial and business functions on the outskirts of the city is gradually advancing, especially in areas such as Saitama, Chiba and Kanagawa prefectures where the railway network is concentrated. Such areas are in the process of becoming new city centers in the suburbs.

INFRASTRUCTURE INVESTMENT

The infrastructure is playing a major role in the development of the Tokyo metropolitan region, with its population of 31 million and concentration of companies. The extremely well equipped railway network is enabling people, living in urban areas within a 70 km radius of the center of the city, to travel in an efficient and highly reliable manner.

Infrastructural work has taken place in three stages. The first stage began during the 1920s with the construction of the railway network. The lines of the national railways which provided links throughout the country together with private railway lines linking suburban regions created a complex web of links in urban areas during the 1950s. The construction of a subway system then resulted in the emergence of an urban region with one of the most thoroughly coordinated railway networks anywhere in the world.

Efforts were directed particularly to road building in order to respond to a rapid increase in the number of motor vehicles on the roads from the 1960s onward. Considerable advances were then made in the construction of expressways during the 1980s. The 1990s have been an age dominated by information technology. The network of digital circuits which has been put in place since the late 1980s has become an important part of the infrastructure underpinning today's global city of Tokyo.

Roads

In comparison with the West, a notable feature of the development of means of transport in Japan was the lack of experience of horse-drawn transport. Since road transport has generally involved walking, roads tend to be very narrow and houses have not traditionally possessed gardens or stables where horses might be kept. This means that, in order to enable roads to be used by motor vehicles, they have to be widened and parking space has to be found. This means that it would have been impossible to cope unless changes had been made in the nature of urban space itself.

The high-level economic growth which was a feature of the Japanese economy from the second half of the 1960s onward had the effect of pushing up income levels. This in turn made it possible for ordinary people to purchase cars and heralded the arrival of the age of motorization. But roads in the Tokyo metropolitan region were relatively poorly maintained. Roads in central Tokyo were built and repaired after the war in the context of national reconstruction policy, but little else was done. It was only after the 1964 Tokyo Olympics that Japan left the age when walking was the principal form of locomotion and entered an age able to cope with the automobile. The year 1964 was also when the first expressways were opened and the national network of expressways began to expand.

There were many difficulties involved in upgrading roads originally intended for pedestrians to roads for the age of motorized transport. Land prices in urban areas were high, and enormous amounts of money had to be spent to acquire the land needed for widening roads. Another factor was that urban areas were highly built up, meaning that large numbers of people had to move house.

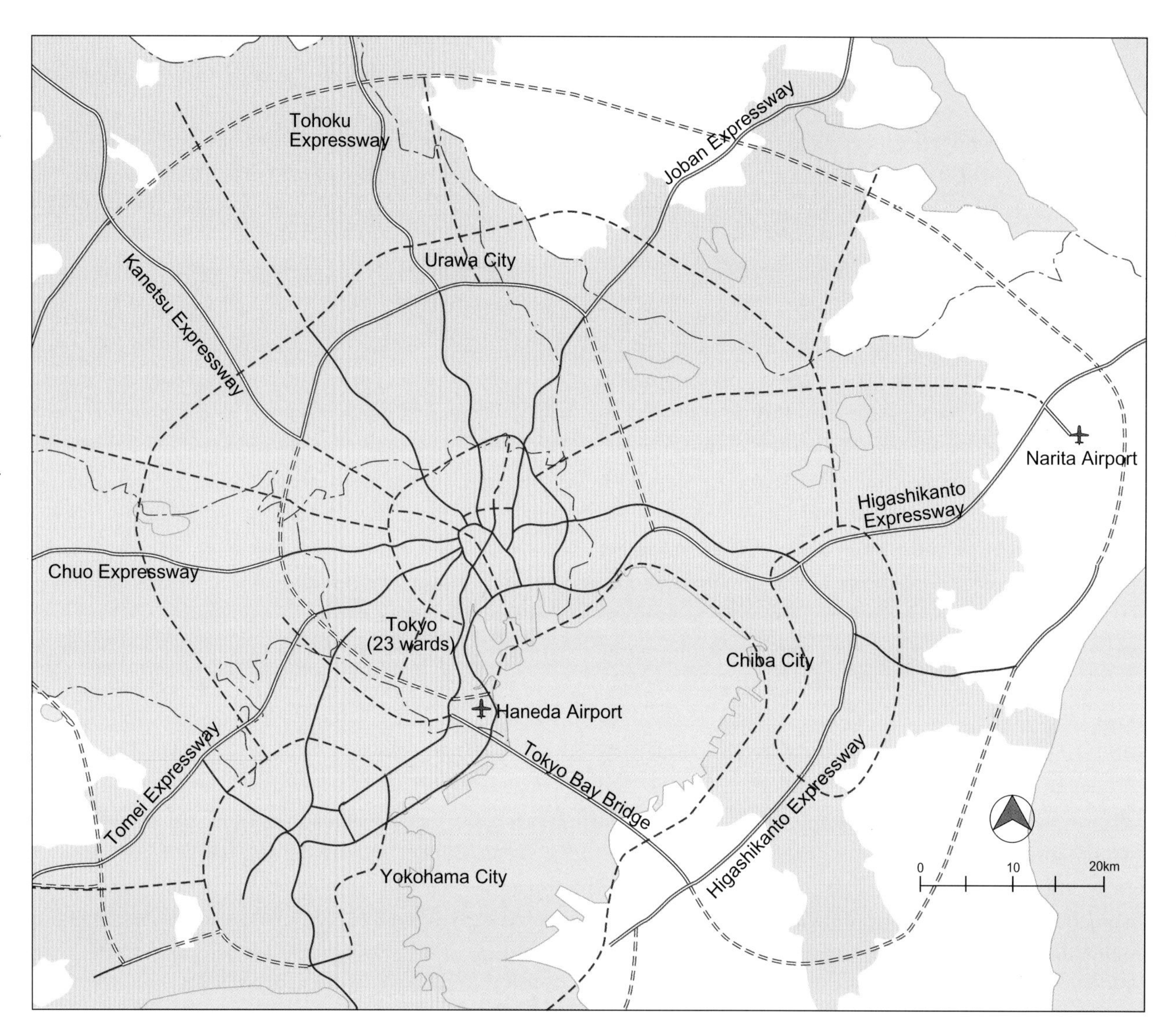

Figure 12.4 Main roads and airports in the Tokyo region, 1995

This inevitably resulted in disputes with local residents. Although road building did not proceed smoothly, the number of cars owned *per capita* by residents of the Tokyo metropolitan region increased from 0.037 in 1960 to 0.487 in 1990, representing a thirteenfold increase and achievement of a level equivalent to that of the United States. This explosive increase in the number of cars on the roads resulted in serious traffic congestion.

Road building is carried out on the basis of a five-year road improvement plan compiled by the Ministry of Construction and including all roads from national highways to municipal roads. The current plan envisages a network of expressways including nine radial roads and three ring roads. The plan is being financed primarily through the fuel tax levied on road users; road building is thus proceeding on the principle that those who benefit should pay the costs. Income from this tax has grown with the increased use of automobiles, but the costs involved in road building are growing rapidly and funding tends to be inadequate.

In contrast to the railways, considerable advances have been made in upgrading roads in the Tokyo metropolitan region over the past two decades. Levels of road maintenance outside central Tokyo are still low and there are considerable differences in level between different areas within the urban region itself. Furthermore, road building is failing to keep pace with the increase in the volume of cars on the roads, meaning that the problem of congestion still remains to be solved. Congestion in the suburbs has become particularly serious. The need for building roads remains as great as ever, but a response is required to environmental problems and spatial limitations must be overcome. Bearing these points in mind, there is a need for road planning linked with appropriate policies for traffic demand management.

Railways

A nationalized rail network which covered virtually the whole of the Tokyo metropolitan region had been created by 1936. With the completion of this network, a privately run rail network with lines stretching into the suburbs and a streetcar system operating in the city center came to be built. These networks provided services in areas not covered by the national railway system and formed part of a total transport network together with the national railways. Completion of this network resulted in the formation of urban areas extending radially out from Tokyo Station. It gave impetus to the rapid development of the suburbs, created urban concentrations centering on railway stations, and defined the fundamental aspect of spatial structure in the Tokyo metropolitan region.

Tokyo is also the center of the rail network which stretches out to every corner of the country. The Shinkansen, which began with the route between Tokyo and Osaka in 1964, subsequently expanded its routes to cover the whole country, centering on Tokyo Station. There are three lines—Tokaido, Tohoku and Joetsu. The Nagano Shinkansen line which is located on the same line as Joetsu has just been built for the Nagano Olympic Games. Construction of these ultra-high-speed railway lines has enhanced Tokyo's position at the center of Japan. It should be noted that Japan National Railways was split up and privatized in 1985.

As to the national railway network linking the regions, enormous advances have been made in medium distance railways such as the Tokaido, Yokosuka, Chuo, Tohoku, Takasaki, Johban and Sobu lines. These lines provide links between the Tokyo metropolitan region and other regions, while at the same time constituting a network of metropolitan commuter services extending 70 km out from the city center. The Musashino, Kawagoe and Saikyo lines, which were originally used only for freight, are now being used for passenger traffic and are proving highly effective in this regard. Plans are under way for the construction of the new Johban line in the northeasterly direction and for the use of lines now used for freight transport to provide access to the Tokyo Waterfront Subcenter.

The streetcars which before the war used to run widely and frequently inside the city center and within the area covered by the Yamanote line were totally closed down in 1967 in order to solve the problem of traffic congestion. Their place was taken by the underground railway or subway system. The first underground railway was constructed in 1927, and by 1965 12 lines had been built to provide links direct to stations on the Yamanote line. From the 1960s onward, links were created between these underground railways and the overground railways which headed into the suburbs. It became possible for suburban trains to use the same stations as those used by trains on the subway system, resulting in a highly efficient railway network. The effect of this was that Shinjuku, Ikebukuro and Shibuya stations on the Yamanote line came to handle enormous flows of traffic and urban functions became concentrated in the immediate vicinity of these stations. Construction of underground railways is continuing today, and a further five lines are planned. Particularly worthy of mention is Tokyo Line No. 12, which will pass in a ring around the center of Tokyo and is expected to alleviate much of the congestion being experienced on the Yamanote line.

As to the private railway network in the suburbs, a process of readjustment is going on centering on the main cities and necessitated as a result of the expansion of the Tokyo metropolitan region. Not only railways but also a city monorail system are being planned and built. Great hopes are being held out for these new systems as ways in which to combat the increase in motorization.

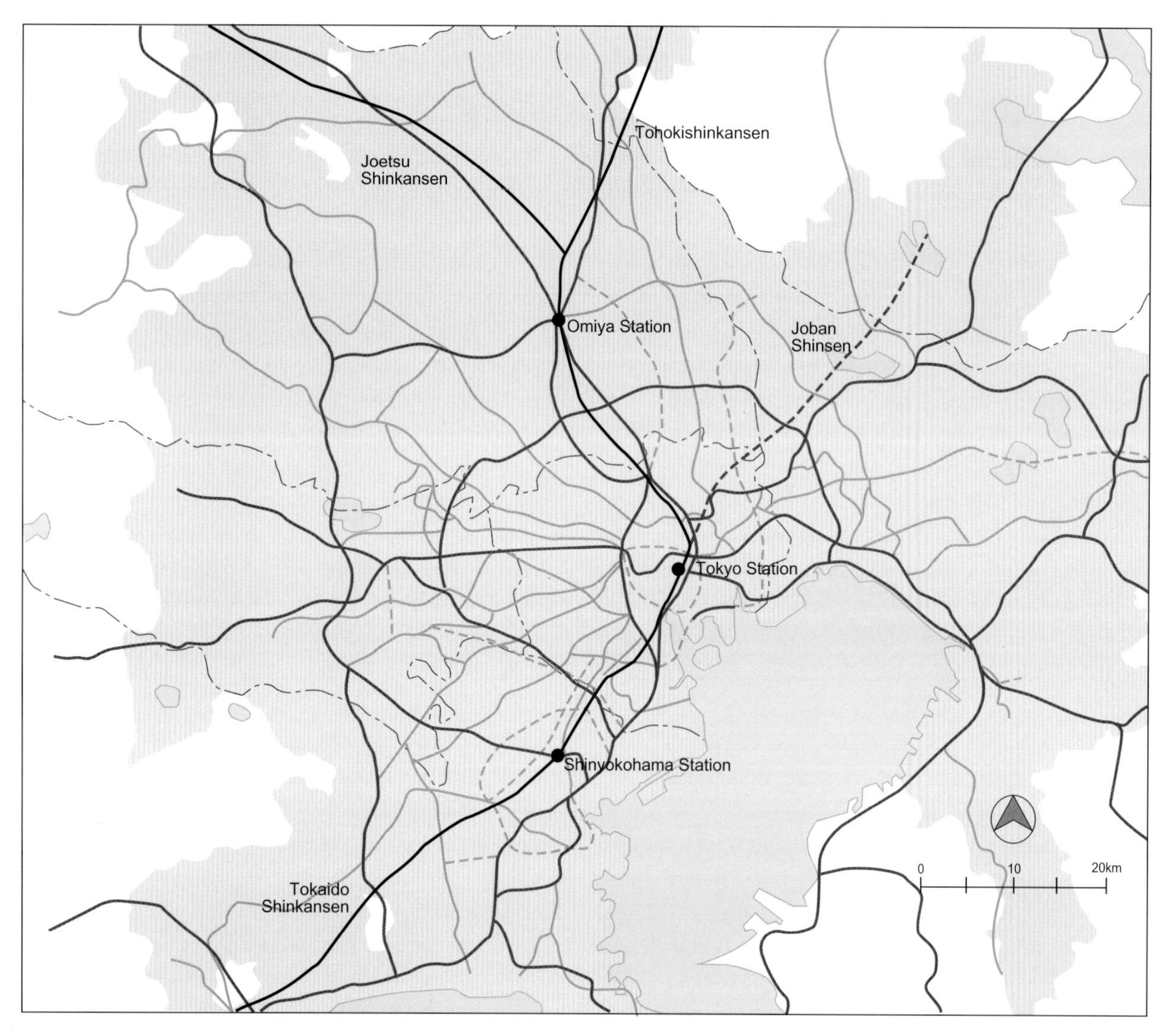

Figure 12.5 Railways in the Tokyo region, 1995

Building of railway networks is dependent upon the construction plans prepared for a railway company by the Transport Policy Deliberative Council, which is an advisory body of the Minister of Transport. The response provided by this council amounts effectively to a railway plan for the Tokyo metropolitan region. The railway network which has been constructed over such an extensive part of the Tokyo metropolitan region is second to none anywhere in the world in respect of its density, the content of the services which it provides, precision and safety. But, in spite of this, the railways continue to be as crowded as ever, and the building of new lines is essential in order to solve the problem.

Airports

The Tokyo metropolitan region possesses two airports, Tokyo International (Haneda) and the New Tokyo International Airport (Narita) (see Figure 12.4). Haneda Airport was returned by the United States in 1958 and improvements were made to it in time for the holding of the Tokyo Olympics in 1964. There was a rapid increase in demand for air transport from the 1970s which resulted in the building of Narita Airport. However, demand is still continuing to grow, and Haneda and Narita airports are currently being used by around 10 million Japanese travelers and foreign visitors every year. These two airports are of central importance to Japan's international aviation system. There has been an enormous increase in the volume of international air freight in recent years, with Narita Airport handling about 1.6 million tons of cargo worth some 12 trillion yen, representing 71.6 percent of all Japanese air freight.

With its single runway, Narita Airport will find it impossible to cope with any further increase in the volume of air freight, and the construction of a second runway is an immediate priority. Facilities for handling freight are being strengthened and, in pace with this development, distribution facilities are being set up in the vicinity of the airport. The two airports are being used annually for journeys within Japan by more than 40 million travelers, representing more than half of total domestic demand. Work on enlarging Haneda Airport has been continuing since 1984. This airport is now capable of handling 320 flights a day, and work on the construction of a third runway is under way.

Building of airports takes place in accordance with a five-year plan formulated by the Minister of Transport. The seventh plan, beginning in 1996, has been drawn up and proposes examination of the possibility of constructing a third airport in the Tokyo metropolitan region in order to solve the problems posed by the limitations of Tokyo's two present airports (see Figure 12.4).

Whereas 4.5 million Japanese and foreign nationals left or entered Japan in 1985, the figure had increased more than twice to about 10 million by 1990. As suggested by this change in demand for air transport, the two airports in the Tokyo metropolitan region are proving instrumental in enabling Tokyo to function as a global city. Narita Airport has hitherto possessed insufficient capacity to deal with demand, but distribution facilities are increasingly being located in the vicinity of the airport. Since Haneda Airport is located close to existing urban areas, there is little influence on the establishment of facilities in the vicinity. However, there are many manufacturing industries making products such as electronic components located in the area, and Haneda is contributing greatly to improving the efficiency of transportation of products suited to conveyance by air. Considerable hopes are being held out of the upgrading of international airports as a way of ensuring that the Tokyo metropolitan region is able to function as a global city.

Telecommunications

The main feature of telecommunication systems in recent years has been the rapid development in the diversification of broadcasting and telecommunications which has accompanied developments in the field of electronics technology. A wide variety of services including telephones, mobile communications, data communications, the internet, satellite broadcasting and cable television are now available. This diversification has been accompanied by a rapid increase in the amount of information actually being communicated: in the 1990s the annual rate of increase was 13 percent.

Telecommunications services in Japan date back to 1869, when telegraph communications were established between Tokyo and Yokohama. However, the telephone grew rapidly in popularity thereafter, to the extent that the rate of telephone ownership in the Tokyo metropolitan region has reached almost one telephone per head of population. Founded in 1952, the Nippon Telegraph & Telephone Public Corporation for many years had a monopoly over telecommunications until the company was privatized in 1985. Many new companies entered the communications market, and costs and charges were lowered, resulting in the provision of a varied range of services. A major influence in this connection was deregulation, which occurred in parallel with privatization, but other contributory factors included progress in digital communications and the laying of fiber optic cables.

Cables used for relay system transmission channels in Tokyo are currently housed entirely underground in accordance with a plan formulated in 1971. The construction of utility tunnels is well advanced along major roads, and four times more work than has so far been carried out is planned according to a basic plan formulated in 1995. The cables can be replaced in a brief space of time by fiber optic cable, and at present 96 percent of the total length of cable throughout Japan of 146.8×103 km consists of fiber optic. There are three relay points on the sea bed in the Tokyo metropolitan region for international telephones, and fiber optic cable is used to provide connections with other Asian countries, the United States, Australia and elsewhere.

Mobile communications began during the 1980s, but it was only after the liberalization of the communications industry in 1994 that they really began to be widely used. Mobile communications have expanded extremely rapidly, the number of devices in use having increased 11.4 times in the space of five years from 1990. A new communications medium which has become noted recently is the internet, which is backed up by the diffusion of personal computers. It is reckoned that there are about 7.3 million users of the internet in Japan.

The infrastructure needed for telecommunications such as fiber optic cable was put together in a very brief space of time. Extremely rapid advances have also been made in the diffusion of information technology, which relies on this infrastructure. It is very difficult to assess what the impact of these developments is likely to be on the Tokyo metropolitan region. But it is clear that phenomena such as the increase in the importance of the Tokyo metropolitan region in the context of the nation as a whole, the specialization of the Tokyo city center as regards economic, financial and administrative functions, and Tokyo's attainment of the status of a global city have all taken place in consort with the spread of information technology.

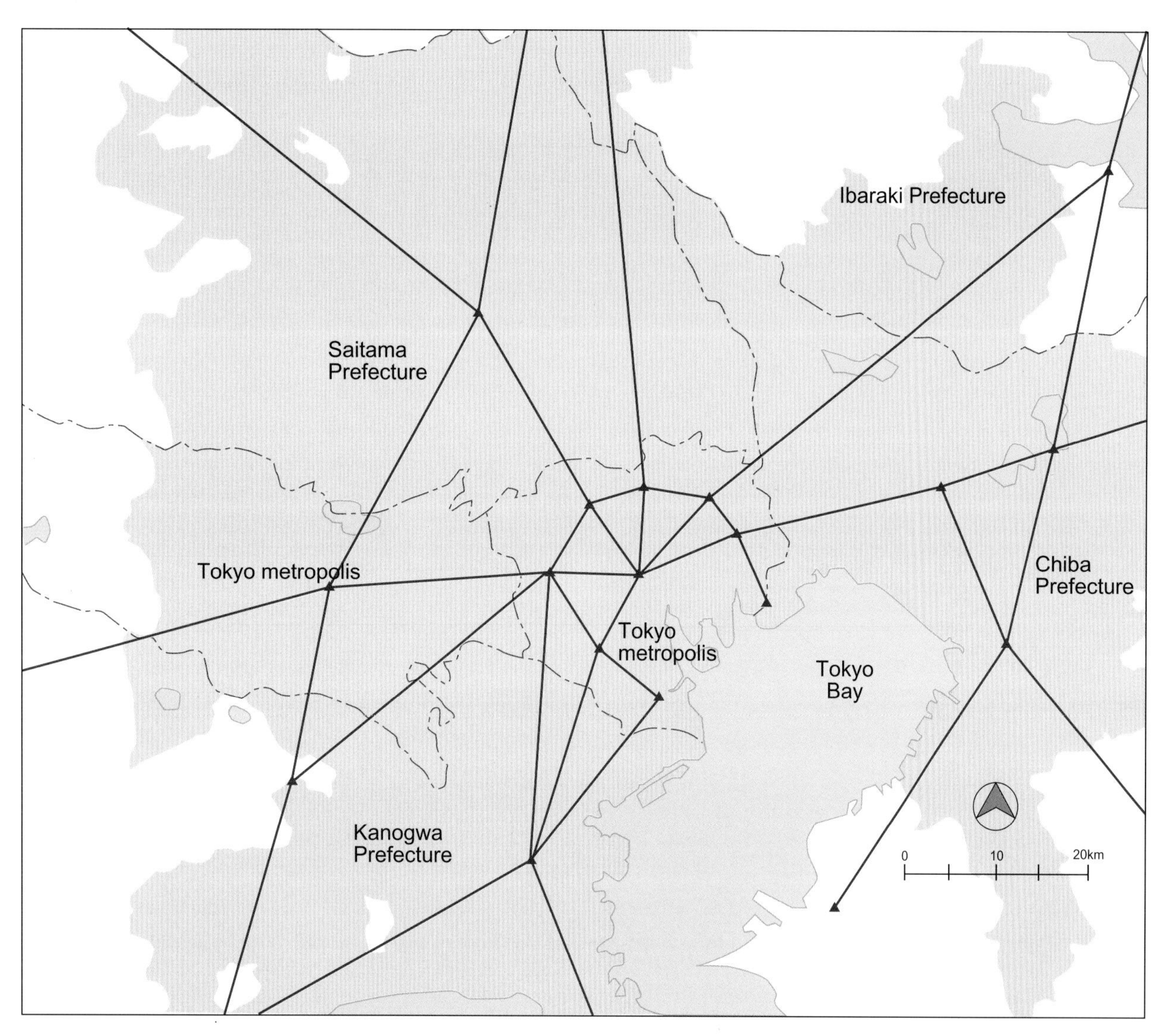

Figure 12.6 Fiber optic cable coverage in the Tokyo region, 1995

Conclusion

Tokyo is a lively and energetic city with plentiful employment opportunities and all the facilities required for everyday living. The most recent information can be easily obtained and manifestations of culture from all over the world are readily available. Although the Tokyo metropolitan region constitutes a vast conurbation, crime rates are lower, fires are fewer, and the city is safer and cleaner than most of the world's major cities. That Tokyo has grown to become the vast city it is today is due to the fact that people have congregated in it because they find it an attractive place to be. But Tokyo also has many problems. One particular problem is the risk of natural disasters such as major earthquakes. Other problems include congestion, which is a feature of road and rail transport, the small streets and cramped living accommodation, the drab urban landscape, and the difficulties experienced by the elderly and disabled in playing an active role in social life. Vast infrastructural improvements have been realized in order to cope with rapid urban growth, as mentioned earlier. In this and other ways, concerted efforts are being made to upgrade the infrastructure in the Tokyo metropolitan region. However, these developments, which far exceeded expectations of what would be necessary, and the failure to cope with them were features of the process of headlong economic growth, urbanization and motorization which occurred at that time. The consequence was that the urban sprawl continued unchecked and the infrastructure continued to be inadequate.

The following measures will need to be taken in order to upgrade the infrastructure in the Tokyo metropolitan region:

- *Formation of an efficient urban region.* Congestion is still very much a fact of life in Tokyo, and the economic loss it causes is enormous. In order to facilitate communication with people all over the world, airports need to be made easier to use and closer relations must be established with the world at large. Although a telecommunications network is in place, demand continues to increase by leaps and bounds and there is a need for facilities of greater capacity.
- *Response to the rapid aging of society.* The Tokyo metropolitan region has seen a rapid increase in aging over the past decade, and the average age of the city's residents is growing much faster than in other world cities. It is essential to create an urban environment in Tokyo which enables the elderly and infirm to lead pleasant lives. Efforts in this direction are only just getting under way.
- *Response to environmental pollution.* Improving the water quality of rivers and Tokyo Bay, decreasing atmospheric pollution and noise, and dealing with refuse are major problems which remain to be solved. A solution needs to be found not merely by purifying any pollution which may have arisen but by removing the root causes of the pollution. The influence that a vast city such as Tokyo may have on the global environment cannot be ignored. It is thus important to get rid of the demand which has caused pollution to occur.
- *Raising safety in connection with natural disasters.* It used to be thought that we had learned from the experience of the great Kanto earthquake of 1923 and that Tokyo was now one of the world's safest cities, but the great Hanshin-Awaji earthquake of 1995 showed that this was a serious mistake. As well as being an extremely large city, Tokyo is also overcrowded. The city must be made safer by raising the seismic resistance properties of buildings and equipment and by creating wide roads and parks in built-up urban areas.

The following questions need to be borne in mind if any attempt is going to be made to upgrade the infrastructure in line with the four approaches referred to above. First, the understanding of local residents with regard to any infrastructural improvements will be required. In the past—the building of Narita Airport being a notable case in point—disputes involving various sectors of society have frequently arisen This emphasizes the point that the way in which infrastructural improvements are made takes insufficient account of the need to gain agreement at the planning stage. Much practical research is going to be needed to determine how the agreement of local communities can best be obtained. Second, there is the problem of how funds are going to be obtained, bearing in mind that there is as much demand as ever for infrastructural upgrading, while at the same time demand for the maintenance and renewal of existing infrastructure is on the increase. It is most unlikely that Japan is going to continue to experience economic growth with the same momentum as over the years 1970–2000. The question of how infrastructure is going to be paid for in such circumstances is one that requires immediate consideration.

LAND USE PLANS AND OTHER INITIATIVES FOR MANAGING REGIONAL DEVELOPMENT

The planning system for the Tokyo metropolitan region consists of plans for improvements in the metropolitan area, comprehensive plans and urban plans drawn up by public organizations in the urban region, and plans for the upgrading of public facilities classified according to sector, such as railways, roads and airports.

Since the Tokyo metropolitan region consists of a vast conurbation which extends way beyond the boundaries formed by administrative entities, when planning railways and roads stretching across the whole of the conurbation not all related problems can be resolved by the local areas concerned. The national government, specifically the National Land Agency, thus formulates an urban region upgrading plan targeted at the Tokyo metropolitan region and the Northern Kanto region located to the north of Tokyo. This plan is the most important within the whole complex of plans relating to the Tokyo metropolitan region. The first metropolitan region plan was compiled in 1958, and the fourth plan is being implemented at present. The current plan envisages a suburban upgrading region in which existing urban areas and their suburbs are upgraded in a planned manner and measures are taken to preserve greenery. Urban development areas have also been established to allow the development of "industrial" and "educational cities" in peripheral regions.

Although maximum priority within the system of planning is being given to this plan, as far as the infrastructure in particular is concerned, the plan is in effect no more than an anthology of the plans compiled by the departments of the central government handling roads and airports (Ministry of Transport, Ministry of Construction, etc.). As well as lacking integrated features, such plans are very weak owing to the fact that the means of implementation are left up to each department. For this reason it is difficult to assess the extent to which this plan has proved useful in shaping the Tokyo metropolitan region since 1958, and in practice it has been the plans compiled by individual departments that have had the most conspicuous influence on the formation of urban regions.

Influenced by the first metropolitan region upgrading plan, a law was enacted prohibiting any new construction or expansion of factories and universities in existing urban areas, the aim being to prevent any further rapid build-up of population and urban expansion. This had the effect of encouraging factories and universities to move out of the city into the suburban urban development areas and indeed in some cases out of the urban region altogether. This was a time when changes in the industrial structure were being accompanied by a move away from heavy and chemical industries in areas close to the sea and from urban types of industry in already established urban areas. More and more factories were being built in inland areas, and this law had an enormous influence on where they located.

Japan's Town Planning and Zoning Act divides urban planning zones into urbanization zones and urbanization control zones. Urbanization zones are zones in which urban development is permitted and urbanization control zones are zones in which development is in principal restricted. The borderlines between these two zones thus function to limit urban growth. However, the continuing inflow of population into the Tokyo metropolitan region and the frequency with which people move home has resulted in an enormous increase in demand for residential land. Urbanization zones were set too large in anticipation of just such an increase. The consequence is that the borderlines intended to limit urban growth have not always been effective in solving the problem of overcrowding in the Tokyo metropolitan region as a whole.

Under the influence of the plan for Greater London, several plans for the construction of large new towns such as Tama New Town and Kohoku New Town were formulated with the aim of providing large quantities of housing. In contrast to the Greater London plan, these new towns were conceived as suburban towns from which people could commute into the Tokyo city center. They played an important role in the context of housing policy in satisfying the demand for housing at a time when the urban population was rapidly rising. On the other hand, they also contributed to the expansion of the suburbs in the Tokyo metropolitan region. The only exception among these new towns is Tsukuba Campus City, which is not a commuting town but a new town located in an existing urban region. It is now home to Tsukuba University, a national research institute.

The concentration of economic functions in Tokyo advanced more rapidly during the 1980s than ever before. More and more high-rise office buildings were erected in the city center, and residential areas close to the city center were converted into office districts. New business centers were built on redevelopment sites vacated by large factories and railway freight yards in existing urban areas as well as on seafront and harbor sites. Such redevelopment strengthened Tokyo's economic status as a world city, although at the same time it highlighted urban problems such as congestion and environmental pollution brought on by a spatial structure characterized by centralization in one area, in this case the Marunouchi district.

A research report commissioned by the Tokyo metropolitan government in 1990 pointed out that it would be impossible to solve the problems of traffic congestion, environmental pollution, inadequate facilities for disposing of waste materials, and long-distance commuting for so long as this process of urban growth and development continued, even if current plans for infrastructure were totally realized. The report advocated the need to introduce powerful growth control policies.

With a view to solving these problems, the fourth metropolitan region upgrading plan advocated a change from a centralized spatial structure to a multi-core, multi-region structure. The following proposals in particular were made:

- While avoiding the overconcentration of facilities in central Tokyo, conditions for enabling that area to display its full potential should be realized while at the same time creating a multi-core structure by developing the metropolitan subcenters.
- Core cities should be developed in areas bordering on central Tokyo. These should become self-supporting urban areas where people could live close to their workplace and which offer a full range of urban services.
- In order to encourage the development of core cities, international, nuclear functions should be attracted to business-centered cities.

Concentration of functions in the Tokyo metropolitan region and especially in central Tokyo is a phenomenon which has occurred under a political, economic and social system which has been in operation in Japan for many years. There are therefore limits to policies aimed at direct and superficial changes in the spatial structure. Changes in the structure of the country itself are therefore going ahead, involving the transfer elsewhere of many of the capital's main functions, administrative reform, devolution, and deregulation. Transfer of the functions of the capital has a target date of 2010 and will involve the construction of a new capital outside the Tokyo metropolitan region to which the National Diet and key administrative and legislative offices will be transferred. It is hoped that, following the transfer of these functions away from Tokyo, the Tokyo metropolitan region will be able to prosper as one of the world's main economic and cultural centers.

CONCLUSION

The Tokyo metropolitan region offers a wide range of opportunities for employment, is adjacent to recreational and cultural facilities, and is a lively city with high levels of productivity. Compared with many of the world's leading cities it is safe and has low levels of crime and racial discrimination. On the other hand, its negative attributes include the constant threat of earthquakes, congestion, environmental pollution, cramped housing, high land prices, and an impoverished external appearance. Problems such as these have been tackled by means of infrastructural improvements, and a city in which 31 million people are able to live has been created. The main topic to be faced by Tokyo city planners in the future must be that of how to build on what has been achieved so far to create a better urban region, and it is important that the aim should be to consolidate Tokyo's position as a global city. To become a global city, it must satisfy three conditions. First, it must be cosmopolitan. Second, there must be a framework for planning the metropolitan region. And third, community development must be encouraged.

It is essential that Tokyo is open to the world and that there is no discrimination, no matter how racially varied the city may become. The future is likely to see a continuing increase in the number of Japanese nationals returning home after extended periods of residence overseas, of students from overseas, of people wishing to seek employment, and of foreigners wishing to settle in Japan. Now problems are likely to arise in a society consisting of a diverse mix of people. The next point is that the construction of Tokyo needs to be conceived in terms of the construction of the whole Tokyo metropolitan region. In this respect, the metropolitan region upgrading plan is, in effect, no more than a plan prepared by a single government department and is lacking in comprehensiveness and practicality. The plan needs to be reconceived as a new framework for the development and construction of the whole region. Another point is that regional development in Japan tends to be centered on physical, tangible aspects. But the trend in the world as a whole is rather toward mental, intangible aspects, toward the establishment of cosmopolitan cities which enable contact with diverse cultures and show tolerance to many different races. Cities in which people of all kinds can live and regard as home are needed. Community development is essential in order to create such cities. This is the third condition.

Looking at the functions of a global city, Tokyo already fulfills the economic conditions which have given it the status of an international financial center. But there are still many inadequacies as regards fulfillment of the above-mentioned conditions. Maturity as an international financial center will come about once Tokyo has achieved true internationalization, has created a framework for planning in the metropolitan region, and has begun to encourage community development. Once these aims have been achieved, Tokyo will be able to develop as a cosmopolitan city to which people can feel a sense of real attachment. These are the aspects that must stand at the foundations of future town planning. By achieving results in this area, the term "world city" when applied to Tokyo will at last take on real meaning and city planning will have become genuinely effective.

REFERENCES

Berry, Brian J. L., and Hak-main Kim (1993) "Challenge to the Monocentric Model," *Geographical Analysis* 25 (1), pp. 1–4.

Castells, Manuel (1989) *The Informational City*, Oxford: Blackwell.

Cervero, Robert (1989) "Jobs–housing Balance and Regional Mobility," *Journal of the American Planning Association* 55 (2), pp. 136–50.

Chang-Hee C. Bae and Richardson, Harry W. (1994) *Automobiles, the Environment and Metropolitan Spatial Structure*, Cambridge MA: Lincoln Institute of Land Policy.

Feagin, Joe R. (1985) "The Global Context of Metropolitan Growth: Houston and Oil Industry," *American Journal of Sociology* 90 (6), pp. 1204–30.

Friedman, John (1986) "The World City Hypothesis," *Development and Change* 17 (1), pp. 69–84.

Garreau, Joel (1991) *The Edge City: Life on the new Frontier*, New York: Anchor Books.

Gordon, Peter, and Richardson, Harry W. (1996) "Beyond Polycentricity: the Dispersed Metropolis, Los Angeles, 1970–90," *Journal of the American Planning Association* 62 (3), pp. 289–95.

Hall, Peter (1988) *Cities of Tomorrow*, Oxford: Blackwell.

Knox, Paul L., and Taylor, Peter J. (1995) *World Cities in a World System*, Cambridge: Cambridge University Press.

Mammen, David (1989) *Making Tokyo a World City*, Tokyo: National Institute for Research Advancement.

Mills, Edwin, and McDonald, J. F., eds (1992) *Sources of Metropolitan Growth*, New Brunswick NJ: Rutgers University Press.

Nilles, Jack (1991) "Telecommuting and Urban Sprawl," *Transportation* 18 (4), pp. 411–32.
Richardson, Harry W. (1988) "Monocentric vs Polycentric Models," *Annals of Regional Science* 22 (2), pp. 1–12.
Sassen, Saskia (1991) *The Global City: New York, London, Tokyo*, Princeton NJ: Princeton University Press.
Scott, Allen J. (1988) *Metropolis: From the Division of Labour to Urban Form*, Berkeley and Los Angeles CA: University of California Press.
Sudjik, D. (1992) *The 100 Mile City*, London: Deutsch.
White, Sammis B., Binkley, Lisa S., and Osterman, Jeffrey D. (1993) "The Sources of Suburban Employment Growth," *Journal of the American Planning Association* 59 (2), pp. 193–204.

In Japanese only

City Planning Institute of Japan (1992) *Tokyo Metropolitan Area*, Shokokusha.
Machimura, T. (1994) *Changing Structure: "Global City" Tokyo*, University of Tokyo Press.
Ministry of Telecommunications (1997) White Paper on Telecommunications in 1997.
Nakamura, H. ed. (1997) *The Infrastructure of Tokyo*, Gihodou Shuppan.
National Land Agency (1997) White Paper on the Shutoken Area.
Okamoto, T. (1994) *Urban Transportation Systems in Tokyo*, Gyousei.
Otomo, A. (1990) *Population and Lifestyle in the Metropolitan Area*, Japan Statistical Association.
Takahashi, N. (1995) *The Big Three Metropolitan Areas of Japan*, Kokin Shoin.
Tokyo Metropolitan Government (1996) Urban White Paper on the Tokyo Metropolitan Area.
Ueda, M. (1992) *Restructuring the Modern Metropolitan Area*, University of Tokyo Press.

13 The West Midlands

STEPHEN WALKER

The West Midlands region has a reputation of bustling towns and cities mixed with rural tranquility and has traditionally been seen as the industrial heart of the UK, being the birthplace of the industrial revolution (at Coalbrookdale). The metropolitan area, composed of six unitary authorities (including Birmingham), is the main center of population and employment (see Figure 13.1) at the crossroads of the national motorway network and the railway network (see Figures 13.6 and 13.8).

The region's historical and industrial past has left it with a rich and costly array of legacies. Physically, the decline of old industries has left vast tracts of contaminated land, preventing rapid reuse because of high costs and uncertainty. Capital restructuring, deindustrialization and government privatization policies throughout the 1980s have littered the inner cores of the built-up areas of the metropolitan county with derelict land and buildings (i.e. National Health Service hospital and infirmary sites; car and motor vehicle manufacturing plants; foundry sites; system-built housing areas) and redundant sites on the urban edge and in the countryside (i.e. collieries, rail marshalling yards and power stations).

Accessibility and locational advantages dictate how quickly such development opportunities are taken up within the region. Sites accessible to the principal rail and motorway networks have been first to be developed by private sector sponsorship, though some sites with less promise have come more quickly to the market whenever EU and other public sector sponsorship has been available. Relative to other European cities, it is clear there has been less development and what development has occurred has tended to be on these brownfield sites. Such increased land occupancy is thus strikingly different from most of the other regions in the study. Populations have remained stable but, as in other parts of the UK, the rate of household formation has led to relative growth.

The competitive advantage of edge of town or out-of-town location is well exemplified by the growing pull of sites located at or beyond the metropolitan area, for example at the M40/M42/M6 motorway interchange, adjacent to the airport and to the west and north of Coventry (Figure 13.6). This growth pole is becoming an increasing threat to the primacy of Birmingham's central business district. At the same time villages beyond the green belt have seen significant rises in population, mostly from higher income in-migrants (Figure 13.4).

Such threats are very difficult to manage and respond to when the nature and scope of government are partial, fragmented and thus weak. The region has only just begun to learn how to benefit from a weak form of regional government; the distribution of local powers has always been shared and thus diluted across many tiers and among many institutions. This is reinforced by the lack of any common boundary between the major statutory authorities, especially covering, for example, electricity and gas suppliers, water supply and treatment, social security or health authorities.

Paradoxically, in the latter part of the nineteenth century and the first part of the twentieth local government was epitomized by a strong sense of local municipal corporatism; in Birmingham this was powerfully led by the Chamberlain family. Over the 50 years since the passing of the 1947 Town and Country Planning Act, autonomy of local government has been increasingly subsumed under even stronger controls of central government. On the other hand, the West Midlands region is now administered rather than managed by a "weak" form of government, which is closer in character to a council of lower-level elected and relatively powerful local governments. Almost the only instruments regional government can use are information strategies, but in the growing age of telematics these can be used to considerable effect. The success of these weak forms of government depends more on their ability to form creative links with business, voluntary groups and local communities throughout their jurisdiction. To date, only Birmingham City Council has excelled in this role.

The election of the New Labour central government in 1997 raises the promise of the creation of Regional Development Agencies, probably operating across the existing government office regions, with the prime objective of coordinating strategies embracing sustainable regional economic, transport and land use planning.

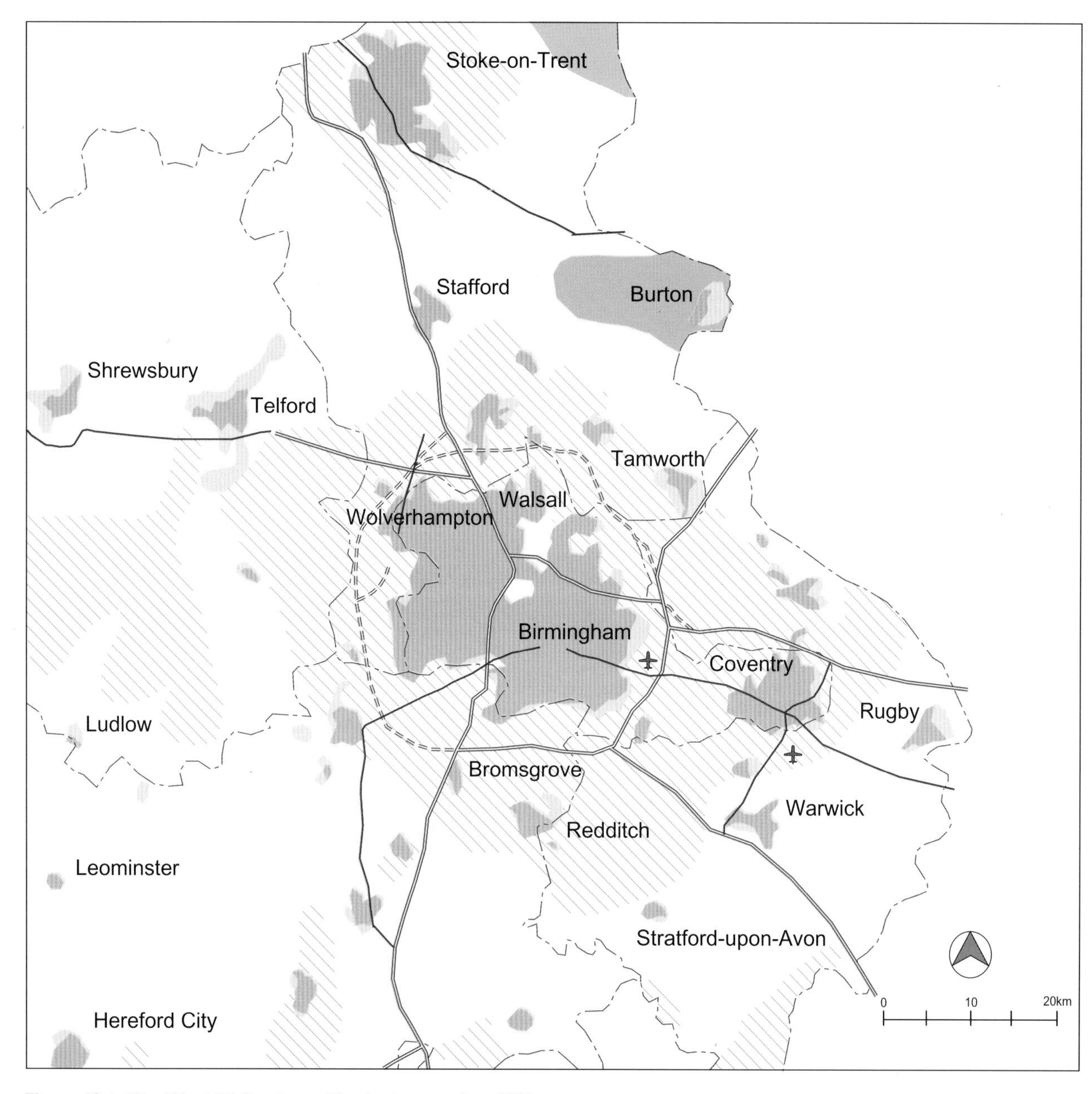

Figure 13.1 The West Midlands, or Birmingham region, 1995

Figure 13.2 The location of the West Midlands

CHANGING ECONOMIC PATTERNS

Metalworking, especially nail and chain making in the Black Country towns of Dudley, Sandwell and Walsall, and the more precision-based engineering trades, such as gun making, sited on Birmingham, became the region's economic base and strength in the nineteenth century. The surrounding shire counties have a strong agricultural history, complemented by pockets of industrial concentration: with carpet making at Kidderminster, ceramics in and around Stoke and car production in Coventry (Figures 13.3 and 13.4).

In the 1960s the pursuit of individual firm growth was frustrated by a distinct lack of internally generated profits. Growth without profits could still be pursued

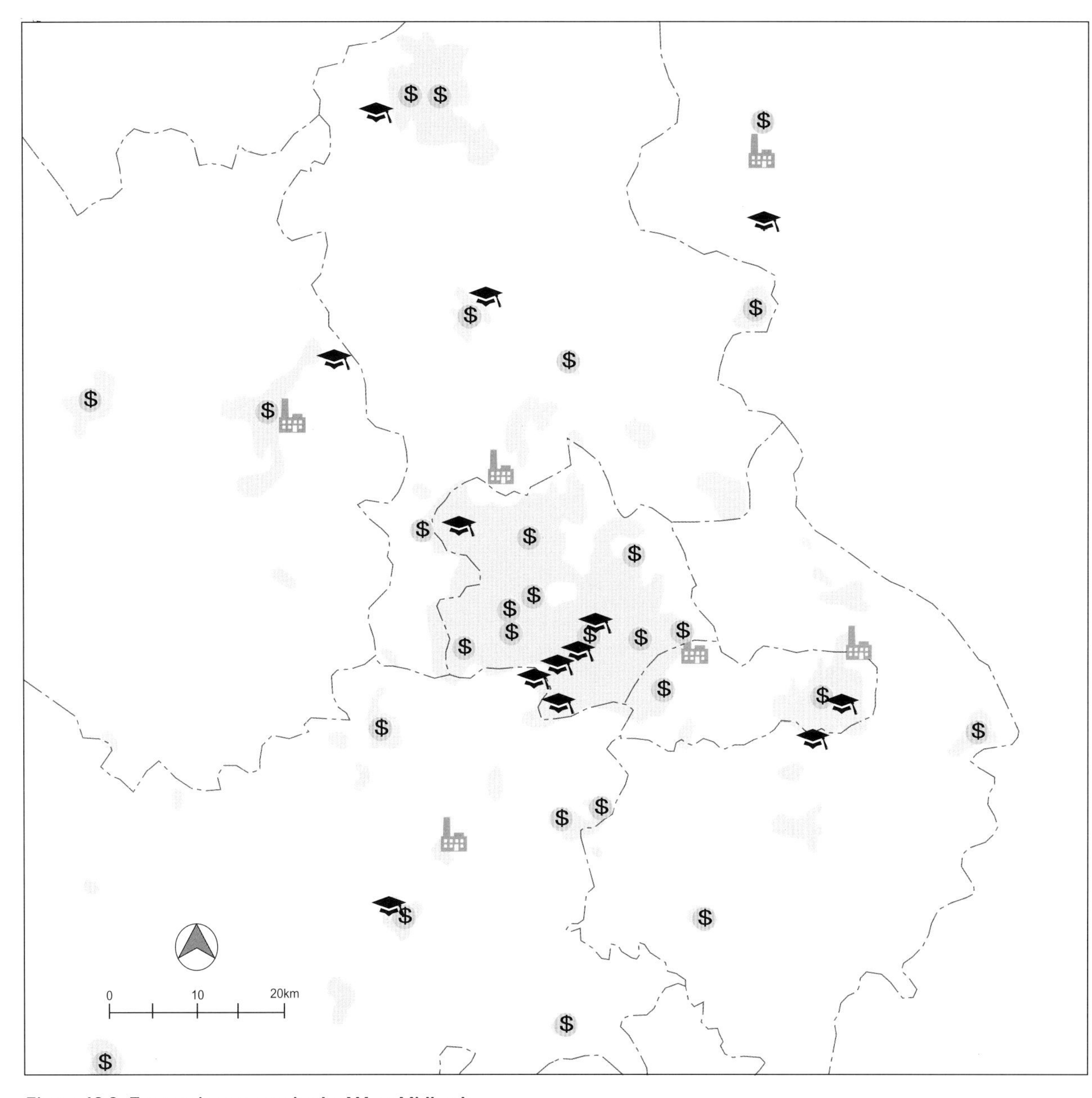

Figure 13.3 Economic patterns in the West Midlands

through mergers and acquisition, which became the common response to check competition, ridding key parts of Britain's industry of overcapacity, and inevitably leading to increasing concentration. Thus, whilst the West Midlands were once characterized by a plethora of small firms, they have become now more dominated by larger-scale enterprises than many other parts of Britain. Motor vehicle and component manufacturers and suppliers, and allied primary and tertiary sectors, provide the bulk of manufacturing jobs in the region: over a quarter of all male employees, and one in 10 female jobs.

As the indicators show, such strength was turned into weakness in the late 1980s when the biggest threat to the region's economy became the massive loss of jobs in its manufacturing base (also see Table 13.1):

- 431,000 jobs lost between 1979 and 1992.
- More prosaically, one in three jobs lost between 1979 and 1984.
- One in four jobs lost between 1989 and 1992.

A brief analysis of the main employment sectors shows a consistently recessionary trend:

- With continuing overcapacity in the *car and other vehicle* markets, the prospects for future growth in and beyond the 1990s are limited, though new technologies and innovations in production and processing may provide better employment opportunities from outsourcing and in research and development enterprises.
- With over 40 percent job losses in *engineering*, the sector is under significant threat from fragmentation (undermining investment and innovation) and increasing competition from international capital. For some còmpanies, relocation outside the region is being planned.

Table 13.1 West Midlands: key employment sectors (000 jobs)

Sector	Actual				Estimated	
	1979	1984	1989	1992	1995	2000
Manufacturing	985.0	709.2	668.0	554.0	565.0	532.0
Services	1,071.0	1,103.9	1,230.0	1,251.0	1,465.0	1,594.0
Other	185.0	167.8	156.0	128.0	198.0	189.0
Total	2,241.0	1,981.0	2,054.0	1,933.0	2,225.0	2,315.0

Sources *Department of Employment and Cambridge Econometrics, 1994.*

- A slimmed-down *ceramics* sector, heavily concentrated in north Staffordshire, is under intense foreign competition at a time when re-capitalization and innovation are needed if the industry is to survive.
- Continuing competition and overcapacity threaten the *metal goods* sector. Firms in this sector are typically located on cramped urban sites, with out-of-date plant and machinery, a poor training record and suffering from product development inertia.
- Only two collieries remain open (at Daw Mill, north Warwickshire, and Littleton, Cannock) in the region; the demise of *coal mining* and jobs have seriously affected ancillary industries and support services. Derelict and redundant sites present specific problems and challenges, especially regarding contamination and reclamation, reskilling and training of workers.
- The *textiles* sector has suffered greatly from intense international competition (low-cost foreign imports) and despite replacement of the majority of labour by new technologies over the years, the last carpet production in Kidderminster relocated to Portugal in 1997.
- *Aerospace, defence electronics and ordnance supply* are important employers in the region. However, these have been subject to rationalization, privatization programs and outsourcing pressures, which have generated significant knock-on effects on the vehicle and engineering sectors in particular. The sector is also characterized by large redundant sites, some in remote locations, which are hampered by lack of viable alternative uses and weak strategic planning tools.
- The *agricultural* sector continues to shed jobs, whilst key product sectors have been (permanently) hardest hit by changes in the Common Agricultural Policy pricing and support systems and now health scares. Agriculture, most important for the peripheral west of the region, is increasingly reliant on part-time farmers, but opportunities to diversify farming activity and their rural economies are limited, though better prospects exist from farm tourism and quiet and passive recreation. The isolated rural areas and villages continue to attract retiring households, whilst low incomes drive those that are economically active (young and educated) to the main employment centers, often outside the region, or to urban cores.

Fortunately, compensatory growth in the service sector has provided some mitigation against such deindustrialization. The service economy has been growing faster than the national average, though it has been from a low and narrow base (see Table 13.1). The narrow service base compared with many of the other regions in this book is possibly due to the West Midlands not being a capital city region but this does not explain why San Diego's (also a non-capital city region) service sector is much lower. Outsourcing, contracting out and competitive tendering have underpinned this resurgence in financial, processing and support services, and increasingly tourism, leisure and recreation. Through new commercial property development, such as the massive Merryhill Centre, which has become a new "town center" for the many small towns on the west of the metropolitan area, major urban regeneration schemes and flagship developments, the region has been responding to these new demands around the region: internationally renowned conference, sports, recreation and leisure facilities in Birmingham's central business district and close to the airport.

CHANGING SOCIAL PATTERNS

Changes and restructuring in the region's economic and industrial base over the last 30 years have left a new imprint on its social geography and demography. With economic growth being primarily concentrated in the rural areas and the new and expanded towns Telford (new), Redditch (new) and Droitwich (Figure 13.3), and economic decline in the metropolitan urban cores, a new division and clarity has emerged between urban areas and rural areas in terms of employment growth and economic opportunity.

Recent studies in Britain reveal that increasing social and economic polarization is now a common attribute, and in respect of the West Midlands two kinds of polarization are relevant:

- A distinction between urban centers and the more rural areas, where the wealthier sections of society tend to live.
- The marked divisions which exist in the urban areas between households with earners and households without.

The consequences of restructuring have impacted directly on people's lives and opportunities to work. The metropolitan core of the region has a large concentration of households with no one in the labour force. Having sharply increased throughout the 1980s and 1990s, the proportion today with no one in work is close to one in three households in key inner-city districts. Indeed, on the official government index of local conditions (deprivation)

Table 13.2 West Midlands: ranking of local conditions (1, worst; 366, best)

Local authority districts	National (1–366)	Region (1–37)
Worst 20%		
City of Birmingham	5	1=
Sandwell borough	9	2=
Wolverhampton borough	27	3=
Walsall borough	43	4=
Coventry city	45	5=
Stoke-on-Trent	64	6=
Hereford city	98	7=
Best 20%		
South Staffordshire	276	31=
Bromsgrove	288	32=
Shrewsbury and Atcham	294	33=
Rugby borough	297	34=
Wychavon	299	35=
North Warwickshire	301	36=

Source Index of Local Conditions, analysis based on 1991 census data (DOE, 1994).

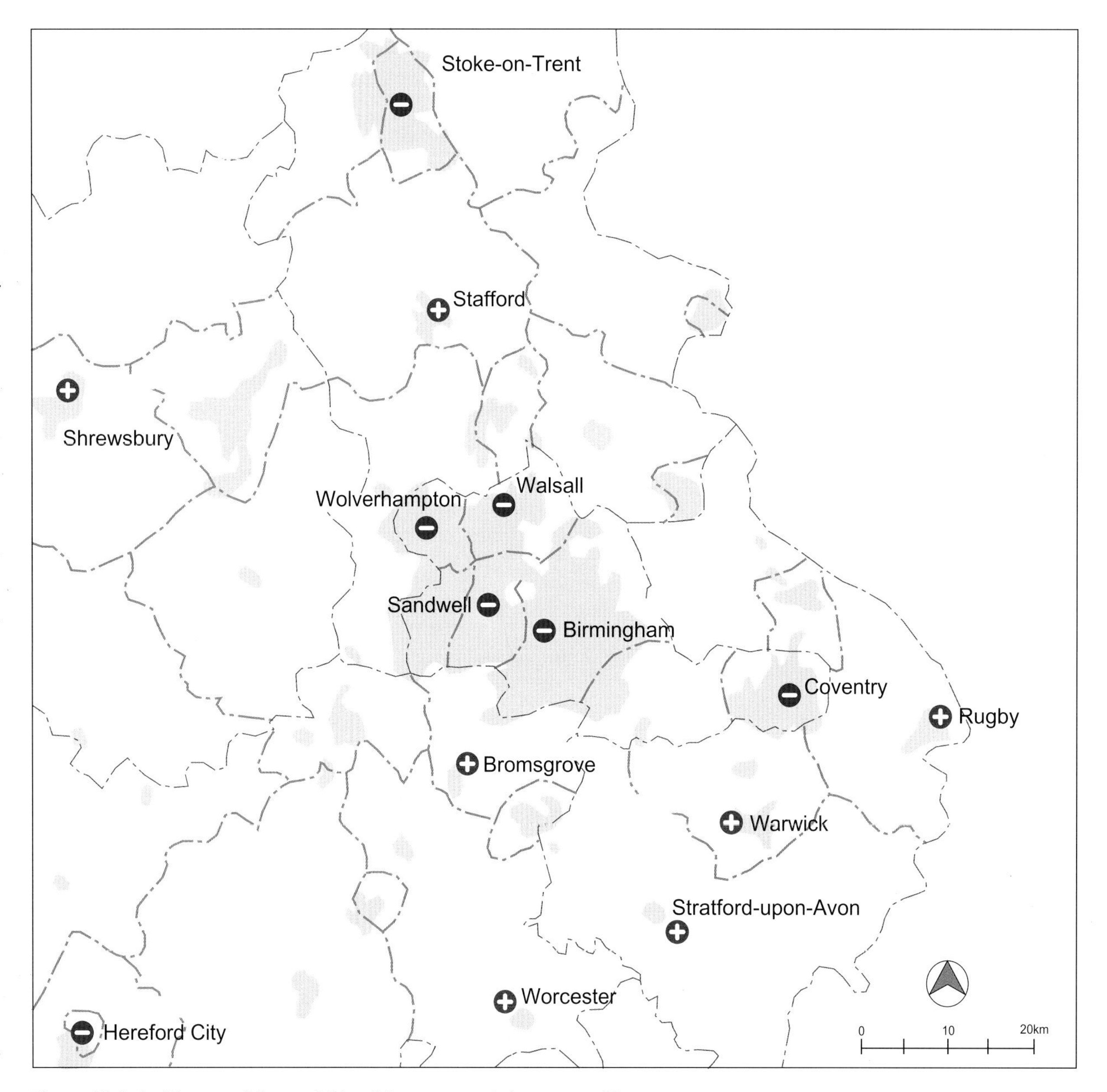

Figure 13.4 Residences of the wealthiest 20 percent and the poorest 20 percent

four out of the seven districts in the central core of the metropolitan area are ranked as some of the most deprived in the whole of England (see Table 13.2). As a result of such deprivation, the districts in the urban core are designated Objective 2 status for funding support from the European Union.

In contrast, some of the most economic and socially prosperous areas in England are predominantly located in six rural districts and in their free-standing towns surrounding the region's metropolitan core (see Figure 13.4).

Economic restructuring has also been generating new forms (and locations) of employment. One facet of this change has been the replacement of traditional employers by new forms of working, primarily in the form of self-employment, working at or from the home, and increasing proportion of part-time, flexible working, especially for women. However, the emergence of self-employment has barely compensated for the loss of traditional employment in the inner urban cores, whilst the outer urban areas have matched or exceeded the national increases. The largest increases have been registered in the rural areas. Indeed, since these areas have gained net population purely through net in-migration, so have more independent ways of working emerged: 27 percent of the economically active are self-employed in Leominster district, in the remoter western part of Hereford and Worcester County, which has the highest proportion of any of the 366 districts in England (see Figure 13.4).

This is not surprising, since recent research and survey evidence show that new technology companies, including teleworking, telecottages and home working, grow significantly faster in rural areas than in traditional employment locations. This apparent success of inward investment and business start-ups masks the structural and local deficiencies of the peripheral areas, specifically suffering from:

- Poor road and rail transport and accessibility.
- A distinct lack of well located, suitable employment sites.
- Intraregional comparative and competitive disadvantage.
- High dependence on regional "export" markets.

The rural counties forming a western and southern crescent around the metropolitan core represent over 70 percent of the region's land area, with agriculture being the dominant employment sector. Yet the peripheral western area beyond Leominster to the border with Wales exhibits many signs of rural decline and deprivation such that it has merited special status under the European Union's Objective 5b designation and as a Rural Development Area under national legislation.

Conflicts are beginning to emerge between promoting enterprise and employment in the countryside, especially if linked with farm and rural diversification initiatives, and conservation and the promotion of more environmentally sensitive, sustainable options.

Today a substantial minority of the population are suffering multiple deprivation and increasing social exclusion in the urban cores, as well as in the peripheral rural areas.

CHANGING SPATIAL PATTERNS

The spread of urban England and its containment has been of great concern to policy makers since the early twentieth century. The increasing tension between the continuing needs of towns and cities for additional land for such uses as housing, industry, commerce and retailing and a desire to protect the countryside and agriculture from excessive encroachment is nowhere more clearly seen than in the West Midlands.

A variety of urban growth management and other policy instruments have been put in place to contain and direct urban growth, including green belts, other restraint designations, and overspill policy, including New and Expanded Towns. In this respect, the region has more than 30 percent of its total land area where there is a strong presumption against development in the form of green belt, Areas of Outstanding Natural Beauty (AONB) and National Parks, including new urban forests (see Table 13.3 and Figure 13.1).

The 1970s and 1980s saw a rise in the propensity of households to move farther from the major centers of employment and for employment itself to decentralize either to the outer or edge of cities or beyond to free-standing towns with locational and competitive advantage on primary transport networks. In spite of this, and with a tendency of leapfrogging, an average commuting time of 23 minutes is still one of the lowest of the regions in the book (see Table 1, p. 19).

Research shows that the differential pace at which land is being converted is strongly influenced by the following factors:

- The statutory planning framework in England and Wales lays particular emphasis on allocating land for employment and particularly housing.
- Housing, as a specific land user, typically accounts for about 70 percent of land in urban areas.
- The demand for complementary services (retailing, leisure, commercial, etc.) and thus the size, location

Table 13.3 West Midlands: designated areas (km²)

Country, by area	National Parks	AONBs	Green belt	Total	Total land area
Hereford and Worcester	0	287	414	701	
Warwickshire	0	0	852	852	5,900
Shropshire	0	777	215	992	
Staffordshire	205	68	911	1,116	6,200
West Midlands	0	0	258	258	900
West Midlands total	205	1,132	2,650	3,919	13,000
England total	9,845	18,460	16,334	40,263	152,500
West Midlands as a proportion of England (%)	2	6	16	10	8.4

Source: Bibby and Shepherd (1996).

and forms of urban development, respond directly to demography and real incomes.

- It is contended that it will be the decentralization of population *rather* than the decentralization of employment that will be leading the evolution of future settlement patterns.

It must also be recognized that the rate of urbanization is not entirely explained by the growth in the number of households or population, since some influences on land conversion are entirely autonomous, being linked with the development of major works of infrastructure, such as power stations, major road interchanges and new rail extensions or upgrading. We also know that previous surveys predicting future levels and rates of urbanization are now exaggerated.

Other kinds of development affecting the rate of urbanization, which particularly characterized urban spatial development in the 1980s and 1990s, at least in England and Wales, are the out-of-town business and retail parks, warehousing and regional distribution centers and major manufacturing plants. We have mentioned the impact of the huge and very successful Merryhill Regional Shopping Centre in Dudley.

Planned decentralization, through the building of New Towns and the development of overspill arrangements with existing towns, has been successfully used to relieve congestion and to provide new homes and jobs. However, over-rapid decentralization of housing and jobs from the inner areas of large cities like Birmingham has been a significant factor contributing to an economic and social decline in the center which has been difficult to overcome. In the West Midlands, Redditch in 1964 and Telford in 1968 were part of a "second wave" of New Towns. These absorbed population overspill and new jobs from the metropolitan core, particularly from Birmingham and Wolverhampton, which had made explicit overspill agreements with the New Towns. The key premises on which this strategy was based were the existence of job surpluses in the inner urban cores, and a net displacement effect caused by the wholesale clearance of dense housing and employment areas, and the creation of new planned housing and shopping areas in the outer areas of the metropolis.

The urban landscapes of the 1960s and 1970s, so clearly visible today, are the system-built low and high-rise housing and retail areas, such as at Chelmesley Wood in prosperous Solihull, which were built by Birmingham City Council. Such mass housing or "grand ensemble" dominates the skyline of the West Midlands, especially from the motorways, and in many cases are or will be the subject of regeneration initiatives in the late 1990s and early years of the new millennium.

Urban land recycling (urban development on land previously in urban use) has and will continue to be a key feature of future development outcomes, especially since strong urban growth management policies are so tightly drawn around the metropolitan core of the West Midlands. However, the counties surrounding the metropolitan core, and especially the western (Shropshire) and southern (Warwickshire) counties forming a crescent of rural areas, have experience of marked recent economic growth and significant development of employment land, reinforced by New Towns policy, for example at Telford in Shropshire.

Significant development pressure exists at the urban fringe, especially along the inner edge of the green belts. These stem from:

- The release or designation of premium employment sites.
- Increasing demand to release more sites for housing to accommodate higher rates of household growth.

- Strategic or infrastructure developments:
  - Adjacent to Birmingham International Airport.
  - Extensions of the National Exhibition Centre.
  - Encroachment on the green belt of science and business parks and transport infrastructure.
  - Motorways: M42, M40, and a Northern Relief and proposed Western Orbital roads.
  - Rail upgrades and new freight terminals at Hams Hall, a former power station (see Figure 13.8).

Equally, high levels of development pressure are to be found in areas immediately beyond the green belt boundaries, and especially if these are along or linked to established or effective transport corridors accessing employment, consumer and trading markets. Thus the new road transport system is the focus of new development pressure in the form of development corridors. In the shire counties, the conversion of land in rural use to urban uses will be generated by significant net gains from retiring in-migrants. Thus high relative rates of urbanization have extended westwards in an arc of counties stretching from Warwickshire through Hereford and Worcester to Shropshire.

In the future, the greatest development pressure appears to be forming on the eastern edge of the metropolitan core, especially in the Coventry, Hinckley and Rugby travel-to-work areas, generated by major new infrastructure investments and upgrading schemes involving road, rail, freight and light rail. In contrast, the far western sector adjacent to the Welsh border, being much more rural and remote, and very much less accessible to the metropolitan core by either road or rail, is likely to continue to experience relative economic decline.

INFRASTRUCTURE INVESTMENT

Given the West Midlands' pivotal and central position at the heart of the country's rail and road networks, autonomous investment in its infrastructure is likely to benefit not only the operational efficiencies of the region itself, but also the national economy as a whole. Given the dissolution of the state monopolies, today businesses pursue corporate goals by maximizing competitive advantage, and thus overriding national or even regional goals of comparative advantage. It makes the task of investment and spatial planning much more challenging, particularly in the pursuit of "sustainable" development.

Strategic planning is now attempting to send a much stronger message in favour of development and settlement growth that is concentrated along transport corridors, and where public transport is given much higher priority. However, there is increasing emphasis on ensuring that these transport corridors permit the efficient movement of people and goods to market without triggering unconstrained urban growth. In this respect, a number of countervailing measures are being implemented to reduce the need to travel by private car, including new bus stations, bus-only lanes, multimode through ticketing, new light rail lines, park-and-ride schemes, taxing business car parking, town center pedestrianization, further restrictions on town-center parking.

The role of infrastructure investment, in particular, greatly influences the overall efficiency in and growth of business, employment demand and real income levels. The pace of investment in infrastructure has a typical staccato rhythm, registering an irregular inventory cycle, since it has been traditionally administered or managed through public sector budgetary and borrowing constraints. This was the case whether it related to the:

- Power industries: coal, oil, electricity or gas.
- Transport network, embracing rail, road or air systems.
- Water supply, sewerage and environmental protection.
- Telephone systems.

In response to the general features of global capitalism and economic recession, witnessed since the beginning of the 1980s, the development strategy of the British government has been explicitly (domestic) deflationary monetarist and export-oriented. This is a break with the past which has dramatically affected the role and position of the public sector, and particularly infrastructure sectors, because of:

- Privatization and exposure to increasing competition.
- Price regulation.
- Industry restructuring and rationalization.
- The creation of private and regional trade-for-profit monopolies quoted on the stock exchange.

The demand management role that these industries have played in the past are now absent from the economic weaponry that governments have traditionally relied upon, particularly in regional development and spatial planning terms. These acts of fractionalization and splintering expose future investment infrastructure decisions to more explicit market appraisal, and make the coordination of complementary investment decision making less certain as regards both input and outcome.

Roads

The existing road network is a product of long-term planning and investment which has shaped regional economic and national geography since the 1950s. In

Figure 13.5 Main roads in the West Midlands, 1967

respect of the West Midlands, the principal road trunk route (M1–M6) linking Birmingham with London was completed nearly 40 years ago in 1959 (see Figure 13.5). Today the region has a network of high-capacity roads which has provided an effective but increasingly congested system of routes for intraregional and interregional car and freight traffic. The existing network comprises a series of interconnecting trunk roads based upon the M1, M6 and M5, forming a triangle of motorways. These have been augmented by the extension of the M40 linking into the M42 in the mid-1980s; the extension of the southern and eastern sections of the M42; and the upgrading of the M69, linking the M6 with the M1 north of Coventry to relieve interregional through traffic from the M1. Today the primary routes along trunk roads and motorways are operating at or near capacity.

Two major roads are planned to complete the two remaining sections of the outer-relief box, shown as a dashed line in Figure 13.6:

- The Western Orbital Route from the M5–M42 interchange at junction 4a to a point on junction 12 on the M6.
- The Northern Relief Road from the M6–M42 interchange at junction 4 to a point north of junction 12 on the M6.

These will be subject to a Private Finance Initiative (PFI) where contracts will be procured under a Design, Build, Own and Operate/Manage arrangement. The Northern Relief Road received permission in 1997; the other proposal, however, continues to be more speculative.

The contribution of local or central public funds to future new road building, upgrading or extensions is now

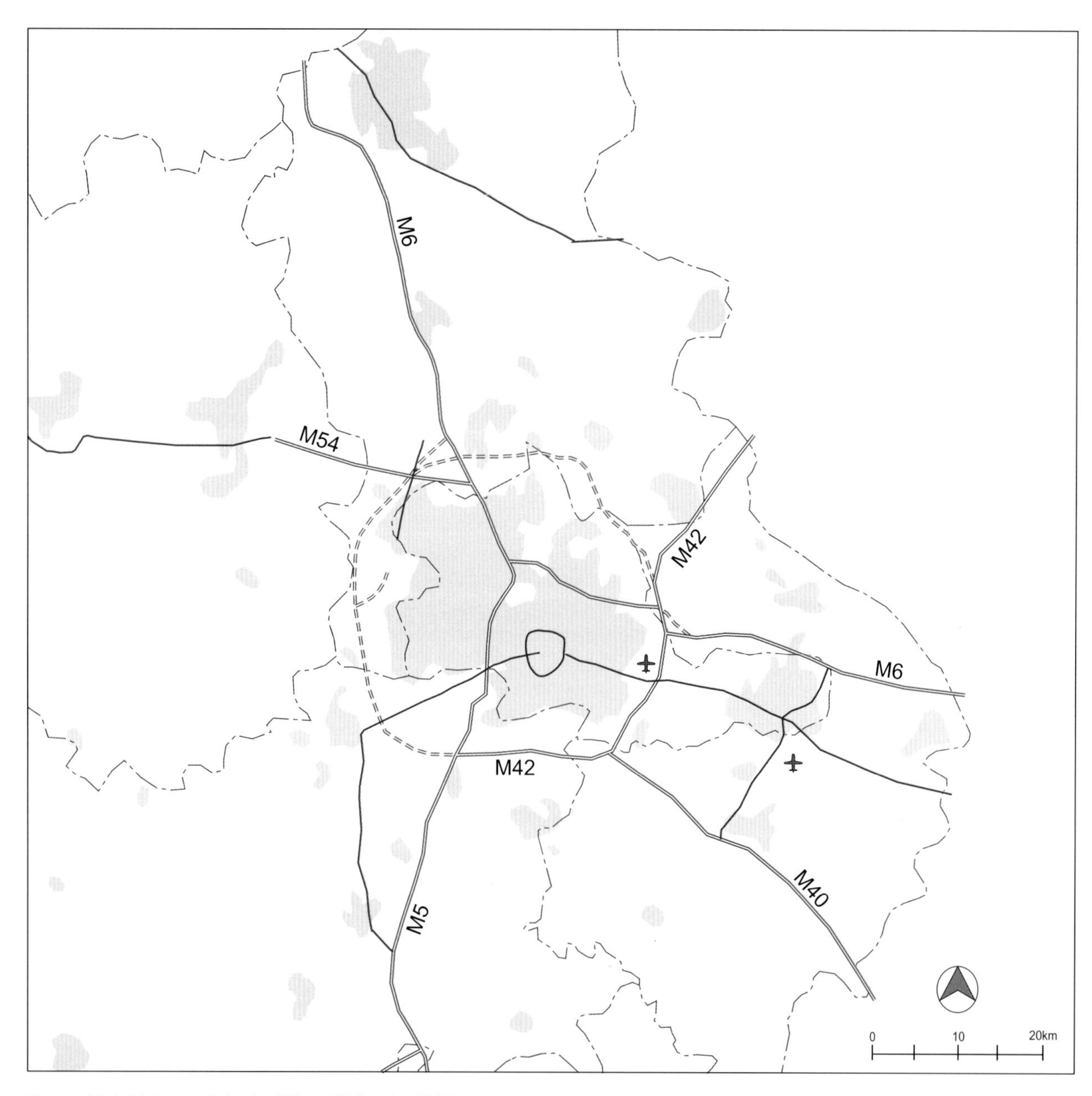

Figure 13.6 Main roads in the West Midlands, 1995

strongly influenced by the primacy of private financing, whether through the PFI or through private contributions via planning obligations (under Section 138 of the Highways Act). This latter financial mechanism is the most frequently used method of paying for the construction of the many bypasses built or planning around towns and villages. As a result, in the future, local and regional transport priorities may be satisfied only if commercial rates of return or private contributions can be secured from related developments.

Railways

The present rail network is largely the product of colossal contraction (37,000 km to 28,300 km) in the intensity of the rail system over the past 80 years. In addition, other changes have affected hundreds of rural branch lines; cuts in the level and frequency of services on others; and reduced and reallocated operational subsidies in consort with financial support from local county councils, to ensure more effective services on the remaining urban and rural networks.

The central position of the region was reinforced nationally by the electrification (in 1964 and 1974) of the west coast main line (WCML), which linked five of the seven largest conurbations, and improved the region's ability to access important local rail routes for employment, business, recreation and tourism throughout the metropolitan core, free-standing towns and remoter rural areas (see Figures 13.7–8).

Until 1994 the rail system had been operated as a unitary service where the infrastructure in the form of track, station development, and rolling stock for passenger and freight services were all under the control and

Figure 13.7 Railways in the West Midlands, 1967

management of British Rail. Since privatization the rail infrastructure (covering the track and signalling) has been split from passenger and freight service operation, and through competitive tendering separate service franchises have been sold off to private operators.

Since privatization a number of new and improved services and new lines are being introduced. In 1995 approval was given for the upgrading of the west coast main line, running from London, Birmingham and Manchester to Glasgow. This includes modernization works involving complete resignalling and comprehensive track renewal, electric power supply and other infrastructure work. A dedicated new station on the main west coast main line has also improved all-round accessibility to Birmingham International Airport for this and other regions.

In 1998 the pattern for future investment will need to respect the following exigencies:

- *Significant spare service capacity on many rail lines*, with the exception of the Birmingham–Coventry line: for example by reintroducing a through service on the Nuneaton–Leamington rail line.
- *Promote better intra-conurbation, cross-route services*, e.g. the Lichfield–Redditch link; install double track on existing single lines, the most critical of innovations if rail is to be able serve the increasingly dispersed movement patterns of today.
- *Reopen old lines and establish entirely new ones for both passenger and freight.* Midland Metro has opened a new Wolverhampton–Birmingham link (Line 1) and two others have been proposed (though not funded): Five ways/Birmingham City Centre to Heartlands and Birmingham International Airport/National Exhibi-

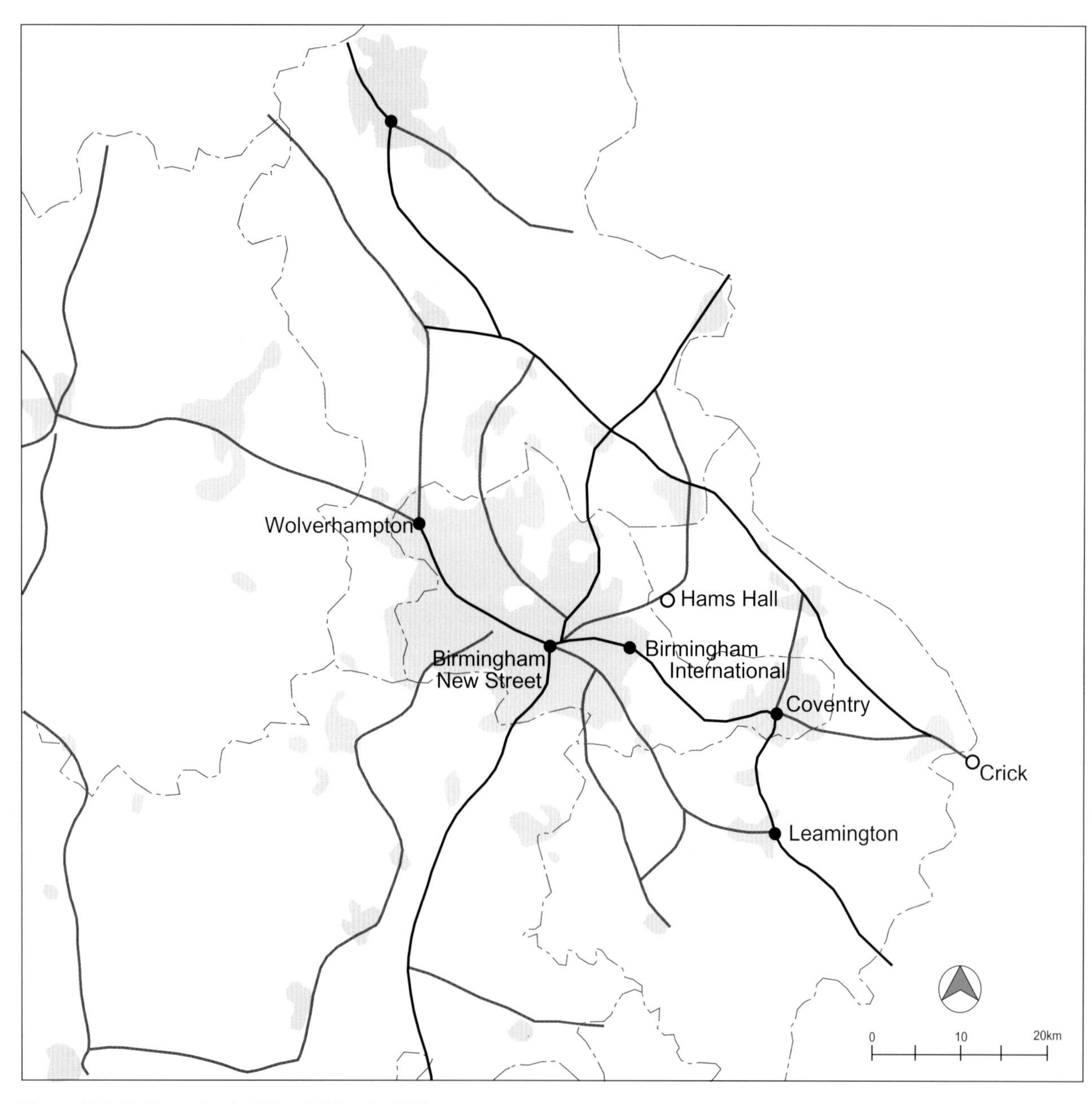

Figure 13.8 Railways in the West Midlands, 1995

tion Centre (Line 2); Wolverhampton to Brierley Hill via Walsall (Line 3). (See Figure 13.8.)

- *Introduce a new light rail system either on new tracks or along existing tracks.* There is a new proposal to link the Regional Shopping Centre at Merry Hill with Brierley Hill by a light rail link.
- *Consistent regional and local ticketing.*
- *Improve access by building new and/or extending existing stations*, extending and improving links and services on the Chiltern line to the West Midlands with the development of Birmingham Snowhill–Moor Street–Smethwick West railway improvement (partially funded by ERDF).

In respect of freight transport, the West Midlands is a region with a high reliance upon manufacturing and the distribution of goods, and throughout a high volume of goods are in transit from other regions to their national and international markets. Though the majority of these goods travel by road, and are likely to continue to in the future, greater use of rail for freight is being promoted through the establishment of two new freight-line terminals. One of these is located on a former power station site at Hams Hall (Figure 13.8), east of the metropolitan area, and a new dedicated freight line along disused passenger lines to provide better freight services to the Channel Tunnel and to east coast ports. (The other is on the region's eastern border at Crick in Northamptonshire; Figure 13.8.) The Coventry/northeast Warwickshire subregion has particular locational advantages for it to become the focal point of very large-scale distribution facilities serving intraregional, interregional and European markets, given the improvements and concentration of existing road, rail and freight networks.

Additional freight and passenger services are being planned as part of a £250 million upgrading of the railway lines between Glasgow and the Channel tunnel, taking a route via the new freight terminal at Hams Hall, Banbury, Oxford and Didcot. This new facility has the capacity to take 400,000 lorry journeys from the roads, using newly designed piggyback wagons.

Airports

In terms of passenger numbers, Birmingham International Airport is now Britain's fifth largest airport. However, the airport is eccentrically located in terms of the load center of its present traffic, and its siting, very close to the edge of the built-up area, will continue to restrict its current operations and achieve its predicted traffic growth level (see Figure 13.1).

The airport is owned by a consortium of local authorities, with the principal interest held by Birmingham City Council. This pattern of ownership and management is a direct legacy of immediate post-war government policy (1945) of devolving responsibility for provincial airports to local authorities, which have lacked the resources to invest in other than piecemeal improvements. This arrangement may no longer be tenable, given the increasing demand for capital for future development, and, given the tight constraints upon local authority budgets, some kind of private equity partnership is expected. Recent liberalization of chartered and scheduled services to North America and its well established links in Europe is reinforcing the increasing importance of Birmingham International Airport as a regional economic and employment growth pole.

Birmingham International Airport has been playing an important role in transforming the city center of Birmingham (as well as the region) as part of a larger "place and regional promotional" strategy to improve the region's national and international reputation. Since the airport has been relieving the pressure on the heavily used air space over London and the south-east, the region is able to offer a number of economic advantages to business, commerce, tourism and delegates, namely:

- The National Exhibition Centre and its extensions.
- Improving the quality of city center public squares.
- A new Hyatt Hotel in Birmingham city center.
- The International Convention Centre.
- The National Indoor Arena.
- Science and business parks linked with established universities.

The region's other major provincial airport is at Coventry; it has been developing into an important center for domestic and Europe-bound freight traffic.

The greatest challenges to the region from increasing urbanization, traffic congestion and future location of development are to be found in this part of the region, particularly in what is known as the Meriden Gap in the green belt between Birmingham and Coventry, since it is easily accessible to the national road and rail systems as well as internationally via the airport.

Telecommunications

The telecommunications sector is a product of national government policy over the last 80 years. Having been transferred from local authorities in the early 1920s, the sector was a public sector monopoly and as such it was wholly dependent for its capital finance on central government. The sector was privatized in the early 1980s and, though it became the first regulated private monopoly, competition from private service providers has substantially increased. New operators (for example, Cellnet, Vodafone, Mercury) have increasingly penetrated British Telecommunications' (BT) business and consumer markets, using the existing trunking systems and new optical fiber and satellite systems

These various systems offer television and telephone services, with the massive potential to offer interactive services such as video-on-demand, home shopping and banking, security and alarm services, electronic mail and remote meter reading. Television channels carried by cable systems include those from a number of satellites, as well as from other sources: thus both local and international channels are now available to people and businesses throughout most of the region.

Local or town franchises have been granted covering two-thirds of the UK population, about 14.5 million homes. In the West Midlands these can be as small as 5,000 homes or as large as 500,000 homes. The rate at which areas are being covered depends upon an assessment of market potential. In the West Midlands the most extensive progress has been in the urban cores and free-standing towns, particularly in Birmingham, the Black Country towns and Coventry. The target market is expected to embrace about 1.54 million homes, which represents about 70 percent of the region's households. However, the proportion of homes actually taking out subscriptions is still quite low: about 4 percent (see Table 1 on p.19). What is clear is the absence of cable provision in vast tracts of the western and remoter rural areas of the region. The economics of cable infrastructure provision require access to high volumes or high densities yet the rural areas cannot match either of these two requirements to generate such business. These remoter areas will be the last to be serviced, if at all.

Satellite-based systems, however, may offer alternative services, but evidence shows that poor-quality reception is hindering mass penetration of these markets, again especially in remoter rural areas. The region has three satellite receiver stations at Warwick (by the M40), Tamworth (by the M42) and Stafford (by the M6). These have sufficient capacity to serve the main concentrations of population in the east and central core of the region.

REGIONAL LAND USE PLANS AND OTHER INITIATIVES TO MANAGE URBAN AND REGIONAL FORM

The relationship between the course of regional growth and change has been inadequately conceptualized by economic theories. Notwithstanding problems in defining the "region," center–periphery or cumulative causation theories directly reflect a long-standing dichotomy in mainstream economics. The former has been rejected as too simplistic in this case, since though the West Midlands is relatively prosperous, several sectors of its population, industrial and employment bases are suffering from deep structural and social and economic decline. In this respect, the central issue regarding regional growth and change is the extent to which the problems in and of the West Midlands are an outcome of unfavourable location as against outdated, narrow or inertia-dominated industrial structures.

Such conditions illustrate marginality and point to the need to overcome a dual adversity. Traditionally, regional and local economic development strategies have been designed to protect industry and jobs, and harness resources for regions, cities and rural areas that are lagging, undeveloped, or suffering from acute deficiencies in demand and economic activity rates. Thus coordinated and complementary European and nationally sponsored regional economic development policies aim to cure the symptoms and prevent a recurrence of the adverse impacts of economic and social change. In this regard, two particular concerns are critically important for effective regional planning in the West Midlands:

- The extent to which economic and industrial growth generated in the region can be harnessed to regional rather than national advantage.
- The growth of and change in pressures expected to be generated along the communications axes passing through the region.

In the final analysis, the problems and potential for growth are measured in terms of the economic and social well-being of the region's population—its people, their work and their quality of life.

The spatial pattern and concentration of development in the West Midlands region have been more the product of a suite of strategic town and country policies managing urban growth than in the majority of the regions in the book. This is no doubt partly because growth pressure has been relatively low and government has provided funds for much of the physical and economic development undertaken, or containment management policies have involved the mutually reinforcing approaches of:

- New Towns, Expanded Towns and overspill policies.
- Urban regeneration and inner-city redevelopment.
- A suite of designated areas where there is a strong presumption against development, including green belts, Areas of Outstanding Natural Beauty, National Parks, Areas of High Landscape Value and Sites of Special Scientific Interest (SSSIs).

These latter restraint policies have had the intention of directing development either to points within the existing urban cores or to free-standing towns beyond the areas of restraint at 30–60 km from the metropolitan core, but along established transport corridors.

The West Midland green belt was established to:

- Check the unrestricted sprawl of large built-up areas.
- Prevent neighboring towns merging into one another (e.g. the Meriden Gap separating Birmingham and Coventry).
- Assist in urban regeneration by forcing growth back into urban areas.
- Preserve the special character of historic towns.
- Safeguard surrounding countryside.

Of the five purposes cited above, the first three are the more important for the West Midlands. The size and extent of the green belt, especially that encircling the metropolitan core of the West Midlands, acts as a *cordon sanitaire* within which development is excluded. For how long this kind of policy and its areal extent can be sustained will depend upon locally generated opportunities and challenges as well the way national government is willing to reappraise both the effectiveness and the efficacy of this kind of growth management strategy. Such challenges and opportunities are expected to embrace:

1. The challenge presented by the "need" to accommodate growth in the demands of private car and

lorry journeys is dramatically put into perspective when national governments have conveniently used the "space" formed by the green belts to build the majority of the trunk routes (the M40 and M42 in the West Midlands, the M25 in Greater London). In the West Midlands two new roads are planned: the Northern Relief Road and the Western Orbital route.

2. A further challenge to the maintenance of the green belt stems from increasing calls for business and household growth to be concentrated along established transport lines or corridors, and along which public transport systems are given much greater priority. In this respect, the green belt would become fractured, producing strategic gaps or green wedges ensuring that any development is strictly contained without generating urban sprawl and agglomeration. The size of such settlements would be relatively small and contained, and would generate a pattern similar to a loosely strung necklace. This is a model receiving increasing support in the professional journals these days.

3. There is increasing pressure to redraw the green belt boundaries. In response to pressure to accommodate urban and economic growth within development boundaries, the inner edge of the green belt has been redrawn outwards in some cases, whilst at the same time its outer edge has also been extended in others. Such changes have been seen as marginal adjustments of boundaries that are expected to be permanent and remain for about 30 years.

4. Evidence from government-sponsored research shows that despite such a presumption against development in the green belt areas, infrastructure investment over the years has been generating a number of significant pressure areas or points around the region:

- South and southeast of the conurbation, in Warwickshire, Hereford and Worcester and within the green belt in Solihull (see Figure 13.1).
- Along the M5 in Bromsgrove district.
- The M54 area north of Wolverhampton.
- The southern part of Lichfield district.
- The Warwick District area related to the M40.

The Solihull/M42 areas, the previously discussed Meriden Gap, relate to possible sites for new employment and industrial development, as do sites along the M5 and M54. Since parts of Hereford and Worcester green belt boundaries are as yet undecided, it is suggested that new housing will have to go on land in the green belt. In addition, there has been a growth in leisure-related development applications, mainly golf courses, theme-related leisure parks (for example, Alton Towers, the Coalbrookdale Industrial Revolution), and rural amenity centers in the form of country parks ("Shakespeare Country," "Elgar Country").

5. Economic forces, and resulting social changes, are putting the urban fringe, land immediately abutting it and the countryside beyond the green belt under development pressure, from a number of influences:

- *Increasingly dispersed patterns of living.* Aided by the ease of car travel, allowing the separation of home and work, the decentralization of people from cities to wider functional economic regions has continued.
- *Agricultural problems.* Once agricultural land was retained under the presumption that productive output should be maximized. Currently, large tracts are being set aside from agricultural production, especially at the urban fringe. Though rural and farm diversification is limited, it would seem important to facilitate such development where it can have wider economic and landscape benefits.
- *Leisure demands* are seen as increasing, particularly where leisure use in the countryside is serviced by car travel: space-extensive sports such as golf and water sports, and some motorized sports. The urban fringe and green belts appear valuable locations for recreation if this could lessen the length of leisure journeys by car, reduce travel for its own sake, and promote greater use of public transport.
- *Environmental degradation.* This embraces a wide range of derelict and degraded land falling out of extractive and other use, and the general neglect of countryside management, especially within the green belt. Mineral extraction and open cast mining continue to be a problem for the urban fringe. Demand for new landfill sites, incinerators and recycling plants is more pressing.
- *Local and rural defensiveness.* Many criticize green belt and policies of promoting a "no growth, no change" philosophy. However, whilst resisting all forms of development, local populations are making higher demands for more local services. The views of farmers and others involved in rural industries, who have traditionally held a more pro-development stance, have been outvoted by local residents. The green belt has become for them a symbol of a life of urban convenience, lived-in surroundings with rural visual attributes and, for all its faults, it commands a great deal of public support.

6. Uncertainties surrounding the impact of new technologies and processes on spatial development, urban form, business and household location, and employment

opportunities and practices. Some researchers contend that innovations in communications and conducting transactions will severely weaken the advantage of the city and metropolitan fabric as well as proffering benefits in terms of reducing the need to travel through new means of working and transacting. Birmingham City Council, for example, now operates a working-from-home policy for its employees. Notwithstanding such differential impacts on employment and economic and social well-being, there are other implications likely in terms of environmental sustainability, particularly relating to resource and energy consumption. These will ultimately depend upon the balance between:

- *Resource and energy-consuming effects* associated with a more spatially dispersed metropolitan form.
- *Resource and energy-conserving effects* associated with the substitutability of physical movements (of people, of goods and services, and of information) and telecommunications equivalents (such as telecommuting, teleshopping, electronic data interchange, videoconferencing).

Some of the existing centers of agglomeration are likely to benefit more, since these areas and locations already possess the advanced complementary infrastructure required for such information-intensive and communications-intensive activities. Where there is competition between providers one would expect prices to fall and perhaps the areas will become more attractive locations for certain companies, especially those thinking of relocating or establishing new businesses based on the new technologies.

Specifically for the West Midlands, an emerging technopole is to be found close to Coventry and Warwick, in the Meriden Gap, close to the airport, to the east of the region's metropolitan core. It reflects the increasing importance of research development and new business and educational alliances to the regeneration of the economy. Research and development capacity is being concentrated around the science park at Warwick University, and at Westwood Business Park in order to achieve a critical mass particularly as a center of excellence for companies involved in advanced manufacturing technology. The science park functions also as a nursery from which expanding firms can migrate to larger units at the adjacent Westwood Park. In total nearly 4,000 jobs have been created to date. Similar initiatives are being pursued at the other universities in the region—all with European funding support and with a mixture of public and private venture capital.

The way business harnesses and utilizes new technologies will ultimately depend upon the role of competition and risk, since it is these features that are generating more important changes affecting economic space, leading to:

- *Flexible specialization* creating patterns of cooperation between enterprises rather than further competition.
- *Strategic alliances and networks*: outsourcing, competitive tendering, partnership funding.
- *Place competition*: city networks.
- As inter-firm competition declines, the importance of *system environment increases*: just-in-time production techniques.

CONCLUSION

Britain's urban growth management strategies (principally the green belt) have been criticized for only containing the physical but not the functional growth of cities. Thus, whilst green belts have tended to generate benefits, by directing and diverting development inwards towards and within the main metropolitan cores, what are being called for are new forms of strategy for the outer parts of the city region which are seen as increasingly separate, in demographic, social and economic terms from the metropolitan cores.

To a high degree these pressures on and criticism of green belts are a reflection of the ineffectiveness of a central–local system of government in delivering regional planning. Many of the possible advantages of compact settlement planning, by adopting policies of local physical containment, have been subverted by the inability to plan for the whole functional extent of individual cities and regions.

Many UK planners are beginning to argue for regional government to be strengthened and planning to be given new powers with new policy instruments. As well as these, there is a need to develop more sophisticated practices, particularly using the "information instrument" more creatively. They claim the challenges being presented by sustainability and environmental capacity issues deem that the following kinds of powers and policy instruments should be available to regional governments:

- A new settlements programme along established transport corridors.
- A system of land and betterment tax to curb development on greenfield sites.
- Target tax breaks to support urban recycling of land and promotion of urban regeneration.
- More efficient and effective land assembly powers, including adequate funding sources.

- A selective review of local green belts, especially in respect of transport corridor development, perhaps the form of strategic gaps, green wedges, or green chains.
- Taxing or prohibiting car parking spaces in town centers, for both residents and business.
- A new regional planning framework as part of some kind of regional government which is more than simply an association of local governments.

These are not extreme demands, since most other cities or regions in Europe already possess such powers and policy instruments. But they do, as discussed earlier, fly in the face of a growing system of investment and development management which is increasingly market-oriented.

REFERENCES

The following texts and journal articles have been drawn on to a greater or lesser extent in compiling and writing this chapter.

Balchin, P. N., and Bull, G. (1987) *Regional and Urban Economics*, Liverpool: Paul Chapman.

Batty, M. (1990) "Intelligent Cities: Using Information Networks to Gain Competitive Advantage," in *Environment and Planning* B, *Planning and Design* 17, pp. 247–56.

Bibby, P., and Shepherd, J., eds (1996) *Urbanization in England: Projections 1991–2016*, Planning Research Programme, DOE, London: HMSO.

Breheny, M. H., ed. (1992) *Sustainable Development and Urban Form*, London: Pion.

Broadbent, T. A. (1977) *Planning and Profit in the Urban Economy*, London: Methuen.

Department of the Environment (1994) *Index of Local Conditions: An Analysis based on 1991 Census Data*, London: HMSO.

Diamond, D., and Spence, N. (1989) *Infrastructure and Industrial Costs in British Industry*, Report to the Department of Trade and Industry, London: HMSO.

Elson, M., Walker, S. and MacDonald, R., eds (1993) *The Effectiveness of Green Belts*, Planning Research Programme, DOE, London: HMSO.

Evans, R. (1994) "Birmingham," in A. Harding, J. Dawson, R. Evans, and M. Parkinson (eds) *European Cities towards 2000: Profiles, Policies and Prospects*, Manchester: Manchester University Press.

Eurostat (1992) *Portrait of the Regions* II, London: Eurostat.

Forecasting Committee for the Construction Industries (1996) *Construction Forecasts 1996–1997–1998* II (3), London: Construction Forecasting & Research.

Gibson, M., and Langstaff, M. (1983) *An Introduction to Urban Renewal*, Built Environment series, London: UCP.

Goddard, J. B., and Champion, A. G., eds. (1984) *The Urban and Regional Transformation of Britain*, London: Methuen.

Government Office for the West Midlands (1995) *Regional Planning Guidance for the West Midlands Region, RPG11*, London: HMSO.

Guy, S., Graham, S., and Marvin, S. (1997) "Splintering Networks: Cities and Technical Networks in 1990s Britain," *Urban Studies* 34 (2), pp. 191–216.

House, J. W., ed. (1977) *The UK Space: Resources, Environment and the Future*, second edition, London: Weidenfeld and Nicolson.

Marshall, T. (1997) "Futures, Foresight and Forward Looks: Reflections on the Use of Prospective Thinking for Transport and Planning Strategies," *Town Planning Review* 68 (1), pp. 31–53.

Martins, M. R. (1986) *The Organisational Approach to Regional Planning*, Aldershot: Gower.

Rodriguez-Bachiller, A., Thomas, M., and Walker, S. (1992) "The English Planning Lottery: Some Insights from a more Regulated System", *Town Planning Review* 63 (4), pp. 387–402.

Valuation Office (1992–96) *Property Market Report*, London: Inland Revenue.

Vickerman, R. W., ed. (1990) *Infrastructure and Regional Development*, London: Pion.

Walker, S., and Grimley, J. R. (1992) *The Use of Planning Agreements*, Planning Research Programme, DOE, London: HMSO.

Walker, S., and Thomas, H., eds (1995) *The Operation of Compulsory Purchase in England and Wales*, Planning Research Programme, DOE, London: HMSO.

Willmott, P., ed. (1994) *Urban Trends* II, *A Decade in Britain's Deprived Urban Areas*, London: Policy Studies Institute.

WMRFLA, *The West Midlands Region: European Development Strategy*, Documents 1–9, Stafford: West Midlands Regional Forum of Local Authorities.

PART 3

Comparing and Contrasting the Cases

The purpose of the research by the consortium was to generate genuinely comparable international data, which could be used by readers to discover how their own region compared with 11 others around the world. The data were also assembled so that they could be contrasted and compared in the search for answers to the research questions outlined in Chapter 1. In this short section we attempt two informal exercises of comparing and contrasting the data in order to answer two specific sub-questions about these city regions:

- How have their spatial patterns been changing over time?
- How have their cultures of governance been changing over time?

14 Infrastructure and regional form

GARY HACK

It has often been said that the twentieth century was the time of two great technological revolutions—the first brought the widespread production and availability of industrial products, and the second saw the emergence of electronic communications and computation. At the turn of the millennium, it is argued, the second is displacing the first in importance, and soon will have a profound impact on urban form.

Another reading of history is that the two have gone hand in hand since the early years of the twentieth century, and are inseparable. When the Singer Sewing Machine Corporation moved its headquarters to a new site in Lower Manhattan in 1908, it was able to forsake a location near its main plants because of the increasing availability of the telephone. This electronic infrastructure enabled its managers to be in constant contact with its production supervisors and an expanding system of railroads and mass transit that allowed easy travel between the various sites. Indeed, the modern form of industrial corporation has developed an overlay of electronic means of communication on its physical infrastructure; neither could exist without the other. Its organizational form has been constantly forced to evolve to account for the new means of communication and control.

And so it has been with cities. Much of the physical infrastructure of the city is currently being reshaped by overlay of electronic aids, including the introduction of intelligent vehicle and roadway systems, sophisticated routing and scheduling systems for delivery vehicles, electronic monitoring and control of traffic, and sophisticated control systems for transit, water and sewer supply. The demand for locations in the city is also shifting in response to the new forms of industrial organizations, new leisure opportunities, new relationships between home and shopping and new communications possibilities. However, cities contain a large stock of durable investments that are not easily reproduced, and the process of change in urban form is likely to be slow. One should also not underestimate the importance of habit and sentiment in maintaining current urban patterns: familiarity exerts a strong hold on urban residents' affections. Thus, rather than imagining cataclysmic change in the form of cities and settlements as a result of the new electronic age, it is more useful to think of the process as one of continuous evolution, in which new means are overlaid on the prevailing physical and organizational infrastructure. New cities, where the capital stock is less committed, can exhibit the new urban forms most rapidly.

Cities are at various points in the evolution of their infrastructure, both industrial and electronic. Developing and finding a basis for maintaining industrial infrastructure (roads with vehicles, mass transit, electrical networks, water supply and waste collection, gas distribution, etc.), is a first requisite for prosperity, although not necessarily assuring it. Over the past three decades, cities in Southeast Asia and Latin America have experienced large-scale industrial development, and have had to face many of the issues addressed earlier by their counterparts. They have had to cope with huge migration to cities from the countryside, inadequate and lagging infrastructure, scattered and uneven development, unimaginable congestion, the need to make room for new commercial enterprises in the preindustrial fabric of the city, loss of valuable agricultural land to urban development and land speculation, and the like. Congestion on roadways is often the driving force of urban development, with the result that development is spreading into fringe areas, demonstrating once again Charles Tiebout's maxim that the land use pattern adjusts itself to even out congestion.

North American and European cities are facing an opposite set of difficulties as a result of deindustrialization.[1] They have a problem in maintaining infrastructure in areas where industries have left, the loss of population in declining areas makes it difficult to maintain essential services, and some vacant land within the city is even being returned to small-scale agriculture. There is an evening out of densities and opportunities across the urbanized realm. Yet even in such cities—Philadelphia, Cleveland, Detroit among them—there is a process of evolution at work, through the expansion of the service economy. The result is islands of prosperity in the central core, and large areas of suburbia that continue to attract jobs and people. Congestion has shifted to the suburbs, and roadways, transit systems and other infrastructure which focus on the core of the metropolitan area often do not fit desired lines.

While the amount of investment on the ground makes the adjustment of urban form difficult, slowly but quite surely older industrial cities are being reshaped to resemble their newer counterparts.

Curiously, while the processes are quite different, the outcomes of urban evolution are quite similar in cities around the world. Growth rates of virtually all major cities have declined, partly as a result of deliberate policies, and partly as a result of scale—the difficulty of accommodating ever increasing populations and economic activities as cities get larger. Migration has slowed, and the fraction of new growth represented by net in-migration has decreased. As Chapters 3–13 have revealed, development is spreading out, with net densities declining in most cities. Spatial segregation of households of different incomes is increasing. Many of the new high income jobs, shopping opportunities and residences are being concentrated in "elite corridors," often but not always in the direction of regional airports and high-speed rail lines. While these emerging forms of transportation are important locational anchors, the most critical factor affecting urban form over the past several decades has been the growth of motorization. Rapidly increasing numbers of private automobiles, coupled with a dramatic shift to truck transportation, has freed the form of the city from dependence on rail and transit systems, and has opened vast areas of land to economic development and housing estates. But the spread of development has also increased the cost of infrastructure, which customarily lags behind development. Local governments are in a desperate race to catch up with the new demands that are created, and a weakening of the control and finances of national and regional entities has placed this burden largely on underfinanced entities.

THE GROWTH OF LARGE CITIES IS SLOWING

The fears over mega-cities absorbing an increasing fraction of the population appear not to be materializing. In fact, quite the opposite is occurring—growth rates of the largest cities are lagging behind intermediate and smaller centers.

The rate of urban growth is quite clearly the reciprocal of the level of economic and social development of a country. When countries are grouped according to the UN scale of human development,[2] the urban population of the lowest ranked countries is growing at a rate roughly four times that of the highest ranked countries. (See Table 14.1.) With only 10 percent of the population of the lowest ranked countries residing in large cities, as opposed to 31 percent in the highest ranked countries, this process is likely to continue at high rates as industrialization occurs. Indeed, the industrialization process takes place largely through urbanization.[3] However, growth rates have slowed considerably in the largest cities of each country, even in countries with low levels of social and economic development. In 1975 the growth rate of the largest cities tended to equal or exceed the overall rate of urbanization of a country, but by 1995 in all categories of countries, from rich to poor, the largest cities were growing at a rate well below other urban areas.[4]

Similar trends can be seen in the 10 cities of various sizes on four continents sampled in the Global City Regions project.[5] (See Table 14.2.) Growth rates in all of the case study cities except Jakarta have slowed to 3 percent or below, with European cities growing at 1 percent or less. Growth in Taipei slowed from 11 percent in the 1960s to 2 percent during the 1990s, and São Paulo from 5 percent to 2 percent.

An important component in the reduction of growth rates has been the significant drop in migration. While

Table 14.1 Urbanization and growth rates of largest cities

	Urban population annual growth rate (%)		Population in cities over 750,000 (%)	Growth rate, largest city	
Countries	**1960–93**	**1993–2000**[a]	**1990**	**1970–75**	**1990–95**
Industrial	1.4	0.7	29		
High HDR (31 countries)	1.3	0.7	31	1.3	0.7
Medium HDR (16)	2.2	1.1	15	2.6	1.3
Developing	3.8	3.5	14		
High HDR (25)	3.5	2.2	31	3.3	1.6
Medium HDR (exc. China) (53)	4.1	3.2	20	4.5	3.2
Low HDR (exc. India) (48)	5.1	5.1	10	6.0	4.8

Source *United Nations Development Report, 1995.*

Notes [a] *Projected; HDR: Human development rank; exc: excluding.*

Table 14.2 Population growth in selected cities

	Year	Bangkok	Madrid	Randstad	San Diego	Santiago	São Paulo	Taipei	Tokyo
Total population	1960	3,312,000	2,510,217	5,144,000	870,700	2,133,252	4,791,245	1,380,010	15,928,189
	1970	4,529,500	3,781,348	5,636,000	1,262,804	2,871,060	8,139,730	3,846,526	22,424,349
	1980	6,644,400	4,685,895	5,789,000	1,736,100	3,735,399	12,558,725	4,627,200	27,365,972
	1990	8,589,900	4,947,555	6,066,000	2,348,417	4,518,057	15,416,416	5,704,400	30,607,845
As % of nation	1990	16	13	40	1	34	10	28	25
Growth rate (%)	1960–69	3	4	1	3	3	5	11	3
	1970–79	4	2	0	3	3	4	2	2
	1980–89	3	1	0	3	2	2	2	1
Migration as % of urban growth	1960–69	74	21	n.a.	55	52	59	57	48
	1970–79	55	18	n.a.	74	33	51	47	25
	1980–89	48	13	n.a.	64	10	–10	44	39

Source Data provided by cities in LILP study.

migration typically represented half or more of the population growth of the case study cities during the 1960s, in many cities it now accounts for less than 20 percent. The exceptions to this are, however, noteworthy. Migration accounted for 64 percent of San Diego's growth over the past decade, helping it maintain one of the highest growth rates of US cities. São Paulo had a net out-migration of 10 percent over the 1980s, lowering its growth rate to only 2 percent.[6]

The interesting question is why this slowdown occurred. As cities get larger it becomes increasingly difficult to sustain high growth rates because of increasing congestion and lack of adequate infrastructure. Increasing regulations on development—such as have occurred in São Paulo—may divert development into jurisdictions beyond the urbanized area. There is also a statistical explanation of reduced growth rates: with an enlarging population base, it takes ever larger increments of growth to maintain the same growth rate. As an example, despite the steep decline in its growth rate, Taipei added almost as many new residents in 1990 as in 1960.

But virtually every country in the world has also been promoting decentralization of growth, through policies which range from bolstering the infrastructure of underdeveloped areas to providing tax incentives for locating industry away from large metropolitan areas to diverting new development to planned new towns. After several decades these strategies may be paying off. More likely, as countries rise on the economic ladder and as national networks of roadways and communications are put in place, there is economic advantage in the decentralization of manufacturing, particularly consumer goods which do not require sophisticated supply chains. Several economists argue that in manufacturing, agglomeration economies do not continue to increase after a city reaches about 300,000 in population.[7]

THE POLYNUCLEATED SPREAD CITY HAS BECOME A REALITY

The spread of settlement has resulted in lower densities in most cities. For the Global City Regions sample, actual built-up areas were measured and gross densities were computed. The results showed that the densities of cities had declined in eight of the 11 city regions.[8] (See Table 14.3.) Some became substantially less dense, particularly European and Middle East cities—Ankara declined from almost 70,000 persons per square kilometer in 1960 to less than 9,000 in 1990, Lyon from 13,000 to less than 5,000, Madrid from 16,000 to about 8,000, and the settled areas of the Randstad from 17,000 to 6,000. The decline is

Table 14.3 Changes in urban form

	Year	Area (km²)	Population	Density/km²	Per / Min Per
Ankara	1960	9	650,000	69528	1.7
	1970	21	1,236,000	59230	1.9
	1980	33	1,878,000	56675	1.9
	1990	288	2,559,000	8882	2.5
Bangkok	1960	103	3,312,000	32151	3.0
	1970	193	4,530,000	23448	3.7
	1980	406	6,644,000	16358	3.8
	1990	429	8,590,000	20004	3.7
Jakarta	1960	224	1,800,000	8031	1.1
	1970	356	4,592,000	12885	1.2
	1980	453	7,393,000	16332	1.2
	1990	423	13,120,000	30999	13.1
Lyon	1960	91	1,199,000	13238	4.8
	1970	252	1,438,000	5713	4.7
	1980	312	1,574,000	5045	5.0
	1990	376	1,703,000	4528	5.3
Madrid	1960	154	2,510,000	16281	3.2
	1970	359	3,781,000	10528	4.9
	1980	455	4,685,000	10295	5.5
	1990	597	4,948,000	8289	6.0
Randstad	1960	295	5,114,000	17317	2.7
	1970	798	5,636,000	7062	4.4
	1980	880	5,789,000	6577	4.6
	1990	1011	6,066,000	5998	4.7
San Diego	1960	420	971,000	2310	4.4
	1970	770	1,263,000	1641	8.5
	1980	1319	1,736,000	1316	11.4
	1990	1525	2,348,000	1540	13.8
Santiago	1960	228	2,133,000	9353	1.6
	1970	322	2,871,000	8927	1.5
	1980	431	3,735,000	8669	1.3
	1990	557	4,518,000	8110	1.7
São Paulo	1960	1038	4,791,000	4614	1.8
	1970	1341	8,140,000	6070	3.2
	1980	1705	12,559,000	7366	4.3
	1990	2038	15,416,000	7566	4.7
Taipei	1960	41	1,380,000	33757	2.2
	1970	65	3,847,000	59543	1.8
	1980	171	4,627,000	27068	2.3
	1990	320	5,704,000	17818	1.3
Tokyo	1960	6628	15,928,000	2403	1.1
	1970	7159	22,424,000	3132	0.9
	1980	8090	27,366,000	3383	1.0
	1990	8402	30,608,000	3643	0.9

Source Maps and data provided by cities

Per/min per—Measure of compactness—perimeter of built up areas divided by theoretical minimum perimeter if one form partly demographic—the reduction of household sizes—and partly the result of new perimeter development.

Development in these cities has also become more scattered. Using a measure we devised to judge the compactness of spatial configurations,[9] all of these cities added considerable non-contiguous development. None, however, come close to the dispersal of San Diego, where densities in developed areas reduced from around 2,300 persons per square kilometer in 1960 to around 1,500 in 1990, while the settlement became about three times more dispersed.

With the spread of settlement has come new large-scale commercial and employment centers in outlying areas. Some of these have begun to rival central areas, particularly in Asian cities, where mega-malls have become the new focal points of cities. Large-scale industry has also typically located on the urban fringe, and industrial enterprises have often taken the lead in assuring that workers' housing is developed nearby, sometimes (as in Bangkok) on the industrial site. The locations of these new concentrations are frequently unplanned, the result of entrepreneurial zeal and the availability of large parcels of land with reasonable levels of infrastructure, meaning typically piped water service and arterial roads.

Cities which saw densities increase are also worth examination, since they run counter to the broad trends. Densities have steadily increased in Jakarta, from around 8,000 per square kilometer in 1960 to around 30,000 today, despite the dramatic spread of development, which now extends 100 km from the historic core.[10] High density housing estates, and seriously overcrowded traditional housing, are the manifestation of this. While migration has slowed and now represents only about 14 percent of new population each year, Jakarta has the highest current growth rate among the case study cities. Its *per capita* GDP is also the lowest. São Paulo appears to have evolved in similar ways, with densities increasing about 60 percent since 1960, even while the city has spread out and become more scattered. Topography seriously limits development, contributing to the breaks in the urban pattern.

Tokyo appears to have increased in density by about 50 percent over the past three decades. However, its form is slightly more compact today than it was in 1960, as a result of deliberate policies. Much of the additional population has been accommodated through redevelopment of low density housing areas. Tokyo has the best developed transit system in the world, and has added a new line on average every three years since 1950. An aggressive land adjustment policy has been pursued to promote development around railway and transit stations. A deliberate policy of creating new metropolitan subcenters, in two rings—an inner ring about 6 km across centering on the Yamanote line, and an outer ring approximately 25 km from the center—has helped focus infrastructure investments. Coupled with significant restraints on the conversion of agricultural land to urban development, the city has been a model of transit-oriented development. The sheer size of the city, however, has meant ever increasing commuting times, now averaging 41 minutes in each direction.

Taipei saw its densities rise initially as a result of large in-migration in the 1960s, but they have declined as the city has expanded outward subsequently. And after several decades of declining densities as the city expanded outward haphazardly, they have begun to rise in Bangkok, probably in reaction to the difficulty of commuting. Average commuting times in Bangkok are 105 minutes each direction, surely among the greatest in the world. In Taipei's case the decentralization was largely planned, through a number of new towns and large-scale planned developments. Bangkok's suburban spread has been largely unplanned, although new regional and metropolitan plans aim to coordinate infrastructure investments.

The case of Santiago is also instructive. While the metropolitan area population has more than doubled since 1960, densities have remained relatively constant (around 8,000 persons per square kilometer) and the development pattern has remained relatively compact. This has occurred in the face of serious political turbulence, which has resulted in shifting policies towards urban expansion. Despite these shifts, the "monolithic character" of the city has been the result of relatively low investment in regional infrastructure (roads and railways), the low rate of car ownership (lowest among our sample of cities) and the restrictive actions of the planners.[11] (Strict urban limits were removed only in 1979.) Santiago remains a relatively low income city without the distribution of resources for widespread motorization.

Motorization clearly plays an important role in determining the form of urban expansion, although many other factors intervene. Each of the case study cities has seen a dramatic growth in the ownership and use of automobiles, but the spread of development varies considerably. Taipei is an extreme case, with the number of persons per automobile decreasing from 127:1 in 1960 to 5:1 today. Yet Taipei remains a relatively compact city, as does Tokyo, which has seen a shift from 27:1 in 1960 to 2:1 today. On the other hand, Ankara, which has the highest number of people per automobile in the sample, has seen the most dramatic spread of development. Clearly, land policies, infrastructure construction, the level of industrialization, and the general level of income of the population have more critical roles in determining the spread of settlement than automobile ownership alone.

ECONOMIC SEGREGATION IS INCREASING

With shifting densities and the outward spread of development, there has also been a significant shift in the locations of rich and poor. Asian and Latin American cities, which had been characterized by fine grained mixing of income groups, are becoming more segregated, partially by design, and partly as a result of economic processes.

In Santiago there has been a deliberate policy of eradicating shanty towns from areas of officially declared "real estate interest." Local government areas (*comunas*) have been redrawn to conform to the boundaries of social and economic groups, isolating the poor from their wealthier counterparts.[12] In Bangkok, infrastructure projects have displaced over 50,000 low income residents over the past few years, and replacement housing is almost exclusively located in outlying areas, poorly served by transit and services. This process is being fueled further by private redevelopment of inner city areas for high income residents and offices, with more of the poor being pushed to the periphery. The segregation of low income residents in US cities is well known, and mapping of the spatial pattern of San Diego shows that virtually all the lowest income neighborhoods are in the southern half of the city, while most of the highest income groups live in the northern half.[13]

New business centers which are evolving in many cities also have the tendency to spur the creation of "elite corridors," with housing, entertainment uses and educational facilities oriented to white collar and high income groups. Virtually every city has such a new center, and often they are located near new regional airports. In Santiago such a cluster is emerging along the Américo Vespucio beltway. In the Randstad the area adjacent to Schiphol Airport is beginning to take this form. In Manila the Makatti area is becoming a new city center, with most of the banks headquartered there along with the city's largest shopping centers, and several gated residential "villages." Tokyo has taken the lead in planning such subcenters, including the ring of new centers on the outer perimeter of the metropolitan area – Makuhari Messe, Tama New Town, Tskuba New Town, MM21 in Yokohama, among them. A new high service center is being planned at Hsintien in Taipei, to begin decentralizing the core of the city. In Bangkok the peripheral land around the Second Bangkok International Airport is being planned to become a multi-use subcenter. Often these new centers are the city's window on the international economy and the preferred location for regional headquarters of multinational corporations.

CONTROL OVER THE FORM OF DEVELOPMENT ON A REGIONAL SCALE IS LESS POSSIBLE

As cities have spread, decision making about urban form has become more diffuse, often involving multiple local governments, states, regional entities and agencies of the national government. The sheer problem of exercising control over development has also increased with the occupied territory. Coupled with this are two important secular shifts since the 1960s—the devolution of responsibilities to local governments, occurring in many countries; and the increased reliance on private organizations for infrastructure and land development.

Each city region has its unique history and institutions, which ultimately influence the way that decisions are made, so one must be cautious with generalizations. None the less, several distinct policy approaches are evident. During the 1960s and 1970s, most cities prepared regional development plans, often aimed at diverting industry, housing and population away from the contiguous built-up area. Some plans included proposals for new towns, others promoted corridors of development leading out from the center, still others promoted "growth poles" based on smaller villages or cities within commuting range of the central city. The 1968 outline plan for Taipei, Tokyo's successive metropolitan regional master plans, Santiago's PRIS-60 master plan, the COPLACO planning for Madrid in the 1970s, the Jabatobek plan in Jakarta prepared in the 1970s, and Lyon's master plan of 1976 are examples. Other cities without a tradition of planning, or where growth materialized later, prepared similar plans in the 1980s—Bangkok's master plan of 1983 (adopted a decade later) is one.

The experience with these master plans was quite similar. They helped shape a number of large decisions on infrastructure, such as the construction of radial and circumferential expressways, the installation of mass transit systems and the construction of new airports. Even though most projects took much longer to materialize than predicted, the announcement of major infrastructure projects often was enough to trigger a wave of development in areas they served.

Most regional agencies preparing plans did not have direct control over land development—it was often in the hands of local governments, which were chronically understaffed and underskilled. There are exceptions, of course, including Tokyo, where tough land use controls were adopted by the national government and mapped and enforced effectively by localities. The London and West Midlands green belts, in England, are other exceptions, where most development was excluded for over 40 years, but the decision to locate major roadways and airports in these areas ultimately undermined their viability as open spaces. However, in Taipei and São Paulo, enforcement of density and building controls has been poor, and in Bangkok almost non-existent, making regional plans largely ineffectual.

Proposals to create new development magnets also have had a mixed history. In a few instances these were carried out by the national government—science cities in the Tokyo, Taipei and Madrid areas are examples. In Lyon a development corporation chartered by the national government carried out the construction of planned new towns. The experience was similar in England, where New Town Development Corporations assumed responsibility for a large fraction of the new peripheral development. But, for the most part, regional agencies could not muster the economic and regulatory powers necessary to see their visions realized.

Proposals to relocate national capital activities out of the major metropolitan area of a country have also had a curious history. Perhaps modeled on Brazil's bold move to open up the center of its vast territory through the construction of Brasilia, Bills have been passed to seek new sites for governmental functions in Japan and Thailand. To date, this has proved more difficult to accomplish than expected. Costs are prohibitive, particularly during a recession; real estate interests fear the loss of their land and property values; and government officials resist the move from familiar surroundings. But debate continues and it is too soon to write these measures off.

More recently a new round of regional plans has been less ambitious, focusing on those structural elements which in a coarse-grained way affect development. These structure plans generally concentrate on major infrastructure elements, areas to be reserved from development, the location of subcenters, and policies that local governments can use to guide their regulatory actions. The Emplasa plan for São Paulo (1993), Bangkok's Metropolitan Regional Structure Plan (1995) and the SANDAG-initiated Regional Growth Management Plan for San Diego (adopted in 1993) are three examples, on different continents.

At the same time that regional planning has focused on a more limited set of issues, political changes have shifted the ground for regional planning efforts. As part of a broad movement to decentralize responsibility, local governments have been enlarged or formed which encompass much of the urbanized city region. In Bangkok the Bangkok Metropolitan Administration area covers 80 percent of the population of the urbanized region, and local taxes and fees provide a growing fraction of expenditure on public infrastructure and services. The city is preparing its first locally drawn metropolitan plan. The region of Madrid government was formed in 1983, assuming many of the responsibilities previously reserved by the central government, including development planning. In Brazil a new national constitution adopted in 1988 decentralized to states most urban development responsibilities, including the creation of new local governments. The result has been the formation of a new Development Council with broad powers to plan and carry out development efforts, which has the potential of overriding local government wishes. While each of these measures holds the promise of creating governments with boundaries and responsibilities that match the city region, they have sometimes been confounded by the low levels of skill among government employees at the local level. This has accelerated the move to privatize functions such as construction of sewer and water systems, major roadways and airports.

When common facilities are created through private concessions, there are important issues of coordination and service that must be faced. Bangkok's experience with private construction of expressways, transit and sewers through contracts and concessions illustrates the point. Decisions about access and routing are made with an eye to capturing the population which can most afford to pay, and timing is determined by the market demand for service. In the case where cross-subsidies from development are expected, construction of infrastructure becomes captive to real estate cycles. There is little incentive to coordinate facilities with others. Before the national government intervened, Bangkok's three transit projects were being planned without transfers between them.

The new localism in dealing with regional issues has also meant increased competition for resources to be used for regional infrastructure. While national governments could justify investments that had a long-term payoff, local elected officials need to balance these against immediate priorities. The result is many more small projects, and fewer megaprojects, since a rough consensus is more easily gained if everyone benefits. In a number of the case study cities there have been conflicts between those advocating investments to capture international business opportunities and those urging attention to immediate local needs. The current mayor of Tokyo, elected on a reform platform, has canceled or slowed several major projects that were a drain on local resources, including Tokyo Harbor Teleport, intended as a new international business center. An administration and mayor of Ankara were voted out of office by a constituency that felt that large-scale projects aimed at the international economy were out of touch with local interests. Similarly, much of the debate over airport and convention center expansion in San Diego has centered on the balance between capturing new business and tourism versus meeting the immediate needs of local residents.

GLOBAL ECONOMIC ARRANGEMENTS AND NEW TECHNOLOGIES ARE LIKELY TO ACCELERATE CURRENT TRENDS

Every major city now believes that it must compete for a position in the international economy. But the degree of connection with international business and trade varies considerably by the country's circumstance. In Singapore, where exports exceed the domestic product (because of large throughputs in its ports), virtually every economic issue takes on an international dimension. In the Randstad few firms of any scale are not international firms, and every manufacturing business must keep an eye on the international marketplace. In the US, by contrast, exports account for only a small fraction of business receipts (around 8 percent), and many large firms survive strictly on domestic sales. But even there, the most significant growth potential may lie in expanding international opportunities—as in the tourism sector in New York and California, in financial and business services, and in specialized fields such as architectural practice. Virtually all the large architectural firms in the US depend upon international markets for a large share of their business.

Where high-quality communications infrastructure is relatively dense and widespread, it may make little difference where businesses locate, although there will usually be a preference for locations near other international businesses. There remain significant agglomeration economies in business services which will help create business clusters. However, where communications infrastructure is lacking, the best public development strategy may be to concentrate efforts on a small number of areas that are large enough to develop as self-contained business centers. This is the approach being pursued in many city regions. Lyon, as an example, is in the process of creating its Cité Internationale, near the city center, and has several ZAC (Joint Planning Zone) projects under way aimed at facilitating international businesses to locate in the city. A current proposal in Bangkok is to create an "intelligent corridor" centered on the outer ring road, where it is possible to install electronic infrastructure along the right of way. Other cities are encouraging airport-related industrial areas, with good air access and excellent communications to allow just-in-time manufacturing. This strategy has been one of the keys to the success of the Subic Bay base redevelopment in the Philippines.

Over time, the number of sectors of any city's economy that are connected internationally are likely to grow. Universities are one portal for this, and areas around universities are attractive sites for the research and development activities of international corporations. Cultural activities such as film production are another avenue. Destinations for international tourism are still another. Heavy manufacturing areas, where there is large export potential, may require improved port facilities, which are increasingly automated and linked through communications ties with other parts of the world.

All of this is likely to continue to promote spread cities, where mobility is at a premium. Automobile ownership rates will continue to rise as incomes grow. Employment in virtually all major cities is now about two-thirds in services, with the balance in manufacturing and agriculture. In the case study cities, the fraction of service employment ranges from, at the low end, Taipei with 62 percent to San Diego at 83 percent, the highest. Since it deals with human resources, service employment is most sensitive to the loss of time through congestion. Thus there will be continued pressure to improve mobility, through improved mass transit, and through better management of roadways. Just-in-time inventorying will create additional demands on roadways; many cities have already seen an explosion of truck use of local streets. Electronic traffic control and management systems hold out the promise of significantly reducing congestion without requiring major capital works, although their value is yet to be proven in center city areas facing extreme congestion.

The quality of life locally is also a significant factor in international business location decisions. Lack of personal safety, poor educational opportunities, pollution and poor environmental conditions all can deter international businesses from locating skilled employees in a city. The physical attractiveness of a city is important, not simply for tourism, but in making an appealing location for business activities. Cities such as Singapore have benefited from strong programs aimed at the quality of life, while cities like Bangkok have been held down by perceptions of congestion and poor environmental conditions.

Ultimately, local improvement efforts are of direct relevance to a city's international competitiveness.

PLANNING NEEDS TO EMPHASIZE THE MICRO RATHER THAN THE MACRO SCALE

What do these new circumstances portend for regional planning? Planning which seeks to influence in detail the location and form of all regional development seems increasingly irrelevant—and increasingly unachievable. The costs of limiting growth through green belts, diverting growth to new towns, even creating growth poles a long distance from major metropolitan areas, are unsustainable in most city regions today. Specific actions to limit development—such as protection of a watershed to preserve a city's water supply (as in São Paulo), or protection of the "green heart" of Holland to preserve its agricultural character, or limiting development in critical areas to protect against major flooding (as in Bangkok)—may in their own right be justified. But managing the overall inventory of land for development, and tightly programming infrastructure development to control the timing of development, is in most cities not a practical possibility. With increased reliance on electronic communications, many more businesses are footloose, and subject to private development decisions.

On the other hand, concentrating efforts on infrastructure location, as many regional structure plans intend, may also fall short of what is needed. Even in highly desirable areas (such as those near airports), the quality of development is often so poor that they lack essential facilities, become congested almost immediately, and soon are seen as unattractive centers. Unless there is a strong regional government in place, municipalities in rapidly developing parts of a city region seldom have the capabilities needed to shape development in a positive way.

This suggests a new role for regional development planners. Rather than focus on regionwide issues, they might be better served by turning their attention to the detailed planning and coordination necessary in critical development areas. These may include areas emerging as new subcenters (such as in outlying areas), areas of critical environmental resources (such as waterfronts), and areas where public and private resources must be closely synchronized (as in areas surrounding airports). The task is to assure that the detailed structure of such areas accommodates human needs, efficiently uses public infrastructure, and has the facilities necessary to be viable over the long term. Someone must be the advocate of the pedestrian, of the low income service employees who may be priced out of desirable areas, of the effective management of the public realm, and of the esthetic character that results from many private building decisions.

Planners quite obviously cannot spread their efforts over the whole metropolitan area, so it will be critical to isolate those locations where they can make a significant difference. In some instances this new regional agenda will be furthered by the creation of special development offices, or development corporations where public and private resources are to be mixed. And this is a task that will require consistent attention over a long period of time. But there will be immediate payoff. The results will be tangible and will do credit to local officials. When cities spread over thousands of square kilometers, small victories can pay large dividends.

NOTES

1 Calling the process "deindustrialization" is a misnomer, since it represents a shift in the portion of the industrial process which is locally dominant. Manufacturing is leaving, but being replaced by other aspects of the industrial process—finance, marketing, operations management, and so on.

2 UN Development Report, 1995, pp. 176–7, 202.

3 Samuel H. Preston, "Urban Growth in Developing Countries: a Demographic Appraisal," in Pradip K. Ghosh (ed.) *Urban Development in the Third World*, Westport CT: Greenwood Press, 1984, pp. 36–56.

4 Ibid.

5 City regions included (but not all in this book) were: Ankara, Bangkok, Jakarta, Lyon, Madrid, the Randstad, San Diego, Santiago, São Paulo, Taipei and Tokyo. City regions were defined to include the area of economically linked settlement. Data were assembled by observers in each of the cities. Observers mapped development patterns, and these have been analyzed by the author, assisted by Andrew Crabtree.

6 While urban limits for São Paulo were drawn quite broadly, settlement began to spill over into adjacent states during the 1980s, as much of the available land for development was either exhausted or withdrawn from the supply by restrictions.

7 Preston, "Urban Growth," p. 44; George S. Tolley, "Market Failures as Bases of Urban Policies," in George S. Tolley and Vinod Thomas (eds) *The Economics of Urbanization and Urban Polices in Developing Countries*, Washington DC: World Bank, 1987, pp. 49–60.

8 Density was computed by dividing the population by the actual urbanized area.

9 Compactness index = actual perimeter of developed areas/theoretical minimum perimeter. The theoretical minimum perimeter is defined as the perimeter of a circle which contains an equivalent developed area. Because of differences in the technique of mapping developed areas (maps were prepared by individual cities), comparisons of compactness index for different time periods in a specific city are more reliable than intercity comparisons.

10 See Budhy Tjahjati S. Soegijoko, "Evolution of Urban Spatial Form in Jabotabek Region: Characteristics and its Policy Implications for Regional Planning," working paper for the Lincoln Institute of Land Policy, September 1995.

11 Sandra Lerda and Francisco Sabatini, "Santiago, Chile: the Context of Urban Development," working paper for the Lincoln Institute of Land Policy, September 1995.

12 Ibid., p. 5.

13 Michael Stepner, "Regional Cities: San Diego," working paper for the Lincoln Institute of Land Policy, September 1995.

15 Emerging cultures of governance

Roger Simmonds

In Chapter 2 we estimated that soon after World War II there were some 10 agencies around the world that had been set up to manage the growth of city regions or what were usually called then "metropolitan regions." We make a very rough estimate that there are 150 of these agencies in the world today. Most began life as commissions of central government, often set up to manage the growth of the national capital, like Berlin in the first decade of the century or London and Paris in the 1930s, or they were set up to manage an industrial region, like the Ruhr in Germany in the 1920s. Gradually most of these earlier commissions of central government have been transformed into agencies which are more directly accountable to the regional population itself. These new agencies, as the data show, have taken on many different forms and levels of power and responsibility. Most have been the subject of constant experimentation, as in Greater London, which has had three quite different institutions of governance in 40 years and is now in the process of setting up a fourth. Of the 11 city regions in this book which have some form of representative government, the Madrid region probably represents the agency with the most power and influence over the affairs of the region. The weakest by some way is the agency for the Boston region.

The first thing to notice about the move to set up management systems for city regions is the way their boundaries have been defined. As discussed, the consortium defined its own "informal" boundaries for these regions, based on "the high level of activity" which they contained. We focused our studies within these informal boundaries. The boundaries of the governments which have actually been set up to manage features of the 11 city regions were, however, based on quite conflicting assumptions. Some boundaries have been drawn tight around the main built up area, as in the São Paulo region, perhaps with the idea of a "metropolis" in mind. Others, like the latest version of the West Midlands region of the UK, have been defined with far-flung boundaries, containing large areas of cultivated land and wilderness, with the idea of a more conventional national region in mind. There is, however, an informal council of governments of the six major municipalities in the region, including Birmingham City Council. Others, as in the case of the Madrid region, are based on historic boundaries often including geographical features, like mountain ranges or rivers.

The growing preoccupation of urbanists with how to define and manage these regions is not just a response to a clearly recognized need. It also reflects a change in the way professionals are approaching the nature of human settlements today. Until very recently urbanists tended to have an image of themselves as "scientists" or "applied scientists" approaching a "natural" phenomenon. This approach has meant that they have been largely uninterested in the institutions of urban governance or management.

Today, however, heavy criticism of this "scientific" approach from a number of different quarters has led to the growing popularity of the perspective which sees human settlements as largely the products of complex patterns of human perception and choice. With this perspective in mind, the focus of social analysis shifts on to the very issues which were ignored in the earlier perspective, namely the process of constructing and deconstructing institutions of urban governance or management. From this point of view, the building of formal and informal institutions of management for global city regions, arguably the dominant (if only half-way coherent) settlements of the age, is the most pressing intellectual and operational task which can be tackled by urbanists today.

Bringing these institutions of management or "cultures of governance" to the forefront of analysis has led to a different kind of inquiry in urbanism, which focuses on how these cultures of governance then constrain, through their form and the content of their decisions, the emerging form of human settlements.

Abandoning the search for grand scientific theories about human settlements, however, does not mean that there is no point in studying them. But it does mean that we will expect to find considerable diversity in the form of global cities and, from the point of view of this chapter, in the way they are managed. The implications of this approach are that we should welcome diversity and abandon any kind of search for an ideal management model to which all global cities ought to conform.

Celebrating or, at least, accepting their diversity does not mean that these institutions should be cast in stone or that there will be no trends in the way all systems are adapting. Some trends will be identified ahead. Some institutions may come to be exposed as inefficient or unfair, even in their own terms. All institutions can and should be improved, and the process of deconstructing and reconstructing these institutions of management should be part of the ongoing task of the population of a global city. It is a process in which one population has much to learn from another.

The purpose of this chapter is thus not to emerge with ideal models, which all global cities will be urged to adopt. The aim is to map out some of the major similarities and differences in the practices of the 11 global cities, giving some sense of their effectiveness in their own terms. It will identify trends which seem to be emerging in all settlements. In short it is aimed to help one global region learn from another rather than encourage all of them to become the same.

THE INSTRUMENTS OF GOVERNANCE

One can look at the management system, or the "culture of governance," of a global city region from a number of different perspectives, focusing on, for example:

- The actors or "players" in the public, private and voluntary sectors and their forms of legitimacy for being involved. This popular perspective today would include the formal and informal relationships between the actors and the power, including the symbolic power, they have to influence policy and action programs.
- The different competences which the formal system of government contains; whether, for example, education is one of these competences or whether it belongs to a different level of governance.
- The "instruments" which are available to the formally constituted systems of governance in the global city region and the instruments which are actually used.

While all these perspectives can throw important light on our broad topic, this chapter concerns itself only with the third: the instruments of governance available to the formally constituted systems of government. It seeks to answer the questions "What instruments are the government systems of the 11 global city regions able to use?" "Of these, what instruments do they favor?" and "How effectively are they using them?"

The main reason for taking this third perspective is that it throws some light on the way government practice is adapting to the special circumstances and characteristics of global city regions. For example, it shows how, in a new "information age," the instrument of "information" is being developed by these governments. Another more practical reason for this focus is that it is a relatively easy topic to deal with in a short chapter because there are only five instruments which government systems can use:[1]

- Own and operate.
- Legislate.
- Use incentives/disincentives.
- Change the legal rights and privileges of land and property owners.
- Use information.

This means that we will not address, except in the way it relates to their use of instruments, the critical issue for all these global cities of the role of the national government in their affairs. It is important to remember that in the case of countries with small populations, like Holland or Chile in Part 2, the capital city region represents a high percentage of the total population and is thus, if given too much freedom from national government, a potential rival to it. The focus of the chapter also means that we will not, except where it impinges on the use of instruments, address another important trend, namely the changing relationship between the public, private and voluntary sectors in the affairs of regions.

If we take the five instruments which are potentially available to these governments, we can distinguish between two crude management systems: (1) "strong" government systems, (2) "weak" government systems. "Strong" systems of regional government, sometimes called "the metro model," are typified by Madrid in the consortium. They are democratically elected and they have their own independent source of income or, at least, they have considerable discretion about how their resources are used. They have the power to acquire land and property, usually under certain limited conditions, and, again under limited conditions, the power of compulsory purchase. They have the power to legislate, again within strictly defined limits. In terms of urbanism, this means they can and are usually required to produce and enforce land use plans. They can use incentives by offering the opportunity to join various programs on condition that certain actions are carried out. In some countries they can offer release from legislation in exchange for certain actions being taken. It is unlikely that they can change the legal rights and privileges of the owners of land or property but they can use their muscle with central government or, in the USA, go straight to the Supreme Court. They can and do use information extensively, but usually as a publicity back-up to the other more powerful instruments. National government departments which are set up to manage regions often have similar powers and are "strong" systems in the sense indicated here.

In short, "strong" government systems in global city regions have the power to use all five instruments. Experience with these governments in Europe, however, shows that over the last 30 years they have tended to favor one instrument over the others. There has been a shift in the popularity of instruments over the years. First the "own and operate" instrument was the most popular, then, when difficulties arose, the emphasis shifted to "legislation." As problems have arisen with the legislative instrument, the emphasis has shifted as far as possible to "incentive/disincentive." This chapter concludes that, notwithstanding the mistake of governments favoring one instrument over the others, we can begin to see signs of the "information" instrument emerging as the favored instrument of the future.

This pattern or trend in favoring instruments is paralleled by a general shift in political persuasion in the West over the 30 year period, from socialist governments, which have tended to favor "own and operate" and "legislate," to governments of the liberal right, which are tending to favor "incentive/disincentive" and "information." This trend, however, is very crude and is moderated by long established tendencies in some countries, like France, to favor strong government and the stronger instruments that are usually associated with that tradition.

"Weak" government systems, represented by the majority of regions in the consortium, are not really governments at all according to most people's understanding of the term. They tend to take the form of councils of municipal governments (COGs). In these situations, the power to use the five instruments lies with the participating lower-level municipalities which make up the council. The only instrument which the council can use directly is "information." It can also, of course, use "incentive/disincentive" in an informal way but seldom has much that it can put on the table by way of incentive. For the purpose of this chapter we will thus say that "weak" government systems can use only the "information" instrument. On the surface, that does not amount to much but, in the changing world of today, the information instrument can be a powerful device, which some of the "weak" systems of government are developing in ways which the "strong" systems seem unable to imagine. We should not forget that the participating municipalities of the weak system are strong systems in their own right and thus the weak system has the opportunity, albeit conditional, to use all five instruments through the powers of its members.

The next section looks at the experience of "strong" systems of government of global city regions. These systems in their directly elected form were pioneered in France in the 1960s to manage metropolitan regions, like those of Paris and Lyon. Later they emerged in London (in the form of the Greater London Council) and, in the chapters above, in Madrid and, initially, in the West Midlands.

The last section looks at practices in "weak" systems of government of global city regions. These emerged, with a major central government presence, in the Ruhr in the 1920s and later in the Randstad in the 1930s. They can be found in the Randstad today and in Taipei, Santiago and Tokyo. They are the systems currently operating in London and the West Midlands, though these are at the point of changing once again. We also look at a new kind of "weak" system which has been emerging in the US, particularly on the west coast, where San Diego and Seattle are particularly important examples. In these systems national and state governments have no formal presence.

"STRONG" GOVERNMENT SYSTEMS

The intention is to look at all five instruments of governance and say something about the lessons which have been learned by "strong" regional governments from using them to manage the way land is used.

Own and operate

Twenty-five years ago the government of the UK passed the Community Land Act. This effectively nationalized all land over a 100 year period. What at one moment consisted of a freehold on a given piece of land was changed to a 100 year lease from the government. This Act, repealed by the succeeding government, was based on the conviction of many at the time that the only way to manage the land use dimension of government policy was to have public ownership of property. City administrations, like Birmingham in the West Midlands, bought up large amounts of land in the city so that, coupled with vigorous building programs, they came to own a high percentage of the land and housing stock. Developers were required to donate a percentage of the land they developed to public ownership so that public open spaces could be built. It was a period when the amount of land in public ownership increased dramatically.

Governments, however, did not often prove to be good managers of land and property portfolios. Manchester, for example, with well over 50 percent of housing in public ownership (the highest in the UK) also had the highest vacancy rate in the country. Land "donated" by developers became badly maintained waste land littering the fringe of cities. This may have been due to the familiar problem of bureaucracy in government. It may relate to the sheer quantity of property which had to be managed, and to the fact that, as ownership increased, the public were not willing to vote extra money for its management and maintenance. This was a particular problem through the recurrent fiscal crises of the 1970s. Probably for all these reasons, this insrument began to fall out of public favor.

This loss of faith in the "own and operate" instrument in city and metropolitan agencies was certainly not the case with central government departments. In all 11 regions central governments continued to supply most of the infrastructure and "own and operate" was the instrument they used. The main problem here has not been with bad management of programs so much as the lack of coordination between one government program and another. This failure of government to coordinate is a cry of pain that rings through almost all of the above cases.

Metropolitan São Paulo and San Diego Association of Governments (SANDAG) appear to have been the only exceptions to this unhappy story. In the case of SANDAG, it came into existence explicitly to coordinate government and state projects for the region. It now officially coordinates 22 of these programs.

With the great popularity of BOT (build, operate, transfer) programs today, used in one form or another by most of the 11 regions above, this problem takes on a different character. In the BOT programs the government still uses its land assembly powers and will eventually end up owning the facility. So "own and operate" is still the most powerful government instrument for generating infrastructure. The big difference is that it is the city or, usually, the regional governments which are managing these programs in partnership with private sector funding, management and construction agencies. Regional governments, like Bangkok, São Paulo, and Madrid are no longer having to wait in line for central government handouts before they build their infrastructure or to suffer the consequences of badly coordinated government programs. But, unless regional governments are willing to commit to very long-term subsidies, their new private sector partners are going to be willing to build only the kind of infrastructure that can turn a substantial profit. This is the powerful reality within which the infrastructures of the 11 regions above are emerging. Its impact is all the more powerful because many of the governments appear to have opted for infrastructure-led rather than plan-led management systems. Also, as the Bangkok case illustrates, governments should not assume that the private sector managers will coordinate their programs any more effectively than the central government agencies did. There is still a major role for agencies like SANDAG.

Legislation

The power to legislate of "strong" government systems involves strict rules about what aspects of land use can be controlled by the regional and municipal governments. These rules are different in all 11 regions. Differences between systems based on case law, like that of the UK, and those based on Roman law, like those of Holland, France, and Spain, and those based on a hybrid of the two, like that of the US, explain a great deal about the differences in the way regional government systems have been set up. Each region has its own accepted but strictly illegal way of getting round the inherent difficulties which all these legislative systems have. All are open to extensive corruption, though the cases above give no evidence of it.

In spite of the variety of forms it takes, the legislative instrument is designed to give each "strong" government of a city region and the municipalities within it roughly the same power, namely to control how privately owned land is used. In practice these systems have been expensive to set up and run and have encountered numerous difficulties.

The first problem is that land use legislation is much more useful when the economy is strong and there is pressure to build than when the economy is weak and governments are trying to stimulate growth. Plans made under the conditions of development "boom" turn out to be of little use in a phase of "bust." In phases of "bust" it is hardly worth making new plans at all but better to promote incentive systems which can include, in countries where it is legal, release from earlier legislative constraint.

The second problem is that land use plans, particularly at a regional scale, tend to push up land prices in exactly those locations earmarked for major investment. This works against the policy which the plan was trying to implement in the first place. It can lead to one region being uncompetitive with others and it was one of the main reasons given for abolishing the metropolitan counties (including the West Midlands and the Greater London Council) in the UK in 1985. In an attempt to counteract this tendency, the last plan for the Madrid region tried to ensure that new infrastructure investment, for example in the first phase of the M50 orbital expressway, passed through the maximum number of municipalities, ensuring competition and lower prices by giving each its own exit from the road and the opportunity to have its commercial and industrial areas related to it. The advantage of this strategy may well be to keep prices down. The cost may be to have too much land earmarked for such uses, leaving large tracts of unused land well into the future.

The third problem has been that, while these land use plans for city regions have been relatively rewarding to make, they have been difficult and frustrating to enforce. It only takes two or three mayors to decide to go against the plan for the policies contained in it to lose credibility. The costs and the length of time it takes to prosecute successfully make this an unattractive option for most governments. If one adds to this the political costs, it is easy to see why so few prosecutions take place and how municipalities get to feel that they can operate almost independently of the plan for the city region.

The plan makers themselves are rarely responsible for any enforcement which is undertaken and, thus, seldom seem to learn lessons from the difficulties encountered. If private consultants, they are engaged in the attractive and remunerative exercise of making plans somewhere else. If they are government employees, they are busily engaged in producing the next plan, which immediately appears to be more "up to date" and superior to the existing one as economic conditions change and new ideas and proposals emerge. This also, no doubt, contributes to the reluctance of elected and professional staff to enforce the existing plan, particularly when there has been a change of government in the process.

To avoid these problems of nonconformity with the plan, "strong" global city governments, as indicated, become ever more deeply involved in consultation with the lower levels of government and local interest groups. This consultation becomes so extensive that the resultant plan begins to be more and more a "consensus document" in which only the policies which everyone can agree to are included. This has been a criticism of the Lyon plan: that it has, in a sense, avoided the difficult decisions which "strong" governments, like itself, are designed to make. It begins, in this important sense, to be almost indistinguishable from the plan of a "weak" government, like San Diego's.

One of the problems of top-down government systems is that they can often limit the capacity of local governments to take the necessary initiatives to help themselves. Local governments are forced into dependent forms of behavior from which very little learning accrues. It does not, in conventional parlance, lead to the development of "social capital" at the local level. In a sense it perpetuates the idea of the benevolent state looking after its "dependencies" rather that the state promoting the capacity for local areas to look after themselves and to innovate and learn from each other, strengthening the region's competitive prospects in the process. As this philosophy begins to take hold in a growing number of regions and in groups of the political left and right, if only because it appears to be the more affordable of two options, "strong" governments are once again forced into behaving like "weak" ones. They are expected to promote policies which will help local governments to take care of their own problems. The story of Lyon is particularly interesting in this regard because it is a "strong" system of governance actively promoting and itself engaging in "contracts" with other lower-level government systems to resolve mutual problems. It looks to an outsider as if something which was designed as a hierarchy is growing into a network.

In this climate of opinion, where local governments are expected to be given room to look after themselves, the role of regional or metropolitan governments to deal only with "strategic" matters has become reinforced. From the descriptions above, however, the definition of "strategic" has been enormously varied. For some, as discussed, it usually means those issues which there is a consensus about among the lower levels of government or among the different interests within a municipality. For others it has come to mean those concrete programs of action which the elected government considers to be the most important for the region as a whole. Most of the "strong" governments in the consortium are in the process of providing new infrastructure, cultural programs, etc., on the grounds that they are of "strategic" importance.

Another common interpretation of the meaning of "strategic" is that policy should be "general," that is, that it should be stated in an abstract enough way so that municipal governments can have some flexibility in the way they incorporate it into their own programs. This sounds sensible enough but the great problem with it has been that policy statements have become so abstract as to be almost meaningless. They have, in effect, such a variety of possible interpretations that they are impossible to enforce. Though the evidence is not available in the 11 cases above, the implication is that one could take any two regional or metropolitan scale plans of the last decade and find their policies so abstract that one plan could almost be interchanged with another. In such plans adjectives like "sustainable" usually play a prominent role.

In response to shrinking budgets for concrete programs

and the perceived failures of exercising control through abstract policy, a relatively new trend is to seek to identify "key indicators" for which desired "performance specifications" are given in the plan. Local governments are expected to achieve concrete and measurable results, i.e. to meet the performance specifications for identified indicators as opposed to conforming to abstract statements. The regional government of Madrid is working with the Île de France (the government of the Paris region) and a number of other European capital city regions to define key indicators which they can agree on and use in a comparative way. The Puget Sound regional government of Seattle, with major inputs from different community groups and single issue parties, has produced one of the better known examples of indicators, though it is still in draft form. Its pamphlet begins with this quote from Robert Kennedy. It is given in full because it reveals the hopes and aspirations which its members have for this "empirical" instrument.

> The gross national product includes air pollution and advertising for cigarettes, and ambulances to clear our highways of carnage. It counts special locks for our doors, and jails for the people who break them.
>
> The gross national product includes the destruction of the redwoods and the death of Lake Superior. It grows with the production of napalm and nuclear warheads. . . .
>
> And if the gross national product includes all this, there is much that it does not comprehend. It does not allow for the health of our families, the quality of their education, or the joy of their play. It is indifferent to the decency of our factories and the safety of streets alike. It does not include the beauty of our poetry or the strength of our marriages, the intelligence of our public debate or the integrity of our public officials. . . .
>
> The gross domestic product measures neither our wit nor our courage, neither our wisdom nor our learning, neither our compassion nor our devotion to country. It measures everything, in short, except that which makes life worthwhile: and it can tell us everything about America—except whether we are proud to be Americans.

This use of indicators has been popular with higher levels of government for a number of years and is now reaching the management of city regions. We can expect a good deal of overlap between the chosen indicators and performance standards of the different government levels. The OECD and the national governments of Holland and the UK, not to mention a host of voluntary associations, have all recently produced advice on "indicators." In the hands of "strong" and "weak" government systems, as discussed ahead, this is a major trend in the management of city regions.

Incentives and disincentives

Though this instrument has been used informally by governments throughout history, it has sometimes been used formally. In the year 1216 the City of London had an incentive strategy to the effect that anyone who was willing to whitewash their thatched roof, and thus prevent the spread of fire, would be able to sit in the front pews at church on Sunday. The first modern version in the West appears to have been the Incentive Zoning instrument of the 1975 Plan for Midtown Manhattan. Developers were offered release from the required floor to area ratio (FAR) in the zoning plan in exchange for providing certain public benefits. Providing a theater in your building could gain you a higher FAR of building. Providing a pedestrian link between two streets could gain you yet higher FAR, and so on. This instrument has been used extensively in suburban areas to encourage conservation of patches of woodland or farmland within urban subdivisions in the US.

Incentive zoning, however, is a hybrid instrument because it depends on the legislation and the incentive instruments being used together. The TDR instrument, discussed ahead, is also a hybrid and one of the conclusions of this chapter is that using instruments in tandem is often more effective than using them in isolation.

A great advantage of the incentive instrument, however, is that, while the legislation instrument is circumscribed in what it can be used for, the incentive instrument can be used for almost anything the government wants. This lack of constraint on the incentive instrument is presumably because individuals can choose whether to participate in incentive schemes or not. In legislative schemes they have no choice but to comply. This choice characteristic is, of course, another reason why the incentive instrument is so popular with governments of the liberal right. A popular strategy, however, is to dress up government coercion as "incentive," pretending that a local authority or an individual has a choice when, in fact, it has no option but to take the "incentive" and thus comply with the requirements.

Another advantage of this instrument is that, unless it is using the incentive of release from legislative constraint (as in the Manhattan example), a government does not have to get tied up in the expensive, lengthy and complex process of formal legislation. Its great popularity with national and state governments today suggests that they have come to similar conclusions.

In the United States the setting up of a system of government for a city region is often the product of an incentive scheme. SANDAG was set up in response to the requirement of the federal government that regions seeking various infrastructure funds must have a system of regional management or government to ensure better coordination with other projects and with the needs of the region. SANDAG, as discussed, now functions in 22 of these state and national programs.

"Strong" systems of regional or metropolitan government are more likely to be able to use this popular instrument successfully because they have their own resources and discretion over how to use them and because they have the power to legislate and can use release from legislation as an incentive in some countries. But resources are thin when compared with state and national governments, unless the government of the city region is also a state government, as is Madrid, with all the associated resources and power.

Changing the legal rights and privileges of land and property owners

The clearest example of how the redefinition of rights of ownership opened up new avenues of local and regional land use management can be found in what has come to be called the "transfer of development rights" (TDR). Its basis is that owners of buildings or land with preservation orders on them should have the same development rights as the owners of equivalent-size plots in the same planned area but without a listed building or preservation order on them. As owners could not sell the actual land for development because of the preservation order, they would be able to sell the "development rights" associated with the land. These could be sold to any developer, who would then be able to build at higher densities than those laid down in the plan.

Instead of the state having to buy up and run these historic buildings or land as a last resort, this instrument allows them to remain in the private sector. Supporters of TDR claim that it can produce three benefits for the public. It raises the necessary private funds to keep the buildings and landscapes in good condition, because a percentage of the money received in selling development rights must go into land and building conservation. It removes the incentive, which the owners of listed buildings and preserved landscapes have, to let them fall into decay or to actively destroy them so that the land can become available for development. The incentive is removed because, once the development rights have been sold, no development rights remain on a given property. All an owner can do is run the building or land in its present state as efficiently as possible or sell it to someone who will. Finally, because it makes no call on limited public funds, there is in theory no limit to how much of the building stock or land of a given region can be put into conservation. At a time when local communities are calling for more and more land to be conserved, while there is less and less money available to buy it, this instrument seems to offer a solution.

There is, of course, a big proviso in all this, and it is that there must be sufficient demand for higher-density development to make it worth while for a developer to buy the rights. Just as in the example of using BOT programs to build infrastructure, regional governments are able to use private sector resources in the achievement of public objectives but, in the process, become ever more drawn into the operation of the land and property market and must take more responsibility for its healthy condition, working to guarantee the profits of its private sector partners and so on.

In San Diego the regional COG is negotiating between independent municipalities to transfer development rights from one to another. In São Paulo TDR is being used in cases where the government wants to acquire land for infrastructure building. Rather than having to pay for the land, the government is trying to persuade owners to transfer their rights by selling them to a developer, who will build at higher densities than the plans allow in another part of the city. In this way it is the private developer who is paying for the land for the new transport corridor while profiting from the process at the same time.

Though the TDR version of this instrument has often proved to be a difficult strategy to work with up until now, it is easy to see why it is popular with the liberal right. It removes the need for ownership by the state and it actually increases the rights and privileges associated with land and property ownership. There are, of course, many more reverse examples of this instrument in use over the last 50 years, where rights of ownership have been decreased. For example in the Community Land Act of the UK, mentioned above, and in the rights acquired by governments all over the world, through land use legislation, to decide what private owners can do with their land.

Information

"Strong" forms of local and regional government have tended, as might be expected, to see the information instrument as back-up to the more powerful instruments of "legislate, own and operate" or, even, use incentives. The public has been informed about these programs. They have been explained and justified in the hope that the public will be encouraged to participate in or, at least, support them.

The best example of an information instrument being used in its own right can be found in the design guides (or design guidelines), which emerged in a number of Western countries in the 1970s. As local governments began to recognize that managing the quality of the built environment could have considerable economic benefits for them, they began to experiment with ways of achieving such quality. At the time "quality" often tended to mean "some kind of conformity with traditional landscapes/townscapes." This made it difficult to quantify or even describe verbally. This, in turn, made it difficult to legislate for. Indeed, local and regional governments in most countries do not have the right to use legislation to promote environmental character except in designated conservation areas.

Design guides were intended, as the name implied, to be guidance to developers and designers and not mandatory. They had to rely on the power of persuasion, not coercion, and, to overcome the problem of articulating exactly what was being suggested in built form terms, the guides gave examples using graphics as their main medium.

The success of these guides in the United Kingdom has much to do with its management system being based in case law. Guides were able to take on a quasi-legislative character which they did not have in other countries. The history of guides in these other countries, like Spain, Brazil and the United States, in the consortium, is one of attempts to build design specifications (often including visual material) into formal land use plans of which the Boston City Plan 1994 is a well known example. The guides contained early experiments with using the now popular "environmental indices" and "performance specifications." Many of these have survived, in somewhat different form, to take on a new life in the latest attempts to produce plans based on key indicators and associated performance specifications, discussed in the last section.

As we shall see in the next section, however, it is really the "weak" government systems which have discovered the true potential of the information instrument.

"WEAK" GOVERNMENT SYSTEMS

We turn now to discuss the practice of urbanism in those government systems which are "weak"; that is, which can really use only one of the five instruments: "information." There are eight of these in the consortium of 11 and, as mentioned, they are not so much governments as councils of lower level governments (COGs).

Most are sandwiched between their participating municipalities, which in all cases are "strong" government systems, and some kind of role of national government, which ranges between mildly and highly interventionist. The Randstad as a form of COG has existed, with variations on this structural theme, for 60 years now. It is most clearly a creature of national government but then it contains something like 65 percent of national economic activity and it involves participating subregions, not just municipal and city governments. Its clear function, however, is to act as a council of lower-level agencies and not as a conduit for national government policies and programs. Taipei and Bangkok are other variations on the same theme. Another example is the group of agencies which have been managing the West Midlands region, replacing the old "strong" West Midlands Metropolitan County, which was abolished in 1985. The formal role played by the national government and its power over the region has, however, been under constant attack from the political left and right since its inception. This is probably the main reason why yet another system of managing the region is being worked out.

The regions of San Diego, Seattle and Boston are the only members of the consortium which are "weak" government systems with no formal role played by national or state governments. The Boston region, with its Town Meeting form of municipal government, which gives the township control over almost all aspects of its affairs, produces a situation where the region can barely be said to have a system of regional government or even regional management at all. Seattle and San Diego are thus the only genuine "bottom up" regional government systems in the consortium. They are typical of a number of new and innovative governments of city regions which are emerging on the west coast of the US. São Paulo's system, however, also has many similarities, the main difference being that it is the state government which sets up and coordinates the metropolitan COG, which is none the less a "weak" government system, working through the consensus of its participating municipalities, including the city of São Paulo.

As discussed, the only instrument these "weak" agencies can use directly is information but, in an information age, that instrument is beginning to become a powerful tool of government. It should not be surprising that it is the "weak" systems of governance, and those forced to rely on it, which are discovering and developing its true potential.

The first function of this type of government is to be a forum of the participating "strong" municipalities. The products of such a forum are almost bound to be "consensus documents," built around aims and objectives which all the participants can subscribe to. No tough decisions will be made about which participating municipality is going to have to take the unpopular land use on behalf of everyone else, unless compensation can be agreed.

Increasingly consensus agreements take the form of commitments by municipalities in a region that they will all meet specified performance standards for identified key indicators. Rather than expressing these in abstract and general terms, the trend today, as discussed in the case of "strong" government practice, is to identify indicators and specify performances for them which can be measured. These indicators stand in for the much more complex characteristics of the whole system which a government is seeking to achieve. By focusing on the "indicator" and its "value" an "indication" about the state of the whole system can be obtained. A clear example can be found in the Puget Sound region of Seattle, discussed above, where a consortium of agencies has proposed a wide range of indicators and associated performance standards. For example, the suggested measurable indicator of "social integration" in the region is "the percentage of minorities who teach in the school system." The suggested indicator of "the quality of fresh water systems" is "the number of wild salmon which swim by identified markers over a specified time period each year." In each case, however, while the indicators have been identified, no performance specifications appear to have yet been agreed and the focus is on trends from one year to the next.

Already SANDAG, the council of governments which manages a growing number of concerns relating to the San Diego region, has begun to monitor the performance of municipalities in meeting agreed performance standards. At present this is a relatively hit-and-miss operation but eventually this monitoring is expected to become a major function of the agency. The agency will publish the results and these will be digested and interpreted by a myriad of private, public and voluntary agencies which, in turn, will publish their conclusions and recommendations through the growing local media outlets. It is often forgotten that the capacity to process quality information must keep pace with its production. Thus the value of the information produced by the regional agency depends on the skill and diversity of the agencies in all three sectors which will receive and process it. Supporters of "weak" systems of regional management will argue that the formal government systems of regions cannot provide the required level of sophisticated analysis without the active participation of the other sectors because the government does not have the required level of expertise and "local knowledge." Without that level of participation, there is no point in producing quality information in the first place because the agency cannot interpret the results on its own.

"Weak" systems of governance have no power to enforce conformity with agreed standards, and for many this renders them ultimately flawed. Yet the simple publication of results of municipal performance must be expected to have a substantial political impact. How long will the local mayor stay in office if the municipality constantly fails to meet standards? Most likely the mayor will seek to learn from a comparable municipality which is meeting the standards. A major function of these regional agencies is to publish information about "successful" municipalities from which others can learn.

It is not difficult to imagine how key municipalities might deliberately break an agreement and opt out of this process—choosing, for example, lower environmental standards and reduced taxes—but this decision will at least be clear to all and the municipality will have to answer to neighbors and other interested parties inside and outside. This "informal" system of enforcing the policy of city regions may turn out to be quite as effective as the "formal," but problematic, system of enforcement associated with the use of the legislative instrument by "strong" governments, which was discussed in the last section. Such claims, however, must remain speculation until these experiments are carried further.

It would be wrong, however, to imagine that SANDAG has no interest in the other instruments of land use management available only to its participating towns. It is actively engaged in brokering the transfer of development rights from one town to another, as discussed, and is coordinating decisions between towns about the conservation of land and townscapes and their enforcement through the land use legislation available to these towns. In this important sense it uses, or promotes, the use of all the available instruments through the activities of its participating towns.

The major function of a Council of Governance, perhaps, is to be a medium through which a participating municipality can work out ways of meeting its own needs. One way is through the building of a consensus, as discussed. Another is to be a medium through which individual municipalities come to recognize their shared needs and opportunities with other individual municipalities. It can facilitate the building of networks of alliances for self-help. "Strong" systems of governance can often work against the formation of alliances between lower levels of governance. In the old resource-rich and "strong" Greater London Council the boroughs (municipalities), though powerful in their own terms, were in competition with each other to have the GLC's resources and powers put to their own advantage. So fixed was their gaze on the upper tier "authority" that alliances between municipalities hardly existed. In the "weak" government system for London which has been in place for 12 years now, alliances between individual municipalities began springing up everywhere, even between those under the control of different political parties. Critics have tended to see these alliances as an unfortunate necessity, due to the lack of a strong central administration for London. Supporters have argued that this is a great moment in the history of the city, indicating that the boroughs have finally kicked the dependence habit and are now actively working to make their part of London an attractive location for investment in competition and collaboration with other areas, so that the whole region is now getting stronger. The clearly expressed function of the management system has been to provide the 32 London boroughs with the information they need so that they have been able to discover what kinds of alliance can be beneficial for them. Equally important, the agency has mapped the way alliances are being put together, with the result that individual municipalities can better plan their own strategies.

A critical issue here is the size of municipalities and its impact on their capacity to learn how to take care of their own affairs, form alliances, etc. Municipalities in the Madrid region are on average only one-tenth the size, in population and land area, of their equivalents in San Diego or the West Midlands. While this must have benefits, it must also have considerable costs for the operational capacity of these local governments. There must be some correlation between the size of a municipality and its capacity to develop strategies for self-help. For this reason, among others, the French government has been experimenting with larger composite municipalities.

The aim, however, is seldom just to promote alliances between municipal governments; it is also to promote alliances between agencies from the public, private and voluntary sectors. This commitment to a "shared power society" has been an article of faith in the last administration of the West Midlands and the London regional administrations. It is based on the belief that systems of governance, "weak" or "strong," cannot function effectively without the close cooperation of the other sectors, providing "local knowledge," technical knowledge, alternative perspectives, resources and, perhaps most important of all, commitment to the long-term future of the area concerned

Not all the regions of the world would wish to be "shared power societies." The voluntary sector is or has often been the origin of antisocial and even criminal activities and it will be a long time before such systems are trusted by the general public. It is also the case that, for a number of possible reasons, some regions do not have well developed voluntary sectors. This also may influence attitudes to the value of "weak" systems of government.

What seems clear, however, is that the institutions which make up the three sectors in any given municipality or city region represent the accumulated "know-how," what is increasingly coming to be called the "social capital," of that region. This social capital will be distributed differently between the three sectors in each region. Depending on where such social capital resides, and where a given population decides it ought to be built up in the future, decisions will be made about what kind of government system a given region should have.

CONCLUSION

A number of general observations can be made about the use of instruments in "strong" government systems to manage the way land is used:

- First, the tendency to rely on only one instrument, particularly land use legislation, is seriously debilitating for urbanism in the new urban epoch. Once it is realized that all of the instruments open to government can be used, they can be deployed in different combinations to manage different kinds of problem. This creates for urbanism a much more powerful and sophisticated range of instruments, which can, at times, overcome the discussed weakness of each single instrument. Composite instruments, like incentive zoning and TDR, seem to have particular potential. This does not mean, however, that different regions will all end up with an agglomeration of composite instruments. There is clear evidence that different global city regions are choosing different kinds of management system, in which different instruments play the lead role. Many are still legislation-led but there are clear signs of infrastructure led and, even, information led systems emergent.
- The second observation is that "weak" systems of government have demonstrated how powerful the "information" instrument can be, if used creatively, both in its own right and in combination with others. "Strong" systems of government have, in this sense, a great deal to learn from the "weak."

- The third observation is highly speculative. It may be that the instrument of "information" will come to dominate the management of the way land is used in the new urban epoch just as the instruments of "own and operate" and "legislate" dominated the control of land use in the last. If this should become the case, we may expect to see "strong" systems of government of city regions metamorphosing into something like "weak" ones.

More government systems for managing city regions are going to be set up in the future because the city region is the only even half-way coherent human settlement of the new epoch. These government systems will be not just for capital city regions or the regions of major conurbations but also for smaller city regions, like the proposed Valladolid–Palencia region in the state of Castilla Leon, Spain. Unless these also happen to be states (or Autonomous Regions as in the Madrid case) another level of government would have to be fitted in between the state and the municipality. It is hard to imagine how another level of "strong" government could function in that space. It would create great problems of duplication and territorial confusion, as appears to be the case in Lyon. "Strong" systems are also much more expensive. Most of these new governments are, therefore, likely to be "weak" systems—taking the form of councils of governments, or COGs, as in the San Diego model. Urbanism, which grew up as a discipline of "strong" government, is having to learn how to be a discipline which can operate effectively in "weak" government. There are some generalizations which can be made about this on the basis of the findings of the last section:

- The first is that, while these systems can "directly" use only the instrument of "information," they use all the other instruments "indirectly" through the activities of their participating "strong" municipalities and towns. Learning how to do this effectively is a major task for "weak" regional governments.
- The second is that, when major structuring decisions have to be taken for a city region, the lack of instruments directly available to "weak" systems is likely to lead to slow and cumbersome procedures and over-compromised programs of action.
- A third is that "weak" systems appear to be more appropriate in "shared power societies," where the actors from the different sectors all have some level of competence and/or access to information and advice. This is less likely to be the case where municipalities are small, where new information and media systems are little used or where the voluntary sector is undeveloped, or largely antisocial, as it is in many parts of the world.

In light of the above, decisions about whether to have a "strong" or "weak" system of government for a given city region will depend not just on cost or efficiency considerations but on where, in the three sectors of a given region, the "know-how" or "social capital" resides and in which sectors the citizens think it ought to reside in the future. For example, if, as is so often the case with governments of the political left and liberal right today, the aim is to break the dependence of municipalities on higher levels of government, the setting up of "weak" systems for city regions may be the first important step to enabling the necessary development of "social capital" at the local level.

We said at the beginning that we should not expect to find, or even go looking for, ideal cultures of governance to which all global cities should conform. On the contrary, while we have identified some trends and speculated about others, different legal and political traditions in which know-how is carried more in one sector than another, will lead to different choices by populations about the kind of institutions of governance they establish. It seems to me that we should celebrate this diversity, not least because it represents a store house of experience which all populations of global cities can draw from, in the ongoing process of deconstructing and reconstructing their own systems of governance.

NOTE

1 I owe this insight to Professor Mark Schuster, with whom I taught a course on urban management, when a visiting professor at MIT in 1986. Many have tried to discover the sixth instrument but I have yet to see a convincing proposal for it.

BIBLIOGRAPHY

Beck, Ulrich (1992) *Risk Society: Towards a New Modernity* (English language edition), London: Sage Publications.

Castells, Manuel (1990) *The Informational City: Information Technology, Economic Restructuring and the Urban Regional Process*, Oxford: Blackwell.

Giddens, Anthony (1990) *The Consequences of Modernity*, Stanford CA: Stanford University Press.

Harvey, David (1989) *The Condition of Postmodernity: An Inquiry into the Origins of Social Change*, Oxford and New York: Blackwell.

PART

Essays about City Regions

The two international conferences were built around the data from the first and second research phases by the 11 consortium teams. We also invited a number of leading thinkers to these conferences to reflect on the emerging city region in the latest age of globalization. We invited speakers who would approach the subject from different points of view. We asked Mel Webber, Pedro Ortiz, and Agustin Rodriguez-Bachiller, who tend to focus on what we called in the introduction the "process of regionalization." We asked Saskia Sassen and David Barkin, who tend to focus on the process of globalization. We asked Christine Boyer, Stephen Graham, and Simon Marvin, who tend to focus on the impact of new electronic technologies. We asked Ralph Gakenheimer to reflect on the future of transportation, a topic which covers in one way or another all three perspectives. Thus the following chapters are written by people who, having attended at least one of its conferences, know the consortium and its mission and who, in their different ways, and overlapping a great deal, represent the three most topical ways of understanding emerging city regions today.

16 Urban management in the global economy

David Barkin

Urbanization is a ubiquitous correlate of globalization. Regardless of where we look, large urban areas are concentrating people, wealth and power. As with virtually every other dimension of social life in the emerging global system, urban space is also suffering from extreme polarization. In this book we argue that a subset of "global cities" have emerged, with key functions in the system. Yet, as is clear from the other chapters, these global regions are far from homogeneous, reflecting the varying positions of their countries and these regions in the global hierarchy, and the local strategies of development from which they have emerged. In their variety, however, there are certain underlying processes, guided by the global economy, that are defining the possibilities and directions for change.

In this chapter we describe some of these common processes affecting all global cities before focusing on some of the specific characteristics that differentiate the cities from each other. Environmental conditions, the historical evolution of these areas, the management approaches used to solve their problems, and the social contract that defines them have combined to produce vastly differing urban areas. In spite of the fact that the homogenizing tendencies of international capital are imposing new restrictions on the variety of development strategies that can be implemented, there is still ample opportunity for local social groups to forge unique alliances that might create different opportunities and responses to global challenges

THE SOVEREIGNTY OF THE GLOBAL MARKET

In the present era, the global marketplace is a powerful instrument for integrating individual countries into a single economic system. If the market itself were not sufficient, the movement towards international economic integration and the emergence of three regional trading blocs is intensifying the pressure for each nation to accept the discipline of the international market in the formulation of economic policy. To reinforce its discipline, international organizations themselves are modifying their structures and operations, privileging the primacy of corporate leadership in a global free market over the parochial demands of local and regional interest groups.

With the ascendancy of private capital and growing international debt burdens, the state is redefining its role in the national economy. In most places the strong state has transformed itself into a financial and regulatory apparatus; rather than building infrastructure and creating basic industries to stimulate economic growth, it now concentrates on creating a favorable climate for private enterprises which are now responsible for the infrastructure investments and even the provision of services needed to promote economic growth and speed national integration into the global economy.

The changes are dramatic. In such disparate regions as Chile and Indonesia, and elsewhere in the developing world, autocratic regimes and dictatorships of various types are being challenged to cede to the demands of the opposition and civilian interests to create more open political systems. Public officials focus their attention on fiscal and monetary management, concerned to maintain attractive conditions for foreign direct and portfolio investment. The global cities in this book differ from other large cities by being in countries now generally accepted as successful or important participants in this global process. To the extent that there are questions about their global character, it is the product of doubts about their ability to attract international capital and effectively complete the restructuring. In the international financial crisis of 1998, domestic difficulties posed a threat to the ascendancy of Bangkok. In contrast, both São Paulo and Santiago consolidated their status in the global economy; they rapidly overcame the complications of the "tequila effect" and remained unperturbed by the crisis of the Asian "dragon."

But, even as global finance creates prosperous centers of modernity in all the cities we examined, many are still mired in a morass of stagnation and poverty. With the notable exception of those societies still able to fulfill their commitment to providing a social safety net for their citizens (e.g. the Netherlands and to a lesser extent Britain), the dominance of financial capital is leaving in its wake growing ranks of un- and underemployed. In much of the Third World regional disparities are growing and the primate city exerts a powerful force, concentrating those discarded by the process of rationalization and integration. Few countries have even tried to resist the tendency towards urban concentration, with the Randstad offering the most extreme example, encompassing one-half of the nation's population. In the poorer nations, structural adjustment policies designed by the International Monetary Fund replaced policies promoting domestic industry and compensatory measures, but the ensuing globalization is incapable of addressing the contradiction between increasing poverty in the midst of accelerated growth.

Integration into the global market is polarizing all dimensions of social existence. In every facet, there is a hierarchy of losers and winners, with the cities examined in this book representing a range of examples of success. Without exception, these cities contain important centers of prosperity, concentrating the corporate services that are indispensable for transnational commodity production (Sassen, 1995). The global centers examined in this book have centralized control of national resources to permit them to dominate the productive system; even as telematics and the revolution in transport permits work centers to be decentralized, in search of low-cost labor, new supplies of raw materials, environmental amenities or financial incentives, the corporate giants are siting their headquarters and regional centers in city regions like those we studied.

In the process, the reorganization of economic activity is having profound effects on local economies throughout the world. Local markets give way to international demand as the engine of growth. The complex structures of protection erected to stimulate economic growth and create jobs are being dismantled to accommodate the imperatives of the mobility of capital and merchandise; only unskilled workers, limited by geopolitical barriers and their poverty, are unable to search freely for opportunities in the global marketplace. Consumer goods are becoming "world" products, with components manufactured around the world to be assembled in numerous countries (global sourcing) for local sale. Even when domestic production can compete successfully, local companies participate in global alliances to strengthen their position and defend against renewed attempts by others to impose new barriers to trade.

The financial sector is a crucial component in modernization. Joining a capability to mobilize local capital with their skill in channeling international flows, new firms are combining the functions of banking, intermediation, insurance and consultancy to forge powerful institutions, whose decisions determine the success or failure of ventures and even of growth strategies themselves. Similarly, real estate development and specialized marketing organizations are reshaping the way business is conducted and how consumers shop as well as their ability to obtain credit. Local capital markets (stock exchanges) enable producers to tap international capital markets and offer global financiers new venues in their search for profit. The privatization of public enterprises, joint ventures and export producers are favored clients for this source of relatively inexpensive credit, further weighting economic growth against smaller companies supplying local markets. These smaller firms are at a decided disadvantage as they become caught up in a vicious circle which makes it difficult for them to attract innovative managers, to invest in the modernization of their plant and equipment, and implement new technological advances. In Chile, where this transformation began early with the creation of a private pension system to which all workers contribute, global companies have found ready access to capital for building industries that specialize in natural resource extraction and agricultural processing for export. In Thailand, Indonesia and Mexico offshore assembly or *maquiladora* operations combine globalized organizational skills and financing with the seemingly limitless supplies of low-cost labor to manufacture consumer products for international and local markets.

In the wealthiest countries and the wealthier parts of the others, globalization has sparked the longest recorded period of prosperity. The financial and corporate services centers are booming as corporate expansion, consolidation and mergers continue their unprecedented advance. Even with the cycles generated by financial problems, as is now occurring in Japan, or in the US a decade earlier, the successful global corporations continue their inexorable pace of growth, compensating for the problem areas by venturing into new markets or diversifying into new products. For those groups who enjoy access to these opportunities and have the required skills or personality, the rewards are generous; this is the brave new world that some consider to be the inevitable future for the whole world.

This form of corporate integration is widening the gap between rich and poor even more as real wages fall and property ownership is further concentrated. Employment in traditional sectors of agriculture and industry is declining; rural communities are being uprooted or simply bypassed, and many find that new opportunities in the global economy simply do not exist. Some policy makers celebrate the creativeness of the new survival strategies as people migrate to new regions or to the "informal" economy, rather than focusing on the considerable deterioration in their living standards or their life-threatening working conditions; even young children are forced into wage peonage.

Employment is growing in export industries, natural resource exploitation and processing sectors, and in export assembly operations. To remain competitive, employers are intensifying the work process to increase productivity while lowering wages. The ready supply of workers and the continuing integration of national economies into a global system forces wages down, not just by raising the supply of workers from other regions and sectors, but also by the threat of competition from more exploited workers elsewhere. To counteract these pressures, an increase in the number of working family members, including a dramatic rise in women's labor force participation rates, has been observed worldwide.

Of course, for many the jobs are simply not available. People are forced to survive in deteriorating conditions. As local economies are integrated into regional and international markets, traditional industries and producers fall victim to global competition. Rural communities were the first to suffer from the lack of local opportunity that accompanied modern industrial growth; even when people could not be productively or safely absorbed into the modern sectors of the economy, they were pulled from their traditional settings; they were transformed into proletarians, losing their ability to be self-sufficient, without gaining any of the rights of the working class to at least legitimately demand employment. With the deepening of the economic crisis in the 1980s, the crisis exploded on to the urban scene and enveloped substantial segments of the populations who were corralled into slum environments (*favelas*, *vecindades*, *villas miseria*, etc.). Not surprisingly, these poor people's settlements are a growing problem, but in Third World cities the residents cannot count on even the most basic social services, like housing, potable water, education, and medical care, that are available in the wealthier countries.

These marginal masses constitute a political problem of varying dimensions in the diverse social fabrics we examined. Anti-poverty programs and welfare systems are effective in minimizing their threat in wealthier countries, where public housing and medical care supplement market opportunities; an expanding group of the working poor now oblige policy makers to rethink past strategies that simply focused on attacking the problem of urban poverty by sending people to work in terrible conditions. In many other countries, however, including some in our study, authoritarian systems are favored over welfare or are used hand in hand to respond to the social unrest that popular opposition occasionally unleashes. With declining budgets, central governments are devolving many responsibilities to lower levels of government, where inadequate tax bases and the dearth of trained personnel make equitable solutions even more elusive.

In contrast, the beneficiaries of global integration—a relatively small number in most countries—are enjoying unprecedented prosperity. For those workers able to obtain jobs in the modern, transnationalized sectors of their economies the rewards are palpable. Their real wages are rising and substantially higher than the national average. Labor policies often offer the most skilled workers opportunities for further training and privileged access to housing and the package of public services which most people cannot hope to obtain. But the real winners are the successful corporate executives, who have become extraordinarily wealthy and powerful. They are constructing a world for themselves, to enjoy their wealth, display their privilege, and expand their sphere of influence.

GLOBAL CITIES IN A POLARIZED WORLD

The cities joined in this study are stellar examples of the possibilities and limitations of individual regions in the world economy. Several of the urban planning exercises in the wealthier countries demonstrate the complexity of the problems they face. In Randstad and San Diego, to cite the most successful, regional plans proved effective instruments to position them to take advantage of the opportunities of globalization. Likewise, São Paulo and Taipei created metropolitan planning processes to construct regional infrastructure programs that would position their cities to meet the challenges and opportunities offered by global capital. In all of these cases, transnational capital is supporting national efforts to transform these countries into important centers of global coordination and production.

In contrast, other cases reflect the difficulty of implementing the best of plans without adequate support from transnational capital. Bangkok is a case in point. It has enjoyed the participation of the finest teams of planners that the international development community could buy. Private capital committed support for grandiose infrastructural programs to transform the metropolitan region into a truly global center. Questions about national development problems, serious environmental degradation, alarming rates of poverty and the lack of a concerted program to face them were ignored or considered irrelevant; the planners thought of the city as a region unto itself, a mistake that became apparent with the unfolding of the Asian financial crisis in 1997; although the ambitious plans are still in place, recent events confirm that more than money and cement are necessary to build a global city.

Similarly, an able team in Jakarta, with less outside support than its neighbor, made valiant efforts to constructing a city model to place the country in the position of global leadership; the plans are proving far more ambitious than the internal contradictions of national development permit.

The global economy is a multifaceted patchwork of inequality. The winners are shining examples of the success of extracting surplus from the backwaters, from the workers and peasants and the resources with which they work to produce. In this hierarchy there are multiple scales of success and failure; many of those with jobs—the assembly workers, the farmers, and the myriad other categories—often feel more fortunate, luckier, than their jobless compatriots, even while the analysts point to the rising concentration of wealth and the declining purchasing power of wages.

The global cities are islands of privilege. They are positioned to be in the forefront of the reorganization of the world economy. Some are home, albeit temporarily, to world-class managers who control a widely dispersed system of exchange and production. These managers depend on their ability to coordinate their decisions with colleagues in other global centers and subordinates dispersed in the isolated points of production, located in an apparently haphazard geographical array that emerged from an intense history of exploration, conquest, pillage, construction, acquisition and merger. These islands of privilege would not exist were it not for the massive investments in infrastructure that allow them to function effectively as command posts in this new empire: dependable airports, sources of energy, fiber optic networks, satellite links and other telematics systems are essential parts of a hardware system that must be in place if the global managers are to settle there.

To develop a successful global city, the planning authorities must also transform a collection of workplaces into a successful center of political, social and even cultural privilege. Herein lies the secret of the flourishing geography of globalized space. It is not sufficient to attract production units: these can be set down wherever there are workers, resources, and a minimum of installations and transport to connect a local unit to the larger logistical network. Technology now allows the enclave economy of the colonial past new levels of integration, with satellite uplinks and air transport to avoid the bottlenecks resulting from local political and bureaucratic limitations. But not only must they have the hardware systems, they must transcend the constraints of local culture and politics, offering the commodities of the emerging international consumption package and the political detachment (in a national context) that being a citizen of the world implies. These centers of power and wealth are truly transnational spaces: although firmly rooted in their hardware systems, their operations are oblivious to the requirements and demands of local place, and sometimes they exacerbate local tensions, even bringing them to the point of crisis.

As hubs of globalized production systems, these command centers often undermine traditional structures and institutions in the national societies and cultural systems that host them. Their mechanisms of control and coordination require a freedom of movement and an access to information that was unthinkable in many of the countries in which they function; their operatives become accustomed to the ability to make unquestioned decisions based on standardized sets of information, completely detached from the institutional context within which they exist. Their primary goal is to maximize worldwide profits, and the literature is replete with examples of managers knowingly making wise corporate decisions that are inimical to local interests.

The very logic and structure of modern production generates the multiple dimensions of polarization noted in the system of global cities examined in this study. Perhaps the most important is the change in the structure of production itself, that leaves most participants more vulnerable as they replace the security of a balanced economy for highly specialized factories tightly integrated into a world trading network. This loss of self-sufficiency is often celebrated as necessary in order to take advantage of the benefits of large-scale production that international trade promises. The ideology of "comparative advantage" preaches that the gains from trade offer important improvements in welfare for all; although the losses from closing any particular plant may be small in comparison with gains elsewhere, the people who are directly affected have no recourse and cannot participate in the benefits.

The pundits of globalization denounce self-sufficiency as a shibboleth of a past era of isolation and inefficiency. As an economic strategy it offered some measure of security to most segments of society, protection against the vagaries of the marketplace and even the natural elements. State systems (national and international) evolved to complement these local institutions with provision for periods of extreme emergency, natural or man-made; unfortunately, state subsides often became excessive, leading to inefficiency. Today these structures are being replaced by the dynamics of the free market that transforms local demands and then supplies them from the far reaches of the global trading system; traditional producers are rendered obsolete, while they themselves and many of their resources become worthless in the new system of values that is incapable of generating sufficient employment and only requires the most productive of the world's resources for its highly intensive but environmentally destructive forms of specialized production (Barkin *et al.*, 1990).

People in many rural areas and urban shanty towns in many parts of the world find themselves relegated to the ranks of the irrelevant. Rural communities no longer can survive simply by producing the basic commodities formerly required for subsistence. Many of these resource-based regions are subjected to the strains of boom-and-bust economics. Individual commodities enjoy periods of high prices, followed by the inevitable plummet as competitive sources or acceptable substitutes are found or invented to reduce the costs of production. Artisans and small-scale manufacturing firms suffer similar fates; mass-produced imitations and cheap consumer imports are driving local producers from their crafts, creating new opportunities for those capable of increasing their production or mass-producing a product that was once hand-crafted. Similarly, local industrialists find the pressure of international competition too intense and have no recourse to agencies designed to help them make the transition to globalization.

As a result of the forces reviewed in this section, social polarization has become a powerful global force. The ranks of the poor are expanding rapidly and are being herded into less advantaged sectors of the leading cities or into secondary areas condemned to slower growth. Modernization is drawing self-sufficient communities into the global economy, subjecting traditional producers to a new calculus of profitability for which they are unprepared. The global cities are generally overwhelmed by the task of adjusting to the opportunities they perceive and the threats from those fleeing the backwaters. These city regions, most of which are mega-cities, face enormous challenges: from transport and air quality to waste collection and removal, from social conflict to community disintegration. The difficulty of managing these cities is rapidly outpacing traditional institutional and financial capabilities; and yet national policies to discourage local initiatives in other regions to strengthen community organization and production have the effect of expelling people and force them to concentrate in these administrative and economic centers. The United Nations (1991) and the World Bank (1991) both make this clear in their strategy papers on urban problems, as do more scholarly works, like those of Remy Prud'homme (1989).

THE CHALLENGES OF PLANNING IN GLOBAL CITIES

In light of the challenges posed by the evolution of the international economy, and the preponderant role of transnational capital in determining the fate of local communities, the question arises as to how priorities should be established and what role government and local organizations should play. Facing the challenges of global integration is important both for communities which are actively participating in the integration process and for those being left behind. Many of the "global regions" in this study are reacting to the opportunities created by international capital, as if they had little or no role to play in influencing these decisions. They focus on providing infrastructure and streamlining their governance procedures to facilitate the expansion of the global corporations into their areas. Most planning they undertake is indicative, designed to anticipate the local manifestations of international trends and incorporate specific zoning and construction programs into a program of local or regional actions to reduce the burdens of local adjustment; rather than initiating a program of local investment, this approach is designed to attract private capital into the region.

Most of these regions, operating in the "eye" of the globalization process, are hoping that this new productive activity will also solve other pending problems. The global cities in the Third World are often those that have attracted large waves of immigrants, from their own hinterlands or from other countries, depending on their location. These are regions that inevitably have fallen behind in offering adequate mass transit systems and road networks. Even a basic service like potable water is often becoming deficient, while other services like education, medical care and social welfare are manifestly inadequate, even in the most affluent of societies, as local governments confront the conflicting demand for diminishing revenues. Globalization is seen as a panacea, offering the promise of growing employment, more tax revenues and an improving "economic environment" that will contribute to overcoming local problems.

For the communities left behind, the problems are often similar, although the difficulties appear insurmountable. Without the benefit of large-scale investments in an expanding global industry, they seem destined to become depressed areas. The commodification of daily life and the incorporation of even local marketing channels into international networks seem to foreclose opportunities for local industries and markets. With shrinking revenue bases, and less support from central governments, domestic programs for "area redevelopment" (as it used to be called in the US) appear to offer ineffective responses.

Local (or regional) government—be it in a global city or in an urban backwater—becomes a passive actor in what it perceives to be a truly global problem. As administrators the local leaders frequently formulate their problem in such a way as to make it insoluble: how to attract the international investments that would somehow take advantage of whatever local resources may exist and turn them to their own advantage while offering benefits to the local society. This is a major concern of European urban leaders (Parkinson *et al.* 1992).

THE OPPORTUNITIES FOR LOCAL INITIATIVES

This vision of the global economy is flawed. Because it focuses all attention on the initiatives of the large corporations, it misses opportunities to mobilize local or regional resources for development. The key to an alternative approach is to identify ways to mobilize available resources with local institutions and entrepreneurs for forging viable enterprises. This is clearly identified in Gilbert's survey of Latin American cities (1994).

Although many programs promoting community development may be conceived in this image, most fail for lack of integration into a broader understanding of the development process. They focus on the local provision of goods to satisfy basic needs; this may involve basic elements in the diet or other aspects of life, such as housing and infrastructure. But it is not sufficient to produce a single product or even organize a local market without taking into consideration the longer-range needs to develop a community capacity for reinvestment for future growth on the basis of product and market diversification.

Thus an effective program for local development requires a multifaceted program that not only responds to the satisfaction of local needs but also encompasses activities that will generate surpluses by successfully marketing products that will produce profits. Such an approach requires a new role for local or regional government: it creates a responsibility for developing mechanisms to identify available investment opportunities in the local resource base or to create new opportunities on the basis of outside technical, financial or commercial resources that might offer a response to local conditions.

These responsibilities require developing a new planning capability at the regional level. This involves more than describing the local resource base or listing available investment projects, as is current practice. Rather a more dynamic process dictates working with local community groups to mobilize untapped or even unidentified resources, to generate new employment opportunities and markets. This vision of the role of active local participation in local planning and implementation is characteristic of many of the more successful broad-based efforts. This approach blends an orientation to service a growing local market with the need to compete successfully in broader regional, national or international markets. Concentrating on regional markets creates added multiplier benefits for the local economy, increasing local employment and strengthening community institutions. Harris (1992) brings together a number of authors who discuss these problems and critically examine past solutions; the journal *Environment and Urbanization*, published in London by the International Institute for Environment and Development, has published innumerable articles that describe specific local-level initiatives designed to increase participation and confront urban problems constructively; see, for example, its special issue on "Sustainable Cities: Meeting Needs, Reducing Resource Use and Recycling, Reuse and Reclamation" (vol. 4 (2), 1992).

By focusing on the impacts of development on the regional economy, planning can create attractive conditions for certain kinds of outside investment while mobilizing local resources that might otherwise be diverted to the international financial system. To accomplish this task, two different approaches to local planning are required. On the one hand, a process of community participation is required to assure as broad an involvement in the conception and implementation as possible. On the other hand, local investment projects must not only build on the opportunities of available markets, but must actively seek out ways in which these resources can meet the challenges of external markets. Local community development can be initiated with an invigoration of local markets, using the traditional tools of development, but it must be understood that, unless they are complemented by mechanisms to ensure further diversified growth, such efforts are likely to fail for lack of sufficient dynamism. This is the challenge of progressive planning in an era of global economic integration. For most regions, and even for the less privileged parts of the global cities, more attention must be directed to the dynamics of local development to avoid the most destructive effects of globalization.

BIBLIOGRAPHY

Barkin, David, Batt, Rosemary, and DeWalt, Billie (1990) *Food Crops versus Feed Crops: The Global Substitution of Grains in Production*, Boulder CO: Lynne Rienner.

Gilbert, Alan (1994) *The Latin American City*, London: Latin American Bureau.

Harris, Nigel, ed. (1992) *Cities in the 1990s: The Challenge for Developing Countries*, London: UCL Press.

Parkinson, Michael, Bianchini, F., Dawson, J., Evans, R., and Harding, A. (1992) *Urbanisation and the Functions of Cities in the European Community*, Brussels: European Commission.

Prud'homme, Remy (1989) "What are Cities becoming the Centers of? Sorting out the Possibilities," in R.N. Knight (ed.) *Cities in a Global Society* (*Urban Affairs Annual Review*, 35), Newbury Park CA: Sage Publications.

Sassen, Saskia (1995) *Cities in a World Economy*, Thousand Oaks CA: Pine Forge Press.

United Nations Development Program (1991) *Cities, People and Poverty: Urban Development Cooperation for the 1990s*, New York: UNDP.

World Bank (1991) *Urban Policy and Economic Development: An Agenda for the 1990s*, Washington DC: World Bank.

17 Crossing cybercities

Boundary problems separating the regional space of the city from the matrix of cyberspace

M. Christine Boyer

The dominant metaphor of cyberspace is the matrix, the web, the net, the lattice and the field. It is a metaphor that includes the distribution of virtual matrices—the bifurcating and diverging of lines and links between points in time and space that define the internet. The periphery now denotes either the space between virtual and actual worlds or those left-over interstitial spaces between the nodes of the matrix, spaces pushed through the Net or left out of the Grid on which we focus. Elaborating on the analogy described in *CyberCities: Visual Perception in the Age of Electronic Communication* between the virtual space of the computer matrix and the material space of physical cities, this chapter will continue to explore the concatenated term of "CyberCities"—moving back and forth with the matrix between virtual and actual reality. *CyberCities* explores the relationship between the imaginary real space which users of computer-mediated information explore and the spatial and temporal experiences of city users. It asks how technological devices such as the computer and its representational metaphors such as the matrix alter perception and direct the formation of knowledge. The analogy between the computer matrix and the city relies on how users organize space, how they lay down routes by which to navigate this space, and build cognitive maps or models in their minds. There are differences to be stressed, however, for cyberspace has no way of treating boundaries, no way to enable users to cross over the threshold separating virtual from actual reality. This problem exists with any mathematicization of space and time, or the assumption that mathematics can model reality, for it always reduces to the formal applicability of these conceptual tools to model real space and time.[1]

The internet or Net will be used in this chapter as the prime example of the electronic matrix of cyberspace, arguing that the relationship between this electronic matrix and the regional city is only an analogy—but a strong one that needs to be explored for its hidden assumptions. The chapter examines the question of democracy on the Net and the new development of virtual public space; it questions the digital divide between those connected electronically and those lag-time places around the world. The chapter as well focuses on the nodes of the matrix, frame-like spaces cut out from the rest of the city and operating as if they were computer algorithms. These decorated nodes with their design codes and simulation rules reinforce the perception that the regional space of the city is a matrix of well defined nodes and interstitial jump-cut spaces left out of the perceptual frame. The issue of cognitive mapping and memory devices is also examined, drawing attention to the distinction between symbolic and associative processes as they map out the territory of cybercities. Finally the space of the Net is explored as a linguistic terrain, examining how electronic writing has begun to move across architectural and urban space.

From the moment that William Gibson announced in his dystopic science fiction *Neuromancer* (1984) that 'cyberspace' looks like Los Angeles seen from 5,000 ft in the air, there has been a predilection for drawing parallels between the virtual space of computer networks and post-urban places of disorder and decay. This matrix is described as a series of city lights receding into the distance, a myriad of connections spreading horizontally and invisibly that define cities in our mind. Bruce Sterling's *Islands in the Net* is a reworking of Gibson's concept of the matrix:

> Every year in her life, Laura thought, the Net had been growing more expansive and seamless. Computers did it. Computers melted other machines, fusing them together. Television—telephone—telex. Tape recorder—VCR—laser disk. Broadcast tower linked to microwave dish linked to satellite. Phone line, cable TV, fiber-optic cords hissing out words and pictures in torrents of pure light. All netted together in a web over the world, a global nervous system, an octopus of data.[2]

Cyberspace has also been called a huge megalopolis without a center, both a city of regional sprawl and an urban jungle. Indeed, what else is the American city of today but a gigantic, boundless metroscape like 'Bama' [Boston to Atlanta]? Its appearance seems to simulate a complex switchboard of plug-in zones and edge cities connected through an elaborate network of highways, telephones, computer banks, fiber optic cable lines, and television and radio outlets. Look at the metaphoric translation of superhighways into the "information highway" to see how this analogy of cybercities determines perception and hides a set of assumptions. William Gibson's ur-matrix "I-95" is in reality the product of massive investments of capital and labor in federally funded highway building programs plus the post-World War II boom in automobile production. Enormous costs were produced in their wake: fossil fuel pollution, neglect of public transit, environmental degradation, and community destruction. Yet the metaphor of the 'information highway' glibly erases this complex set of costs, assuming a technological mind set that we can remake the world without paying attention to consequences. While the task of bringing America on-line will not generate the same set of charges, it will determine a new set of power/knowledge relationships that should be taken into account. Presented as a natural development of science and technology, the narrative logic of the "information highway" assumes that we can extrapolate from the present into the future based on the evolutionary progress in software and hardware technologies that will inevitably lead to revolutionary improvement.[3]

Drawing an analogy between cyberspace and the regional city, in addition, settles Christopher Alexander's 1965 argument that "A City is not a Tree." Alexander felt that a tree structure, representing a hierarchical and linear arrangement of divisions [or bifurcations] dictating the organization of knowledge or urban places, was too rigid, too reductive. Instead he proposed that the space of the city be reconceptualized as a semi-lattice: lacking hierarchy, each point in this abstract structure could be linked to any other point, not just to the branches above or below it. Instantaneous accessibility and connectivity replace the hierarchical tree structure terms. Certainly the concept of the Net or semi-lattice does away with center/periphery arguments and the notion of sub-urbs that depend on a central urb. A net or matrix is open-ended, potentially connected to any point on its grid. As it spreads laterally throughout an invisible ethereal space, it is capable of generating infinite complexity. Deleuze and Guattari have criticized the tree structures that have dominated Western thought from botany to philosophy. "We're tired of trees. We should stop believing in trees, roots and radicles. They've made us suffer too much. All of arborescent culture is founded on them, from biology to linguistics."[4] So let us explore the realm of the regional matrix and the metaphorical analogies embedded in cyberspace.

THE DEMOCRATIC PERFORMANCE OF CYBERSPACE

Thinking of cybercities as a matrix or net covers up a multitude of erasures and avoidances. What does it mean that this electronic imagery of the matrix generates a unique mental ordering that seems to parallel, but not represent, reality? What significant effects result from the fact that textual universes of postmodern accounts conjure up fictional worlds that disavow any link with material reality, any connectivity with a shared community? Of course, "shared community" is open to criticism: perhaps it is too nostalgic for a lost public sphere or assumes erroneously that democracy is based on Enlightenment principles—of open discussion, of normative behavior, of rational purposive action. We need to digress and ask if old concepts of freedom of speech and individual rights ruled by law can be used to analyze new forms of electronic communication, public assemblage, and decentralized dialogues taking place across the globe on the Net. The internet is a decentered communications system—a product of Cold War policies that included non-hierarchical communications networks that would survive a nuclear attack if their hub was eliminated.[5] Now the Net consists of a network of networks—a heterotopia of discourses that exists as pixels on a screen generated at remote locations by individuals who will probably never meet face to face (f2f). What does this say about a "shared community"?

Does the internet constitute an increase in democracy, as many suggest? Anyone can access the Net from their computer terminal. But central authorities still have to recognize that namespace in order for others to find it. This entry point to the Net is controlled in America by two private companies: AT&T, the telecommunications giant, and SAIC, or Scientific Applications International Corporation, a firm that specializes in military, police and government intelligence contracts.[6] Albeit a non-hierarchical cooperative mode of communication, the Net is highly centralized and controlled. For example, the federal government commands the root server A which distributes any new address information to other root servers around the world. Furthermore, a private company, Network Solutions, was awarded an exclusive government contract in 1995 to administer this crucial root server and to register domain names such as .com, .org, .net. This profitable monopoly has enabled Network Solutions to generate millions of dollars in profits from registration fees as the internet itself has grown bigger and bigger. Such monopoly control flies in the face of those who believe the internet to be an open-ended cooperative and egalitarian enterprise.[7]

Although the Net is often referred to as an information

highway, will it be a toll road or a freeway? Will the traffic that streams across it be controlled or not? Will the market dominate the Net? Will it be commercialized or free to those who can afford a telephone and computer? How do the answers to these questions relate to physical space?

As formerly independent telecommunication, computer, media and entertainment industries merge into transnational communication corporations, they have set their sights on controlling the global information and entertainment network. The CEO of Walt Disney Company has suggested that his company's prospective growth is based on the fact that its "nonpolitical product" does not threaten any political regime around the world.[8] Meanwhile public sector communications are being dismantled and their independent voices—both journalistic and cultural—are increasingly quiet. Communication, a free flow of information, is essential for a lively democratic political culture, but will uncontrolled networks of information, with universal access and open discussion, remain without some form of government or market regulation, or some form of public scrutiny? And what should that form of regulation or scrutiny be?

In spite of what many advocates of cyberspace believe, universal access is far from guaranteed. Estimates made in 1996 claim that over 25 million people communicate on the internet, a figure that grows yearly. Yet a 1995 estimate asserted that, although one-third of US households owned computers, many of them had no access to the internet, and in poor neighborhoods at least one-third of households were without basic telephone connection. Hence the computer could become another device that increases economic and educational disparity. According to Mitchell L. Moss and Anthony Townsend of New York University's Taub Urban Research Center, 50 percent of all internet hosts that connect computers to the internet are located in just five states and, within these five, concentrated in a few metropolitan regions. Furthermore, 30 percent of these hosts are clustered along the northeast corridor between Maine and Virginia (not quite BAMA). If California is added, then almost half of all the hosts have been included. Internet hosts are also concentrated in certain regional cities: the most highly concentrated exist in Silicon Valley, California outside of San Francisco, then along Route 128, the high-tech corridor outside of Boston. Next comes Los Angeles County. Manhattan continues to dominate its region, owing to the enormous number of information-intensive financial and media businesses centered in the city. There are cities that have no internet hosts: Houston, Miami, Detroit and New Orleans, for example. These are information black holes, and no doubt their economic growth and well-being will be inhibited in the twenty-first century's information society.[9]

Stephen Doheny-Farina in *The Wired Neighborhood* (1996) explored the creation of electronic neighborhoods, the virtualization of community. He remains critical of the absolute dependence these new communities place on a technology that is created, provided and sustained by others. Rather than the euphoria of technological liberation, independence and self-sufficiency he sees these virtual communities as a sign of containment and domestication.[10] We still do not know the real effects: whether these virtual communities strengthen community ties, provide community education, or counteract the fragmenting tendency of privatization. Can they reduce the cost of delivering government services or update education and bring children into the twenty-first century regardless of school system, income level, geographic location and ethnic background?

Other critics complain that the new telecommunications technology centralizes control over cultural production, homogenizes cultural consumption by peddling the same cultural products worldwide, and makes government irrelevant. This position argues that community networks will lead to an information dystopia—isolated and alienated citizens locked together within their electronic prisons—while a powerful technical elite gains actual mind control over society through panopticon surveillance. Silent surveillance results as communications are scanned for selected key words then stored as a virtual profile characterizing each discussant.

A more supportive approach to the new democratic and egalitarian Net is Neil Guy's "Community Network: Building Real Communities in a Virtual Space" (1991). He studied a set of computer-based communication systems called Free-nets or public access networks created out of community computing centers, civic networks, and telecommunities. Owned by non-profit organizations, these networks utilize the internet for community welfare. They provide an open forum for citizen discussions and bring fractured communities together. This connectivity enables communities to perceive things in different ways: they know more about what is going on and they change their behavior in relation to each other. But there are limits to these virtual communities: most community organizers rely on face-to-face contacts and some are not computer-literate.[11]

There is also a mounting digital divide between those connected and those disconnected from the electronic matrix: two-thirds of the world's population are excluded from cyberspace, for they have yet to make their first telephone call and, even if they were connected electronically, the Net is predominantly an English-speaking realm that limits accessibility. Moreover the microtechnology on which the Net depends is produced in Third World countries often by exploited labor. Just look at the figures and facts: 90 percent of all Net users live in North America or Europe because 80 percent of the world lacks basic telecommunication devices (i.e. telephones). Access to the Net is 12 times more expensive in Indonesia than in Rome. Singapore, China, Iran, and Vietnam want to limit uncontrolled access to the Net. Singapore, for example, is trying to prohibit its internet providers from distributing "material that spreads 'permissiveness or promiscuity' or that 'depict(s) or propagate(s) sexual perversions such a homosexuality, lesbianism and paedophilia'" (Singapore Broadcasting Authority, 1996).[12]

The international telecommunications quadrennial meeting, Telecom 95, held in Geneva in 1995 adopted the slogan "Connect!," referring to the rapid eradication of boundaries that separate the telephone, computer and media industries. Clearly this slogan was directed at only the top 50 developed countries, not the 48 poorest. The poorest nations have fallen further behind in the potentially liberating effects of telecommunications. Investors are unwilling to share the risk of developing telephone service in Africa, for example, because of political instability in much of the continent.[13] Of course the hope is held out that the internet would offer "a great leap forward in Africa," the poorest continent, but Africa is crippled by unreliable communication systems on the one hand and prohibitively expensive telecommunications on the other. Manhattan has more telephone lines than exist in the total of three dozen sub-Saharan countries.[14]

There are information "have-nots" at home in the US as well. Blacks are far less likely to use the Net than whites, and anybody who is poor is in trouble as well. The Department of Commerce notes that about 20 percent of America's poorest families do not have telephones and only a fraction of those that have them can afford the computers and peripherals needed to participate in the information age. In the South Bronx in New York City the problem is how to get poor people wired: 25 percent of the participants in Lifeline, the local telephone company's program to provide basic phone service to families receiving some kind of public assistance, live in the South Bronx. Less than 5 percent of all households in that area of New York have computers, and even if more households could afford to buy computers they lack the skills and training to operate them. The New York Public Library has introduced LEO, Library Entrance On Line, for local libraries that will allow a user to search the library's 50 million holdings and to explore the Net. But on-line time will be limited and eventually the user will have to pay for print-outs.[15]

Considering the democratic performance of cyberspace, we have also to question the creation of both hypothetical communities and hypothetical identities on the Net. There are elaborately constructed fantasy worlds created on the Net known under a variety of acronyms such as MUD, MUSH, MOO, MUSE, and MUCK—the MU*:= defines a multi-user, network-accessible user interface that is entirely textual.[16] These domains are highly interactive computer-based extensions of fantasy role-playing games developed in the 1980s in which players invent a fictional character or "handle" and the characters are moved about as if they were puppets on a string. Often actions are prefaced by comments such as IC:= (in character) or OOC:= (out of character), to stress a difference which is important to the play, but it is difficult to ascertain the boundary that has been crossed. It has been argued that these fantasy games are important, for they allow extravagant experimentation with the definition and self-invention of subjectivity, but there is an addictive quality to the games as well and a sense of dwelling in a metaphor without living the experience.

We need to examine these emerging relations on the Net, for mobile identities undermine the notion of authority and normative behavior. Since the Net is primarily a language-based realm, we should become aware that language acts, words can wound, speech or language can constitute injury. As the Nobel Prize winning author Tony Morrison has said, "oppressive language does more than represent violence, it is violence."[17] The problem appears to lie in the metaphorical term "cyberspace," for considering the Net as space masks the fact that subjectivities on the Net are dissociated from their bodies, or disembodied. Hence there is a tendency to downplay responsibility and/or agency. As the internet decreases our awareness of reality and increases privatization, there arises a vacuum of responsibility to an on-line community. "Netiquette" rules have yet to appear. Furthermore, on the internet, gender, race and class become irrelevant and constructed at will.

In the "ecstasy of communication" obscenity begins. As Pamela Gilbert reports in "On Sex, Cyberspace and being Stalked," aggressive behavior is routinely displayed on the Net, for it is constituted "merely" of words. Hence there is a tendency to use aggressive words, to fight or flame at the least provocation and to act out invasive or provoking behavior.[18] An entire vocabulary has developed to describe this excitable speech: *flame* is a message posted as an insult—and usually elicits a response. The result is a "flame war": a name-calling free-for-all of fighting words. A *troll* is a deliberately provocative post, targeted to an audience it hopes to annoy; it is a flame bait intended to provoke a war of words. On the other hand, an indiscriminate posting, aimed at the widest possible group, is called *spam* and generally sets up a cacophony, drowning out any hope of intelligent discourse.[19]

Stalking on the Net utilizes many of these harassing procedures but adds another dimension, as Pamela Gilbert has described. After she had terminated a relationship with a former colleague he began to stalk her on the Net, violating her sense of personal space. He started to show up on 'listserves' where Gilbert was active. He began searching her e-mail and obsessively tracing her log-ons and whereabouts on the Net. She had a feeling of being watched every time she was posted or posted a message. There was nowhere on the Net she could safely go without being watched or stalked. Then he threatened to send pornographic photographs which he had collected of her to her colleagues, and to universities' search committees where she was seeking a job. She felt as violated and unprotected on the Net as if she had taken a walk late at night down some dark and dreary city street. The Net, like any physical space, has its noir side that is far from safe.

On-line harassment appears to be a gatekeeping device that limits the extent to which women feel comfortable participating in cyberspace. Rowdy group flaming discourse deters women, who tend to prefer semi-private e-mail discussions. With any new communication technology there is always a backlash problem of allowing the wrong kind of communication to take place. In America this often refers to indecent material available to children under the age of 18, cyberporn, or the proliferation of sexually explicit material—and so we have the federally legislated Communication Decency Act, passed in 1996. Having been discussed by the Supreme Court, this Act has been deemed by the high court of the land to be detrimental to freedom of speech, which is protected by the first amendment of the constitution. The question before the court rested on the decision of whether the Net was to be considered to be like radio and television or like the telephone and the newspaper. The former are so pervasive in the home that they require strict scrutiny and censorship. While the latter are considered to be discrete pieces of information or discourse, not emitted from a central location, and hence they constitute speech that must be protected. But still questions remain: is cyberspace a closed-off closet space beyond the range of social norms and common decency or what kind of regulation might help this electronic space become truly democratic and open?

THE FRAMED CITY MATRIX

Let us turn to look at the nodes and interstitial spaces of the matrix of cybercities. It appears as if Michel Foucault's spaces of enclosure, at least metaphorically, have been turned inside-out in cyberspace. The marginals—however they are defined—are left outside the protected zone of the shopping mall, the campus, the walled community and outside the internet, the credit-card/ATM system, or the privileged trade nation agreement. These outsiders haunt and invade the interior. The marginal has become our postmodern Monster, beyond the norm and increasingly invisible. This fear has caused an outpouring of *walled cities* in which the wall represents a boundary, a partition, a border that encloses and excludes, much the way cells of a matrix do.

Here, again, we can continue to deploy the analogy between the electronic matrix of cyberspace and the actual space of cities, but now make a counterclaim that the purity, the cleanliness, the synthetic quality of cyberspace—that is, the visual matrix of space in the clean machine of the computer memory—have been set up in opposition to the dirt and seediness of real city space. There is a tendency to introduce into real spaces of the city the synthetic purity of cyberspace, filling in only the nodes of the matrix. These imaginary assemblages and decorated places are the result of our taste for the artifice, the simulation, and the computer-generated model.

Marvin Minsky, one of the early explorers of artificial intelligence, conceived of mental images as active structures or frames which help us organize reality. In *A Framework for Representing Knowledge* (1974) he wrote:

> Whenever one encounters a new situation (or makes a substantial change in one's viewpoint) one selects from memory a substantial structure called a frame. This is a remembered framework to be adapted to fit reality by changing details as necessary. A frame is a data-structure for representing a stereotyped situation, like being in a certain kind of room, or going to a child's birthday party. Attached to each frame are several kinds of information. Some of this information is about how to use the frame. Some is about what one can expect to happen next. Some is about what to do if these expectations are not confirmed. . . .
>
> Collections of related frames are linked together into frame systems. The effects of important actions are mirrored by transformations between the frames of a system. . . .

> The frame systems are linked, in turn, by an information retrieval network. When a proposed frame cannot be made to fit reality—when we cannot find terminal assignments that suitably match its marker conditions—this network provides a replacement frame. . . .[20]

Minsky's frames revolve around memory—an individual selects a remembered framework—but there is also a geographical analogy: a network of places that enables thought to move from one frame to another. One's behavior is modified by the fear of being outside a frame in a non-typical situation and so one's sense of reality is organized into preestablished frames, making only small and gradual updates to the system. In a world of accelerated change, inevitably there will be dislocations of meaning and failed correspondence with framed structures of knowledge yet there is a general tendency for individuals to hold on to unrevised interpretive frames, no matter how discontinuous and divergent from reality they may be, until new frames of reference are accepted.

In an analogous manner we find many framelike zones—rule-driven simulations or representations by structured correspondence—in our regional cities. They produce what Ada Louise Huxtable in an article entitled "Living with the Fake, and Liking it," calls "the real, real space" of the city—a surrogate experience, a synthetic setting, an artifice. In this blurring of boundaries, she argues, the spectator of city spaces cannot make a distinction between the real and the false, or tell the difference between the real fake and the fake fake. Now we find that the authentically unauthentic has become a new urban design frontier.[21] So it is said, "history repeats itself neither as farce nor as tragedy but as themed environment."[22] The question has to be asked, nevertheless, what this categorization of the real and the fake masks? Huxtable bemoans the loss of "connoisseurship"; that is, the training of the eye, the informing of taste by direct contact with the real thing and the true work of art. She specifies this contact as "the related sequence of close knowledge and informed taste by which works of art can be accurately understood, compared, defined, judged and enjoyed. There is no replacement for this primary experience—the direct connection. . . ."[23]

Why this nostalgic cry for contact with the real thing at the very moment when computer-generated simulation has confused our sense of authenticity? Are we actually afraid that the image of the city has been tampered with by simulated copies or is this a cover-up for more fundamental fears? Huxtable confuses the distinction between imitation and simulation. Imitation holds out the belief in an authentic origin, but simulation goes further. It generates the semblance of a non-existing reality and often reveals the very apparatus of its own creation. Is not the projection of an image that we fear is false, that is not real or optically true, such as a theme park image or the image of New York in Las Vegas, or Disney World, a fear that we are losing control or mastery over the object world? In other words, in the edgy alliance between the actual and the virtual, the material and the immaterial, the imitated and the simulated, critics find that the projection of an image of the city that is believed to be false, that is not based in reality, nor optically true, questions our symbolic or imaginary possession of space.[24] To be more precise, as the status of the photographic image as documentary evidence is destabilized, and its relation to memory and history disassembled, interesting questions are raised about how we perceive and apprehend the world in which we live (that is, questions of epistemology, representation, and truth[25]).

Photographic documentation used to serve as a reality test. It was evidence that something actually happened, that reported events were true. (Photographic coverage of the Vietnam War or the pro-democracy movement in Tiananmen Square are two good examples.) But the computer has had a major impact on photographic veracity. With electronic imaging, photographs are no longer sacrosanct from editorial modification. Digital manipulation of an image can add or subtract elements, enhance its lighting or color on command, so that its "truthfulness" or its reliability as a record of reality becomes problematic. Computers offer the image maker the ability to transform, change, and move images about. This same information system, with its mathematical models and algorithms, can generate a "realistic" image, "reinventing the world from scratch." While a computer image may still appear realistic, its referent is not, because reality is no longer being represented but modelled and mimicked. Electronic visualization—either computer-manipulated or computer-generated—constructs artificial domains and simulated environments. This image-space appears to be completely autonomous, a surrogate reality that can no longer be judged for either its authenticity or its accuracy. So why do we worry about the authenticity of urban space?

Returning to these artificial zones, image-schema or frames, a major claim is made here that urban space is transformed in some manner by cybernetic, representational space. Since the matrix of cyberspace is a cognitive map, that is, a mapping of conceptual space, the more features that are elaborated the more the mind can navigate and negotiate the space inside its well articulated nodes. Hence the matrix of cyberspace becomes the way we accept and/or legitimate what has happened to cities, as we no longer question an image of the city parceled into zones: BIDs (business investment districts), CIDs (common interest developments), theme parks, malls, historic districts, Special Urban Design Districts, and so on. Since the move into cyberspace favors models of decentered, dispersed and discontinuous sprawl juxtaposed against self-contained zones or theme parks, it allows the interstitial areas of silence, estrangement and decay to remain outside the Grid. Cyberspace and city space seem to go very much hand-in-hand here, enabling the viewer to forget the in-between, interruptive spaces. This is the effect, reiterated once again, when the space of the city and cyberspace is conceptualized as that of the matrix.

Another effect is the production of fortified enclaves or walled cities as framed and privatized zones of the regional city where the boundary between surveillance and city spaces breaks down. By the late 1980s, according to Evan McKenzie, about 40 million Americans lived in common interest developments—that is, about one person in eight. CIDs are also called "gated communities" or "walled-in communities" and include cooperative apartments, condominiums, and new towns. They will be the predominant form of housing by the twenty-first century.[26] Lawyers call CIDs "association-administered servitude regimes": communities in which residents own or control common areas or shared amenities and a regime because they impose reciprocal rights and obligations enforced by a private governing body. An owner has to abide by a variety of covenants, contracts and restrictions: they may dictate the minimum or maximum age of residents, hours and frequency of visitors, color of paint on a house, style and color of draperies hung in windows, size of pets and number of children, parking rules, patio and landscaping controls.[27]

These are planned as spatially segregated communities and on a small scale they simulate the functional order of the modernist city. They set aside discrete areas for residences, work, leisure and the necessary transportation corridors that link together these places. Look at Irvine, California, on the southern edge of the regional sprawl of Los Angeles. With a gross domestic product of $60 billion in 1989, Irvine is economically among the top 30 countries in the world, ahead of Argentina, Austria, or Denmark. The map of Irvine looks like a matrix with its grid of highways and its series of well designed nodes or theme parks, for, after all, we should not forget that Irvine is only 10 or 15 miles south of Disneyland. It has a master plan that allocates residential communities, open spaces, commercial and industrial areas to zones, with emphasis given to "city identity" in each of its residential areas, where the values of nature, family and work are bound together.[28]

The Irvine Company is in charge of developing this regional city and targets its image to two markets: businessmen working in the fields of advanced technology or luxury goods and residents with medium–high incomes who are firmly attached to the region's economic system, are lovers of nature, active in sports and want to live in an extremely homogeneous social and economic environment.[29] Each residential nodal point is publicized as a tourist village where everything is designed for a resident's well-being. Neighborhoods become the basic organizing unit of this New Urbanism—a model limited in area, revealing a well defined edge and structured around a defined center of activity. The optimal distance from center to edge is a quarter of a mile, and each neighborhood center contains shops and businesses and may also have a post office, a meeting hall, a day-care center and sometimes religious or cultural institutions. A fine network of streets and paths connect all these neighborhood spaces together.[30]

As the *image* of the *city* becomes important for high-income-generating citizens in well designed nodes of the city matrix, it simultaneously bears the marks of exclusion as it withdraws from the spaces left outside of its grid. Thus strategic control over this image becomes important and conflict dramatically increases within the interstitial spaces of alterity. There are several ways to contain these problems in their own specified zones. One is the creation of social control districts where criminal and civil code enforcement merges with land use controls; that is, special anti-graffiti districts, anti-red-light zones, new nuisance uses such as garage sales in Los Angeles, homeless districts in Miami, and drug enforcement zones on the Lower East Side of New York. In these zones the definition of nuisance has been extended from covering health, safety and general welfare issues that historically controlled the location of noxious industries or the placement of sweatshops and manufacturing uses to people's behavior, even though people cannot be fixed in place in the manner that land uses can.

In order to protect the rights of the homeless in Miami, Florida, for example, a federal judge ordered the city to create 'safe zones' where the homeless could sleep, eat, bathe and cook without being arrested. City police usually drove the homeless from public places and arrested them for harmless life-sustaining acts. The judge found this police action violated their constitutional rights: "Miami's policy of using ordinances on vagrancy, loitering, curfew and disorderly conduct to bar the homeless people from public areas violated the constitutional provisions of due process, equal protection and freedom from cruel and unusual punishment."[31] In the special zones that had been set aside the police were expected to act with restraint. Lawyers for the Homeless, however, believed that the homeless still would be arrested for sleeping or eating in public places that were not in one of the two designated safe zones because the homeless were categorized as an eyesore. They smelt as well, and discouraged investment and tourism. Some city officials also argued that such safe zones should not exist: you cannot create areas, the mayor said, where certain people are immune from regulation.[32] Shutting out homeless people in the end is but the inverse of shutting ourselves up within protected domains of the Framed City matrix because anything confused, unpredictable and random, without an assignable place, threatens the analytical order.

MATRICES AND MAPS

Returning to the analogy between matrices and the regional city, much of the theory of cyberspace assumes implicitly or states explicitly that a profound mutation has taken place that displaces the traditional Western space of geometry, of work, of the road, the building, and the machine. Instead, novel forms of diagramming, bar graphs, spreadsheets, matrices and networks are expressive of "a new etherealization of geography" in which the principles of ordinary space and time have been altered beyond recognition. Michael Heim, in "The Erotic Ontology of Cyberspace," writes that "[f]iltered through the computer matrix, all reality becomes patterns of information. When reality becomes indistinguishable from information, . . . the computer culture interprets all knowable reality as transmissible information."[33]

The pattern of information forming the architecture of computer memories is based on Boolean logic outlined by the English logician George Boole in his 1850s book *The Laws of Thought*. He demonstrated how thinking follows clear patterns and rules that can be mathematicized.[34] Boolean logic has become the metaphor for the computer age: it shows how we interrogate information, how we scan through flows of data. This Boolean search guides our subconscious when we interact with the computer interface: this is how we begin to model the world as Yes/No, On/Off 0s/1s. In the digital arts, files are stacks of information, searched by key words based on the Boolean algebra of "and" (*x*, *y* are both present), "or" (either *x* or *y* is present) and "not *x*" (*x* is not present). Furthermore, this binary logic is displayed graphically by Venn diagrams —images that classify things and then shuffle them into the appropriate set of boxes. In the end, Boolean logic is the governing relationship that determines inclusion or exclusion among terms.

Inevitably, direct experience declines, for the operations of Boolean logic are removed from subject matter and involve an abstract formal detachment having no inherent connection with things we directly perceive and experience. Michael Heim notes that:

> Boolean search logic cuts off the peripheral vision of the mind's eye. The computer interface can act like the artificial lens that helps us persist in our preconceptions. . . . We may see more and see it more sharply, but the clarity will not hold the rich depth of natural vision. The world of thought we see will be flattened by an abstract remoteness, and the mind's eye, through its straining, will see a thin, flattened world with less light and brightness.[35]

Cyberspace devotees assume they are jacked into this binary matrix of information flow. Yet they make a rhetorical jump, crossing boundaries from the technology based on binary logic to the fictional realm of a seamless human/machine symbiosis. These boundary crossings are based on the belief that the world can be understood by mathematics. It is an idealized projection of an underlying order whose mathematical substructure reveals the coherence, not of a material world, but of an objective realm of ideal forms.[36] In other words, cyberspace is a complex idealization. It offers the alluring fiction of limitless possibilities and connections, rather than a stale recasting of oppositional binary logic, but its principles of self-organization remain mathematical and Boolean.[37] Whatever way the denial is posed, cyberspace is based on binary structures that characterize traditional views of Western thought: the mind/body, idea/matter oppositions that have been around for centuries yet oppositions that cyberspace advocates seek to overcome.

The problem is that the real world is blurry and logic is incapable of dealing with new and unanticipated types of situations. Nor does logic deal with pattern recognition or activities that involve visual perception, abstraction and comparison. In Boolean set theory, an element is either in or out of a set (0/1), but in reality there are fuzzy sets, where things lie neither in nor out but somewhere in the middle. In order to include fuzzy thinking, connectionist models of cognition or associative memory and image-based modes of thought need to be examined.

Assemblages represent a form of associative thinking. Created by the liberal use of xerox, photocopy machines, silk screen printing, Polaroid cameras, an assemblage suggests that categorization is based on human experience and imagination. Thus associative grammars are erected on strategies of analogy and circumlocution, facilitating unexpected juxtapositions and overlapping images which make suggestive conjunctions. Associative thinking is not linear, progressive, rational, or conclusive. It is engendering, utilizing recursive reflexivity, loops, and returns. Furthermore, associative memory is based on storing a given piece of information next to similar information, not the standard pigeonholes of the library grid or a tree-structured encyclopedic recall. The latter are networks based on Boolean logic or matrix mathematics.[38] Rather than focusing on nodal points and linkages in the matrix, it is the oscillation between the contents of the nodes that becomes the concern in associative grammars.

How does associative thinking relate to mapping or imagining the physical form of regional cities where matrix mathematics seems firmly in control? Returning to Deleuze and Guattari, who described a different kind of map from the one we normally utilize as our conceptual tool to order and hierarchialize the actual territory of the city, we find their virtual postmodern map:

> is open and connectable in all of its dimensions; it is detachable, reversible, susceptible to constant modification. It can be torn, reversed, adapted to any kind of mounting, reworked by an individual, group, or social formation. It can be drawn on a wall, conceived of as a work of art, constructed as a political action or as a meditation. . . . it always has multiple entryways . . .[39]

Indeed, this ideal of connectivity and malleability produces unpredictable conjunctions capable of bonding virtually anything. It holds out the alluring fiction of limitless possibilities and endless connections.[40] It is part of the fiction of cyberspace that participants exist in " 'dynamic interaction with information' and consequently 'space (and experience) are pervasive rather than dualistic' . . . 'both/and inclusions rather than either/or dichotomies.' "[41]

Thus electronically mediated existence or the virtual reality of cyberspace becomes a means to imagine infinite productivity, the limitless possible metaphors of information and exchange.[42] The problem is the conjunctive hinge between virtual reality and, for want of a better word, actual reality. Cyberspace has no way of treating boundaries, no way to cross from virtual into actual reality. This problem exists with any mathematicization of space and time. It always reduces real space and time to the formal applicability of these conceptual tools. Take any virtual reality machine: it has to process vast amounts of data and feed back responses that can be translated into sensory experience. Obviously, simplified processes have to be employed in order to reduce the complexity of reality to manageable form.[43]

The argument being developed here makes a distinction between different computational models of cognition, and this relates to how we map or imagine the form of a regional city. The conventional model on which computers are currently based takes cognition to be the manipulation of symbols in accordance with preexisting computational rules. Kevin Lynch's image of the city is based on such symbol-manipulating procedures of cognitive mapping. On the other hand, the connectionist or associative network model operates as a parallel processor and has yet to be materialized as the architecture of a computer memory. This cognitive map more adequately expresses the complexities and nonlinear dynamics of regional cities. The latter model figures cognition as the spread of activities across a network of interconnected units. The connections between these units, rather than the units *per se*, take on the pivotal role in the functioning of the network.[44] Traditional theories of cognitive functions assume that information flows in a linear and sequential manner. Connectionist models move away from causal linearity towards a web of interconnections. Thus cognitive processes are supposed to be distributed and parallel, not sequential and linear. Von Neumann's machine, the grandfather of computation theories, was based on a series of rule-governing processes that were literally written out in propositional logic and stored inside a computer program. They established a hardware/software distinction in which the software determined cognitive functions and the hardware was simply a machine on which the program was implemented. Connectionist models reject this software/hardware distinction. There is no central processing unit, no stored rules. Cognitive functioning is controlled by the difference in weights between units, the general wiring of units, and a series of learning rules. Knowledge is no longer stored in locatable pigeonholes of an electronic memory, the nodal points of the matrix, but in the links/connections, the interstitial spaces between units where memory becomes the effect of differences between units and across the network.[45]

Perhaps we should turn to Italo Calvino's *Invisible Cities* for a demonstration of associative memory and the argument against a fixed spatial form (like the matrix) being used as a cognitive map of the city. Calvino notes that the computer provides a theoretical model for the most complex processes of memory, mental associations and imagination. Being based on rational thought, it simultaneously opens up towards multiple routes and unbounded wanderings. Finally realizing the *ars combinatoria* proposed by the medieval monk Raymon Lull, electronic brains make instantaneous calculations of unthinkable complexity, a "triumph of discontinuity, divisibility, and combination over all that is flux, or a series of minute nuances following one upon the other."[46] Calvino's mathematical structure spreads his tales of 55 cities over nine sections and classifies them into eleven sets of city types (such as "Cities and Memory," "Cities and Desire," "Cities and Names" . . .). A rotating device determines that after the fifth appearance of a tale from a given city set that type is retired and another one is born ("Cities of Memory" is finished and "Trading Cities" begins). Since the referent of these cities is invisible, their meaning must appear on the surface as signs change places and regroup. The reader must focus on the literal reading of the arrangement of tales, in spite of the fact that the abstract nature of this serial play tends towards accumulation and incompleteness.[47] Poor Kublai Khan desires a location map to link these cities together, a map he can master so that he can control all of this space. Yet he is confined to follow the author's open-ended process that moves in indeterminate directions. Thus he declares: "I will put together, piece by piece, the perfect city, made of fragments mixed with the rest, of instants separated by intervals, of signals one sends out, not knowing who receives them."[48]

WRITING ON THE NET

Finally let us turn to explore the establishment of a textual virtual environment on the Net. As one internet site advises the user who enters its space, "You are your words," underscoring the fact that the Net is predominantly a territory circumscribed by sentences, phrases and words skittering across cyberspace in different chat rooms, home pages, and electronic mail.[49] Your body enters this "space" as a form of writing, it literally becomes a cybertextual body. Because language wraps the internet, the entire environment becomes a textual projection. In this wordspace of electronic culture a work of art (be it verbal or visual) undergoes perpetual transformations and desubstantiations. Indeed, electronic writing is deeply playful; it focuses attention on the rhetorical surface, becoming an art intended to persuade. Its game of play depends on locating attention and emphasis through its use of topics, preformed arguments, phrases, discrete chunks of verbal boilerplate, which can be cut, pasted and repeated at will.[50] The conventions of reading from left to right, from top to bottom are challenged by diverting these norms and instead rotating lines, inverse mirroring of words and sentences, and ignoring the familiar grid of the page.[51] Once again, cyberspace pushes us to think beyond the matrix or the grid that has dominated Western conceptualization since the beginning of writing.

Look at several pages of the Times Square BID booklet, designed by Two Twelve Associates, and examine the parts of the message that are marked and those that are not.

"TIMES SQUARE
is as much an
(idea)
as it is
a place."

"The slightly **Eccentric**,
MAGNIFICENTLY artful
EXCITEMENT
and thrilling variety of . . .
TIMES SQUARE."

The first text, by shifting type and altering scale, not only directs attention but plays with the relations of greater and lesser than: it presents the amusing thought that Times Square is an idea first and secondly a place. The second text, by shifting typefaces, styles, sizes, positions, turns the simple statement into a series of zoned and ranked activities. These zones are linked to the actual space of Times Square, which is full of excitement, certainly magnificent, possibly eccentric and slightly artful. Placing the emphasis on rhetoric more than syntax, like *Learning from Las Vegas*, this form of writing allocates emphasis and directs attention in a nonlinear system of statements aimed at describing the confusion of everyday life in the public space of Times Square.[52]

The gestural language that encompasses the advertising billboard seems to swirl around the proclamations of Robert Venturi, Denise Scott Brown and Steven Izenour in *Learning from Las Vegas*.[53] Back in 1968 they acknowledged the rhetorical surface of the cityscape, noting that the successful text in the commercialized culture of the late twentieth century was the one that combined high-speed communication with maximum information.[54] While *Learning from Las Vegas* was concerned with architecture in the age of television and the automobile, Venturi has since turned his attention to new modes of electronic communication. Venturi's latest book, *Iconography and Electronics: Upon a Generic Architecture*, is primarily concerned with language of the direct address and with the manner in which statements communicate.[55] Architecture, Venturi proclaims, involves shelter and symbol; it "embrace[s] signs, reference, representation, iconography, scenography, and trompe-l'oeil as its valid dimensions."[56] But rather than examining the signs of Las Vegas and exploring the iconography of the commercial strip, as once was

Figure 17.1 **"We also have a very nice bridge." San Francisco advertisement, *New York Times*, February 5, 1989, p. 58**

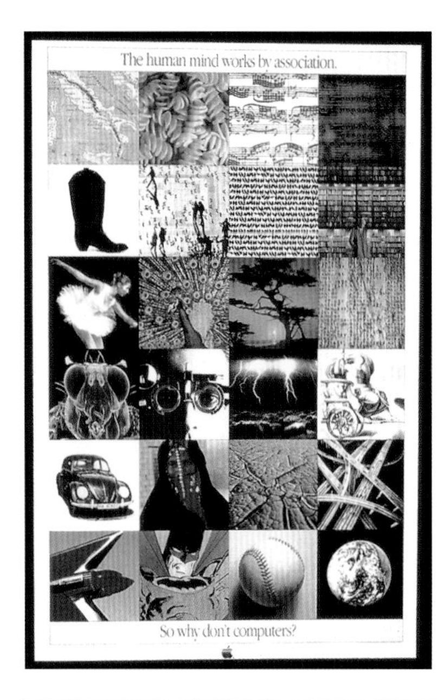

Figure 17.2 **"The human mind works by association, so why don't computers?" *Graphics 259*, January 1989**

Figure 17.3 **Twenty-first century course system: satellite seminars, live interactive teleforums. *Graphics 259*, January 1989**

Figure 17.4 **Nodes of desire. Cover of *Smithsonian*, February 1998**

Figure 17.5 **The electronic city. *Lusitania* 7, p. 89**

Figure 17.6 **Disney on Forty-second Street. *New Yorker* magazine, April 4, 1994, p. 71**

the focus, now Venturi is intent on studying the electronic images displayed on Jumbotrons and LED (light-emitting diode) mosaics emitting their messages day and night. The Las Vegas Strip reveals dramatic changes since 1968: it has been urbanized, its linear strip settlement recomposed in superblocks, its parking lots either filled in with large hotels or converted into front lawns and its traffic so congested that its streets will soon be pedestrianized. Signs have evolved into scenography and neon has been replaced by LED matrices of ever changing images and graphics.[57]

Venturi's underlying question is clear: what will be the future relation of electronic technology to writing, architecture and urban space if the former transposes the latter? The answer requires renegotiating the entire word/image —or alphabet/icon—relationship. This revolution in the material form of writing impacts architecture and urban space, since they become the public surface on which electronic texts are displayed. It offers new forms of expressivity, new relationships with the word and with typography, and new intellectual techniques of cognition. Electronic writing searches for ways to bring the comical and play into the seriousness of print and design; it aims to make communication interactive, not reliant on conventional or canonical expressions.

Lessons can be learned from Times Square/42nd Street because this public space has always been famous for its electronic one-liners: the strip zipper blurting out news bites on the Times Building was put in place in 1924. Textual artists such as Jenny Holzer over the last two decades have been preoccupied with these one-liners, what language poets call aphorisms. Her "Truisms" (1977–1979) were a series of "mock clichés" or throwaway paste-up texts like those she found scattered about Times Square warning men to stay away from the vice in the area, exclaiming how they would get leprosy if they overstepped a magic circle drawn around the place. She was amazed at how the word "leprosy" on a poster stopped her short. This led her to experiment with her own short texts, posting them in public space wherever she wanted. At first Holzer did not exploit the expressive potential of various typefaces or construct her texts in zones of activity. Her aphorisms were stereotypical one-liners typed on white paper in black ink. Alphabetically arranged line by line, her "Truisms" crossed over the border from literary to visual art, raising many questions in their wake. How do we read the following lists?

> Abuse of Power comes as no Surprise
>
> Action causes more trouble than thought
>
> Alienation produces eccentrics or revolutionaries"

Are they a manual for operating in contemporary times? Are these alphabetical wordspaces to be compared with other verbal orderings of experience, such as lists, associations, fragments, those "structures of accretion" that pile up disparate things and only slowly begin to make contradictory and complicated sense? Are we browsing through catalogues—flipping, scanning, scrolling or linking through mobile electronic texts—as the eye and the mind catch similar or dissimilar meanings and thoughts? They seem to be a form of nonlinear associative thinking where meaning is intended to slip in and out of focus. Meant to provoke and to prod the spectator to stop and to read, in the end these aphorisms problematize communication and stand on the edge of chaos.

Venturi's writing has also been involved with one-liners and utilizes forms of direct address. In *Complexity and Contradiction* (1966) he told the reader that "Less is a bore" and "I like elements which are hybrid rather than 'pure', compromising rather than 'straightforward,' ambiguous rather than 'articulated,' . . . inconsistent and equivocal rather than direct and clear."[58] By stressing the words he dislikes—"pure," "straightforward," "articulated"—Venturi highlights his own double-coded preferences for mundane objects stripped of all pretensions yet wildly productive of a multivalent, multivocal architecture. Such was his rhetorical intent: to bring the noisy materiality of the outside world of the street and the billboard inside the clean and distilled realm of modern architecture and shatter its tranquility like an explosive device.

Venturi's attack continues in *Iconography* and *Electronics*, where he opens on a "sweet and sour" note. There is particular sweetness in the Information Age where electronic signage transforms words into evanescent, instantly transformable signs and opens on to a variety of languages both vulgar and tasteful. But there are sour notes as well, a tone that dominates his one-liners presented as a list of "Mals Mots: Aphorisms—Sweet and Sour—By an anti-hero Architect."[59] Venturi develops a "flaming" critique of the *retardataire* avant-garde American architects who have transformed architecture into a theorized and immaterial form. His rhetorical play enables formal pleasure to balance conceptual thought, self-conscious stylistics to alleviate theoretical despair.[60] Hearing echoes of Jenny Holzer—for it is difficult not to see these statements flashing across a spectacolor board, flung down at the reader as so many "Truths"—Venturi uses forms of public address to express personal feelings, ambivalences, even insecurities mimicking the self-conscious manner of electronic space.

There are a cluster of volatile statements entitled "Valid Rantings" which display posturing, suggestibility and play.

> I am always out of step.
>
> I am an exhibitionist: I go around exposing my thoughts.
>
> It is better to be good than in—I think.
>
> Challenge me, don't harass me!
>
> Am I being sour? Yes, but also sweet as that combination works to illuminate.
>
> It's OK to be cranky if you're perky too.
>
> Am I the marginal nerd?
>
> Remember, my positivity complements my negativity, and I hope, embraces wit.

Eventually Venturi reaches his goal and presents "Iconography and Technology":

> Viva iconography *and* scenography in architecture.
>
> Can we learn from the vivid art of advertising of today?
>
> Iconography is all over tee shirts—why not buildings?
>
> Billboards perversely represent the civic art of today—to be cherished 100 years from now as significant elements for historical preservation; Houston will be for billboards what Williamsburg is for Colonial.
>
> Today's fear of electronic technology for evolving iconographic surfaces in architecture resembles yesteryear's fear of engineering technology for a machine aesthetic.
>
> And now, from decorated shed to virtual box . . .
>
> Light is our essential material—more than bricks (and even wire frame guy wires.)
>
> Light is our essential medium—not as "veiled" and "luminous" planes that are electric but as vivid iconographic decor that can be electronic.
>
> Virtual variety.
>
> Iconography as graffiti glorified . . .[61]

Which brings us back to the city and in particular to urban spaces such as Times Square that are filled with writings on the wall. Zooming in and out of an image, reversing the traditional figure/ground relationships or playing with ornamental/purposive features, electronic writing allows the writer to shift scales at will. The viewer/reader looks at writing as a material surface or a series of pixel patterns. Just as Roy Lichtenstein's 1960s comic book paintings forced the viewer to look at the surface pattern of dots as a design motif, so Venturi envisions the gigantic blown-up surface of electronic writing as the nonlinear public space we enter into, where writing becomes the interactive and volatile iconographic surface we must learn to playfully traverse and enjoy.

CONCLUSION

The analogy between the computer matrix and regional cities—or the spatial orderings that cybercities erect—asks us to make a qualitative leap from virtual to physical space, erroneously assuming that the boundaries separating these spaces can be crossed with ease. Behind all the hype surrounding cyberspace and the internet, challenges must be faced: about the future of democratic public space, whether virtual or real; about increasing privatization, commercialization, and hierarchical control that create a new periphery—those locked out of the zones of cyberspace—or those left behind in the digital divide between the well defined frames and zones of cybercities. There is the problematic construction of subjectivity or the self in computer-mediated communications that needs to be scrutinized. And there are challenges to face concerning the basic assumptions of mathematics that sustain both the architecture and the language that control events in cyberspace. In the interface between writing and architecture we need to keep in mind both the materiality of space and its representational images as they oscillate back and forth in the construction of meaning and as they open us to new explorations and playful reformulations.

The hybrid condition of cybercities challenges the long held privileged status of Cartesian geometry, the map and the matrix or grid. Infrastructural links and connectors, information exchanges and thresholds, become the dominant metaphors used to examine the boundless extension of regional cities. We need to look at the space of the city in a different manner in order to envision the thresholds and loops it now represents. A map with its pictorial icons and static spatial relationships cannot represent the nonlinear and interactive flows of information that cybercities contain. On the edge of chaos, the contemporary city may no longer be readable, in the manner that Kevin Lynch proscribed in *The Image of the City*.[62] Yet there will always remain the need for some conceptual filter to make sense of the confusion of turbulent urban conditions. Standing on the threshold between fixity and relativity, the natural and the artifice, the real and the imaginary, the liminal space of cybercities still waits to be imagined.

NOTES

1 Robert Markley, "Boundaries: Mathematics, Alienation and the Metaphysics of Cyberspace," in Robert Markley (ed.) *Virtual Realities and their Discontents*, Baltimore: Johns Hopkins University Press, 1996, pp. 55–77.

2 Bruce Sterling, *Islands in the Net*, p. 17, quoted by Peter Fitting, "The Lessons of Cyberpunk," in Constance Penley and Andre Ross (eds) *Technoculture*, Minneapolis MN: University of Minnesota Press, 1991, p. 299.

3 Markley, "Boundaries," pp. 76–7.

4 Gilles Deleuze and Félix Guattari, *A Thousand Plateaus*, quoted by Michael J. Ostwald, "Structuring Virtual Urban Space: Arborescent Schemas," in Peter Droege (ed.) *Intelligent Environments: Spatial Aspects of the Information Revolution*, Amsterdam: Elsevier, 1997, p. 451.

5 Neil K. Guy, *Community Networks: Building Real Communities in a Virtual Space?* <www.vcn.bc.ca/people/nkg/ma-thesis/title.html>

6 SAIC's board of directors is composed of retired defense and intelligence officials. Guy, *Community Networks*.

7 Amy Harmon, "Internet Group Challenges U.S. over Web Addresses," *New York Times*, January 26, 1998, p. D5.

8 Robert W. McChesney, "The Internet and U.S. Communication Policy-making in Historical and Critical Perspective", *Journal of Communication* 46, (1) 1996, p. 115.

9 Mitchell L. Moss and Anthony Townsend, "Leaders and Losers on the Internet," September 11, 1996). <http: www.nyu.edu/urban/research/internet/interent.html>

10 A review by Steve Cisler of Stephen Doheny-Farina, *The Wired Neighborhood*, New Haven CT: Yale University Press, 1996, <sac@gala.apple.com>

11 Guy, *Community Networks*.

12 Quoted by ibid.

13 Mark Landler, "Haves and Have-nots Revisited," *New York Times*, October 8, 1995, p. D4.

14 Howard W. French, "In Africa, Reality of Technology Falls Short," *New York Times*, January 26, 1998, pp. D1, D0.

15 "Information Democracy," *New York Times* editorial, November 20, 1945, p. A14.

16 Guy, *Community Networks*.

17 Quoted by Judith Butler, *Excitable Speech*, New York and London, Routledge, 1997, p. 6.

18 Pamela Gilbert, "On Sex, Cyberspace and being Stalked," *Women and Performance* 9 (1) 1996, pp. 125–49.

19 Guy, *Community Networks*.

20 Quoted by Klaus Bartels, "The Box of Digital Images, the World as Computer Theater," *Diogenes* 41 (3), 1993, p. 50. Also see Michael Johnson, "Swamped by the Updates Expert Systems, Demioclasm, and Apeironic Education," *Stanford Humanities Review* 4 (2), 1995, pp. 86–7.

21 Ada Louise Huxtable, "Living with the Fake, and Liking it," Sunday *New York Times*, March 30, 1997, Section 2, pp. 1, 40.

22 Aaron Betsky, "Las Vegas' New York, New York" quoted by Huxtable, "Living with the Fake."

23 Huxtable, "Living with the Fake."

24 Sarah Kember, "The Shadow of the Object: Photography and Realism," *Textual Practice* 10, 1996, pp. 145–163.

25 Kevin Robins, "Into the Image: Visual Technology and Vision Cultures," in *Photo Video*, London: Rivers Oram Press, 1991, p. 58.

26 Evan McKenzie, *Privatopia*, New Haven CT: Yale University Press, 1994. See also Dennis R. Judd, "The Rise of the New Walled Cities," in Helen Liggett and David C. Perry, *Spatial Practices*, Thousand Oaks CA: Sage Publications, 1995, pp. 144–66.

27 Judd, "New Walled Cities," p. 157.

28 "Il ranch di Irvine a Organe County: la città che non imita la città" (Irvine Ranch of Orange County: the City which does not Imitate the City), *Lotus* 89, 1996, pp. 52–99.

29 Ibid., pp. 76–7.

30 Andres Duany and Elizabeth Plater-Zyberk, "The Neighborhood, the District and the Corridor," in Peter Katz, *The New Urbanism: Toward an Architecture of Community*, New York: McGraw-Hill, 1994, pp. xvii–xx. For another example, look at the regional grid plan for Madrid, 1997–2017. Here the radio-centric model of a spread city, or the concentric ring theory of circumferential highways, has been replaced by an orthogonal mesh as the orienting paradigm of the region's structural growth. "The units of this grid, network, mesh or reticulum, represented on an analogue Plan, . . . offer a new vision of regional land . . ." The grid plan is based on the notion of sustainable growth throughout the entire region and is thought to be able to transfer the pressure of growth towards new adjacent spaces as opposed to the hypertrophy and congestion implicit in earlier development models. Comunidad de Madrid, *Land Strategy Regional Plan Basis 1996*, Madrid: Dirección General de Urbanismo y Planificaión, 1996, p. 12.

31 Larry Rohter, "Miami ordered to create Homeless Zones," *New York Times*, November 18, 1992, section A, p. 16.

32 There have been similar ordinances on vagrancy, begging and park curfews related to homelessness in Atlanta, Chicago, Las Vegas and San Francisco. Chicago swept all of the homeless from its airport, and New York has a state law prohibiting begging in the streets, a case that advocates for the homeless have declared to be unconstitutional, since begging is a form of speech and cannot be barred.

33 Michael Heim in "The Erotic Ontology of Cyberspace," in Michael Benedikt (ed.) *Cyberspace: First Steps*, Cambridge MA: MIT Press, 1992, p. 65.

34 Douglas R. Hofstadter, "On Seeing A's and Seeing As," *Stanford Humanities Review* 4 (2), 1995, pp. 109–21.

35 Michael Heim, *The Metaphysics of Virtual Reality*, New York: Oxford University Press, 1993, p. 25.

36 Markley, "Boundaries," p. 67.

37 Ibid., p. 69.

38 Maureen Caudill, *In Our Own Image: Building an Artificial Person*, New York: Oxford University Press, 1992, pp. 73–88.

39 Gilles Deleuze and Felix Guattari, *A Thousand Plateaus*, trans. Brian Massumi, Minneapolis MN: University of Minnesota Press, 1987, p. 12.

40 For a full definition of the conjunctive "and' see Marcus Doel, "A Hundred Thousand Lines of Light," *Society and Space* 14 (4), 1996, pp. 421–40.

41 William Bricken, *Extended Abstract: A Formal Foundation for Cyberspace*, quoted by Markley, "Boundaries," p. 65.

42 Markley, "Boundaries," p. 75.

43 Ibid., p. 59.

44 Elizabeth A. Wilson, "Projects for a Scientific Psychology: Freud, Derrida, and Connectionist Theories of Cognition," *Differences* 8 (3) 1966, pp. 21–52.

45 Wilson, "Projects."

46 Italo Calvino, *The Uses of Literature*, New York: Harcourt Brace, 1986, p. 9.

47 Carol P. James, "The Fragmentation of Allegory in Calvino's *Invisible Cities*," *Review of Contemporary Fiction* 6 (2), 1986, pp. 88–94.

48 Italo Calvino, *Invisible Cities*, trans. William Weaver, New York: Harcourt Brace, 1974, p. 164.

49 Quoted by David S. Bennahum, "I got E-Mail from Bill!," *New York Times Book Review*, February 16, 1997, p. 23.

50 Richard A. Lanham, *The Electronic Word Democracy, Technology and the Arts*, Chicago: University of Chicago Press, 1993.

51 Craig Douglas Dworkin, " 'Waging Political Babble': Susan Howe's Visual Prosody and the Politics of Noise," *Word and Image* 12 (4), 1996.

52 Johanna Drucker, *The Visible Word: Experimental Typography and Modern Art, 1909–1923*, Chicago: University of Chicago Press, 1994.

53 Robert Venturi, Denise Scott Brown and Steven Izenour, *Learning from Las Vegas*, Cambridge MA: MIT Press, 1972.

54 Marjorie Perloff, *Radical Artifice: Writing Poetry in the Age of Media*, Chicago: University of Chicago Press, 1991, p. 93.

55 Robert Venturi, *Iconography and Electronics: Upon a Generic Architecture*, Cambridge: MIT Press, 1996.

56 Ibid., p. 3.

57 Ibid., pp. 123–8.

58 Robert Venturi, *Complexity and Contradiction in Architecture*, New York: Museum of Modern Art, 1966, p. 16.

59 Venturi, *Iconography and Electronics*, pp. 299–329.

60 Ibid., pp. 2–16.

61 Ibid., pp. 325–8.

62 Kevin Lynch, *The Image of the City*, Cambridge MA: MIT Press, 1960.

18 The future of transport

Mobility and infrastructure

Ralph Gakenheimer

Table 18.1 Rates of motorization in Third World countries

Country	Year	No.	Year	No.	Year	No.	Year	No.	Increase (%)		
Least motorized (30 vehicles or less per thousand population)											
Burundi					1980	10	1990	16	60		
Bhutan					1980	2.2	1985	3.7	68		
Chad					1980	9.5	1985	14	47		
Nigeria			1975	200	1985	600	1990	300	200	–50	
Ghana					1985	40	1990	100	150		
China			1975	1,000			1990	6,000	500		
Egypt		1975	300	1985	800			160			
Indonesia		1975	500			1990	2,700	440			
Intermediate motorization (31–100 vehicles per thousand population)											
Ecuador			1975	120	1985	325			170		
Jordan			1975	40			1990	190	375		
Thailand					1985	1,350	1992	3,200	137		
Chile			1970	250	1980	700	1992	1,000	180	42	
Syria			1970	50	1980	175	1985	280	250	60	
Korea					1983	750	1990	4,200	460		
More motorized (101–200 per thousand population)											
Poland			1970	900	1985	4,500	1993	7,900	400	75	
Costa Rica			1970	55	1980	160	1992	260	190	63	
Hungary	1960	50	1970	400	1980	1,100	1990	2,100	700	175	91
Mexico			1970	2,000	1980	6,000	1991	10,800	200	80	

This is an effort to look ahead to transportation issues of the future in the developed and developing worlds. In doing so it is unavoidable to perceive the prospects of the future from the trends and perspectives of the present. I do this in the light of four themes: (1) increasing affluence in most countries of the world during the next decades, (2) a forceful concern for the protection of the environment, (3) an increasing role for telematics in human transactions, and (4) new transportation technologies.

INCREASING AFFLUENCE

The most important force for change and adjustment in urban transportation is the rapidly increasing number of motor vehicles in the world. Table 18.1 shows the remarkable increase of vehicles in selected countries. The number is increasing rapidly in nearly all the developing countries, including those with currently very low motorization rates (less than 30 vehicles per 1,000 population) and those which at up to 200 are nearly in the developed category. As Table 18.2 shows, East and Southeast Asia are in a phase of especially rapid growth, even countries we think of as consciously controlling motorization, such as Singapore and Japan. The most dynamic environment of motorization at the present time is China, where the growth of motor vehicles is 15 percent per year, that of cars 25 percent per year, and that of private autos over 50 percent per year. Of course current levels of motorization there are very low, but with a population of over a billion the compounded growth will soon rise to daunting figures.

Vehicle ownership tends to rise with income. The fit of the regression curve in Figure 18.1 indicates the close relationship between the annual income of upper income groups and the level of national motorization. This curve is for the lower income developing countries. For countries with higher *per capita* income the fit is not as good. For the developed countries this relationship is entirely useless.

Table 18.2 Growth in the number of motor vehicles in Southeast Asia (per thousand population)

Country	1988	1992	Increase (%)
Thailand	35	54	54
Hong Kong	35	49	40
Taiwan	79	112	42
Singapore	90	102	13
Japan	250	313	25

The overall picture is one of very rapidly rising motorization in the developing countries, often exceeding 5 percent per year; that is, doubling every twelve years. In the developed countries registrations tend to be rising slightly, but distance traveled per person is rising too.

Cities are growing as well, so the increasing traffic is distributed over space, but high demand destination areas are bound to create very serious congestion. This is the case because urban structure, personal origin–destination needs and infrastructure supply cannot possibly adjust quickly enough to the rapidly increasing travel demand. As a result it is essential that cities undertake strong immediate solutions such as traffic management and road pricing while also planning carefully for longer-term solutions such as access-oriented land use policy and expansion of the transportation infrastructure capacity.

PROTECTION OF THE ENVIRONMENT

The geography of policy priorities across the world varies greatly, but it is clear that environment is important in many countries and gaining hold in others each year. There are two different types of issues. The first is local pollutants and particulates, which are causing increasing irritation to urban dwellers, especially in cities where high concentrations and microclimatic conditions exacerbate the problem. Concern for this problem is not as great in the developing world as in the developed countries, except in cities with particularly acute problems such as Mexico and Santiago. But the concern is observably expanding rapidly. In recent years the problem has become much more important in Bangkok and new importance was signaled in India with special attention in *India Today* news weekly, with a cover picture and several technical and news articles on the subject.

The second set of issues relate to global warming. As a policy issue global warming is very intractable. Although it is clear that the use of internal combustion engines is disturbing the distribution of ozone and will gradually change the climate at some rate, it is not clear how

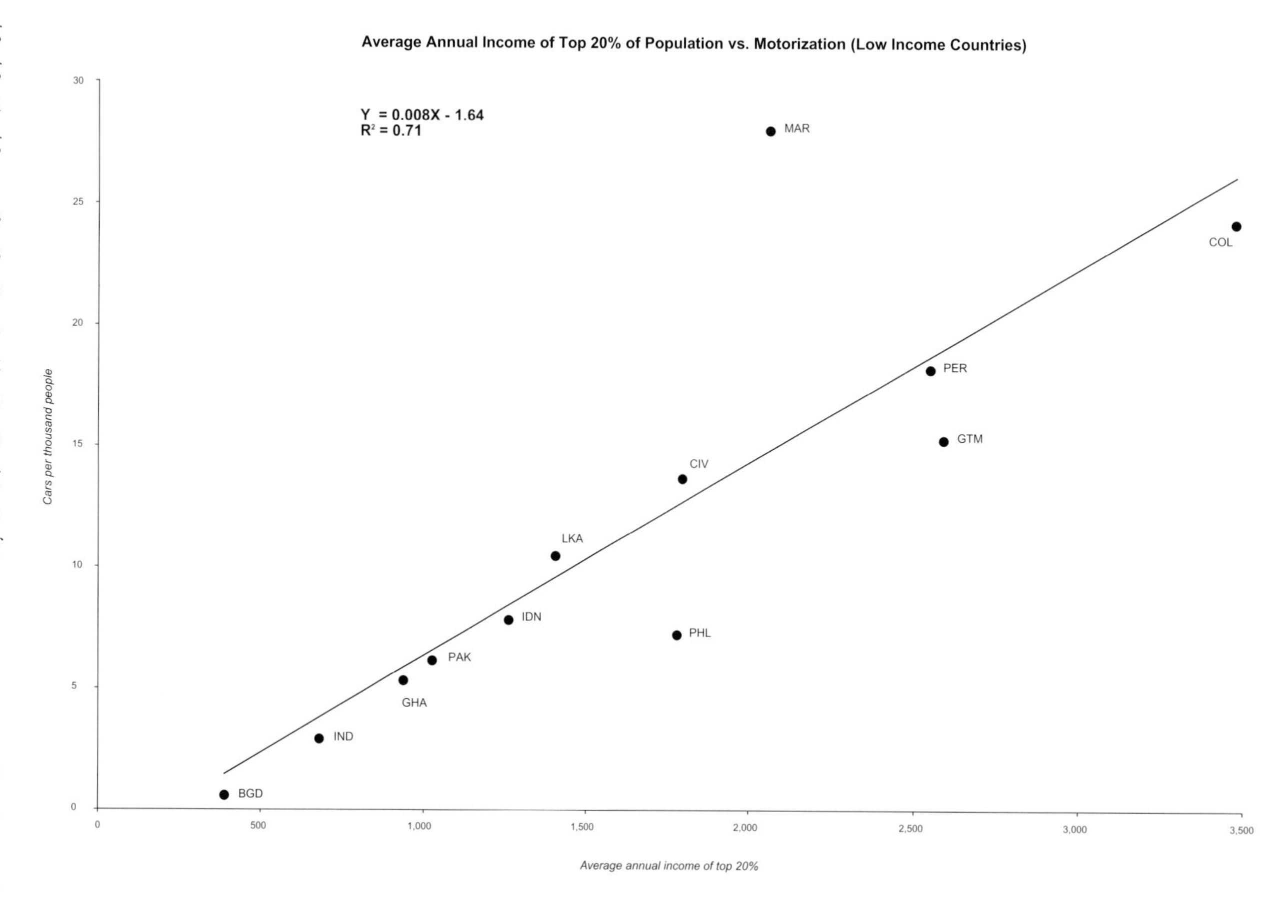

Figure 18.1 Average annual income of the top 20 percent of the population vs motorization in low income countries

immediate the problem is or what the earth's capacity to adjust to it will be. As a result, while it is a very serious policy issue to some groups, government attention is likely to be quite unpredictable. Global warming is none the less suspended behind policy discussion as a veiled threat that takes some toll on the outcomes.

The result is an increasingly intense concern for engine technologies, fuel technologies and vehicle kilometers traveled. Vehicle and fuel technologies are getting constructive attention at the national level. The principal local attention is to reduce trip making. This is one of several forces toward the enactment of traffic management and congestion pricing actions.

These concerns have already been, for a number of years, one of the principal reasons why it is virtually impossible to build new highways in most American cities. Even more broadly, the US Environmental Protection Agency requires that new highways have the projected effect of reducing total pollution rather than increasing it. In Central Europe there are all kinds of actions in place to restrict the use of motor vehicles, including parking restrictions, pedestrianization, vehicle registration limits, and traffic calming measures.

THE ROLE OF TELEMATICS

Advanced electronic communications are very rapidly growing technologies. They will surely have a profound effect on transportation. The question of foreseeing what effect they will have, however, is remarkably difficult. Indications in the US according to research on telecommuting are to anticipate only limited response. Telecommuters are a quite small and not rapidly growing portion of the work force. As a result, professional opinion concerned with travel behavior tends to minimize the trip-making impact of telematics.

But there are incipiently visible indications that serve to guide our expectations. First we concede that advanced communications do not result in a net decrease of travel—so far. Communications result in increased acquaintance and associations that lead eventually to travel. Videos result in increased interest in the cinema, and more visits to movies. Well televised sports provide much superior images of the game than are available in the stadium, but they also dramatize the excitement of being in the stadium and thereby stimulate attendance. The final result is that trip making does not decrease, but it dramatically changes in structure. There is an increasing number of professionals who have specialized schedules. They live in remote locations and spend three days a week at an office in the major city. They never drive at rush hour.

Further developments will have substantial effect. The use of telematic substitution for travel has not yet become sufficiently widespread to be a competitive factor. That is, there are few cases in which telecommuting workers have a competitive edge over traditional commuters because of the time they save by not traveling. There are not enough of them to be a factor in the labor market. This issue is bound to rise. Competition arising from technological advantage may take a long while to influence lifestyle but its impact is eventually felt. Recall that in most Western cultures people once returned home for a long lunch at midday, but the practice eventually collapsed because two work trips were not competitive. The last of the work communities with this practice, for example in Latin America, have by now nearly all adjusted to the competitive continuous work day. In addition, management needs to adjust to the demands of telecommuting with adequate arrangements for telematic meetings, management control of employees at remote locations, etc. Also suburban communities have to adjust to meet the needs of people who will seldom leave them. Note that we are really still adjusting to the full use of the simple telephone as part of our work environments, a full century after beginning to use it. Technological change happens fast, but significant lifestyle behavioral adjustment happens slowly. What is the future timing and shape of telematics in work? It is not hard to envision an all-day heavy travel demand that is roughly level for most of people's waking hours, with slight peaks at hours of commuting and convenient meeting.

Another aspect is the future of telematic innovation in personal transactions of all kinds. There are fragments of behavioral impact we can count on.

1. Increasing numbers of workers with jobs that do not require continual interface with site-specific conditions, jointly used equipment, or interpersonal transaction will live at remote locations. They will gather at workplaces on a regular basis, but only for part of their work week. They will transform their residential localities into fuller living environments. The overall effect, unfortunately, will probably be increased social homogeneity of individual settlements. It will mean lower densities because of less frequent trips to work. But the total mileage of work travel will be quite high. This trend will be spurred on by the competitiveness of telecommuting, as it saves time, saves working space and includes some services at hand that could not be provided at office sites.

2. People will increasingly belong to special interest groups sustained by electronic networks. This includes hobbyists, for example, who collect stamps from the Cameroon, make historical reproduction furniture in the

Jacobean style, or read the works of an obscure nineteenth-century English novelist. But there will be also highly focused professional interest groups—who are interested in non-motorized, two-wheeled public transport vehicles, computer software for designing a certain class of carburetors, and so forth. To any extent that these groups include high-income people or manage sufficient propinquity they are likely to hold meetings once in a while that may create big aggregations at particular locations.

3. Shopping will be gradually rationalized. Rather than walking the streets among stores, it will be possible to see a much larger assortment of merchandise in a class of interest. Michael Dertonzos (in *What Will Be*) foresees that we will shortly have means by which the individual can be physically measured for size by a program that is stored, making it thereafter possible to examine a clothing choice by illustrating the shopper him/herself modeling the garment. This probably requires rapid movement of merchandise for inspection purposes into the hands of shoppers and back to sellers. As a result it may well increase the freight component of travel demand. This is an effect somewhat parallel to freight traffic increases through just-in-time delivery made necessary to achieve the low-stock holding advantages made possible by electronic inventory records.

4. Education is a good candidate for transition in certain ways. All the basic activities of education are easily transferred to electronics. Listening to lectures and asking questions, holding a seminar discussion, accessing library materials, submitting a paper, taking an examination—none of these requires personal attendance. All this excludes an extremely important element, however, the personal development part. The educational process for a young person is very important because of its socialization role, and is conducted during precarious times in the personality development of the student. It is hard to say now what activities that implies during a process of computerizing education, but chances are it will surely involve travel.

5. Recreation is another sector where transitions of travel demand will be hard to follow. On the one hand, television plainly provides a better way to experience an athletic event than being there. By being present one sacrifices the instant replay, the multiple camera angles, the zoom capability. There is probably not a large market for sacrificing these advantages in order to be part of the crowd except for very special occasions. On the other hand, the amplitude of coverage of the media may increasingly drive people to participation in new recreations. Increasing numbers may take up squash, cross-country skiing, jai-alai, or beach soccer. That produces travel to play sites.

The details, especially as far as urban travel is concerned, are difficult to anticipate. It does appear, however, that the future will see increasing decentralization of residence and work. It will also include more long-distance travel (relative to familiar commuting distances) and a less peaked daily travel demand.

Superimposed on all these adjustments, of course, is the impact of intelligent transportation systems (ITS). Serious efforts to examine the impacts of ITS on mobility are only beginning to take place. It is hard to foresee the outcome. Most of the innovations in driver advisory systems are likely to result in only modest increments of mobility. They may encourage modest numbers of drivers to choose non-congested hours for trips and to take substitute routes during obstructive highway incidents. Perhaps the greatest ITS impact will come through electronic tolling, for the first time making it possible to toll urban highways. That leads the way toward the commercialization of urban highways that could facilitate their expansion and, perhaps, toward congestion pricing.

NEW TRANSPORTATION TECHNOLOGIES

During recent years there has been relatively little interest in new technologies that promise increased urban mobility. It may reflect the fact that in the developed countries urban growth has been modest in most regions and, while miles traveled have grown impressively, government concern has been more focused on responding to the externalities of transportation. Accordingly, most technological research on vehicles has been applied to fuel and engine design as means of reducing pollutants.

There are exceptions. The principal one is the current recovery of interest in automated highways. The idea of a highway in which the driver puts the vehicle in the hands of a system that assures efficiency and safety, taking his hands off the steering wheel, has been recurrent during the last four decades. It is problematic because of the need for so much simultaneous innovation and because of the jeopardies of lawsuits in the case of system failure. None the less, several of the largest auto manufacturing companies are investing in it, and we should watch it.

Though not really innovative, the recent increase of light rail systems on independent rights of way and elevated transitways in the developing world merits attention. These are possible at modest expenditure. Transitways (mostly for buses) have the advantage of incremental implementation. They can be built in increments as congestion makes them necessary or as funds are available, leaving the bus at street level for the rest of its route.

There may also be a new life for heavy urban rail systems (metros). The international transportation community has been generally opposed to metros in developing countries, on account of their very high capital costs. But there are indications that they may reconsider the possibilities of metro based on its capabilities for making the overall transportation system work under circumstances of intense congestion in cities of the developing world, and its, by now demonstrated, effect in retaining the economic strength of city centers. The apparent success of the 15 or so new metros in developing countries during the last 25 years in preserving city centers is becoming a factor.

Perhaps the only firm generalities that can be concluded from the trends pictured in these commentaries on urban transportation are that (1) pollution per vehicle and probably also in aggregate will decrease, (2) the daily peaks in traffic will continue to decline, and (3) individual trip length will increase on the basis of continued, maybe accelerated, decentralization.

OPTIONS AND EVENTUALITIES

What are the major actions that can, and may, be taken to improve mobility during the next years? Here are some possibilities.

1. *Infrastructure extension.* Building more highways under circumstances of rapid decentralization is partly effective. Houston, Texas, has managed to reduce congestion during the past several years by a combination of highway construction and HOV emphasis. Analysts at the World Bank concluded that the traffic conditions of Bogotá have remained more or less constant over the past years as a result of decentralization and highway building under the rapid growth of motor vehicle registrations. There is, however, a resistance to the construction of new highways in much of the world, and no means to build highways in much of the world. Also, a policy of this kind may well doom the city center to deterioration.

2. *Spatial and temporal repression of independent travel.* This approach, traffic demand management (through traffic management or pricing), has made important impacts in certain areas—such as in Singapore and the cities of China. Traffic demand management is the only tool that can gain sufficiently high yield results under conditions of rapid population and vehicle increase to make a real impact on the problem of congestion. European cities have kept the impacts of auto travel under control by these techniques in an impressive manner.

3. *Increase the efficiency of urban travel.* Techniques of traffic management and advanced electronic methods have made modest improvements in the efficiency of movement. Certainly they should be prudently employed to make the most of the infrastructure, but they will not make significant gains on the problem under circumstances of rapid growth.

4. *Make substantial investments in mass transit.* The likelihood of any significant progress by this means in the heavily auto-oriented countries—such as the United States and Australia—is small. In Central Europe the transit share of travel is increasing on the strength of resolute policy and maybe will continue to grow if investment keeps pace. The low-income countries have a chance to keep transit viable while automobiles increase, principally by controlling the use of cars rather than making increases in transit they cannot afford. The upper-income developing countries, on the other hand, have a real possibility of making gains in the use of transit through building attractive infrastructure and charging fares that enable it to at least approach paying its operating costs. Their cities have simultaneously the income level to pay the fare and the market for transit. Accordingly, Malaysia, Korea, Singapore, Brazil and other upper-income developing countries have reached important solutions of this kind.

5. *Rationalize land use for mobility.* Across the world metropolitan planning generally attempts to implement the same single scheme to produce higher levels of amenity and access. It is a plan that decentralizes the extremely dense pre-automobile city and accommodates the current decentralization of a highly motorized city. This plan proposes clusters of new development that concentrate trip ends and make more efficient travel modes possible. There is little doubt that this program is better than the unstructured decentralization that would otherwise take place. It may not be the optimal land use pattern, but among good ones it is the only one with a chance of implementation. None the less, this planning is in most cases futile because of the lack of land development powers on the part of government.

One way to handle this is for the government of a developing country to intervene by choosing sites outside the current wave of development and providing the basic infrastructure. Then developers who urbanize the land are attracted to such localities by their superior public services. The developers are then required to pay a share of the infrastructure cost. A group of MIT faculty under the leadership of Professor Gary Hack planned such centers for metropolitan Bangkok, as shown in Figures 18.2–3.

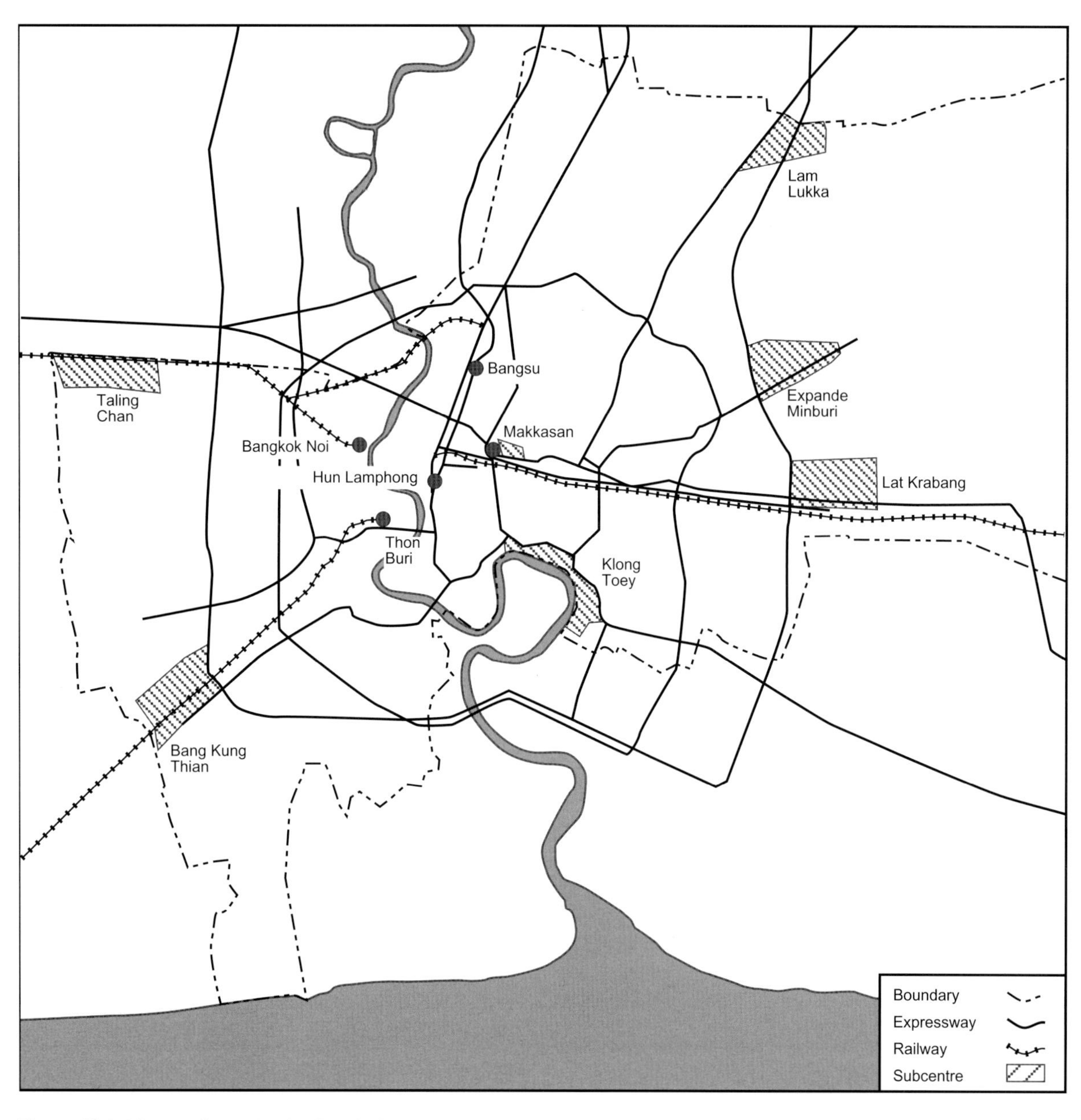

Figure 18.2 Metropolitan plan for Bangkok

Another version of this plan has been designed by the Urban Development Authority of Sri Lanka, as indicated in the Colombo Plan. In this case the new connecting roads link the coastwise centers with one another and with the city center. (See Figure 18.4.)

Significant improvements in the mobility of cities are hard to achieve. They require a firm sense of the problem and a commitment to solve it by means strong enough to make a difference. During the coming years most cities that try will probably fail. But there are opportunities for resourceful governments to make a genuine difference in a future otherwise burdened by inefficient mobility.

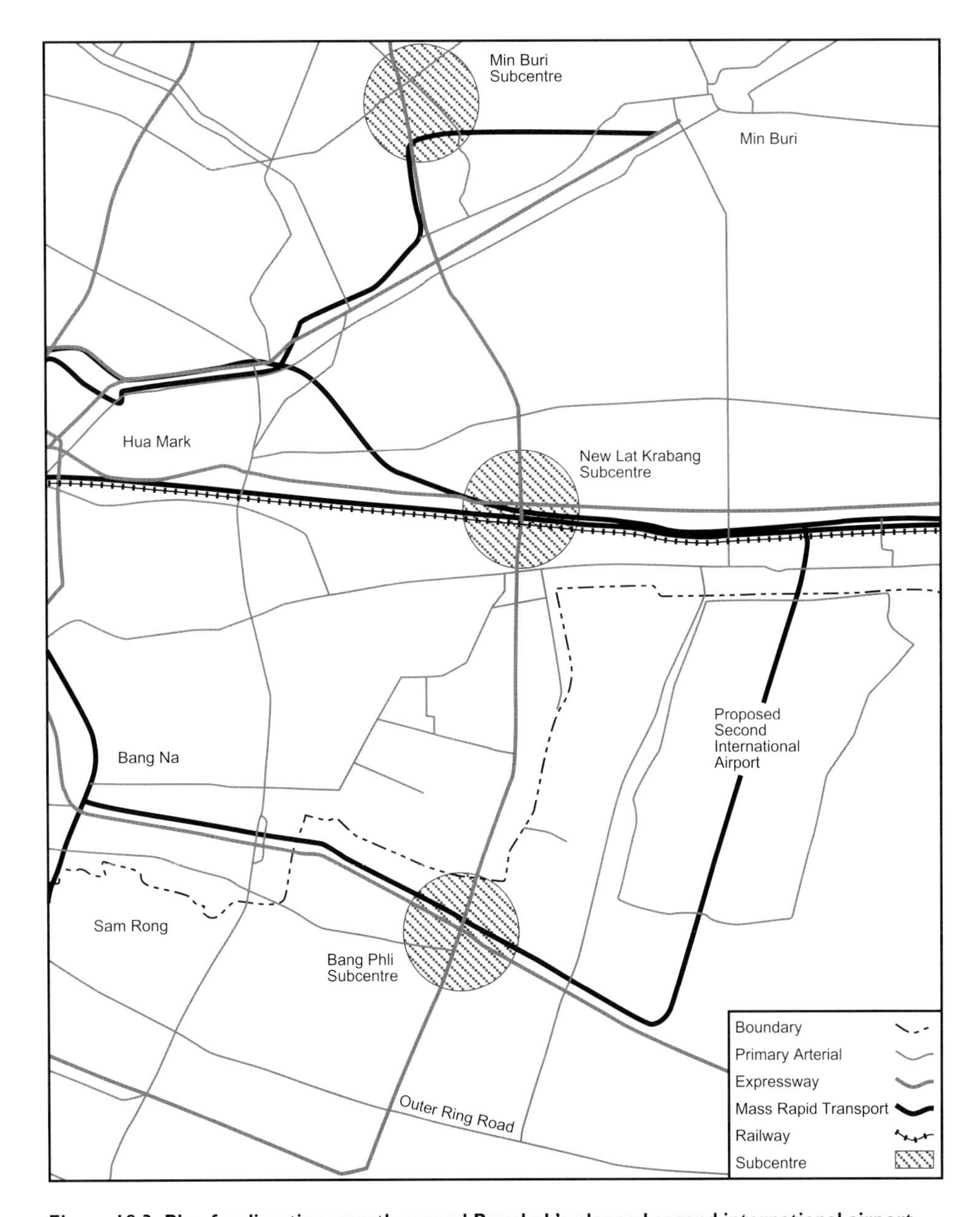

Figure 18.3 Plan for directing growth around Bangkok's planned second international airport

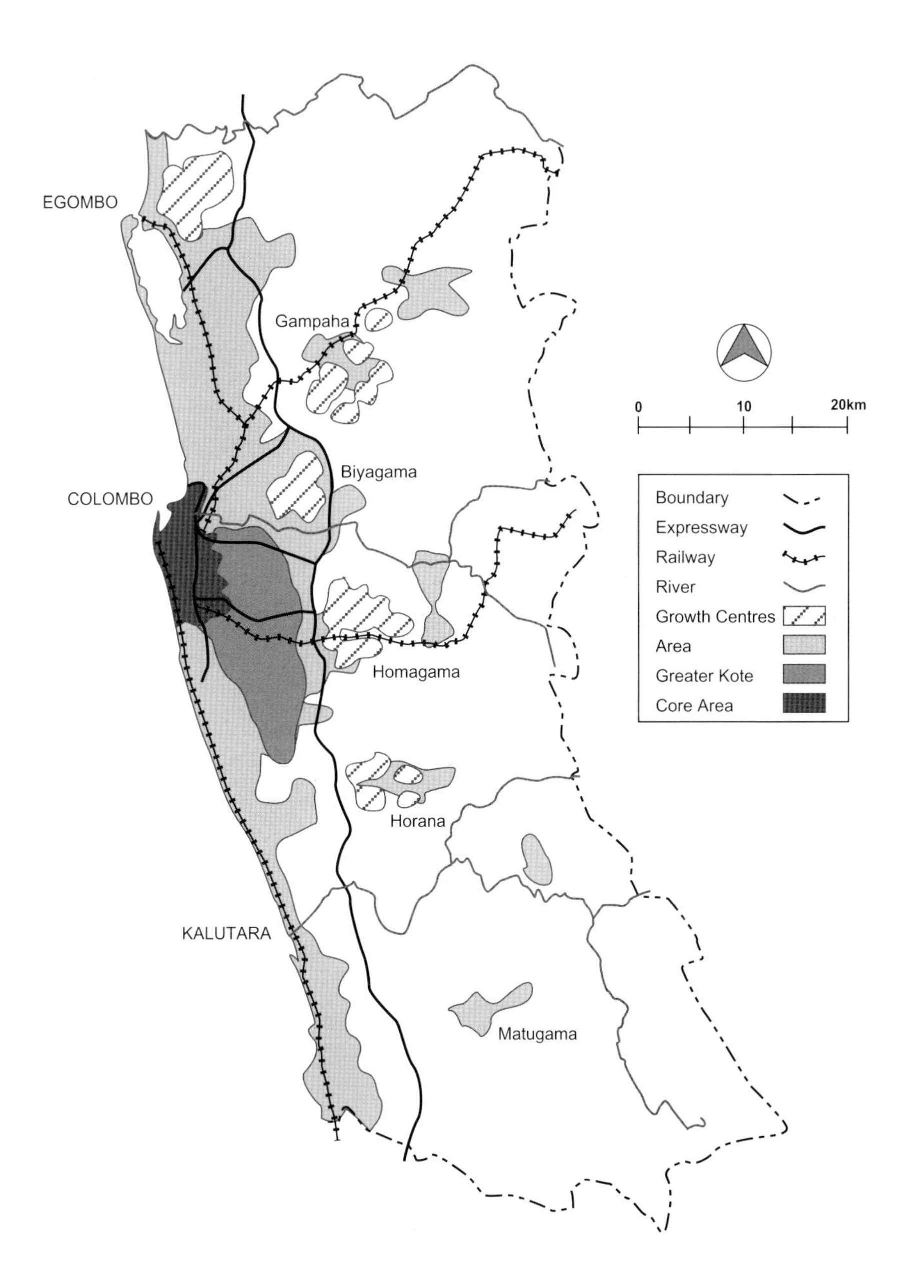

Figure 18.4 The plan for Colombo

19 Planning cyberplaces

Stephen Graham

TOWARDS "TELE-MEDIATED" CITIES

Global city regions, and the corridors between them, are being permeated with widening arrays of telecommunications grids—conventional 'phone networks, wireless and radio systems, cable networks, satellite systems, internet, data and video networks. These silently and (usually) invisibly underpin rapidly increasing flows of voice, data, video and images across all walks of city life and development, and at all geographical scales. Indeed, every aspect of the life of our cities is now cross-cut with all manner of computerized and "tele-mediated" communication, exchanges and transactions, most of which are now based on digital principles (meaning that they are based on the streams of zeroes and ones used in computers).[1] As Geoff Mulgan once put it, "The redefinition of the city as a system for producing and switching information is highly visible."[2]

IT and telecommunications networks are becoming, in a real sense, the very sinews of our globalizing society. For profoundly urban or urbanizing societies, and for the whole gamut of actors, agencies, policy makers, organizations and individuals who depend on cities in various ways, there is, arguably, no more important issue than the relationship between new media and telecommunications technologies and the future of city regions. But what does this "digital age" really mean for our cities? What future is there for city regions as more and more of the traditional roles and functions which first generated the need for urban concentration seem likely to be possible across distance via advanced telecommunications links? Will our cities face some electronic requiem, some nightmarish *Blade Runner*-style future of decay and evisceration? Or can they be global powerhouses of economic, social and cultural innovation in the new electronic media? Finally, what roles are there for urban policies, plans and strategies, and for urban design and community development, within the shift to a so-called "tele-mediated" urban life, based more and more on all types of on-line interactions?

These questions are the concern of this chapter. In it I aim to suggest future directions for urban policy, by exploring the linkages between telecommunications, the future of cities and an emerging range of innovations in urban policy and planning based fundamentally on exploring the use of telecommunications and IT networks as policy tools.

NEW TECHNOLOGIES AT WAR WITH THE CITY? PREDICTIONS OF URBAN DECLINE

Answering questions about cities and telecommunications is actually extremely difficult. As soon as one poses them the story quickly turns deeply problematic. For there has been very little critical and informed debate or research about the future of cities, and the kinds of urban strategies that are appropriate to the shift to the "tele-mediated city". This does not mean, of course, that analysts and commentators have been silent on questions of technology and cities: there have been countless attempts to describe the "future city" over the past 20 years. But most of them have been characterized by simplistic assumptions about how future cities will simply be "impacted" by new communications technologies in some linear, cause-and-effect way. New information and communications technologies are usually seen as some disembodied, external "wave" of change. Their urban "impacts" are usually seen to follow inevitably from their effective "collapse of distance" as a constraint on human life.[3] Worse still, such scenarios usually suggest that all cities (say Los Angeles, London, Bangalore, Charleroi and Santiago) will somehow all be "impacted" in the same ways. Such so-called "technological determinism" is attractive because it creates powerful scenarios and clear stories, and because it accords with the dominant experience in the West, where, as Stephen Hill puts it, the pervasive experience of "technology is one of apparent inevitability".[4]

In fact, much of the current rhetoric about the "information age" is actually made up by suggestions that the need physically to congregate and interact in cities, or to travel, is about to become little more than some quaint anachronism. Instead, in an economy, culture and society of generalized, on-line and speed-of-light interactivity, any activity will soon be possible from any place and at any time. Everything will be "one click away".[5] All activities will become possible, from the "tele-home" or the "electronic cottage", located in the idyllic rural or suburban environment of one's choice. Power and control will inevitably be shifted from centralized cities, bureaucracies and institutions towards physically and organizationally-decentralized networks based on electronic inter-connections.

The inevitable results, many allege, will be a society based largely on tele-mediation: tele-voting, electronic transactions, tele-education, tele-health, tailored media services, and virtual friendships and communities. The emerging message is clear. Our reliance on urban places, urban infrastructures and transport flows, with all their messy ambivalences, their congestion, poverty, crime, pollution and social problems, can easily (and thankfully) be transcended. We will substitute for them blossoming electronic interactions over ever more sophisticated fiber optic grids and, increasingly, within ever more realistic "virtual" environments and realities, accessible from anywhere. Crudely put, the pure, clean and limitless realm of "cyberspace" will rescue us from the dirty, polluted, contested, finite city. A new, effectively post-urban age will be ushered in, allowing the ruralized utopias of Frank Lloyd Wright and Alvin Toffler to be achieved.[6]

Consider, for example:

- The urbanist Anthony Pascal's suggestion that "the era of the computer and the communication satellite is inhospitable to the high density city. With the passage of time [will come] spatial regularity; the urban system converges on, even if never quite attains, complete areal uniformity."[7]
- The pronouncement of the *Independent*'s architecture critic, Martin Pawley that "in urban terms once time has become instantaneous, space becomes unnecessary. In a 'spaceless city', the whole population might require no more than the 30 atom diameter light beam of an optical computer system."[8]
- The architectural commentator Shafraaz Kaba's question: "Why would you want to drive for an hour, get stuck in traffic, and be scolded by your boss, when work is a few keystrokes away from the comfort of your home-office?" "Why", he continues, "even *build* in reality? If the sensations of space provoke the same emotion in virtual reality as they do in 'real life', why go through the expense of construction, building and maintenance? Nothing degrades in cyberspace!"

It is widely assumed that such shifts will inevitably disperse or fragment cities to the extent where we can no longer assume that, internally, their relations will be any stronger to those linking them instantly with the outside world. As the eminent French philosopher and critic Paul Virilio put it, "the city of the past slowly becomes a paradoxical agglomeration in which relations of immediate proximity give way to interrelationships over distance".[9] Such rhetoric and logic inevitably pit new technology *against* urban areas in some simple, dualistic way. The whole position is summarized well by Kaba, to whom "the future will be a war between the city of bits and the city of atoms".

THE NEED FOR MORE SOPHISTICATED POLICY PERSPECTIVES

Unfortunately, such implications and assumptions of urban dissolution are, quite simply, both empirically false and dangerously misleading. At the very least, they offer partial, onesided and often self-interested accounts of very complex pictures. As a result, they provide a poor basis for critical and sophisticated consideration of the ways our cities are developing, and of how urban change relates to technological change. They radically overestimate the degree to which what goes on in cities, with their rich textures of communication, interaction, symbolic exchange, life, and meaning, can somehow be simply pushed on-line and replaced by electronic flows. Consequently, such images and ideas are extremely pessimistic about the prospects of urban economies, cultures and society in the "digital age".

I take a very different starting point from the widespread images and icons suggesting urban dissolution, technological determinism and the transcendence of place. I recognize that new communications technologies will be involved in the important current transformations of our cities. But I want to counter the pervasive and deterministic pessimism about cities and telecommunications. In fact, I seek to demonstrate the opposite case: that our metropolitan regions are, in fact, central to all aspects of innovation in information and telecommunications technologies, and to the "information society" more broadly. As the sovereignty of nation states is "hollowed out" by globalization, and subnational urban and regional strategies articulate more directly with global forces, it is increasingly obvious that metropolitan regions are the fundamental buildings blocks of the emerging global "information" economy, society and culture. Information technologies, in fact, are a profoundly urban phenomenon. New technologies are centrally involved in the emergence of a new type of urban world (based on subtle combinations of tele-mediated and place-based exchanges) rather than a post-urban world (based purely on tele-mediated exchanges).

This is not to say that the transition to the "tele-mediated" city will not raise many problems, challenges, even crises; like all major urban changes, it will be profoundly uncertain, problematic and probably divisive. Nor do I disagree that more and more sophisticated telecommunications will support richer and richer telemediated interactions, of all sorts and across all geographical scales. But I would stress the ways in which applications of new communications technologies actually resonate with, and are bound up within, our urban-based lives, and the changing nature of our cities. They do not spring from some external source of technological "impacts", to simply erase the profoundly urban nature of our civilization, however much commentators and advertisers may want this to be so (or may benefit from suggesting that it is so).

Following the communications scholar H. Sawhney, I would criticize what he calls the "very transmission-oriented view of human communication" in cyberspace debates. In these, he argues, "the purpose of human communication is reduced to the transfer of information and the coordination of human activity. The ritual or the communal aspect of human communication is almost totally neglected."[10] Without exploring how cities and places support meaning through communal, ritual, trustful, even playful, bodily, face-to-face and corporeal interactions—which are, by definition, very difficult to sustain over on-line links—we will fail to understand the economic, cultural or social resilience—indeed, centrality—of city regions in the so-called "information age". When we do acknowledge the subtle, qualitative communicational roles of urban places, it quickly becomes apparent that cities are actually *co-evolving* with advances in communications and information technology.

Current advances in telecommunications are a phenomenon which is overwhelmingly driven by the economic dynamism of cities, particularly larger, internationally oriented, metropolitan regions. City regions have important assets in an internationalizing economy, based more and more on flows of information, services and "symbolic" products like media, advertising, cultural services, software and electronic entertainment (as well as the movement of people, goods, and commodities). They support face-to-face interactions, especially for higher-level decision-making functions, in a world of fast flows and great volatility. We should not forget the sheer infrastructural advantages of cities. Cities also have the high-quality physical, service and telecommunications infrastructure to extend access efficiently to distant places and markets. Whilst remote rural areas may still have the old-fashioned and poor-quality analogue telecoms infrastructure of the old monopolies, many main city centers now have three or more separate, high-capacity digital systems competing on price and quality (with many others selling specialist services). The City and West End of London have four superimposed optic fiber grids and countless other specialist service providers who deliver over these networks. Eighty percent of investment in French telecommunications goes to the Paris region.

But cities offer unrivalled place-based, as well as electronic, contact potential. Today's uncertain and globalizing economies make trust, constant innovation and "reciprocity" more and more important, which can be fully forged only through ongoing face-to-face contact. Stressing "the extraordinarily social nature of modern economies", the geographers Nigel Thrift and Kris Olds write that "it is clear that face-to-face interaction has not died out. Indeed, in some sense it has become more important as reflexivity (including an enhanced ability to see oneself as others see us) has become built into economic conduct."[11] Tony Fitzpatrick, of Ove Arup, argues that:

> cities reflect the economic realities of the 21st century. Remote working from self-sufficient farmsteads via the Internet cannot replace the powerhouses of personal interaction which drives teamwork and creativity. These are the cornerstones of how professional people add value to their work. Besides, you cannot look into someone's eyes and see that they are trustworthy over the Internet.[12]

On the consumption side, too, the whole range of consumer services now so important in urban economies—tourism, shopping, visiting museums and leisure attractions, eating and drinking, sport, theater, cinema, etc.—are all growing and seem likely to resist any simple, substantial substitution of "on-line" equivalents.

In fact, as the value added in IT industries shifts from the zones dominated by hardware production to places that can sustain innovation in software and content, so the focus of the industries may actually be shifting Silicon Valley-like research and development campuses to central, old-city, locations. In the cultural industries the creative small firms that dominate internet software, digital design and worldwide web services, far from scattering towards rural idylls, seem, in fact, to be concentrating into (a small number of) gentrifying metropolitan "information districts" like SoHo and Trebeca in New York, Shoreditch in London and Temple Bar in Dublin. As well as having good (broadband) telecom connections and tailored, "internet-ready" office spaces, such districts are thriving through processes analogous to those that spawned the first industrial districts in nineteenth-century cities. But the raw material of such industries is the sort of informal networks, high levels of creativity and skill, tacit knowledge and intense and continuous innovation processes that become possible in an intensely localized culture, based on ongoing, face-to-face contacts supported by public spaces.

Most important here, the internet, with its "spiralling mass" of information, communication, transactions and specialized media flows, is now weaving into support every aspect of urban functioning in contemporary city regions. Such trends are most advanced in the US, which demonstrates the strong metropolitan bias of both the production and the consumption sides of the internet. On the *production* side, for example, downtown New York's "Silicon Alley" has emerged, along with districts in downtown San Francisco and other large cities, as a remarkable concentration of micro and small firms, based on digital art and design, web production, and digital and multimedia services. These draw on the city's unparalleled arts, cultural industries and literary traditions. One of the main motors of the recent economic renaissance in Manhattan, Silicon Alley encompasses over 2000 new media firms which rely on intense, informal local contacts to sustain continuing innovation and interaction. Interestingly, urban planning and policy are beginning to find ways of supporting this new information district. It must be stressed, however, that only a relatively small number of urban districts are being redeveloped in this way and that such "organic" spaces are very difficult to develop "artificially"—that is, in the absence of an existing appropriate high-skill and innovative entrepreneurial culture.

On the *consumption* side, too, there are many opportunities for weaving "access points"—internet and service kiosks—into the fine-grained fabric of cities, to animate, enliven and inform what goes on in the public and private realms of cities and metropolitan regions. Whilst there are many problems here to do with the high cost of technologies, highly uneven social access and skill levels, and dangers of oppressive surveillance, a growing range of initiatives at the urban level are currently experimenting with new media solutions to support the improved delivery of public services, support community networking and enhance local economic, social and cultural development.

But such public initiatives are far outweighed by the sheer *economic logic* of the internet industry starting to develop a coherent, and legible, relationship with the metropolitan regions that constitute the vast bulk of its commercial web pages, social interactions and information sources. Again, Manhattan, by example, has twice the "domain density" (i.e. concentration of internet hosts) of the next most "internet-rich" US city—San Francisco—and six times the US average.[13] In fact, the urban dominance of the internet in the US is actually growing rather than declining. The top 15 metropolitan core regions in the US in internet domains accounted for just 4.3 percent of the national population in 1996. But they contained 12.6 percent of the US total in April 1994, and by 1996 this had risen to almost 20 percent as the internet became a massly diffused and corporately rich system. As Moss and Townsend suggest, "the highly disproportionate share of internet growth in these cities demonstrates that internet growth is not weakening the role of information-intensive cities. In fact, the activities of information-producing cities have been driving the growth of the internet in the last three years."

EMERGING URBAN TELECOMMUNICATIONS INITIATIVES

Such are the imperatives of addressing the complex interlinkage between cities and telecommunications across the world that, despite the many analytical and conceptual problems inhibiting such policies, it is now becoming possible to identify an emerging style of planning that attempts to start addressing the relations between new media and the different dimensions of the "new urbanism". Early examples can be drawn from a *bricolage* of evidence, drawn from cities in the US, Canada, Malaysia, Europe, the UK and elsewhere around the world. These examples have not yet coalesced around a coherent new paradigm of urban policy. Many can be criticized as technologically determinist, environmentally problematic or socially exclusionary. But I would argue that, together, they point to new emerging styles of planning and urban policy. Within the confines of space here I want to look in more detail at three emerging styles of policy: city-level new media strategies, urban corridors and "online" economic spaces, and so-called "information districts" and "urban televillages".

Urban new media and IT strategies

The first broad emerging policy area is urban new media strategies. IT strategies for community networking, local economic development and public service delivery have been under way in many UK, European and American cities for a decade or more. Following American experience, community networks like Free-nets, the Manchester, Kirklees and Nottingham Hosts, and the Newcastle NewNet system, based on the internet, have emerged which try to use computer communications to support grass-roots local economic and voluntary activities.[14] Many local authorities are also experimenting with public Internet systems, electronic kiosks and smart card systems to deliver information on public services, and aim to improve the services themselves. In the UK there are proposals to wire up both schools and libraries as places where ICT networks can be made widely available to local communities. Local services have developed patchily on the new urban cable networks developing across the UK. And virtually all major cities in Europe, North America and Asia now have a presence on the internet, where so-called "virtual cities" range from simple tourist promotion and local databases to sophisticated spaces which attempt to add coherence to all local activities on the internet, to widen local access and skills, open up interactive services for local debates, and develop information and communication services which feed back positively on to the development of the home city.[15] Interestingly, the most innovative virtual cities use the analogies of city "spaces", "squares" and "districts" so that the many services they offer relate directly to their counterparts in physical urban space. The most sophisticated of these in the UK currently is virtual Bristol, supported by a partnership of the city council, Universities and Hewlett Packard, launched in April 1997. Not to be left out, BT is exploring the concept of "urban intranets"—internet services that are accessible only to specified local communities.

This disparate range of local new media initiatives has two problems, however. First, they have tended to be isolated "IT islands", largely ignoring each other. Second, they have usually been developed with little or no respect for how they relate to the physical urban realm or to the broader development dynamics and geographies of their subject cities. Thus the challenge for cities is to shape coherent partnership-based strategies aimed at harnessing all types of new media applications—internet, cable, kiosks, telephone, infrastructure—to their economic, social and cultural development needs. Such issues need to begin with social, geographical and institutional issues and policy needs and move on to how new technologies might meet these needs—rather than the other way round. Institutional solutions need to be found that harness the entrepreneurial energies of the new media industries, and their growing interest in market-based local initiatives (like the booming commercial metropolitan internet sites in the US). At the same time, they must link creatively and positively to the fragmented sets of agencies involved, in the broadest sense, in the governance of cities (local authorities, development agencies, health, education and information institutions, firms, schools, the community and voluntary sector, etc). Clearly, urban media "master plans" will be impossible: what is needed are strategic frameworks so that the innumerable local media investments and initiatives emerge to be more than the sum of their parts.

Finally, and most important from the point of view of this chapter, there needs to be a much more thoroughgoing attempt to link urban media strategies with the development of cities themselves, so ensuring that, wherever possible, synergies can be developed between media and place-based exchanges. Progress is being made here, however, at both the urban and the regional levels. At the city level, strategic planners in cities like Amsterdam and Lille have already attempted to integrate new media into future urban visions. In dozens of cities across the world "teleports" and "telezones" have been designated in particular urban districts, blending advanced office and business space and sophisticated telecommunications facilities. Edinburgh, marketing its world-class BT infrastructure, now markets itself as a "telezone". In the US ambitious "smart city" new media strategies are tentatively starting to consider land use planning and urban policy issues—as our discussions of strategic urban corridors and information districts demonstrate. Already, in some affluent communities, like Palo Alto, California and Blacksburg, Virginia, very high levels of internet and e-mail access and use have begun to transform the communicational fabric of urban areas. Predictably, in a private sector-led planning process, the consultancies engaged in "smart city" planning argue that "cities unprepared for these [new media-based] changes risk being consigned to geopolitical obsolescence before they even know what hit them".[16]

In the United Kingdom the packaging of IT infrastructure with individual land use developments—business parks, "tele-cottages", "wired villages", etc.—is increasingly common. But efforts are also starting to link broader urban media strategies with urban-wide development strategies. After a period when grant, training and technological support was "pepper-potted" through the city, Manchester is increasingly gearing its broad telematics initiatives to specific urban redevelopment and reuse projects, and to strategic discussions about combating social exclusion. A widening range of new physical projects have emerged linked into the network services on offer: the Electronic Village Halls (linked with community centers and initiatives through the city), existing managed work spaces in New Mount Street and others proposed in the "Northern Media Quarter", and a center for multimedia development and applications in Hulme.[17] A similarly broadly based ICT strategy, known as the

Gemesis project, is under way in adjacent Salford, backed by a broad partnership between the cable company, IT firms, local universities and training providers. In partnership with its university sector, Manchester/Salford, like German cities such as Berlin and Bochum, is also building a new broadband Metropolitan Area Network (MAN) infrastructure ring that aims to spur efforts to regenerate the inner city, especially through science-related initiatives.

New urban corridors and "on-line" economic spaces

The second area where new media policy is becoming directly linked with policies for particular urban spaces is the emergence of new master-planned IT-based communities and economic spaces. In the US, cities like Orlando, Florida, are the focus of large-scale private "wired city" experiments. In these, media, cable and telecom firms are experimenting with the generation of "broadband" (i.e. high-capacity) home media infrastructures, testing the viability of services like video on demand, home shopping, video phones and the like. Across the US, new master-planned communities, targeted at affluent "knowledge workers", are now routinely provided with high-capacity telecom infrastructures from the outset.

On the economic front, most large dynamic cities already have their campus-like "technopoles", developed to house science parks, corporate R&D centers, and university business, science and engineering schools, usually located in greenfield, peripheral zones.[18] Cities like Lille, Cologne and Sunderland have gone further and have developed high-profile "teleports" which connect local industries directly with advanced services and satellite ground stations. All over the world new urban business zones are being constructed and tailored to the widening array of firms that effectively deal in flows of digital information. Many examples are emerging here: digital financial dealing spaces in the international financial capitals like London, Paris, New York and Tokyo; "intelligent office parks" where routine back-office, electronic commerce and telesales operations are locating (in peripheral cities like Milwaukee, Sunderland and Newcastle); and "Digiport", tax-subsidized investment zones in countries like India, Jamaica and the Philippines, where transnationals are locating their back-office, data-crunching and customer support operations. Such dynamics, in fact, are creating their own complex networked urban geographies strung out across the world. For example, in cities like Bangalore in southern India—colloquially termed India's Silicon Valley—a whole new cycle of frantic urbanization is emerging, fueled by the influx of global technology firms eager to access the cheap, highly skilled IT professionals available there.

But giant among the emerging generation of urban, new technology-based planning initiatives is the Multimedia Supercorridor (MSC) in Malaysia. Here, in effect, at the heart of the burgeoning "miracle economies" of the ASEAN block in Southeast Asia—until the financial collapse of 1998 Malaysia was growing at 8 percent per annum—a whole national development strategy has effectively been condensed into a single grandiose urban plan for a vast new urban corridor. Whilst the plan has been substantially downgraded with the economic crisis, the aim of the MSC remains nothing less than to replace Malaysia's manufacturing-dominated economy by a booming constellation of service, IT, media and communications industries, by turning a vast stretch of rain forest and rubber plantations into "Asia's technology hub" by the year 2020. The MSC starts in the center of the capital, Kuala Lumpur—itself a booming city symbolized by the new Petronas twin towers, momentarily the world's tallest buildings. It ends 30 miles south at an immense new international airport strategically placed on the routes to Singapore.

Information districts and urban televillages

Finally, building on the debates about "urban villages" in Europe, and the so-called "new urbanism" movement supporting denser, less auto-dependent urban neighborhoods in the US, interest is also growing rapidly in how media infrastructure and services can be designed and managed to sustain and feed back on to particular urban districts. In California the concept of the "TeleVillage"—an integrated urban place supported by a whole suite of ICT infrastructures and services—is gaining support. The first example, the Blue Line televillage, a two square mile area on one of the new public transit corridors in Los Angeles, is based on a holistic strategy to manage land use, transport trips and electronic communications so that synergies emerge between the three, creating a "livable" community with reduced automobile use, higher community-based activities and higher urban densities than in the usual LA suburbs. Physical places for supporting IT training and services—community centers, computer centers, telework centers, IT links in schools, hospitals, transport facilities and libraries, and electronic kiosks in public and semi-public spaces—are integral to the plan, which is backed up by a broad, public–private–community partnership and an extensive array of on-line public services. In partnership with the public transport operators in the LA region, a new fiber network is being developed to link together whole constellations of tele-villages across the region. Different packages of ICT infrastructure and services are being offered for different land uses; "distributed" organizations are being encouraged; and attempts are being made to include more marginal social groups. The philosophy is that IT-based retrofitting in existing US urban areas will mean that many urban problems may be addressed with very little new physical construction and no dramatic changes in density.

The other emerging example of combining new media and urban regeneration at district level is the concept of the "information district". Here the emphasis is on creating urban "milieux" that sustain economic growth in new cultural and "symbolic" industries, where informal face-to-face contact is essential, whilst also providing high-capacity on-line linkages with the wider world. Most often, information district strategies emerge organically, as in the cases considered above—New York's Silicon Alley, Dublin's Temple Bar and Manchester's Northern Quarter—where clusters of such industries emerge spontaneously in inner urban districts. Then the challenge is to intervene to further support the growth of small and micro firms in the relevant sectors, whilst also ensuring appropriate property is available and that efforts are made to improve the broader urban realm and the contribution of the industries to the economic and social revitalization of the city as a whole. Thus both New York and Los Angeles have offered grant schemes and tax exemptions to small and micro firms in the new media sectors. Backed by the powerful New York New Media Association (NYNMA), specialized multimedia centers, offering managed work spaces and high-level telecoms bandwidth, have also started to emerge in Silicon Alley, as have dedicated venture capital funds and orchestrated events and programs to encourage local face-to-face networking.[19] Elsewhere in the US, the city of Spokane, in Washington state, has wired up much of its downtown to attract multimedia firms.

In Europe, Dublin's Temple Bar district is backing up its physical regeneration efforts, weaving a parallel infrastructure for electronic multimedia exchange. And in London's Soho media core a specialized telecommunications network was constructed by a consortium of film companies called Sohonet. This system links the tight concentration of film and media headquarters in the district directly to Hollywood film studios, allowing on-line film transmission and editing over intercontinental scales, via highly capable digital broadband connections. The network is seen as a critical boost to the broader global ambitions of the UK film and cultural industries.

CONCLUSION: ENVISAGING PROGRESSIVE TECHNOLOGICAL FUTURES FOR GLOBAL CITY REGIONS

With the above examples I have started to map out the emergence of what promises to be a major shift in conventional urban strategies. Reviewing a set of new planning practices, it is apparent that attempts are now being widely made to incorporate integrated concepts of communications within the management and planning of urban places, supported by fully "relational" perspectives of how land use and the urban realm, transport, face-to-face contact and telemediated connections weave together in subtle and synergistic ways.

At this early stage, too little is known about the effectiveness of the above strategies to provide full evaluations of them. Indeed, initially, it is important to raise serious warnings against *overstating* the potential role of telecommunications and information technology in urban strategies. There is the danger that urban strategies are uncritically embracing the transformational rhetoric that characterizes contemporary notions of technology "impacts" upon the city that I touched on at the start of this chapter. To date, the new styles of urban planning have often been characterized by a very narrowly drawn set of powerful participants, pursuing grandiose and probably socially regressive spatial practices. As a result, new spatial concepts often powerfully reflect the interests of private sector producer interests—telecommunication providers, developers and landowners aiming to add value, high-tech symbolism and kudos to their spatial "products." Often, as part of wider trends towards the physical and social fragmentation of city regions, the resulting spaces are narrowly designed for elite on-line groups and corporate users, whilst being carefully fortressed from incursion from "undesirable," non-on-line, social groups. Too many planners have already been seduced into investing public funds and municipal support into high-tech "mega" projects by the technological symbolism and "quick fix" discourses promulgated by global property, technology and media firms. The social, environmental and economic merits of many such strategies often remain highly dubious.

Despite these caveats, however, I would argue that there exists much potential for creatively rethinking our urban concepts through a careful, critical and systematic integration of telecommunications and IT into our ideas about the development, planning and management of global urban regions. Otherwise, traditional planning concepts and approaches risk being made less and less relevant, in some "paradigm crisis", to the relational, time-space dynamics of the "networked" or "tele-mediated" city.[20] It is time for a thoroughgoing and critical consideration of how urban policies and strategies may creatively and progressively engage in the complex articulations betwen urban places and "electronic spaces".[21]

But such a debate must start by fully recognizing the starkly uneven social and geographic patterns of access to IT; the ways in which new technologies are being used to enhance the powers of social elites and corporate actors; and the dangers that such technologies may support further the splintering and fragmentation of urban spaces. Envisaging how urban IT strategies might sustain or renew social cohesion, how they might strengthen or build up the urban public realm, and how they might support more progressive and inclusive processes of urban policy making and governance should be the essential starting points for analysis here.[22]

NOTES

1 See S. Graham and S. Marvin, *Telecommunications and the City: Electronic Spaces, Urban Places*, London: Routledge, 1996; M. Castells, *The Rise of the Network Society*, Oxford: Blackwell, 1996.

2 Geoff Mulgan, "The Changing Shape of the City" in Stuart Hall and Martin Jacques (eds) *New Times*, London: Lawrence & Wishart, 1991.

3 "The Death of Distance," *Economist*, Telecommunications Survey, September 30–October 6, 1995.

4 Stephen Hill, *The Tragedy of Technology*, London: Pluto, 1988.

5 Shafraaz Kaba, "Building the Future: an Architectural Manifesto for the next Millennium", *Web Architecture Magazine*, April 1996.

6 Alvin Toffler *The Third Wave*, New York: Morrow, 1980.

7 Anthony Pascal, "The Vanishing City", *Urban Studies* 24, 1987, pp. 597–603.

8 Martin Pawley, "Architecture, Urbanism and the New Media." Mimeo, 1995.

9 Paul Virilio, "The Third Interval: a Critical Transition" in V. Andermatt-Conley (ed.) *Rethinking Technologies*, Minneapolis MN and London: University of Minnesota Press, 1993, p. 10.

10 H. Sawhney, "Information Superhighway: Metaphors as Midwives", *Media Culture and Society*, 18, 1996, pp. 291–314, at p. 309.

11 N. Thrift and K. Olds, "Refiguring the Economic in Economic Geography", *Progress in Human Geography* 20 (3), 1996, pp. 311–37.

12 T. Fitzpatrick, "A Tale of Tall Cities", *Guardian On-Line*, February 6, 1997, p. 9.

13 M. Moss and A. Townsend, "Manhattan leads the Net nation", http://www.nyu.edu/urban/ny_affairs/telecom.

14 See Graham and Marvin, *Telecommunications and the City*.

15 See S. Graham and A. Aurigi, "Virtual Cities, Urban Social Polarization, and the Crisis in Urban Public Space", *Journal of Urban Technology* 4 (1), 1997, pp. 19–53.

16 *Smart Cities Guidebook*, 1997.

17 D. Carter, "'Digital Democracy' or 'Information Aristocracy'? Economic Regeneration and the Information Economy" in B. Loader (ed.) *The Governance of Cyberspace*, London: Routledge, 1996.

18 See M. Castells and P. Hall, *Technopoles of the World*, London: Routledge, 1994.

19 D. Hill, "Cultural Industries in the Digital City". Unpublished MA Dissertation, Manchester Metropolitan University.

20 S. Graham and P. Healey, "Relational Concepts of Place and Space: Issues for Planning Theory and Practice", *European Planning Studies* 7(5), pp. 623–46.

21 See Graham and Marvin, *Telecommunications and the City*, chapter 2.

22 This chapter is adapted from the paper "Planning Cybercities? Integrating Telecommunications into Urban Planning", *Town Planning Review* 70(1), pp. 89–114 by S. Graham and S. Marvin.

20 Telecommunications and sustainable cities

Simon Marvin

Global environmental change has stimulated interest in the development of local policy initiatives designed to reduce the ecological impact of resource flows through cities (Breheny, 1992; CEC, 1990; Douglas, 1983; and Elkin *et al.*, 1991). But as cities attempt to develop new ways of improving the environmental performance of their older water, waste, energy and transport infrastructure very little interest has focused on the role of the latest form of urban infrastructure—telematics and telecommunications networks. Most assessments of the environmental role of telecommunications have tended to assume that telematics technologies are inherently environmentally benign and that they can easily be manipulated to deliver wider environmental benefits. For instance, Lee argues that telecommunications networks are "in harmony with nature . . . are environmentally sound, non-polluting and non-destructive of the ecology" (1991: 30). Yet Toffler goes further, stating that "the growth of the telecommunications society would relieve some of the population pressure on cities. It could greatly reduce the pollution, raise the quality of life, and lessen the drudgery of commuting" (1980: 192).

But if telecommunications have so much to offer the urban environment we might have expected to find a close degree of engagement with urban environmental studies and policy making. Despite the growth of academic and policy interest in both the urban environment and the links between telecommunications and cities, little attention has focused on the interface between the two sets of issues (Marvin, 1993, 1994). The urban environmental research and policy communities have tended to ignore the telecommunications sector—at best they may mention the potential environmental benefits of substituting the telephone for travel. Research and policy development in the telecommunications sector has focused on the technologies' role in urban economic restructuring, the spatial development of cities or the changing nature of social and cultural life in cities. In contrast there is relatively little interest in the wider environmental issues raised by telecommunications, with the consequence that we have little insight into the technologies' potential role as a *cause* of environmental problems or as part of the *solution* to the challenge of developing more sustainable forms of urban life.

Competing ideas about the environmental role of telecommunications are largely based on differing conceptions of the type and direction of the linkages between "electronic" and "physical" flows and spaces within cities. Are they simply equivalents in which electronic flows of information displace physical movements of goods and services? Does the electronic re-creation of the physical city in telebased services signal the dissolution of the physical city? Alternatively, are there other types of relationship in which electronic flows generate new demands for physical travel? This chapter addresses these issues by critically reviewing environment–telecommunications interactions. Rejecting simple notions that telecommunications are either inherently environmentally benign technologies or that they simply and unproblematically promote the development of more sustainable cities, we take a more critical view, accepting that the relations between telecommunications and the urban environment are often complex and contradictory.

TOWARDS THE DEMATERIALIZATION OF CITIES?

A powerful discourse assumes that electronic flows and spaces actually undermine the need for physical spaces and flows, eventually leading to the *dematerialization* of cities. Electronic forms of communication and a range of telebased services simply displace the need for physical movement between home and work, while urban functions will no longer have a physical presence as services are delivered in electronic form. Telecommunications simply substitute for, displace and inevitably lead to the eventual dissolution of the physical city, underpinning powerful utopian and technological deterministic views of telecommunications as an environmentally benign technology that can easily be manipulated to improve conditions in cities. Such a scenario clearly envisages an enhanced role for electronic over material flows and resources and the rapid decentralization of activities rather than the need for close physical proximity and face-to-face contact in the city.

Empirical studies have "provided evidence of the postulate of declining material (and energy) intensity over time and with increasing GDP" (Bernardini and Galli, 1993: 433). Dematerialization is the product of three sets of factors.

- The changing nature of demand characterized by the gradual shift of output towards the production of goods with higher unit value and lowering material content. In particular, the shift towards information services means that income is increasingly spent on goods that have a low materials content to value.
- At the same time technological innovations lead to improvements in the use of materials and energy through miniaturization, design and quality control and improved logistics that also cut waste and increase recycling.
- The final trend is the substitution for energy-intensive materials of alternatives such as glass and plastics that reduce both the material and the energy content of manufactured products.

Societal development will be based on new infrastructure built around natural gas, information systems, telecommunications and satellites. The physical requirements related to this growth are "certain to be less material-intensive" than the industrial phase of development (Bernardini and Galli, 1993: 447). Although there have been few attempts to verify these concepts empirically in an urban context, both utopian and critical commentators have argued that telecommunications are powerful dematerializers of cities.

Much of the early work on telecommunications and cities argued that the technologies could displace or substitute for the physical movement of people and information freight (Harkness, 1977; Meyer, 1977; Toffler, 1980). This perspective has helped underpin the view that telecommunications are an environmentally benign set of technologies inevitably and logically leading to the dematerialization of cities. The dematerialization concept is based on the assumption that telecommunications would dissolve the very glue that holds cities together. Cities were originally established to make communication easier by minimizing space constraints to overcome the time constraints of travel. The boundaries of the early city were based on walking distance, with urban functions located in close proximity. Improved modes of transport facilitated the dispersal of cities as motorized transport enabled functions to be located farther away from the urban core but within reasonable travel times. The substitutionist perspective argues that telecommunications are able to displace and substitute for physical transport.

This view has two important implications for the dematerialization of cities. The first set of issues are concerned with the replacement of physical flows by electronic flows. This is based on the assumption that telecommunications can substitute for the physical movement of people and information freight—the so-called telecom–transportation trade-off (Kramer, 1982; Kramer and King, 1982). The environmental implications of this trade-off could be quite profound (Tuppen, 1992). There are clearly much lower direct energy inputs required for telecommunications than for any other form of communication. This has led the proponents of teleworking to argue that trade-offs could have substantial environmental benefits by saving huge amounts of energy and resources consumed in physical travel, saving time commuting and potentially solving the problems of urban congestion (Toffler, 1980). These potentials have stimulated considerable interest in the environmental potential of telecommuting, teleworking and teleconferencing (Nilles, 1988). The second linkage between telecommunications and the physical city concerns the potential for dispersal of urban functions. Without the constraints of travel time and distance telecommunications could help facilitate the dispersal or break-up of the city. Toffler (1980) argues that the *electronic cottage* could be the basis of a new form of decentered home life in which the potential of telebased work and services means that home and work can be separated by long distances. Toffler assumes that these trends will have important environmental implications because transport becomes less significant. Taken together, these two aspects open up the potential of new forms of decentralized urban environment in which functions can be many miles apart but communication takes the form of electronic flows. In this scenario electronics create the potential dispersal of urban space and substitution of physical movement along telecommunication networks.

A parallel claim is that cities are increasingly being reconstructed in new forms of electronic space. For Paul Virilio, telecommunications now mean that the distinction between departure and arrival is increasingly lost—"where motorized transportation and information had prompted a *general mobilization* of populations . . . modes of instantaneous transmission prompt the inverse, that of a *growing inertia*" (1994: 11, original emphasis). Telebased services allow the world to be shrunk so that the distinction between a global and personal environment is increasingly lost as individuals interact through the capacities of telematic receivers and sensors. While Virilio does not speculate about the implications of these transformations for the physical form of cities it is clear that the home becomes the focus for electronically mediated forms of interaction subject to a form of "domiciliary inertia . . . and behavioural isolation."

A range of different approaches, from the technological deterministic to highly critical perspectives, envisage a wider dematerialization of the city through the substitution of physical flows and spaces. Although it is not clear what the result will be, most attention has focused on the home as a battleground for the future. While Alvin Toffler presents a utopian vision of the electronic cottage this contrasts strongly with Paul Virilio's vision of an inert and sedentary society. Yet both views seem to suggest that environmental problems are dissolved through a very simple one-way relationship between the physical and the electronic which leads to the substitution or dissolution of the city. But is all the traffic one-way?

URBAN ENVIRONMENT—TELECOMMUNICATIONS: PARALLEL TRANSFORMATIONS

Alternative views of the relationship between electronic and physical environments would stress that there are still major environmental problems associated with cities. For instance the growth in movement and mobility has stimulated a reappraisal of the relationship between electronic and physical flows, focusing on the potential for synergistic relations. In this scenario electronics can generate or induce changes in the physical environment rather than simply displacing or substituting for it. These linkages can take a number of different forms.

First, *electronic flows are able to act as powerful generators of physical flows*. For instance, the ease of electronic communications based on decreasing cost and increasing availability of telecommunications networks can generate new demands for physical transport (Mokhtarian, 1990; Saloman, 1986). As e-mail, fax, telephone effectively increase the number of participants in a business or recreation network this can then create demands for higher-level forms of interaction between the participants in the network based on face-to-face interaction. This creates a demand for close proximity, leading to new forms of physical travel. Although it is difficult to assess the strength of these effects, it is clear that telecommunications do not simply displace physical travel.

Telecommunications technologies have actively facilitated both the centralization and the decentralization of cities (Sola Pool, 1977). In the early part of the century the development of skyscrapers was underpinned by the telephone, without which communication in multi-storey towers would have been a logistic nightmare. Later the telephone, together with increased access to public transport, facilitated movement to the suburbs. These trends have continued, with telecommunications allowing functions, such as back offices, to disperse out of cities to new locations in rural areas. Increasing separation between activities has helped to generate increasing and longer trips. As Herman *et al.* (1990: 337) argue, "the spatial dispersion of population is a potential materializer." Highly dispersed settlement patterns with the increasing separation of functions in physical space underpinned by the communication abilities of electronic telecommunication networks have facilitated resource-intensive mobility patterns and the need for more energy and waste infrastructure.

The second effect is the role of *telecommunication networks in the enhancement of physical movement*. The new control, supervision and data acquisition role of telecommunications can increase the attractiveness of travel (Cramer and Zegveld, 1991). For instance, computerized systems of booking and payment for travel make it very easy to obtain information and pay for air travel. In turn, more effective methods of managing travel networks can help increase the efficiency of transport networks at all levels—road, rail, air—lowering costs and increasing the attractiveness of travel as an option. It has become increasingly clear that the new technology of road transport informatics provides ways of overcoming the problems of congested road networks and increasing the effective capacity of those networks at a fraction of the cost of constructing entirely new transport infrastructure (Gianopouloos and Gillespie, 1993; Hepworth and Ducatel, 1992). In this sense the retrofitting of electronic networks over relatively old and polluting physical transport networks can enhance the efficiency, capacity and attractiveness of those networks.

The third effect is the *uneven electronic displacement of physical movement*. Electronic–physical interactions are much more complex than the simple substitutionist view. Empirical assessments of the environmental role of substitution are extremely complex and contingent on the particular locations and contexts where experiments have taken place. For instance, many Californian telecommuting initiatives have an explicitly environmental set of objectives designed to improve air quality. A legislative framework ensures that companies have to meet targets to reduce physical movement and teleworking is promoted as an electronic alternative (California, 1990; Grant, 1994). But teleworking has environmental benefits in this particular context partly because the commutes to work are so long. A study in the UK reached very different conclusions. Because the length of commutes is lower the energy savings were relatively low, particularly when compared with the increased demands for heating and powering the home (BT, 1992). Decentralization of work also created new difficulties, with recycling of products much more feasible in centralized offices. While working from home may save commute trips it can also allow workers to live farther away, resulting in a longer trip when workers do need to be at the workplace. The time saved through not commuting may also create the potential or desire for other trips that might previously have not taken place or been combined with the commute to work. For these reasons the substitution perspective is not as simple as previously supposed.

Finally, *does absolute or relative substitution take place?* There is potential for telecommunications to displace trips and that this does have clear environmental benefits, particularly when teleworking or teleconferencing is substituting for a long commute. But it appears that, rather than absolute displacement, telecommunications are simply taking a larger share of increases in all forms of communication. If the amount of communications was to remain stable and electronic forms of communication took an increasing share, then absolute displacement would take place. But if all forms of communications increase absolutely then little displacement effect takes place. It appears that telecommunications and travel have increased in parallel and are not currently substituting for each other. Long-run analyses of the relationship between telecommunications and travel have found little evidence of a substitution effect. Instead they show that "due to the diffusion of new telecommunications technologies there will be no reduction in passenger travel, instead considerable growth is likely to occur" (Grubler, 1989: 258).

CONCLUSION

Relations between telecommunications and the urban environment are much more complex and contradictory than is often assumed. Rather than simply substituting electronic for physical flows, telecommunications technologies have a number of effects which can lead to demands for new physical spaces, generate new physical flows and increase the effective capacity of infrastructure networks. Consequently it is not possible to make any simple assessment of the environmental role of telecommunications. Where does that leave us? Is it possible to define a role for telecommunications in environmental policy? While there do appear to be dematerialization effects in the production of manufactured goods there are contradictory trends around demands for increased mobility. Telecommunications technologies are firmly implicated in both sets of changes, simultaneously increasing the efficiency of production processes and reducing the need for material inputs but also allowing physical spaces and flows to be reconstituted, generating environmental problems through dispersal, and the generation and enhancement of travel. Urban environmental policy needs to develop a new conceptual framework that starts to include the conflicting and complex role of telecommunications. Without such changes researchers and policy makers will fail to develop a more complete understanding of urban environmental problems or develop relevant policy responses.

REFERENCES

Bernardini, O., and Galli, R. (1993) "Dematerialization: Long-term Trends in the Intensity of Use of Materials and Energy," *Futures* 25 (5), pp. 431–48.

Breheny, M. J., ed. (1992) *Sustainable Development and Urban Form*, London: Pion.

British Telecom (1992) *A Study of the Environmental Impact of Teleworking*, report by BT Research Laboratories.

California, State of (1990) *The California Telecommuting Pilot Project: Final Report*, Sacramento CA: Department of General Services.

Commission of the European Communities (1990) Green Paper on the Urban Environment, Com (90) 218, Brussels: EU.

Cramer, J., and Zegveld, W. C. L. (1991) "The Future Role of Technology in Environmental Management," *Futures* 23 (5), pp. 451–68.

Douglas, I. (1983) *The Urban Environment*, London: Edward Arnold.

Elkin, T., McLaren, D., and Hillman, M. (1991) *Reviving the City: Towards Sustainable Urban Development*, London: Friends of the Earth.

Giannopouloos, G., and Gillespie, A., eds (1993) *Transport and Communications Innovation in Europe*, London: Belhaven.

Grant, W. (1994) "Transport and Air Pollution in California," *Environmental Management and Health* 1, pp. 31–4.

Grubler, A. (1989) *The Rise and Fall of Infrastructures*, Heidelberg: Physica-Verlag.

Harkness, R. C. (1977) "Selected Results from a Technology Assessment of Telecommunication–Transportation Interactions," *Habitat* 2 (1–2), pp. 37–48.

Hepworth, M., and Ducatel, K. (1992) *Transport in the Information Age: Wheels and Wires*, London: Belhaven.

Herman, S., Ardekani, S. A., and Ansubel, J. H. (1990) "Dematerialization," *Technological Forecasting and Social Change* 38, pp. 333–47.

Kramer, K. L. (1982) "Telecommunication/Transportation Substitution and Energy Conservation" I, *Telecommunications Policy*, March, pp. 39–99.

Kramer, K. L., and King, J. L. (1982) "Telecommunications/Transportation Substitution and Energy Conservation" II, *Telecommunications Policy*, June, pp. 87–99.

Lee, M. (1991) "Social Responsibilities of the Telecommunications Business," *IEEE Technology and Society Magazine* 10 (2), pp. 29–30.

Marvin, S. J. (1993) "Telecommunications and Environmental Debate," working paper 20, Newcastle upon Tyne: Department of Town and Country Planning, University of Newcastle.

Marvin, S. J. (1994) "Green Signals: the Environmental Role of Telecommunications in Cities," *Cities* 11 (5), pp. 325–31.

Meyer, S. L. (1997) "Conservation of Resources, Telecommunications and Microprocessors," *Journal of Environmental Systems* 7 (2), pp. 121–9.

Mokhtarian, P. L. (1990) "A Typology of Relationships between Telecommunications and Transportation," *Transportation Research* 24A (3), pp. 231–42.

Nilles, J. M. (1988) "Traffic Reduction by Telecommuting: a Status Review and Selected Bibliography," *Transportation Research* 22A (4), pp. 301–17.

Salomon, I. (1986) "Telecommunications and Travel Relationships; a Review," *Transportation Research* 20A (3), pp. 223–38.

Sola Pool, I., *et al.* (1977) "Foresight and Hindsight: the Case of the Telephone" in I. Sola Pool (ed.) *The Social Impact of the Telephone*, Cambridge MA: MIT Press.

Toffler, A. (1980) *The Third Wave*, New York: Morrow.

Tuppen, C. G. (1992) "Energy and Telecommunications: an Environmental Impact Analysis," *Energy and Environment* 3 (1), pp. 70–81.

Virilio, P. (1984) "The Third Interval: a Critical Transition" in V. A. Conley (ed.) *Rethinking Technologies*, Minneapolis MN: University of Minnesota Press.

21 Regional grid planning

Pedro Ortiz Castaño

We are on the verge of a quantum leap in the evolution of the metropolis. The pressures of growth are the subject of continual public debate not confined to professional circles. It is a wide-ranging debate involving the entire make-up of the social fabric, and the inability of cities to manage the integration of all the functions required has become a central political issue. Professionals lack the ability to solve these growth problems at least in the terms required by society.

On one hand, we find that there is insufficient land available for housing, not only in quantity, but also in quality and price. This saturation has its impact on the final product, which suffers from the same deficiencies in quality and price. On the other hand we also find that there is a lack of land to support all the public and social facilities that society requires. This impacts the economy's capacity for industrial as well as tertiary production. It leads to congestion, overcrowding, pollution, noise. We can add to this the misuse and destruction of the natural environment and the failure of the system to respond to the needs of accessibility.

The professional argument propounded by some is that this is the first time that this particular set of circumstances has occurred in the history of mankind. Some like to see in this uniqueness the beginning of an apocalyptic flash. Others merely use it as an argument to explain why we have not found a solution. Most think that there is no solution. Some give solutions of such a drastic nature and so alien to the "system" that they lead us into pure theories more relevant to social utopias than to the response of the urban professional.

We are at a stage of expansion of our economies which, seen in a wider context of several decades, gives us cumulative figures with amounts of an "explosive" more than an "expansive" nature. We are not talking about growth in population, a debate which took place in the 1960s. It is surprising and significant to see professionals and academics falling into this trap. We are talking about growth without growth in population, at least in the most developed countries, although in the developing countries both phenomena impact on each other. It is important to understand this phenomenon, because it gives focus to the fact that growth will be continual, and growth is here to stay. We have to prepare a strategy and not just *ad hoc* measures in order to respond to it and take account of it in our urban and regional structures.[1]

The reason for this phenomenon is very simple: economic growth of 2 percent per annum gives over 20 years accumulated growth of almost 50 percent. The key factor is that a component of economic growth is spatial consumption and urban investment. For town planning that is the issue which has to be understood. The wealthier an economy, the more space for construction it uses, produces and consumes. SEPES, the Spanish public enterprise for the creation of industrial land, some years ago used the ratio of 50 jobs per industrial hectare; now it creates industrial sites with 20 jobs per hectare. This means that each job occupies two and a half times more land and industrial construction than a few years ago. For the same number of employees it is necessary to generate two and a half times more industrial land and built space. In a few years, without any growth in active population, a need for urban industrial growth of 250 percent has arisen.

The private motor vehicle is reaching saturation point in the strongest markets. In Europe the ratios of car ownership of 0.6 and/or 0.7 are not increasing significantly; there is only a process of renewal of the stock. But, owing to the greater geographical spread of business and homes, an increase is occurring in the use of these vehicles.[2] Without an increase in the motor vehicle "population", the growth in space consumed and produced will be 65 percent. In the tertiary, commercial and leisure sectors, the figures for growth are still more important in a region like Madrid. These extra trips by car are difficult to satisfy by public transport which is principally radial in form and requires higher density of use.

In the residential sector the phenomenon is similar.[3] The growth in the economy, and in the purchasing power and wealth of the population, leads to increased consumption of dwelling space per inhabitant. Sometimes this phenomenon occurs through the effects of a reduction in the size of the family, in such a way that "those who remain" have more square meters of house for themselves and "those who leave" to form a new home are those who consume the new residential areas produced.[4]

This is a process that will go on. In the Madrid region the size of a family in the year 2016 will be 2.5 members. The outgoing members, 0.5 per family, will form a new home which will take up space in one of the 25,000 dwellings per year which are being completed. This means an increase in residential space occupied per citizen from 21 m^2 to 25 m^2 in the next 20 years.[5] That is to say, an increment of 25 percent of the stock and residential space taken up in 20 years. The urban surface will increase by 50 percent, 50 percent of the urban area produced in 400 years. In 20 years.

A point will come when the average family size will stabilize, but not the use of residential space. From that moment, instead of a process of production of new dwellings, there will occur a process of replacing certain segments of the housing stock with dwellings of greater size and better living conditions, especially in those dwellings which because of their size cannot meet the current minimum standards and enter into the category of slum dwellings. If those dwellings have heritage value, the process will have to be one of rehabilitation; if they do not, it will be by replacement.

When Spain reaches the 30 m^2 per inhabitant of Italy, Italy will have reached the 34 m^2 per inhabitant of France and that country the 37 m^2 per inhabitant of Germany. Right now the only threshold of saturation which we can glimpse is that of Canada, with 51 m^2 per inhabitant. We do not know if, or when, we will catch up with the others, Canada will have figures unthinkable at this moment. What does it mean to reach the threshold of Canada? For many, it means that we have to face up to a territorial revolution of great proportions. It means that we must produce a system for growth, a model which enables us to respond to urban expansion on a scale unknown until now.

Is this a process of "sustainable" growth? I do not believe that we can give a definitive reply to this question, but we can carry out an exercise full of reservations, and with a touch of humor. If the whole of mankind, which is estimated to reach a population of 10,000 million persons by the year 2050, were to live in families of an average size of 2.5 persons, occupying 50 m^2 per person, the Canadian space standard, in a typical single-family attached dwelling, with an intensity of use of 20 dwellings per hectare in plots of 250 m^2, and with as much space again of public areas for facilities, infrastructure and green spaces, the whole of mankind would occupy an urban area of 2 million km^2.

The surface of the earth, *terra firma*, is 150 million km^2. We would consume, therefore, 1.3 percent of the earth's surface. Two million km^2 is the area of a country like Sudan: the whole of urbanized humanity would occupy a total area such as that of Sudan, leaving the rest of the planet, 98.7 percent, free from urbanization, "deserted". It is up to every one of us to consider this argument and/ or decide whether reaching the Canadian threshold is sustainable or not in terms of urban invasion and degradation of the planet's environment.

In any case, and for those who may decide that this urban future is not sustainable, I dare ask them to seek a political formula by which national governments can explain, convince or impose on their populations the fact that they should give up the aim of reaching the levels of residential comfort achieved by other countries, even though they possess the money and economic capacity. All this for the sake of environmental standards which are desirable but not shared homogeneously by all nations. It will be difficult to convince a population when some have reached these levels but others have to be prevented from being able to reach them.

Lacking this political formula, those of us who are the professionals and academics in urbanism have to provide solutions to the problems which society confronts us with. We have to assume that, even in the absence of population growth, and with stable long-term economic growth, urban growth in the future will be important, rapid and permanent. Growth is here to stay and we must find the formula, the method, the right system to make room for this explosion and give a sustainable response to it, adapting the process in a non-congestive and non-limiting way. Not providing for it will just mean chaotic, unsustainable development.

ORBITAL AND GRID

These are the basic systems of territorial colonization that we have used throughout history. We may think that both systems, the orbital and the grid, have continued to succeed each other at random throughout our urban history, but that is not so. Societies have chosen one or the other depending upon their economic, social and, consequently, urban evolution. Let us examine the particular features of each system and we will understand the reason for their choice. Comparing both systems we can see the strengths and weaknesses of each.

Orbital

The radial/orbital system is the formula for expansion of many natural processes. The economy of surface tension, which can be projected on urban processes, produces this type of growth. If the natural way is good, the orbital way must be good. Besides being good, it would be easy. Orbital growth, which is incrementalist, accumulative, unimposed, disjunctive and occurs unconsciously, involuntarily, without the need for control but through a natural order, appears to have all the attributes desirable to be adopted in a natural way. On the other hand, with the grid system growth requires a conscious effort of structured implementation. It is the result of a rational process which requires control and even the appearance of a governing body to carry it out. It is an unnatural process, and, therefore, should be approached with caution.

The orbital system arises from a point of growth. The connection between two points creates the line which is the second of the most primary systems. The axis of growth, on the line which joins two points, is a process equally natural, which does not require public intervention unless it is to provide fixed capital to improve the use of this route. But even without public intervention, without capital investment, the process occurs.

As opposed to the line as a natural primary system, the grid system requires the introduction of the abstract concept of infinity. It requires, therefore, a more complex and difficult level of intellectualization; to understand that, with the concept of infinity, appear qualities of isomorphism or capacity for productive reproduction by repetition or standardization, so that a further stage of complexity is reached.

The orbital system has, besides, an urban effect: it produces hierarchy. Every point of the system has a relative position with respect to the center which confers upon it an attribute of rank or value. This individualization in some way contributes to a sense of belonging or a *genius loci* essential in reinforcing urban identification.

On the other hand, the grid system does not produce a hierarchy. It creates that isomorphous space in which every point has equal opportunities to be the "center". There is no reference point in respect of an undeniably higher rank, as can occur in the circle. This absence of relative identity, translated into an absence of own identity, can produce effects of alienation and can even become psycho-perceptively neurosis-producing.

Grid

As a counter to this series of positive elements of the orbital system, it would have to be said that it can become an intrinsically speculative system. The center is scarce and has more value. Because it is a limited resource, it can bring about processes of the withholding of supply. The limited value retained generates an increase in prices and speculation. If the circle and the center are provided with public investment there also occurs a private appropriation of profits generated by public capital.

On the other hand, the grid system distributes centrality. There can be many centers, or the center can be everywhere. Accessibility is homogeneous and with a distributed accessibility the value of the land is also distributed. Having a more distributed accessibility throughout a wider territory, the sum of these is superior and its economic contribution through the value of the land also turns out to be superior. Land provided with accessibility is more plentiful and, therefore, supply exceeds demand. The supply depends only upon a factor of production which is the creation of infrastructure and not upon a scarce primary resource which is centrality. This means that there cannot be speculative processes of withholding of land as a scarce resource. The supply can meet demand at all times. Because the production of land is more directly linked with investment in the infrastructure, this investment can stem from the private sector itself, which in this way manages to direct its investments internally into the added value of the land.

The orbital system is congestive. The struggle for the center produces an accumulation of uses, activity and, consequently, congestion. Businesses, the economic activity, have to use important resources in the battle between each other to obtain the land with centrality/accessibility, adding these costs to the production process. The congestion produces diseconomies of scale. The more activity that sets up in the center, the greater the harmful effect on the existing businesses. The sum of the harmful effects is much greater than the positive effect obtained by the newly set up business. It is the very definition of congestion. The saturated infrastructure ceases to produce an economic effect proportional to the investment. Cost effectiveness decreases and a process of decreasing marginal return is reached, with waste of infrastructure and waste of resources and investment. It can happen that there is an effect of loss of value of the center owing to congestion, bringing about processes of decline, as we can see in the effects of the American "loop".

The grid system provides for multiple centrality, which should not necessarily be identified as dispersed. There are subcenters, but it is not necessarily a diffuse isomorphism. The system of multiple centrality breaks up congestion over a wider territory. It unties the great knot into an assembly of distributed centers. Besides, it allows mobility of these multiple centers. Centrality shifts become a process implicit in the system without the need to alter or modify the system, as occurs in the orbital system. The urban history of New York is an example of this process of relocation of business as an integral part of the urban process. By distributing centrality the intensities of use are distributed, avoiding congestive processes. The congestion itself disperses automatically if there are alternatives of equivalent location.

With regard to congestion, the orbital system has a balance which is unstable. The grid is a system in stable equilibrium. The orbital system is fragile: traffic and movements have one sole optimum route. Any alternative entails significant excess distances, of 200 percent or 300 percent. When a center–periphery radius of access breaks down, all the orbital rings with access to that radius also break down. The congestion spreads progressively to the whole system. In a radial-orbital system there are no alternatives or equivalent routes and one is slave to the system. Congestion generates congestion. It is a system which auto-induces congestion.

The grid system is robust. Traffic and movements have a multiplicity of routes. Any two points have a journey distance with a maximum of 142 percent excess. The diagonal, which serves a different function from the radius, can even reduce this effect over long distances. When a segment of the grid breaks down, any other can serve the same function. The congestion disperses naturally. In a grid system there are a large number of alternative routes, all equivalent, and one has the liberty of choice within the system. The congestion disperses itself. It is a congestion self-dispersing system.

Besides all these mechanistic aspects of the two systems, one must be aware of the social consequences that arise. An orbital system creates marginalization and social injustice, since we can identify the result of location in the center with factors of price, worth and power. The periphery, on the other hand, acquires a residual function, with reduced accessibility, lower price and worth, and marginalized locations. Originally the grid system is isomorphous. There exists an equality of opportunities for all the pieces of the system. There is no handicap from the outset, accessibility is equal to all. Competition between all the pieces is under the same conditions. Inequalities appear only when each cell begins to differentiate itself from the others by means of capitalization and the functions which arise in each of them.

From this social approach we can reach a political interpretation of the two systems. From what has been described, a grid system would appear to be more "democratic". Let us remember that centripetal, orbital, radial systems, all of them revolving around the center, as a concept have been used as an allegory of monotheistic and absolutist systems. Let us remember that in architecture and urban design the radial-orbital system, under the designation of panopticon, has been used almost exclusively in four types of construction: hospital, cemetery, park and prison. In none of the four is the customer free to choose. The patient, the corpse, the tree and the prisoner depend upon a will alien to their own.

The orbital system displays a center–periphery antagonism which suggests a confrontation (of classes?) in which the periphery, although more voluminous, is always subordinate to, and dependent upon, the center. Even if it "kills off" the center, its own systematics regenerates it. It regenerates it implicitly. Even though it wants to give itself a toroidal (i.e. a ring) structure: the "donut". The center is always present, even if it is a hole, a loop, a degraded downtown.

On the other hand, the grid system appears as a multipolar system (multiclass?), in which the different poles and centers interact between themselves in a multiplicity of alternatives and possibilities. One must draw a distinction, however. Although initially the isomorphous space appears to suggest a homogeneous system (without classes), soon there will appear differentiations which determine subcentralities with a polynucleation (multiclass system), which suggests the appearance of relative positioning and belonging.

It is possible that some readers will identify current ideological tendencies in this social interpretation of historical processes that we are undergoing. Others will even see strategic values of security in a network system, in a net in which the absence of a hierarchy and of a center makes it less vulnerable to an endogenous or exogenous crisis of whatever type. We are not talking about "military" threats, but we are talking about strategies which may have arisen from defensive preoccupations such as the internet itself.

Rem Koolhaas (1978) analyses very well, in his book on the "delirium" of New York, the metalanguage of the grid. The grid is for him, above all, a conceptual proposal. Its apparent neutrality supports a complete intellectual proposal. The indifference to topography, to what exists, is a celebration of the intellectual construction of the human brain faced with reality. One could begin to see a resurgence of neoplatonism in this focus in opposition to empiricist attitudes. Koolhaas comes to see in the grid a desire for domination, even annihilation, of nature. This would entail even a Nietzschean trace in its reading. However, one realizes rapidly that the new dialectics that the net requires is a different intellectual and social process. As he himself says:

> All blocks are the same. Their equivalence wipes out, at a stroke, all the principles of articulation and

individualisation that have guided the design of traditional cities. The grid makes irrelevant the whole history of architecture and urban planning. Power to the constructors of the city to develop a new system of formal values, to create new strategies to differentiate one block from another.

This idea of "the history of architecture and urban planning" is not true, since that history is, above all, the history of the grid. But Koolhaas is right when he says that the rigid two-dimensional discipline of the net opens up the door to the most anarchic liberty in the third dimension. The dialectic between control and lack of control acquires a background of equilibrium. It must be said that this "dialectic" between the orderly state of the plane and the shaky state of height, of the "metropolis of a rigid chaos", does not reach the values of the process of Hegelian synthesis. It does not reach it in the New York of Koolhaas, but it opens the door so that others indeed can see and reach it.

Koolhaas also fully understands the "democratic" nature of the polycentricity of the grid. He argues that, with the grid, the city stays definitively inmunized against any attempt at totalitarian domination. For him, the block is the maximum unit that can fall under one-party control. The block is the maximum limit of urbanistic-architectural egocentricity. In this way, any "urbanistic ideology" can be imposed only in the restricted framework of a single block.

Orbital plus grid

The balance appears to be strongly swayed in favour of the grid system. Why, therefore, has the orbital system been applied so often and with such success? Is one really better than the other? Are they compatible? Are they opposed? It is all a question of scale.

The orbital system is more effective in the origin of the creation of the urban system. These are principles derived from geometrical mechanics. The minimum length which contains a maximum area is the circle. When at the beginning of an urban phenomenon we are producing a costly infrastructure, an investment in fixed capital which requires a significant effort on the part of the society that produces it, the system of least cost/greatest benefit is the circular one. A wall of protection, a stockade and a ditch protect and give service to a greater surface of land if they are circular.

The maximum economic return per unit of capital invested is obtained with an orbital system. We can even quantify it. For each square metre of area served, the square requires 4 m of perimeter, the circle only 3.54 m: 13 percent more length and, therefore, 13 percent more investment and effort than the circle. The square is 13 percent more inefficient than the circle (see Figure 21.1); "efficiency" of the square = perimeter of the square / perimeter of the circle:

"E" = 4.00 / 3.54 = 1.13

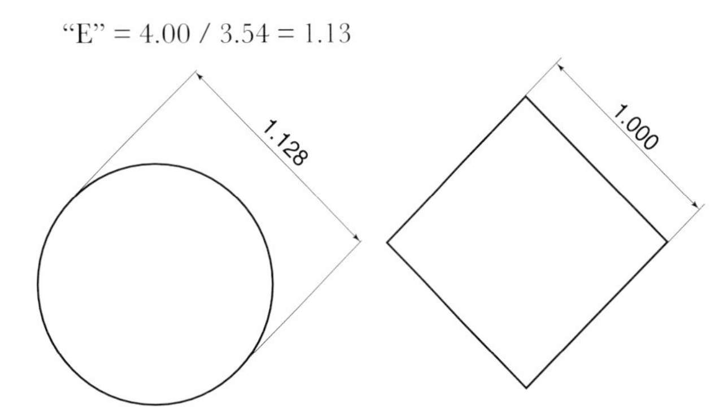

Figure 21.1 The square is 13 percent less efficient than the circle

But as the dimension of the urban area increases, these differences reduce. A bigger city, with a greater territorial expanse, needs an internal system of infrastructure as well as that of the perimeter. With a minimal radial system, that is to say, only two perpendicular diameters, the length of infrastructure necessary to service this surface unit, diameters plus circumference, is 5.8 linear units.

This same surface unit, served by a system of square with medians, that is to say, an incipient grid system, requires a length of infrastructure of six linear units; the reticular system, six linear units; the orbital, 5.8 linear units. The grid (reticular) system requires 3 percent more investment and effort than the orbital. The reticular is 3 percent more inefficient than the orbital. But before, in a more primary system, it was 13 percent more inefficient. As can be seen, the difference reduces as the city increases in size (Figure 21.2).

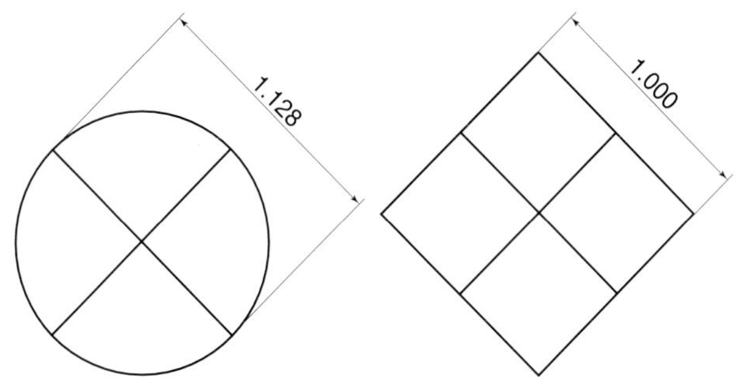

Figure 21.2 Incipient grid: the square is 3 percent less efficient than the circle

Even making other, more complex evaluations of aspects such as the overall accessibility from every point the result is that the grid system has come to be the most efficient as regards the territorial dimension, and the length of infrastructure, as the scale of investment has increased. In the orbital system, the most efficient on a small scale, diseconomies of scale have arisen which are overcome by a change to the grid system.

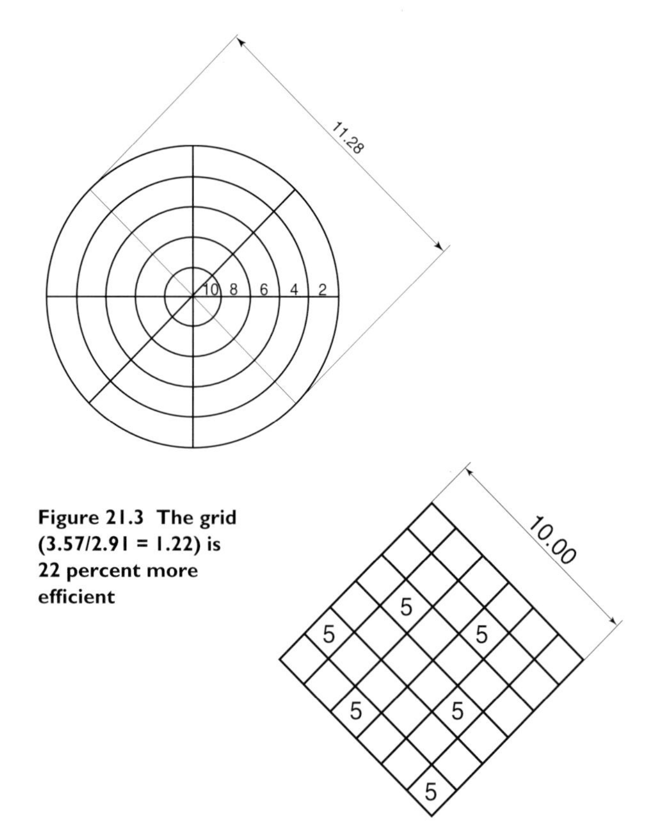

Figure 21.3 The grid (3.57/2.91 = 1.22) is 22 percent more efficient

PRAXIS

A change which is difficult, a change which is painful, a change which is revolutionary. The switch of systems is without risk. When a city has initiated its historical formation in an organized way, in an orbital system, it requires a certain level of technical, economic, social and political awareness to take responsibility for the future and take this qualitative leap. Mankind has done it many times without our having properly appreciated it in our analyses of history. Let Madrid and Barcelona in 1854 and 1864 serve as examples.

But it was not by any means the first time that mankind took this qualitative leap. Prehistoric man made his hut round, with a conical roof of straw. I do not imagine he made it like that after a thorough econometric analysis, seeking to maximize the marginal cost effectiveness of his investment. But there must have been something of this, since in view of his limited technological capacity, as we have seen, it was the best solution. His villages acquired the same circular shape, in order to maximize the stockade or wall. There occurred, as a result, also, a maximum economic efficiency and social return from the collective effort, the most direct of contributions through personal work, in the orbital solution for the village.

With technological development in agriculture and settlement on the land, more complex urban systems start to appear, requiring a greater extent of infrastructure and investment, both public and private. The urban grid articulation appears 3000 years BC in Mohenjo-Daro in an empirical form and in the workers' village of Akhenaton (the revolutionary pharaoh) in Tell el-Amarna in Egypt.

From then on, the history of the colonization of territory by man has been the history of the evolution of the grid in its urban application. The Greeks, with Hippodamus of Miletus. The Romans, with their military camp, which is the basis of the great number of cities around the Mediterranean. The new towns (*villanuevas*) of medieval times. The ideal cities of the Renaissance are an exception, because in the quest for neoplatonic perfection the circle appeared to offer, erroneously, a better ideal frame. Few were established, because they were implicitly doomed to failure. The baroque urban development, in which the diagonal should not be confused with the radius of the orbital system. Spanish urban development in Latin America from the sixteenth century on. Anglo-Saxon development in North America in the eighteenth century, almost like an early premonition of industrial urban development.

Let us dwell a little more on the most recent history, the analysis of which can give us the key to the present. It is in the nineteenth century that we encounter one of the more important crises of the orbital system. The technological developments of the eighteenth century bring about a transformation of the systems of production and their social organization. It is what has been called the industrial revolution, which appears in the most advanced countries from the start of the nineteenth century. European cities start to grow at a vertiginous pace, at rates similar to those we are currently suffering, and the orbital system on which they were historically structured was not capable of responding to the necessary speed of these needs and this growth.

The traditional disjunctive incrementalist system had neither the speed nor the scope required. Two phenomena occurred: overcrowding in the consolidated center, with decline in quality of housing, and chaotic accumulation on the periphery with settlements based on the structures of agricultural plots, which will not be able, in the long term, to support the civic structures which a city requires. Numerous literary descriptions of nineteenth-century realism describe these processes to us, as well as the social and political analyses of authors such as Engels in Manchester. However, you do not need to go to written works. Our cities still bear today living evidence of this phenomenon.

Only from the middle of the nineteenth century does the problem receive an adequate response on the part of urban professionals. Only from the 1850s does the professional, economic, social and political capacity necessary to make the qualitative leap arise, passing from the orbital system to the grid. Only from this leap forward do "extensions" (*ensanches*) begin to occur in European cities. Extensions which, thanks to the grid, resolve congestion, allow standardization of production processes and regulatory homogenization, in such a way that the law and the rules of urban life become applicable to all.

Industrial society finds expression in the grid system the same way as—how curious—it had been encountered by all the sociopolitical systems which had previously adopted it throughout history. Urban grid extensions appear in Stockholm, Amsterdam, Rome, Florence, Vienna and many other cities. Madrid and Barcelona are paradigmatic cases.

Madrid carries out its extension in 1854. Castro delivers a grid extension which overcomes the limitations of the radial/orbital system the historical city inherited. But he lacks the final spark of talent and ends up circumscribing the grid in an octagonal polygon which reintroduces the principle of limitation of territory, and with it, once again the orbital problems. Beyond the outer routes the disjunctive and incrementalist chaos recurs in suburbs such as Tetuán or Cartagena, and this becomes the origin of the problems of lack of response which Madrid has demonstrated throughout the twentieth century. (See Figure 21.4.)

Barcelona carried out its extension in 1864, ten years later. But Cerdá, perhaps through the experience learnt by

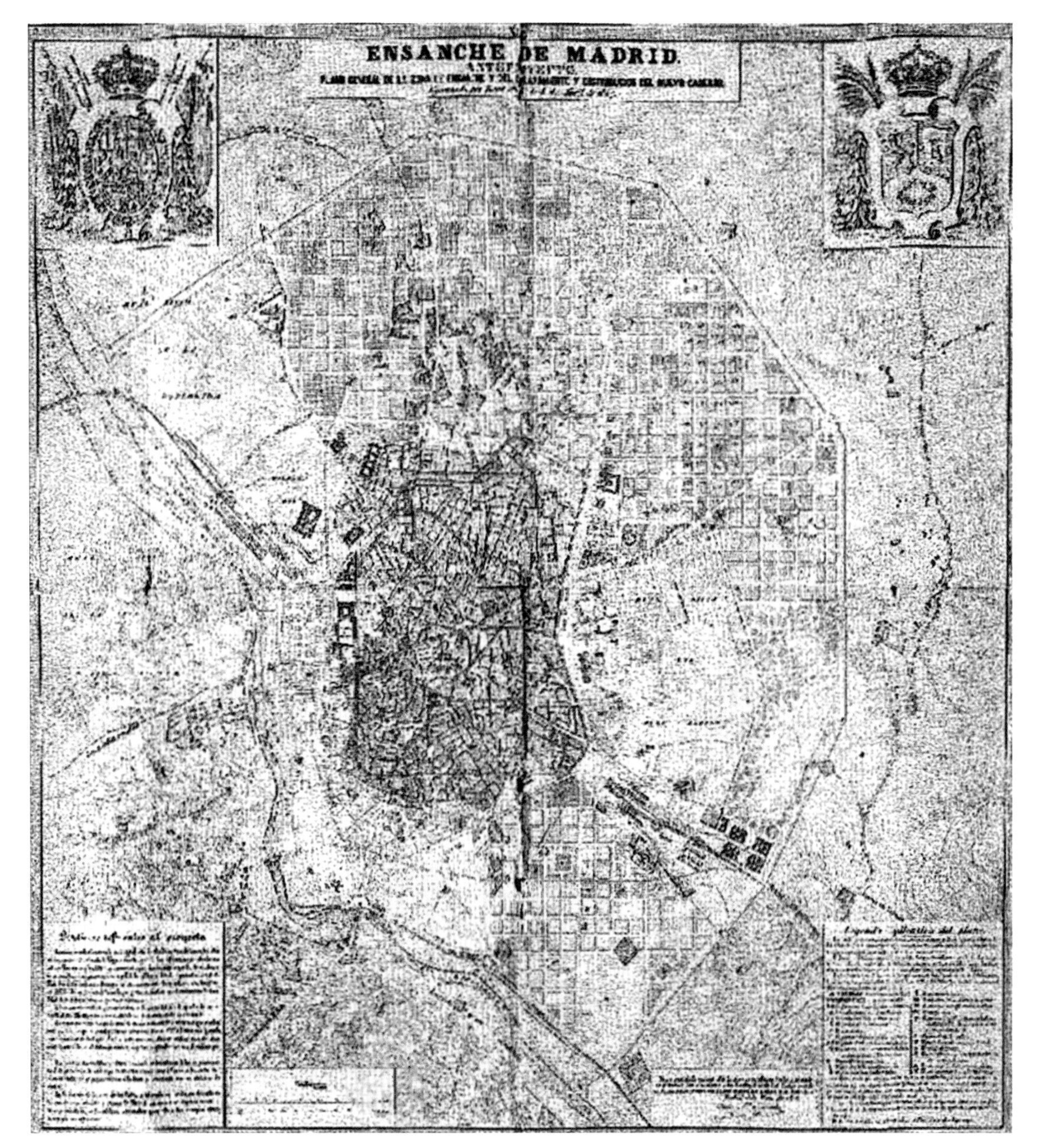

Figure 21.4 Castro's grid extension of Madrid, 1854

the profession in other cities such as Madrid, demonstrates the ability to understand the concept of infinity which is implicit in the grid system (parallel lines, etc.) and delivers a vision of Barcelona without orbital exhaustion. (See Figure 21.5.) One must appreciate in this context the superiority of Cerdá's proposal over the other competitors in the Barcelona tender. One must recognize in both Castro and Cerdá the ability to surmount the hurdle of contemplating significant growth, in volume as well as spread. We could even say explosive growth, in the long term. So farsighted was it that the territory defined by the Castro plan was not saturated until the 1940s in Madrid, and some zones of the Cerdá plan have still not been built upon. A vision of urban planning which projected 90 and 150 years into the future. An example to follow.

The story does not end there. Grid systems continue to be used in the twentieth century for new developments, such as the urban plans for Milton Keynes in the United Kingdom or regional plans like those for Padania (1964)

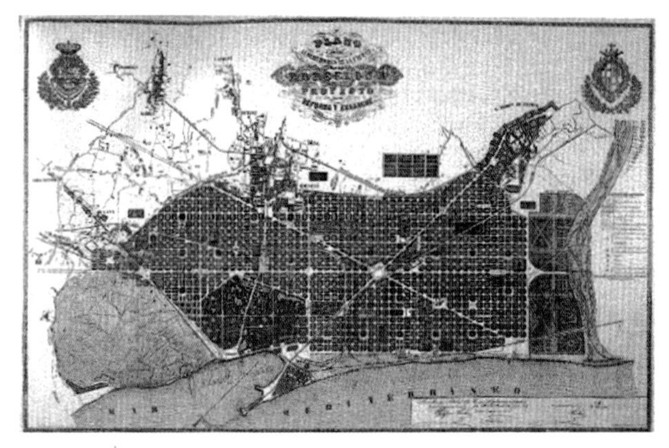

Figure 21.5 Cerdá's grid extension of Barcelona, 1864

in the north of Italy. The developments of metropolitan road systems in the United States since the 1940s are also an example of the use of territorial grids. Miami, Silicon Valley, territories in which a strong lineal geographic determinant, i.e. the coast, generates directionalities in parallel and perpendicular gradients.

The second half of the twentieth century generated a phenomenon comparable with that which we have described in the nineteenth century of explosive growth. It can be summed up in the following way. The post-industrial revolution has generated the need for new and greater urban spaces and a dispersion of their territorial location. Information technologies cause each employee to occupy a greater area of production space. The increase in wealth, counter-intuitive perhaps, results in each citizen taking up a greater residential, commercial and leisure area. The revolution in transport means that settlements occupy increasingly more extensive territory in dispersed and diffused growth. However, the problems deep down do not change. The distances associated in each epoch with the existing transport technology, which in Miletus were 30 m on foot, in the extensions of the nineteenth century were 130 m on horseback, are now 5 km at 120 km per hour. Journey times to work are kept constant.

In this grid system each cell must make the most of the characteristics of its location to establish a differential strategy with reference to the other squares of the grid. Each municipality, each type of settlement, must fit in with the assembly of the other pieces in a coherent whole, knowing what its possible activities are in the framework of a minimum set of rules, as well as its own objectives in the application of the said rules. Tactics and strategy, in each piece, in a framework of unity.

We could suggest a metaphor in the game of chess to understand how the pieces operate on the board of territory and what the methodology of the grid order of this territory may be like. Each piece of the territory has rules of structure, rules common to all the like pieces, which establish the general rules for their development: where industry, public transport stations, communication towers, etc. are sited. These rules, which we call "intra-zonal", belong to the domain of tactics; in chess they would be equivalent to the possible moves of each piece. But besides this, it is necessary to define where each of the pieces is located on the board to form the global strategy of the game of the territory. These rules of relationships between pieces belong to the domain of strategy.

The pieces on our board, the municipal councils, normally prefer to play draughts rather than chess: they all want to have everything, they resist the diversity of strategic movements that a territory requires. However, each piece, as in chess, must adopt its strategy in the global sphere of the game. There cannot be an airport or university in every square. Each piece must develop its strategy depending upon the possible moves, which are different in the short, medium and long term. (See Figure 21.6.)

The regional whole must be the summation of the particular strategies of each piece, which requires an organization for the coordination of this "summation", an organisation which must seek the objective of being an "integral". Whatever the case, it must be understood that within an urban region the game is not one of every piece against the others, because what regional coordination must aim for is a complementarity of the pieces in a strategy of unity. Competitiveness comes in at the supra-

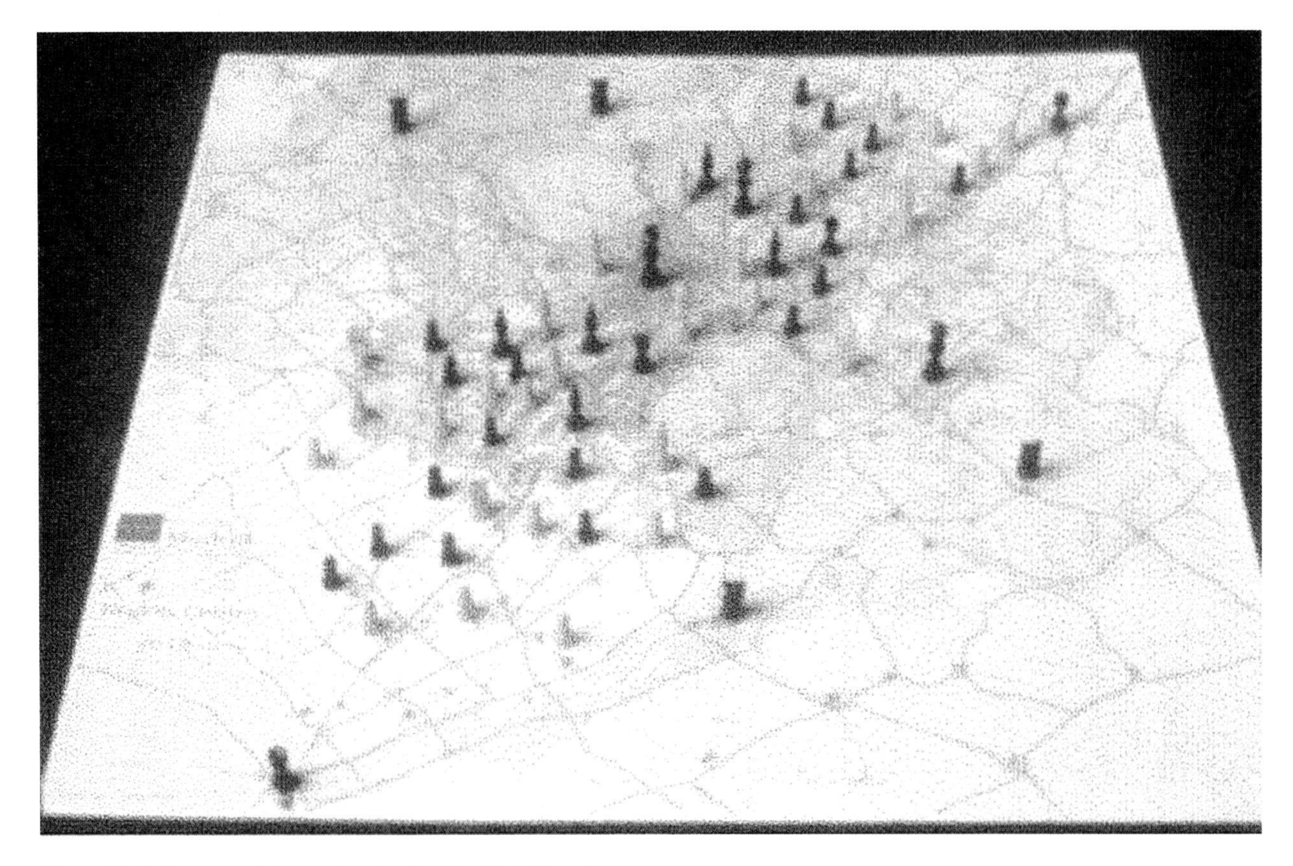

Figure 21.6 A game of chess: the plan for the Madrid region

regional level, as is in fact occurring now in the competition of international regions, in a valid and creative struggle for the international positioning of each of them.

The regional plan for Madrid develops and fulfills these objectives, these strategies, these tactics and this methodology. In Madrid we have stopped playing darts, all trying to land in the limited and congested center, and moved on to playing chess, in which each square and each piece has equivalent possibilities differentiated only by the playing capacity of each one in the whole. (See Figures 21.7–9.)

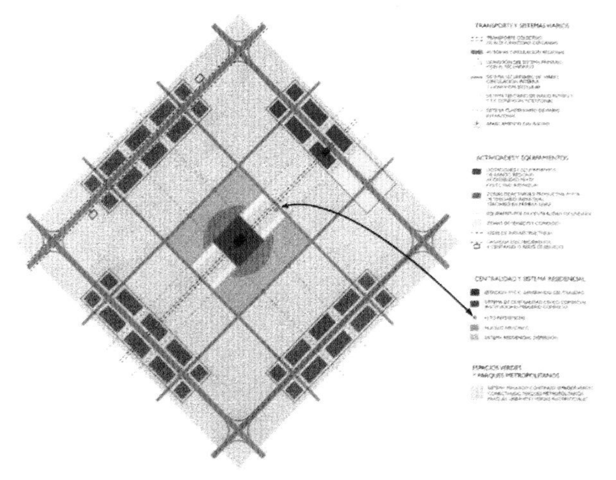

Figure 21.7 One of the grid squares of the regional plan for Madrid

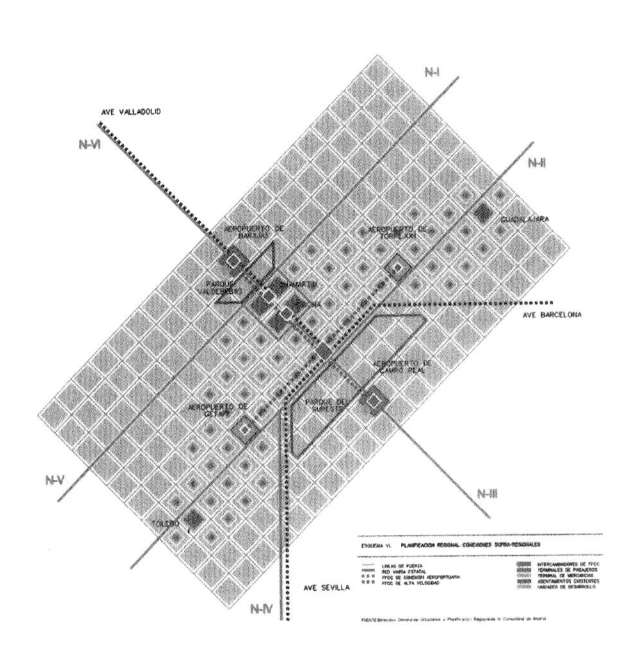

Figure 21.8 The regional plan for Madrid, showing occupied squares and those planned in the next 20 years

Figure 21.9 The regional plan for Madrid to the year 2018

NOTES

1. In the 1980s and 1990s the population of New York grew by 8 percent whereas its urban surface grew by 65 percent. Chicago's population grew by 4 percent and its urban surface by 46 percent. Cleveland's population declined by 8 percent whereas its urban surface increased by 33 percent. The population of Madrid will increase by 4 percent in the first 20 years of the twenty-first century and its urban surface by 50 percent, figures in line with those for Chicago.
2. So Paris in its regional plan to the year 2015 has predicted stability in the number of cars and an increase of 65 percent in their use in kilometers per traveler. Does this mean that it is necessary to increase the infrastructure by 65 percent to maintain the level of service? The extrapolation is not so direct but we can retain this figure.
3. Recent data on residential consumption in Europe are: Spain 20 m^2 per inhabitant, Italy 30 m^2 per inhabitant, Austria 33 m^2 per inhabitant, France 34 m^2 per inhabitant, Germany 37 m^2 per inhabitant, Denmark 43 m^2 per inhabitant, Sweden 45 m^2 per inhabitant, Norway 48 m^2 per inhabitant. These figures may be supplemented by those of 50 m^2 per inhabitant in the United States and 51 m^2 per inhabitant in Canada and contrasted with those for Japan, 7 m^2 per inhabitant, in a wealthy economy but with limited consumption, China, with 6 m^2 per inhabitant, in an economy with a strong rural element, or Russia, 5 m^2 per inhabitant, with a low-consumption economy.
4. So that if in Madrid the average family of five members occupied an average dwelling of 60 m^2 per person in 1974, giving a figure of 12 m^2 per person, today that same family, with only three members, will occupy 20 m^2 per person in the same dwelling. The other two will have left to form new homes and are the consumers of the 40 m^2 of new space produced since 1974, 66 percent more dwelling space.
5. Austria has gone from 22 m^2 to 33 m^2 in 20 years.

REFERENCE

Koolhaas, R. (1978) *Delirious New York: a Retroactive Manifesto for Manhattan*, London: Thames & Hudson.

22 Discontiguous urban growth

Edge cities, global cities, or both?

Agustin Rodriguez-Bachiller

This chapter began life as a discussion of the papers presented at the conference on "Global City Regions: Their Evolution and Management" held at the Lincoln Institute for Land Policy in Cambridge, Massachusetts, in September 1995, the theme of which can be summarized by reference to two now classic books which appeared in 1991: Joel Garreau's *Edge City* and Saskia Sassen's *The Global City*, and it is probably right to say that the underlying theme of that conference—and of the research project that preceded it—came from the idea that maybe the two phenomena these books brought to light might be related, and that it was certainly a possibility worth exploring empirically. My discussion here is based on looking across the evidence presented on those cities studied as part of that research project and presented at that conference, trying to generalize from that and tell the "story" that I see emerging from that evidence and which, as I will elaborate below, does *not* point in the direction of a clear link between edge city and globality.

GLOBAL CITIES OR JUST LARGE CITIES?

The first general comment that comes to my mind when looking at these cities is that I do not see much which is really new and unexpected according to the "classic" models of urban growth. I find it fascinating to see how some good, simple, and basic ideas retain their validity for an incredibly long time: I am thinking of the American tradition of Urban Ecology of the 1920s and 1930s, and the models they suggested for cities: the radial-growth model, the concentric-ring model, and the multi-nucleated model; these are often treated as competing models, fighting for supremacy in the description of a particular city—in a typical modernist tradition—but I prefer to see them as complementary, as showing different aspects of city form (maybe in a more postmodern approach) and, in particular, as illustrating *different stages* of urban growth:

- The pre-industrial city is essentially compact and organized around a series of focal points of religious, political or civic relevance, almost in a kind of "compact multi-nucleated" pattern.
- With industrialization, cities first grow radially away from the original nuclei along main arteries of communication, often guided by lines of collective transport. Certain activities which generate heavy externalities (positive or negative) "mark" certain directions and make them their own, and they will remain so for considerable time:
    - The wealthy middle classes.
    - Ethnic groups guided by language/cultural externalities, as we still see in Boston today.
    - Industry and its typically negative externalities (the sign of this externality can also change)
    - So called "marginal" settlements of squatters can sometimes behave in the same way.
- As the growth of car ownership opens up the wider space in between those main arteries, a ring-like pattern begins to appear, and an important point here is that this is not a contiguous pattern but that these "rings" are really conceptual abstractions of sprawling growth.
- The sprawl can with time coalesce into larger nuclei, leading to a "dispersed multi-nucleated" structure at a supra-urban scale, and the cycle is completed and can maybe restart at a higher level.

We can say that *the city grows first by sectors, then by rings and then, in doing so, it becomes something else:* maybe a "galaxy of settlements" (Lynch, 1962), maybe a metropolitan area in its various definitions (Gibbs, 1961), maybe a "non-place urban realm" (Webber, 1964).

Transportation infrastructure (for mass transport or for the private motor car) is crucial in guiding development throughout this process, be it at the stage of radial growth or at the stage of sprawl. But at a later stage, as communication begins to replace transportation in an increasing number of urban activities like shopping, working from home, tele-conferencing (Graham and Marvin, 1996), the "non-place" character of urban expansion is reinforced by the new kind of *footloose infrastructure* that makes this communication possible (cable and fiber optics), which is so cheap and easy to install that, instead of being a "fixing" factor for development (as transportation infrastructure was), it can *follow* development wherever it goes.

Of course, this process is not a historical invariant, and there are intervening variables; in particular, this process can be modified or even prevented by certain types of *constraints*:

- *Physical:* topography, or the existence of special natural areas (Tokyo, Taipei).
- *Political:* what Gary Hack referred to as the "culture of governance" can be in some cities (or countries) one of *containment*, coupled with a political situation which gives it enough strength to actually implement such containment: in the Randstad we see such culture based on conservationist/environmentalist ideas, in Santiago de Chile it was the strength of the political regime that kept it quite compact, in the United Kingdom strong conservationist and agricultural pressure groups have historically joined forces with town planners to produce the pattern of containment well documented in Peter Hall's classic book (1973).

But my starting point is that—with the variations introduced by these constraints—industrializing cities *do* follow this general process, even if, at the moment when we look at them, they may show different patterns, simply reflecting the fact that they are at different *stages* in that process. I think that both the edge city and the global city simply reflect the last stage of this process and, in order to say something about them, we should go back to look at how they got there.

TERTIARIZATION

Another generalization from the empirical evidence—this time in *functional* terms—can be that cities seem to follow a process of industrialization first, and then tertiarization, reaching a typical pattern of jobs of a third to a quarter industry and two-thirds to three-quarters services (Figure 22.1), present in many of the cities being discussed.

As before, some variations appear, and they come from the political dimension. *Capital cities* may show (not always) early tertiarization due to the development of the administrative function linked with government, and such cities approach the pattern mentioned before from a different angle: instead of industry increasing first and then decreasing as services replace it, it is the other way around, with industrialization growing—after tertiarization—to fill the gap and diversify the local service economy, sometimes even linked with a slight decrease in the service sector (as in Jakarta or in Santiago).

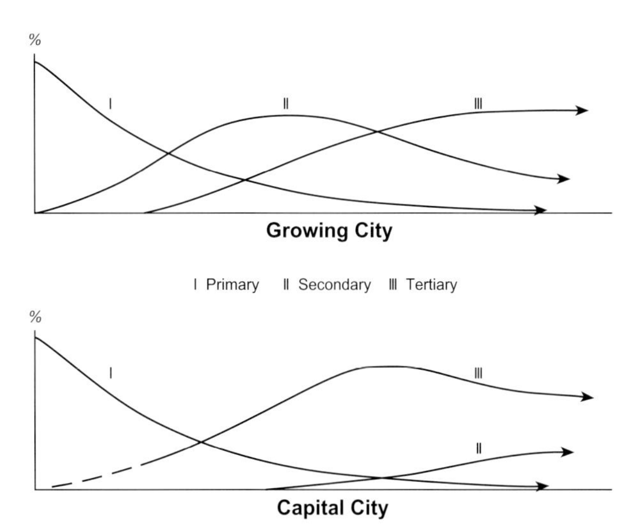

Figure 22.1 The functional breakdown of growing cities

But in all cases (including that of capital cities), another regularity seems to be that *immigration*, which played a crucial role during the heavy sprawling period, slows down or even disappears, and the city carries on growing only by vegetative growth.

DISCONTIGUITY IN URBAN GROWTH

Going back to the spatial point of view, the issue of discontiguity becomes central to the process presented above from quite an early stage. This phenomenon can originate from a variety of sources, and it is worth commenting on them, first to show the considerable variation in their nature (see Rodriguez-Bachiller, 1986, for a systematic review of the economic literature) and second, but most important for our discussion here, to see if these sources can be linked with the notion of "globality" we are addressing. I shall group these *sources of discontiguity* into two categories:

- Some are based on the needs associated with the particular land uses being developed (the "users") and their requirements; I call these *demand-based*.
- Others are based on the process of developing the land uses in question, and the particular needs of those intervening in that process (the "producers"); I call these *supply-based*.

Although the two are necessarily related (some would say, they are two sides of the same coin: the market), it is useful to separate them in that they represent very different challenges to policy and they often come from different theoretical perspectives:

Demand-based sources of discontiguity

First, some land uses may have a certain *preference for separation*:

- A first and well documented source of discontiguity in urban growth can be referred to under the generic heading of *the jump of the middle classes*—who tended to occupy central areas in the pre-industrial city, and reappear at the outer suburbs as urban growth progresses—over the working classes who were originally located on the outskirts of the city (Caplow, 1952; Schnore, 1965). This "flight to the suburbs" can be caused by "push" factors like the need to escape the increasing congestion and pollution of city centers (Schuler, 1974; Richardson, 1977) or by "pull" factors like William Alonso's "preference for space" over proximity (Alonso, 1960), but it is a process that seems to be ever-present (Madrid, the Randstad, Santiago, and many others).
- Also, a body of literature appeared in the 1970s on the effect of *social prejudice and aversion* in both the "symmetrical" and the "asymmetrical" case: when prejudice is mutual, this can lead to the segregation of land uses (Yellin, 1974) and even the appearance of "gated communities", expressed economically by depressed "bid rent" levels around the frontier between the two prejudiced groups (Rose-Ackermann, 1975, 1977; Courant and Yinger, 1977; Yinger, 1978; White, 1977a; Rosser, 1978) which can potentially lead to gaps in location patterns.
- Another phenomenon which can generate discontiguity is that of *squatters* and what are often called generically "marginal" developments, which tend to show three typical location patterns (well illustrated in the evidence considered here): (1) occupying existing buildings, as in São Paulo; (2) as "shanties" in intra-urban interstitial locations, in the small gaps (often in quite central locations) left by other land uses: Bangkok, and (3) extra-urban, "over the hill" locations hiding from view (Laboratorio de Urbanismo de Barcelona, 1971), normally associated with much more extensive (and organized) occupations of land, as we saw in São Paulo or in Jakarta. It is this third type of location pattern that, by definition, generates a spatial gap in the growth pattern of the city; the other two don't.

Second, some land uses have *preferences for accessibility* that point them away from urban locations:

- Households with multiple points of reference for their locational decisions (as opposed to locating by reference only to the central business district, as in the classic model): *two-worker households* have been seen in the economic literature (White, 1977b; Curran *et al.*, 1982) as potentially preferring locations accessible to both job markets, thus leading to possible location patterns *in between* city centers and not necessarily adjacent to any of them. And accessibility to out-of-town shopping centers can also produce a similar effect on household location (Brueckner, 1979), even with one-worker households.
- The *regional and out-of-town facilities* themselves (shopping centers, leisure centers, etc.), which try to cater for a transurban market, tend by definition towards locations "in the middle of nowhere".
- The *need for external functional linkages* outside the urban area, typically affecting footloose industrial or office developments, which can then prefer locations near a motorway or rail network. A typical example is that remarkably repetitive case of the "motorway corridor to the airport" (Taipei, Bangkok, Santiago, San Diego, Boston, Madrid), another may be the attraction shown by intersections of peripheral motorways (Madrid, Boston), both usually identified with remote links with distant places: of all these accepted causes of discontiguity we are discussing here, *this is probably the only one that is clearly identified with some notion of "globalization" of the urban economy*.

Supply-based sources of discontiguity

First, the nature of *certain types of developments* (or of the controls imposed on them) can produce patterns of physical discontiguity:

- What Conzen (1960, 1962) called *fringe belts* on the urban periphery of alternating high and low intensities of land use, linked to the ups and downs of the economic cycle (Whitehand, 1972a, b): in the downward part of the cycle, extensive land uses involving large plots and low densities tend to be developed; in the upward part of the cycle, intensive uses tend to be developed, leading to an alternation of dense and sparse rings at the periphery of the city.
- Also, *very low-density developments* produced by what in the US is sometimes referred to as "large-lot zoning" can depress the attraction of certain areas (White, 1975) and potentially create gaps in the urban fabric.
- *Green belts* can act as extreme cases of the restrictive zoning mentioned above, making new development "leapfrog" over them or, if any development is allowed

within the green belt, it is only to reinforce the pattern of existing (isolated) villages (Elson, 1986).

Second, *landowners* have been seen as a direct cause of discontiguity, mostly through the withholding of land:

- *Large landowners* can have as an explicit strategy to start developing (or selling for development) their large properties from the end farthest away from the existing urban area (Lombardini, 1963), so that development itself contributes to the appreciation of the rest of their land in between. Such landowners (often corporate landowners) will "focus" the market on their properties by holding *auctions*, where and when their plans for the release of the land dictate.
- *Different types of landowners* with different time preferences: owner-investors who have bought the land as an investment may be located closer to the urban fringe, while family owners (more willing to sell if an offer is made to them) may be located farther away from the edge of the city (Brown *et al.*, 1981), thus producing temporary gaps.

Third, the behaviour of *developers* themselves, as a logical result of their deliberate strategies:

- *Myopic foresight* (what we could call "miss-calculation" on the part of developers): development at a distance from the urban edge can take place in anticipation of urban growth (Mills, 1981) and whether long-term gaps appear or not may depend on the total magnitude of urban growth taking place: if it is much less than expected, new development will not fill the gap, and discontiguity will persist.
- *Political opportunism* by developers: sometimes small municipalities around a larger (central) one are more eager to get jobs and to improve their tax base—therefore less anxious to control development—than their central counterpart and, in such context, developers can take advantage of the difference by moving a short distance farther away and applying pressure on land just over the municipal boundary, still quite close to the large urban area but within the jurisdiction of the more accommodating authority, leaving a gap between the new development and the large urban area. This has been one of the traditional arguments for having a metropolitan-wide authority to control development but, historically, one of the side effects of increasing deregulation of urban management in the last 20 years has been a decrease in the strength (and often the dissolution) of such authorities.
- *Imperfect competition in the residential land use market* (by far the most important "city-forming" land use): rather than looking at sprawl as the result of some kind of "deviant" behaviour on the part of landowners or developers, I want to look now at a source of discontiguity in urban growth based on the economic logic of those involved in development (just as the opportunism discussed above was the result of their political logic) in a realistic economic context of so called "imperfect" competition—away from the idealized theoretical assumptions of perfect competition typical of the models normally found in the literature—which reflect much more realistically the conditions of development markets. I want to suggest that, even when the situations discussed above that could cause discontiguity are not present—even when landowners are all similar and "normal" in size, even when developers are politically "straight" and accurate in their foresight—discontiguity is likely to result just from the normal operation of the residential land use market. I want to extend this argument further than when discussing the other causes of discontiguity listed above, and propose a model of "normal" discontiguous urban growth under conditions of so called "imperfect" competition.

IMPERFECT COMPETITION AND DISCONTIGUOUS URBAN GROWTH

Looking at markets as "imperfect" means among other things making the assumption (quite realistic in the case of urban development) that the numbers of consumers or producers are not so large that they are all "price takers", so that the behaviour of each one has some degree of influence over the market price. Consumers are not forced any more to make the highest bid they can afford (because otherwise someone else will), producers are not forced to lower their prices as much as they can (because otherwise someone else will), but they all adjust their bids—or their acceptance of bids, if they are sellers—according to their relative *market power* (Mills, 1980), which can be measured by how limited the number of other individuals in their same situation is (other buyers if they are buyers, other sellers if they are sellers), in other words, their decisions will be a function of the probability (not the certainty, as in the perfectly competitive case) of someone else outbidding them. Mills compares for the land market the extreme case of a single monopolist owner in an area, with the case of several owners, and shows that the monopolist is likely to get higher rents. From this perspective, the perfectly competitive case can be seen as a *limiting theoretical case*, and the actual prices will deviate from the theoretical ones depending on the relative strength (numbers) of buyers and sellers in that particular market.

We shall concentrate this discussion on the markets for *residential* development as the most important "city-forming" land use and, as the first building block of our model, we must separate the "development" market into two: the *land market* in which landowners provide land to developers at a price, and the *floor space market* where developers provide floor space to consumers (the land users), also at a price.

Applying what we said at the beginning of this section to the *floor space market* first, we can probably say without too much fear of overgeneralization that in a growing city of the kind we are discussing here the residential floor space market is a *sellers'* market with many more buyers than sellers, so that we should expect the prices being paid for floor space to tend towards the maximum that consumers can afford. This situation may vary with the size of the development, and the market may be less clearly dominated by smaller developers (of whom there are many more), but only comparatively speaking; the general balance of supply and demand seems to favour residential developers across the city, who can develop whatever and wherever suits them best in the near certainty that they will be able to sell it in the market (Clawson and Hall, 1973).

With respect to the *land market* the situation is more complex, and our argument is based on considering the situation separately in the built-up area and in the undeveloped periphery:

- In the central, reasonably compact built-up part of the city, because of its nature, there is relative scarcity of developable land, putting the landowners in a strong position in the land market, which can be expected to be a *sellers'* market where landowners are likely to be able to extract maximum land rents from developers.
- As we leave the built-up area, however, the situation changes quite rapidly: the amount of land available grows *exponentially* with distance, while the number of developers doesn't (they are quite ubiquitous), so that the land market changes rapidly into a *buyers'* market, bringing the prices of land down—quite fast as distance increases—from what would be its theoretical value in the competitive case.

We can now look at the overall situation (both markets together) in these two parts of the urban area:

- In the *built-up area* both are sellers' markets and, in this type of situation, developers are likely to be able to extract from consumers maximum rents for their floor space, while at the same time landowners are likely to be able to extract maximum land rents from developers, and we are looking at a situation very much like that described by the classical *competitive* Alonso-type bid-rent model, where developers' profits are tight and land rents absorb all potentially excessive profits. It is well known that this type of model generates a *compact* pattern of urban growth, so that additions to the urban fabric will happen adjacent to the built-up area or at the interstices in it. If we consider a simple representation of the situation in terms of bid-rent curves for both markets, the land bid-rent curve will represent the profile of variable costs to the developer, while the floor space bid-rent curve will represent his revenue and, assuming for the sake of simplicity the developer's profits to be a function of the difference between revenue and variable costs, we can see how the *maximum profits* will tend to appear closer to the center (tending towards M_1 in Figure 22.2).
- At the *urban periphery*, on the other hand, the floor space market is still a sellers' market but the land market becomes a buyers' market increasingly with distance so that, while the developer is still likely to extract maximum prices for his floor space, he can expect to pay lower and lower prices for land as he moves away from the urban edge, and the profile of his profits will show a different shape, with a *maximum at a distance from the edge* (M_2 in Figure 22.2). In this situation, developments large enough to be self-sustaining will take place at a distance from the edge, leaving a gap, and only those developments too small to detach themselves will have to accept suboptimal profits and locate next to the edge of the city, extending its compact perimeter.

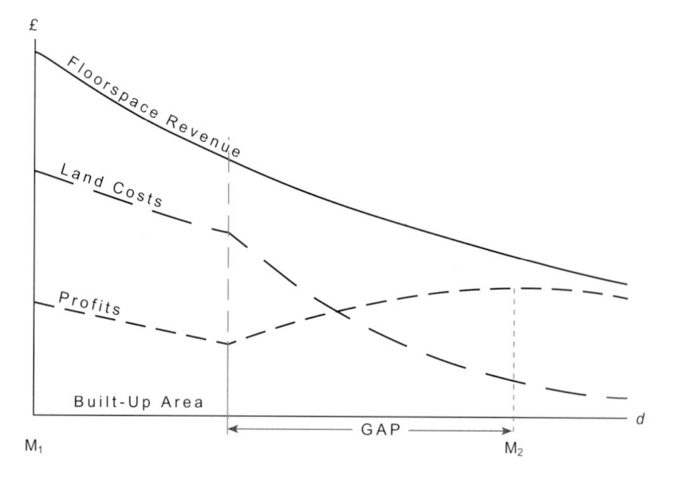

Figure 22.2 Developers' profits at the urban edge

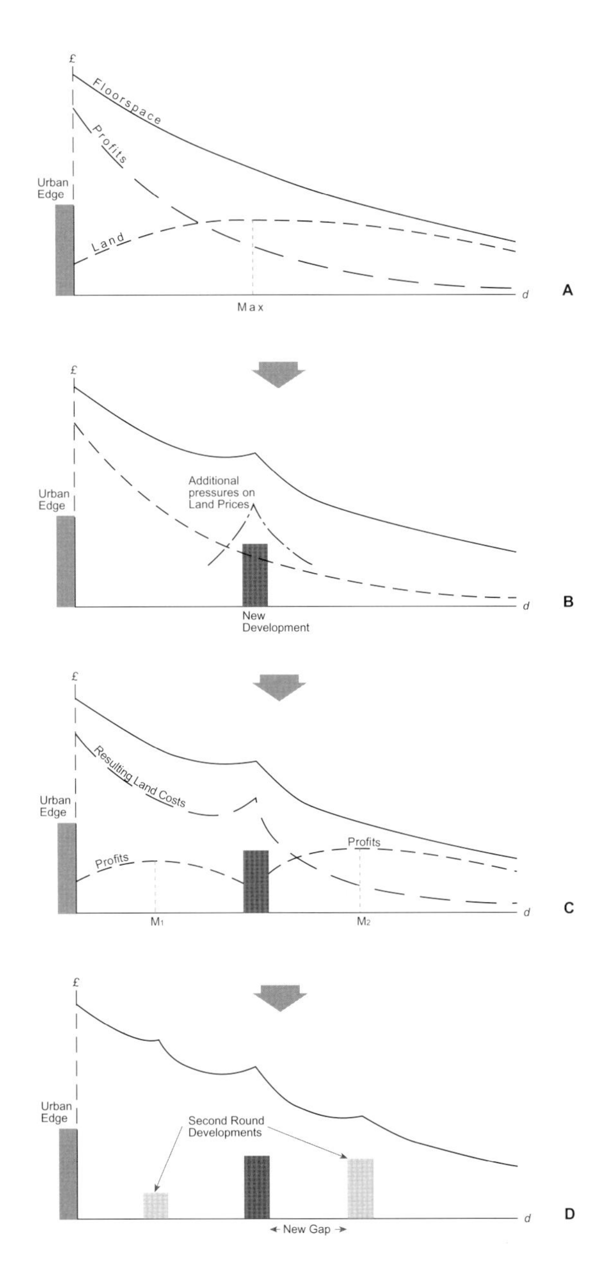

Figure 22.3 The dynamics of discontiguous development

We can extend the dynamics of this same process to further "rounds" of development (Figure 22.3). The new development will in turn produce a turmoil of readjustment of bid-rents around where it is located (Figure 22.3b), probably in the form of "peaks" in land values reaching towards their theoretical (competitive) values at that point, with—again—rapid decreases in all directions as we move away from that point. This will mean that, for the next round of development, the structure of profits for the developer is likely to show *two maxima*, one in the gap between the previous development and the old city, and the other farther away from the newly developed area (Figure 22.3c), and that is where the next round of development is likely to appear, and so on (Figure 22.3d).

A final point worth making about this process is that it would not necessarily be one of "jump and infill" (making discontiguity only temporary) because, despite the locations of some development in successive rounds in the middle of previous gaps, infill is unlikely to result, because as the gaps get smaller the expectations of landowners grow and their numbers drop (making them more competitive), reaching a point where land prices do not get depressed enough to compete with other land beyond the outer fringe, and developers will rather jump into open land (and extend the leapfrogging) where they can make greater profits. Paradoxically, it is land speculation itself that will prevent many landowners in those gaps from ever selling their land as long as there is further open land beyond the urban fringe.

As a result of this kind of process, the overall pattern of land prices in the urban edge can be visualized as consisting of at least three distinct parts (Figure 22.4):

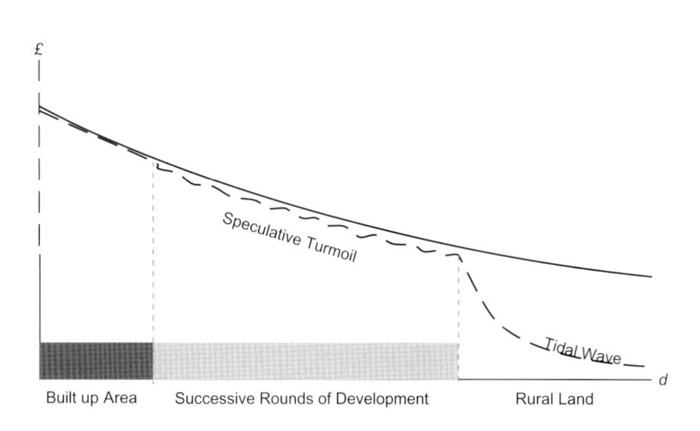

Figure 22.4 Land prices on the urban edge

- In the built-up area, prices will be near the levels suggested by the standard competitive market model.
- In between the built-up edge and the outermost developments (what we can call the "urban fringe"), successive developments create an artificial climate of expectations and land scarcity (some would call it just "speculation") that pushes prices up towards their theoretical maximum, in a combination of peaks and depressions, the former reducing the importance of the latter as the number of developments increases, but never reaching their expected competitive maximum—as developments will never reach complete in-fill. It is in this area that informal sector and "marginal" developments like squatters are likely to appear.
- Beyond the most outward development, a rapid depression of land prices with distance, what has been called before the "tidal wave" of land prices (Blumenfeld, 1954; Boyce, 1966).

This is a relatively simple model based on two general assumptions: that the floor space market tends to be a sellers' market practically everywhere (and certainly in and around urban regions), and that the land market changes in nature depending on the part of the urban region we are considering: while it is also a sellers' market in urban cores where land is relatively scarce, it changes rapidly into a buyers' market as we move out into the open land beyond the urban fringes of these regions.

If the city is not on a "featureless plain" the general pattern remains, even if specific locations may vary: for instance, it is typical for fringe developments "in the middle of nowhere" to gravitate towards *secondary road junctions* (as in the case of Madrid), even if the overall accessibility they provide is not actually very high at the time of the development.

According to this model, discontiguity should be expected to be the "normal" outcome of urban growth rather than the exception, in-fill being relatively small compared with the extension of the urban fringe, and it is the case of compact cities that needs explanation and not the other way around. Compactness can be explained maybe by the constraints mentioned before, or maybe by the operation of planning policies (like special zoning or green belts) that constrain the availability of cheaper land beyond a certain point, although these policies will always be subject—of course—to the political will (and strength) to implement them.

SOME CONCLUSIONS

Global edge city?

To finish, we are now going back to the main thread of our argument (the phenomenon of "edge cities" and their possible connection with the emergence of the so-called "global city"), which raises two basic questions: the possible causality between the two (are edge cities global?) and the evaluation of this phenomenon (are edge/global cities good?) to be left for the next section.

Starting with the issue of causality, we have spent some time showing the considerable variety of ways in which discontiguity (at the root of edge cities) can come about, and we have seen how only one of the many sources of discontiguity (what we referred to as "the need for external functional linkages") was potentially linked with the globalization of the urban economy, and an obvious conclusion from this should be that *discontiguity has actually relatively little to do with globality*: not only is a small fraction of discontiguous urban growth likely to originate from globalization, but global functions are known to appear in downtown locations as much (if not more) as on peripheral locations, so that globalization seems to be happening anyway, discontiguously or not.

Maybe we are watching two phenomena which happen to coincide in only a few (limited) situations, and the scientific community cannot resist applying to that coincidence a paradigm of causality, while it is clear from the evidence discussed here that (1) globality does not cause much of the discontiguity present, (2) nor does discontiguity seem in itself to cause the globality we see emerging in these cities.

Maybe discontiguity and globality are two phenomena happening simultaneously but caused by totally different sets of circumstances: discontiguity caused by the physical growth of the city and the factors affecting it, and globality caused by its functional growth and increased integration into the world economy, each taking advantage of the opportunities the other offers, but not involved in any causality links between them.

Good edge/global cities?

To conclude, and independently of what causes this "edge/global city", fundamental questions of *evaluation* arise (are edge/global cities good?):

First, and referring specifically to the "globality" issue, there is the question of the *contrast* between the global part of the city and the "residual" city it leaves behind, raising the issue of possible "dualization" of the city (a point already hinted at in Castells, 1984) and the effect that the globalization of one part is likely to have on the rest:

- Is it going to be *beneficial* by adding to the economic base of the city and promoting further development of its economy to support the expanding global sectors, in some sort of "trickle-down" model?
- Will it be *detrimental*, with the global sectors attracting the most dynamic elements of the urban economy and generating its benefits in other parts of the global network but not necessarily in that particular city?
- For the sake of completeness, we can consider the possibility that it might be just *indifferent*.

Second, the more general question of the *quality* of the (global) edge city itself. Looking at the evidence from the cities studied here, it is remarkable how similar their problems seem to be when expressed by the researchers (so that it may not seem worth while to look at diferences among them) but I cannot help feeling that this is because each team compares its situation with its own targets and the demands of its own culture. If, on the other hand, we take a step back and try to compare the quality of these situations not by what the analysis teams say but by the information they provide, a more differentiated pattern emerges, and I find it inescapable to conclude that, in addition to all the analytical issues discussed about all these cities, we should consider the fact that *there is "good" edge city and there is "bad" edge city*.

I would identify with the notion of *good* edge city (exemplified by cities like San Diego, Lyon or Toronto) peripheral developments characterized by:

- *Balanced land uses*: a good mix of land uses (housing, industry, shops, offices) in each of the peripheral clusters of development that form the edge city, and a parallel mix of social groups (rich and poor), all produced by a cumulative steady process, creating functional "mini-cities" with the potential to become real satellite centers.
- Large unoccupied gaps in between urbanised areas, with still a lot of *free environment*.
- Happening in urban regions integrated with *other similar regions* in a national structure.
- In relatively *rich economies* with higher standards of living, construction, planning controls.

I would label as *bad* edge city (exemplified by São Paulo), situations where:

- The new peripheral developments are *uni-functional*, often just industry, new job centers which only increase commuting (what are called in Chapter 8 "pieces of city").
- *Explosive growth*.
- Leaving only *small gaps between developments*, leading to a poorer environment.
- Only happening in *isolated urban regions*.
- In *poorer countries* with lower standards.

A simple dichotomous model like this requires some modification to account for notable exceptions—for instance, to include cities which are *in transition* from one type to the other. Santiago is one example, Madrid another, coinciding with the overall modernization it has been undergoing.

Finally, to finish this tentative evaluation at another level, there is the question of the relationship between the "good" and "bad" edge cities—in so far as they are connected with each other in some way by some element of globality—and their *relative balance of power* (another version of the issue of "contrast" discussed earlier). In this "global partnership" between comparable elites, is their relationship symmetrical, or are there *dependences* of the "bad" on the "good"? If this were the case, then maybe applying a *colonial* model to the analysis of the global city might prove quite productive, adding a much needed critical element to the discussion of this pervasive phenomenon.

REFERENCES

Alonso, W. (1960) "A Theory of the Urban Land Market," *Papers of the Regional Science Association* 6, pp. 149–58.

Blumenfeld, H. (1954) "The Tidal Wave of Metropolitan Expansion," *Journal of the American Institute of Planners*, Winter, pp. 3–14.

Boyce, R. R. (1966) "The Edge of the Metropolis: the Wave Theory Analog Approach," *British Columbia Geographical Series* 7, pp. 31–40; also in L. S. Bourne (ed.) *Internal Structure of the City*, London: Oxford University Press.

Brown, H. J., Phillips, R. S., and Roberts, N. A. (1981) "Land Markets at the Urban Fringe: New Insights for Policy Makers," *Journal of the American Planning Association* 47, pp. 131–44.

Brueckner, J. K. (1979) "A Model of Non-central Production in a Monocentric City," *Journal of Urban Economics* 6, pp. 444–63.

Caplow, T. (1952) "Urban Structure in France," *American Sociological Review* 17 (5), pp. 544–9.

Castells, M. (1984) *Towards the Informational City?* Working paper 430, Berkeley CA: Institute of Urban and Regional Development, University of California.

Clawson, M., and Hall, P. (1973) *Planning and Urban Growth*, Resources for the Future, Baltimore MD: Johns Hopkins University Press.

Conzen, M. R. G. (1960) *Alnwick, Northumberland: A Study in Town Planning Analysis*, Transactions of the Institute of British Geographers 27.

Conzen, M. R. G. (1962) "The Plan of an English City Centre," in K. Norborg (ed.) *Proceedings of the IGU Symposium in Urban Geography*, Lund Studies in Geography, Series B, No. 24, pp. 383–414.

Courant, P.N., and Yinger, J. (1977) "On Models of Racial Prejudice and Urban Residential Structure," *Journal of Urban Economics* 4, pp. 272–91.

Curran, C., Carlson, L. A., and Ford, D. A. (1982) "A Theory of Residential Location of Two-worker Households," *Journal of Urban Economics* 9, pp. 102–14.

Elson, M. J. (1986) *Green Belts: Conflict Mediation in the Urban Fringe*, London: Heinemann.

Garreau, J. (1991) *Edge City: Life on the New Frontier*, New York: Doubleday.

Gibbs, J. P. (1961) *Urban Research Methods*, New York: Van Nostrand (Part I, "Urban Units, their Nature and Boundaries").

Graham, S., and Marvin, S. (1996) *Telecommunications and the City*, London and New York: Routledge.

Hall, P., Thomas, R., Gracey, H., and Drewett, R. (1973) *The Containment of Urban England*, London: Allen & Unwin.

Laboratorio de Urbanismo de Barcelona (1971) "Teoria y experiencia de la urbanizacion marginal," in the Spanish edition of D. Lewis (ed.) *El crecimiento de las ciudades* (The Growth of Cities), Barcelona: Gustavo Gili.

Lombardini, S. (1963) "La normalizzazione dei mercati delle aree e degli allogio attravesso la nouva legge urbanistica," *Urbanistica* 38.

Lynch, K. (1962) "The Pattern of the Metropolis," in R. Rodwin (ed.) *The Future Metropolis*, London: Constable.

Mills, D. E. (1980) "Market Power and Land Development Timing," *Land Economics* 56, pp. 10–20.

Mills, D. E. (1981) "Growth, Speculation and Sprawl in a Monocentric City," *Journal of Urban Economics* 10, pp. 201–26.

Richardson, H. W. (1977) "On the Possibility of Positive Rent Gradients," *Journal of Urban Economics* 4, pp. 60–8.

Rodriguez-Bachiller, A. (1986) "Discontiguous Urban Growth and the New Urban Economics: a Review," *Urban Studies* 2, pp. 79–104.

Rose-Ackerman, S. (1975) "Racism and Urban Economics," *Journal of Urban Economics* 2, pp. 85–103.

Rose-Ackerman, S. (1977) "The Political Economy of a Racist Housing Market," *Journal of Urban Economics* 4, pp. 150–69.

Rosser, J. B. (1978) "The Theory and Policy Implications of Spatial Discontinuities in Land Values," *Land Economics* 54, pp. 430–41.

Sassen, S. (1991) *The Global City: New York, London, Tokyo*, Princeton NJ: Princeton University Press.

Schnore, L. F. (1965) "On the Spatial Structure of Cities in the two Americas," in P. M. Houser and L. F. Schnore (eds) *The Study of Urbanization*, New York: Wiley.

Schuler, R. E. (1974) "Air Quality Improvement and Long-run Urban Form," *Papers of the Regional Science Association* 33, pp. 133–48.

Webber, M. M. (1964) "The Urban Place and the Non-place Urban Realm," in M. M. Webber, J. W. Dyckman, D. L. Foley, A. Z. Guttenberg, W. L. C. Wheaton, and C. Bauer Wurster (eds) *Explorations into Urban Structure*, Philadelphia PA: University of Pennsylvania Press.

White, M. J. (1975) "The Effect of Zoning on the Size of Metropolitan Areas," *Journal of Urban Economics* 2, pp. 279–90.

White, M. J. (1977a) "Urban Models and Race Discrimination," *Regional Science and Urban Economics* 7, pp. 217–32.

White, M. J. (1977b) "A Model of Residential Location Choice and Commuting by Men and Women Workers," *Journal of Regional Science* 19, pp. 41–52.

Whitehand, J. W. R. (1972a) "Urban Rent-theory, Time Series and Morphogenesis: an Example of Eclecticism in Geographical Research," *Area* 4, pp. 215–22.

Whitehand, J. W. R. (1972b) "Building Cycles and the Spatial Pattern of Urban Growth," *Transactions of the Institute of British Geographers* 56, pp. 39–55.

Yellin, J. (1974) "Urban Population Distribution, Family Income, and Social Prejudice: 1. The Long, Narrow City," *Journal of Urban Economics* 1, pp. 21–47.

Yinger, J. (1978) "The Black–White Price Differential in Housing: some Further Evidence," *Land Economics* 54, pp. 187–206.

23 Cities in the global economy

Saskia Sassen

Why and how do cities matter in today's global economy? Is there something different about their role today from 20 or 30 years ago? This is, inevitably, one particular angle into the question of the importance of cities today, since most cities have probably had few interactions with the global economy and have felt only minor repercussions from its growth. But it is an important issue to pursue because many experts and policy makers appear to be convinced that globalization and the new information technologies mark the end of the economic importance of cities.

The dispersal capacities emerging with globalization and telematics — the offshoring of factories, the expansion of global networks of affiliates and subsidiaries, the move of back offices to suburbs and out of central cities—led many observers to assert that cities would become obsolete in an economic context of globalization and telematics. Indeed, many of the once great industrial centers in the highly developed countries did suffer severe decline. But, against all predictions, a significant number of major cities also saw their concentration of economic power rise. Why?

One way of summarizing my answer to this question and the argument I will develop here is to say that place is central to the multiple circuits through which economic globalization is constituted. One strategic type of place for these developments, and the one focused on here, is the city. Other important types of places are export-processing zones or high-tech districts such as Silicon Valley.

The combination of geographic dispersal of economic activities and system integration which lies at the heart of the current economic era has contributed to new or expanded central functions and the complexity of transactions has raised the demand by firms for highly specialized services. Rather than becoming obsolete owing to the dispersal made possible by information technologies, a critical number of cities:

- Concentrate command functions.
- Are post-industrial production sites for the leading industries of our period, finance and specialized services.
- Are national or transnational marketplaces where firms and governments can buy financial instruments and specialized services.

How many such cities there are, what is their shifting hierarchy, how novel a development they represent, are all subjects for debate. But there is growing agreement about the fact of a network of major cities both in the North and in the South that function as centers for the coordination, control and servicing of global capital.

Introducing cities in an analysis of economic globalization allows us to reconceptualize processes of economic globalization as concrete economic complexes situated in specific places. A focus on cities decomposes the nation state into a variety of subnational components, some profoundly articulated with the global economy and others not. It also signals the declining significance of the national economy as a unitary category in the global economy.

THE NEW ROLE OF SERVICES IN THE ECONOMY: IMPACT ON CITIES

This new or sharply expanded role of a particular kind of city in the world economy since the early 1980s basically results from the intersection of two major processes. One is the sharp growth in the globalization of economic activity. This has raised the scale and the complexity of economic transactions, thereby feeding the growth of top-level multinational headquarter functions and the growth of services for firms, particularly the growth of advanced corporate services. The second is the growing service intensity in the organization of the economy, a process evident in firms in all industrial sectors, from mining to finance. This has fed the growth of services for firms in all sectors, and for both nationally and internationally oriented firms.[1]

The key process from the perspective of the urban economy is the growing demand for services by firms in all industries and the fact that cities are preferred production sites for such services, whether at the global, national or regional level. The growing service-intensity in economic organization generally and the specific conditions of production for advanced corporate services, including the conditions under which information technologies are available, combine to make some cities once again a key "production" site, a role they lost when mass manufacturing became the dominant economic sector. They are the world cities or global cities that are the focus of this chapter.

While the decline of industrial centers as a consequence of the internationalization of production beginning in the 1960s has been thoroughly documented and explained, until recently the same could not be said about the rise of major service cities in the 1980s. Today we have a rich new scholarship, replete with debates and disagreements, on cities in a global economy.

There are good reasons why it has been more difficult to understand the role of cities as production sites for advanced information industries. Advanced information industries are typically conceptualized in terms of the hypermobility of their outputs and the high levels of expertise of their professionals rather than in terms of the work process involved and the requisite infrastructure of facilities and non-expert jobs that are also part of these industries. Along with the hypermobility of their outputs there is a vast structure of work that is far less mobile and, indeed, requires the massive concentrations of human and telecommunication resources we find in major cities.

The specific forms assumed by globalization over the 1990s have created particular organizational requirements. The emergence of global markets for finance and specialized services, the growth of investment as a major type of international transaction, all have contributed to the expansion in command functions and in the demand for specialized services for firms.

A central proposition here is that we cannot take the existence of a global economic system as a given, but rather need to examine the particular ways in which the conditions for economic globalization are produced. This requires examining not only communication capacities and the power of multinationals, but also the infrastructure of facilities and work processes necessary for the implementation of global economic systems, including the production of those inputs that constitute the capability for global control and the infrastructure of jobs involved in this production. The emphasis shifts to the *practice* of global control: the work of producing and reproducing the organization and management of a global production system and a global marketplace for finance, both under conditions of economic concentration. The recovery of place and production also implies that global processes can be studied in great empirical detail.

Two observations can be made at this point. One is that to a large extent the global economy materializes in concrete processes situated in specific places, and that this holds for the most advanced information industries as well. We need to distinguish between the capacity for global transmission/communication and the material conditions that make it possible, between the globalization of the financial industry and the array of resources—from buildings to labor inputs—that makes it possible; and so on for other sectors as well.

The second is that the spatial dispersal of economic activity made possible by telematics contributes to an expansion of central functions in so far as this dispersal takes place under the continuing concentration in control, ownership and profit appropriation that characterizes the current economic system. More conceptually, we can ask whether an economic system with strong tendencies towards such concentration can have a space economy that lacks points of physical agglomeration.

A NEW GEOGRAPHY OF CENTRALITY AND MARGINALITY

We can then say that the global economy materializes in a worldwide grid of strategic places, uppermost among which are major international business and financial centers. We can think of this global grid as constituting a new economic geography of centrality, one that cuts across national boundaries and across the old North–South divide. It signals, potentially, the emergence of a parallel political geography. An incipient form of this is the growing intensity in cross-border networks among cities and their mayors.

The most powerful of these new economic geographies of centrality at the interurban level binds the major international financial and business centers: New York, London, Tokyo, Paris, Frankfurt, Zurich, Amsterdam, Los Angeles, Sydney, Hong Kong, among others. But this geography now also includes cities such as São Paulo, Buenos Aires, Bangkok, Taipei and Mexico City. The intensity of transactions among these cities, particularly through the financial markets, transactions in services, and investment has increased sharply, and so have the orders of magnitude involved. At the same time, there has been a sharpening inequality in the concentration of strategic resources and activities between each of these cities and others in the same country.

One might expect that the growing number of financial centers now integrated into the global markets would have reduced the extent of concentration of financial activity in the top centers.[2] One would further expect this given the immense increases in the global volume of transactions. Yet the levels of concentration remain unchanged in the face of massive transformations in the financial industry and in the technological infrastructure that industry depends on.[3]

The growth of global markets for finance and specialized services, the need for transnational servicing networks due to sharp increases in international investment, the reduced role of governments in the regulation of international economic activity and the corresponding ascendance of other institutional arenas, notably global markets and corporate headquarters—all these point to the existence of transnational economic processes with multiple locations in more than one country. We can see here the formation, at least incipient, of a transnational urban system.

The pronounced orientation to the world markets evident in such cities raises questions about their articulation with their nation states, their regions, and the larger economic and social structure in such cities. Cities have typically been deeply embedded in the economies of their regions—indeed, often reflecting the characteristics of the latter, and mostly they still do. But cities that are strategic sites in the global economy tend, in part, to disconnect from their region. This conflicts with a key proposition in traditional scholarship about urban systems, namely, that these systems promote the territorial integration of regional and national economies.

Alongside these new global and regional hierarchies of cities is a vast territory that has become increasingly peripheral, increasingly excluded from the major economic processes that fuel economic growth in the new global economy. A multiplicity of formerly important manufacturing centers and port cities have lost functions and are in decline, not only in the less developed countries but also in the most advanced economies. This is yet another meaning of economic globalization.

But also inside global cities we see a new geography of centrality and marginality. The downtowns of cities and metropolitan business centers receive massive investments in real estate and telecommunications while low-income city areas are starved of resources. Highly educated workers see their incomes rise to unusually high levels while low or medium-skilled workers see theirs sink. Financial services produce superprofits while industrial services barely survive. These trends are evident, with different levels of intensity, in a growing number of major cities in the developed world and increasingly in some of the developing countries that have been integrated into the global financial markets (Sassen, 1996: chapter 2).

THE URBAN ECONOMY TODAY

This is not to say that everything in the economy of these cities has changed. On the contrary there is much continuity and much similarity with cities that are not global nodes. It is rather that the implantation of global processes and markets has meant that the internationalized sector of the economy has expanded sharply and has imposed a new valorization dynamic, often with devastating effects on large sectors of the urban economy. High prices and profit levels in the internationalized sector, e.g. finance, and its ancillary activities, e.g. restaurants and hotels, made it increasingly difficult in the 1980s for other sectors to compete for space and investments. Many of the latter have experienced considerable downgrading and/or displacement; or lost economic vigor to the point of not being able to retake their economic space when the recession weakened the dominant sectors. Illustrations are neighborhood shops catering to local needs replaced by up-scale boutiques and restaurants catering to new high-income urban elites. The sharpness of the rise in profit levels in the international finance and service sector also contributed to the sharpness of the ensuing crisis. These trends are evident in many cities of the highly developed world, though rarely as sharply as in major US cities. (See, for example, *Le Débat*, 1994, for Paris; Todd, 1995, for Toronto, etc.)

Though at a different order of magnitude, these trends also became evident towards the late 1980s in a number of major cities in the developing world that have become integrated into various world markets: São Paulo, Buenos Aires, Bangkok, Taipei, Mexico City are but some examples. (See for more detail the series edited by Milton Santos on São Paulo; Sassen, 1994; Knox and Taylor, 1995). Central to the development of this new core in these cities as well were the deregulation of financial markets, the ascendance of finance and specialized services, and integration into the world markets, real estate speculation, and high-income commercial and residential gentrification. The opening of stock markets to foreign investors and the privatization of what were once public sector firms have been crucial institutional arenas for this articulation. Given the vast size of some of these cities, the impact of this new economic complex is not always as evident as in central London or Frankfurt, but the transformation has occurred.

Accompanying these sharp growth rates in producer services was an increase in the level of employment specialization in business and financial services in major cities throughout the 1980s. There is today a general trend towards high concentration of finance and certain producer services in the downtowns of major international financial centers around the world: from Toronto and Sydney to Frankfurt and Zurich to São Paulo and Mexico

City we are seeing growing specialization in finance and related services in the downtown areas. These cities have emerged as important producers of services for export, with a tendency towards specialization.[4] New York and London are leading producers and exporters in financial services, accounting, advertising, management consulting, international legal services and other business services. (For instance, out of a total private sector employment of 2.8 million jobs in New York City in December 1995, almost 1.3 million are export-oriented.) Cities such as New York are among the most important international markets for these services, with New York the world's largest source of service exports.

There are also tendencies towards specialization among different cities within a country. In the United States, New York leads in banking, securities, manufacturing administration, accounting and advertising. Washington leads in legal services, computing and data processing, management and public relations, research and development, and membership organizations. New York is more narrowly specialized as a financial and business center and cultural center. Some of the legal activity concentrated in Washington is actually serving New York City businesses which have to go through legal and regulatory procedures, lobbying, etc. These are bound to be in the national capital.[5]

It is important to recognize that manufacturing remains a crucial economic sector in all of these economies, even when it may have ceased to be so in some of these cities. This is a subject I return to in a later section.

THE FORMATION OF A NEW PRODUCTION COMPLEX

The rapid growth and disproportionate concentration of producer services in central cities should not have happened according to standard conceptions about information industries. As they are thoroughly embedded in the most advanced information technologies they could be expected to have locational options that bypass the high costs and congestion typical of major cities. But cities offer agglomeration economies and highly innovative environments. Some of these services are produced in-house by firms, but a large share are bought from specialized service firms. The growing complexity, diversity and specialization of the services required make it more efficient to buy them from specialized firms rather than hiring in-house professionals. The growing demand for these services has made possible the economic viability of a free-standing specialized service sector.

There is a production process in these services which benefits from proximity to other specialized services. This is especially the case in the leading and most innovative sectors of these industries. Complexity and innovation often require multiple highly specialized inputs from several industries. One example is that of financial instruments. The production of a financial instrument requires inputs from accounting, advertising, legal expertise, economic consulting, public relations, designers and printers. Time replaces weight in these sectors as a force for agglomeration. That is to say, if there were no need to hurry, one could conceivably have a widely dispersed array of specialized firms that could still cooperate. And this is often the case in more routine operations. But where time is of the essence, as it is today in many of the leading sectors of these industries, the benefits of agglomeration are still extremely high to the point that it is not simply a cost advantage but an indispensable arrangement.

It is this combination of constraints that has promoted the formation of a producer services complex in all major cities. This producer services complex is intimately connected with the world of corporate headquarters; they are often thought of as forming a joint headquarters–corporate services complex. But it seems to me that we need to distinguish the two. While it is true that headquarters still tend to be disproportionately concentrated in cities, many moved out in the latter years of the twentieth century. Headquarters can indeed locate outside cities. But they need a producer services complex somewhere in order to buy or contract for the specialized services and financing they need. Further, headquarters of firms with very high overseas activity or in highly innovative and complex lines of business tend to locate in major cities. In brief, firms in more routinized lines of activity, with predominantly regional or national markets, appear to be increasingly free to move or install their headquarters outside cities. Firms in highly competitive and innovative lines of activity and/or with a strong world market orientation appear to benefit from being located at the center of major international business centers, no matter how high the costs.

But what is clear, in my view, is that both types of headquarters need a corporate services complex to be located somewhere. Where is probably increasingly unimportant from the perspective of many, though not all, headquarters. From the perspective of producer services firms, such a specialized complex is most likely to be in a city rather than, for instance, a suburban office park. The latter will be the site for producer services firms, but not for a services complex. And it is only such a complex that can handle the most advanced and complicated corporate demands.

CORPORATE HEADQUARTERS AND CITIES

It is common in the general literature and in some more scholarly accounts to use headquarters concentration as an indication of whether a city is an international business center. The loss of headquarters is then interpreted as a decline in a city's status. The use of headquarters concentration as an index is actually a problematic measure, given the way in which corporations are classified.

Which headquarters concentrate in major international financial and business centers depends on a number of variables. First, how we measure or simply count headquarters makes a difference. Frequently, the key measure is size of firm in terms of employment and overall revenue. In that case, some of the largest firms in the world are still manufacturing firms and many of them have their main headquarters in proximity to their major factory complex, which is unlikely to be in a large city owing to space constraints. Such firms are likely, however, to have secondary headquarters for highly specialized functions in major cities. Further, many manufacturing firms are oriented to the national market and do not need to be located in a city's national business center. Thus the much publicized departure of major headquarters from New York City in the 1960s and 1970s involved these types of firms. If we look at the Fortune 500 largest firms in the United States (cf. "*Fortune* Magazine 500 list") many have left New York City or other large cities. If instead of size we use share of total firm revenue coming from international sales, a large number of firms that are not part of the Fortune 500 list come into play. For instance, in the case of New York City the results change dramatically: 40 percent of US firms with half their revenue from international sales have their headquarters in the New York metro area.

Second, the nature of the urban system in a country is a factor. Sharp urban primacy will tend to entail a disproportionate concentration of headquarters no matter what measure one uses. Thirdly, different economic histories and business traditions may combine to produce different results. Further, headquarters concentration may be linked with a specific economic phase. For instance, unlike New York's loss of top Fortune 500 headquarters, Tokyo has been gaining headquarters. Osaka and Nagoya, the two other major economic centers in Japan, are losing headquarters to Tokyo. This is in good part linked with the increasing internationalization of the Japanese economy and the corresponding increase in central command and servicing functions in major international business centers. In the case of Japan, extensive government regulation of the economy is an added factor contributing to headquarter location in Tokyo in so far as all international activities have to go through various government approvals.

CONCLUSION

The massive trends towards the spatial dispersal of economic activities at the metropolitan, national and global level which we associate with globalization have contributed to a demand for new forms of territorial centralization of top-level management and control operations. National and global markets as well as globally integrated organizations require central places where the work of globalization gets done. Further, information industries require a vast physical infrastructure containing strategic nodes with hyperconcentration of facilities; we need to distinguish between the capacity for global transmission/communication and the material conditions that make it possible. Finally, even the most advanced information industries have a work process that is at least partly place-bound because of the combination of resources it requires even when the outputs are hypermobile.

This type of emphasis allows us to see cities as production sites for the leading information industries of our time and it allows us to recover the infrastructure of activities, firms and jobs necessary to run the advanced corporate economy.

NOTES

1 Services for firms are usually referred to as producer services. The producer services, and most especially finance and advanced corporate services, can be seen as industries producing the organizational commodities necessary for the implementation and management of economic systems. Producer services are intermediate ouputs; that is, services bought by firms. They cover financial, legal, and general management matters, innovation, development, design, administration, personnel, production technology, maintenance, transport, communications, wholesale distribution, advertising, cleaning services for firms, security, and storage. Central components of the producer services category are a range of industries with mixed business and consumer markets; they are insurance, banking, financial services, real estate, legal services, accounting, and professional associations (For more detailed discussions see, e.g. Noyelle and Dutka, 1988; Daniels 1991).

2 Furthermore, this unchanged level of concentration has happened at a time when financial services are more mobile

than ever before: globalization, deregulation (an essential ingredient of globalization) and securitization have been the key to this mobility—in the context of massive advances in telecommunications and electronic networks. One result is growing competition among centers for hypermobile financial activity. In my view there has been an overemphasis on competition in general and in specialized accounts on this subject. As I have argued elsewhere (Sassen, 2000a: chapter 7; 2000c), there is also a functional division of labor among various major financial centers. In that sense we can think of a transnational system with multiple locations.

3 Much of the discussion around the formation of a single European market and financial system has raised the possibility, and even the need if it is to be competitive, of centralizing financial functions and capital in a limited number of cities rather than maintaining the current structure in which each country has a financial center.

4 All the major economies in the developed world display a similar pattern towards sharp concentration of financial activity in one center: Paris in France, Milan in Italy, Zurich in Switzerland, Frankfurt in Germany, Toronto in Canada, Tokyo in Japan, Amsterdam in the Netherlands and Sydney in Australia. The evidence also shows that the concentration of financial activity in such leading centers actually increased over the 1990s. Thus, in Switzerland, Basel used to be a very important financial center but is now completely overshadowed by Zurich. Montreal was certainly the other major center in Canada two decades ago, and has now been overtaken by Toronto. Similarly, Osaka was once a far more powerful competitor of Tokyo in the financial markets in Japan than it had become by the late 1980s.

5 The data on producer services are creating a certain amount of confusion. For instance, the fact of faster growth at the national level and in medium-size cities is often interpreted as indicating a loss of share and declining position of leading centers. Thus one way of reading these data is as decentralization of producer services: major centers losing share of all producer services in a given country. Another way is to read it as growth everywhere, rather than a zero sum situation where growth in a new location *ipso facto* is construed as a loss in an older location. In my reading the second is the correct interpretation: these patterns point to the growing service intensity in the organization of economies nationwide.

REFERENCES

Abu-Lughod, Janet Lippman (1995) "Comparing Chicago, New York and Los Angeles: Testing some World Cities Hypotheses" in Paul L. Knox and Peter J. Taylor (eds) *World Cities in a World System*, Cambridge: Cambridge University Press, pp. 171–91.

Alegria, Tito Olazabal (1992) *Desarrollo urbano en la frontera Mexico–Estados Unidos*, Mexico City: Consejo Nacional para la Cultura y las Artes.

Amin, A., and Thrift, N. (1992) "Neo-Marshallian Nodes in Global Networks," *International Journal of Urban and Regional Research* 16 (4), pp. 571–87.

Berner, Erhard, and Korff, Rudiger (1995) "Globalization and Local Resistance: the Creation of Localities in Manila and Bangkok," *International Journal of Urban and Regional Research* 19 (2), pp. 208–22.

Body-Gendrot, S. (1993) *Ville et violence*, Paris: Presses Universitaires de France.

Borja, Jordi (1996) "Cities: New Roles and Forms of Governing" in Michael A. Cohen *et al.* (eds) *Preparing for the Urban Future*, Washington DC: Woodrow Wilson Center Press, pp. 242–63.

Brake, Klaus (1991) *Dienstleistungen und raumliche Entwicklung Frankfurt*, Oldenburg: Department of Town and Regional Planning, University of Oldenburg.

Browning, Harley I., and Roberts, Bryan (1980) "Urbanization, Sectoral Transformation and Utilisation of Labour in Latin America," *Comparative Urban Research* 8 (1), pp. 86–104.

Burgel, Galia, and Burgel, Guy (1996) "Global Trends and City Politics: Friends or Foes of Urban Development?" in Michael A. Cohen *et al.* (eds) *Preparing for the Urban Future*, Washington DC: Woodrow Wilson Center Press, pp. 301–35.

Carrez, Jean-François (1991) *Le Développement des fonctions tertiaires internationales à Paris et dans les métropoles régionales*, report to the Prime Minister, Paris: Documentation française.

Castells, Manuel (1989) *The Informational City*, Oxford: Blackwell.

Castells, Manuel, and Aoyama, Yuko (1994) "Paths towards the Informational Society: Employment Structures in G-7 Countries, 1920–90," *International Labor Review* 133 (1), pp. 5–33.

Chen, Xiangming (1995a) "The Evolution of Free Economic Zones and the Recent Development of Cross-national Growth Zones," *International Journal of Urban and Regional Research* 19 (4), pp. 593–621.

Cohen, Michael A. (1996) "The Hypothesis of Urban Convergence: are Cities in the North and South growing more alike in an Age of Globalization?" in Michael A. Cohen *et al.* (eds) *Preparing for the Urban Future*, Washington DC: Woodrow Wilson Center Press, pp. 25–38.

Cohen, Michael A., Ruble, Blair A., Tulchin, Joseph S., and Garland, Allison M., eds (1996) *Preparing for the Urban Future: Global Pressures and Local Forces*, Washington DC: Woodrow Wilson Center Press.

Competition and Change 1 (1), Philadelphia PA: Harwood Academic.

Daniels, Peter W. (1991) "Producer Services and the Development of the Space Economy" in Peter W. Daniels and Frank Moulaert (eds) *The Changing Geography of Advanced Producer Services*, London: Belhaven Press.

Le Débat (1994) *Le Nouveau Paris*, special issue (summer), Paris: Gallimard.

Drennan, Mathew P. (1992) "Gateway Cities: the Metropolitan Sources of US Producer Service Exports," *Urban Studies* 29 (2), pp. 217–35.

Dunn, Seamus, ed. (1994) *Managing Divided Cities*, Keele: Keele University Press.

Ernst, Rainer W., Borst, Renate, Krätke, Stefan, and Nest, Günter, eds (1993) *Arbeiten und Wohnen in städtischen Quartieren*, Berlin: Birkhauser.

Eurocities (1989) *Documents and Subjects of Eurocities Conference, Barcelona, April 21–2.*

Friedmann, John (1995) "Where we Stand: a Decade of World City Research" in Paul J. Knox and Peter J. Taylor (eds) *World Cities in a World System*, Cambridge: Cambridge University Press, pp. 21–47.

Frost, Martin, and Spence, Nigel (1992) "Global City Characteristics and Central London's Employment," *Urban Studies* 30 (3), pp. 547–58.

Futur antérieur (1995) *La Ville-monde aujourd'hui: entre virtualité et ancrage*, special issue, ed. Thierry Pillon and Anne Querrien, 30–2, Paris: Harmattan

Hall, Peter (1988) *Cities of Tomorrow*, Oxford: Blackwell.

Hardoy, J. E., and Satterthwaite, D. (1989) *Squatter Citizen: Life in the Urban Third World*, London: Earthscan.

Holston, James, ed. (1996) *Cities and Citizenship*, special issue of *Public Culture* 8 (2).

Journal of Urban Technology (1995) *Information Technologies and Inner-city Communities*, special issue, 3 (1).

Kasarda, John D., and Crenshaw, Edward M. (1991) "Third World Urbanization: Dimensions, Theories and Determinants," *Annual Review of Sociology* 17, pp. 467–501.

King, A. D., ed. (1996) *Representing the City: Ethnicity, Capital and Culture in the Twenty-first Century*, London: Macmillan.

Kloosterman, Robert C. (1996) "Double Dutch: Polarization Trends in Amsterdam and Rotterdam after 1980," *Regional Studies* 30 (5).

Knox, Paul L., and Taylor, Peter J., eds (1995) *World Cities in a World System*, Cambridge: Cambridge University Press.

Kowarick, L., and Campanario, M. (1986) "São Paulo: the Price of World City Status," *Development and Change* 17 (1), pp. 159–74.

Kowarick, L., Campos, A. M., and de Mello, M. C. (1991) "Os percursos de desigualdade" in R. Rolnik, L. Kowarick and N. Somekh (eds) *São Paulo: crise e mudança*, São Paulo: Brasiliense.

Kunzmann, K. R. (1994) "Berlin im Zentrum europäischer Städtnetze" in Werner Süss (ed.) *Hauptstadt Berlin* I, *Nationale Hauptstadt, europäische Metropole*, Berlin: Berlin Verlag, pp. 233–46.

Kunzmann, K. R., and Wegener, M. (1991) *The Pattern of Urbanisation in Western Europe, 1960–90*, report for Directorate General XVI of the Commission of the European Communities as part of the study *Urbanisation and the Function of Cities in the European Community*, Dortmund: Institut für Raumplanung.

LeGates, Richard T., and Stout, Frederic, eds (1996) *The City Reader*, London and New York: Routledge.

Logan, John R., and Swanstrom, Todd, eds (1990) *Beyond the City Limits: Urban Policy and Economic Restructuring in Comparative Perspective*, Philadelphia PA: Temple University Press.

Meyer, David R. (1991) "Change in the World System of Metropolises: the Role of Business Intermediaries," *Urban Geography* 12 (5), pp. 393–416.

Meyer, David R. (unpublished) "The World System of Cities: Relations between International Financial Metropolises and South American Cities," Providence RI: Department of Sociology, Brown University.

Mittelman, James, ed. (1996) *Globalization: Critical Reflections*, *International Political Economy Yearbook* 9, Boulder CO: Lynne Rienner.

Noyelle, T., and Dutka, A. B (1988) *International Trade in Business Services: Accounting, Advertising, Law and Management Consulting*, Cambridge MA: Ballinger.

Petz, Ursula von, and Schmals, Klaus M., eds (1992) *Metropole, Weltstadt, Global City. Nue Formen der Urbanisierung*, Dortmund Beiträge zur Raumplanung 60, Dortmund: University of Dortmund.

Portes, A., and Lungo, M., eds (1992a) *Urbanizacion en el Caribe*, San Jose, Costa Rica: Facultad Latinoamericana de Ciencias Sociales (FLACSO).

Portes, A., and Lungo, M., eds (1992b) *Urbanizacion en Centroamerica*, San Jose, Costa Rica: Facultad Latinoamericana de Ciencias Sociales (FLACSO).

Portes, A., Castells, M., and Benton, L., eds (1989) *The Informal Economy: Studies in Advanced and Less Developed Countries*, Baltimore MD: Johns Hopkins University Press.

Pozos Ponce, Fernando (1996) *Metropolis en reestructuracion: Guadalajara y Monterrey 1980–89*, Guadalajara, Mexico: University of Guadalajara.

Roberts, Bryan R. (1995) *The Making of Citizens: Cities of Peasants Revisited*, New York: Arnold.

Rodriguez, Nestor P., and Feagin, J. R. (1986) "Urban Specialization in the World System," *Urban Affairs Quarterly* 22 (2), pp. 187–220.

Rolnik, R., Kowarick, L., and Somekh, N., eds (1991) *São Paulo: crise e mudança*, São Paulo: Brasiliense.

Rosen, Fred, and McFayden, Deidre, eds (1995) *Free Trade and Economic Restructuring in Latin America*, New York: Monthly Review Press.

Rotzer, Florian (1995) *Die Telepolis. Urbanität im digitalen Zeitalter*, Mannheim: Bollmann.

Sachar, A. (1990) "The Global Economy and World Cities" in A. Sachar and S. Oberg (eds) *The World Economy and the Spatial Organisation of Power*, Aldershot: Avebury, pp. 149–60.

Sanchez, Roberto, and Alegria, Tito (1992) "Las ciudades de la frontera norte," Tijuana: Department of Urban Studies, Colegio de la Frontera Norte.

Sandercock, L., and Forsyth, A. (1992) "A Gender Agenda: New Directions for Planning Theory," *APA Journal* 58, pp. 49–59.

Sassen, Saskia (1996) *Losing Control? Sovereignty in an Age of Globalization*, New York: Columbia University Press.

Sassen, Saskia (2000a) *The Global City: New York, London, Tokyo*, Princeton NJ: Princeton University Press.

Sassen, Saskia (2000b) *Cities in a World Economy*, Thousand Oaks CA: Pine Forge/Sage Press.

Sassen, Saskia, ed. (2000c) *Cities and their Cross-Border Networks*, Tokyo: UNations University.

Savitch, H. V. (1996) "Cities in a Global Era: a new Paradigm for the next Millenium" in Michael A. Cohen *et al.* (eds) *Preparing for the Urban Future*, Washington DC: Woodrow Wilson Center Press, pp. 39–65.

Simon, David (1995) "The World City Hypothesis: Reflections from the Periphery" in Paul L. Knox and Peter J. Taylor, eds (1995) *World Cities in a World System*, Cambridge: Cambridge University Press, pp. 132–55.

Smith, David, ed. (1992) *The Apartheid City and Beyond: Urbanization and Social Change in South Africa*, London: Routledge; Johannesburg: Witwatersrand University Press.

Social Justice (1993) *Global Crisis, Local Struggles*, special issue, 20 (3–4).

Stren, Richard E. (1996) "The Study of Cities: Popular Perceptions, Academic Disciplines, and Emerging Agendas" in Michael A. Cohen *et al.* (eds) *Preparing for the Urban Future*, Washington DC: Woodrow Wilson Center Press, pp. 392–420.

Stren, R. E., and White, R. R. (1989) *African Cities in Crisis: Managing Rapid Urban Growth*, Boulder CO: Westview Press.

Taylor, Peter J. (1995) "World Cities and Territorial States: the Rise and Fall of their Mutuality" in Paul L. Knox and Peter J. Taylor, eds (1995) *World Cities in a World System*, Cambridge: Cambridge University Press, pp. 48–62.

Todd, Graham (1995) "'Going Global' in the Semi-periphery. World Cities as Political Projects: the Case of Toronto" in Paul L. Knox and Peter J. Taylor, eds (1995) *World Cities in a World System*, Cambridge: Cambridge University Press, pp. 192–214.

Toulouse, Chris (1993) "Politics, Planning and Class: The Sociology of Inner City Development in London and New York, 1977–92," Ph.d. dissertation, New York: Columbia University.

UN Conference on Trade and Development, Program on Transnational Corporations (1993) *World Investment Report, 1993: Transnational Corporations and Integrated International Production*, New York: United Nations.

Ward, Kathryn B., ed. (1990) *Women Workers and Global Restructuring*, Ithaca NY: ILR Press.

World Bank (1991) *Urban Policy and Economic Development: An Agenda for the 1990s*, Washington DC: World Bank.

24 The joys of spread-city

MELVIN M. WEBBER

SOME WORLDWIDE TRENDS

Similarities among metropolitan areas revealed here may seem surprising in light of the widely varied cultures, politics, and economics that mark the world's regions. The dominant technologies vary among them as well, along with their stages of economic development, levels and distributions of wealth, and the internal compositions of their economies. How can it be true, then, that the figures in this book look so much alike?

I suspect the prominent cultural differences have been masking their increasing commonalities, leading us to see their idiosyncracies instead. But, today, when history is speeding up, nations everywhere seem to be racing to become more like each other. Visibly apparent samenesses are accompanying inherited and long-standing differences.

Some universal forces seem to be at work around the world. Among the underlying influences shaping metropolitan societies are the overriding global traits of modernity—increasing specialization of labor and resulting interdependencies among persons and industries; monetization of economies; acceptance of modern technologies; rising wealth; and rising consumer purchasing power. In turn, modernization has meant expansion of the nonextractive industries and urbanization of the national populations. Resulting economic betterment, in turn, is making for greater capacity to consume—to consume houses, cars, and the accoutrements of modern life—and to enjoy greater ranges of individual consumer choice. These in turn foster rising aspirations and ever higher standards of living. Established and new middle classes everywhere are acquiring free-standing housing surrounded by adjacent open land, typically spacious enough to hold all sorts of modern appliances. Residence-serving services and new industrial plant are following them, reinforcing low-density expansion at the metropolis's growing edge.

Declining roles of extractive industries are paralleled by increasing emphasis on information-rich products whose raw materials are knowledge and intelligence instead of ore, soil, and oil. Transmission of data, information, money, and other nonphysical commodities relies on telephones, computers, television, and wireless radio channels that have become worldwide in scope. Physical commodities are transported ever more easily and rapidly, making for greater mobility of resources, both natural and human. Typically, current modes of transport are worldwide in their operations. They include ocean-going container ships and high-capacity jet aircraft, nowadays sharing tightly coordinated schedules with ground-based trucks and railroads and permitting geographically extensive accessibility, mobility, and just-in-time manufacturing. As equipment for communication and transportation is improved and installed worldwide, both households and business establishments are becoming increasingly footloose. Activities that once had but few locational options—that once had to locate near sources of raw materials and energy, or at transport junctions, or adjacent to a resident labor force—can now locate almost anywhere and still have ready access to those resources. Besides, they can operate with comparable effectiveness, even if physically removed from their associates, suppliers, and customers.

The outcome is increasing internationalization of firms and whole industries. Rapid diffusion of innovation and high mobility of capital, technology, and managerial capabilities is making for rapid industrialization, even among societies that were preindustrial only yesterday. In turn, increasing skills, incomes, and capacities to consume mean ever more rapid modernization around the globe, typically led by firms conducting their business in many countries simultaneously.

Most of them have chosen to locate in the midst of the world's large metropolitan areas where business services, transport, and labor are readily available. The magnetic attraction of jobs has induced population migration from rural areas and transformed regional subcenters into megacities. Accumulating business services, improved communication and transport, and available manpower at those sites has, in turn, made these urban places increasingly attractive to new industries, foreign and domestic. The effect is a seemingly unending process of mutually reinforcing growth.

Internationalization of cultural traits and preferences follows, making for similarities of wants in newly industrializing and postindustrial countries alike. That has been so despite initially wide cultural differences among the world's nations and regions. So, even though Bangkok residents may differ from Europeans and Americans in basic values, religious beliefs, and behavioral patterns, we can predict directional changes in some of their consumption and living styles by looking to places like San Diego and Randstad which are further along the developmental path.

Despite some emerging gross similarities across cultures (similarities, not homogeneities), we can also expect increasing cultural diversity over future time. As new ideas are generated and percolate through society we should expect new literatures to emerge everywhere. New music, new belief systems, new religions, new sports, new organizational forms, even new philosophic systems and new modes of governance are the likely products of increasing education, interchange, and exposure to the knowledge, customs, and thoughtways of other societies. That is to say, despite increasing similarity, but abetted by increasing intercourse, we can expect increasing innovation and difference too.

SPATIAL ATTRIBUTES

All 11 metropolitan areas reviewed here are marked by peripheral expansion. San Diego's map probably reflects the most diffused spatial pattern, however. Among the megalopolises in developing countries, Jakarta's and Bangkok's patterns seem most like San Diego's. In contrast, the Randstad's may show fewest signs of scatteration, even though it too seems to be acquiring San Diego-like propensities. Despite internationalization of technologies, business enterprises, and lifestyles, it is apparent that some striking differences remain among them. How can we account for these differences?

Surely their relative stages of modernization are responsible for a lot of the diversity. Because high income levels and widespread auto and home ownership must contribute to the spread-city form, we can expect metropolitan areas in wealthy post-industrial economies to be widely scattered outside their metropolitan cores. Thus it is no surprise that San Diego, Los Angeles, Phoenix, and others in the American west and south are spatially dispersed over wide areas. In contrast, we may expect a metropolis in a newly developing country to be more compactly structured. São Paulo, Bangkok, and Jakarta would seem to fit the compact model. And yet their maps are already looking like San Diego's, while the Randstad's dispersion has been slower to evolve.

Perhaps the sources of these disparities lie in their different cultures of governance. The Dutch are renowned for the rigor of their regulations over land use. Built-up towns literally stop at a town's legal boundary or at its plan-designated edge. Green land is presumably inviolate. The Netherlands equivalent of zoning more closely resembles a constitutionally stable law than a flexible statute or regulation. Certainly, changes there are not readily for sale.

In the United States, and probably in most rapidly developing countries where virtually everything is negotiable, there are active markets in modifications of land use regulations. At a price, one can get any rules revised or rescinded. Besides, because US government is so highly decentralized and because no central authority can coordinate decisions or controls over land use, the Americans rely heavily on the workings of land markets and political markets. Markets in turn reflect the revealed wants and demands of participating citizens.

The report from Thailand suggests that governance in Bangkok somewhat resembles America's in these respects. If so, it is not surprising that the geographic edge of Bangkok is coming to resemble the edge of San Diego—and of virtually every other American metropolitan area as well. Developments in many other places reflect the workings of land markets rather than the precepts of formal plans. As such, they reflect consumer preferences; builder preferences; emplaced infrastructure for transport, water supply, waste disposal, and communications; and, *inter alia*, the vicissitudes of *who* happens to be in political-governmental office at a given time. In truth, land use regulations in many cities scarcely warrant the label "regulation." They are so irregular, so flexible, and so adaptable to political pressure, they are more like "nominal guides" than regularizing controls.

The dispersed settlement surrounding so many of the global metropolises discussed in this book directly reflects land market responses to continuing in-migration of population and industry. It also reflects political acquiescence in that migration. The accompanying spatial dispersion has attracted much negative criticism, owing to the higher costs associated with lower density—especially the higher capital costs of infrastructure and the higher operating costs of travel. But the *benefits* deriving from the dispersed (and seemingly messy) pattern of the San Diego model may equal, if not exceed, the benefits deriving from concentrated patterns, such as that of the Randstad several decades ago—or of London or Paris today.

To be sure, San Diego is surrounded by a lot more empty land than is available anywhere in the Netherlands. So San Diego, Los Angeles, Phoenix and the other highly dispersed metropolitan areas of the American west can afford to spread across the landscape, virtually uninhibited. In turn, that sprawled pattern is wholly compatible with most of the population's ability to pay—to pay for low-density housing, for multiple cars per household, and for the associated high costs of infrastructure and public services that attach to spatial dispersion. Given the public's ability and willingness to pay the costs of the spread-city, and given their apparent preference for these living and working patterns, there is no gainsaying the wisdom of building more cities from that mold.

It looks as though spread-city is the form of the modern city—the form that closely matches societal modernization; current levels of income and wealth; industrial mix; retailing and consuming patterns; modes of travel and communication; and preferred lifestyles during this time in history.

Although aficionados may find spread-city aesthetically unacceptable, although economists may judge it overly costly, although it may violate traditional canons of urban design, it *is* the form that seems to work best with cars, wealth, and wide consumer choice. Four associated problems are genuinely troublesome, nevertheless.

FOUR PROBLEMS WITH SPRAWL

1. Not everyone can afford those costs. Large segments of every nation's urban population do not enjoy the high-paid jobs, high-quality housing, the high level of accessibility associated with individual automobiles, and the rest. Residents living in the *favelas* of this world may not be worse off *because* the middle classes are enjoying more specious residences and ease of travel, but they are surely not better off. Where much of the metropolitan fringe holds shanties built by recent in-migrants, as in much of Latin America, the costs are largely borne by the lowest-income residents. Having to spend inordinate amounts of time and money just getting to and from such jobs as they can find in the metropolitan center, they are surely far worse off than people living near employment sites. Despite life's miseries among poor migrants, continuing migration to the megacities suggests that life in the rural village must be harder still. Until such time as migrants acquire the requisite urban and industrial skills and until relocation of jobs or improved transport reduces their isolation, prospects for their integration into the economic and social life of the metropolis will be limited.

2. No metropolitan area charges the full costs of infrastructure and services to the users of the facilities and services. So others are paying for the benefits enjoyed by those users, and these cross-subsidies make for profligate, noneconomic overconsumption by some. Where funding comes from low-income sources and benefits redound to upper-income recipients, where environmental degradation is concentrated in districts already marked by severe poverty, the redistributive effects can scarcely be justified. There can be but limited tolerance of a metropolitan spatial structure whose costs fall unduly upon those least able to sustain them.

3. Expanding populations, increasing numbers of automobiles, and limited road capacity have led to traffic congestion and ever rising costs of movement and loss of access, compounded by air and noise pollution. It is something of a paradox that the city's fundamental attraction has always been the promise of accessibility among interdependent persons and groups. And yet, by concentrating large numbers of persons and cars into limited space, access is reduced, if not erased. In some places, business and social life is locked up by traffic jams that extend for much of the day, owing to inefficient spatial distributions of activities and to inadequate transport capacity. Because accessibility is the *sine qua non* of the city, accessibility must be ranked as the dominant criterion against which alternative spatial patterns must be judged. That spatial form and density pattern that make for the most access and hence the freest social and economic intercourse should be the structure most worth striving for.

4. In the absence of studied concern for the quality of the natural environment and associated ecologic systems, urban developments are likely indiscriminately to spread on to land that is best kept open and undisturbed. And yet land markets are notoriously insensitive to environmental attributes that are judged valuable but are not accountable in normal market transactions. Some sites having unique natural features, or providing habitat for endangered species, or having other special qualities, justify retention as undeveloped places. Yet these may be caught up in the normal processes of suburbanization and used as building sites instead. They may then be lost to future use as parks or other public-service areas unless explicitly removed from the normal commercial land markets.

These are serious matters, especially in developing countries where poverty is widespread and deep-seated and where the urban economies are most fragile. But, apart from these issues in redistributive social justice, spatial accessibility, and environmental quality, I see little cause for concern regarding the spread-city form.

SOME BENEFITS OF SPREAD-CITY

If costs are commensurate with services received and ability to pay, *if* persons have free access to opportunities for jobs and free social intercourse, *if* producers have ready access to sources of raw materials and markets, *if* economic transaction and social interaction are not unduly constrained by distance, *if* sites that are valued for nonurban use can be reserved: *then* the spatial pattern of the urban settlement is, *per se*, almost irrelevant. That is to say, it matters not whether mapped patterns are concentrated or dispersed—whether densities are high or low and whether activities occur in centers or at scattered sites—so long as the valued operating criteria are satisfied.

Further, to the degree it fosters a high standard of living, high efficiency of the urban economy, high levels of social interaction, and satisfies the preferences of consumers and producers, as it seems to do in wealthy metropolitan areas, spread-city must be judged a desirable form.

The success of America's extensive suburbs (especially in the new and modern cities of the south and west) is clear evidence of the spread form's merits. The economic viability of this arrangement is exemplified by the industrial success of the Los Angeles metropolitan area—spread-city *par excellence* which became the largest manufacturing concentration in a highly industrialized country. It continues to attract millions of migrants from around the country and around the world, people seeking a better life, with most of them finding it there in that extensively spread-out metropolis.

The evidence reported in this book suggests that many of the world's large cities are also expanding in Los Angeles-type or San Diego-type or Bangkok-type or even São Paulo-type dispersed and low-density patterns. That trend suggests either that this arrangement has something powerful going for it, or that it is being compelled by some powerful, worldwide technological and institutional imperatives that most societies have so far been unable or unwilling to restrain. I suggest it is both.

DISSOLUTION OF GEOGRAPHY

Modern transport and communication technologies are rapidly dissolving geographic space, and we have probably seen only the early stages of that dissolution. As the effects of information exchange are realized, the costs of overcoming distance will collapse even further.

Highly specialized and affluent persons already live in nonplace societies. Rather than relying primarily on face-to-face interaction, people already communicate largely through print on paper and through telephones connected to fiber optics, radios, and satellites. Increasingly, they are communicating through the internet and e-mail—worldwide. Urban life is already, in large measure, lived in electronic channels that are essentially freed from geographic constraints. That trend toward unimpeded intercourse suggests that spatial location will be less important in the future metropolis than it is today—that the spatial pattern of the metropolitan development will be of lessening importance.

It is clear that no metropolis is any longer, in any sense, an independent entity. All of them are increasingly and intricately engaged with all other metropolises around the world. They are constantly exchanging information, goods, ideas, money, customs, and personnel.

In the language of this book all metropolises are "global." There is no such thing any longer as a provincial metropolis. It is no longer fitting to consider a single metropolis as a unitary place—to treat a metropolis as a place-defined phenomenon. Indeed, its place-specific characteristics are anachronistic, hence of ever lessening relevance. All metropolises are connected with all others in real time. They are all economically interdependent. They are all interlinked parts of an integrated international urban system.

Despite their geographic separation, Bangkok's economy is a subset of the world economy in which San Diego, São Paulo, Tokyo, the Randstad, and the rest are also subsets. So Bangkok is effectively a part of (*not merely a partner of*) San Diego and the Randstad and all the other metropolises examined here. Similarly, inside the dispersed settlement pattern of any metropolitan area, the social, political, and economic activities in any one district are integral with those of all other districts, making even the idea of a separate business district or a separate suburb anachronistic.

Spatial dispersion is occurring at all geographic scales, propelled by that long array of factors I have referred to: automobiles, telephones, the internet, international corporations, international finance, rising incomes, and rising aspirations. Even in the Netherlands!

We have all seen data indicating that the long-augured megacities of megamillions may turn out to be exaggerations, because migration to the largest metropolises is declining. If that is really so, does it imply lessened productivity of the national economies, given that the biggest metropolis has traditionally been the most productive and efficient center within each country? Or, rather, does it imply *increased* productivity within the national economy? I suspect the latter, so long as outlying urban centers are highly accessible to each other and to the primary metropolis.

In retrospect, it should be no surprise that migration trends are shifting. Declining cost of overcoming geographic space means that functional proximity is no longer dependent on spatial propinquity. Persons and forms within a given urban settlement have long been adapting to the costs of density and congestion by moving to the outskirts of town. They are now also able to move away from the metropolis, even to towns considerably distant.

The counterpart of spread-city is dispersed-urban-region. Populations and functions, once constrained to the metropolis by high costs of interaction and transaction, are now able to prosper no matter where they happen to locate within the national landscape. If that is really so, we can expect increased productivity to follow the greater dispersion of urban activities across the landscapes of the Third World. Experience in the United States points the way. Following installation of transportation and communication systems, urbanization quickly spread from the eastern regions to places like Los Angeles and San Francisco, and, more recently to such places as the mountains of Colorado and Montana.

The US metropolitan region occupies the entire continental space from the Atlantic to the Pacific. Urban activities are located at sites throughout the national space—and beyond—integrated into a coherently functioning *national urban system*, that is, in turn, integrated into the coherently functioning *global urban system*.

Rather than focusing on settlement patterns within limited metropolitan areas, perhaps we should be directing our sights to settlement patterns within countries, or global regions, or, more appropriately, the globe!

THE COURSE OF FUTURE PROGRESS

The trends I have been discussing represent progressive improvements over conditions in the recent past. So-called Third World nations are urbanizing rapidly—modernizing rapidly. That is, they are industrializing, then building high-level *service economies* accompanied by rising living standards. The standards are not yet high enough for *all* their citizens; but increasing proportions of them are enjoying enriched lives, with the prospect of ever wider diffusion of benefits to higher proportions in the future. (Witness the successes of the so-called Tigers of East Asia with their escalating GNP, narrowing distribution of income and wealth, and expanding middle classes.)

I suspect that spatial arrangements inside metropolitan settlements are far less determining of the course of progress than are the organization of industry and patterns of governance. I am suggesting that what matters most is accessibility among partners to interaction and transaction and then the volume and distribution of benefits and costs—not spatial form. I suggest, further, that trends toward spatial dispersion are symptoms of greater productivity, and wider distribution of wealth—that spatial dispersion is a sign of progress. Moreover, I suspect these spatial trends are unstoppable—that there's little, if anything, any society can do to deter them. If I'm right about that, the spread-city is here to stay—in Bangkok, San Diego, the Randstad, and all the other places this book reviews.

In celebration, I propose we all exclaim a loud and joyous Hallelujah!

Index

Page numbers in italic denote illustrations